SOCIAL DEVELOPMENT AND PERSONALITY

**American Educational Research Association
READINGS IN EDUCATIONAL RESEARCH**

Merlin C. Wittrock, EDITOR OF THE SERIES

PHILOSOPHY OF EDUCATIONAL RESEARCH
Harry S. Broudy | Robert H. Ennis | Leonard I. Krimerman

INTELLECTUAL DEVELOPMENT
Pauline S. Sears

SOCIAL DEVELOPMENT AND PERSONALITY
George G. Thompson | Francis J. DiVesta | John E. Horrocks

LEARNING AND INSTRUCTION
Merlin C. Wittrock

EDUCATIONAL ORGANIZATION AND ADMINISTRATION
Donald A. Erickson

RESEARCH DESIGN AND ANALYSIS
Raymond O. Collier, Jr.

EVALUATION AND CURRICULUM DEVELOPMENT
William W. Cooley

SOCIAL DEVELOPMENT AND PERSONALITY

Edited by George G. Thompson
Department of Psychology
OHIO STATE UNIVERSITY

With the collaboration of
Francis J. Di Vesta
Department of Educational Psychology
PENNSYLVANIA STATE UNIVERSITY

and

John E. Horrocks
Department of Psychology
OHIO STATE UNIVERSITY

JOHN WILEY & SONS, INC.
New York • London • Sydney • Toronto

Copyright © 1971 by John Wiley & Sons, Inc.

All rights reserved. Published simultaneously in Canada.

No part of this book may be reproduced by any means, nor transmitted, nor translated into a machine language without the written permission of the publisher.

Library of Congress Catalogue Card Number: 77-146673

ISBN 0-471-86005-0

Printed in the United States of America

10 9 8 7 6 5 4 3 2

Series preface

MERL C. WITTROCK

This book is one of a series entitled "Readings in Educational Research," sponsored and prepared by the American Educational Research Association (AERA). The tentative titles of the seven projected volumes are:

1. Philosophy of Educational Research
2. Intellectual Development
3. Social Development and Personality
4. Learning and Instruction
5. Educational Organization and Administration
6. Research Design and Analysis
7. Evaluation and Curriculum Development

The object of this preface is to state the purposes of the series, to describe briefly the history of its development, and to acknowledge the people who created the series. For several years they donated their time and considerable abilities to its preparation.

The two purposes for publishing the series have in common the liberal theme of building understanding across the different areas and specialties of educational research and of preventing insularity among educators and educational researchers. The major purpose is to promote a systematic development of the quickly growing field of educational research. A multivolume series encompassing different fields of educational research, such as educational administration and research design and analysis, is one appropriate way for AERA to further the cohesiveness of educational research. The second purpose of the series is to make available to students, teachers, researchers, and administrators a comprehensive, useful, and organized set of outstanding published papers representing major fields of educational research.

These two objectives have guided the editors in their selection of the papers and articles that comprise the series. Each paper is included in the series because it contributes to the two purposes mentioned above. Each paper makes important points about significant issues or problems of education and each complements the logical organization of the series and the volume editor's conception of the significant divisions of his field of research.

Lee Cronbach conceived the idea for the series. He is absolved of any inadequacies it may have. When he was president of AERA, he appointed a committee to investigate the advisability and value of having AERA sponsor the series. The members of this committee were John DeCecco, Arthur P. Coladarci, Leland K. Medsker, David G. Ryans, and M. C. Wittrock, chairman.

The committee recommended that the preparation of a multivolume series of readings was an appropriate endeavor for AERA, provided that the series encompassed several major areas of educational research. The series would not then compete with individual researchers' single-volume treatments of their fields of educational research. More important, the series would help to accomplish the objectives mentioned above.

A second committee was then appointed to provide a tentative design for the series and to select a Board of Editors to prepare the series. The second committee consisted of Luvern Cunningham, Ellis Page, Ole Sand, George Thompson, Robert Travers, and M. C. Wittrock, chairman. This committee nominated people to serve as the Board of Editors.

The Board of Editors was then appointed with the responsibility of designing and preparing the seven volumes. This board consisted of nine people, seven of whom each took senior responsibility for preparing a volume: Harry S. Broudy, Raymond O. Collier, William Cooley, Donald Erickson, Pauline S. Sears, George G. Thompson, and M. C. Wittrock. W. W. Charters, Jr. and Robert Travers worked at large with the preparation of all the volumes.

Lack of space allows me to mention only a few of the other people involved in the preparation of the series. Dr. Richarr Dershimer and the Central AERA staff were of invaluable help. The successive presidents of AERA, Lee Cronbach, Benjamin Bloom, Julian Stanley, John Goodlad, Roald Campbell, and Robert Gagné, and their respective Association Councils were, without exception, highly supportive of the series and most helpful in its development. The staff members of the Center for Advanced Study in the Behavioral Sciences at Stanford, California also gave extensively of their time to the completion of several manuscripts for the series. Joseph F. Jordan, of John Wiley, was consistently helpful whenever he was needed.

It is my hope that *Readings in Educational Research* helps to accomplish the goals set for it by the Board of Editors. We have prepared it to further the development and organization of educational research and to provide its readers with intellectual stimulation that will warrant its continued use in coming years.

March 1971

M. C. Wittrock
Editor of the Series
Readings in Educational Research

Preface

Why a volume of readings on research and theory related to the social development of boys and girls? In attempting to answer this question, we must acknowledge that man is, first and foremost, a highly social animal. Individuals expend considerable time and energy to meet and be near each other—to look and wonder, to admire and imitate, to converse, to compete in peaceful ways, and to engage in aggressive actions that again are initiated primarily by social concerns. If we hope to influence the goals and the means-ends programs of social interactions among individuals, communities, states, nations, and the alliances of national groups, it has become increasingly clear to social scientists and professional educators that it will be necessary to initiate the beginnings of such changes with the very young.

As the many findings presented in this volume demonstrate, social actions, social preferences, social motivations, social learnings, and the internalization of social controls make their appearance, become shaped and organized into styles of living at a very early age. Certainly, educational procedures related to some of the most important dimensions of social living are introduced (often unwittingly) during the first two years of the child's life. The educational processes that define some of the unique aspects of social development in a particular culture become more obvious during the preschool years, and by school age many of them have been codified into the rules, regulations, and traditions that are consistent with the aims and goals of our educational institutions.

The papers included in this volume provide convincing evidence that we have begun to identify some of the important variables that either influence, or are coordinate with, some of the more obvious features of social development during childhood and adolescence. We have invented and adapted some rather ingenious methodologies that appear to have a minimum effect on the social behavior being observed. Psychologists have extended and elaborated some of the older theories of social development and have begun a more extensive and meaningful colloquy with theorists in sociology and cultural anthropology who also are interested in social development but who have different perspectives on the processes and different evaluations about the most relevant and influential sets of variables. These trends seem promising.

All of the foregoing, well represented in this book of readings, are indicators of scientific progress—and are so interpreted. But how far have we hacked our way into the forest of knowledge, how well have we charted the primitive paths and their various crisscrossings, and how well have we guessed about the nature of the terrain ahead and the unexplored pockets of ignorance on every side? How much do we know about the ecology of this forest of knowledge, its seasonal variations, its relation to adjoining territories, and its special sensitivities to deviations from the "normal" in terms of over- and under-abundance of certain natural contributions? Without being either unduly optimistic or pessimistic, about all that we can say is that the current state constitutes a beginning. We have made some discernible progress, and we are continuing to recruit more and more workers who are willing to devote themselves to research in this area. A trickle of cross-cultural research findings have begun to appear. Some cross-disciplinary communications have already broadened our theoretical ventures. And parents and teachers of the large numbers of boys and girls who frequently reject almost all of the old values and rebel against almost all established institutions and forms of authority are beginning to welcome and support research that promises to lead to a better understanding of the antecedents of social behavior and development. These are some of the major omens of the good things that may come to pass—hopefully, at an accelerated rate—in the near future. I will not dwell on the possible stumbling blocks, because they are well illustrated in the problems that the investigators have been forced to bypass in order to conduct the truly excellent research studies presented in this volume.

This volume of research and theoretical papers includes representative and important contributions in the area of social development and some wise criticism and advice on important omissions by some colleagues whose judgments are especially respected. It includes a typical sampling of the research literature and also supplies enough information on theory, methodology, and substantive findings to enable the reader to become a knowledgeable amateur even if he should not have the time or inclination to read further. A substantial body of references is presented at the end of the book and we hope, of course, that some readers will be stimulated to study the papers listed there.

In organizing the material we adapted or abridged many of the papers to suit the purposes of this book. Of course, we made as few changes in the selections as possible. Most of our alterations were deletions of secondary findings on interesting variations of the main argument or research design. A reader who is especially interested in the contents of an article that has been abridged extensively should consult the full original text.

We thank Willard Hartup, Wayne Holtzman, and Sheldon White, as well as the colleagues and graduate students (too numerous to mention here), who made many valuable suggestions that helped to make this book a better balanced treatment of social development.

We thank the contributors and publishers who gave us permission to use adapted and abridged versions of their articles.

Because this volume is part of a larger educational program to serve the scholarly interests of members of the American Educational Research Association (a nonprofit and internationally respected professional organization) as well as of students in professional education, the original publishers of the papers presented here waived all charges for the privilege of reproducing them. We are grateful for the understanding and generosity of the following publishers: Academic Press, American Association for the Advancement of Science, American Orthopsychiatric Association, American Psychological Association, British Journal of Educational Psychology, Chandler Publishing Company, Duke University Press, Edwards Brothers, Harper and Row Publishers, International Journal of Psychology and Dunod-Publisher, Journal Press, Ronald Press Company, Society for Research in Child Development, Tavistock Institute of Human Relations, and University of Chicago Press.

In the compilation of this book, there was truly an equal division of labor among the editors. The work of adapting and abridging the papers in order to keep them within the allotted space and of writing the introductions to the individual papers was shared by the three of us. I thank my coeditors, Francis J. Di Vesta and John E. Horrocks, for devoting their time to this important project.

Finally, I thank the AERA Committee on a Series of Readings, and all the individuals who became involved in this venture, for generous assistance and helpful counsel.

GEORGE G. THOMPSON
Columbus, Ohio

Contents

CHAPTER 1
Primary Dimensions of Socialization 1

   1. PATTERNS OF CHILD REARING
      Robert R. Sears, Eleanor E. Maccoby, &
      Harry Levin 4

   2. STANDARDS OF SOCIAL BEHAVIOR AMONG SCHOOL
      CHILDREN IN FOUR CULTURES
      Robert R. Rodgers, Urie Bronfenbrenner, &
      Edward C. Devereux, Jr. 13

   3. PSYCHOLOGICAL ECOLOGY OF A NURSERY SCHOOL
      Myrna Beth Shure 26

   4. THE CULTURALLY DEPRIVED CHILD
      Frank Riessman 38

CHAPTER 2
Interactive Processes During Socialization 49

   5. THE INFLUENCE OF CHILDREN'S BEHAVIOR ON
      PARENTAL BEHAVIORS IN SOCIALIZATION
      Richard Q. Bell 55

   6. BIRTH ORDER AND ITS SEQUELAE
      William D. Altus 67

   7. SOCIAL REINFORCER EFFECTIVENESS AS A FUNCTION
      OF THE RELATIONSHIP BETWEEN CHILD AND ADULT
      Norma McCoy & Edward Zigler 75

8. JUSTIN AND HIS PEERS: AN EXPERIMENTAL ANALYSIS OF A CHILD'S SOCIAL WORLD
Donald J. Cohen   86

9. THE CHILD AS A DETERMINANT OF HIS PEERS' APPROACH TO HIM
Martin Kohn   96

10. A STUDY OF REPUTATION: CHILDREN'S EVALUATION OF THEIR PEERS
Read D. Tuddenham   104

CHAPTER 3

Personal-Social Motives and Incentives   115

11. THE PSYCHOSOCIAL ORIGINS OF ACHIEVEMENT MOTIVATION
Bernard C. Rosen & Roy G. D'Andrade   121

12. CHILDREN'S TEXTBOOKS AND PERSONALITY DEVELOPMENT
Irvin L. Child, Elmer H. Potter, & Estelle M. Levine   136

13. DELAY OF GRATIFICATION, NEED FOR ACHIEVEMENT, AND ACQUIESCENCE IN ANOTHER CULTURE
Walter Mischel   148

14. ACHIEVEMENT MOTIVATION TRAINING FOR UNDERACHIEVING HIGH SCHOOL BOYS
David A. Kolb   158

15. SOCIAL NORMS IN TEENAGE BOYS' PEER GROUPS
Barry Sugarman   168

16. THE SOCIAL CONTEXT OF AMBITION
Ralph H. Turner   179

CHAPTER 4

Growing Responsiveness to Socially Administered Rewards   189

17. EFFECTS OF SOCIAL CLASS AND RACE ON RESPONSIVENESS TO APPROVAL AND DISAPPROVAL
David L. Rosenhan   196

18. THE EFFECT OF SOCIAL REINFORCEMENT ON THE PERFORMANCE OF INSTITUTIONALIZED AND NONINSTITUTIONALIZED NORMAL AND RETARDED CHILDREN
Harold W. Stevenson & Leila S. Fahel   204

19. SOCIAL ISOLATION: A PARAMETRIC STUDY OF ITS EFFECT ON SOCIAL REINFORCEMENT
Michael Lewis   213

20. IMITATION OF A PEER AS A FUNCTION OF REINFORCEMENT FROM THE PEER GROUP AND REWARDINGNESS OF THE MODEL
Willard W. Hartup & Brian Coates   222

21. SOCIAL REINFORCEMENT UNDER NATURAL CONDITIONS
Phyllis M. Scott, Roger V. Burton, & Marian Radke Yarrow   233

22. EFFECTS OF SOCIAL REINFORCEMENT ON ISOLATE BEHAVIOR OF A NURSERY SCHOOL CHILD
K. Eileen Allen, Betty Hart, Joan S. Buell, Florence R. Harris, & Montrose M. Wolf   243

CHAPTER 5

Imitation and Identification—Semi-Autonomous Steps Toward Social Maturity   253

23. THE CONCEPT OF IDENTIFICATION
Jerome Kagan   259

24. LEARNING OF GENERALIZED IMITATION AS THE BASIS FOR IDENTIFICATION
Jacob L. Gewirtz & Karen G. Stingle   267

25. IMITATION IN CHILDREN AS A FUNCTION OF PERCEIVED SIMILARITY TO A SOCIAL MODEL AND VICARIOUS REINFORCEMENT
Mary A. Rosekrans   281

26. A COMPARATIVE TEST OF THE STATUS ENVY, SOCIAL POWER, AND SECONDARY REINFORCEMENT THEORIES OF IDENTIFICATORY LEARNING
Albert Bandura, Dorothea Ross, & Sheila A. Ross   291

27. CONFORMITY AS A FUNCTION OF AGE LEVEL
Philip R. Costanzo & Marvin E. Shaw   302

28. EFFECTS OF COMMITMENT TO SOCIAL ISOLATION ON CHILDREN'S IMITATIVE BEHAVIOR
Ralph Epstein   308

CHAPTER 6

Role-Playing, Role-Taking, and Role-Commitments   317

29. DEVELOPMENTAL CHANGES IN THE SELF-CONCEPT DURING ADOLESCENCE
Barbara H. Long, Robert C. Ziller, & Edmund H. Henderson   322

30. MODELS AND HELPING: NATURALISTIC STUDIES IN AIDING BEHAVIOR
James H. Bryan & Mary Ann Test   331

31. ROLE-TAKING IN CHILDHOOD AND ITS CONSEQUENCES FOR SOCIAL LEARNING
Eleanor E. Maccoby   343

32. SEX ROLE LEARNING IN THE NUCLEAR FAMILY
Miriam M. Johnson   357

33. SEX-ROLE CONCEPTS AND SEX TYPING IN CHILDHOOD AS A FUNCTION OF SCHOOL AND HOME ENVIRONMENTS
Patricia P. Minuchin   371

34. EFFECTS OF PATERNAL ABSENCE ON SEX-TYPED BEHAVIORS IN NEGRO AND WHITE PREADOLESCENT MALES
E. Mavis Hetherington   388

CHAPTER 7

Learning to Understand and to Live with Others   397

35. SOCIAL PERCEPTIONS AND ATTITUDES OF CHILDREN
Marian Radke, Helen G. Trager, & Hadassah Davis   401

36. INTERPERSONAL RELATIONS IN PRESCHOOL CHILDREN AND AVERAGE APPROACH DISTANCE
M. G. King   408

37. A COMPARISON OF RACE AWARENESS IN NORTHERN AND SOUTHERN CHILDREN
J. Kenneth Morland   416

38. PREJUDICE AMONG NEGRO CHILDREN AS RELATED TO PARENTAL ETHNOCENTRISM AND PUNITIVENESS
Ralph Epstein & S. S. Komorita   424

39. RACE AND BELIEF: AN OPEN AND SHUT CASE
David D. Stein, Jane Allyn Hardyck, & M. Brewster Smith   432

CHAPTER 8

Acquiring Culturally-Approved Controls over Aggressive Behavior   445

40. ADOLESCENT AGGRESSION
Albert Bandura & Richard H. Walters   451

41. NAME-MEDIATED AGGRESSIVE CUE PROPERTIES
Russell G. Geen & Leonard Berkowitz   461

42. SOCIAL CLASS, PARENTAL PUNISHMENT FOR AGGRESSION, AND CHILD AGGRESSION
Leonard D. Eron, Leopold O. Walder, Romolo Toigo, & Monroe M. Lefkowitz   469

43. PATTERNS OF AGGRESSIVE BEHAVIOR IN EXPERIMENTALLY CREATED "SOCIAL CLIMATES"
Kurt Lewin, Ronald Lippitt, & Ralph K. White   479

44. CHILDREN'S AGGRESSION, PARENTAL ATTITUDES, AND THE EFFECTS OF AN AFFILIATION-AROUSING STORY
Jesse E. Gordon & Edward Smith   489

45. CONTROL OF AGGRESSION IN A NURSERY SCHOOL CLASS
Paul Brown & Rogers Elliott   497

CHAPTER 9
Internalizing General Behavioral Controls   503

46. THE DEVELOPMENT OF SOCIAL RESPONSIBILITY
Nevitt Sanford   507

47. SOCIAL CLASS DIFFERENCES IN CONSCIENCE DEVELOPMENT
Leonore Boehm & Martin L. Nass   517

48. SOME RELATIONSHIPS BETWEEN CONSCIENCE AND ATTENTIONAL PROCESSES
Paul F. Grim, Lawrence Kohlberg, & Sheldon H. White   528

49. THE ORIGIN OF SELF-CRITICISM
Justin Aronfreed   552

50. RELATIONSHIPS BETWEEN SHAME AND GUILT IN THE SOCIALIZATION PROCESS
David P. Ausubel   568

51. THE LEARNING OF SHARING BEHAVIOR
Dilman J. Doland & Kathryn Adelberg   585

CHAPTER 10
Striving Toward Idealized Goals   593

52. MORAL REASONING OF YOUNG ADULTS: POLITICAL-SOCIAL BEHAVIOR, FAMILY BACKGROUND, AND PERSONALITY CORRELATES
Norma Haan, M. Brewster Smith, & Jeanne Block   597

53. THE DEVELOPMENT OF MORAL VALUES IN CHILDREN: THE CONTRIBUTION OF LEARNING THEORY
H. J. Eysenck   618

54. CHILDREN'S CONCEPTS OF JUSTICE: A COMPARISON WITH THE PIAGET DATA
Dolores Durkin   631

55. CHILDREN'S JUDGMENTS OF THEFT FROM INDIVIDUAL AND CORPORATE OWNERS
    Frederick J. McDonald   640
56. EGOCENTRISM IN ADOLESCENCE
    David Elkind   651
57. CHILD-REARING PRACTICES AND MORAL DEVELOPMENT: GENERALIZATIONS FROM EMPIRICAL RESEARCH
    Martin L. Hoffman   661

References   685
Author Index   723
Subject Index   731

SOCIAL DEVELOPMENT AND PERSONALITY

CHAPTER 1

Primary Dimensions of Socialization

Few contemporary psychologists, sociologists, or professional educators would agree in defining the primary dimensions of socialization. Even fewer would agree on the structure and dynamics of the socialization events that occur within the different dimensions of rearing and educating our young. These disagreements and, in many instances, misunderstandings among professionals reflect the infantile state of the contributing sciences. Although this must be discouraging to the practitioner, who would like to be able to find the "true answers" to his daily problems, the confusions and the issues involved in scientists' debates are obviously stimulating to the average investigator and theoretician, who characteristically loves puzzles and the challenges of trying to discover some of the "secrets" of nature.

Interested readers may be encouraged and stimulated by the papers selected for this volume to do some arguing, theorizing, and scientific investigating of their own. And to the extent that they are genuinely inquisitive and well informed (but not too heavily indoctrinated with the impression that currently popular theories and research techniques are necessarily the most fruitful), their contributions may be among those that will stand as basic markers for significant steps forward as viewed by the eyes of posterity. Also, it may be well to remember that there have been many scientists down through the centuries (far more than the often-quoted example of Gregor Mendel) who worked diligently and creatively simply to satisfy their curiosity about some apparently minor variation in nature that they happened to find especially interesting. The team approach to science and the analytic aids provided by the digital computer have proved to be useful advances in helping modern man solve *some* problems; however, the creative and analytic minds of individual investigators continue to be the most valuable "tools" for advancing the sciences and their related applied arts. Thus two of the reports selected for this first chapter lean heavily on the output of especially creative personalities rather than on a completely internally consistent system of ideas (the latter is a rare, if not totally nonexistent, phenomenon in any branch of science—for example, even Euclid relied on some "obvious truths" that were eventually proven to be neither obvious nor necessarily "true").

In choosing an example of an important personality who has had much to say about the primary dimensions of socialization, one cannot ignore the many contributions of Robert R. Sears. The work presented here represents only a very small portion of his voluminous writings and will give the reader only a tiny bit of the flavor of the creative and provocative conceptions of this internationally esteemed developmental psychologist. But even in this modest excerpt from one of his influential books, the reader will find something of the broad scope of Sears' panoramic views of the complexity of socialization processes. Sears, his colleagues, and numerous graduate students—many of whom have grown to have comparable influence in developmental and educational psychology—have been true leaders in their efforts to identify and measure the structure and dynamics of the socializing processes. In his theoretical conceptions, Sears has been able to produce a happy productive blend of psychoanalytic and neo-behavioristic concepts, and to develop experimental and observational procedures that have given these concepts conceptual and operational meaning in his many research studies with children. Like a magnet, he attracted young men and women with drive and talent to become his collaborators. The short excerpt included here, from his and Drs. Maccoby and Levin's pioneering and now classic book on *Patterns of Child Rearing* will, hopefully, arouse the reader's interest to a point where he or she will want to read the book for one early interpretation of the primary dimensions of socialization.

One other paper was especially selected for this introductory chapter because of the strong influence of one of its authors, as well as for its highly significant social content. Urie Bronfenbrenner, along with his collaborators, Drs. Rodgers and Devereux, in this particular report, have forced American psychologists to recognize the fact that parents in different civilized nations have a variety of aspirations for their children and often rear their offspring very differently—all of which may alter the structure and dynamics of the principal dimensions of socialization, as well as the observed social outcomes. There are some scientists who are willing to overlook all but a very thin slice of nature to avoid confusing themselves about what they consider to be the important nucleus of the problem. There are other scientists who believe equally strongly that the thin slice cannot be studied in isolation because its relevance and significance are importantly determined by the other thin slices that make up the whole (including the "field" relationships and ecology for these component dimensions). Bronfenbrenner has consistently emphasized the latter scientific outlook in such influential ways that psychology and education have greatly benefited from his strong commitment to this perspective on scientific strategy. His is a truly comprehensive and cosmopolitan view which is definitely needed in helping social scientists to identify and describe the primary dimensions of socialization.

In an era where almost every conscientious citizen is worried about water, air, and land pollution, the eventual effects of chemicals for eliminating "undesirable" flora and fauna, and other "balances" in nature, it seems perfectly reasonable that the social scientists and professional educators should also be concerned about the ecological conditions most desirable for man's happiness and welfare. The report by Myrna Shure shows that even preschool-aged children are influenced by the "psychological ecology" of their behavioral settings. It would seem foolish, indeed, to believe that institutions, mores, folkways, and other established social forms are not vital in the primary dimensions of socialization. The research findings of Shure remind us of this, and the research methods also remind us that much can be learned about socialization by well trained human observers who may be able to manipulate the environmental setting in only minor ways.

The last paper in this warm-up chapter of the present volume is an excerpt from the writings of Frank Riessman and was included because it represents some interesting and unusual thinking about what happens when the "normal" processes of socialization within a given setting are upset, altered, or disturbed by the larger social forces of a culture. When the father is absent from the home (and this may occur for many different reasons), does this alter one or more of the primary dimensions of socialization? If so, are the social effects of such alterations always psychologically undesirable under all social conditions for all individuals? This type of question will be raised again and again in the papers presented in the subsequent chapters of this book, because such questions constitute one of the reasons why man conducts research, theorizes, and consistently wonders what lies beyond the horizon as he continually struggles to find conceptual and instrumental means for reaching higher ground. The scientist's struggle to see beyond the known is largely motivated by his desire to gain a superior vantage point for observing new phenomena and for reasoning and guessing at the possible meaning of all that has been newly discovered.

1. PATTERNS OF CHILD REARING

Robert R. Sears, Eleanor E. Maccoby, & Harry Levin

More than two decades ago the first author of the following report gave his presidential address to the American Psychological Association on the significance and dynamics of some components of diadic relationships. The following discussion is a continuation of that interest. It is concerned with attempting to unravel some of the strands of the complex relationship between acting-and-interacting mother and preschool-aged child. This portion of a comprehensive study by Sears, Maccoby, and Levin was truly a pioneer contribution in inferring the consequences of the middle-class mother's impact on her four- to five-year-old child. As the reader may note, this investigation was marked by productive intermingling of neo-behavioristic and psychoanalytic concepts. Although this research has some admitted weaknesses in its experimental methodology, it has had a sustained and substantial impact on subsequent studies of the mother-child interaction. Moreover, all three authors have continued to contribute significantly and generously to this body of the psychological literature.

The following excerpt from their now classic book summarizes some of the more important concepts involved in the interpretation of this influential study. The reader's attention is called especially to the authors' interpretation of the probable effects of punishment. Even as we move out of an extremely permissive era of child rearing, the authors' conceptual analysis of the effects of punishment have not, as yet, had to be substantially altered. As a matter of fact, the following discussion, despite the several

SOURCE. Adapted and abridged from pp. 457-466 of Robert R. Sears, Eleanor E. Maccoby and Harry Levin, *Patterns of Child Rearing*. Evanston, Illinois: Row, Peterson, and Co., 1957. (With permission of the authors and Row, Peterson, and Co.)

years that have elapsed since its publication, still stands as an insightful and remarkably modern interpretation of the principal dimensions of early socialization within the home environment.

Child rearing is not a technical term with precise significance. It refers generally to *all the interactions between parents and their children*. These interactions include the parents' expressions of attitudes, values, interests, and beliefs as well as their caretaking and training behavior. Sociologically speaking, these interactions are one separable class of events that prepare the child, intentionally or not, for continuing his life. If a society survives beyond one generation, it quite evidently has cared for some of its offspring, and has provided opportunity for them to develop the values and skills needed for living. Some of this learning comes from parent-child interaction, and much does not. Relatives, neighbors, and peers play an important role, too, as do teachers or others specifically charged with the training function. Once he is beyond infancy, a youngster's personality is always a product of more social experiences than just those offered by his parents.

Not all parent-child interactions are intended, by the parents, to train the child. Some are simply for caretaking, such as feeding and cleaning and protecting. Others are expressions of love or annoyance, of concern or pride—reactions that have no significant purposes for the child's future nor even for his control at the moment; but they are nonetheless elicited by the child and impinge on him when they occur. Child rearing includes all such interactions, for they all affect his behavior, and, whether by intention or not, change his potentialities for future action.

To understand the implications of these defining statements about child rearing, one must examine the apparent mechanisms by which parents and children influence one another. There are two ways. One is with respect to action and the other to learning. Action is what a person is doing on any given occasion; a theory of action attempts to define the conditions under which specified kinds of action do or do not occur. Anything a parent does to or with a child that has as its aim *control*, i.e., the changing or maintaining of a particular form of behavior, is an influence on action.

Learning, on the other hand, is the changing of a person's potentialities for acting in the future; a theory of learning attempts to define the conditions under which a second presentation of a given situation will produce a different reaction from that elicited by the first presentation of the situation. Learning is the process involved in personality development. Parental behavior that is intended to *train* the child, to change his customary way of acting, is an influence via learning.

This distinction between action and learning is not always clear either to a mother or to a child. In one way this is just as well, but in another it leads to confusion. Actually, every interaction between two people has an effect both on their present actions and on their potentialities for future actions. An affectionate hug or a testy reprimand not only influences what the child is doing at the moment, but adds a small change into his expectations of what will happen on future similar occasions. This expectancy, in turn, increases or decreases the probability that he will act the same way in the future. Likewise, a mother's discipline—which she may view strictly as a method of training for the future—has some immediate impact on the child and leads to a change in his behavior at the moment.

However, when a child has developed adequate language skills, it is possible for a mother to make clear what her intentions are, whether to control for the moment or to modify permanently. This verbal understanding helps a child discriminate somewhat the difference between his "now" behavior and his "next." Better discrimination of his mother's intent leads to more efficient learning.

The most convenient way to view behavior is not simply as action, but as re-action. Every motion is a function of some immediately preceding state of affairs. Some of these antecedent conditions are internal to the person, such as thirstiness or a desire for affection. These include the various organic drives as well as a good many wishes, ideas, desires, or knowledge that can only be inferred to exist—sometimes from what the person says, sometimes from other things he does, and sometimes simply from a knowledge of what experiences he has had in the past. (It is safe enough to infer, for example, that an adolescent who has gone four hours without food, in the afternoon, has internal instigation to eat!)

Still other antecedents of behavior can be observed directly by an outsider—a smile or a request or a spank or a warning look. Not all those that affect a child are equally noticeable to a disinterested stranger, of course. When two people live closely together, they become sensitive to each other's expressions, to postures, manners of movement, and expressions of tension or mood. Even a husband may not note all the little signs of a mother's impending actions that a child does. Or at least not the same ones.

One can distinguish two functions of the conditions which precede action: to *direct* behavior and to *impel* it. Some conditions have more importance for the former purpose and others for the latter, while some do both equally (e.g., a slap). By *directing* is meant giving a signal as to what to do next. A child must move around in his world, and manipulate it to a certain extent, if he is to stay alive and get satisfaction from living. He must reach for the food in front of him, accept or refuse the glass of water for drinking, comply with his mother's "no!" or suffer uncomfortable consequences. In the life of a young child, a mother provides a great many directive signals. Her words and her gestures, even the faint and intangible expressions of mood in her gait or her posture, help him to find his way around in his world and interact with it in the most effective fashion.

But there must also be some *impulsion* to action. Even a chocolate pie has little directive effect on a child already full-fed: it does not make him reach for it. The strongest impulsions in the beginning come from bodily needs—the so-called primary drives. These are native and universal, and some of them are referable to reasonably well understood physiological processes. They initiate action with varying degrees of specificity. In the newborn infant, for example, hunger and thirst may produce no more than a general thrashing about and crying. In an older child they set off quite specific actions of asking for food or water, or of turning on a tap, or opening the bread box. The primary drives include hunger, thirst, sex tensions, fatigue, need for activity, waste elimination, optimum temperature maintenance, pain, and probably a number of metabolic ones. Also, the internal states of affairs reflected by the emotions of rage and fear probably belong in the same category. The impelling quality of primary drive states is a constitutional characteristic of the organism. The directed behavior with which the organism satisfies its needs is (in man) almost entirely learned. Furthermore, through learning, the child comes to want and need certain conditions, such as the presence of the mother. Learning is a crucial process underlying not only the child's actions in pursuing a goal but his choice of goals themselves. A brief consideration of the learning process, that is, of the principles by which life experiences change the child's potentialities for action, appears to be in order.

For purposes of description, it is convenient to break up the continuous flow of a person's behavior into segments called *action sequences*. These are somewhat arbitrary units that have the following qualities in common. Each starts with some impelling state of affairs, such as the state of being hungry (the hunger drive), and ends with a consummatory (goal) response (e.g., eating) that reduces the drive. Between the beginning and the end, there is a series of instrumental acts which puts the person in such contact with his environment that he can make the goal response; for instance, a child runs to his mother and asks for a sandwich. Actions that lead to gratification (whether conscious or not) are learned, and may be expected to occur more quickly, more skillfully and more customarily on future occasions when the child finds himself in a same or similar situation.

It is not only the acts immediately preceding gratification that are learned, however. For most activities, especially those that involve social interaction, there are intermediate (or concurrent) events that must be produced in order that the goal may be achieved. For example, a two-year-old child who is hungry needs co-operative action by his mother in order to perform his own goal response of eating. He may cry, or gesture, or ask in words for help. Whatever instrumental techniques he uses, the necessary event must be the same—his mother's giving him food. And he must learn to perform the necessary acts to produce her response. As time goes on, the child develops a "want" for any object, person, or social situation that happened to be associated with the original satisfying experience, and he will learn to perform whatever actions are necessary to produce the desired state of affairs.

It is important to keep in mind that this learning process is, in at least one respect, a highly *mechanical* one. The child learns to want *whatever events regularly occur* in the satisfying context. He does not discriminate between those that are physically efficacious and those that are simply inadvertent accompaniments. For example, the mother must nearly always be present when a child is fed; she orients herself toward him physically, looks at him, often smiles and talks while she is giving food. To the observer trying to decide which of the mother's acts are relevant to the child's food-seeking behavior, the mere handing out of food may seem all that is essential. But the orientations and other actions of the mother nearly always occur, too, and hence the child learns to want them as much as the giving of food. To him, they are part of the whole pattern accompanying the satisfaction of his hunger, and he learns to want the entire pattern. A new item has been added to the list of things the world can do for that child to make him happy—it can be labeled as "mother looking at me and smiling and talking."

When one considers the myriad situations in which children are rewarded throughout childhood, the variety of actions their mothers perform in the process of child rearing, it does not seem surprising that there are so many sub-goal systems of this sort. Or that there should be a unique set of them for each child. Every mother has her own temperament, her own attitudes, her own methods of rewarding and punishing. It is these ways of behaving that her child learns to want. If she is warm and loquacious, he will treasure demonstrativeness; if she is reserved, he will seek her normal reserved expressions toward him. It should be evident now why the term child rearing includes *all* the interactions between parents and their children, not just the ones which directly satisfy primary drives, or those that are consciously *intended* to have a training effect.

The problem of punishment must be raised in connection with both these kinds of learning. Punishment, in its broadest sense, is the inflicting of pain or anxiety. Such an act may be intentional on a mother's part, or it may not. From the standpoint of its effect on the child, any maternal act that hurts or shames or frightens the child is punishment. This is the technical, not the ordinary, use of the word.

The effects of punishment are relevant to both ongoing action and learning. Punishment motivates a child to do something which will reduce the pain created by the punishment; for example, something which will get him away from the source of pain. In the beginning, when there are only reflexes available, infants cry and thrash about. Gradually they learn to move away from external sources of discomfort, mainly sharp things and hot things. But when the source of pain is a punishing parent, the problem cannot be solved merely by avoidance, for the child is dependent upon the parent's presence for the gratification of many of his needs.

There are many kinds of behavior the child can learn in response to punishment that emanates from his mother. Those responses will be selected and retained which serve best to reduce the discomfort. What kind of behavior by him will placate the mother will depend to some extent on her personality characteristics. Sheer flight may work—if the mother has lost her temper or is irritably nagging. Passivity may help, or a counterattack may do the trick. If the mother's punishing actions are accompanied by some indication of what behavior she *does* desire from the child, then he can follow this clue. And then his reaction to the punishment likely will be effective in reducing the pain.

Once a child develops a repertory of responses to threatening or punishing situations, he will use those that are appropriate to any specific instance. This does not mean that what he does will actually work. Many of the reactions to punishment that are learned in early childhood are quite ineffectual in later years. Bursting into tears may be useful at four, but it is less likely to be so at ten or twelve. Passivity toward a mother may be established because she stops punishing under those circumstances, but passivity in a threatened adult is often quite the least useful form of response. But usefulness or "sensibleness" is not the only determiner of behavior; both actions and desires are the products of previous learning experiences, and which ones are activated at any given moment depends on what situation is present.

Whether a particular action is effective for achieving its aim depends on what may be called the *response qualities* of the environment, that is, what reaction the environment can make to the actions the person imposes on it. A child may learn, as a great joke, to pummel his father's knee when his father is reading the newspaper. He learns to do this because his father always responds affectionately, rewardingly. If the child does the same thing to a newspaper reader on a train, he may get the same friendly response or he may get a swat on his behind. It depends on the response qualities of the man who, in this instance, is the relevant "environment" of the child. The effectiveness of a given action is only as great as is the similarity of the response qualities of the environment in which the behavior was originally learned. Since it is always possible for aspects of the new situation (man on train reading a newspaper) to resemble those of many previous ones, without there being any similarity in the environment's response qualities (the man is *not* tolerant and affectionate to this child at this moment), much human social behavior inevitably is maladaptive and "senseless."

We have said little about the intentional training that is a part of child rearing. From a mother's standpoint, there is much to teach a child, or to help him learn. There are all the motor activities that will enable him to manipulate his environment and to get around in it. There are eating habits, toileting, independence, responsibility. Speaking and understanding of speech must be developed. He must learn what are desirable things to have, what to avoid. He must develop proper control of his aggressive impulses and his sex drive. He must learn what is good and what is bad. He must learn the names and functions of things, and the proper techniques of behaving toward other people. And much of this learning is not simply the adding of new responses to the collection he already has: it requires the replacing of undesired actions or attitudes or desires with ones the mother conceives as more appropriate.

Teaching is a delicate and complex process. It requires the selection of appropriate kinds of behavior for the child to perform, the providing of sufficient opportunity for him to practice them, the introducing of adequate motivation to induce him to do the practicing, and the insuring that he enjoys the rewards of his labors so that he will be inclined to repeat them. This is all there is to teaching—in theory. In practice, there is a serious stumbling block. A child often knows what he wants to do, knows how to do it in some degree, and insists on doing it. If his existing action patterns do not coincide with those his tutors would like to teach him, the teacher must undertake an additional task—eliminating his old actions. This is what makes the theoretically simple process so difficult. No child is ever a *tabula rasa*; he always has a repertory of actions that need replacing. Many of them he likes and does not want to change. Any one can teach a person whose desire to learn comes from being dissatisfied with what he already knows. But the socialization of children is not so easy. Many an action a mother wants to introduce comes in conflict with actions the child already has. She must find a way of eliminating the old before she can establish the new.

There is one infallible way to stop a child from doing what he is doing: start him doing something else. Like all panaceas, however, this one has a joker in it. *How* do you start him doing something else? Actions occur because the child wants something, and certain situations have impinged on him— situations to which he has learned to react with a specific kind of behavior. To change these actions, new wants or new situations must be introduced.

Much of the maternal control and teaching in child rearing is accomplished by manipulating the child's wants. Mothers quickly learn that a youngster can be induced to do all manner of things if these are a part of some pleasurable sequence of activities. If she joins him in cleaning up the toys, he works like a Trojan with her just to have her company and to gain the sense of being useful in an adult fashion. He can relish the wash-up job if she shows him how much fun it is to slop and squeeze the fluffy soapsuds. He will attend seriously to his table manners if she calls this "the grown-up way." To the extent that a mother can introduce new actions into already existing motivational systems, or can contruct new goals and values by associating them with such desirable achievements as being *mature* or *big* or *strong* or *beautiful*, to that extent is child rearing made easy, and the inculcation of new actions made a pleasure for both teacher and learner.

But not *always*, with *every* child, can a mother think up an effective way of doing this. She has trouble during temper tantrums, some frights, some stubborn spells. When children have strong emotional reactions, they are not easy to control. But the real problem is not with the unmodifiability of the child, but with the fact that mothers are not always themselves calm or rational or profound. They get angry, frightened, tired, and neither their wit nor their wisdom can ever be perfect. The upshot of it is that they are not infrequently driven into interaction with children on a basis that has little to do with teaching. But teaching or not, the continuing interaction has a lasting effect on the child, in the sense that it affects his potentialities for future action as well as his present behavior.

Obviously not all, or perhaps even very much, of a mother's interaction with her child is of an intentional teaching variety. But the need to ensure the child's development, to socialize him, is always present and creeps into expression whenever the mother observes a kind of action, on the child's part, that she wishes to see modified.

It is these various changeworthy actions that cause the trouble. Some of them relate to eating habits or table manners, some to speech and language. Some involve cleanliness or neatness or orderliness or noise or play habits or interests. A large proportion, however, have to do with the child's relation to other people. After all, the word *socialization* does have a social reference. It means, in large part, the development of socially appropriate behavior, the proper (i.e., adult) kinds of interactions with others.

Child rearing is a continuous process. Every moment of a child's life that he spends in contact with his parents has some effect on both his present behavior and his potentialities for future action. Happily, the importance of many of these moments is small, but those that provide repetitions of common and consistent experiences add up, over the years, to the production of consistent ways of behaving toward the kinds of people he knows.

So much for the mechanics of interpersonal influence. Left at this, the process would seem to dictate a unique personality for each child. Every mother behaves differently, and hence even without constitutional variation every child should be different. Strictly speaking, this appears to be the case. Although the process by which learning occurs is the same for everyone, the specific environmental conditions that determine just what wants and actions will be learned are unique to each human being.

The researcher's task is not as impossible as this conclusion may suggest, however. He does not have to study every living human being, for his interest is in those aspects of personality that are common to many. There are quite a few dimensions of this kind. Our interest has been largely in those that describe mothers' child-rearing activities. These represent a part of mothers' personalities, just as our measures of eating problems, enuresis, aggressiveness, and other aspects of children's behavior are indicators of children's personalities.

2. STANDARDS OF SOCIAL BEHAVIOR AMONG SCHOOL CHILDREN IN FOUR CULTURES

Robert R. Rodgers, Urie Bronfenbrenner, & Edward C. Devereux, Jr.

Scientists tend to study and do research with those materials and events which are nearest at hand. This universal tendency is also found in psychology where some critics have charged that most of the research data on human learning are drawn from the responses of college and university freshmen and sophomores. Furthermore, the largest amounts of information about infrahuman behavior are heavily loaded with the response tendencies of the albino rat. Somewhat similar charges can be made about the sources of knowledge concerning socialization processes. Information here is remarkably provincial in that it is only very infrequent that data based on subjects other than white, native American born offspring is included in textbooks of child development and psychology published within the United States. During the last decade this picture has fortunately been changing a bit. One professional leader who has raised our sights and broadened our vision to the truly heterogeneous child-rearing practices employed in different cultures of the world is Bronfenbrenner of Cornell University. In the following report, he and his colleagues, Rodgers and Devereux, have examined the standards for acceptable social behavior within four different western cultures: American, English, Soviet Russian, and Swiss.

Although the findings of this investigation are important in their own right, the significance of the research is further augmented by the sheer

SOURCE. Adapted and abridged from Robert R. Rodgers, Urie Bronfenbrenner, and Edward C Devereux, Jr., "Standards of social behavior among school children in four cultures," *International Journal of Psychology*, 1968, Vol. 3, 31-41. (With permission of the authors and the *International Journal of Psychology*.)

fact that it was conducted at all. It is one of the few cross-national surveys of this important dimension of socialization consequences. The authors were impressed with the similarities found across the sexes and the cultures in the overall ordering of the importance of the following behavioral standards: telling the truth, keeping clean, being punctual, and being good in sports. The American children, more than any others, gave greater importance to telling the truth. The English, more than any others, gave greater importance to a standard of masculinity involving both a stoical boyish ideal and some opposition to adult authority. The Soviet children placed greatest emphasis on overt propriety of behavior as measured by a "manners" factor obtained through factor analysis. The Swiss appeared to place great emphasis on the substantive and constructive Calvinist virtues of individual industry and achievement. These research findings constitute only a beginning. Much more information on socialization antecedents and consequences in different countries of the world is sorely needed.

Each generation attempts to pass on to its successor a set of standards for acceptable social behavior. That these standards differ by time and place has troubled the parent and the traveler at least since the days of Sophocles and Herodotus. That there are also universal values and norms of conduct has been the assumption of philosophers and more recently of some anthropologists (Kluckhohn, 1953; 1954, p. 952). As part of our cross-cultural research on processes of socialization we have elicited children's value judgments of standards of social behavior. We are interested not in cultural differences *per se* but in the effects of different techniques and agents of socialization on the development of social behavior and personality. The observations by students of national character, as well as our own preliminary observations (Bronfenbrenner, 1963), suggest that children differ in their standards of acceptable social behavior, not only among cultures, but also by age, sex, socioeconomic status, and other factors operating within societies.

PROCEDURE

It was to substantiate these impressions with objective data that children of four cultures, American, English, Soviet Russian, and Swiss, were asked to evaluate the importance to themselves of a variety of standards by responding to a questionnaire. In the United States and England we sampled children who lived at home with their parents and attended public day schools. In both nations the influence of a semi-autonomous peer group sub-culture on socialization has been observed. In the Soviet Union and Switzerland we sampled children who lived in boarding schools under the supervision of trained adults. The Soviet setting differed from the Swiss in the greater emphasis placed on the rationalized peer collective as a means of socialization and social control. The responses of 1,459 children were analyzed.

While the sets of items in the questionnaires varied slightly from culture to culture, 18 were given to all four samples (Table 1). All of the behaviors were plausibly desirable to some degree. The responses of the samples most likely to differ, the English and the Soviet, were factor analyzed, separately for boys and girls. In each case the unrotated first common factor approximated a general factor. The rotated varimax factor loadings are shown in Table 1. Coefficients of congruence (Harman, 1960, p. 257) among the four samples averaged .84 among the first factors, .71 for the second factors, and .18 between first and second factors. This indicated sufficient similarity among the samples to warrant selecting sets of items to represent these factors The five items chosen for each factor were simply those with the highest average loadings across the four samples. Factor one was labeled «manners» and factor two labeled «masculinity».

We made the assumption that values are ordinal variables, hierarchically organized within the individual, having a motivational and potentially affective component. Among an array of desirable values or standards, not all of them can be simultaneously maximized by the individual's behavior. For this reason it was decided to use an operational measure of the children's responses which would to some degree represent this state of affairs. The scores used in the analyses are, for the two factors and the remaining eight items, z-scores based on each individual's own mean response level to all eighteen items. From this point of view the mean response level (MRL) represents either a measure of drive state or of social desirability response set. That this response process was not merely a statistical artifact is suggested by the tendency toward a general factor noted above, and by cultural differences in MRL to be described below.

While this rationale lends theoretical support to the use of ipsative scores, there was also a practical reason for their use. The Swiss and Soviet children had rated the importance of the standards on a four-point scale while the responses of the American and English children were on a five-point scale. In order to compare the two pairs of cultures a standardized measure was essential. The dependent variables in the study, included the two factors each measured by the sum of responses to five items, the eight remaining items common to all four samples, and the MRL. The independent variables included: sex, culture, age, coeducational *vs* single-sexed boarding homes (in the Swiss sample), classroom or school differences within cultures, and parental socioeconomic status (in the American and English samples).

RESULTS

Similarities Across the Four Cultures

With respect to the question of the universality of standards of behavior there are two lines of evidence that point to cross-cultural similarities among

TABLE 1

Behavior Standards Items in Order of Importance for All Samples Together (With Rotated Factor Loadings for First Two Factors, English and Soviet Samples)

	English				Soviet			
	Boys		Girls		Boys		Girls	
Items	I	II	I	II	I	II	I	II
1. Always telling the truth	.43	—.11	.19	—.14	.72	.04	.35	—.13
2. Keeping hands, face and clothing clean (Factor I)	.34	.02	.57	.07	.70	.16	.45	—.05
3. Having good table manners (Factor I)	.56	.01	.54	.05	.63	—.06	.70	—.07
4. Asking questions about things you don't understand	.14	.21	.18	.01	.17	.11	.30	.09
5. Not using bad language (Factor I)	.47	.04	.57	.02	.94	.08	.64	—.09
6. Being on time for everything	.30	.20	.47	.16	.48	—.22	.48	—.29
7. Knowing how to work with your hands	.19	.39	.22	.43	.02	.23	.64	.01
8. Doing things on your own	.23	.21	.24	.03	.24	.29	.61	.27
9. Keeping your things in good order (Factor I)	.58	.06	.52	.01	.23	—.05	.58	—.17
10. Being good in sports (Factor II)	.14	.40	.05	.68	.04	.26	.09	.13
11. Doing something useful in your spare time, instead of just playing	.42	.07	.48	.28	.30	.28	.14	.25
12. Speaking up about your own ideas, no matter what grown-ups may think (Factor II)	—.01	.48	—.08	.14	.04	.60	.27	.18
13. Being quiet in front of grown-ups, and not speaking until you are spoken to	.47	—.07	.49	.05	.14	.10	—.05	.04
14. Telling grown-ups if you don't like their ideas (Factor II)	—.08	.46	—.12	.19	.19	.41	.49	.37
15. Fighting back when someone picks on you (Factor II)	—.17	.48	—.11	.30	—.03	.46	—.12	.36
16. Talking and playing quietly (Factor I)	.52	.05	.60	.04	.80	.21	.52	.00
17. Not asking for help	.25	.23	.19	.23	.17	.35	.23	.24
18. Not crying (Factor II)	.00	.49	.04	.50	.06	.43	.45	.05

children when they are asked to rate the importance of standards. The first of these is in the overall hierarchy or value ordering given to the 18 standards. Correlations were computed between rank orders of the raw score means of the items, across and within sexes and cultures. All of the correlations were statistically significant, and those between sexes within the same culture (averaging .88) were not much higher than those between cultures within the same sex (boys average .66, girls average .78), or even those across both sexes and cultures (averaging .67). This is impressive evidence that children in these four industrialized societies have, in spite of the cultural differences to be described below, much in common concerning the hierarchy of value which they give to these standards of social behavior.

The second similarity we have documented only for English and Soviet samples, based on the coefficients of congruence used to assess the degree of similarity among the arrays of factor loadings. The congruence of the same factors between boys and girls within each culture averaged .85, that between cultures within sexes averaged .73, and that across both sex and culture also averaged .73. Coefficients between first and second factors indicated an appropriate absence of congruence, whether within or across sexes or cultures. Thus there is evidence for these two cultures that not only do the children order these standards similarly but also they respond to similar implicit dimensions of behavior implied by the content of the items—those dimensions which we have called "manners" and "masculinity." The only possible exception are the Soviet girls whose coefficients with the other samples are somewhat lower.

Overall Sex Differences

In Table 2 (Columns 1 to 4), are given the means of the z-score for the total sample, for boys and girls, and the overall sex differences in the eight items and two factor scores. Overall means across cultures for MRL could not be included because of the differences between four- and five-point response scales, mentioned above. In calculating the means of the z-scores each culture's was given equal weight regardless of the number of cases by averaging individuals within classrooms, classrooms within cultures, and cultures within sexes. The differences between boys and girls were tested against the interaction of sexes and cultures.

Turning to the results, not surprisingly we find that, across cultures, girls exceed boys in the relative value given to the "manners" factor, while boys give greater relative importance to the "masculinity" factor. Among the remaining items, girls give greater relative importance to telling the truth, being quiet in the presence of adults, doing something useful in their spare time, and doing things on their own, while boys give greater relative value to being able to work with their hands.

TABLE 2

Unweighted Mean Ipsative Standard Scores on Selected Behavior Standards Items and Factors I and II

		Across Cultures				Within Cultures			
	Total	Boys	Girls	Difference Favoring Boys	American	English	Soviet	Swiss[a]
Individuals	1149	617	532		249	497	135	268
Class & Schools	46	46	46		10	16	3	17
6. Tell truth	0.673	0.608	0.738	−0.130**	0.826	0.785	0.483	0.597
18. Ask questions	0.442	0.428	0.456	−0.028	0.548	0.600	0.179	0.441
Factor I: "Manners"[b]	0.251	0.189	0.313	−0.124***	0.194	0.193	0.452	0.166
2. Be on time	0.240	0.211	0.272	−0.061	0.061	0.030	0.436	0.435
12. Work with hands	0.239	0.299	0.178	0.121**	0.107	0.143	0.412	0.293
16. Do things on own	0.144	0.109	0.180	−0.071*	0.252	−0.023	0.074	0.273
13. Do something useful	−0.034	−0.117	0.049	−0.166*	−0.026	0.119	−0.470	0.239
Factor II: "Masculinity"[b]	−0.404	−0.299	−0.509	0.210***	−0.371	−0.334	−0.392	−0.518
1. Be quiet with adults	−0.417	−0.514	−0.321	−0.193**	−0.259	−0.136	−1.421	−0.146
17. Don't ask for help	−0.465	−0.417	−0.513	0.096	−0.624	−0.577	0.005	−0.663
Mean response level	—	—	—	—	3.736	3.597	3.458	3.242

* p less than .05; ** p less than .01; *** p less than .001.
[a] Children from coeducational homes.
[b] Means divided by five to put them on the same scale as single-item variables.

Cultural Differences

The mean standard scores within the American, English, Soviet, and Swiss samples, for both sexes together, are also shown in Table 2 (Columns 5 to 8). Tests of significance were computed between pairs of cultures based on the unweighted means of classrooms, homes, or internats. Since we have frequently found significant differences among schools or classrooms for similar variables obtained from questionnaire responses, the cultural differences were tested against an error term of the mean square between classrooms. The Swiss single-sexed homes were not included in these comparisons, because only coeducational groups were used in the other three cultures. Following the procedure outlined by Ryan (1959), for each array of four means the extremes were tested first followed by tests of progressively less extreme values until a non-significant difference was found, at which point no further tests were made within that array. Nominal significance levels of .01 or less per comparison were set as indicating cultural differences. Based on that level, the error rate per "experiment," *i.e.*, the expected number of false indications of a cultural difference per array of four means, is .06 (Ryan, 1959, Table 1, p. 37). There is, of course, some redundancy in the results, since the use of ipsative scores results in lack of complete independence among the variables.

The results of comparing samples from four cultures, both sexes together, are as follows:

—1. Always telling the truth has greater relative importance for the American children than for the Soviet or Swiss children.—2. Asking questions about things that are not understood is of greater relative importance to American and English than to Soviet children.—3. The relative importance of "manners" is greater for Soviet children than for Swiss, English or American children, who do not differ among each other.—4. Doing things on their own has greater relative importance for American and Swiss than for English children.—5. The relative importance of doing something useful in spare time, rather than just playing, is greatest for Swiss, intermediate for American, and least for Soviet children.—6. The relative importance of "masculinity" is greater for English than for Swiss children.—7. The relative value placed on being quiet in the presence of adults is greatest for the Swiss children, intermediate for American and English, and least for Soviet children.—8. Not asking for help is given greater relative value by Soviet than by Swiss, American, or English children, who do not differ among each other.—9. While it was not possible to compare all four cultures on MRL because of the difference between four- and five-point scales, it was possible to compare pairs of cultures having the same scale form. American children have a higher MRL than English (p less than .05), and Soviet children have a higher MRL than Swiss (p less than .05).—10. There were no cultural differences in the value ascribed to being on time or to knowing how to work with one's hands.

Sex Differences by Culture

Differences between boys and girls within each of five samples are shown on Table 3. Only in the American and English samples were there extensive

TABLE 3

Differences Between Boys' and Girls' Mean Standard Scores on Selected Standards Items and Factors I and II (Items are Presented in Descending Order of Difference Favoring Boys from Table 2)

	American	English	Soviet	Swiss[a]	Swiss[b]
Classrooms	10	16	3	17	7 et 12
Boys	125	256	74	162	134
Girls	124	241	61	106	176
Factor II: "Masculinity"[a]	0.336***	0.272***	0.103	0.128	0.067
7. Work with hands	0.109	0.237*	0.063	0.074	0.022
17. Don't ask for help	0.050	0.016	0.138	0.178	−0.039
4. Ask questions	0.043	−0.145*	−0.018	0.012	−0.058
6. Be on time	−0.183	−0.029	0.063	−0.093	0.062
8. Do things on own	0.061	−0.233*	0.007	−0.121	−0.068
Factor I: "Manners"[c]	−0.244***	−0.155**	−0.031	−0.068	−0.008
1. Tell truth	−0.217	−0.172**	−0.107	−0.023	0.091
11. Do something useful	−0.342**	−0.011	−0.257	−0.057	−0.185*
13. Be quiet with adults	0.014	−0.265**	−0.247	−0.274	−0.120
Mean response level	0.007	0.001	−0.057	−0.004	−0.086

* p less than .05; ** p less than .01; *** p less than .001.

[a] Children from coeducational boarding homes.

[b] children from all-male and all-female boarding homes.

[c] Mean differences for factors I and II divided by five.

and reliable sex differences. In both cultures greater relative value is given to "manners" by girls and greater relative value is given to "masculinity" by boys. In addition, American girls valued doing something useful in their spare time more than did the boys, while English girls differed from their classmates in giving more relative importance to being quiet in the presence of adults, always telling the truth, doing things on their own, and asking questions about things they did not understand. The sexes do not differ, either within cultures or within pairs of cultures having the same response scale, in their mean level of response to the questionnaire. There is also no sex by culture interaction in this variable.

Reliable overall interactions of sex and culture were found only for the two factor scores. The results were similar for both factors. In each case the greatest sex difference was in the American sample, followed in descending order by the English, Swiss, and Soviet. The directions of sex difference were of course opposite for the two factors, being in favor of girls for "manners" and in favor of boys for "masculinity". In addition to the overall interaction across the four cultures, comparison of pairs of cultures showed that the sex difference in the importance of "manners" was greater for American children than for Swiss or Soviet.

That this ordering of the cultures in degree of sex difference might reflect the difference between boarding schools and day schools must be emphasized. Both the Soviet internats and the Swiss "homes" were coeducational boarding schools, while the American and English subjects were obtained from day schools. In order to explore this factor further, the responses of Swiss children who resided in single-sexed boarding homes were also analyzed (Table 3, Column 5). On five of the eight items and on the two factor scores, the sex difference was smaller among children from the single-sexed homes than in the coeducational ones. However, it was not possible to test this interaction directly because of the incomparability of error terms used in the two analyses, as well as the unequal numbers of children and of homes. Both boys and girls in single-sexed homes gave greater relative value to "manners" and less to "masculinity" than their peers of the same sex living in coeducational homes, although these differences were non-significant. While this comparison does not directly attack the question of coeducational boarding schools *vs* day schools in producing sex differences in values, it does suggest that for the values of "manners" and "masculinity" it may be the pattern of group living away from parents rather than the specifically coeducational nature of the group which minimizes sex differences in these standards (assuming that the effect of culture itself were held constant).

Variation in Standards Among Classrooms and Schools

In each of the four cultural samples the variance among clasrooms, boarding homes, or internats was tested against the variance of individual differences within groups for all variables. The results clearly showed that classroom variation was more often significant in the English than the American sample, and that boarding school differences were more often significant in the Swiss than the Soviet sample. Not only were individual items and the "manners" and "masculinity" factors sensitive to group variation in English and Swiss samples, but the MRL also differed among classrooms and boarding homes. To anticipate results described below, controlling for either age or socioeconomic status of parents had very little influence on these group differences within cultures.

The Influence of Age and Socioeconomic Status

Our data do not permit a meaningful analysis of the effects of age or socioeconomic status because of the generally restricted range of these variables in our samples. Average ages within cultures varied from 11.3 for the English to 13.6 for the Swiss. Age ranges were limited to three years in the English and American samples, four years in the Soviet, and seven years in the Swiss. Socioeconomic status data were not available for children in either Switzerland or the Soviet Union, where the majority came from broken homes. Occupational data for the fathers of the English and American children showed both samples to be skewed toward high status. To control for possible influences of age and social status, co-variance analyses were carried out within cultures. Controlling for either of these variables had no effect on sex differences in any of the four cultures, and only minor effects on differences among classrooms or schools. There was some evidence that status had an effect on values in the English sample where higher status children gave greater value to "manners" while lower status children gave greater relative value to "masculinity".

DISCUSSION

We may begin our discussion by examining cultural differences in the general tendency to ascribe importance to behavior standards, reflected by the MRL. Comparisons between members of pairs of cultures responding to comparable scales show that the tendency to give socially desirable answers was stronger in American than English children and in Soviet than Swiss children. Given our knowledge of these cultures, this suggests that the inclination to give socially desired responses varies directly with the general value in the culture given to conformity *vs* individualism. Ascribing importance to standards in general may also be associated with the context of peer group socialization, as shown by significant variation among English classrooms and among Swiss boarding homes. In fact, the results lead to the suggestion that when there is subcultural variation from group to group within a society, there is also less likely to be a high level of importance ascribed to behavior standards in general.

The factors of "manners" and "masculinity" emerged consistently in the factor analyses of the responses of English and Soviet children. They were especially clear in the ratings made by boys. "Manners" is the larger factor and is correlated with MRL in all cultures. The two rotated factors have low positive coefficients of congruence with each other, evidence pointing to orthogonality (Harman, 1960, p. 257). In their content they are similar to the semantic meaning dimensions of evaluation ("goodness-badness") and potency ("strength-weakness") (Osgood, 1962). Peterson (1965, p. 57) has pointed out how diverse forms of ratings of various social objects—the self, parents, peers—all tend to split into these dimensions plus an "activity-passivity" dimension. The evidence from this study is that evaluations of abstract forms of social behavior also tend to cluster on these dimensions.

That "goodness" and "strength" preferences should be different for boys and girls is not surprising. That this should hold only in English-speaking samples of children living with their parents and not for Swiss or Soviet boarding school pupils is perhaps less expected. What seems to have happened is that girls from each of the four cultures place about the same high value on "goodness" and low value on "strength". Although boys also give greater relative value to "goodness" than to "strength", it is only boys in the Soviet and Swiss boarding school samples who make as great a distinction as the girls between these two qualities. Boys from England and America who were socialized by their families (and children from broken homes were excluded from these two samples) give relatively less weight to the type of visible conformity expressed in the "manners" factor, and relatively more weight to the "all boy" and counter-dependent qualities contained in the "masculinity" factor.

We are suggesting that boys raised in institutional settings are likely to be more conforming to adult authority and less individualistically aggressive or self-assertive than their counterparts raised in intact families. In interpreting the results as a function of socialization context we are obviously going beyond what we can prove at present. We may also suspect selective recruiting into the Swiss and Soviet boarding schools—more children from broken homes, for example—as well as cultural differences independent of the context of socialization. We must also recognize that it may not be the specifically coeducational nature of the institution which makes boys more docile. If anything, the opposite may be true for boys (and girls) being raised in single-sex Swiss boarding homes since they tended even more in this direction than those in the coeducational homes. Thus it is possible that coeducational settings may provide a better basis for the development of traditional sex-role differences than all-male or all-female collectivities.

That the relative importance of these two standards of behavior varies among classrooms and boarding schools, for both sexes, within the English and Swiss societies, reminds us that other, more molecular processes also influence the relative value placed on "goodness" and "strength". Observation of teachers and boarding school directors points to individual differences in their standards and values and in their interaction with pupils, as a source of group differences. On the other hand, a separate analysis made of the American sample revealed that the sex of the teacher did not account for classroom differences in "masculinity" among boys, but indicated that residual classroom variation within the sex of the teacher may be associated with the school or school district, pointing to the community ecology of the classroom unit as a source of variation in standards of behavior. It is apparent that much remains to be done to further our understanding of the development of divergent group norms.

Turning to the specific items of the questionnaire, we have obtained results contributing to our understanding of both sex and cultural differences in standards of social behavior of children. Above and beyond these effects, however, is the impressive similarity across sexes and cultures in the overall ordering of the importance of these standards. We are reminded that our respondents were *school* children, engaged at least formally in the learning enterprise by the fact that telling the truth, asking questions, and being on time were among the more highly valued behaviors, and not asking for help was one of the least important. It is reasonable to suspect that the student role and the fact that we gathered our data in the school setting may have contributed to the similarities in value hierarchies across cultures.

The Four National Culture Samples

1. *The American.* Our approximately 250 sixth-grade boys and girls from ten public school classrooms in the suburbs of a northeastern city of about 200,000 averaged 11.9 years of age. They, more than their English contemporaries, rated behavior standards in general as important. There were large sex differences in the relative importance of "manners" and "masculinity", girls valuing the former more and boys the latter. There was little difference among classrooms, and differences in age and parental status were not generally associated with differences in standards. These children, more than those from the other societies, gave greater importance to telling the truth and (with the English) to seeking intellectual understanding.

2. *The English.* These 497 boys and girls from sixteen day school classrooms averaged less than eleven and one-half years old, the youngest of our samples, and attended schools extending from the southern edge of London through the suburbs into semi-rural Surrey. They tended to be less responsive to behavior standards in general. Their views of the importance of various standards were the most differentiated by their personal characteristics of the four samples. Not only were there extensive differences between boys and girls, but also there was much variation among classrooms and among socioeconomic status levels within classrooms. Overall, they differed from the other cultures in assigning greater importance to a standard of masculinity or strength involving both a stoical boyish ideal and some opposition to adult authority. Also (with the Americans) they valued telling the truth and seeking understanding.

3. *The Soviets.* Residing in three "internat" boarding schools in the vicinity

of Moscow, these 135 boys and girls averaged 12.2 years of age. Like the Americans, they tended to attribute strong importance to behavior standards in general. In keeping with the aims of Soviet collective educational philosophy, differences between sexes and age levels, and among schools, were minimal. In comparison to the other three cultures, these Soviet children placed greatest emphasis on overt propriety of behavior as measured by the "manners" factor—orderliness, cleanliness, and other forms of the control of disordered behavior—and relatively less emphasis on telling the truth and seeking intellectual understanding.

4. *The Swiss.* These 268 boys and girls were residents of coeducational boarding homes representing a variety of philosophies of socialization. They ranged in age from ten to seventeen with an average of over thirteen and one-half. They were less likely than Soviet children to rate all standards as important. While there were no sex differences in the importance of the various standards, there were extensive differences among the boarding homes. Differences in values among age levels were slight and did not account for differences among homes. Overall, these children respect adult authority and place less value on aggressive masculinity, but they also express preference for the substantive and constructive Calvinist virtues of individual industry and achievement—spending their time usefully and doing things on their own.

3. PSYCHOLOGICAL ECOLOGY OF A NURSERY SCHOOL

Myrna Beth Shure

Ecology is a science that deals with the mutual relations between organisms and their environment. An example of the concerns of this science is the finding that some organisms will thrive in one setting but perish in only a slightly different milieu. *Psychological ecology* is a relatively recent offshoot of the parent discipline, a new branch with its own proto-theories and rudimentary methodology, all oriented toward describing broadly defined environmental impacts on the behavior patterns of individuals and groups. For example, it is averred that in certain specifiable ways individuals behave church-like in churches, school-like in schools, playground-like on playing fields, and so on through many culturally defined correlations between environmental settings and appropriate behaviors.

The following question is typical of those asked by psychological ecologists. In what ways does the psychological ecology of contemporary nursery school, with its characteristic equipment and curricula, dictate the play activities of four-year-old boys and girls? This and many other interesting questions are raised and tentatively answered in the following study by Dr. Shure. For example, when four-year-olds are in the presence of art materials they are more likely than not to engage in activities relevant to artistic manipulation and production. Similarly, when boys and girls are in the presence of dolls and related equipment, they engage most frequently in those complex social interactions commonly associated with the dramatic make-believe of home and community living. Furthermore, boys and girls

SOURCE. Adapted and abridged from Myrna Beth Shure, "Psychological Ecology of a Nursery School," *Child Development*, 1963, Vol. 34, pp. 979-992. (With permission of the author and the publisher, Society for Research in Child Development.)

at four years of age are already responding to their environment in sex-appropriate ways. Sex differences concerning what is proper behavior in what situations are clearly evident by age four.

Educators who may be interested in influencing the behavior and life styles of children during the nursery school years will find many provocative leads in the findings of this study. For those with more methodological interests this investigation clearly demonstrates that the naturalistic method of inquiry can generate extremely useful information when imaginatively designed and rigorously applied.

Psychological ecology is the systematic investigation of physical-environmental influences on the behavior of individuals and groups. Barker and Wright (1954) have reported an extensive investigation of behavior in various physical settings in a small town in the Midwest. Their purpose was to describe as accurately as possible the frequency, duration, and complexity of selected behaviors. Psychological ecologists state that individuals perceive settings as appropriate for specific kinds of behavior and that certain behaviors occur year after year in spite of the changing personnel involved. For example, a level area, such as a football field or a school gymnasium, is often seen as a place "for running and romping in organized, exuberant activity". The size and arrangement of a room and the distribution of furniture and equipment are factors influencing behavior, allowing locomotion in some directions and providing obstacles in others. No study has been made of the psychological ecology of a nursery school.

The present study investigates the influence of some of the situational factors studied by Barker and Wright on the spontaneous behavior of preschool children as it occurs within certain areas of the indoor nursery school setting.

More specifically, interest is centered upon providing some basic descriptive and comparative data within the art, book, doll, games, and block areas in the 4-year-old section of a university nursery school. The study seeks to answer specific questions regarding:

1. Population density, as measured by the number of appearances within an area. Area is defined as a perceptually segregated physical location with designated appropriate activities.
2. Mobility, as determined by the frequency with which children move in and out of an area.
3. Appropriateness of an activity to a locale.
4. The quality of emotions.
5. The complexity of social participation.
6. Amount of constructiveness with play materials.
7. Sex differences in each of the items above.

The first four items are among those studied by Barker and Wright. They were chosen because they seemed applicable to a nursery school setting. The fifth item is a term used by Barker and Wright, but a slight revision of Parten's (1932) social participation categories (explained below) seemed more appropriate for preschool children. "Penetration of social interaction" as used by Barker and Wright (1954, p. 69) is more appropriate for the study of children of all ages in a small town. The constructiveness category was added to discover if certain play materials elicit more destructive behavior than others. Are there psychological forces in the block area, for example, that would suggest knocking down the blocks more often than, say, the amount of throwing puzzles off a table in the games area?

DESIGN AND PROCEDURES

Subjects

The subjects used in this investigation were seven boys and seven girls from the 4-year-old group enrolled in a university laboratory nursery school. With the exception of one boy and two girls, all of the children had also attended the same school during the preceding year.

Setting

The indoor areas for art, books, dolls, games, and blocks were chosen. The first four of these were located in one room. The block area was an adjoining room, and the largest of the areas. The art area was second in size, followed in descending order by the games, doll, and book areas.

The areas were equipped with materials typically found in American nursery schools. The physical structure of the areas and the placement of materials and equipment remained constant through the period of data collection. New materials were not presented, helping to reduce usage due to a novelty factor. The science corner was not studied as it was found during preliminary observations that appearances were very sporadic and usually due to unfamiliar materials brought to that area. Teachers were asked not to bring science materials during the periods of recording.

Observational Sampling Procedure

During the early morning free play period between 9:15 and 10:30, observations based on a systematic time-sampling technique were recorded beginning November 7, 1960, and ending March 20, 1961.

Each of the five areas was observed in prearranged order for 5 minutes and divided into 1-minute periods. The 1-minute segments were recorded in order to obtain more samples of behavior as well as to determine area mobility. After the last area was observed, the process was repeated so that each area was observed for 10 minutes during a recording session. Data collection continued until a total of 200 behavioral samples were obtained for each area, or 20 actual days of observation. Systematic rotation of areas was employed for each new day of recording.

Three other observational controls were utilized in this research. Recordings were not made for a period of one week before or after school vacations in order to minimize the effect of absence from school upon behavior. With the exception of only one day, the head teacher was always present to maintain as much consistency as possible regarding teacher effect upon behavior. Further, in order to obtain a representative picture of the group, at least 10 of the 14 children were present on each day of observation.

DEFINITIONS OF BEHAVIOR CATEGORIES

Participation

Relevant. The child is engaged in an activity or use of equipment appropriate to an area. Use of equipment not belonging to an area is considered appropriate if its use is related to an appropriate one. A child may be putting dolls on a "chair" made in the block area. Assigning roles of "mother" or "father" without actual use of equipment is considered an activity appropriate to the doll corner.

Irrelevant. The child is engaged in an activity or use of equipment inappropriate to an area. A child may dress a doll on the floor in the block area.

Absent. The child is not engaged in any activity, but is standing around, walking, or talking to others. He has no physical contact with materials.

Affect

Positive. The child is exhibiting a happy, cheerful mood as seen in action, facial expression, or verbalization. This includes laughing, smiling, humming, or singing, whether or not he is engaged in an activity.

Neutral. The child shows indifference or lack of concern.

Negative. The child is exhibiting a depressed unpleasant mood. This includes crying, whining, or pouting. "I don't like this," "You can't come in here," and hitting another child accompanied by overt signs of displeasure are included.

Constructiveness

Constructive. Any activity beyond merely holding or actually upsetting objects is included, such as building, molding, painting, placing objects from one place to another.

Neutral. The child is merely holding or touching an object.

Destructive. There is intentional throwing over or upsetting of any object.

This includes knocking down blocks, tearing up a painting, throwing objects such as a doll.

Absent. There is lack of contact with play materials or equipment.

Social Participation (modified Parten [1932] categories)

Unoccupied, solitary, solitary-same, onlooker, parallel, associative, and cooperative.

Recording Procedure

The numbers of each child occupying the area being watched were recorded in a vertical row. The first child was coded across all four major categories before the next child was begun, in order to obtain the behaviors as they were emitted simultaneously. This process was done within 60 seconds and repeated five times before beginning the next area.

Reliability

After a training period of one week, reliability was established in terms of how consistently two observers could classify each individual response as defined. Independent but simultaneous recordings were made three times at the beginning of the observational period and two times one month before the end of data collection. The formula

$$\frac{2 \text{ (number of agreements)}}{\text{number of judgments of A} + \text{number of judgments of B}}$$

yielded an agreement of 95 per cent. The total number of interobserver recordings made indicated almost perfect agreement between the raters.

RESULTS

Population Density

Table 1 reveals that for both the total number of appearances made as recorded minute by minute and for the number of different children appearing in the various areas, more time was spent in the block area with 772 total appearances and 143 different children as totaled over the 20 days. The art area was second with 490 and 116, respectively, with the book area being the least popular choice during the free play period with only 205 total appearances and 47 different children appearing over the total period of observation.

With the exception of the games area, all areas showed some noticeable sex differences in regard to both the total number of appearances and appearances by different children. Time spent by boys was greatest in the block area with 342 more total appearances than the girls and total time spent by girls was greatest in the art area with 236 more appearances than boys. Considering

TABLE 1
Population Density by Area and by Sex

	Art	Book	Doll	Games	Block
Total Number of Appearances					
Total group	490	205	316	323	772
Boys	127	77	110	166	557
Girls	363	128	206	157	215
		$\chi^2 = 892.54$; $df = 4$; $p < .01$			
Number of Appearances by Different Children					
Total group	116	47	87	99	143
Boys	37	19	33	51	86
Girls	79	28	54	48	57
		$\chi^2 = 83.34$; $df = 4$; $p < .01$			

appearances by different children, 42 more girls appeared in the art area than boys and 29 more boys appeared in the block area than girls. The doll corner and the book area ranked third and fourth respectively.

A chi square test on the differences between the number of actual observations of different boys and girls was not significant at the .05 level indicating that the null hypothesis that there are no differences between observations of different boys and girls cannot be rejected. This is important since it was the area that was observed, and the similarity of total observations for each sex makes it possible to compare the differences among areas. Chi square on over-all differences among both areas and differences by each sex within the different areas, with 4 degrees of freedom, was significant at less than the .01 level.

Area

Interest is now centered on differences in behavior emitted in the various areas. In comparing behaviors in the areas, deviations in the areas from the total behavior observed in the study were measured by the chi square test. Table 2 shows that in each of the four comparisons made the areas differed significantly among themselves, with probabilities in each case less than .01.

Participation

Of the total sample of the quality of behavior observed, all of the areas elicited more relevant activity than irrelevant or lack of activity (Table 2). However, the art area elicited the most relevant (84 per cent) while in the block area only 65 per cent of the play was appropriate to that locale. By the same token, the relative proportion of irrelevant and absent activity in the

TABLE 2

Frequency of Categories of Behavior by Area

	Art		Book		Doll		Games		Block		Total
	N	%	N	%	N	%	N	%	N	%	N
Participation											
Relevant	412	84	161	79	218	69	227	70	503	65	1521
Irrelevant	37	8	36	18	51	16	41	13	149	19	314
Absent	41	8	8	4	47	15	55	17	120	16	271
Total	490	100	205	101	316	100	323	100	772	100	2106

$\chi^2 = 76.50;\ df = 8;\ p < .01$

Affect											
Positive	167	34	74	36	154	49	107	33	327	42	829
Negative	18	4	3	1	21	7	5	2	52	7	99
Neutral	305	62	128	62	141	45	211	65	393	51	1178
Total	490	100	205	99	316	101	323	100	772	100	2106

$\chi^2 = 58.60;\ df = 8;\ p < .01$

Constructiveness											
Constructive	402	82	170	83	205	65	219	68	400	52	1396
Destructive	6	1	3	1	11	3	9	3	51	7	80
Neutral	34	7	8	4	51	16	31	10	154	20	278
Absent	47	10	24	12	49	16	64	20	167	22	351
Total	489	100	205	100	316	100	323	101	772	101	2105

$\chi^2 = 193.42;\ df = 12;\ p < .01$

Social Participation											
Single child	101	22	38	19	62	19	116	36	215	28	532
Awareness	237	49	100	49	50	16	113	35	167	22	667
Social interaction	149	30	66	32	200	63	87	27	378	49	880
Total	487	101	204	100	312	98	316	98	760	99	2079

$\chi^2 = 223.91;\ df = 8;\ p < .01$

block area was about twice as great as in the art area. The proportion of absent activity was lowest (4 per cent) in the book area.

Affect

The quality of affect did not differ markedly from area to area (Table 2). The proportion of positive affect in the doll corner was slightly greater than in the art, book, and game areas. The proportion of neutral affect was least in the doll corner and slightly greater in the block area. The amount of negative affect was negligible in all areas.

Constructiveness

There was more constructive use of materials than destructive or neutral handling in every area (Table 2). The proportion of constructive use of materials was greatest in the art and book areas. The block area elicited the lowest proportion of constructiveness. Neutral handling of materials occurred one fifth of the time in the block area, with the doll corner showing only slightly less. The relative frequency of occupancy in the games and block areas without any use of materials was twice as great as such activity in the art and book areas. Destructive use of materials was negligible in amount in every area.

Social Participation

The subcategories were grouped for statistical analysis. Play involving a *single child* unaware of others includes the solitary and solitary-same subcategories. Play that displays *awareness* but lack of social interaction includes the onlooker and parallel subcategories. Play involving complex *social interaction* includes the associative and cooperative play subcategories. The behaviors tallied as "unoccupied" were omitted, since there were only 26 in the total sample.

Play involving a single child was exhibited most often in the block and games area (Table 2). In the former area, this was predominantly solitary-same behavior; in the latter, predominantly solitary. About half of the play in both the art and book areas was simple awareness, predominantly of a parallel quality. The proportion of awareness, only, was less in the other areas. Complex social interaction occurred most often in the doll corner. Half of the play in the block area was of this quality, mostly classified originally as associative.

Sex Differences

In participation the boys and girls differed significantly in the art, doll, and block areas. The boys engaged in irrelevant activity proportionately more often than the girls in the art and doll areas; the girls more often than the boys in the block area. In the art and doll areas the girls engaged in more relevant behavior than the boys while in the block area the reverse was true. Comparing the girls among themselves in the five areas, the proportion of time spent in the block area irrelevantly was about four times greater than the proportion of irrelevant behavior in the other areas. The boys were most often irrelevant in the doll area.

Comparing boys against girls as to affect across all areas, the difference was statistically significant. The boys showed more positive affect and the girls less in the games and block areas to a significant extent. The boys expressed more content in the doll corner, but the amount of positive affect did not differ greatly from area to area. Girls were content almost twice as often, proportionately, in the doll as in the games area and showed an inverse proportion of neutral behavior in the two areas.

Because expected frequencies of destructive behaviors were so small in three of the areas, it was necessary to combine destructive and neutral behaviors in the statistical analysis. Sex differences in constructiveness were statistically significant only in the doll and block areas. The boys showed more destructive behavior in these two areas than in the others. The girls were constructive in the doll area, but more "absent" in the block area.

Boys engaged in a greater proportion of associative play than girls in the doll corner, the difference being greater than in any other area. Girls engaged in more cooperative play than boys, but the proportion of associative play was almost as high by girls in that area. Girls emitted more cooperative play in the doll corner than in any other area. The amount of parallel behavior by girls was comparatively greater than boys in the book area, with onlookers activity much less in that area than in any other. Girls emitted almost three times as much solitary play, proportionately, in the block area as compared to the boys.

DISCUSSION

Behavior within Areas as Suggested by Selection and Arrangement of Play Materials

During the free play period from 9:15 to 10:30 at the university nursery school, when the children were most likely to be found in the different areas, more children occupied the block area than any other area studied, with the art area being second. Since it was the *area* being studied, rather than the direct use of play materials, the findings will not be compared to earlier studies regarding specific materials. In the present study, the children may have been engaged in activity other than direct use of the materials. For example "playing house" in the doll corner was considered a relevant activity for that area, but if no actual play materials were being used it was scored as *absent constructiveness*. Blocks were found to elicit the least amount of constructiveness as compared to materials in the other areas. However, there was three times as much neutral handling without actual manipulation of materials in the block area as compared to the art. It is possible that in the block area the high population density may have stimulated the higher proportion of onlooking activity as compared to the other areas, making it difficult to manipulate the materials with which they had previously been engaged. Therefore, they may hold the materials until the activity they were watching has terminated. Thus, it appears that, while in the present study the children were found in the block area more often, the children were constructive with the art materials a greater proportion of the time. Further, the relatively high proportions of neutral handling and absent constructiveness (lack of use of materials) in the block area may be due to the high proportion of complex social interaction in that area. The children may have spent a large proportion of the time talking to or playing with each other in activities not involving play materials such as dancing or jumping. Notice that the proportion of irrelevant activity (possibly without use of materials) is high in comparison to most of the other areas. Further, the presence of the lockers and piano near the block area may have stimulated social interaction without actual use of materials.

Physical Space, Arrangement, and Size of Equipment

More children occupied the block area than any other area studied. In addition, they remained there for the greatest length of time, with the exception of the book area. It happens that the block area is the largest in physical size, meaning that possibly more children can occupy in comfortably. At the same time, the book area, with the smallest population density, is the smallest in physical size. Since they were also stable, it may be that the number of children in an area is related to physical size, but not how often they move in and out. The high social interaction in the doll corner may be partly a function of the small size of the area, bringing the children in close physical proximity. The relatively high proportion of associative activity in the art area may be partly due to the close physical proximity when the children are sitting at the art table.

Perhaps Parten's (1932) definition of parallel play is, indeed, a function of the size of the area. According to Parten, parallel play involves playing *near* another child with the same or similar play materials. However, a child may have been playing with the same or similar play materials and yet not be near another child. This would be possible in the larger areas. When such behavior occurred, it was classified as solitary-same in the present study. In the largest locale, the block area, there was almost five times as much play classified as solitary-same as parallel, whereas Parten would have classified all such play as parallel. Conversely, in the book area, the smallest in physical size, there was almost seven times as much parallel as play of the solitary-same quality.

Certainly there are other explanations influencing children's choice of activity. For example, in relation to sex-role conditioning, Brown (1958) reports that girls may play with toys typically associated with male activities but the boys are discouraged from playing with toys associated with female activities. He found that boys of all ages showed a strong preference for the masculine role between the ages of $3\frac{1}{2}$ to $5\frac{1}{2}$. This may account for the present finding that girls chose the block area as their second choice but that boys chose the games area as their second choice (not typically associated with female activities). Fauls and Smith (1956) add that boys especially choose occupations as perceived appropriate by the parent of the same sex. Also, friendship groups must influence choice of activity.

Some of the numerous questions that could be asked of further research imply causal factors in relation to situational factors. Would a rearrangement or addition of equipment change some of the frequencies of the behavior found in this study? For example, in the doll corner, boys' activities were irrelevant more often than girls' in this area. Perhaps more masculine play materials relevant to the area could be used such as men's hats, shoes, and pipes as suggested by Hartley, Frank, and Goldenson (1952). This may also increase constructive use of materials. The influence of use of irrelevant materials in areas would be interesting. For example, does the location of one area in relation to another influence the frequency of any particular interdependence of areas? Would a placement of the doll corner near the block area influence more play by girls in constructive, if irrelevant activity in the block area? Or, would such a placement even influence more girls to actually play with blocks? Further, how would the size of an area affect the complexity of constructiveness? Would smaller areas be more frustrating to the children, thus reducing complexity as suggested by Barker, Dembo, and Lewin (1943) and Wright (1942)?

In relation to social participation, would larger areas reduce the amount of parallel play and do smaller areas enhance complex social interaction? Or, would large areas with few play materials increase the need for social interaction and reduce the amount of solitary play?

SUMMARY

Based on a study of the psychology ecology of a small town by Barker and Wright (1954), the present research was designed to describe and compare patterns of behavior as they occurred in the naturalistic physical environment of five indoor areas (art, book, doll, games, block) of a nursery school. The subjects consisted of seven boys and seven girls from the 4-year-old group. Systematic observations of 200 behavioral samples at 5-minute intervals were recorded in each area during the free play period of 9:15 to 10:30, when the children were most likely to be found in the different areas. Interest was specifically centered upon the number of appearances in each area, their mobility, whether activity was relevant to an area, the children's affect, the constructiveness of the behavior, and the complexity of social participation.

The most important results are:

1. Of the five areas sampled, the block area was most popular, especially for boys, and the art area second, preferred by the girls. The book area was the least populated during the free play period. With the exception of the games area, all showed some sex differences in regard to frequency of appearances.

2. For the total sample, the games area was the most mobile, while the book and block areas had the least number of children moving in and out of them.

3. All of the areas elicited more relevant activity than irrelevant or lack of activity. A greater proportion of boys' play than girls' was irrelevant in the

art area and doll corner. Girls, on the other hand, spent a greater proportion of time in irrelevant activity than boys in the block area.

4. While positive affect was slightly more evident in the doll corner, neutral affect was most marked as a whole while negative affect was negligible in all the areas. Boys emitted more expression of content than girls in the games and block areas.

5. Constructive use of materials occurred most frequently in every area, especially in the art and book areas. Girls had the least amount of contact with materials when in the block area.

6. The doll corner elicited the greatest proportion of complex social interaction, with boys engaging in more associative activity and girls in more cooperative play. The proportion of play involving a single child was relatively more frequent in the block and games areas. The block area, however, also elicited a high proportion of complex social interaction. The proportion of play involving awareness of others without interaction, predominantly of a parallel nature, was greatest in the art and book areas.

The relatively high proportions of simple holding and lack of use of materials in the doll and block areas may be a function of the high frequency of complex social interaction when the children played in those areas.

4. THE CULTURALLY DEPRIVED CHILD

Frank Riessman

At the time of this writing, there is a strong social concern for the victims of poverty, political disenfranchisement, unstable social conditions, prejudice, and so on through the series of what are regarded generally as deleterious conditions for comfortable, civilized living. The conscience of the average American citizen has been sorely pricked by the realization that his culture is not without its serious social inequities. The sting will not go away and the thoughtful American has currently resolved to take action toward correcting some of these social evils. There is an old saying that the road to Hell is paved with good intentions. Will our good intentions and new programs of social action, all designed to correct as many social inequities as possible, lead us up the road to righteousness, or may we unknowingly create equally troublesome conditions for living by our ignorance of what is good and what is bad in the situations we are trying to reform? The following analysis of some of the strengths and weaknesses inherent in the "underprivileged" family shows clearly that we must be continuously on our guard against throwing out the good with the bad when we seek to ameliorate the social disadvantages experienced by members of underprivileged families.

In this era of what some critics have called a time of pervasive alienation, it would be foolish to overlook the advantages of psychological support provided by the extended family that is frequently found among the underprivileged. The debits of broken, overcrowded homes must be balanced

SOURCE. Adapted and abridged from pp. 36-48 of Frank Riessman, *The Culturally Deprived Child*. New York: Harper and Co., 1962. (With permission of the author and Harper and Co.)

against children's reliance on each other in these situations, and their obvious enjoyment of each other's company. Overprotection which is characteristic of so many middle social-economic homes must be balanced against the neglect but resultant self-reliance in the underprivileged homes.

The negative side of the underprivileged family is easy to see: the family may be prematurely broken by divorce, desertion, and death; the home is overcrowded, the housing facilities inadequate; considerable economic insecurity prevails; both parents frequently work, and thus the children may be neglected; and typically the irritable, tired parents use physical punishment in order to maintain discipline.

But there is another side of the family which should not be ignored. Two things stand out immediately: there are many children, and there are many parents or parent substitutes. The home typically includes aunts, uncles, and grandparents, all of whom may, to some degree, play a parental role. This pattern is technically known as "the extended family." In the Negro family the grandmother often plays a most decisive role. This is well portrayed in the play, "A Raisin in the Sun."

The key to much of the family life is security and protection. The large extended family provides a small world in which one is accepted and safe. If help is needed, the family is the court of first resort and will provide it, at least to some extent. Time and energy, rather than money, are the chief resources provided. Hand-me-down clothes may be passed on to needy members; the mother's sister may work a little extra to supplement the limited budget. But it is in the providing of the services of helping with children or in the household generally that major aid is provided.

One of the reasons why some underprivileged parents like to have many children seems to be related to the role the family plays as a security-giving agency. The family is seen as a major source of strength in a difficult, unstable world.

Many commentators have placed considerable importance on broken homes as the source of emotional instability, mental illness, juvenile delinquency, and the like. The broken home, however, may not, among the deprived, imply family disorganization (nor does it necessarily have the same implications for a deprived child that it might in a middle-class home). To think of the underprivileged family as consisting of a father, mother, and children alone is to miss vital aspects of this family today.

THE FAMILY-CENTERED HOME

The home is a crowded, busy, active, noisy place where no one child is focused upon. There are too many children for this, and the parents have too little time. Consequently, the children spend much more time in each other's company and with the relatives. Individualism and self-concern on the part of the children is much less likely to emerge and is, in fact, discouraged in this more family-centered home.

Intense parent-child relationships are infrequent, and while the danger of parental rejection is present, overprotection is out of the question.

The atmosphere is much more communal and, to some extent, cooperative. For example, it is not at all uncommon to see a six- or seven-year-old child taking his younger brother across the street, holding him by the hand and watching for cars. Nor is it rare to see a mother buy an ice cream cone which she passes from one child to the other to share.

Sibling rivalry and fear of a new baby brother seem to develop somewhat less here. Perhaps this is because the children never have had that much attention in the first place, and have less to lose. Perhaps, also, the fact that the children depend so much on contact with each other, rather than being overly dependent upon the parents, plays a decisive role. Whatever the reason, there does appear to be far less jealousy and competitiveness.

In light of the different structure of the family and the lack of intense parent-child relationships, many of the classic psychoanalytic formulations, such as the Oedipus complex, may have to be revised when viewing the underprivileged.

DISCIPLINE AND LOVE

While the last ten years have produced conflicting evidence and opposing interpretations of various aspects of the child rearing of the deprived, there is one area, at least, in which all the evidence agrees. This concerns the parental use of physical punishment as a major source of discipline. This, of course, reflects the traditional approach to life, as well as the physical style of the deprived.

The possibly deleterious effects of punishment have been well argued: it may result in a negative attitude toward the person who administers the punishment; it generally does not develop a flexible, reasoned understanding of why the proscribed behavior is wrong; frequently it is ineffective in halting the forbidden practice; it can be debasing to the dignity of the recipient; it can eventuate in deep, frustrated feelings and latent aggression. Undoubtedly many of these potential consequences affect the deprived child in the expected fashion.

But in recent years the attitude of psychologists toward punishment has changed somewhat. Dr. Benjamin Spock writes:

> In the olden days children were spanked plenty, and nobody thought

much about it. Then a reaction set in, and many parents decided that it was shameful. But that didn't settle everything.

If any angry parent keeps himself from spanking, he may show his irritation in other ways, for instance, by nagging the child for half the day, or trying to make him feel deeply guilty. I'm not particularly advocating spanking, but I think it is less poisonous than lengthy disapproval, because it clears the air for both parent and child (Spock, 1957).

Psychological research now indicates that under certain conditions punishment can be effective and anticipated negative consequences may not necessarily occur. This is true if the punishment is not too severe or overpowering, and if alternative actions are available to substitute for the punished acts (Morgan, 1956, p. 115).

In their recent study, Miller and Swanson found that it is mixed discipline (a combination of physical and psychological forms of discipline) that has the best consequences. They state that boys trained in this manner are more "realistic," "are neither uncontrolled or overly constricted." Their data indicate that while the underprivileged use more physical punishment, and the middle class more psychological techniques (e.g., withholding of love), the mixed form of discipline occurs more frequently among the deprived (Miller and Swanson, 1960, pp. 399, 426).

Since physical punishment is part of the everyday pattern among the disadvantaged, there is probably considerable adaptation to it and it is not perceived as a major threat to the ego; as physical punishment and aggression generally are expressed rather easily and directly, it is unlikely that they have the sadistic overtones that often produce the negative correlates of punishment.

Although the consequences of punishment may not necessarily be bad, the question of its effectiveness as a deterrent to proscribed behavior is a different issue. Punishment is apparently ineffective in deterring aggression. Not only does it fail to halt aggressive behavior in deprived children, but in some cases it actually leads to an increase in this behavior. On the other hand, punishment seems to be successful in stopping masturbation, thumb sucking, dependency, and numerous other behaviors disapproved by lower socio-economic groups.

Since punishment appears to be so effective in these areas, why is it notoriously ineffective in preventing aggression among the underprivileged? A number of possibilities suggest themselves in light of the culture of the deprived. First, there seems to be considerable ambivalence toward aggression in this culture. While it is rejected as a form of response to the parents and family, it is expected that the child will stand up for himself, and fight if necessary, in the outer environment. Secondly, the parents themselves express anger in administering physical punishment. In a sense, they provide a model for imitation. Although they tell the child not to be aggressive, they themselves are aggressive in punishing him. They appear to be saying, "Do as I say but not as I do."

Why do underprivileged parents use punishment so freely? This practice is frequently interpreted as restrictive and unloving. However, with the peculiar problems that plague their lives, with large families often crowded into small apartments, and with both parents working, the problem of discipline becomes a difficult one. Popularly held notions of permissiveness cannot easily be applied. Respect and obedience without a lot of arguing and "reasoning" is probably much more convenient when the parents come home tired from a hard day's work. They are in no mood to cajole the children and they resort much more quickly to physical punishment—not sadistic beatings, but a quick slap and a strong tone.

A number of studies have noted that deprived individuals strongly, and more frequently, support the statement that "the most important thing a child should learn is respect and obedience to his parents" (Riessman, 1955). Not only parents, but older people in general are to be obeyed and respected. After all, if neighbors and relatives, including grandparents, are to take part in child rearing, respect for older people is important.

Underprivileged people do not see discipline as inconsistent with love; that is, they do not feel when they punish a child that this might indicate a lack of love for him.

"Love," the keynote of middle-class child rearing, plays a much less central role among the deprived, where it is taken for granted and not something that the child must win, nor something that he loses by disobeying. If the child is "bad" he gets a "belt" rather than a conversation. He is not told that "Mommy won't love him if he isn't good."

Control of children is not exerted by the withholding of love but through punishment. A child is expected to do what he is told, not because he wants to demonstrate love for his parents; rather, he does it because it is expected, and if he does not do it he will be punished. He does not accrue love by doing, nor lose it by not doing.

The meaning of love is different where it must be earned and where it is regarded as involved in all one does. A reprimand can then seem to indicate a lack of love by the parent. It need not have this meaning where parental authority is unquestioned and children are expected to perform their roles without the reward or deprivation of love.

When a child disobeys and his mother "whacks" him, he knows what he is being punished for, and it is soon over. His mother has indicated that she disapproves of his behavior but, because she has not threatened him with the loss of love, it would seem the child is assured of her continued feeling for him.

FUNCTIONAL RESPONSIBILITY

Davis and Havighurst found that middle-class parents expect their children to learn to cook, sew, help in the house, and generally assume responsibility at an earlier age than do underprivileged parents (Davis and Havighurst, 1952). Other studies also indicate that the deprived child is not expected to pick up his own toys, or put away his own clothes, at as early an age as his middle-class counterpart. Middle-class respondents when interviewed stated that the child should be on his own as early as possible.

These findings are surprising in light of the fact that deprived children are expected to get jobs after school at an earlier age, and often they appear older and more mature. Moreover, since both parents work and are likely not to be at home as much, one would expect that the children would be given more household assignments as part of the division of labor that characterizes the extended family.

How then can the findings of Davis and Havighurst be explained? The authors themselves have an illuminating interpretation.

> The explanation probably lies in a tendency on the part of middle-class people to train their children early for achievement and responsibility, while lower-class people train their children to take responsibility only after the child is old enough to make the effort of training pay substantial returns in the work the child will do. Middle-class parents can afford to use time to train children ... at such an early age that the children cannot repay this training effort by their actual performance, although they may repay it by adopting attitudes of self-achievement and responsibility. (Davis and Havighurst, 1952, p. 549.)

The deprived apparently are more concerned with what might be termed functional responsibility rather than symbolic training for the future.

Another indication of functional responsibility training is found in a study reported by Bronfenbrenner.[1] Here middle-class children were taught to *start* dressing and feeding themselves at an earlier age than deprived children.

---

[1] Bronfenbrenner does not share Davis and Havighurst's view of the data on responsibility. He simply summarizes all the data showing that the middle-class parents, in general, expect their children to pick up their toys at an earlier age, cook earlier, etc. As the majority of the items are in this direction, he is able to conclude that the lower class demands less responsibility. It is only by observing contradictions among the items that Davis and Havighurst were able to develop their interpretation. See Urie Bronfenbrenner, "Socialization and Social Class Through Time and Space," in *Readings in Social Psychology* by Eleanor E. Maccoby, Theodore M. Newcomb, and Eugene L. Hartley, third edition, (New York: Henry Holt, 1958), pp. 400–425.

However, the deprived child was able to *completely* feed and dress himself earlier than the middle-class child. The mother of the underprivileged child apparently introduced the training at an age where it could be effective, while the middle-class parent was satisfied to have the child make some effort at dressing and feeding, in a sense, looking responsible and independent even though this served no immediate functional purpose.

THE QUESTION OF SEX

The attitude of the deprived toward sex is something of an enigma. Much of the evidence is, on the surface, contradictory. On the one hand there is Kinsey's (1948) well-known data which indicate that premarital intercourse is far more frequent among lower socio-economic groups. Teachers' observations that pregnancy is more common among teen-age girls in culturally deprived areas is in the same direction. Common-law marriages and broken homes are certainly more frequent also. On the other hand, there is evidence that does not fit into this picture as neatly. Doctors working in poor neighborhoods have told us that these women have a more puritanical, inhibited attitude toward sex. This seems to be confirmed by a recent study in Chicago by Lee Rainwater (1961). Moreover, Kinsey's data show that the women, unlike the men, do not have more frequent premarital sex relations.

Various studies indicate that deprived parents are much less likely to permit their children to walk around naked in the house, and they are less apt to appear unclothed in front of their children (Sears, et al., 1957). The studies also reveal that these families, far from encouraging indulgence of the child's sexual play with himself, are more concerned than middle-class parents with preventing masturbation. (This effort *may* be undesirable, but it certainly does not indicate any easy indulgence of the impulses of the child.) The deprived child is much more likely to be punished for masturbatory acts than is the middle-class child (whose parents may be more attuned to the new demands of permissive upbringing).

Some recent research has brought into question another attitude toward sexual practices. It has been widely accepted that illegitimacy is more widespread among lower socio-economic groups. The California studies of Clark Vincent (1954) on unwed mothers raise some doubt about this belief. Vincent found that illegitimacy among the deprived was far greater than among the middle class, if one examined the public hospital records, but that *illegitimate births among middle-class individuals were far* more frequent when data were collected from private doctors. Data on abortions are, of course, much more difficult to obtain, although Kinsey's data suggest that abortion has become a common practice in all classes.

After examining these contradictory findings and impressions, it is most difficult to arrive at any clear-cut, unambiguous conclusion, but a few tentative intrepretations are possible. The attitude toward nudity in the home can perhaps best be explained in terms of the crowded living conditions characteristic of deprived life. If the parents and children sleep in the same room, and a number of children sometimes sleep in the same bed, a permissive attitude toward nudity might prove dangerous. Similarly, the strong parental inhibition of masturbation may be rooted in the close living arrangements of the family.

These attitudes indicate a strong taboo against sexual behavior. If this is true, how can we explain the frequently observed pregnancies among adolescent girls? This is a difficult question. In attempting to answer it, perhaps first we should assume that the conditions of deprived life—limited supervision of children, crowded homes—produce a strain toward sexual behavior at an earlier age. To some extent the parents may recognize this danger and attempt to counteract it. This effort is expressed in their attitudes toward nudity, masturbation, and the like. But sometimes the life conditions are too powerful and overcome the inhibitions. When this takes place, and pregnancy results, the attitude seems to be one of resignation and both the girl and the child are accepted as part of the family.

Recently at a P.T.A. meeting, a Negro woman made a distinction about illegitimacy which many of us may not be aware of. In her eyes the worst thing an unwed mother could do would be to surrender the child to an adoption agency. Abortion also was looked upon with some disfavor. Keeping the illegitimate child and accepting the responsibility was the most favored solution to this difficult problem. It is not to be covered up, "hypocritically denied," once the mistake has been made. Unfortunately this is often misunderstood by the outside observer, who sees illegitimacy as going hand in hand with a light and "irresponsible" attitude toward marriage. The deprived, just as the middle class, prefer legitimate children in legitimate marriages. When something goes wrong, and this apparently occurs in all classes according to the statistics, the deprived prefer to incorporate the child in the household and to accept the attendant responsibilities.

There are a few other dimensions to the attitude toward sex. The traditionalism of the underprivileged is an important factor in contributing to the more puritanical attitudes, and to the patriarchal feature expressed in the greater freedom for the male (evidenced by Kinsey's findings). To some extent, the traditionalism is counterbalanced, particularly among the younger groups, by the search for excitement, and sex is a well-promoted avenue for this search.

Another consideration is the fact that the deprived adolescent is far more of an adult in that he is already employed or anticipates working in a short time, and he is much less dependent on his parents. Under these circumstances it is more likely that he will engage in adult sexual practices at an earlier age.

Finally, there are sub-groups differences among the deprived that have to be taken into account in understanding the sexual mores. For example, a large section of the Negro group has a matriarchal family structure where the mother and grandmother play powerful roles. The attitude toward sex is likely to be somewhat different in this setting than in the more typically patriarchal cultures.

While we feel we have shed some light on the sexual attitudes of the deprived, it must be confessed that there is still much that is unclear.

ACTION IMPLICATIONS

Teachers, P.T.A. leaders, and school administrators should recognize the significance of the "extended" family and utilize it in the attempt to effect changes in the child. For example, in considering college for the economically deprived child, guidance counselors should recognize that the family will frequently pool its resources and take extra jobs in order to send *one* of the children to college.

Instead of absorbing blame, the family, if worked with properly, can perhaps play a powerful role in combating juvenile delinquency. Thus, strong efforts should be made to enlist the aid of members of the extended family.

Juvenile delinquency is often explained, in an oversimplified manner, as resulting from broken families and insufficient love and attention. If we recognize the role of the larger family we cannot accept this explanation quite so readily.

The teacher should work closely with the family, and through respecting it, build a basis of mutual respect which the parents can help transfer to the child. Suggestions from the family should be encouraged and *acted upon*. Too often suggestions are elicited from parents in the course of attempting to establish good relations with them, only to be forgotten or ignored later. A great deal can be learned from the parents about the community, ethnic differences, and cultural traditions.

In this connection, a new position has been developed in a number of school systems, called School-Community Coordinator, whose job it is to interpret the school to the parents, and interpret the *parents to the school*. To be successful, he has to be a two-way communicator.[2]

RESPECT VS. LOVE

While underprivileged children strongly desire physical warmth, it would be a mistake to believe that they want intense affection. Very often teachers

---

[2] In some areas there is a Puerto Rican Community Coordinator, whose special function it is to integrate the school and the Puerto Rican community, interpreting each to the other. In some cases these coordinators are not highly trained people, but rather "informal leaders" who have close ties to the neighborhood and its traditions.

from a non-deprived background misread a child's desire for physical expression and assume that it is "love" that he wants.

Deprived children need respect rather than "love" from their teacher. The teacher need not be a substitute parent! Love is not a major issue in the deprived home; it is not used as a discipline technique, and the child generally does not feel that he must win love or that he can lose it. Respect, on the other hand, is something that the child is not likely to have received in the culture at large. This lack of respect is closely connected to his feelings of alienation and resentment. Too many people (in society at large) deprecate him and laugh at him. He himself knows that he is ignorant. He needs a teacher who will stand by him, someone on whom he can depend. For him to be accepted despite his initial hostility and defiance is paramount.

THE PROBLEM OF PUNISHMENT

The fact that the parents of deprived children employ physical punishment as a major source of discipline presents a serious problem for the teacher because this practice is rightly condemned in the school system. Probably the best way the teacher can emulate the parental discipline, without employing corporal punishment, is by being definite, authoritative, "strict." (Classroom "rebellion" is more a reflection of the child's feeling of alienation from the school than a basic reaction to authority.)

The parents of deprived children often punish them by restriction of privileges, and this pattern can easily be imitated by the teacher. The great danger to be avoided is the protracted reasoning and arguing about rules and regulations that is so popular in modern homes, but is most ineffective with the deprived child who has had little of this type of experience. On the other hand, there is a technique that has been employed successfully, which does allow for the discussion of rules. This is the "mock court," in which other children try the offender in a make-believe classroom court. Here the laws can be argued and justice can be explained. But this has to be used carefully, with full preparation of the children involved; otherwise it can become a farce, where the teacher attempts to impose *her* justice.

THE LIMITS OF TRADITIONAL PSYCHOTHERAPY

There is now considerable evidence that the standard psychological approaches are not attractive to most deprived people, and, in fact, may be somewhat inappropriate for them. Psychoanalytic formulations in particular require considerable modification in order to be applicable to deprived individuals. Most psychoanalytic therapy is based on the assumption of a middle-class, love-oriented childhood pattern and its presumed repetition in the therapeutic situation. In the light of the different emphasis on love in the deprived family, this may be a misleading assumption. The fact that this family includes many adults ("parent substitutes"), a less intense relationship of child to parent and more sibling contact, also has bearing on psychoanalytic concepts and treatment.

Most psychiatric practice takes place either in the well-furnished office of the therapist, or in a hospital setting. Recently it has been observed that home visits by the psychiatrists to the families of the deprived have led to much improved rapport between patients and doctors. Moreover, the psychiatrists report that they see the problem in a different light when it is observed in the family setting.

BALANCE SHEET: STRENGTHS AND WEAKNESSES

Drawing up a balance sheet listing strengths and weaknesses of the underprivileged is not an easy task. Although some traits have fairly clear positive or negative consequences, others are more ambiguous. On the liability side of the ledger are: narrowness of traditionalism, pragmatism, and anti-intellectualism; limited development of individualism, self-expression, and creativity; frustrations of alienation; political apathy; suggestibility and naïveté; boring occupational tasks; broken, over-crowded homes.

On the asset side are: the cooperativeness and mutual aid that mark the extended family; avoidance of the strain accompanying competitiveness and individualism; equalitarianism, informality, and warm humor; freedom from self-blame and parental over-protection; the children's enjoyment of each other's company, and lessened sibling rivalry; the security found in the extended family and in a traditional outlook.

Much more unclear are the effects of the quest for excitement, the alienation, the stubbornness, the desire for strong leadership, the early marriages, the attitudes toward sex, the role of love, the parent substitutes in the home and the development of Oedipal resolutions, and the effects of corporal punishment.

CHAPTER 2

Interactive Processes During Socialization

An important product of socialization is the mastery of social skills involved in interacting with others. The child must learn expectations about given social situations and how to differentiate among them. Through interpersonal interaction, he learns the ways in which he can express himself in these situations, the ways in which he can adapt to them, and the ways in which he can modify them constructively. Simultaneously, general behavioral tendencies are acquired that become reflected in the way these skills are implemented. Thus, one may observe that the dominant behaviors which characterize the child's personality might be dependent or independent, aggressive or unaggressive, withdrawn or outgoing, and so on. In the main, these complex processes are acquired informally, nevertheless their acquisition is not a matter of chance. Socialization is part of a cultural plan which can differ radically from culture to culture and from subculture to subculture; but there are always agencies and institutions to regulate, in formal and informal ways, the execution of this plan.

Within the social context, the child is sometimes considered the *object* of socialization and the parent, teacher, or other influential person in the process is the *agent*. Several steps may be hypothesized to occur, in this relationship, that will affect the child's social skills: Initially, there is a period during which he is wholly dependent on the adult. He quickly adopts some relatively primitive behaviors for obtaining help that are reinforced by gratification from the mother. Then there is a growing social bond between the two. With further development, absence of the adult may cause consternation and the presence of an unfamiliar person may provoke anxiety or worry. This dependent relationship makes available a broad spectrum of social responses acquired through a variety of processes including reinforcement and imitation in playful situations with adults and peers. These behaviors are then channeled for use in appropriate situations and are used even more selectively in adapting to novel situations.

There are environmental factors that are also to be considered. There is a great deal of similarity among people within a given social milieu. Some characteristics of the environment are unchanging. Physical laws, for example, work the same way for all people, so behaviors learned in adjusting to these will be very similar for all people. In the social realm there are relatively constant demands, too. Societies not only provide opportunities but they also place constraints on behavioral expression. Thus, while change may be permitted it is generally possible to do so only around a relatively stable fulcrum of normative behavior even during periods of revolutionary change.

The kind of model described thus far for examining interactive processes is a relatively static one. There was a time in the history of developmental psychology, however, when it appeared to provide a sufficient explanation of socialization. In general, there was an object to be molded into a given pattern and there was an agent who was the instrument of this change. It was natural, from this viewpoint, to place a great deal of emphasis on child-rearing practices. At first such practices as time of weaning and the characteristics of toilet training were considered important variables. Later, broader practices such as amount of permissiveness, democratic control, or warmth proved to provide more fruitful descriptions of family climate with predictable effects on the child's developmental status. As helpful as these early explanations were, it became apparent that an elaborated model would be necessary to account for the stability of trends in personality development as well as the similarities to be found from person to person.

In more current socialization models, it is still accepted, of course, that the object, instruments, and agents of socialization occur in a somewhat orderly social context. The social environment is organized according to relatively explicit sets of formal rules. However, they are rarely organized in any specifically prescribed fashion by the individual whose behavior, nevertheless, is structured by them. Among these are the parent behaviors employed to govern the child's behavior in accordance with cultural demands which are, thereby, informally passed on to the child. He in turn also manages his own behavior in accordance with these rules, not as they are stated, nor as they are interpreted by the parent or other person, but in terms of his own perceptions and interpretations. Such processes result in sometimes subtle, sometimes radical transformations of the socialization goals. It would appear that, in any one generation, such goals undergo at least two transformations: one made by the adult and one made by the child. The interpersonal relationship is always a dynamic one with the child playing a role in determining which behaviors will be employed and what the nature of these behaviors will be.

The interpersonal dynamics in this process emphasize the complexity of social interaction between two persons even if one is a child and the other is an adult. Viewed as a whole, socialization appears to consist of a cycle in which initial child-rearing practices (interpersonal interactions) are interpretations of cultural requirements. These become modified or transformed by the stimuli provided in the child's unique characteristics. Such alterations in modes of dealing with the child are responsible for further differences in his behavior. Thus, as the parents' impressions of the child change, the child's reaction tendencies to the adult will also change. Accordingly, any behavior of the adult, including his use of rewards and punishments become more or less effective than might otherwise have been the case. Socialization, viewed in this way, is not discontinuous or unidirectional. The process is controlled by environmental factors but it is at the same time self-seeking in that it also allows for modification of the environment.

In view of the intricate network of variables involved in social interaction processes and the widely varying conditions under which socialization is accomplished, investigators have found it necessary to employ a variety of research methods to uncover the important relationships that will eventually become a part of socialization theory. The papers in this chapter describe a number of useful research methods. Some have examined child-rearing practices through interview techniques and then have searched for correlates in the child's behavior. Others have taken a given characteristic (for example, eminence) and looked for some characteristic such as birth order, that might be associated with it. Inferences are then made about antecedents of the relationships found. The experimental method can be used to discover differential reactions of persons to experimental treatments as, for example, the way first- and later-born children react to anxiety. Although observation can be used for some purposes, under certain circumstances it modifies the behavior of the child to make it a virtually worthless procedure. This is the kind of situation that exists where one wishes to identify the child's reputation among his peers.

These papers are especially unique in revealing the complexities of interpersonal interactions in socialization. They are highly provocative papers since their substance departs from traditional views in their explanations of the interactive process as well as in the research methods suggested for its study.

Bell's paper points out some of the difficulties that are involved in explaining the origins of behavior. He suggests that correlational data are often used to infer that cause-effect relationships in socialization occur uniformly in the parent-child direction, and that this assumption may be incorrect. Accordingly, findings from the literature on child-rearing practices, experimentation with animals, differences between identical and fraternal twins, and the like are reinterpreted to show that cause-effect relationships can also occur in the child-parent direction—that is, the child's unique characteristics do provide stimulus control of the parents' behavior. The model he proposes implies that parental control is analogous to a homeostatic mechanism: The stimulus characteristics of such behavioral traits as hyperactivity or overaggression serve to evoke parental behavior that reduces the level of activity. The opposite characteristics lead to parental behavior that will tend to stimulate the level of activity toward the parents' interpretation of the societal norm. He reasons further that to explain such behaviors as maternal hostility in terms of a reaction to an aggressive child is just as plausible an explanation as the more common explanation that the child's aggression is a reaction to maternal hostility. Bell clearly indicates, however, that while he makes a case for the child to parent direction of effects it is mainly for the purpose of indicating that such effects do exist. A complete model of socialization must include both sides of the picture.

The paper by Altus examines the origins of behavior by selecting a given variable, birth order or ordinal position of the child in the family, and concentrates primarily on its behavioral consequences. It then attempts an explanation of the antecedents of the effects. In the initial studies in this area some of the characteristics of men of eminence were analyzed. First-born sons outnumbered later-born sons to a greater degree than would be expected by chance in this group. Analyses of other data by Altus, including data of his own, show that ordinal position is related to abilities and attitudes as well as to attendance in graduate school and college. The enduring personality characteristics of the first-born children also differ. This group tends to be characterized by fear, conscientiousness, and dependency conflict. When things are going well for them they work alone but when faced with anxiety they seek out the help of others. In the middle class, at least, they also tend to have higher need for achievement. The mere fact of being born first in a family somehow has profound effects on at least some people in the group. Altus indicates that proportionately fewer attempts to study differences in socialization experience associated with sibling order have been made than have attempts to find personality differences. However, he speculates that some of these differences may be attributed to the greater insecurity of the parents with the first child, the first child's lack of opportunity to associate with a peer, greater availability of the parents to the first-born child, and the later appearance of a sibling with its consequence of displacing the first-born.

The effective use of reward and punishment, as mechanisms for shaping the child's behavior in socialization, is investigated in a study by McCoy and Zigler. From their viewpoint every such interaction between the child and an adult is a conflict situation. Since parents sometimes use rewards, positive reaction tendencies toward the parents are developed; because they also use punishments, negative reaction tendencies are developed. The child's reaction to rewards in any situation is the net effect of these two tendencies. Thus, a parent who has acquired more negative reaction-tendencies may be less effective since the child will approach him more cautiously than he will to a parent who has more positive reaction tendencies. The use of rewards does not preclude an all-or-none effect. Rather, it changes the stimulus value of the one who dispenses the rewards.

An extension of the use of rewards to the shaping of complex social behaviors is described in a study by Cohen. By use of differential reinforcement procedures, the subject, Justin, interacts with his mother or one of several peers in sequences of induced cooperation and competition. This study is an excellent demonstration of the way complex social behaviors can be defined, manipulated, and experimentally controlled. The method used is called the free-operant analysis of behavior. The study here relates Justin's behavior in the experimental setting to his differential history of experience with other significant figures in his life. His previous history of competition, domination, and cooperation with them is demonstrated to affect Justin's ability to assume leadership or cooperative roles when interacting with them. In this study it can be seen that effective social interaction requires the interpretation of cues given by the other person but that this interpretation is affected by one's experiential history.

Early socialization practices, the use of rewards, and the like have their effect on the child's personality. Basic trends in behavioral manifestations can be observed at an early age. Once such trends have been established, Kohn's data indicate that they tend to determine or elicit behavior in others that reinforce existing trends. In a real sense, the child establishes a social climate congenial to the continuation of existing personality tendencies. The outgoing child establishes more contacts with other children; as a result he becomes the object of more contacts by his peers. Presumably, other behavioral traits such as friendliness or hostility are similarly affected.

The dynamic nature of interpersonal interaction is highlighted still differently in Tuddenham's study. He points out quite clearly that the trends in the child's personality become reflected in his reputation among his peers. These impressions are shown to be relatively stable at the first grade level, and can be identified by the number of "votes" a child receives from his peers for such behaviors as being the most helpful, the quietest, the friendliest, or the most popular in a class or other group. Obviously, such reputations will vary as a function of the composition of the group making the ratings, but these differences can be useful for diagnostic purposes. The notion of "impression" suggests the child has some stimulus value to his peers, and, accordingly, will affect their reactions to him. His opportunity for further interaction, and his social development will be influenced accordingly as Tuddenham illustrates in a short case study.

These papers provide novel insights into the dynamic interrelationships to be found as the child interacts with his peers and with the important adults in his life. Within the social matrix that provides the context for socialization, the child is seen to be not only an object of socialization, but also a stimulus to influence, however inadvertently, his developmental pattern. As complex as these processes may appear to be, they are shown to be within the reach of further understanding by the many research methods, represented in these papers, either as they stand or as stepping-off points for more refined techniques.

5. THE INFLUENCE OF CHILDREN'S BEHAVIOR ON PARENTAL BEHAVIORS IN SOCIALIZATION

Richard Q. Bell

The research on socialization is based largely on correlations between parent and child behavior. As an illustration, there is the finding that maternal hostility is related to the child's aggressive behavior tendencies. The typical interpretation tends to emphasize the effect of the parents' behavior on that of their children. Thus, it might be concluded that children's aggression is a reaction to maternal hostility. However, causal relationships, implying direction of effects, can only be *inferred* from correlational data. Even evidence that a behavior is modifiable under specified experimental conditions does not necessarily provide an explanation of its origin.

In this paper, Bell reinterprets data from many recent studies in terms of a revised model of the socialization process. He reasons that a model indicating only the effect of a parent on the child is too limited a view of socialization and that the child's inherent characteristics do influence the parents' reactions to the child.

According to this model, the possibility that children's aggression leads to maternal hostility is an entirely plausible one. Parent-child interaction is viewed as a homeostatic mechanism whereby equilibrium between the parents' standards and the child's behavior is achieved. Specifically, some parental behaviors are used to reduce the behaviors of the child that exceed parental standards; others are used to escalate behaviors that are below parental standards. A parent might employ verbal appeals or physical

SOURCE. Adapted and abridged from Richard Q. Bell, "A Reinterpretation of the Direction of Effects in Studies of Socialization," *Psychological Bulletin*, 1968, Vol. 75, pp. 81–95. (With permission of the author and the publisher, the American Psychological Association.)

means to arrest the level of activity of a highly aggressive or hyperactive child; on the other hand, he might use urging, prompting, or demanding appeals to stimulate assertiveness in the overly submissive child. By comparison, a traditional point of view, hypothesizing only a parent-child direction, would suggest the one-sided interpretation that the parent oriented toward the upper limit is "punitive" or "restrictive" and that the one oriented toward the lower limit is "demanding."

Bell presents a series of convincing reinterpretations of the sort described above together with suggestions for approaches that might be used in further studies. His arguments indicate the potential of an expanded model for understanding the socialization process in which both the child-parent and the parent-child directions of effects are considered.

The prolonged helplessness of the human infant, in comparison to the early competence of some other animal infants, fits in with the picture of an organism designed to be taught and modified by the parent in the early years. It seems plausible to visualize the human parent as the vehicle for the transmission of culture and the infant as simply the object of an acculturation process. The parent is the initial agent of culture, the child the object.

This paper summarizes data indicating that a unidirectional approach is too imprecise and that another formulation is possible which would accommodate our social philosophy as well as new data from studies of man and other animals. In the ordinary interaction of any parent and child we can speak only of an event sequence. However, by experimental operations we can isolate parent effects and child effects. In the remainder of this paper a child or parent effect will refer to such a derivative of an experimental operation. No implication about origin of the behavior need be drawn in this case since such studies can take as their starting point any behavior which is available at the time in the repertoire of parent or child.

We must also keep in mind that demonstration of a child effect indicates only that it plays *some* role in parent behavior. The development of the parent behavior is not explained by such a demonstration. In the same vein, Epstein (1964) has pointed out relative to studies of learning that evidence of the modifiability of a response provides no explanation of its origin.

RECENT DATA DISCORDANT WITH PARENT-EFFECT MODEL

Discordant data at the human level are still meager. This is because most research efforts have been directed to the task of testing parent effects and have not always been designed so as to permit clear interpretation of "negative" results. It will be necessary to rely upon informal observations and data generated unintentionally.

Rheingold (1966, pp. 12–13) has pointed to a compelling fact observable under ordinary circumstances in any human group containing an infant. "The amount of attention and the number of responses directed to the infant are enormous—out of all proportion to his age, size, and accomplishments." The effect of the appearance of helplessness and the powerful stimulus of distress cries were also noted. "So aversive, especially to humans, is the crying of the infant that there is almost no effort we will not expend, no device we will not employ, to change a crying baby into a smiling one—or just a quiet one."

Studies of variations in parental behavior with different children provide one other kind of data discordant with a parent-effect model. Yarrow (1963, pp. 109–110) has reported that the same foster mother showed differences in behavior with infants assigned to her at different times. In one particularly dramatic case extreme differences in maternal care existed for two infants of the same sex and age assigned to a foster mother at the same time. Characteristics of the infants appeared to have evoked very different behavior in this foster mother and in other members of her family.

Reports of lack of uniformity of behavior of parents towards their children are not confined to intensive case studies. Stott (1941) reported a correlation of only .22 between sibling reports of a positive or negative home environment. Lasko (1954, p. 111) correlated maternal characteristics across 44 sibling pairs and found that mothers were not consistent in affection but were in restrictiveness, a finding which is in agreement with the report on the quadruplets. In a parent-effect model, it is easy to explain differences between the behavior of two parents with the same child, but awkward to accommodate a difference in the behavior of one parent toward two children. The latter difficulty is due to the fact that the parent-effect model assumes a fixed and invariantly applied repertoire. The usual method of explaining differences in behavior of a parent with different children is to postulate effects associated with ordinal position or sex of siblings. The reports on infants in foster homes could not be explained this way.

Research on lower animals provides stronger evidence of the stimulating and selective effect of the young. A volume edited by Rheingold (1963) covers maternal behavior from the deer mouse to the baboon and provides a number of observations on the importance of the young in shaping interactions. The clinging of rhesus infants with nonlactating females induced maternal responsiveness and biochemically normal lactation (Rheingold, 1963, pp. 268–269). In some studies offspring effects have been manipulated experimentally. Lactation in the rat has been maintained for long periods by supplying new litters of pups; number and age of pups were effective parameters (Bruce, 1961). A study by Noirot (1965) supports the hypothesis that changes in the interest of the female mouse in the litter from birth to weaning depend mainly upon changes in stimuli coming from the young. Pups from one strain of mice induced more retrieving and licking behavior than pups from another strain (Ressler, 1962).

In a classic study, Beach and Jaynes (1956) manipulated appearance and behavior of offspring so as to identify specific classes of stimuli controlling parent behavior. Visual, olfactory, tactile, thermal, and movement cues from rat pups were shown to be capable of inducing maternal retrieving, being effective individually and in combination.

There are many implications of this research on animal behavior. For the present purpose two are most salient. If variations in offspring behavior affect animal parents from which we expect fairly rigid patterns, even greater effects would be expected on human parental behavior, which is presumably more plastic and susceptible to all classes of influence. The other point is brought out by the variety of offspring stimulus parameters being opened up by animal studies; it should not be difficult to accept the notion of offspring effects if we consider the fact that offspring are at least sources of stimuli. Some stimulus control of human parental behavior should be expected since we take for granted the general likelihood of finding stimulus control over behavior in general.

MODIFIERS OF PARENT RESPONSE

Congenital Determinants

Three propositions concerning congenital determinants of later behavior will be advanced in this section. The objective is to take the first steps toward developing an alternative to existing socialization theory. A limited scheme which is merely plausible and parsimonious will serve the purpose. Provisional acceptance of this scheme will make it possible to provide concrete illustrations of how some recent findings in the research literature may be reinterpreted.

It will first be assumed that there are congenital contributors to human assertiveness, which will be taken to mean maintenance of goal-directed behavior of high magnitude in the face of barriers. Reasoning, threat of withdrawal of love, and appeals to personal and social motives can all be used to arrest ongoing child behavior in excess of parental standards, providing the child is not extreme in assertiveness. With a child who is strongly assertive a parent may more often fall back on quick tangible reinforcement or nonreinforcement. At times when the child, the parent, or both are stressed, the parent falls back further to distraction, holding, frightening verbalization, and physical punishment. The foregoing effects on parent behavior also are considered likely to issue from the behavior of hyperactive, erratic, and unpredictable children, and it is assumed that there are congenital determinants of this kind of behavior as well.

It is further assumed that a different kind of behavior is shown by parents of children congenitally low in assertiveness, activity, or sensory-motor capability. Drawing attention to stimuli, rewarding an increase in behavior, urging, prompting, and demanding are examples of parent response to these child characteristics.

It is also assumed that there are congenital contributors to differences in person orientation. Children high in person orientation attend to the behavior of their parents and reinforce social responses emanating from them. Children low in person orientation induce less nurturance from parents, and their behavior is controlled less by variations in social response of parents. They are interested in physical activity and inanimate objects. Their stimulus characteristics primarily mobilize those elements in the parent nurturance repertoires pertaining to providing and withholding physical objects and activities. Since love-oriented control techniques are less useful with these children and material reinforcers cannot always be flexibly applied, their parents more frequently show further recourse to physical punishment.

Some specific ways in which congenital factors may affect person orientation can be suggested on the basis of data from other studies. Schaffer and Emerson (1964) concluded that avoidance by some infants of being held, carried on the lap, stroked, or kissed was not accounted for by propensities of the mothers, but was due to the infant's restlessness and negative response to the restraint involved in these contacts. Infants who avoided contact showed lower intensity in later social contacts, though neither timing nor breadth of contacts was affected. There was a nonsignificant tendency for those who avoided early contacts to be males. The study is suggestive rather than conclusive because the sample of infants who avoided contacts was small.

Moss (1967) reports from day-long naturalistic observations in the home at 3 and 12 weeks that male infants were more irritable (crying, fussing), and slept less than females. This would mean that, on the average, the mother-son interaction was more one of physical caretaking, the mother being engaged in a variety of efforts to soothe males. There are many reasons for expecting that greater irritability in the males would not favor development of social responses positively valued by parents (i.e., smiling, visual regard, noncrying vocalizations): (a) appearance of the mother at the time of crying could lead to an increase in the rate of crying, as reported for institutional infants by Etzel and Gewirtz (1967); (b) ministrations which follow the mother's appearance would necessarily contain some stimulation of an aversive nature, as in diaper changing or efforts to release ingested air, a point made by Rheingold (1966, p. 11); (c) nonaversive reinforcing elements in caretaking would be less likely to reinforce the infant's positively valued social responses since an irritable infant probably emits less of this behavior; (d) the mother would have less time available for purely social stimulation, and might simply wish to avoid the infant when he is quiet.

These possibilities are all consistent with Moss' (1967) finding that by the 12th week, mothers provided less stimulation of an interactional-social nature (imitation) for male than for female infants. It might also be argued that mothers imitated female infants more because of the earlier maturation of social responsiveness in females, an alternative explanation in congenital terms. Mothers could have begun differential sex-role training in social responsiveness sometime in the intervening period, but a ready explanation for initiating such training in just this period is not available. The data do not permit decisions on these different explanations, but the one selected for the present thesis seems at least as defensible as the others: Greater irritability in males led to less stimulation from mothers of the kind which should produce positively valued social responsiveness. Goodenough's (1957) report of sex differences in object and person orientation is typical of many other reports in the literature which indicate that males show less social orientation by the preschool period.

The research of Pasamanick, Rogers, and Lilienfeld (1956) provides evidence that complications of pregnancy and delivery are associated with later behavior disorders of children, including hyperactive behavior, and that males are more frequently affected. The foregoing studies permit an inference that there is a congenital contributor to early response to social reinforcement. If hyperactive or restless infants do not respond as well as other infants to some of the early social reinforcers, it would be reasonable to expect that their later behavior would be controlled less adequately by use of love-oriented techniques which depend for their efficacy on the strength of the social bond. It could also be inferred that they would be less person-oriented, as a consequence of the less intense primary social bond.

Stechler (1964) lists a number of recent prospective studies which confirm the general validity of Pasamanick's approach, and reports his own finding that neonatal apnea was associated with low developmental quotients in the first 2 years of life. Higher irritability or crying during the newborn period and lower developmental quotients later in infancy have been reported for infants whose mothers reported fears or anxiety during pregnancy (Davids, Holden, & Gray, 1963; Ferreira, 1960; Ottinger & Simmons, 1964).

To summarize there is direct evidence of congenital factors contributing to two classes of child behavior which are likely to have very different effects on parents: impaired sensory-motor development, and behavior disorders involving hyperactivity. From twin studies there is evidence of a congenital contributor to person orientation and to facets of behavior which appear related to assertiveness. On the other hand, the evidence for congenital contributors to sex differences in person orientation and assertive behavior is mostly inferential.

Differentiation of Parent Response

Two types of parent control repertoires must be differentiated. *Upper-limit control behavior* reduces and redirects behavior of the child which exceeds parental standards of intensity, frequency, and competence for the child's age. *Lower-limit control behavior* stimulates child behavior which is below parental standards. In other words, parent control behavior, in a sense, is homeostatic relative to child behavior. To predict interaction in particular parent-child pairs it is necessary to know the behavior characteristics of the child, the cultural demands on the parent, and the parents' own individual assimilation of these demands into a set of expectations for the child. Nonetheless, for purposes of illustration we might say that the average parent would show an increase in upper-limit control behavior in response to excessive crying in the infant, or in response to impulsive, hyperactive, or overly competent or assertive behavior in the young child. These widely different behaviors are only considered similar with respect to their effect on upper-limit control. Parental lower-limit control behavior would be stimulated by lethargy in the infant, by low activity, overly inhibited behavior, and lack of competence in the young child. Again, these are different behaviors but are assumed to be similar in effect.

It is customary to observe or rate parental behavior without reference to stimulation provided by the young. When this is done, a parent showing extreme upper-limit behavior in several areas is likely to be described as "punitive," or "restrictive," one showing extreme lower-limit behavior as "intrusive," or "demanding." Both could be considered "controlling," but according to the present conceptual scheme designed to accommodate child effects, the history of preceding interaction sequences could be quite different.

REINTERPRETATION OF RECENT LITERATURE

The child-effect system of explanation which has just been developed states that parent behavior is organized hierarchically within repertoires in the areas of social response and control. Reasonable bases exist for assuming that there are congenital contributors to child behaviors which (a) activate these repertoires, (b) affect the level of response within hierarchies, and (c) differentially reinforce parent behavior which has been evoked.

This system will be applied next to current findings in several major areas in which parent and experiential family effects on children have been given almost exclusive consideration. The findings in most cases are from recent studies which replicate or are consistent with previous studies, or in which results are more defensible than usual because of careful attention to sampling, procedural controls, and measurement. In most cases the authors of these papers were careful not to claim that causes and effects could be clearly differentiated. The question of direction of effects may be raised nonetheless, to ascertain whether the findings are relevant to the theory which motivated the research.

Though in the discussion which follows the evidence is organized to support the validity of a child-to-parent effect, this should not be taken to mean that an "either-or" approach to the study of parent and child effects is preferred to an interactional view. This reinterpretation is only an expedient considered necessary to direct attention to the possibility of child effects. If this possibility is admitted we can than begin the task of thinking of parent *and* child effects. The primary goal of an expanded model of the socialization process is to uncover interactions of child and parent effects as well as main effects attributable to either source.

Lefkowitz, Walder, and Eron (1963) found in 8-year-olds that peer ratings of aggression were highest and parent reports of the child's use of confession lowest where use of physical punishment was reported by the parents. Bandura and Walters (1959) reported more physical punishment used in a group of male 15- to 16-year-old repeated offenders than in nondelinquents. One theory being tested in each case was that use of punishment in the home produces frustration and conflict or affords a model of aggression which in turn produces aggressive behavior in the child. An alternative explanation is that these children were congenitally assertive. Congenital assertiveness activated upper-limit control repertoires in parents and techniques within the repertoire were escalated toward physical punishment. Congenital hyperactivity could produce similar results.

Reviewing the area of moral development, Hoffman (1963) found consistent results in studies dealing with reaction to transgression. His interpretation was that an internalized moral orientation, indicated by confession, guilt, or reparation efforts, was fostered by an affectionate relation between the parent and child, in combination with disciplinary techniques which utilized this relation by appealing to the child's personal and social motives. One alternative explanation is that the children showing little internalization of a moral orientation were congenitally low in person orientation. Because of this their mothers were less affectionate and did not appeal to the child's personal or social values.

A study of sex-role development by Mussen and Rutherford (1963) reports findings which replicated those in a previous study. Boys 5–6 years old scoring high in masculinity in comparison with lows, revealed high father nurturance, punishment, and power in doll play. A high power score indicated that father figures were both highly rewarding and punishing. These findings generously supported all major contending theories: developmental identification, defensive identification, and role-theory. A congenital explanation would be that the highs were more masculine in the sense that they showed lower person orientation and higher assertiveness. The father responded with affection because the son's assertiveness and interests in physical activity and toys were sex appropriate, reinforcing his own identification vicariously through his boy. Much as he felt affectionate toward his masculine boy he found he retreated to punishment frequently because the child, being assertive and less responsive to social stimuli, could not be controlled readily by love-oriented techniques.

In the area of intelligence, Bing (1963) found that mothers of children who showed higher verbal than spatial or numerical ability had a more close and demanding relation with their children both in interviews and observation situations than did mothers of children who showed discrepant nonverbal abilities. These findings confirmed the hypothesis that discrepant verbal ability is fostered by a close relation with a demanding and somewhat intrusive mother, discrepant nonverbal abilities being enhanced by allowing the child a considerable degree of freedom. An alternative explanation would be that the high-verbal children were high in person orientation and low in assertiveness. This is a reasonable combination of characteristics if one assumes that congenital determinants of assertiveness and person orientation are independent or at least not highly positively correlated. These children reinforced their mothers' social responses and elicited nurturant behavior. The resultant interaction intensified verbal expression because this is the primary channel of communication. The fact that these children were low in assertiveness led to lower-limit control behavior reflected in the mother's demanding and intrusive behavior.

Schaefer's (1959) summary of his own work and that of others indicates that a major portion of the variance in parent behavior can be accounted for under two dimensions described as love-hostility and autonomy-control. This is a useful finding, offering the possibility of descriptive parsimony, regardless of the question of direction of effects. However, the two-dimensional model might represent a system of effects of children on parents. The hostility extreme of the love-hostility dimension (strictness, punishment, perceiving the child as a burden) could be characterized as a parent upper-limit control pattern in response to overly assertive, unpredictable, or hyperactive behavior. The love extreme could reflect positive evaluation of children showing more modal behavior but not behavior extreme in the opposite direction.

The autonomy extreme of the autonomy-control dimension might reflect parents' granting autonomy to children who conform to parental expectations of capability and assertiveness. The control extreme (intrusiveness, anxiety, achievement demand, anxiety relative to the child's behavior and health) would be considered parental lower-limit control behavior in response to children low in assertiveness or sensory-motor capability. In support of this we find that mothers of male and female inactive children during the period 9–14 years were rated as intrusive and as high in achievement demand, but low in granting autonomy to the child. All relations cited from this study (Schaefer & Bayley, 1963) were consistent for both sexes and significant beyond the .05 level for combined male and female samples.

Another area receiving considerable attention in the research literature is that of family structure effects such as birth order, sex of siblings, and family size and density. Data from several studies would support the assumption that differences in parent behavior with different children in the family may be primarily due to increased experience and change in availability to children as the family grows (Conners, 1963; Lasko, 1954; Waldrop & Bell, 1964). However, this does not make it possible to dismiss the possibility of child effects. Second- or later-born neonates show higher skin conductance than firstborn (Weller & Bell, 1965). There is collateral evidence that this indicates heightened arousal and greater maturity in this early period, though there is no information available on later development. Another paper summarizes data indicating that the physiology of pregnancy and delivery is quite different for the mother with her first versus later births (Bell, 1963), raising the possibility that some differences in parent behavior with first- versus later-born children may be a response to congenital differences in the child.

A similar child effect could be operative with increases in family size and density. Since greater dependency was found in preschool children coming from large families with short intervals between siblings it was assumed that these children were simply more deprived of maternal attention (Waldrop & Bell, 1964). While this may have been true in part, further study revealed that newborns from large dense families were more lethargic (Waldrop & Bell, 1966). In this case information on later development was available and the finding was that measures of lethargy in the newborn period were correlated with later dependency. In short, there may be congenital factors operating in determining family structure effects, and credence cannot be given to an interpretation solely in terms of experiental factors until influences identifiable in pregnancy, delivery, and the newborn period are isolated.

EXAMPLES OF STUDIES DIFFICULT TO REINTERPRET

In contrast to these studies, there are others yielding data which could not be reinterpreted as a function of congenital effects contributed by the child. For example, there are studies which substitute experimenters for parents and assign children at random to experimental groups in which different "parental" treatment is administered. In one study, experimenters played the role of parents who did or did not control access to food and toy resources in familylike interactions with preschool children (Bandura, Ross, & Ross, 1963): Children imitated parents who controlled resources. In a study of moral development, experimenters behaved with different groups of children in such a way as to create differences in the child's control over punishment and in the cognitive clarity of a task which preceded a contrived transgression (Aronfreed, 1963). Self-critical and reparative responses following transgression were maximized by prior cognitive clarity and child control. These studies used a flexible approach which can be applied to a wide variety of parent-effect parameters very rapidly. One limitation is that we do not obtain data on the cumulative effects of parents on children. The other problem is that of ownness. It is encouraging in this respect that Stevenson, Keen, and Knights (1963) in studies of social reinforcement with 4- and 5-year-olds, found effects common to fathers and male experimenters, and effects common to mothers and female experimenters. This reassures us that at least with young children it may be possible to produce results with experimenters similar to effects parents have on their own children.

One other approach involves experimental manipulation of the behavior of parents and measurement of the effects on children. This is an approach that is only slightly less flexible than the foregoing and can be carried out very rapidly. Merrill (1946) manipulated parent behavior by providing mothers in two matched groups with different feedback relative to the behavior of their children. As in the previous approach which substituted experimenters for parents, the possibility of pseudo-parent effects being produced by latent child effects is minimal where the children are assigned to experimental groups at random, or on the basis of some relevant matching variable. On the other hand, since the parent is present in the interaction, the child may respond in terms of past expectancies rather than to the manipulated behavior of the parent as such. This operates against obtaining differences in child behavior in different treatments, but where differences are obtained they can be interpreted as free of child effects.

Offspring effects can also be isolated. An example is provided in a summary of a series of studies carried out by Siegel (1963). Retardates aged 10 and 15 were classified into high- and low-verbal ability groups. Children in each group were then placed in brief interaction situations with adults who had had no previous contact with them. The adults were to assist children in learning how to assemble a puzzle. Generally, adult responses and questions with low-verbal children were more frequent but shorter and more redundant. Labeling children of similar verbal ability as high or low had no effect on the adult behavior. Support was provided for the hypothesis that linguistic level of children exerts a control over adult verbal behavior.

A second variant of the first design is suggested by the research of Yarrow (1963), already discussed, which took advantage of the assignment of young infants to foster mothers for temporary care while adoption procedures were pending. It is necessary only to measure infant characteristics prior to assignment to foster mothers and then make the assignment systematically so that each foster mother's behavior with at least two different kinds of infants could be measured.

One other approach would make it possible to obtain effects with natural parents. Clinicians frequently report that successful medication of children who are hyperactive and impulsive produces pronounced reactive changes in parent and even total family behavior. Addition of pre- and postmedication measures of parent-child and family interaction to a well-controlled study of drug effects should make it possible to evaluate this and other possible child effects.

Other approaches have been mentioned in the introductory section of this paper (Bell, 1964; Levy, 1958). A detailed discussion of all possible research designs is beyond the scope of this paper, which is primarily concerned with a substantive question of how studies of socialization may be interpreted. This brief recapitulation of designs is to serve the purpose of emphasizing the fact that offspring and parent effects can be separately identified and experimentally manipulated. This will require less reliance on correlation studies of parent and child behavior upon which theories of socialization have been largely based up to the present. Even correlations obtained between parent and child behaviors from longitudinal studies offer no means of ascertaining the direction of effects, unless specially designed for the purpose. Kagan and Moss (1962) have pointed out that the problem of whether maternal hostility is a reaction to child aggression or vice versa is not solved by the demonstration of long-term relations between these maternal and child behaviors in follow-up studies.

6. BIRTH ORDER AND ITS SEQUELAE

William D. Altus

Nearly a century ago Galton produced the first formal report on the observation that first-born sons were more highly represented among men of eminence than one would expect by chance. However, so common is the observation that first-born children somehow differ from laterborns in their behavior that it is probably safe to say many differences were noticed, informally, centuries before Galton. It is a psychologically meaningful question to ask, "What is the nature of these differences?" And, based on the existing evidence any answer must say that personality, social, and intellectual behaviors are affected. For example, first-borns, more often than later-borns, tend to be anxious; they seem to profit from affiliative tendencies; and they tend to be more highly represented in graduate schools.

The mere fact that ordinal position is related to some index has no explanatory value. Accordingly, recent research in this area has been directed toward identifying the significance of, and the reasons for, this effect. Among the important antecedents are differences in the kind of child-rearing practices used by the parent for first- and later-born children and in the opportunities afforded first- and later-born children for interaction with a peer. Thus, for example, it might be inferred that the first-born is the charge of inexperienced, and oversolicitous parents who, simultaneously, push him prematurely into adultlike responsibilities. The consequences are manifested later in achievement-oriented behavior, conflict relationships

SOURCE. Adapted and abridged from William D. Altus, "Birth Order and Its Sequelae," *Science*, 1966, Vol. 1151, pp. 44–49. (With permission of the author and the publisher, the American Association for the Advancement of Science.)

with parent-figures who may be sources of anxiety, and seeking out the help of others in times of difficulty.

Since the causes of ordinal position effects can only be identified by inference there is difficulty in arriving at definitive conclusions; a difficulty that is compounded by the variety and complexity of studies that must be examined. Often superficially similar studies appear to yield inconsistent results that sometimes can be resolved only after detailed examination. Furthermore, the birth order effect appears, in some instances to interact with other factors, for example, sex. Consideration of such factors as these leads investigators to be conservative in deducing the antecedents of sequelae associated with ordinal position.

The relation of order of birth to achievement has been investigated for nearly a hundred years. The first known data appear in Sir Francis Galton's *English Men of Science*. Galton selected his scientists according to objective criteria, such as being a Fellow of the Royal Society, and then asked them for biographical data, including their order of birth. He found more only sons and first-born sons among them than his calculations showed chance should have allowed. This finding he thought easy to interpret: Through the law of primogeniture, the eldest son was likely to become possessed of independent means and to be able to follow his own tastes and inclinations. Further, Galton argued, parents treated an only child and a first-born child (who is also an only child for a period of time) as a companion and accorded him more responsibility than other children were given.

In his dissertation on the nature and nurture of American men of letters, E. L. Clarke (1916) reported that eldest and youngest sons appeared in greater than chance numbers. He rationalized his findings in a somewhat different way from his predecessors:

> First-born and last-born children frequently enjoy greater educational opportunity than do their intermediate brothers and sisters: First-borns often succeed in getting a start before adversity befalls the family, or before the expense of caring for an increasing family of young children becomes so great that it is necessary to curtail the education of some of the older children.

Anne Roe (1953) analyzed data on 64 eminent scientists, selected for their distinguished contributions by the elder statesmen in their respective specialities. Thirty-nine, or 61 percent, were first-born. But the evidence for primogeniture of talent is even more overwhelming, according to Roe:

> Of the 25 scientists in my groups who were not first-born, five are oldest sons, and two of the second-born were effectively the oldest during their childhood because of the death of older sibs, one at birth, one at age two.

Therefore, Roe concludes, some 46 of the 64—72 percent—were actually or effectively the oldest sons in their respective families. Roe's data corroborate in an accentuated way all the evidence which has been marshalled on the topic of birth order and eminence, beginning with Galton's study in 1874. No study has been found that shows trends divergent from those here reported.

BIRTH ORDER AND INTELLIGENCE

Terman's findings (1925) which indicate that—at least among the very bright—birth order may be of some significance, have to my knowledge never been checked on a large sample until quite recently. Robert C. Nichols, of the National Merit Scholarship Corporation, analyzed data on 1618 high school students who were finalists in the National Merit competition and who earned exceptionally high scores among this restricted group. Nichols reports the average score of this selected group of finalists to be "almost three standard deviations above the mean of the general population," which would imply an aptitude at least in the top 0.5 percent of the general population. This level of aptitude is superior to that of Terman's gifted group. Nichols reported that of the 568 representatives of the two-child family, 66 percent were first-born. Of the 414 from three-child families, 52 percent were first-born: the other two ranks obviously contributed 48 percent. Of the 244 students from four-child families, 59 percent were first-born, the other three ranks contributing 41 percent. Of the 85 representatives of the five-child family, 52 percent were first-born, the other *four* birth ranks contributing 48 percent.

In summary, nearly 60 percent of the Merit Finalists who came from families of two, three, four, and five children were first-born. Here is intellectual primogeniture with a vengeance! But Nichols shows that birth order is effectively linked to aptitude *only at the top level*. In the very large number of high school students who took the first round of tests before any were eliminated, birth order does not appear to be related to the scores earned.

BIRTH ORDER AND COLLEGE ATTENDANCE

Given the data on birth order and eminence and birth order and aptitude, one would expect to find some degree of correspondence between birth order and college attendance. During the 4 years, 1960 through 1963, annual data were gathered for all—or nearly all—students matriculated for the first time on the Santa Barbara campus. Of the 1817 representatives of the two-child family, 63 percent were first-born. The figures for men and women are almost exactly alike. During the same period, 1299 representatives of the three-child family matriculated; 50.5 percent of these were first-born, 30.8 percent were second-born, 18.7 percent were third-born. Matriculants from four-child families numbered 538, of whom 50.5 percent were first-born, 25.8 percent second-born, 14 percent third-born, 9.7 percent fourth-born. The youngest is not favored over the intermediate sibling; he is at the bottom step in the progression.

Are the data on college attendance and birth order thus far reported merely a parochial accident? Sufficient data are not at hand for a definitive answer, but there is some evidence that it would be no. At Yale, 61 percent of an undergraduate sample proved to be first-born (Altus, 1965), at Reed College 66 percent; at the University of Minnesota, slightly over 50 percent (Schachter, 1963). The differences in percentages may be a function of the degree of selectivity exercised by the various institutions—the more stringent the standards for admission, the higher the percentage of first-borns. This inference is based, of course, upon what has been found in the realm of aptitude testing.

Mary Stewart (1962) reported a study of 7000 boys and girls in grammar and modern secondary schools in a London borough. The grammar school is mainly college preparatory and is entered by virtue of passing a state examination, the "11 plus." Those who do not pass may attend the modern school. Stewart found the first-born to be overrepresented in the grammar school, and the later-born in the modern school. However, of those who remain in school after the legal attendance requirements have been met at age 15, roughly the same proportion of first-borns is found in both schools, when the ratio of the first- to the later-borns becomes slightly greater than two to one. It seems clear that birth-order influences on schooling are present in England and are just as sharp as they are here.

Schachter (1963) reported data from colleges and certain professional schools in the United States which show that at the graduate level, also, the first-born is overrepresented. This overrepresentation holds not only for the ratio of all first-born to all later-born, but also for families of any given size.

BIRTH ORDER AND PERSONALITY

Alfred Adler believed that order of birth was influential in the channeling of the socially very significant power drives. The first-born, he said (1928) is a "power-hungry conservative." The foregoing data suggest that the later-born may come out poorly in competition for position in our technological society, but it does not necessarily follow that industrial or professional achievement derives from a hunger for power. As to the allegation that the first-born is a conservative, one is unable to find convincing evidence on the college campus. At Santa Barbara the first-born is somewhat more likely to say he attends church services than is the later-born, but this bit of evidence is about all that links the first-born with conservatism. None of the measures of liberalism-conservatism tried out thus far show consistent trends related to birth order.

Sears, Maccoby, and Levin (1957) came to the conclusion that the first-born shows greater "conscience" development than does the later-born. They thought that the differences they found in children were probably due to differences in handling of the first-born by parents, that the first-born had more metes and bounds set to his behavior and was more likely to be punished for transgressions. The father, it was noted, often participated in the disciplining of the first-born, a practice he did not usually continue with the later children. Dean (1947) found the first-born to be more cooperative and more given to curiosity, the later-born to be more pugnacious and also more affectionate. This latter finding—that the later-born are more affectionate—may have a sequel in a recent report by Schachter (1963) that first-born were not so well liked as later-born by their fraternity brothers in the University of Minnesota.

Koch (1956) found in her study of 5- and 6-year-old boys and girls from two-child families that the sex of their siblings together with birth order could influence their social behavior. For instance, a boy who is junior to a sister close to him in age (within 30 months, say) will often be rather "sissy" in comparison with a boy who has an older brother. The boy with the not-much-older sister will more commonly admit to liking to play with girls and with dolls than will boys reared in other sibling relationships. Recently some similar evidence has been found among college students. Male students with older sisters close to their own age were significantly less masculine on two measures of masculinity-femininity than were other males from two-child families.

Schachter (1959) concluded from a series of studies conducted over several years that the first-born is more driven by "affiliative needs" than is the later-born, especially when danger threatens. If the first-born feels that danger or pain lurks in the offing, he wants to share his anxiety by being with others; the later-born shows considerably less need to be with other people under similar circumstances. In this sense, the first-born is more dependent on others. These generalizations of Schachter's derive largely from studies of women undergraduates at the University of Minnesota.

Capra and Dittes (1962) have reported that among Yale undergraduates first-borns were more likely to volunteer for a psychological experiment than were later-borns. In a study concluded on May, 1965, first-born males showed up for voluntary experimental testing in somewhat greater proportion than did later-borns. The differences among the female undergraduates were in the same direction but were not statistically significant. It may be that there is a sex factor here; it is also plausible that the nature of the experiment influences the ratio of volunteers. More research is certainly necessary to determine the significant parameters, if any, relating to birth order and volunteering for experimentation. If first-born do tend, even though only under certain circumstances, to offer themselves as subjects with greater alacrity, this would have great significance for those who base research on samples drawn from college students, especially where the first-born is already considerably overrepresented. Social scientists, in particular, who often use college populations in their studies, would have to control another parameter in their experimental designs.

AN ATTEMPT AT A SYNTHESIS

In England and in the United States, there appears to be an indubitable relation of birth order to the achievement of eminence, however it has been defined. The dice are loaded in favor of the first-born. There is also some evidence that in the *quite bright* segment of our population the first-born are not only present in greater numbers, but are also somewhat more verbally able. The first-born is overrepresented among college populations, and there is some indication that the more selective the college, the greater the overrepresentation. It seems reasonable to believe that the aptitude data and the college attendance figures must be interrelated, and it seems equally reasonable that both sets of data are linked, quite possibly in a causal way, to the numerous data on eminence that have been presented.

Cattell observed (1917) that the preeminence of the first-born was "probably due to social rather than to physiological causes." In my opinion the most prominent of the presumed social "causes" is likely to be the differential parental treatment accorded children of different ordinal positions, to greater "conscience" development, greater dependence on adult norms, and higher expectations of achievement falling to the lot of the first-born. Parents tend to be stricter with the first-born child. Later-born children tend to be treated in a more relaxed, permissive way. This difference in rearing practices may explain why Dean (1947) found the first-born to be more dependent upon adults and the later-born more physically aggressive—that is, less hampered by social restraint. She also reported that the first-born showed more curiosity—that is, he asked more questions—and that he sought adult attention more frequently. Finally, one further difference which sets the first-born apart is that he is the only child who has access for an indeterminate period of time to parental interaction which he does not have to share with a sibling.

The foregoing data suggest fairly strongly why the first-born may do better in school. His curiosity, dependence upon adults, and greater conscience development doubtless make him respond more affirmatively to the teacher and to the school. He should thus more frequently win the teacher's approval, which should serve to augment further his tendencies to do that which is expected of him as a student. If this inference is correct, it is easy to understand why the colleges attract such a high proportion of the first-born.

Schachter (1963) argues that the greater predilection of the first-born for college explains his greater eminence: his superior educational attainments make the achievement of eminence easier for him when he competes for place and position with the less well-trained later-born. This would appear to be unquestionable today, at least as regards eminence in science and technology. One would suspect, however, that in creative writing, sculpture, painting, music—the arts generally—the dependence on college training is not nearly so marked. Furthermore, it would seem that a century ago it was easier to achieve eminence, however defined, without having gone to college. Still, the greater incidence of the first-born among the eminent must have somewhere its origin: Educational attainment cannot be discounted as an important source of the observed differences in eminence among the birth orders.

The intellectual superiority of the first-born noted by Terman, by Altus, and by Nichols among the very bright segment of the population deserves further comment. Hunt (1961), who has summarized the literature on the development of intelligence, leaves room to believe that the child can increase his intelligence by hard intellectual work. If the first-born, by virtue of his different treatment in the home, takes to school more readily, works harder, persists longer (as the college attendance figures attest), then it might be expected that he may well increase his intellectual stature in the process. The first-born who arrives at college has given himself a boost, as it were, by hard tugging at his intellectual bootstraps.

Finally, one must grapple with this problem: If differential treatment of the first-born by his parents makes him a better prospect for higher aptitude, for college training, and for eminence, why does it affect relatively few of the total available first-borns? McClelland (1961) who has given two decades to research on motivation and achievement, has generalized his findings on optimal home influences thus: "... what is desirable ... is a stress on meeting certain achievement standards between the ages of six and eight." The child is given, he continues, training in independence and mastery, and he is held in warm regard by both parents who are ambitious for him but not too dominating, and who have a strong, positive attitude toward education.

Not many parents would fill this bill of particulars in all details. Even when they do, their offspring must have an initial aptitude for learning that places them in the upper half of the total pool of children, if the parental impetus toward achievement is to have the desired result. It seems to me that the preceding considerations impose sufficient restrictions to ensure that only a minor portion even of the relatively fortunate first-born will attain a college degree. And to the extent that aptitude and eminence are a product, even partially, of the educational process, they would tend to vary with education.

In conclusion, the viewpoint embodied in this paper may be fairly summarized by a single sentence: Ordinal position at birth has been shown to be related to significant social parameters, though the reasons behind the relations are as yet unknown or at best dimly apprehended.

7. SOCIAL REINFORCER EFFECTIVENESS AS A FUNCTION OF THE RELATIONSHIP BETWEEN CHILD AND ADULT

Norma McCoy[1] & Edward Zigler

Most psychologists accept the principle of reinforcement as relevant for understanding the acquisition and maintenance of a behavioral tendency. Behaviors that result in the attainment of positive reinforcers are strengthened. Those that achieve negative reinforcers are, at the least, suppressed; and those that are unreinforced are extinguished. Among the many stimuli that can function as reinforcers are verbalizations such as the words "good" or "bad." So apparent are these effects that most people use them at one time or another in attempts to control the behavior of others.

The fact that such social reinforcers are used with varying degees of success implicitly suggests that the social situation complicates the factors contributing to their use. Their action is not as automatic as Thorndike had once supposed it might be.

McCoy and Zigler, in this study, assume that whenever a child is in a situation where he receives reinforcement from an adult, a conflict is created. Adults, because they have been associated with primary or secondary reinforcers, elicit generalized positive reaction-tendencies; because they have been associated with aversive stimuli (i.e., punishing events) they also elicit generalized negative reaction-tendencies. Whether an adult is an effective reinforcing agent, that is, whether or not the child will respond freely to him in order to receive positive reinforcement, depends upon which of the two tendencies is the stronger. The net potential, of course, is determined by the child's history of experience with the person.

SOURCE. Adapted and abridged from Norma McCoy and Edward Zigler, "Social Reinforcer Effectiveness as a Function of the Relationship Between Child and Adult," *Journal of Personality and Social Psychology*, 1965, Vol. 1, pp. 604–612. (With permission of the authors and the publisher, American Psychological Association.

[1] Now Norma McCoy Irons.

These assumptions receive convincing support in the experiment described. They can be used to account for the apparently contradictory finding that strangers were more effective than parents in some studies but less effective in others. Thus, parents are more effective reinforcers to the extent that they elicit greater positive reaction tendencies than do strangers. These investigators note, in their discussion, that the child's feelings toward an adult also seemed to be a sufficiently important variable to invite further research into its interaction with the reaction tendencies elicited by an adult in his role as reinforcer.

Considerable evidence has now been presented indicating that a number of verbal responses, for example, "good," "right," emitted by adults are effective in influencing children's behavior. Although the effects of a number of variables have been demonstrated, the process or processes by which these verbal responses of an adult acquire their reinforcing properties are far from clear. Social reinforcers do not operate in an automatic or mechanical manner, nor is the key variable simply the number of pairings that these reinforcers have had with primary reinforcement. It would appear, rather, that the reinforcing agent and the responses he makes are complex stimuli which activate a variety of emotional, motivational, and cognitive responses. Depending upon the particular measure of reinforcer effectiveness employed, the responses of the child thus activated can result in either a facilitation or an attenuation in the effectiveness of the adults' supportive comments. Thus, the reinforcing adult is best conceptualized as being both a general reinforcer and a complex cue eliciting a wide array of responses. The history of every child is such that any adult elicits both a positive (approach) and negative (avoidance) reaction tendency. Thus, every interaction between an adult and child is viewed as a conflict situation for the child. Stating that the reinforcing adult elicits a positive-reaction tendency in the child is simply another way of asserting that the history of all children is such that adults have been paired with primary or secondary reinforces frequently enough to make adults general-positive reinforcers. What has received minimal attention in the literature is that parents and adults are not only general-positive reinforcers but through their history of pairings with punishing events, are general-negative reinforcers as well. Thus, how reinforcing the adult is for the child will depend on the interaction between both these positive and negative tendencies. Clearly, then, the relative magnitude of the tendencies will depend on the relative amount of positive and negative experiences the child has had with adults. Within such a framework the child minimally affected by social reinforcers would not necessarily be viewed as having low motivation for social reinforcers; he could be one whose negative-reaction tendency inhibits him from freely responding in order to secure positive reinforcement.

In the present study, the hypothesis was tested that the child's positive- and negative-reaction tendencies interact in determining an adult's effectiveness as a reinforcer. The assumption was made that the magnitude of these tendencies is affected by the general quality of the relationship existing between the reinforcing adult and the child. Three experimental conditions were employed. In the first, the reinforcing adult was a stranger; in the second, she was a familiar but neutral person; and in the third, she was a familiar and positive person. The general prediction tested was that the adult would be least reinforcing in the first condition, more reinforcing in the second condition, and most reinforcing in the third condition. This prediction was derived from the position that the strange adult would elicit the child's negative-reaction tendency which in turn would reduce the adult's effectiveness as a social reinforcer. In the familiar-neutral condition, the child would have learned that this particular adult was not a punishing agent; and this knowledge would reduce the child's negative-reaction tendency towards the adult prior to the reinforcing situation. The familiar-positive condition was viewed as one in which not only the negative-reaction tendency would be reduced but one in which the positive tendency would be enhanced as well.

A test of this position demands independent measures of both the child's positive and negative tendencies. As in previous studies (Zigler, 1961; Zigler, Hodgden, & Stevenson, 1958), the total time the child elected to play a two-part satiation task was employed as the measure of his positive-reaction tendency. A cosatiation index, that is, a score reflecting the relative amount of time spent playing each part of the game, was employed to assess the child's negative-reaction tendency. That this score is a valid measure of a child's negative-reaction tendency is suggested by a number of earlier studies in which relatively low cosatiation scores were found for subjects whose life histories were characterized by a high incidence of negative social encounters (Kounin, 1941; Zigler, 1961; Zigler et al., 1958). The rationale of this measure as advanced by Zigler (1961) is as follows: If the child has no negative-reaction tendency, he should play the first part of the game until he is satiated on the social reinforcers being dispensed. Such a child should play the second part for a shorter period of time than the first. The greater the negative-reaction tendency of the child, the shorter should be the time he spends on the first part. However, during the first part he is socially reinforced: he learns that the adult is not punishing and furthermore, he discovers upon the termination of the first part that he can indeed end the interaction whenever he likes. This should reduce the negative-reaction tendency with which he begins the second part. How long such a child plays the second part depends upon how large a negative-reaction tendency was present to be reduced during the first part. The greater the child's initial negative-reaction tendency, the greater the likelihood that he will play the second part longer than the first.

Further evidence that the cosatiation index is a valid measure of the child's negative-reaction tendency was provided by Shallenberger and Zigler (1961). These investigators found that both normal and retarded children who received the negative pretraining condition prior to the two-part game had lower cosatiation scores than children in a positive pretraining condition. For normal children, evidence to date suggests that the reduction in the negative-reaction tendency during Part I of the game is balanced by the satiation effects. Such children play Part II for about the same length of time as Part I. Thus, employing the two-part cosatiation procedure, the specific prediction made was that children in the stranger condition should play Part II about as long as Part I, while both familiar groups should show a marked decrease in playing time from Part I to Part II.

METHOD

Subjects

The sample consisted of 36 first- and second-grade boys attending the Edgewood Elementary School in New Haven, Connecticut. The school was located in a middle-class neighborhood having a predominantly Jewish population. Subjects were picked at random from all first- and second-grade boys with the restriction that no boy was included who was judged a behavior problem by the teacher or principal. The mean age of the group was 7.2 years. The sample was restricted to boys in order to avoid the complications of sex effects.

Experimental Manipulations

The sample was divided randomly into three groups of 12 boys each with the restriction that the mean CA of the groups be approximately equal. The three experimental conditions were:

Stranger (St). The experimenter had no contact with any of the subjects in this condition prior to the administration of the experimental task.

Familiar-Neutral (FN). On three occasions the 12 subjects in this condition were taken from the classroom in two groups of 6 subjects each. The three sessions were separated by intervals of 1 week. Each group of 6 subjects was taken to an empty classroom and given drawing paper and attractive art materials consisting of pastels in 12 colors in Session 1, felt-top markers in 6 colors in Session 2, and presto paints in 6 colors in Session 3.

The instructions were as follows:

> Hello. As you remember [Sessions 2 and 3 only] my name is Miss
> ———, and I've brought some things for you to have some fun with.
> I will give each of you some of these pastels [markers, paints] and
> some paper and you can make a picture of anything you like. You can
> begin as soon as you get some materials.

Following the instructions the experimenter distributed the art materials and told the subjects that she was going to be busy at her desk (located in the front of the room) and requested that they work quietly until it was time to return to their classroom. Any further comments by a child were reacted to minimally or not at all. Questions were answered briefly and the child was reminded to work quietly because the experimenter was very busy. If the children attempted to interact among themselves, the experimenter again requested that they work quietly. Very few children made more than one attempt to interact with the experimenter, and very little effort was required to keep the children quiet.

Familiar-Positive (FP). The initial procedure for this group was the same as for the FN group. Following the instructions, however, the experimenter responded at some length to all questions and comments as she passed out the materials. As the children began to work, the experimenter approached each boy individually and talked with him about what he was drawing. The experimenter then continued to interact with each subject attempting to establish a warm, positive relationship by being complimentary, helpful, and responsive. By the end of the three sessions the experimenter was employing the subjects' first names in her interactions with them. One boy in the group was absent for Session 3 but was retained in the study. Another boy was withdrawn from school during the course of the study; and this group, therefore, had 11 rather than 12 subjects.

Experimental Game (Marble-in-the-Hole)

The experimental game was a two-part satiation task consisting of a simple monotonous repetitive game called Marble-in-the-Hole which has been described previously (Zigler, 1961, 1963a). The game was made up of a wooden box having two holes on top. Inside the box was a chute connecting the holes with a single opening at the bottom of the box. The opening was filled with green and yellow marbles, thus insuring the subject a steady supply of marbles. The apparatus was automated so that it recorded the length of time the child played and the number of marbles he inserted. The subject's task was to insert a marble of one color into one hole and a marble of another color into the other hole.

Part I. The game was placed in front of the subject with the experimenter directly behind it and facing the child. The experimenter said:

> Hello. As you remember [with FN and FP subjects only] my name is Miss ——, and we are going to play some games today. This is a game we call Marble-in-the-Hole. I'll tell you how to play it. You see these marbles. Some of them are green and some of them are yellow. They go in these holes. The green ones go in this hole [the experimenter's left] and the yellow ones go in this hole [the experimenter's right] [the experimenter pointed to the appropriate holes]. Now show me a green marble. Put it in the hole it goes in. Now show me a yellow marble.

Put it in the hole it goes in. You can put as many marbles in the holes as you want to. You tell me when you want to stop. Remember, when you want to stop just tell me. OK, ready? Begin.

The subject then played the game until he indicated that he wished to stop, either by telling the experimenter he wanted to stop or by not inserting a marble for 30 seconds. A 15-minute time limit was used.

Part II. After the subject indicated that he wished to stop, the experimenter said:

Now I'll tell you how to play *this* game. This time we put the yellow marbles in this hole [the experimenter's left] and the green marbles in this hole [the experimenter's right]. Put a yellow marble where it goes. You can put as many marbles in the holes as you want to. You tell me when you want to stop. Remember, when you want to stop just tell me. OK, ready? Begin.

The subject again played the game until he indicated that he wished to stop, either by telling the experimenter he wanted to stop or by not inserting a marble for 30 seconds. A 15-minute time limit again was employed.

Procedure

The St subjects were administered the Marble-in-the-Hole game prior to any contact between the experimenter and FN and FP subjects. This was done so that none of the St subjects would become familiar with the experimenter by seeing her in the school or by hearing about her from subjects in the other groups. The FN and FP subjects were administered the Marble-in-the-Hole game 1 week following their third experimental session.

The subjects were tested individually in a small conference room. The subject was verbally reinforced twice a minute for as long as he played either part of the game. (The decision to verbally reinforce the child rather than to employ attention alone as a reinforcer was made in light of studies which have indicated that an attention-only condition has differential effects depending upon the reinforcement condition that has preceded it—Crandall, 1963; Stevenson & Snyder, 1960. While it might appear that an attention-only condition would provide the purest measure of the child's reaction tendencies, the particular contrast effects introduced by such a procedure mitigated against its use.) Reinforcements were administered approximately at the 15-second and 45-second points within each minute. Five statements were used: "You're doing very well," "That's very good," "You know how to play this game very well," "That's fine," and "You're really good at this game." These statements were made in a predetermined random order established separately for each subject. The experimenter was warm and friendly, smiling and nodding when administering the praise, but she did not respond to any attempts by the subject to engage her in conversation. If the subject dropped a marble on the floor, he was told not to pursue it but simply to continue playing the game.

RESULTS

The three groups' time scores are presented in Table 1 and Figure 1. Since the means and variances of these scores were correlated, a logarithmic transformation of the time scores (log $X + 1$) was made. The log times spent by each group on each part of the game were subjected to a Lindquist Type I analysis of variance (Lindquist, 1956). The method of unweighted means was used to handle the unequal number of subjects in three groups. The results of this analysis yielded significant effects due to Conditions ($F = 8.87$, $df = 2/32$, $p < .001$); to Parts ($F = 13.51$, $df = 1/32$, $p < .001$), and to the interaction of Conditions by Parts ($F = 4.28$, $df = 2/32$, $p < .025$).

As can be seen in Figure 1, the significant groups effect supported the prediction concerning how the groups would differ in the total time spent on the

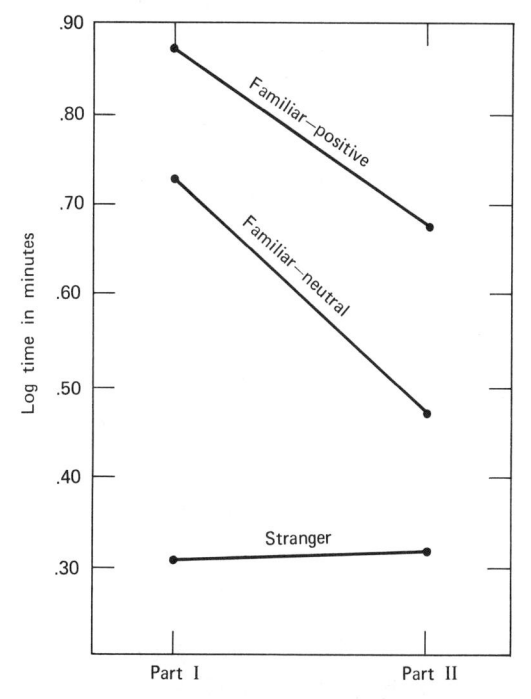

FIGURE 1. Mean log time spent by the three groups in Part I and Part II of Marble-in-the-Hole game.

TABLE 1
Performance of the Three Groups on the Experimental Game

Group	N	Mean time								Part I—Part II	Part I − Part II / Part I + Part II
		Part I		Part II		Total				
		Minutes	Log minutes	Minutes	Log minutes	Minutes	Log minutes			
Stranger	12	1.22	.3095	1.31	.3193	2.53	.6288	−.10	.0071
Familiar-neutral	12	6.72	.7327	2.85	.4702	9.57	1.2029	3.87	.3203
Familiar-positive	11	7.96	.8725	5.39	.6315	13.35	1.5540	2.56	.2455

game. Further analyses of the total log-time scores using the between-subjects mean square as the estimate of error variance revealed that each group differed significantly from the other two. The FP group played significantly longer than both the FN ($t = 2.23$, $p < .05$) and St ($t = 5.88$, $p < .001$) groups. The St group also differed significantly from the FN group ($t = 3.73$, $p < .001$). The significant Parts effect reflected the overall tendency of the three groups to play Part I (M log $= .6315$) longer than Part II (M log $= .4849$). However, the St group did not contribute to this effect; and it was the failure of this group decrease from Part I to Part II that resulted in the significant Conditions $\times$ Parts interaction. The performance pattern of the three groups on the two parts of the game supported the prediction that the two familiar groups would evidence a greater decrease from Part I to Part II than would the St group.

The prediction concerning the decrease from Part I to Part II was tested further through a direct examination of difference scores for each subject. A variation of Kounin's (1941) cosatiation index was employed to compute relative difference scores (Part I — Part II/Part I $+$ Part II). Mean relative difference scores for each of the three groups are presented in Table 1. A simple one-way analysis of variance of these scores was significant ($F_{2/32} = 3.64$, $p < .05$). Further analyses revealed that the FN group had a significantly ($t = 2.59$, $p < .02$) greater decrease from Part I to Part II than did the St group. The difference between the FP and FN groups was not significant ($t < 1$), while the difference between the FP and St groups reached a borderline level of significance ($t = 1.93$, $p < .10$).

An examination was made of the number of subjects in each group who played Part II longer than Part I. As noted earlier, this pattern has been found in socially deprived children and in normal children who had negative experiences with an adult prior to being reinforced on the Marble-in-the-Hole game. The number of children playing Part II longer than Part I in the St, FN, and FP groups was seven, one, and two, respectively. The familiar groups were combined and a 2×2 contingency table was set up. Employing the Fisher exact test, this difference was found to be significant ($p < .01$). However, one subject in each of the familiar groups played both parts of the game for the total time allowed (15 minutes). Since it was possible that these two subjects might have played Part II longer than Part I had longer playing times been permitted, the analysis reported immediately above was recomputed with these two subjects excluded. The resulting differences remained significant ($p < .02$).

DISCUSSION

The findings of the present study clearly indicate that the nature of the relationship between a child and an adult influences how effective the adult will be in reinforcing the child's behavior. The experimenter was found to be significantly more reinforcing in the FP than in the FN condition. In turn, the experimenter was significantly more reinforcing in the FN than in the St condition. The significant differences between the groups in the decrease in playing time from Part I to Part II lent support to the view that one factor resulting in an increase in an adult's effectiveness as a social reinforcer is a decrease in the child's negative-reaction tendency, that is, wariness of and/or reluctance to interact with an adult. However, the total pattern of performance of the three groups on the two parts of the game indicated that the enhanced effectiveness of the adult cannot be attributed solely to the reduction of the negative tendency.

If a reduction in the negative tendency were the only pertinent factor, then the FP group would show a greater decrease from Part I to Part II than would the FN group. However, the FP group not only played the total game longer than the FN group but also did not evidence any greater decrease from Part I to Part II. The overall findings thus suggest that the increased effectiveness of the adult in the FP condition was due to both a reduction in the negative-reaction tendency and to an increase in the positive-reaction tendency. It would appear that the reinforcers dispensed by the experimenter take on increased reinforcement value if the adult has been associated with warm, positive experiences in the child's recent past. This seems to be such a straightforward explanation that one is tempted to explain all the findings in terms of a differential increase in the positive tendency.

Thus, one could argue that the differences in total time found between the three groups reflect differences in the positive-reaction tendency and that the large decrease between Part I and Part II found for the familiar groups reflects nothing but fatigue and other satiation effects caused by playing Part I of the game so long. However, the finding that over half of the subjects in the St group play Part II longer than Part I constitutes strong evidence against this more simple view. The very nature of the game is such that one would expect every child to play the second part of the game for a shorter period than the first due to satiation and fatigue effects. No argument employing the positive tendency alone is capable of encompassing the finding that the majority of the children in the St group played Part II longer than Part I. As demonstrated by Shallenberger and Zigler (1961), playing the second part longer than the first is the clearest indication that a negative-reaction tendency is present. It would thus appear that the most appropriate conclusion derivable from the findings is that the treatment conditions differentially affected both the positive- and negative-reaction tendencies of the groups.

The results of the present study appear capable of shedding light on the effectiveness of parents versus strangers as social reinforcers. If it is assumed that parents have been more frequently associated with punishing events than have strange adults, then one would expect the negative-reaction tendency elicited by parents to be higher than that elicited by strange adults. It would be quite possible for this negative tendency to interfere with the parent's effectiveness as a reinforcer and given our usual experimental procedures, make him appear less effective as a social reinforcer than he really is. Given differences in the age of their children, their procedures, and the actual parents employed, it is not surprising that investigators have found that parents can be either negative or positive reinforcers (Stevenson et al., 1963). Certainly the context in which the parent serves as a reinforcer for his child and the particular child-rearing practices that have been employed by that parent would be factors influencing the magnitude of the child's negative-reaction tendency during the experimental task.

One final note is in order. Throughout this study longer playing time of the child has been interpreted as being due to the greater reinforcer effectiveness of the adult. The argument can be made that while longer playing time may reflect a heightened positive tendency towards the adult, it does not necessarily indicate that the adult has taken on greater social reinforcer effectiveness. The central issue here is whether the adult is effective only in maintaining the child's interaction with him or whether the adult has acquired a generally enhanced reinforcer effectiveness in respect to specific responses of the child. The investigation of the relationship between the child's positive or negative feelings towards an adult and that adult's effectiveness in shaping various behaviors of the child would appear to be an inviting area of future research.

8. JUSTIN AND HIS PEERS: AN EXPERIMENTAL ANALYSIS OF A CHILD'S SOCIAL WORLD

Donald J. Cohen

Unlike the use of the interview, survey, or observation methods where the investigator is a bystander to ongoing activity, some psychologists describe and analyze behavior by active experimental intervention. Their experiments enable them to identify the operations necessary to initiate, change, maintain at a given level, or otherwise control the organism's responses, often for long periods of time. The results of such experiments provide the bases for statements of principles describing the relationship between some feature of the controlling environment and the behavior. The rigor of this method, known as the experimental analysis of behavior, is reflected in the fact that a principle is considered sound only if it can be applied to influence the behavior of all individuals in the same way.

Within this framework, the social behaviors of cooperation and competition can be defined as team behaviors. In cooperation, *all* members of a team are reinforced provided there is interdependent participation. In competition, only those individuals who reach a given criterion, such as surpassing all others, are reinforced. Thus, these behaviors are said to be under the control of differential reinforcement contingencies.

By controlling which member of a two-person team gets "paid-off" for responding in cooperative or competitive ways, Cohen uses the experimental analysis method to describe the social behavior of Justin, a precocious, physically mature, 13-year-old boy. In this clever experiment, the other member of the team, in separate sessions, was a stranger to Justin, or his

SOURCE. Adapted and abridged from Donald J. Cohen, "Justin and His Peers: An Experimental Analysis of a Child's Social World," *Child Development*, 1962, Vol. 33, pp. 697–717. (With permission of the publisher, Society for Research in Child Development.)

sister, mother, brother, or friend. The variations in reinforcement contingencies, paralleling those described in the preceding paragraph, were effective in directing Justin's behavior as a cooperative leader, as a cooperative follower, or as an individual competitor. The behavior of the other member of the team was similarly controlled.

An important finding was that the effects of experimental manipulations were modified by extraexperimental influences; that is, the characteristics of the behavior generated in competition and cooperation depended, in part, on Justin's history of experience with the other team member. For example, he was dominated in the cooperative sequence by a mother who was typically aggressive; he had difficulty in taking leadership from a competitive brother; and turned a typically competitive situation into one in which he alternates leadership when with his friend.

The methods of free operant conditioning allow for a sensitive control of particular variables and for analysis of changes in behavior through time. This experimental approach is thus methodologically suitable for the study of social transactions which are continuous (Argyle, 1957, pp. 112–117) and which can be shown to be related to particular classes of environmental events.

The first free operant experimental analysis of human social behavior Azrin & Lindsley, 1956) demonstrated the possibility of generating cooperative behavior in young children through the scheduling of candy reinforcements. The cooperative behavior could be extinguished by withholding the reinforcements and regenerated through the rescheduling of the reinforcements.

In this present paper, a new instrument for the experimental analysis of social behavior is briefly described. The results of analysis of the social behavior of a particular young person are discussed. These results demonstrate that the young man behaves differently towards people with whom he has different nonexperimentally determined relations.

METHOD

Subject

The social behavior of Justin, a normal 13-year-old, is studied in relation to people with whom he has different relationships. The five people involved in this analysis of Justin's social profile are his brother (age 16), sister (age 14), close friend (age 13), mother, and a stranger (age 14).

Apparatus

The experimental environment employed throughout the experiments was two adjacent 6-ft. square rooms. Each room was equipped with a standard

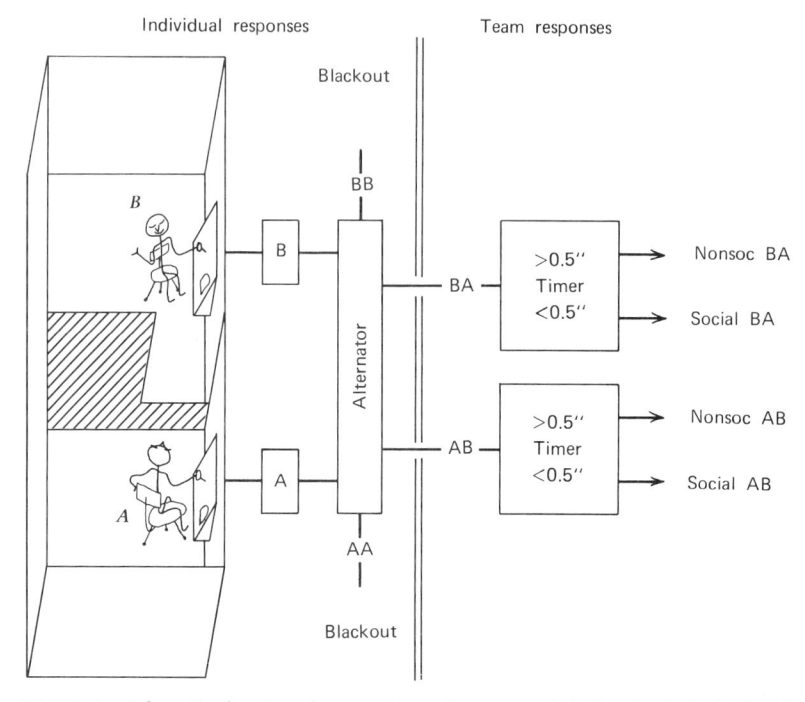

88 SOCIAL DEVELOPMENT: READINGS IN EDUCATIONAL RESEARCH

FIGURE 1. Schematic drawing of apparatus and response definition for individual and team responses. Each room is equipped with a metal plunger; movement of the plunger produces an electric impulse which is electrically defined into individual and team responses as shown in the block diagram.

operant conditioning panel on one wall (Figure 1) as described by Lindsley (1956). Mounted on each panel was a metal plunger and a small bin into which the reinforcements (pennies and candy) were dropped. The two adjacent rooms were separated by a clear plexiglass window through which the subjects could see each other when seated in front of the operant panels.

Controlling and recording apparatus was located behind the experimental rooms in an adjoining area from which the experimental rooms were observed through concealed periscopes. A white noise generator delivered covering noise to concealed speakers in each room. The noise was maintained just loud enough to prevent any discussion between the subjects.

Response Definition

There are two major response definition categories: team responses and individual responses (Figure 1). The latter involves only one subject, the former requires the participation of both. All response categorization was performed automatically by switching circuits. As individual A pulled his plunger, an impulse shortener converted the movement into an electric impulse of .06 sec. duration. Similarly, B's response was converted into an electric impulse. The impulses were fed into a sequence analyzer which categorized the responses into four groups: A followed by B (AB); B followed by A (BA); A followed by A (AA); B followed by B (BB). AB and BA were team responses; AA and BB were individual responses.

In order to facilitate the study of socially defined, or team, behavior, the individual responses were mildly punished. The punishment for an AA consisted of A's room being darkened for 2.5 sec. during which a pure tone (500 cycles) was sounded through his speaker. When either A or B was being blacked out, no responses entered the sequence analyzer.

The team responses are further defined on the basis of the temporal relationship between the two responses. An A response followed within .5 sec. by a B response is a *Social AB*. An A response followed within any period of time greater than .5 sec. is a *Nonsocial AB*. *Social BA* and *Nonsocial BA* responses are defined analogously.

Reinforcement Contingencies

Cooperation is operationally defined in this study as behavior in which both subjects are involved and in which both are reinforced. Competition is defined as behavior in which both subjects are involved and only one is reinforced. That is, cooperation and competition are team responses which are differentiated on the basis of the reinforcement, or "pay-off," contingency.

Experimental Situation

The two subjects were brought to the laboratory together by the experimenter. They were given a minimal amount of information concerning what was to take place, with instructions limited to the following: "You are going to play a game. You can keep all you get." The subjects were then placed in the adjoining rooms in which the lights were dimmed. No other information was given the subjects at any time during the experimental session. All changes in behavior thus were generated by specific, controlled changes in the experimental conditions or resulted from the "dynamic" aspects of social interaction.

To clarify the experimental procedure, the first few moments of a *characteristic* experimental session will be outlined. The subjects were placed in the adjacent rooms; they sat down in front of the panels. The room lights went from dim to bright.... The subjects waited a minute or two and then explored the operant conditioning panels. They pulled the metal plungers. The initial reinforcement contingency was uncontrolled leadership during cooperation; that is, regardless of which subject led, so long as the other pulled his plunger within .5 sec., both were reinforced. A pulled his plunger; B pulled his within .5 sec. This constitutes a Social AB response. The room lights dimmed and a light went on in the reinforcement bin on each panel (conditioned reinforcer). A penny (reinforcement) fell into the reinforcement bin in each room and the lights remained dim for 5 sec. (the conditioned reinforcement cycle). The room lights brightened. B pulled his plunger and A followed within .5 sec. This is a Social BA. The rooms were dimmed and a reinforcement delivered to each bin. When the lights brightened again, B pulled his plunger twice in a row (BB). A sequence of two responses by the same subject (individual responding) was mildly punished. B's room darkened while a pure tone was delivered to his speaker for 2.5 sec. (black out B). When the lights went on again, either A or B could have led, and, so long as the other followed within .5 sec., both were reinforced by a penny dropping into both bins.

EXPERIMENTAL RESULTS

Justin and His Brother

Justin is the third born of seven children of an upper-middle class, professional family. He has grown quite rapidly and, because of his imposing size and intellectual precocity, is thought of by his teachers and schoolmates as a "very unusual and special youngster" who is a "natural-born leader."

The firstborn child of Justin's family is 16 years old and a high school junior. Justin's brother is as tall as Justin, but he is withdrawn, has difficulty with any type of social situation, in general is unsure of himself, and, according to his parents, has lived a life overshadowed by his precocious younger brother. The mother's comments on the relationship between Justin and his brother are of the following nature: "They are friendly, but in a competitive way;" "not very likely to cooperate;" "Justin's older brother is easily annoyed." Throughout this session the brothers could see each other and also see a red light flash when the other pulled his plunger.

Uncontrolled leadership during cooperation. Regardless of which brother led, so long as the other followed within .5 sec. both were reinforced. For the first 11 min. of the first segment Justin's brother *(A)* led significantly more often than he followed. There was a dramatic change, however, after 16 min. when Justin very strongly took the leadership. Justin's assumption of the position of leadership after the period of leadership-instability represents a dynamic change in the social behavior of the team. That is, no experimental conditions were changed that can account for this emergence of Justin as the leader in this situation.

Asocial or individual responses occurred only during the time that the leadership was unstable or changing. With the emergence of Justin as the leader and the resulting stability of leadership, the AA responses dropped out and the number of team responses increased.

Controlled leadership during cooperation: Brother (A) leads. No signals or other indications were given to the subjects between segments; for them the entire experimental session was continuous. A new segment of the experiment is considered to begin every time the conditions were changed, and the conditions were changed when the social behavior of the subjects reached some stable or steady state. In the second segment, only those team responses in which the brother *(A)* led and Justin *(B)* followed were reinforced (Soc AB). No reinforcements were presented for Justin's leadership (Soc BA). After 4 min. Justin no longer at attempted to lead. However, there was not an immediate increase in the number of brother-leading team responses. Instead, for about 20 min. the brother frequently blacked himself out with individual (AA) responses. In the middle of the segment the brother assumed the leadership position and both subjects received a high number of reinforcements. During the time that the brother was blacking himself out neither subject received many reinforcements. The first part of this segment contains a high number of Nonsocial AB responses. These frequent Nonsocial AB responses represent Justin's hesitancy at following his brother.

Controlled leadership during cooperation. Justin (B) leads. After having led Justin, Justin's brother was not ready to follow his younger sibling. There were 272 Soc AB responses, for which no reinforcements were delivered. This can be contrasted with 76 Soc BA (Justin leading) responses in the previous segment where Justin gave up the leadership fairly quickly. In this segment the brother persisted in attempting to be the leader for 19 min. At the end of the segment there was acquisition of the reinforced leadership pattern.

The total responses for the session were as follows: 561 Soc AB; 451 Soc BA; 123 Nonsoc AB; 42 Nonsoc BA; 175 AA; 44 BB. *A* responded a total of 1527 times, *B* a total of 1265 times. Both received about 640 reinforcements.

Justin and His Friend

Justin and his friend are the same age and in the same grade in school. They are friendly at school, play together after school, and serve together at church. The boys consider each other as "best friends" and were quite happy to come to the laboratory as a team.

Uncontrolled leadership during cooperation. Justin *(B)* led in 112 of the team responses (Soc BA) and the friend *(A)* led in 39 team responses (Soc AB). The distribution of the team responses in which the friend led is interesting to note. Justin would lead for an extended run of team responses (Soc BA); then the friend would lead for several team responses (Soc AB). The friend's several attempts at leadership were cut short by Justin. The friend's attempts at leadership, quickly met by Justin's self-assertion, represent the dynamic aspect of their confrontation in the experimental situation.

Controlled leadership: Friend (A) leads. The differential control of leadership was quite rapid; immediately following the extinction of Soc BA (Justin leading), the friend assumed the leadership and maintained the leadership throughout the segment. The rapid increase in the number of Nonsoc AB responses during this segment, a total of 78, is indicative of Justin's unwillingness to respond after his friend responded. Justin showed this same tendency in the experimental session with his brother. His hesitancy to respond is apparent in both cases although Justin did not attempt to lead when not being reinforced for leading.

Therefore, there are two major social behavioral expressions of "unwillingness" to follow: (a) the continued leadership of the subject while this leadership is being extinguished; (b) the hesitancy to follow as expressed in increased nonsocial responses.

Competition. After cooperative responding was fully acquired and leadership experimentally reversed, competition between the two friends was programed. What emerged, however, was a complicated form of cooperation in which leadership was alternated between the friends. The alternation of leadership allowed for an even distribution of reinforcements between the subjects with each receiving only 50 percent of the number of reinforcements that could have been received on a cooperative schedule. The sequence of responses that permitted the subjects to convert a programmed competitive schedule to a complex form of cooperation was of this order: A responded and then B responded within .5 sec.; B was reinforced for this Soc AB. Then B responded and A followed within .5 sec.; A was reinforced for this Soc BA. The nonsocial responses (Nonsoc AB and Nonsoc BA) were considered as "mistakes" by the two subjects and were "made up" to provide an even distribution of reinforcements.

Justin and the Stranger

The stranger used in this experiment is the brother of Justin's friend. Justin did not know the stranger before they met at the laboratory. The difference between the stranger and the friend to Justin was, of course, their previous social relationships.

Competition. Initially the competitive schedule produced competition of an asymmetric type. Justin *(A)* received reinforcements by quickly responding after the stranger *(B)* responded; for Soc BA, A is reinforced. The stranger, however, received his reinforcements by distracting Justin. By shouting or waving at Justin, the stranger generated a number (44) of Nonsoc BA responses, for which he *(B)* was reinforced. In distracting Justin, the stranger was relying upon Justin's slowness of movement or the possibility of "catching him offguard" or "asleep."

The stranger led 146 times to Justin's leadership of 59 times.

The initial competition was eventually transformed into the complex form of cooperation by alternating leadership as described above. There were few Nonsoc BA and a fairly even alternation of leadership giving each subject an equal share of the reinforcements.

Uncontrolled leadership during cooperation. Here the strength of the stranger's *(B)* leadership was clear. Throughout the segment the stranger led Justin, although they would have been similarly reinforced if Justin had taken the leadership.

The stranger *(B)* remained the very strong leader, although several reinforcements were delivered for team responses in which Justin *(A)* was the leader.

Blackouts occurred only infrequently during the experimental session.

Justin and His Sister

Justin's sister is a 14-year-old, first year high school student. She was characterized by her mother as being "aggressive, maternal, and not too dependable." Justin's sister attempts to "mother" him, which he reported he does not very much care for.

Uncontrolled leadership during cooperation. From the first moments of the experimental session Justin's sister took the leadership.

Controlled leadership: Justin (B) leads. Only Soc BA team responses were reinforced. The Soc AB (sister leads) data were characterized by the occurrence of bursts of several responses in which Justin's sister *(A)* led indicating the sister's attempts to regain the leadership. The fact that these could be observed via the methodology employed demonstrates the sensitivity of the method to subtle, dynamic properties of unstable leadership.

Competition. In this segment Justin *(B)* received 97 reinforcements to his sister's *(A)* 26.

Unlike the teams of Justin and his friend and Justin and the stranger, the competitive contingency did not produce cooperative alternation of leadership between Justin and his sister. Instead, the programmed contingency produced competition.

Justin and His Mother

Justin's mother "believes in directing the children in their homework;" along with her husband, she is presently engaged in studying college catalogues to determine the best schools to which to send the children. She believes that Justin is the most exceptional of her children and she is very concerned about his future.

Uncontrolled leadership during competition. Before entering the experimental room Justin instructed his mother on several occasions to pull her plunger *after* he pulled his. On entering the rooms, Justin led for the first several team responses. However, his mother quickly took the leadership and maintained it throughout the first three experimental segments. Justin signalled his mother to let him lead. She, however, signalled back that she was trying to but that he was not responding fast enough.

Controlled leadership: Justin (B) leads. The data clearly indicated the differential control of leadership. Justin's mother attempted to regain leadership throughout the segment, as indicated by the bursts of Soc AB responses similar to those occurring in the experimental sessions with Justin and his sister.

Controlled leadership: Justin's mother (A) leads. There was very rapid acquisition of the reinforced leadership during this segment. The Soc BA data did not indicate any bursts of Justin's leadership during this segment.

There was a significant change in the leadership direction through differential reinforcement in which only those team responses in which Justin *(B)* led were again reinforced. The bursts of mother's *(A)* leadership indicate that she is in fact not as good a follower of Justin as Justin is a follower of her, regardless of her statements to the contrary.

Competition. The programmed contingency of competition was converted into alternation of leadership. This alternation adds greater strength to the "validity" of the competition recorded for the team of Justin and his sister.

QUESTIONNAIRE RESULTS: BRIEF SURVEY

Each subject was asked to answer an informal questionnaire composed of sentences to be completed and several direct questions. The quotations in this paper attributed to the subjects are drawn mainly from the answers given to this questionnaire.

SUMMARY AND DISCUSSION

All the subjects in these experiments have asked if they could return to the laboratory. Sensitive behavioral analysis requires such highly motivated behavior.

Justin led those people with whom he had previous nonexperimental experience of leadership, his brother and his friend. His sister who "mothers" him and his mother look strikingly similar during cooperation: both were strong leaders during uncontrolled leadership and both exhibited resistance to following him by bursts of inappropriate leadership responding when they were not reinforced for leading. With Justin and the friend, the stranger, and his mother, the competitive contingency was converted into complex cooperation. Justin and his sister displayed strong competition.

The Justin-sister and Justin-brother family interactions are reflected in the experimental analysis by the slow development of cooperation and control of leadership (Justin-brother) and the strong leadership accompanied by true competition (Justin-sister). The experimental analysis is validated by such statements as Justin's mother's in relation to her children: "They are the most competitive, aggressive group you ever met." The experimental analysis has successfully evaluated the type of expression given the "competitive, aggressive" family spirit.

Justin and his friend had a long history of extra-experimental cooperation. Their experimental behavior is fully cooperative with immediate alternation of leadership during programmed competition. Justin and the stranger had no history of extra-experimental cooperation; after initial competition during programmed competition, their experimental behavior changed into the more complex form of cooperation. Justin and his brother had a long history of competition and aggression; their experimental behavior is marked by a large number of nonteam responses, long periods of acquisition, persistence of nonreinforced leading, and the other occurrences noted above.

The results of these experiments clearly demonstrate that Justin's social behavior is differentially controlled by reinforcement. However, the dynamic properties of his social behavior are controlled by his previous extra-experimental relations with his teammates. Different patterns with different teammates prove that the method is sensitive to different social relationships.

CONCLUSIONS

The experimental determination of five different dynamic patterns of cooperative and competitive leadership between a young man and five other persons clearly demonstrates the sensitivity of this free operant method to important social variables. The close similarity between the experimentally measured patterns and the extra-experimental relationships as determined by questionnaires and interviews demonstrates that these experimental masures have high validity. The method permits a laboratory analysis of a child's social world.

9. THE CHILD AS A DETERMINANT OF HIS PEERS' APPROACH TO HIM

Martin Kohn

There is a continuity in interpersonal skills despite the fact that an individual grows in a constantly changing environment. These two, somewhat contradictory events may be understood if one considers the possibility that a child is more than a passive participant, to be buffeted and molded by whatever situational patterns he may encounter, in the socialization process. Indeed, a growing body of evidence suggests that the child actively seeks and fosters a given social climate in his interactions with peers.

An aspect of the dynamic interplay between the person and others' reactions to him was described in Bell's report (see page 55). His analysis implied that the child's initial behavioral tendencies can influence parental behaviors, and, consequently, the kind of psychological environment the parent establishes for the child.

Kohn, in a similar vein, demonstrates that preschool children are instrumental agents in creating a social climate that will maintain an established trend in social skills. For example, a hostile child tends to elicit hostility from others; a child who initiates activity toward others is the recipient of activity by others. The reciprocity of congruent behaviors provides a confirmation of his ongoing behaviors. Since most situations provide a wide range of friendship opportunities, the selection of friends further permits him to construct an environment most congenial to his existing dispositions.

A moderate rate of initiating contacts with others appears to be related

SOURCE. Adapted and abridged from Martin Kohn, "The Child as a Determinant of His Peers' Approach to Him," *The Journal of Genetic Psychology*, 1966, Vol. 109, pp. 91–100. (With permission of the author and the publisher, The Journal Press.)

to a greater proportion of positive, constructive, social behaviors. Rates that are too low tend to inhibit self-expression. High rates were found to be related to a greater proportion of negative, unconstructive behaviors.

The provocative results of this study help in understanding how interpersonal integrations are established and maintained. However, as Kohn aptly notes, the general conclusion needs to be confirmed in a variety of other settings, and with larger samples.

Previous research has yielded evidence that indicates that children tend to be instrumental in bringing about the kind of approach that their peers make to them. Bott (1934) found a rank order correlation of .91 between amount of verbal and motor contacts initiated and verbal and motor contacts received. With respect to quality of behavior, Anderson (1939) found that dominative behavior invited domination in return; similarly, integrative behavior invited integrative approaches in return.

These findings are important in relation to personality development and pyschotherapy. In his relationship to his peers, the child may create for himself a particular kind of environment that will foster and continue his development in a given direction. Longitudinal research is beginning to yield considerable evidence that many aspects of personality show continuity over relatively long periods of time [see Kagan and Moss (1962)]. Such continuity may be, in part, a function of the kind of response that the individual can call forth in others: i.e., existing personality trends are strengthened when they consistently evoke congruent responses from others.

The area of personality development can benefit when such repetitive patterns, or these tendencies to bring about given kind of interpersonal constellation, can be subjected to systematic research. An intensive pilot study of children in their first year in school provided an opportunity (a) to re-examine the correlation found by Bott on frequency of contact initiated and received and (b) to examine the relationship between quality of contact initiated and quality of contact received under conditions that differed in two main respects from Anderson's work. In the present study, the children's responses were studied over a long period of time (covering almost a full year), as compared to the brief experimental session from which Anderson derived his findings. Moreover, the conditions of the present study were closer to life than the conditions in Anderson's study; the children had the opportunity to select their peers from the total classroom groups, whereas in the Anderson study they were paired experimentally.

METHOD

Subjects

The subjects were 11 children (six boys and five girls, eight from middle-class and three from working-class families). The median age of the children was 5 years, 11 months; the range from 5 years, 5 months to 6 years, 3 months.

Although the sample of children is small, the results on each child are based on many hours of observation carried on over an entire school year, and the categories of analysis are highly reliable.

Criteria for selection of the children were as follows: (a) that the home be intact; (b) that the child be an only or the oldest child, without prior nursery school experience (so that this would be the first school-entry experience of the family); (c) that the family be middle-class or working-class and the home be English speaking.

The children were chosen from two classrooms: six children (three boys and three girls) from a relatively tight, rigid kindergarten that emphasized preparation for first grade; and the remaining five (three boys and two girls) from a relatively free setting with emphasis on play and learning through here-and-now activities. Each of these kindergartens contained 20 to 25 children. These kindergartens as settings have been described in previous publications (Kohn, 1962; 1963).

Procedure

The findings of the present study are based on half-hour nonselective observations of individual children. The observer's main function was to follow one study child for a half-hour in order to obtain a complete picture of this child and his life space for this time. The specific focus was on the child's way of relating to people, materials, tasks, and routines with which he was involved. The observers were instructed to note what the child did or failed to do (where a response might normally be expected), what his emotional responses were, and how he interacted with the people and objects in the classroom environment.

These observations were carried out during four different periods during the school year. Observation Period I was from the middle of September through the end of October, Observation Period II during the first three weeks of December, Observation Period III for a total of three weeks preceding and following the spring vacation, and Observation Period IV for a three-week period at the end of the school year.

Analysis of Data

As a first step, the records were subdivided into units. A unit covers a designated school activity from beginning to end; it covers a range of time that is teacher-structured. If the activity was in progress when the record began, the unit begins with the beginning record. Similarly, when the activity continued beyond the end of the half-hour, the unit ends when the record ends. These units cover the various phases of kindergarten life—playground, organized games, free play, milk time, and rest period. The main purpose of the units was to permit matching, so that the types of activities analyzed were the same from child to child. An average of 17 units were picked for each child, eight from the first observation period and the balance equally distributed among the remaining three observation periods. The 17 units covered an average of five and one-half hours' observation time per child (range, four hours, 18 minutes to seven hours, 28 minutes).

A unit, as described above, was analyzed to determine the number and kinds of interactions of each study child with every other child with whom he interacted. Each act initiated by a child was scored as a *positive action* (for example, child directs, leads, controls kindly; child asks for guidance and advice; child assists in a kindly constructive manner; child evaluated another child in a positive way; child extends invitation for interactions to another child; child initiates a new idea or extends the idea of another child, etc.), or, as a *negative action* (for example, child structures in a bossy and domineering way; child helps in a domineering way; child evaluates another child negatively; child acts in a provocative and aggressive manner towards another child; child takes property of another child, etc.).

The interactions in all the units analyzed were counted and two types of measures were calculated for each child:

1. *Rate:* (a) the rate on an hourly basis at which the study child initiated activity towards others, and (b) the rate on an hourly basis at which others initiated activity towards the study child.

2. *Per cent positive:* (a) the per cent of behavior initiated by the study child to others that fell into the positive category, and (b) the per cent of behavior initiated by others towards the study child that fell into the positive category.

Reliability

The classroom analysis categories from which the present categories were adapted had been subjected to an intensive reliability study. Two scorers independently categorized 2008 incidents, and there was exact agreement in 86 per cent of the instances. Since the refinements made for the individual child analysis were all obliterated by the pooling of the items into two groups (positive and negative), no further item-by-item reliability study was undertaken. However, the children's per cent positive scores during the first two observation periods were correlated with their per cent positive scores during the Observation Periods III and IV. The rank order correlation was .78 ($p < .01$).

RESULTS AND DISCUSSION

The results of the study are presented in Tables 1 and 2. The data on the 11 study children that comprised the sample are presented in Table 1; specifically

(a) the rate and per cent positive of each study child's initiation towards others, (b) the rate and per cent positive with which others initiated towards the study child, and (c) each study child's rank within the group on these four measures. At the bottom of Table 1, the median scores of the group on these four measures are presented.

Table 2 presents the Spearman Rank Order Correlations (rho) among the various measures. In two of the correlations (Numbers 6 and 8), three ranks were tied; these correlation coefficients were corrected for these ties.

Three types of results will be discussd: (a) the median scores and their significance; (b) "Within-study-children" correlations (the relationship between rate and per cent positive within the same child as well as the effect of age on rate and per cent positive); and (c) "Between-children" correlations (the relationship between the study-children's rate and per cent positive, and the rate and per cent positive directed towards them by others).

The median per cent of positive acts in the present study was 86 per cent for the study-children to others, and 75 per cent for others to the study-child. Mengert (1931), using a friendly-unfriendly dichotomy, found that friendly behavior constituted approximately 80 per cent of the total, roughly similar to the present findings.

1. "Within-Children" Relationships

Table 2 shows that within the relatively narrow age range of the children in the study, no significant relationship was found between either per cent positive or rate and the age of the study-child; therefore, none of the results presented below can be accounted for in terms of the age factor.

Table 2 also shows a rank order correlation of $-.69$ ($p < .05$) between a child's rate of activity and the per cent of the activity that is positive. In other words, in this particular sample, the more active child was also the less constructive one. These results make sense in terms of our more general knowledge of the children studied. The three children with the highest per cent positive were rather meek and inhibited; they seem to have considerable difficulty expressing any aggression. On the other hand, two of the three children with the highest initiation rate were rather hostile and seemed to be under a great deal of inner pressure to express themselves in domineering and bossy ways. The children whose constructiveness scores were between 80 per cent and 90 per cent seemed to be the best functioning ones. In general, they had a moderate degree of initiation rate, were on balance constructive, but not to the extent that it restricted their self-expression.

2. "Between-Children" Results

Results presented in Table 2 show a high degree of correlation between the rate at which the child initiated acts towards others and the frequency with

TABLE 1
Study-Child Initiates to Others and Others Initiate to Study-Child

Study-child	Study-Child Initiates to Others				Others Initiate to Study-Child			
	Rate	Rank of rate	Per cent positive	Rank of % constructive	Rate	Rank of rate	Per cent positive	Rank of % constructive
A	32.0	1	82	7	17.0	1	75	6.5
B	28.2	2	58	10	11.0	5	65	10.
C	24.2	3	56	11	10.5	6	75	6.5
D	20.0	4	86	6	12.2	4	82	3.5
E	20.2	5	89	5	13.4	3	74	8.5
F	19.7	6	65	9	9.9	7	58	11.
G	17.8	7	96	2	14.7	2	82	3.5
H	17.4	8	81	8	8.3	9	74	8.5
I	13.8	9	94	4	9.8	8	83	2.
K	12.9	10	98	1	7.3	10	81	5.
L	3.7	11	95	3	5.9	11	90	1.
Median	19.7		86		10.5		75	
Range	3.7–32		56–96		5.9–17		58–90	

TABLE 2
"Within-Children" and "Between-Children" Relationships

Relationships	r	p
"Within-Children" Relationships		
1. Relationship between constructiveness of study-child and rate of initiation by study-child	−.69	<.05
2. Relationship between age of study-child and rate of initiation by study-child	−.26	n.s.
3. Relationship between age of study-child and constructiveness of study-child	−.14	n.s.
"Between-Children" Relationships		
4. Relationship between rate of initiation by study-child and rate of initiation by others to study-child	.77	<.01
5. Relationship between rate of initiation of study-child and constructiveness of other children	−.45	n.s.
6. Relationship between constructiveness of initiation of study-child and rate of initiation to him by others	−.18	n.s.
7. Relationship between constructiveness of study-child and constructiveness of others to him	.68	<.05
8. Relationship between constructiveness of study-child and ratio of rate of others to study-child to rate of study-child to others	.80	<.01

which they initiated acts towards him ($r = .77$, $p < .01$). These findings are in line with the previously mentioned results obtained by Bott (1934).

There is also a significant correlation between the per cent positive acts a child initiates to others and the proportion of positive acts others initiate towards him ($r = .68$, $p < .05$). These findings, although based on somewhat different measures than Anderson's, generally express the same type of relationship and indicate that the correlations that Anderson found to be true for a relatively brief experimental session also hold for increased time periods.

No significant relationship was found between the proportion of positive acts the study child initiated to others and the rate with which others initiated to him ($r = -.18$, n.s.).

There is, however, an inverse relationship between the rate with which a study-child initiated to others and their per cent positive score towards him ($r = -.45$, $p < .10$); in other words, the children who were most active tended to receive somewhat more negative contacts from others. This finding may be due, in part, to the previously reported results which showed the more active study-children tended also to have the lower per cent of positive acts.

In order to parcel out this factor, the author tested the assumption that the more constructive in his approach the child is, the more his rate of initiation to others would be matched in a one-to-one way by their rate of initiation to him. In other words, given two children of equal activity rate, the one who had a greater proportion of positive acts should have proportionately more activity initiated towards him than the one who initiates a low proportion of positive acts. Therefore, per cent positive was correlated with a ratio of the rates of others initiating towards the study-child to the rate at which he initiated towards them. This correlation was highly significant ($r = .80$, $p < .01$).

These results suggest that both with respect to quantity and quality, the child gets what he puts out; that, in other words, the child creates his own environment. Thus, the hostile child is the recipient more frequently of hostile activity from others than is the unhostile child; this then validates his being hostile to begin with. It is quite likely that this is one mechanism through which continuity of personality development is maintained. The child manages to bring about that kind of approach from the world that validates, in a sense, his own approach to it. Basic here is the assumption that through his behavior the child is a causal agent in bringing about a given kind of psychological environment. Alternative explanations, however, are possible: for example, a child may be physically attractive to others, be contacted by them frequently and, in turn, contact them frequently.

An important feature of the present study very likely was the opportunity that the children had to choose among many playmates. A classroom is a setting that offers choice among a wide variety of children—some passive, some active, some with a constructive approach, others with a more destructive approach. The rate and constructiveness of the interactions that a child draws to himself reflect no doubt, in part, his choice of peers from among the children in the classroom. The variety of children available probably offers the individual child sufficient choice to enable him to construct the kind of environment which will keep constant his prevailing mode of adaptation. The mild-mannered, low-initiative child will, in all likelihood, select the nice children who will collaborate with him to maintain his preferred equilibrium between himself and the environment.

The findings of this study are based on a small number of children studied over an extensive period of time (one school year). They are highly suggestive but need to be confirmed with a larger sample.

10. A STUDY OF REPUTATION: CHILDREN'S EVALUATIONS OF THEIR PEERS

Read D. Tuddenham

Both the objective realities of a person's behavior toward another, and the subjective interpretations of these behaviors by each person are important components of interpersonal relationships. The person's adjustment to his peers is undoubtedly influenced most by the latter, that is, by his stimulus value, or by the more or less stable impression he makes on others; in short, by his *reputation*.

Since reputation undoubtedly affects the child's acceptance in his group it also affects, indirectly, his social development. Peer groups provide a reference for normative behavior, for testing social skills, and for developing a peer identity at different levels (e.g., star or isolate, leader or follower). Thus, reputation determines not only whether the child will be afforded, or denied, opportunities to participate in significant socialization activities but it determines in which activities he will participate.

The *Reputation Test*, described by Tuddenham, is a way of gaining information about this important bit of social behavior. It arrives at a pupil's reputation by asking such questions as, "Who is the most popular boy in the class?" of those who are directly responsible for the formation of reputation in the first place: the child's peers, the adults with whom he associates, reference groups, and himself.

In this article, one is cautioned that the test must be short enough that the child does not become bored in taking it and the questions must not make the respondents defensive or anxious. Reliability is examined and

SOURCE. Adapted and abridged from Read D. Tuddenham, "Studies in Reputation: I. Sex and Grade Differences in School Children's Evaluations of Their Peers. II. The Diagnosis of Social Adjustment," *Psychological Monographs*, 1952, Vol. 66, 1, Whole No. 333. (With permission of the author and the publisher, the American Psychological Association.)

found to be sufficiently high to justify its use for research purposes. Since reputation ratings may vary as functions of the size and composition of the group doing the rating, both teachers' and pupils' ratings are compared. The usefulness of the test for differentiating among groups on the basis of their reputational characteristics is demonstrated by comparing how girls and boys were rated at three grade levels. Finally, the possibility of using reputation information for diagnostic purposes is illustrated in a case history.

In studying child personality, most investigators utilizing rating procedures have depended upon the impressions of adults-parents, teachers, or psychologists. However, the influence of other children constitutes a major component of the social milieu to which the child must adapt, and his behavior with them may differ in many ways from that which he exhibits in other groups. This important domain is peculiarly inaccessible to the adult observer, whose very presence alters the situation under study. In order to investigate those aspects of child personality which are revealed in the social relationships obtaining among children, a method is needed which permits the children themselves to express their attitudes toward one another in a manner which is adapted to their capacities, which avoids disturbing them or provoking undesirable attitudes of "tattling" on their associates, and which meets the practical criteria of ease of administration, quantifiability, and reliability of measurement.

To meet this need, Hartshorne, May, and Maller (1929) devised the "Guess Who" test in connection with their investigations of service and altruism among school children. This test consisted of a series of short word pictures presented with the instructions that the children "guess" which of their classmates were most nearly like the persons described. This procedure successfully circumvented the practical difficulties of securing a measure of reputation, and achieved a high degree of reliability in the final ratings by pooling the extreme judgments of a large number of judges.

The method has subsequently been used to study children's social adjustments, sex differences in judgement patterns of adolescents, and adolescent personality values. Results of these investigations have indicated that reputation testing offers a promising approach to a variety of problems in personality development, and further, that the method supplies a type of information which is not obtainable by means of the more common devices which secure ratings by adult observers.

PURPOSE

The purpose of this study is to explore the possibilities of the Reputation Test as a device for studying social aspects of personality development in children of elementary school age.

The present report is restricted to the study of group differences in reputation as related to age and sex for the light they throw on the general process of social development during this period of childhood. Findings were analyzed not only for their significance as norms for diagnosis but also for their reflection of the social demands to which the individual child must adjust. On the level of qualitative diagnosis, we have investigated the usefulness of the Reputation Test in locating the socially atypical disliked, or withdrawn children who need special help, by means of a comparison of "blind" interpretations of individual records with relevant data from other sources.

In a domain in which speculations are more numerous than facts, the supplying of normative data and the refinement of method are necessary preliminaries to the more crucial tests of theory. At the risk of violating a major criterion of scientific respectability, the present investigation has been formulated not as a statistical proof or disproof of any explicit hypothesis, but rather as an exploration of methods for studying this area of personality and its developmental sequences.

METHOD

The test used to explore these problems was constructed to measure children's attitudes toward each other on certain aspects of personality which they could readily observe in each other, which they could judge without emotional disturbance, and which were of significance to the clinician. In form, the test consisted of pairs of short questions, one item in each pair being considered favorable for adjustment and the other unfavorable. Examples are:

(+) "Which children are good sports and always play fair?"
(—) "Which children aren't very good sports, the poor losers?"

The children were asked to supply the names of those of their classmates who they thought best fitted each description. They were allowed to make as many nominations as they wished, to omit items if they could think of no one deserving mention, and to name themselves as often as they pleased. The teacher of each class also supplied data in this form on her pupils.

Subjects

The data upon which this investigation is based were obtained as a part of the Guidance Study of the University of California Child Welfare Institute (MacFarlane, 1938). The Reputation Test was administered in the public schools of Berkeley, California, in order to secure material on the social adjustment of these 250 Study cases, but since the test can be given only to an entire room, reputation data were secured also on the classmates of these children. Hence, the findings reported here are based on a much larger total population. The effect upon the sampling of selecting only classrooms containing Guidance Study cases is unknown; but the size of the group and the fact that the testing was carried on in all the elementary schools of Berkeley, make it seem likely that the population was quite typical of the entire elementary school population of that city during the years the data collection was in progress (1936–1939). Classrooms in all six grades were tested, but the group analyses reported here were performed only at the alternate grade levels I, III, and V.

Administration and Scoring of Test

For the first four grades, the children's opinions were obtained in individual interviews. In Grades V and VI the test was given to an entire class at one time, and the children requested to write down their nominations in test booklets. The number of mentions given to and received from others, self-mentions, and mentions made by the teacher were tabulated by sex and grade and used in the various analyses.

To obtain the reputation scores for each child, the number of mentions on each item (excluding self-mentions) was divided by the number of classmates who might have mentioned him. Scores on each dimension (composed of the positive and negative items of each pair) were obtained by dividing the algebraic sum of positive and negative mentions by the number of classmates.

RESULTS AND DISCUSSION

The objective of the initial analysis of the data was to identify group differences in reputation. The results of this analysis are presented in Table 1 where the means and standard deviations of votes received by boys and girls, in each of the three grades, on each item pair are summarized.

So far as votes *received* are concerned, it was found that on the majority of items girls enjoy much more favorable status in the eyes of their classmates than do boys. The average girl was judged to be QUIET, POPULAR, FULL OF FUN, NOT QUARRELSOME, a GOOD SPORT, a LITTLE LADY, GOOD-LOOKING, NOT A SHOW-OFF, TIDY, and FRIENDLY. The average boy was mentioned on the items WIGGLY, QUARRELSOME, BOSSY, SHOW-OFF, TAKES CHANCES, NOT BASHFUL, GOOD AT GAMES, and REAL BOY. Although aggressive was regarded as typical masculine behavior, the unfavorable connotations of such qualities as BOSSY, SHOW-OFF, QUARRELSOME, etc. suggest that boys are subject to much more disapproval than are girls in learning their appropriate sex role.

Age differences in reputation were less marked than the sex differences cited above, but a tendency with increasing grade level for girls' scores to grow less favorable and for boys' scores to improve operated to reduce the magnitude of the sex differences. The scores of both boys and girls were determined primarily by the opinions of judges of the same sex. Nevertheless, in the first

TABLE 1 Means and Standard Deviations of Boys' and Girls' Scores on the Various Item-Pairs of the Reputation Test*

Titles of Item Pairs	Grade I Girls (N = 49) Mean	Grade I Girls S.D.	Grade I Boys (N = 70) Mean	Grade I Boys S.D.	Grade III Girls (N = 340, items 1–25) (N = 178, items 26–31) Mean	Grade III Girls S.D.	Grade III Boys (N = 352, items 1–25) (N = 194, items 26–31) Mean	Grade III Boys S.D.	Grade V Girls (N = 306) Mean	Grade V Girls S.D.	Grade V Boys (N = 322) Mean	Grade V Boys S.D.
Quiet	**7.6**	12.4	−3.9	14.5	**5.2**	13.9	−3.8	15.1	**6.9**	17.1	−4.3	16.6
Popular	**7.6**	14.4	−1.1	15.4	**4.7**	14.3	−.8	14.9	4.8	20.7	3.0	17.3
Full of Fun	5.9	11.2	1.3	10.3	2.4	10.3	1.3	9.0	3.2	12.1	3.2	11.4
Not Quarrelsome	**6.9**	12.2	−5.7	10.9	**3.9**	9.6	−4.4	14.4	4.4	**15.5**	−.7	16.2
Takes Chances	1.8	7.2	3.3	12.7	−.2	7.2	4.1	**11.0**	−1.9	10.4	**3.9**	15.2
Not Bossy	1.4	7.3	−2.9	9.6	**1.3**	10.0	−1.9	9.3	.8	13.1	−.9	14.5
Good Sport	4.7	11.8	1.6	11.7	3.2	9.3	1.2	13.0	3.5	12.1	2.6	14.4
Not Bashful	.6	7.1	2.6	8.7	1.3	9.0	2.1	7.5	.6	16.1	3.7	11.9
Good at Games	4.9	10.9	1.1	11.8	1.2	10.6	3.4	14.9	1.0	15.3	**5.8**	20.8
Doesn't Get Mad	2.2	6.8	−1.4	9.9	**2.4**	10.5	−2.0	10.6	2.2	13.2	−.1	14.2
Real Boy			2.6	16.1	4.2	16.4	4.6	16.7	3.2	23.0	8.6	23.2
Little Lady	6.7	15.7			5.6	5.2	5.4	4.9	6.7	5.4	6.5	5.4
Best Friend	5.8	6.7	5.3	4.7	**3.6**	13.0	−.5	6.9	3.0	19.7	−.5	12.7
Good-Looking					**1.4**	9.3	−1.9	9.9	**2.8**	12.9	−3.8	15.9
Not a Show-Off					1.0	5.0	1.9	9.7	.1	11.6	.9	13.7
Leader									**8.0**	14.5	−1.2	14.4
Tidy									2.8	**8.6**	−2.2	17.4
Doesn't Fight									5.0	12.6	1.4	10.1
Friendly									1.3	8.7	2.3	8.9
Can Take a Joke												
Mean (all dimensions)	4.7	10.3	.2	11.4	2.8	10.2	.6	11.2	3.1	13.8	1.5	14.4

Note: In this table, the titles refer to the favorable–unfavorable item-pairs of which the titles indicate the "favorable" poles. A Positive Mean indicates that the average score is on the favorable side of the indifference point. A Negative Mean indicates the unfavorable side. The item not presented for each of the item-pairs shown are, respectively: Wiggly, Not Many Friends, Serious, Quarrelsome, Doesn't Take Chances, Bossy, Poor Sport, Bashful, Not Good at Games, Gets Mad Easily, Sissy, Tomboy, no opposite for Best Friend, Not Good Looking, Show-Off, Not a Leader, Untidy, Fights, Not Friendly, and Can't Take a Joke.

* Boldface means indicate items on which the sex represented is judged significantly more "favorably" than the other.

grade, girls' scores were determined relatively more by boys than vice versa, while by the fifth grade, the situation was reversed and boys' scores were determined relatively more by girls. Since sex differences in reputation were so conspicuous even in the first grade, and since the picture for girls was so markedly favorable and for boys so markedly unfavorable, it seems likely that these findings reflect not only behavioral differences between boys and girls, but also the stereotype that little boys are aggressive and dominant, little girls docile and well-behaved.

Group Differences in Judgment

Marked differences in the volume of voting on different items were found in teachers' mentions and in children's mentions of each other and of themselves. Both teachers and children made more nominations on favorable than on unfavorable items, and insofar as children's judgments of each other are concerned this tendency grew more pronounced in higher grades. However, the trend for self-mentions was in the opposite direction, self-judgments being made almost exclusively on favorable items in the first grade, but only slightly more frequently on favorable than on unfavorable items in the fifth grade.

Older children voted more heavily for others (and markedly more for themselves) than did younger children, but at all grade levels considerably more than half of the judgments concerned persons of the same sex as the judge. Certain qualities, especially WIGGLY, QUARRELSOME, FIGHTS, and SHOW-OFF, were customarily attributed to boys by judges of each sex, while others such as QUIET, NOT QUARRELSOME, and GOOD-LOOKING were more frequently used to describe girls. Self-mentions were made most often on items correlated with popularity for children of the sex concerned, the girls choosing items connoting amiability and docility, the boys those connoting athletic skills and daring.

In several respects, the judgment habits of girls and of boys stand in contrast: girls voted more for others than did boys at all three levels studied, but boys made more self-evaluations than did girls. Also, girls judged others of the same sex more favorably than did boys, but gave less favorable self-evaluations. Since these differences between boys' and girls' habits of judgment parallel those between younger and older subjects, the tentative conclusion is offered that girls are more "mature" in the pattern of judgments they make than are boys.

Group Differences in Agreement Among Judges

In order to measure the pervasiveness of opinion among classmate judges, the latter were divided into two halves and correlations computed between item-pair scores received from one half, and scores received from the other half. These "agreement" coefficients increased on the average item-pair from

.55 in Grade I to .72 in Grade III and .81 in Grade V, indicating considerable community of group opinion.

Disagreement in classmates' judgments was extremely infrequent concerning children whose scores differ markedly from the average, but was very common in the scores of children who received few votes. On the average dimension about 20 per cent of the children received a dimension score of zero, and of these about half were completely disagreed about (i.e., received equal numbers of favorable and unfavorable votes). Of those receiving a definite characterization on one item or the other of the average dimension, approximately 30 per cent in Grade I and 50 per cent in Grades III and V were identified without any dissenting mentions on the opposite item. If those receiving only one dissenting vote are included in the group agreed about, the proportions are increased by about 15 per cent. In general, there was more concurrence in the scores of boys identified on negative items, and in the scores of girls identified on positive items.

Agreement was quite poor between self-mentions and scores received from a pool of classmates, although the agreement improved with the age of the subjects concerned. Agreement between classmates' opinions and the teacher's judgment was somewhat better, but even here it was not until the fifth grade that the mean score of children mentioned by the teacher on the average item was significantly greater than the mean score of children not so mentioned. Hence, self-nominations, teacher mentions, and classmate judgments cannot be considered equivalent in the information they yield concerning the individual child. However, all may be useful in evaluating the adequacy of his social adjustment and the social climate to which he must adjust.

AN ILLUSTRATIVE CASE RECORD

The case record of James is described because his record illustrates the capacity of the Reputation Test to disclose difficulties in peer-relationships which may escape for a time the notice of adults.

It should be made explicit that such case interpretations constitute illustrations of the diagnostic potentialities of the Reputation Test rather than a "validation" of it. Further, it is not possible to be sure that the case material gives an unbiased picture of the child in question, since the total volume of life history data accumulated from birth is very large and only condensed excerpts from it could be included here. To minimize the degree of distortion from this source, the case summary was written without reference to the Reputation Test interpretations and prepared by a routine selection of data from several sources.

Reputation Test Interpretation

James is a member of a fifth-grade class containing almost twice as many girls as boys. More than half of the children enjoy reciprocal friendships with other members of the class. Although there are four "stars" of exceptional popularity, no complex clique groupings can be discerned. In this group James chooses as BEST FRIEND a boy who in turn chooses him, but neither received any votes from anyone else. James' mention of a BEST FRIEND of a girl (who, however, doesn't mention him) is sufficiently uncommon to deserve mention. On the test as a whole, James is mentioned by fewer boys and by fewer girls than the average fifth-grade boy, but he mentions considerably more than the average. (See Table 2.)

TABLE 2
Reputation Test Record of James

Sex—Male	Age 11 Yrs., 1 Mo.	Grade—High Fifth
Girls Present in Class —25.	Proportion mentioning James— 52%	(Norm = 64%).
Boys Present in Class —14.	Proportion Mentioning James— 69%	(Norm = 79%).
Girls Enrolled in Class—25.	Proportion James Mentioned — 72%	(Norm = 49%).
Boys Enrolled in Class—14.	Proportion James Mentioned —100%	(Norm = 79%).

The votes James receives on negative items both from boys and from girls, are almost twice as numerous as are his favorable mentions. However, since he is relatively inconspicuous, the total number of unfavorable judgments is not large, and on no item-pair is the boy's standard score larger than —.80. His more deviate scores are received on the items NOT A LEADER (—.80), SISSY (—.80, although three girls considered him a REAL BOY), BEST FRIEND (—.70), DOESN'T TAKE CHANCES (—.60), NOT GOOD AT GAMES (—.50), and SERIOUS (—.50).

None of these items is correlated with REAL BOY and its associated variables. The implication is plain that James is, if not somewhat effeminate, at least not as masculine as the average. This impression is substantiated by the fact that the items on which he received a favorable standard score (QUIET, NOT QUARRELSOME, NOT BASHFUL, TIDY, and DOESN'T FIGHT) are traits more valued by girls than by boys.

James' teacher mentions him as POPULAR, FULL OF FUN, A GOOD SPORT, A REAL BOY, FRIENDLY, and most significant, as her BEST FRIEND, an item usually omitted by teachers. This wholly favorable picture is quite at variance with that drawn by his classmates. It suggests that James gets along better with adults than with children, and probably presents a pretty bland front to the former. In this case it may be that the boy is suffering mild hostility from his classmates as the result of being too well liked by his teacher. It is further possible that the approval he receives from his teacher indicates that he is brighter academically than most of his group.

Despite his favorable and secure position from the point of view of his teacher, some evidence of insecurity is offered by the fact that he names himself only on unfavorable qualities, and makes the next to the most such mentions of any boy in class. (The average boy is more prone to name himself for favorable qualities.) Some of his self-mentions, viz., DOESN'T TAKE CHANCES, NOT GOOD AT GAMES, and NOT A LEADER, indicate his awareness of being less venturesome and ascendant than other boys. His other self-votes (GETS MAD and FIGHTS) are not in harmony with the opinion of the class, and may indicate aggressive wishes or a fantasy of being more aggressive than he really is. In any event, he seems franker and better able to verbalize his problem than most boys in similar circumstances.

James is relatively more interested in or at least more aware of the personalities of girls than of boys. He casts more votes for girls than any other boy on seven items, and the next to the most on four more, although on no item is he correspondingly extreme for mentions made of boys. Not only does he cast more votes for girls than for boys, but relatively more of them are favorable. He casts the most votes of any boy for girls both on BOSSY and on NOT BOSSY, and makes a similar extreme number of mentions of girls on the GOOD AT GAMES-NOT GOOD AT GAMES pair. On the other hand, in mentioning boys, he names only one as BOSSY and one as NOT BOSSY, omits GOOD AT GAMES (usually an item eliciting heavier voting than any other in the test), and names only one boy as NOT GOOD AT GAMES. These facts taken together suggest quite strongly that he does not play much with boys but rather enters, or at least tries to enter, into the girls' games where he is sometimes rebuffed by the "bossier ones." However, the fact that he makes six nominations on the REAL BOY item indicates that this is an important dimension for him and possibly one concerning which he feels sufficiently uneasy to omit a self-mention on either pole.

Summary based on reputation data. James is probably a bright, polite boy, more attractive to adults than to other children, though not actually unpopular with anyone. He is not very masculine, is a follower, cautious, unaggressive, and lacking in athletic skills. He is probably open and outgoing but quite insecure, and may harbor aggressive wishes which he is unable to carry into action. He seems to know more about girls than boys, and to esteem them more highly. However, he is not too well thought of by members of either sex. Fortunately, he has one close friend in the class who may give him considerable support. He may be headed for an unhappy time in adolescence. Efforts to improve his physical skills might well be expended on his behalf.

Excerpts From the Case History

a. Physical development. James is slightly above average in height, but very obese (girdle adiposity). Sex maturation definitely below average. He has had a kidney disorder of long standing, and in consequence his physical activity has been curtailed on medical advice.

b. Mental test results. (Stanford, Form L) IQ = 149. (This has varied from 137 to 149.) Comment of Examiner: "Interested in success but not upset by failure. Friendly, relaxed, and gracious. Cooperative and kindly. Good insight —a few show-off mannerisms, but quite well poised."

c. Teacher's comments. "Very friendly and well liked, witty and humorous —self-reliant, quite courteous. A leader admired by others, has ideas they accept. Enjoys excelling, and does. Grades good or excellent. Doesn't join in hard games because of physical condition. Quite a thinker and reader—can converse on adult level. A well-adjusted child."

d. From an interview with James. With reference to social adjustment: "I used to be shy but I have lots of friends now. I always arrange to meet Robert (named as friend on the Reputation Test) at recess." (Q) "We don't play much—just walk around."

With reference to teasing: "Sometimes kids say, 'Hi-ya, fatty?' but I don't let it get under my skin unless they do it too much."

With reference to scholastic work: "I always get a good card but not better than most." (Note: One year later James commented that he knew lots of people but didn't have bosom friends. He admitted that he was not popular, but he thought boys like him better than girls.)

e. Case worker's comments. "Is overdependent upon mother. Demands attention and is lazy. Very sensitive to remarks about his size. Too cautious, never wants to try anything new. Is friendly, expressive, and spontaneous. Dislikes quarrels and keeps out of them. Good-natured—gets along well with adults and children. Prefers to win, but isn't too disturbed by failure. High energy level, a verbal child with an adult vocabulary. Seems to be quite content with his lot in life."

Comment

James's major problem, apart from his physical handicap, seems to lie in the field of social adjustment to his contemporaries. It seems obvious that his difficulties are related to his inability to participate in active sports, but a solution to them is difficult. It is interesting that the Reputation Test revealed James's rather poor status at a time when adults were giving this polite and verbal child a much more favorable characterization, and a year before the boy himself admitted the true state of affairs.

CONCLUSION

An illustrative clinical interpretation has been presented based on the Reputation Test records of a subject chosen to represent one of the more deviate patterns obtained in the Guidance Study. Teachers' mentions, self-mentions, reputation *with* and votes given *to* other classmates were considered in relation to the norm for the appropriate sex and grade level, and to the pattern of friendships revealed by the BEST FRIEND item.

The adequacy of a clinical characterization of a child based on his reputation record depends, apart from the insightfulness of the interpreter, upon how deviate the child is in his group and upon how full his record is. However, an extremely scant number of votes given and received may itself be indicative of a withdrawn personality. Behavior which is not correlated with that elicited in the school situation cannot be predicted on the basis of the Reputation Test, and nonsocial aspects of personality are also difficult to get at. Statements about more obvious personality characteristics can be made quite accurately, within the limitations noted above, on the basis of the reputation data taken alone. Inferences about a child's areas of tension derive from his reputation, and in addition from his pattern of voting (i.e., from the projective aspect of the test), but the significance of the latter can be evaluated only in relation to the former.

Although the Reputation Test is limited both as to areas of personality which it can reveal and as to the types of questions which it is expedient to include in a classroom setting, it is nevertheless useful in diagnosing a child's adjustment to his classmates, and can throw some light on his social maturity and on his areas of sensitivity and conflict. Since the Reputation Test yields information that is not always directly accessible to teachers making judgments from an adult point of view, it frequently reveals problems making for social maladjustment much earlier than they are ordinarily detected by adult observers. Hence, it may make a practical contribution to counselors and school administrators, both in locating children who are having psychological difficulties in the field of social relationships, and in measuring the effectiveness of efforts on their behalf.

CHAPTER 3

Personal-Social Motives and Incentives

Incentives are goals, objects, or states of well-being that can take the shape of material things, events, or ideals. However, the constructs of motive and incentive, as employed in discussions of human behavior, are sometimes difficult to separate. In this regard, a clarification by Atkinson (1957, p. 360) will prove to be helpful. Motive is defined by him as a striving for certain satisfactions implicit in the attainment of incentives. Personal-social motives, as well as other motives, are given names that represent the class of intrinsic incentives which, when achieved, produce similar kinds of satisfactions; the power motive produces a feeling of being in command and of being influential; the *affiliation* motive produces a sense of belonging through being received and accepted by others; and the *achievement* motive yields satisfaction through accomplishment.

This definition implies that incentives have the characteristics of being expectations of satisfactions; of directing behavior toward their attainment; and of having some degree of probability that they will be reached. There must be some assurance that the goal will have some *value* when it is attained; or, at least, it must have positive *valence* (attractiveness) for the person before it is attained. If not, there would be little sense in working to acquire it. Personal-social incentives, by this definition, are typically intrinsic events which, as expectations, are antecedents of behavior that increase effort and provide direction to behavior; as consequences, they function as rewards by strengthening the responses they follow.

The personal-social incentives differ radically from those typically associated with the primary drives. They always involve interaction with other people and in this sense they are unique. For example, imagine that a student is asked the question, "Why did you go to the football rally?" He might reply, "Because everyone else went." No physiological need was satisfied, there was no threat to his survival, but energy was expended for the expectation of satisfaction from social-interaction. Affiliation incentives involve relating to people by being with them, enjoying their companionship, getting along with them, and acting in ways that obtain their approval. Incentives reflected in achievement-striving tendencies involve relating to people on a competitive level; prestige, status, and self-esteem are gained by comparison of oneself with others or by standards set by them, by rivalry or competing with them, and by surpassing them. In either case, people, as social objects, are influential facets of other-people's incentives.

The derivation of personal-social incentives has been a central issue for many psychologists as illustrated in the history of theory and investigations about the achievement motive, which, incidentally, has been a concern of most major developmental-personality theories. There may be good reason for the speculation that this and other social motives are innate or intrinsic. However, on balance, most theories suggest it is acquired. The Freudian school indicates that the sex drive can be channeled, via sublimation, into a drive for mastery. The neo-psychoanalytic school takes issue with the dominance of sexual motives, but agrees that accomplishment is fundamental to feelings of personal satisfaction, worth, and well-being. Lewin, whose work was in the field-Gestalt tradition, spoke of the striving nature of man's aspirations and of the way challenges, successfully met, enhance further striving. Personality theorists have thought of social motives as being derived from association with the comforts provided by the mother's care, and eventually becoming functionally autonomous. That is, the functioning of a motive eventually becomes independent of its relationship with comfort. The neo-behaviorist's constructs of secondary drives and secondary rewards are based on very similar notions. A complete discussion of the innate or derived character of incentives and motives is beyond the scope of this introduction. But is is clear that some goals *do* get channeled or transformed to take on personal-social features through initial social-emotional experiences in the family. Once they have been so canalized they can be further modified or intensified by the nature of other socialization experiences.

The articles in this chapter deal primarily with the achievement motive, aspirations, and ambition. They have been selected as representatives of the kind of research conducted on the variables affecting the development of social motivations and all have implications for understanding influences affecting the value of personal-social incentives.

The major impetus to investigations of the achievement motive was provided by McClelland, although one of the articles below antedates his work by several years. His theory and method for measuring achievement motivation was founded on the notion of achievement imagery. The subject, after viewing a picture for twenty seconds, writes a four-minute story, in answer to four questions about the characters in the pictures. This procedure is repeated with each of three other pictures. The resulting protocols are then scored for expressions of desire for achievement goals, achievement-oriented activity, or successful goal attainment. These scores, weighted appropriately according to a standardized scoring system, provide an operational definition that reflects McClelland's construct of achievement motivation as *a concern with competing successfully with some standard of excellence.* The standard of excellence, it should be added, can be imposed by one's membership group, reference group, family, personal standards, or by an arbitrary norm. This definition is not at all unlike that used by Henry A. Murray in his classic studies in the exploration of personality where he described the achievement motive as the rapid mastery of difficult tasks which involved the surmounting of obstacles and surpassing the accomplishments of other people. More recently, Robert White has suggested a similar notion in his construct of the competence motive as an intrinsic motivation to interact effectively with one's environment.

The initial output of studies that followed McClelland's introduction of a theory and measurement device for studying achievement motivation was mainly oriented toward establishing the reliability, validity, and correlates of the scores and assumptions. A new momentum was provided this effort when studies were redirected toward understanding the antecedents of the achievement motive, particularly those involved in child-rearing practices. These relationships were soon to be extended by theories and evidence relating family antecedents to the Protestant ethic and to economic development in a book entitled *The Achieving Society* (McClelland, 1961).

What influences are responsible for the development of personal-social motives? The answer is to be found in the practices employed by the societal institutions responsible for the transmission of values. Among these, parental influences are, of course, especially important. The mother's role appears to be particularly related, for example, to the achievement motivation of her sons. One of the first studies in this area, by Winterbottom (1957), showed that mothers of sons with high need for achievement scores, more than mothers of sons with low scores, place independence demands on the child at an early age, usually before he is seven or eight years old. They expect him to be self-reliant and to make his own decisions in those areas in which he is capable of doing so: making his own friends, finding his way around the neighborhood, running errands, performing simple tasks, and engaging in hobbies and other interests of his own accord. When he successfully performs these behaviors the mother rewards him affectionately and warmly. Compared to the mothers of low-achievers, they place fewer restrictions on their children's attempts at self-initiated behavior.

These studies were based on mothers' reports of their child-rearing practices and yielded correlates with high achievement. Thus, there may be more fundamental or other, unidentified reasons why these practices produce differences in motivation. Nevertheless, they do imply, together with the ideas produced in other theoretical orientations described above, that the development of personal-social motives shares some of the characteristics of imprinting behavior in lower organisms. There appears to be a critical period in which such motives are most easily formed. Early experiences, probably those up to late childhood take precedence over later, more recent experiences. Once the motive is formed it becomes functionally autonomous, that is, it is persistent and does not extinguish easily. Finally, motives function in pervasive fashion in behavior. While they do not supplant physiological drives, they do seem to be persistent, yielding only temporarily to the satisfaction of other drives.

The paper by Rosen and D'Andrade is one of the few attempts to go beyond correlations of mothers' reports of child-rearing practices with measures of achievement motivation. Complete nuclear family units, comprised of mother, father, and son, from both the lower- and middle-socioeconomic strata were engaged in a realistic setting. Thus, the behavior of *both* the mother *and* father were observed as their son performed difficult and challenging tasks. The report of these observations permits the reader a somewhat formal glimpse at what parents actually do when interacting with their high, or low, achievement-oriented child.

The article by Child, Potter, and Levine extends our understandings of influences affecting the achievement motive. These investigators systematically examined the influence of children's textbooks on the development of various personal-social incentives. It preceded the work based on McClelland's currently popular theoretical approach but shows that achievement orientations were clearly presented to the young third grade pupil as associated with the male rather than female role. Children's readers do provide strong value orientations and, as the authors of the article conclude, their findings imply that the selection of readers warrants careful attention. This classic study is all the more interesting when its conclusions are recognized to complement those found in more recent studies. For example, McClelland (1961) found that he was able to tell more about economic growth of a country through children's readers than he could from population and economic data.

What are people with ambition, people who seek incentives associated with achievement, like? They tend to aspire to reasonably high goals but not goals that are beyond their capacities to reach. They display self-initiated effort and seem to be self-reliant, confident, and independent in these efforts. They take reasonable risks where such risks are challenges to their ability rather than matters of chance or luck. They are more receptive to knowledge of progress than to knowledge about how well they get along with others. Since they are more task- than other-person oriented they prefer working partners who are knowledgeable resource persons over socially attractive friends.

Achievement-oriented people are also able to *delay gratification*. This relatively new construct is introduced, in this set of papers, in the article by Mischel. The concept implies that time perspective is an essential part of the socialization process if personal-social incentives are to emerge in functionally useful ways; striving requires postponement of more or less trivial outcomes that could be achieved immediately for the important ones that require more time to acquire. The hypothesized relationship of delay of gratification with measures of achievement motivation were examined in the Trinidad society. Support for this hypothesis suggests the generality of these constructs and their importance in developmental processes.

Is enough known about motives to change them in programs deliberately intended to do so? A unique training program devoted to promoting increases in achievement-oriented values of underachievers is described in the interesting paper by Kolb. The program provided models with whom the boys could identify, counseling to increase expectations of success, instruction designed to help translate achievement imagery into behavior, and opportunities to practice the necessary instrumental behaviors. The subsequent school achievement of boys from the middle-class was increased but the school achievement of the lower-class boy was unaffected. This study indicates the requirements necessary to design programs of instruction for objectives of concern to educators but which are ordinarily considered to be beyond the scope of the typical curriculum. For the researcher, it points out the necessity for additional analytic investigation of the variables responsible for whatever changes in motives were actually accomplished.

Sugarman's study of pupils in English schools views still another aspect of social influences, also of importance to the school, on learning of personal-social incentives. He clarifies how sanctions are imposed in closely-knit peer groups to affect the aspirations of individual members for achievement in school. Perhaps one of the most interesting findings, in this very extensive study, is the interaction found between the peer-group's norms and opportunities provided in the home; that is, boys from homes with fewer opportunities for intellectual stimulation were more influenced by peer groups in which achievement was the norm than were boys from homes where more opportunities were available.

Turner's paper extends the findings related to normative influences, to the development of ambition, within the context of the broader social structure, as it occurs during a major transition period in the socialization cycle. He reports on the nature of strivings by youths of both sexes during the last years in high school, when separation from earlier friendship patterns and embarkation on new careers take place. The problems encountered by the mobility-ambitious pupil are similar to those of the marginal-man. They must leave the security of traditions associated with their stratum of origin for the less well-defined values associated with the stratum of destination. These problems are avoided by those with eminence ambition, that is by those pupils who aspire to occupations within their original social class and who achieve satisfaction by moving upward within such occupations.

In this chapter, then, there are represented studies demonstrating the effect of socialization agents including the media, the family, the peer group, and the society on development of incentives that involve interactions with people. These influences may be effective at any time in the person's life-span but appear to be especially critical in the formative years before late childhood. Training programs directed toward the modification of strivings may be pragmatically efficacious and if carefully controlled will provide further analysis of the variables contributing to this aspect of social development.

11. THE PSYCHOSOCIAL ORIGINS OF ACHIEVEMENT MOTIVATION

Bernard C. Rosen & Roy G. D'Andrade

The parents' strategic role in the origin of the achievement motive had been all but neglected in research investigations until Winterbottom's (1957) study was reported.[1] The mothers of boys with high and low achievement motivation were interviewed about their child-rearing practices. The mothers of highly motivated boys reported employing practices that appeared to be directed toward independence training. They defined the child's role accordingly, that is, they emphasized expectations of self-reliance.

Parents of boys with high achievement motives also use practices that imply an achievement orientation; they encourage the child to do well. These parents are themselves characterized by high need for achievement and by their behavioral example suggest that the child should and can emulate them. When the child is engaged in achievement-oriented activities he invites his mother's affection and encouragement. Her demands and involvement are less directed toward what the boy is to do than it is toward the necessity for doing something and doing it well. If either independence training or achievement training are to be effective, sanctions must be employed and the child must be permitted to perform autonomously. Neither, by itself, appears to be a sufficient condition for the development of achievement motivation. These relationships between training practices and motivation are highly correlated and have been replicated by a number of

SOURCE. Adapted and abridged from Bernard C. Rosen and Roy D'Andrade, "The Psychosocial Origins of Achievement Motivation," *Sociometry*, 1959, Vol. 22, pp. 185–218. (With permission of the authors and the publisher, the American Sociological Association.)

[1] Based on Marian R. Winterbottom's Ph.D. dissertation, University of Michigan, 1953.

investigators. However, they are based primarily on interviews. Furthermore, these interviews have been mainly with the mother, and rarely with the father.

Thus, it is an interesting question to ask, "Just how do parents react to their sons' efforts at challenging tasks?" The study by Rosen and D'Andrade is especially interesting because it is based on direct observations of each parent's reactions toward the child as he performed several problem-solving tasks. Each task was structured to invite verbal participation by the parent. The three member family interaction permitted the observation of the nature and intensity of parental behaviors and the sanctions they imposed on the boy. The mothers and fathers of highly motivated boys compared with parents of low motivated boys were effusive in their praise and approval, provided more encouragement, urged the boys to reach for high scores, and generally required more of him. The fathers actually were *less* demanding than fathers of low-motivated boys. The latter were more direct, and more authoritarian in the assistance they provided the boy. These data are still primarily correlational and, hence, can only be suggestive of the origins of achievement motivation. As the reader will have noticed, too, the subjects in these studies were always boys. Inquiry into the development of girls' achievement motivations is much needed.

Studies of the origins of achievement motivation have been built around the notion that training in independent mastery is an antecedent condition of n Achievement (McClelland & Friedman, 1952; McClelland, Atkinson & Lowell, 1953). This approach grew out of McClelland's and his associates' theory of the nature and origins of motivation. They argue that all motives are learned, that "they develop out of repeated affective experiences connected with certain types of situations and types of behavior. In the case of achievement motivation, the situation should involve 'standards of excellence,' presumably imposed on the child by the culture, or more particularly by the parents as representatives of the culture, and the behavior should involve either 'competition' with those standards of excellence or attempts to meet them whch, if successful, produce positive affect or, if unsuccessful, negative affect. It follows that those cultures or families which stress competition with standards of excellence or which insist *that the child be able to perform certain tasks well by himself* . . . should produce children with high achievement motivation" (McClelland et al., 1953).

Two distinctly different kinds of child-training practices are implicit in this theory. The first is the idea that the child is trained to do things "well"; the second, the notion that he is trained to perform tasks "by himself." The former has been called *achievement training* (Child, Storm & Veroff, 1958) in that it stresses competition in situations involving standards of excellence; the later has been called *independence training* in that it involves putting the child on his own. The failure to disentangle these two concepts has resulted in a focus of attention upon independence training largely to the exclusion of achievement training, although the former is primarily concerned with developing self-reliance, often in areas involving self-caretaking (e.g., cleaning, dressing, amusing, or defending oneself). Although both kinds of training practices frequently occur together, they are different in content and consequences and needed to be examined separately. We believe that of the two training practices, achievement training is the more effective in generating n Achievement.

There is another component of independence training—one which is explicit in the idea of independence—that needed further exploration: *autonomy*. By autonomy, we mean training and permitting the child to exercise a certain amount of freedom of action in decision making. The operation of both components tends to increase the power of independence training to generate n Achievement, since in itself high parental expectations for self-reliance may cause rebellion, feelings of rejection, or of apathy on the part of the child, while autonomy without parental expectations for self-reliance and achievement may be perceived as mere permissiveness or indifference.

In association with parental demands that the child be self-reliant, autonomous, and show evidence of high achievement, there must be sanctions to see that these demands are fulfilled. Winterbottom found that mothers of children with high n Achievement gave somewhat more intense rewards than mothers of children with low n Achievement. Little was known about the role of negative sanctions, or of the relative impact of sanctions from either parent. Further study was required of the degree and kind of sanctions employed by both parents to see that their demands are met.

Methodological. This study departed from two practices common in studies of the origins of n Achievement. The first practice is to derive data exclusively from ethnographic materials; the second, to obtain information through questionnaire-type interviews with mothers. Interviews and ethnographies can be valuable sources of information, but they are often contaminated by interviewer and respondent biases, particularly those of perceptual distortion, inadequate recall, and deliberate inaccuracies. There was a need for data derived from systematic observation of parent-child relations. It is not enough to know what parents *say* their child-rearing practices are; these statements should be checked against more objective data, preferably acquired under controlled experimental conditions, that would permit us to *see* what they do. In this study, experiments were employed which enabled a team of investigators to observe parent-child interaction in problem-solving situations that were standardized for all groups and required no special competence associated with age or sex.

An equally strong objection can be raised against the tendency to ignore the father's role in the development of the child's need to achieve. Apart from an earlier study of father-son power relations, no efforts had been made to determine the father's contribution to achievement and independence training—a surprising omission even granted the mother's importance in socializing the child in American society. Although we were not prepared to take a position on the nature of the role relationships between father, mother, and son with respect to this motive, we deliberately created experimental conditions which would enable us to observe the way in which the three members of the family interacted in a problem-solving situation. Finally, this study incorporated in one design the variables of group membership, child-training practices, and motivation, variables that heretofore had not been studied simultaneously. In so doing we hoped to establish the nexus among class membership, socialization practices, and achievement motivation.

EXPERIMENTAL PROCEDURE

The subjects selected to provide data for the testing of these hypotheses about the origins of achievement motivation were 120 persons who made up 40 family groups composed of a father, mother, and their son, aged nine, ten, or eleven.

The forty boys, matched by age, race, IQ, and social class were white, native born, and between nine and eleven years of age; the average was ten years. Half of the boys had high n Achievement scores, half had low scores, according to the method developed by McClelland and his associates (1953). In each achievement motivation category, half of the boys were middle class, half were lower class, according to a modified version of the Hollingshead Index of Social Position (Hollingshead & Redlick, 1953) which uses the occupation and education of the chief wage-earner—usually the father—as principal criteria of status.

It can be seen that the study was designed in such a way that the subjects fell into one of four cells, with the achievement motivation level of the boys and the class position of the parents as the classificatory variables. Within each cell there were ten families. This four-cell factorial design was constructed so as to facilitate the use of the analysis of variance technique in the statistical analysis of the data.

Experimental Tasks

After the boy was selected, appointments were made to visit the families. There were two teams of observers, each composed of a man and woman. Both teams had been trained together to ensure adequate intra- and inter-team reliability.

A pair of observers visited each family group, usually at night. When rapport had been established, the parents and their son were placed at a table—usually in the kitchen—and it was explained that the boy was going to perform certain tasks.

The observers wanted to create an experimental situation from which could be derived objective measures of the parents' response to their son as he engaged in achievement behavior. Tasks were devised which the boy could do and which would involve the parents in their son's task performance. The tasks were constructed so that the subjects were often faced with a choice of giving or refusing help. At times they were permitted to structure the situation according to their own norms; at other times the experimenters set the norms. In some situations they were faced with decision conflicts over various alternatives in the problem-solving process. The observation of the parents' behavior as their son engaged in these experimental tasks provided information about the demands the parents made upon him, the sanctions employed to enforce these demands, and the amount of independence the child had developed in relations with his parents.

In creating the experimental tasks an effort was made to simulate two conditions normally present when boys are solving problems in the presence of their parents: (1) tasks were constructed to make the boys relatively dependent upon their parents for aid, and (2) the situation was arranged so that the parents either knew the solution to the problem or were in a position to do the task better than their son. In addition, tasks were created which tapped manual skills as well as intellectual capacities, although intelligence is a factor in any problem-solving situation. It was for this reason that the experimenters controlled for I.Q.

Pretesting had shown that no single task would provide sufficient data to test all hypotheses. Hence, five tasks were constructed, each designed to attack the problem from a somewhat different angle and yet provide certain classes of data that could be scored across tasks. The tasks used in this study are: block stacking, anagrams, Koh's block patterns, and a ring-toss game.

Category System

A brief description of the category system for scoring is shown in Figure 1. Most of the subjects' verbal and some of their motor behavior (e.g., laughing, hand-clapping, scowling) was scored in one of twelve categories. In eight of these categories were placed acts involving relatively strong affect. Four additional categories were used to distinguish between various kinds of statements—either giving, requesting, or rejecting directions—which contained very little or no affect. A distinction was made between negative and positive affective acts. Affective acts associated with explicit or implicit evaluations of the boy's performance which aimed at motivating or

+X	Expresses approval, gives love, comfort, affection
+T	Shows positive tension release, jokes, laughs
+E	Gives explicit positive evaluation of performance, indicates job well done
+P	Attempts to push up performance through expression of enthusiasm, urges, cheers on
N	Gives nonspecific directions, gives hints, clues, general suggestions
S	Gives specific directions, gives detailed information about how to do a task
aa	Asks aid, information, or advice
ra	Rejects aid, information, or advice
−P	Attempts to push up performance through expressions of displeasure; urges on indicating disappointment at speed and level of performance
−E	Gives explicit negative evaluation of performance, indicates job poorly done
−T	Shows negative tension release, shows irritation, coughs
−X	Expresses hostility, denigrates, makes sarcastic remarks

FIGURE 1. The system of categories used in scoring parent-child interaction.

changing his behavior were scored differently from affective acts which involved reactions to the boy and only indirectly to his performance.

EXPERIMENTAL FINDINGS

The fundamental hypothesis of this study is that achievement motivation develops out of repeated affective associations with two kinds of experiences: achievement training and independence training. It was hypothesized that high n Achievement scores were most likely to be found among children whose parents (1) gave them *achievement training* (i.e., imposed standards of excellence upon tasks, had high expectations for their son's achievement, and indicated that they evaluated highly his competence to do a task well), (2) who gave them *independence training* (i.e., expected high evidences of self-reliance while at the same time permitting relative autonomy in decision making), and (3) employed sanctions to reinforce appropriate behavior. Data to test these hypotheses were derived from an examination of parental estimates and choices and from the observation of parent-child interaction.

From these data several measures of achievement and independence training and sanctions were constructed. We turn now to an examination of the manner in which these measures were derived and their relationship to achievement motivation.

Parental Aspirations and Evaluations

The parents' estimates of how well their son would do in the Block Stacking task are considered measures of their aspiration for and evaluations of him. In this case the estimates were made against a stated norm. The parents' first estimate, unaffected by any previous performance in this task, is conceived to be primarily a measure of parental aspirations for the boy. Undoubtedly, this estimate is somewhat affected by the parents' evaluation of the boy's competence, for aspiration and evaluation levels are often intricately mixed. Nonetheless, since presumably the parents had never seen their son perform a block-stacking test with one hand while blindfolded, we believe the element of aspiration level to be dominant in this measure.

We began by comparing the fathers of boys with high n Achievement with the fathers of boys with low n Achievement, and the mothers of high n Achievement boys with the mothers of boys with low n Achievement. It had been predicted that the parents of the boys with high n Achievement scores would give higher estimates than parents of boys with low scores. And in fact the data are in the predicted direction; the fathers and mothers of boys with high n Achievement scores on the average give higher estimates, but the differences are not statistically significant. However, when father's and mother's scores are summed together the differences between parental groups is significant ($F = 4.09, P < .05$).

Parental estimates for the second and third trials of this task were combined to form a combined score considered as a measure of the parents' aspiration-evaluation of the boy as affected by his performance against a given standard of excellence. The data show that the mothers of boys with high n Achievement scores give considerably higher estimates for the second and third trials of this task than do the mothers of boys with low scores ($F = 10.28, P < .005$). The differences between the fathers, although in the predicted direction in that the fathers of boys with high n Achievement scores tend to give higher estimates, are not statistically significant.

The Patterns task was designed to provide additional and supplemental measures of parental aspiration-evaluation levels. In this situation the parents were not asked to estimate how well their son would do, but actually to select three tasks, graded in difficulty, for their son to perform. Since all three choices were made before their son began the problem, these scores could be considered as performance-free measures of the parents' evaluation of the boy's capacity to do the task, plus their aspiration for him to do the more difficult task in a situation structured by degree of difficulty with no stated norm or group average.

Each subject's three choices were combined by simple addition (no transformation of scores was necessary) to provide a single score for each person. We had expected that the parents of boys with high achievement motivation scores—in keeping with their tendency to have higher aspirations for and evaluations of their boys—would choose the more difficult patterns for their sons. The data indicate a difference in this direction, but the differences are small and not significant for either fathers or mothers.

Parental Standards of Excellence

In the two experiments just described some parents would very likely have imposed standards of excellence upon the tasks even if the experimenters had not done so. However, since they had been asked to make their estimates or choices in situations where standards were explicit (as in the Block Stacking task where a group performance norm had been given, or in the Patterns task where the complexity of the patterns had been clearly graded by the experimenters) it could not be clearly seen from these experiments whether parents differed in their tendencies to impose standards upon the problems their children were expected to solve. The Ring Toss experiment was devised for this purpose. In this experiment no norm or group standard of excellence was set by the investigators. Each parent was asked to make ten choices of "the best place for your son to stand." After each choice the boy threw three rings at the peg. A measure of the height of the standard of excellence each parent sets for the boy was derived by summing the choices (number of feet the boy is asked to stand from the peg) of each parent.

We hypothesized that parents who imposed standards of excellence upon this normless task would be most likely to structure tasks generally in these terms. Our expectation was that the parents of boys with high motivation scores would be more likely to impose standards of excellence upon this task in that they would place their sons farther from the peg than would parents of boys with low scores. The data tend to support this expectation: the fathers and mothers of high n Achievement boys, on the average, chose positions further from the peg than the parents of children with low achievement motivation. The differences, however, are significant only in the case of the mothers ($F = 5.47$, $P < .025$). The combined scores of fathers and mothers were significantly different for the two groups ($F = 6.99$, $P < .01$).

The Anagrams experiment involved another task for which the investigators had set no explicit standard of excellence, the parents and boy merely being provided with lettered blocks out of which words could be made. This experiment had been designed primarily to provide measures of independence training. The parents shared three letters which could be given to the boy at any time to help him. The sum of the time at which new letters were given by both (or either) parents was treated originally as a measure of self-reliance training, i.e., the longer the parents delayed in giving the boy new letters the more was the indication that they expected him to work longer and harder at a problem on his own. This experiment revealed a clear difference between parental groups but not in the direction we had predicted: the parents of high n Achievement boys gave new letters *sooner* than the parents of boys with low n Achievement ($F = 6.28$, $P < .025$).

This finding, so different from what had been expected, prompted a re-evaluation of the task and a further (albeit ex post factum) interpretation of the data. We believe, now, that we were mistaken in assuming that this task would only measure self-reliance training. Rather, our observations indicate that this experiment elicited from some parents a type of achievement training in which the element of competition with a standard of excellence was very strong. The parents (especially the mothers) of boys with strong achievement motivation, it appeared, tended to perceive the task not so much as one which their son should do on his own, *but as a challenge to do well*. They reacted to this experiment with more emotion and competitiveness than displayed toward any other problem. The mother, in particular, was eager for her son to do well and often became anxious when he stopped making words. Both parents typically showed keener pleasure and disappointment at the boy's success or failure than was ordinarily displayed by the parents of boys with weak achievement motivation. The boy with strong motivation tended to receive letters sooner, we believe, because his parents were eager to see him make words and because of their reluctance to frustrate him to a point where his motive to excel in this important area would be destroyed.

Achievement Training and Performance Levels

The behavior of people with high achievement motivation is characterized by persistent striving and general competitiveness. It would follow from this, other things being equal, that boys with high achievement motivation would perform better than those with low motivation—and in fact this proved to be the case. Boys with high n Achievement tend to build higher towers of blocks, construct patterns faster, and make more words in the Anagrams task. The differences are significant in the case of the Block Stacking task ($F = 8.16$, $P < .005$), but not for the Patterns and Anagrams experiments. In the latter two tasks the individual's performance is very greatly affected by his intelligence. Since I.Q. score was one of the variables controlled in this study (there were no differences between the mean I.Q. scores of boys with high n Achievement and their peers with low achievement motivation), even these small differences are surprising. The superior performance of high n Achievement boys appears to be more a function of greater self-reliance and zest in competitive activity than of intelligence. Thus, boys with high achievement motivation tend to ask for less aid (aa), are more likely to reject offers of help from their parents (ra), and appear to get more pleasure out of participating in the experiment.

Sanctions

Typically, positive and negative reinforcements are associated with any learning situation—rewards for success and punishment for failure. We had predicted that the parents of boys with high achievement motivation would score higher on Warmth (positive affect) and lower on Rejection (negative affect) than the parents of low n Achievement boys. *The data show that the mothers of high n Achievement boys score significantly higher on Warmth than the mothers of low n Achievement boys* ($F = 8.87$, $P < .01$). The differences between fathers, although in the predicted direction, are not significant ($F = 4.13$, $P < .10$).

Fathers of boys with high n Achievement tend to score lower on Rejection. The reverse is true for the mothers: *the Rejection scores are higher for mothers of high Achievement motivation boys than for the mothers of low n Achievement boys*. None of these differences in Rejection, however, is statistically significant.

Parental Profiles and Motivation

The split plot type of analysis of variance was next employed to permit the examination of all variables simultaneously for each parent. All scores were transformed into standard scores, and in the case of four variables (S, Pushing, Rejection, and Autonomy) where low parental scores for parents had been hypothesized as producing high n Achievement the direction of the scores was reversed. Hence, we have labeled these as "Fewer Specific Statements," "Less Pushing," "Less Rejection"; a high score for Autonomy means that the parents have given their son a relatively high amount of autonomy. This was done in order to make it possible to sum across all variables and arrive at a meaningful figure for each parent. A mean score for each variable for fathers and mothers was computed and the distance from the mean in standard deviations was plotted; the profiles for fathers are shown in Figure 2, for mothers in Figure 3.

A Split Plot analysis of variance reveals that there are significant differences *in levels* between the profiles of the parents of boys with high achievement motivation and the parents of boys with low n Achievement. The difference in levels for fathers is greater ($F = 10.09$, $P < .005$) than for mothers ($F = 4.77$, $P < .05$). By difference in level we mean that when the scores for each variable are summed for each parent, the parents of high n Achieve-

Personal-Social Motives and Incentives 131

```
Fewer specific directions

More nonspecific directions

Fewer pushing statements

More autonomy

Less rejection

More warmth

Total choice, Ring Toss

Total estimates, Patterns

2nd & 3rd est., Block Stacking

1st estimate, Block Stacking
```

         1   3/4   1/2   1/4   x̄   −1/4 −1/2 −3/4 −1
              Mean difference in standard deviations
                    ——— High n achievement group
                    ——— Low n achievement group

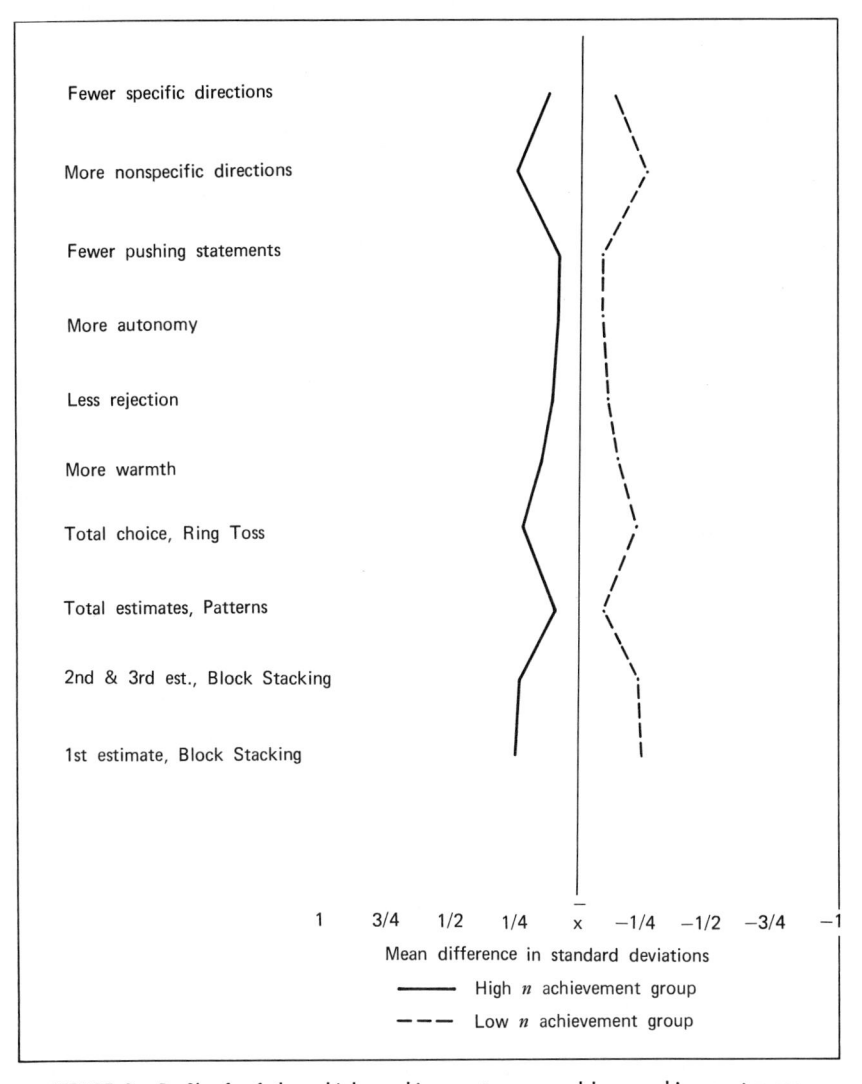

FIGURE 2. Profiles for fathers: high n achievement group and low n achievement group.

ment boys have a significantly higher *total* score than the parents of low n Achievement boys.

In Figure 2, where the fathers' profiles are compared, it can be seen that the mean scores for the fathers of boys with high achievement motivation are higher for every variable, where "highness" was predicted as being positively related to high n Achievement. The interaction between n Achievement groups and test variables was not significant ($p > .05$).

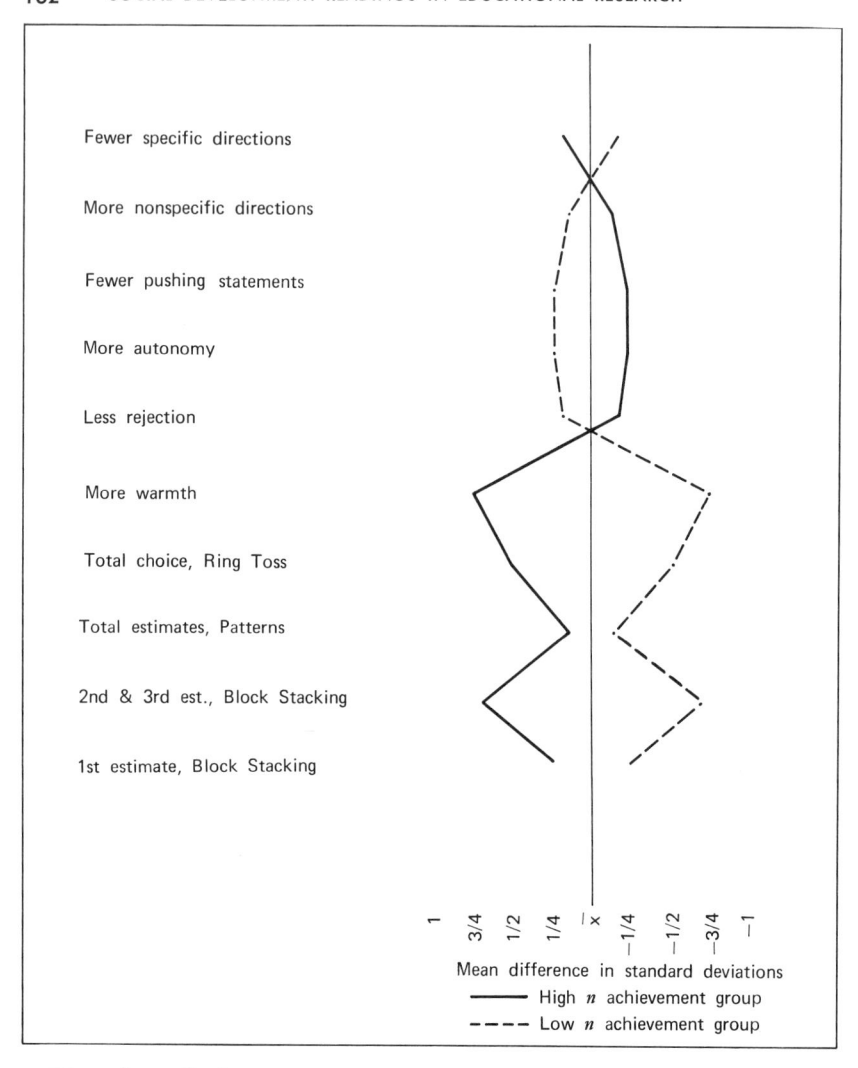

FIGURE 3 Profiles for mothers: high n achievement group and low n achievement group.

The profiles for mothers are not parallel so that even when level differences are taken out the profiles for the mothers of high *n* Achievement boys remains significantly different from that of the mothers of low *n* Achievement boys (F = 2.30, P < .025). There are even some reversals in that mothers of high *n* Achievement boys give fewer nonspecific directions, more pushing statements, and are more dominant than the mothers of low *n* Achievement boys.

Social Class and Child-Training Practices

The research design made it improbable that the class differences in training practices would be great, for the sample was selected in such a way as to make both classes equal with respect to the dependent variable. That is, the n Achievement scores of lower class boys were on the average equal to the scores of middle-class boys—a situation known not to be true for the more general universe of middle- and lower-class boys. Hence, if the independent variables examined in this study are necessary and sufficient causes of n Achievement, and the measures of these variables valid, there should be no significant differences in the training practices of the middle- and lower-class parents *in this sample*. Significant class differences would be found only if these variables were noncausally related to n Achievement but associated with social class—a conclusion which had not been apparent when the original hypotheses were formulated. This was confirmed in the analysis since the data, though sometimes in the direction predicted, indicate that the training practices of middle-class parents are not on the whole markedly different from those of lower-class parents.

DISCUSSION AND SUMMARY

The question of how achievement training, independence training, and sanctions are related to achievement motivation may be rephrased by asking, How does the behavior of parents of boys with high n Achievement differ from the behavior of parents whose sons have low n Achievement?

To begin with, the observers' subjective impressions are that the parents of high n Achievement boys tend to be more competitive, show more involvement, and seem to take more pleasure in the problem-solving experiments. They appear to be more interested and concerned with their son's performance; they tend to give him more things to manipulate rather than fewer; on the average they put out more affective acts. More objective data show that the parents of a boy with high n Achievement tend to have higher aspirations for him to do well at any given task, and they seem to have a higher regard for his competence at problem solving. They set up standards of excellence for the boy even when none is given, or if a standard is given will expect him to do "better than average." As he progresses they tend to react to his performance with warmth and approval, or, in the case of the mothers especially, with disapproval if he performs poorly.

It seems clear that achievement training contributes more to the development of n Achievement than does independence training. Indeed, the role of independence training in generating achievement motivation can only be understood in the context of what appears to be a division of labor between the fathers and mothers of high n Achievement boys.

Fathers and mothers both provide achievement training and independence training, but the fathers seem to contribute much more to the latter than do the mothers. Fathers tend to let their sons develop some self-reliance by giving hints (N) rather than always telling "how to do it" (S). They are less likely to push (P) and more likely to give the boy a greater degree of autonomy in making his own decisions. Fathers of high n Achievement boys often appear to be competent men who are willing to take a back seat while their sons are performing. They tend to beckon from ahead rather than push from behind.

The mothers of boys with high achievement motivation tend to stress achievement training rather than independence training. In fact, they are likely to be more dominant and to expect less self-reliance than the mothers of boys with low n Achievement. But their aspirations for their sons are higher and their concern over success greater. Thus, they expect the boys to build higher towers and place them farther away from the peg in the Ring Toss experiment. As a boy works his mother tends to become emotionally involved. Not only is she more likely to reward him with approval (Warmth) but also to punish him with hostility (Rejection). *In a way, it is this factor of involvement that most clearly sets the mothers of high* n *Achievement boys apart from the mothers of low* n *Achievement boys:* the former score higher on every variable, except specific directions. And although these mothers are likely to give their sons more option as to exactly (fewer Specifics) what to do, they give them less option about doing something and doing it well. Observers report that the mothers of high n Achievement boys tend to be striving, competent persons. Apparently they expect their sons to be the same.

The different emphasis which the fathers and mothers of high n Achievement boys place upon achievement and independence training suggests that the training practices of father and mother affect the boy in different ways. Apparently, the boy can take and perhaps needs achievement training from both parents, but the effects of independence training and sanctions, in particular Autonomy and Rejection, are different depending upon whether they come from the father or mother. In order for high n Achievement to develop, the boy appears to need more autonomy from his father than from his mother. The father who gives the boy a relatively high degree of autonomy provides him with an opportunity to compete on his own ground, to test his skill, and to gain a sense of confidence in his own competence. The dominating father may crush his son (and in so doing destroys the boy's achievement motive), perhaps because he views the boy as a competitor and is viewed as such by his son. On the other hand, the mother who dominates the decision-making process does not seem to have the same affect on the boy, possibly because she is perceived as *imposing her standards* on the boy, while a dominating father is perceived as *imposing himself* on the son. It may be that the mother-son relations are typically more secure than those between father and son, so that the boy is better able to accept higher levels of dominance and rejection from his mother than his father without adverse affect on his need to achieve. Relatively rejecting, dominating fathers, particularly those with less than average warmth—as tended to be the case with the fathers of low n Achievement boys—seem to be a threat to the boy and a deterent to the development of n Achievement. On the other hand, above-average dominance and rejection, coupled with above-average warmth, as tends to be the case with mothers of high n Achievement boys, appear to be a spur to achievement motivation. It will be remembered that the fathers of high n Achievement boys are on the average less Rejecting, less Pushing, and less Dominant—all of which points to their general hands-off policy.

It is unlikely that these variables operate separately, but the way in which they interact in the development of achievement motivation is not clear. Possibly the variables interact in a manner which produces cyclical effects roughly approximating the interaction that characterized the experimental task situations of this study. The cycle begins with the parents imposing standards of excellence upon a task and setting a high goal for the boy to achieve (e.g., Ring Toss, estimates and choices in Block Stacking and Patterns). As the boy engages in the task, they reinforce acceptable behavior by expressions of warmth (both parents) or by evidences of disapproval (primarily mother). The boy's performance improves, in part because of previous experience and in part because of the greater concern shown by his parents and expressed through affective reaction to his performance and greater attention to his training. With improved performance, the parents grant the boy greater autonomy and interfere less with his performance (primarily father). Goals are then reset at a higher level and the cycle continues.

12. CHILDREN'S TEXTBOOKS AND PERSONALITY DEVELOPMENT

Irvin L. Child, Elmer H. Potter, & Estelle M. Levine

The acquisition of motives, values, and attitudes associated with such distinctive behaviors as those involved in sex-typing is clearly affected by the social influences of parents, teachers, and peers. Though its role in socialization is considerably less apparent, reading material is among these influences. Textbooks portray lifelike characters through which are communicated many of the behaviors implied by cultural norms.

How much a child's behavior patterns is governed by exposure to the models presented in textbooks and other media is difficult to judge. However, as Child, Potter, and Levine hypothesize in this classic investigation, verbally presented behaviors can be readily rehearsed in thinking and thereby becomes available as a regular part of the child's behavioral repertoire. Character portrayals typically coincide with the pupil's other experiences, too, and so can influence awareness of a value or motive that previously may have been lying dormant.

Through an analysis of thematic units (each consisting of a character, circumstance, behavior, and consequence) identified in children's textbooks, these investigators have delineated an impressive picture of the social relationships and adjustments communicated to the child. In the reading material they analyzed, learning was emphasized but intellectual activity was not; discovery and exploration were rewarded mainly where

SOURCE. Adapted and abridged from Irvin L. Child, Elmer H. Potter, and Estelle M. Levine, "Children's Textbooks and Personality Development: An Exploration in the Social Psychology of Education," *Psychological Monographs*, 1946, Vol. 60, No. 3, Whole No. 279. (With permission of the senior author and the publisher, the American Psychological Association.)

the child resorted to authority; males were portrayed as wise, assertive, strivers; females were depicted as docile, unmotivated, and unaggressive persons; and, the importance of success in social relationships was emphasized but the lesson of how to cope with failure was not taught.

Some of the "model" behaviors represented in these early textbooks will undoubtedly succumb to the influence of changing times. Values do change from one era to the next; from individual striving and competition in one era, to affiliation and nurturance in another, and to social responsibility in another. The salient values reflected in textbooks are thus sure to change. Nevertheless, the contribution of this investigation to our understanding of the socialization process will remain for many years and should encourage systematic investigation into the social influence of all the media. The methods employed are unique, especially in their application. They can serve as valid models for analysis of today's communications with reference to today's concerns.

In the application of psychology to the study of formal education in our society, attention has been directed primarily at intellectual aspects of education. A few notable studies such as those by the Character Education Inquiry (Hartshorne & May, 1928) and by Jones (1936), have been concerned with the development of ideals and morals in the school situation. But for the most part, psychologists have directed their attention to the study of intellectual aptitudes and achievements—their measurement, the factors influencing them, and their predictive value.

Yet intellectual achievements and aptitudes are only one aspect of the child's behavior that schools are capable of influencing. Also of tremendous importance is another aspect: the motives that children develop, the ways they learn to satisfy their motives, the expectations they acquire about the consequences of trying to satisfy their motives in various ways. It is around this motivational aspect of the educational process that this study is centered.

The motivational influences of education are significant both in themselves and in relation to intellectual development. They are important in themselves because education should be directed at training children to become well-adjusted and responsible adults as well as adults equipped with intellectual skills. But a person's very acquisition of information and understanding, and most of all the use he will make of it, depends upon motivational aspects of his personality. Hence the attainment of the intellectual aims of education is itself dependent upon the motives developed in children.

This study represents, then, one of several beginnings that have been and are being made in the social psychology of education in our society—the study of the role of the educational system in shaping not merely the intellect but the general personality of children.

The specific objective of this study is the analysis of certain content of the world of ideas which confronts children in the process of education, from the point of view of the probable effect of that content on the motivation of their behavior. Just what that means will be made clear through the discussion, in the rest of this chapter, of the way the content was analyzed.

METHOD

We chose for our purpose all of the general third-grade readers we were able to find which had been published since 1930. (Excluded were third-grade readers intended primarily to teach special topics such as science, social studies, or arithmetic, and one reader which deviated greatly from all the others in containing considerable material on religion.) In all, 30 books were included in the analysis; they are listed in the references at the end of this monograph.

Selection of Content From the Books

The first step in the process of analysis of the readers was the selection of those stories which were to be analyzed. Since the purpose of the analysis was to determine what effect the readers might have on the socialization of the child, only those stories were chosen in which the content could conceivably affect the child's behavior. The general criterion for selection was that the story contain characters in action, since the child's behavior would be affected only by his generalizing from that of individuals in the stories to his own behavior.

The content which was included in the analysis was those stories in which characters appeared who presented distinctive behavior that could be analyzed according to the method described below. The material analyzed included well over three quarters of the books. Altogether, 914 stories were analyzed.

Analysis

The method of analysis applied to the thema found in the readers was based on the following considerations:

It is assumed that in reading a story, a child goes through symbolically, or rehearses to himself, the episode that is described. The same principles, then, are expected to govern the effect of the reading on him as would govern the effect of actually going through such an incident in real life. The principles that seemed important for this study are those of reinforcement and of avoidance learning.

It is assumed that when a sequence of behavior is shown as leading to reward, the effect will be to increase the likelihood of a child's behaving in that way under similar conditions in the future. Among the kinds of behavior that may be learned in this way are motives, for they are to be regarded as being produced largely by a subject's own behavior.

When, on the other hand, a sequence of behavior is shown as leading up to punishment, it is expected that the incident will contribute to the probability of the subject's avoidance of such behavior in the future. Again, among the effects of such avoidance can be the reduction of the strength or the likelihood of the appearance of a motive.

This reasoning suggested the analysis of the content in accordance with the following general scheme:

1. *Character* whose behavior is represented in the thema: children, adults, animals, or fairies (i.e., all supernatural creatures).
2. *Behavior* displayed by the character, classified according to Murray's (1938) categories (see Table 1).
3. *Circumstances* surrounding the behavior.
4. *Consequences* of the behavior (for the character himself): reward, punishment, or no consequence.
5. *Type of story* in which the incident occurs: fairy, animal, hero, or everyday stories.

The actual technique used in recording the data was to read each story in a given book and determine whether it was suitable for the purposes of the analysis. If it was found to be suitable, all the separate thema in the story that fitted the pattern of analysis were identified and a file card was prepared for each one. It was labeled appropriately to identify the story and the book and then the following information was entered on it:

1. The type of story.
2. Whether the character was central or anti-social.
3. The classification of the character according to age, sex, humanity, etc.
4. The behavior displayed, classified according to Murray's system of needs.
5. Notes on the circumstances surrounding the behavior.
6. The classification of the consequences of the behavior.

RESULTS AND DISCUSSION

The treatment of various categories of behavior in children's readers can leave no doubt that this treatment is such as to encourage the development of certain motives and to discourage others. A tabulation of the percentage of reward, punishment, and no consequence for the various categories of behavior, presented in Table 1, brings out this general point quite clearly. The categories are arranged here in order of relative frequency of reward, and

TABLE 1

Percentage of Reward, Punishment, and No Consequence for Each Category of Behavior (in All of the 3,409 Thema Which Were Analyzed)

Category of Behavior	Percent of Thema in Which the Behavior Is Rewarded	Percent of Thema in Which the Behavior Is Punished	Percent of Thema in Which Behavior Results in No Consequence (i.e., Neither Rewarded Nor Punished)
Construction	96	1	3
Sentience	96	4	0
Elation	95	4	1
Cognizance	86	9	5
Succorance	84	10	6
Affiliation	82	8	9
Nurturance	82	5	12
Achievement	80	10	9
Recognition	79	13	8
Activity	74	9	16
Dominance	74	16	8
Blamavoidance	71	15	14
Imaginality	71	6	23
Order	70	2	28
Acquisition	64	31	3
Passivity	54	26	20
Deference	52	10	38
Harmavoidance	49	39	12
Autonomy	48	40	12
Retention	42	48	10
Aggression	35	52	11
Rejection	14	62	24
Infavoidance	8	74	18
All categories	71	17	12

this order may be taken as one indication of the degree of encouragement or discouragement of the development of each one. In considerable part, of course, this order reflects general cultural norms—for example, in the high value placed on affiliation, nurturance and cognizance, and in the frequent punishment of aggression, retention and rejection.

But the entire impact of cultural forces on personality manifested in these readers is not shown in a simple listing of the treatment of the several categories separately. There are also certain generalities which can be found running through the whole series of categories, generalities about particular ways of achieving ends which are most likely to lead to success or to failure.

Perhaps the most striking case of this sort is the repeated reward of effort or work as a way of reaching goals. Here certainly are some of the forces leading to the development of a motive to work or put forth effort. This motive is sometimes very important in adults or older children, and may activate them for a long time, even when the effort leads to no external reward. The motive is doubtless developed in large part through social learning, and we have in this reading matter an example of the kinds of social influences that lead to its development.

Another special emphasis is on the acquisition of skills, on learning. Despite this emphasis on learning, there is in these third-grade readers little encouragement of intellectual activity as such. The cognizance is usually directed at simple isolated information rather than a quest for understanding.

It should be noted, moreover, that the acquisition of skills or knowledge which is rewarded is generally that which is dependent upon other persons in a superior position—for example the gaining of knowledge by children through questioning parents or teachers. In this sense, too, there is less emphasis on intellectual activity than might appear, since there is relatively little encouragement of original thinking on the part of the central character.

Problems of Adjustment

A major defect of the readers is what might be called their unrealistic optimism. Behavior directed at affiliation and nurturance, for example, is almost always rewarded in the readers. There are very few cases of failure. It is impossible to compare the proportion of success here with that obtaining in children's everyday life. Yet from the point of view of contributing to the solution of problems of everyday life, failures ought to receive a larger proportion of attention, for it is they that pose problems.

Children's reading matter might be quite useful in furthering satisfactory adjustment if it were able to pose models for the child of ways to satisfy these needs when they are prevented from the most direct and immediately satisfactory expression. While there are certainly some incidents which might be useful in this way, the general tendency in the readers is, instead, for these needs simply to be overlooked in the child characters. It is as though the writers were inclined to solve problems of aggression and acquisition in children by trying to convince children that they do not have these needs, that they are experienced only by adults, animals and supernatural creatures. To a certain extent the child's real social environment may be cooperating with the readers in this direction, through a tradition that children do not hate or covet and are basically nice unless they are led to be otherwise. But the fact probably is that every child does hate and does covet, and that in his efforts to do so he is being repeatedly rebuffed by the more powerful persons in his environment. Those persons are apt often not to have the psychological insight necessary for redirecting these interests of the child into channels where they can have more success. Here then is a valuable potential role of children's reading matter.

Another possible inadequacy of the reading matter, one much more difficult to judge, is concerned with maturity. It is notable in the content of these readers that independent action initiated by child characters, and indeed by anyone, is more likely to be punished than similar behavior which is performed under the direction of a superior. Cognizance, for example, is rather frequently punished when it is undertaken on the child's own initiative and leads to pursuit of knowledge directly by the child's own exploratory behavior, whereas it is almost always rewarded if knowledge is gained through dependence upon authority. Autonomous behavior, too, is generally punished except in the case where the kind of autonomy is that desired by the child's elders.

Differential Treatment of the Sexes

Perhaps the most striking single finding of this study is the extent to which a differentiation is made between the roles of male and female in the content of these readers. To the extent that boys identify with male characters, and girls with female characters, this difference both in itself and as a reflection of facts that hold true of many other sources of influence on children, must have a profound significance on the differential development of personality in the two sexes.

Some of the differentiation can be seen in the mere frequency with which the two sexes appear among the characters displaying the various categories of behavior, as presented in summary form in the first part of Table 2. Female characters, for example, are relatively more frequent among those displaying affiliation, nurturance, and harmavoidance. On the other hand, females are less frequent, relatively, among characters displaying activity, aggression, achievement, construction, and recognition. Girls and women are thus being shown as sociable, kind and timid, but inactive, unambitious and uncreative.

This picture is further added to by considering the relative proportion of male and female characters among the subsidiary characters who are objects related to the satisfaction of the needs of the central characters. The facts here are summarized in the last columns of Table 2. The most important findings here refer to nurturance and cognizance. The persons nurtured by a central character are in the majority female, suggesting that females are in a relatively helpless position. The persons who supply information to central characters who are seeking for knowledge are, in contrast, predominantly male. It will be recalled that even among unrelated adults who supply knowledge to children, the majority are male despite the obvious fact that the most important such persons of the real environment are the child's

TABLE 2 Sex of Characters: Frequency Distribution for Each Category of Behavior

Category of Behavior	Sex Distribution of Central and Anti-Social Characters Appearing in the Thema						Sex Distribution of Characters Appearing in Thema As Social, Objects, Cooperators, etc.[b]					
	Frequency Distribution			Percentage Distribution[a]			Frequency Distribution			Percentage Distribution[a]	
	Male	Female	Mixed	Male	Female		Male	Female	Mixed	Male	Female
Construction	43	7	18	86	14		7	7	26	46	54
Achievement	126	25	30	83	17		17	3	77	85	15
Recognition	75	16	32	82	14		29	20	96	59	41
Aggression	74	21	8	78	22		54	30	29	64	36
Activity	116	32	61	78	21		47	20	101	70	30
Sentience	30	9	25	77	23						
Passivity	71	22	15	76	24						
Autonomy	52	17	18	75	25		21	22	31	49	51
Cognizance	156	54	85	74	26		97	41	43	70	30
Dominance	75	27	18	74	26		40	23	39	63	34
Acquisition	84	33	18	72	28		40	27	31	60	40
Deference	86	33	30	72	28		48	46	39	51	49
Imaginality	15	6	9	71	29						
Succorance	73	35	19	68	32		59	23	31	72	28
Infavoidance	17	8	3	68	32		5	7	15	42	58
Blamavoidance	36	18	8	67	33		20	16	11	56	44
Affiliation	142	74	78	66	34		119	55	124	68	32
Harmavoidance	77	40	19	66	34		39	10	3	80	20
Nurturance	116	65	42	64	36		51	67	39	43	56
Elation	20	14	13	59	41						
Order	17	12	8	59	41						
Retention	14	10	3	58	42		8	2	7	80	20
Rejection	4	4	7	50	50		4	3	4	57	43
Total	1519	582	567				704	422	746		
Percentages for total				72	28					63	67

[a] In the calculation of these percentages, the characters (groups) of mixed sex were omitted.
[b] There are no entries in these columns for those behavioral categories in which there were no social objects or cooperators, etc.

143

teachers, who are mostly women. Males, in short, are being portrayed as the bearers of knowledge and wisdom, and as the persons through whom knowledge can come to the child.

In all of these respects, a distinction in role is being made between the sexes which may indeed have a certain validity as of our society of the present time, but which seems much more a survival of former practices. The many schoolgirls who will at some future time have to make their own living are failing, if they identify with female characters, to receive the same training in the development of motives for work and achievement that boys are receiving. To the extent that this distinction is characteristic of many other aspects of the training the child receives from his environment, it should cause little wonder that women are sometimes less fitted for creative work and achievement than men of similar aptitude, for there is certainly much difference in the motivational training they receive for it. It has been a common assumption that the education of the two sexes is virtually the same in American public schools, except for differences in vocational training. Here is clear evidence that the education is not the same, even at early levels of grammar school and even when the boys and girls are mixed together, as they usually are, in the same classroom. Not only does the informal training of boys and girls at home and in the community differ, but even the formal education they are receiving in the classroom differs.

The most striking fact of all, however, about the difference between the sexes is that the female characters do simply tend to be neglected. There can be no excuse for this greater attention to males in the claim that males have achieved more in society and hence that there is more to write about them. These stories are, with few exceptions, not about individuals of outstanding achievement but simply about the life of everyday people. The implication of this difference for a girl is that being female is a pretty bad thing, that the only people even in everyday life who are worth writing about or reading about are boys and men. If the content of these readers is typical of other social influences, small wonder that girls might develop for this reason alone an inferiority complex about their sex.

Differential Treatment of Adults

There are great differences in the relative frequency of the various categories of behavior for the human characters, divisible into adults and children. Children are much lower than adults in the incidence of aggression and acquisition. In adults, aggression and acquisition are the most frequently appearing categories of behavior, whereas in children these two are of very low incidence.

It is of interest that this contrast shows the children as conforming more closely than adults to socially approved behavior. The same tendency is found in certain other comparisons that can be made between children and adults.

That children are shown as more socialized is demonstrated also by the relative frequency of different kinds of rewards. It appears from the data summarized in Table 3 that children receive internal rewards in more than twice as large a proportion as do adults.

TABLE 3

Kinds of Rewards for All Categories of Behavior: Percentage Distribution in Each Character Type

Character Type	Percentage Distribution of Kinds of Reward in Each Character Type			
	Internal	Social	Material	Automatic
Children	34	23	36	6
Adults	16	26	53	4
Animals	24	18	50	8
Fairies	16	34	43	8

Now internal rewards are dependent upon socialization, for they are rewards that a person administers to himself because he is well socialized, because he is able to feel good or virtuous at having done the right thing, even if no reward is offered by an external agency. The content of the readers, however, is likely to point out to children certain rewards and punishments that, for them, follow upon the display of approved or disapproved behavior and to suggest that these rewards and punishments may stop when they grow up to be adults. Such a lesson, which to be sure is also often made in a child's everyday life, may be satisfactory for the short-sighted parent or teacher, who knows that his immediate responsibility for the child will cease when the child becomes an adult. But as a background for educational policy it seems deficient to anyone who looks at child-rearing or education as a task of preparing children to become adequate adults.

Treatment of Animals

Animals are usually portrayed as anthropomorphic characters endowed with speech, and their relationship to the physical and social environment closely approximates the subordinate position in which children also find themselves.

The pattern of their behavior is in most instances similar to that of children: they, like the child characters, are shown as rewarded for dependent, socially conforming behavior.

To a certain extent, the animal characters seem to furnish an outlet for the expression in child-like characters of aggressive and rebellious tendencies. Since these needs are predominantly punished, the animal characters serve the function of teaching the lesson that whenever asocial tendencies are expressed, they are punished. Thus they have a double purpose: they remove the necessity of showing child characters as exhibiting undesirable behavior, while at the same time yielding an object lesson as to the results of such behavior should it be manifested. It is as though the writers felt that, to a child reading animal stories, the behavior is detached enough from the child so that he would not copy it, and yet plausible enough for him to accept the moral that aggressive and autonomous asocial behavior leads to certain punishment. (Because of the low incidence of fairies as central or anti-social characters, no detailed comparison with the other types of character can be made, and few general conclusions as to their treatment can be drawn.)

Indirectly, then, the readers do admit the existence of aggression in young persons. Yet here too, there is little constructive suggestion as to how to handle such tendencies. When characters are shown as aggressive, punishment follows, without an indication of suitable substitute outlets.

Significance of Various Story Types

The distribution of types of character in the various types of story is of interest from the point of view of their realism to children. The four types of stories—everyday, hero, fairy, and animal—vary decidedly in the nature of the central characters appearing in them. However, analysis did not show that the categories of behavior manifested by any type of character vary significantly from one kind of story to another. The relative frequency in children, for example, of the various categories of behavior is about the same in each type of story.

It is apparent that the various types of stories do serve a function, and that this is related to the types of characters appearing in them. The stories represent various degrees of realism in portraying behavior, from the prosaic everyday story, through the idealized hero story and the humanized animal story, to the frankly unrealistic fairy story. It is significant, therefore, that most of the behavior of the children is portrayed against a realistic, everyday background. For if the children are able to differentiate between the real and the unreal, they will tend to be more influenced by behavior which is possible for them. And even where they do not make this distinction, the very fact that such behavior more closely resembles theirs is likely to make for greater generalization to their own behavior. It is important to note, therefore, that the pattern of behavior for children in the readers, which was summarized earlier in this chapter, is the one pattern of behavior for any character type that is most consistently presented realistically. It is reinforced and emphasized by the medium of its presentation—the everyday story.

Since animal stories are composed almost exclusively of animal characters, the interpretation of them is similar to that for the characters: they permit the expression of rebellious and asocial tendencies in a situation where the child will not be very likely to copy such undesirable behavior.

Hero stories occur so infrequently that few general statements can be made about them. The emphasis here is on nurturance, and as the characters are usually historical figures with whom the child is presumably already familiar, they can be considered as tending to equate greatness with generosity and kindliness.

13. DELAY OF GRATIFICATION, NEED FOR ACHIEVEMENT AND ACQUIESCENCE IN ANOTHER CULTURE

Walter Mischel

People with a behavioral tendency to delay gratification are said to have acquired a higher *net* valence for delayed rewards than for immediate ones. They have learned to weigh the prospect of an *immediate* goal of a *given* value with reference to and in favor of a *promised* goal of *higher* value. This is not a simple response pattern. The farther goal must be perceived as attainable within a reasonable period of time. For most people the distant goal must be seen to depend less on chance than on one's ability, though there are individual differences in the extent to which the perceived locus of control guides the person's behavior. There must also be confidence that the delayed event will materialize.

This tendency, like other behavior tendencies, is acquired through learning: work and effort become attractive after being linked to the increased rewards they bring, and impulse gratification tendencies are "punished" when their resultant losses, relative to what might have been gained, are recognized. Especially important in the socialization experience is the acquisition of expectations whether they are hypothesized to take the form of fantasies, images, or verbal mediators. These are the stepping-stones that keep the child (and adult) in cognitive-contact with the reward during the delay period.

Within this theoretical orientation, Mischel examines delay of gratification as it is related to the need for achievement, to acquiescence (that is,

SOURCE. Adapted and abridged from Walter Mischel, "Delay of Gratification, Need for Achievement, and Acquiescence in Another Culture," *Journal of Abnormal and Social Psychology*, 1961, Vol. 62, pp. 543–552. (With permission of the author and the publisher, the American Psychological Association.)

a general tendency to agree), and to the child's reputation for social responsibility. An important assumption in this study is that scientific understanding of a construct like delay of gratification can be enhanced by predicting other events with which it will be positively correlated, negatively correlated, or uncorrelated. Out of a series of such studies, among which the present study would be one, there would evolve a network of correlations linked by theoretical considerations. This study is especially interesting, and its value augmented, because the generality of findings regarding the delay of gratification is extended to children of another culture.

Relationships between overt behavior on important psychological dimensions and relevant motives are much sought foundations in personality research. This paper explores the relationship between a person's choice preferences for immediate, smaller (ImR) as opposed to delayed, larger (DelR) reinforcement and his motive system. It thus seeks to extend our knowledge of preference for delayed gratification, some antecedents and correlates of which have already been investigated (Mischel, 1958, 1959, 1961). Here choice behavior with respect to preference for ImR or DelR is related to the need for achievement (n Achievement) as scored from fantasy material in the manner described by McClelland and his associates (McClelland, Atkinson, Clark, & Lowell, 1953).

The central aim is not primarily to elaborate the network of correlates of n Achievement, but rather, to clarify some of the variables relevant to preferences for ImR or DelR by relating such choices to a motive that is logically relevant and whose measurement and empirical correlates appear relatively firm. If this can be done, research on delay of gratification with human subjects and in choice situations, in which smaller, immediate gratifications are pitted against more long term, larger gratifications, should be somewhat more solidly anchored, albeit only on a correlational basis, to the data of other more elaborated domains of personality research.

The present study is part of a larger research program that approaches the problem of delay of gratification by using direct measures of preference for ImR or DelR in particular choice situations. Thus far, with children from other cultures as subjects, preference for DelR as opposed to ImR has been found to relate positively to social responsibility and to accuracy of time statements, negatively to delinquency (Mischel, 1961), positively to intelligence (Melikian, 1959), and positively to the presence (as opposed to the absence) of the father within the home under some conditions (Mischel, 1958, 1959).

Consistent with past theorizing and research on n Achievement, high n Achievement should be related to preference for DelR as opposed to ImR. The essence of the definition of n Achievement is "competition with a standard of excellence" (McClelland et al., 1953). Implied in such striving is the ability to delay and postpone the relatively trivial but immediately available for the sake of later but more important outcomes. Clearly there can be little realization (and thus little maintenance) of the motive to compete with a standard of excellence unless the person is able to delay immediate but smaller gratifications and to choose instead larger future rewards and goals.

A direct and positive relationship between preference for DelR and n Achievement is to be expected for the following reasons. It has been argued (Metzner, 1960) that one of the crucial conditions that facilitates the development of the ability to delay gratification is the acquired reward value of working itself. Learning to delay starts when behaviors based only on the pleasure principle are either frustrated or punished. Then, fantasy becomes an acquired primary process substitute and work a secondary process detour, both of which are rewarded by eventual (larger) gratifications, thus ultimately becoming rewarding activities in their own right. Liking to work for its own sake is generally assumed to be a basic ingredient of the high n Achievement pattern. Presumably, persons high in n Achievement have learned to like work, and they have learned this in part as a response to demands to forego immediate gratification in favor of more long-term goals. That is, they have learned to tolerate waiting periods and in the course of such socialization have built up a general readiness to delay when it is demanded by conditions or people. Consequently, when persons high in n Achievement are given choices between immediate, smaller rewards and delayed, larger ones, the balance between the negative valence of waiting and the positive valence of the delayed, larger reward is weighted in favor of the latter because the former is relatively minor for them. This is in contrast to the state of affairs with persons who have not learned work as a response to the delay situation, or who have not acquired intrinsic interest in achievement (i.e., persons low in n Achievement). The anticipated positive relationship between preference for DelR and n Achievement does not depend on an absolute preference by individuals high in n Achievement for the delayed alternative, but, rather, applies equally to relatively less nonavoidance of the delayed alternative on their part.

Two personality syndromes related to simple acquiescence or "agreeing tendency," are conceptually germane to the present distinction concerning preference for ImR-DelR. "Yeasayers were shown to be individuals with weak ego controls, who accept impulses without reservation, and . . . easily respond to stimuli exerted on them. The naysayer inhibits and suppresses his impulses . . ." (p. 173). The former "can freely indulge in impulse gratification" whereas "the egos of naysayers take over the controlling functions of the parents, and the suppression of impulses is subsequently self-maintained and self-rewarded" (p. 173). A cluster of scales including impulsivity and dependency characterized the positive end of the agreeing tendency; the disagreeing tendency was defined by scales including ego strength, responsibility, and trust. Further, in interviews, yeasayers (in contrast to naysayers) described themselves as ". . . unreflective, quick to act, easily influenced, and unable to tolerate delays in gratification" (p. 170).

Clearly, these two personality syndromes are directly relevant to preference for ImR-DelR. "Trust," or the expectancy that the promised delayed reward is forthcoming, is a basic factor in preference for DelR, and empirically have related preference for DelR to social responsibility (Mischel, 1961). It is to be expected that DelR preference should be related to naysaying and ImR preference to yeasaying and to the personality syndromes associated with each.

Lastly, data were also collected on social responsibility, as measured by an independently validated scale (Harris, 1957), substantially correlated with other measures of adjustment and maturity. Replication was thus sought for a previously established positive relationship between measures of preference for DelR (as opposed to ImR) and social responsibility (Mischel, 1961) and to determine the extent of interrelationship between social responsibility and the other variables measured in this study.

The over-all methodological aim is to aid the development of relatively simple but quantifiable techniques for testing psychological hypotheses in cultures much different from our own in which measures developed in the United States are inappropriate or excessively cumbersome. Such techniques are needed if the generality of psychological principles established on United States samples is to be extended to grossly different populations.

METHOD

Subjects

A total of 112 Trinidadian Negro children (68 boys and 44 girls), all in the age group 11–14, with a modal age of 13, were tested in a government school located near the capital city. The school contained children from the urban environs, primarily from the lower middle and lower socioeconomic strata of the society.

Measures of Preference for ImR or DelR

Three preference measures (a behavioral choice and two questionnaire items) were used to elicit preference for ImR or DelR. These were selected on the basis of earlier research with comparable Trinidadian samples. The general procedures used in the pretesting and selection have been described in detail (Mischel, 1959, 1961). Briefly, the behavioral measure consisted of a choice between ImR or DelR in the form of a small candy bar (costing approximately 10 cents) available immediately *or* a much larger candy bar (costing approximately 25 cents) for which the subject must wait one week.[1] The reward choice was administered as the last item in the total procedure and was structured as a way of "thanking" the subjects for their cooperation. The two verbal items, one inserted near the beginning, the other near the middle of the procedure, were:

1. I would rather get ten dollars right now than have to wait a whole month and get thirty dollars then.
2. I would rather wait to get a much larger gift much later rather than get a smaller one now.

Following the procedure used earlier (Mischel, 1961), subjects were divided for purposes of data analysis into "Consistent ImR" (ImR preference over the three measures), "Consistent DelR" (consistent DelR preferences over the three measures), and "Inconsistent R" (one ImR and two DelR responses, or the reverse). Although the predictions center on differences between the Consistent ImR and Consistent DelR groups, results are also presented in terms of the number of DelR choices out of the total three possible made by the subject, i.e., 3 DelR, 2 DelR, 1 DelR, or 0 DelR.

Measures of n Achievement

Two measures of n Achievement were used. The first was the standard group-administered procedure developed by McClelland and his associates (1953), using five TAT-type cards. The second measure was an innovation, in the form of an open-ended aspiration question. The latter was introduced in the context of "let's pretend there is a magic man": "Now let's pretend that the magic man who came along could change you into anything that you wanted to be, what would you want to be?" Subjects were instructed to answer in one word.

Measure of Acquiescence

The measure of acquiescence or conformity—suitable for large scale research in other cultures—consisted of the following instructions, administered orally by the experimenter:

"I have something in mind. I am closing my eyes and concentrating and thinking of it . . . it is something that you might agree with or that you might disagree with . . . you might disagree with what I'm thinking of or you might agree with it . . . if you agree put down a *Y* for Yes; if you disagree put

---

[1] The size of the immediately available reinforcement used here was deliberately greater than that used in past work (Mischel, 1961) in order to increase the probability of a more equal dichotomy in the immediate, smaller versus delayed, larger choice distribution.

down a N for No. (This was repeated twice, reversing the position of Y and N in the sequence of instructions.) Now I'm concentrating on it (closing eyes); go ahead."

Measure of Social Responsibility

The Social Responsibility Scale (SRS) was designed to "discriminate children who have, with their peers, a reputation for responsibility as contrasted with children who have little reputation for responsibility" (Harris, 1957, p. 326). The scale was administered in the modified form described earlier (Mischel, 1961).

Procedure

The experimenter was introduced as an American from a college in the United States interested in gathering information on the children in the various schools of the island. To help with this the subjects were asked to answer a number of questions. The details of the instructions are similar to those previously reported (Mischel, 1961). Subjects were seated sufficiently far apart from each other to give reasonable assurance that their choices were made independently. All testing was done in group settings in large classrooms, with two sessions. All measures except the TAT and the candy choice were given in the first session.

RESULTS AND DISCUSSION

Examination of both sex and age in relation to preference for DelR or ImR revealed no differences approaching statistical significance and consequently the male and female data and all age groups were treated collectively in subsequent analyses.

n Achievement and Preference for Delayed Reinforcement

Comparison of subjects with respect to delay of reinforcement patterns as they related to n Achievement was done as follows. Subjects were first divided into Consistent ImR, Consistent DelR, and Inconsistent R, to categorize their choices with respect to the three measures of preference for ImR or DelR, the choice preferences with respect to DelR also being shown in terms of the number of DelR choices made by the subject out of the three total possibilities. Thus the Consistent ImR group contains all subjects with 0 DelR choices, the Inconsistent group is further subdivided into subjects with one as opposed to subjects with 2 DelR choices, and the Consistent DelR group contains all subjects with 3 DelR choices.

Table 1 presents the means and standard deviations of n Achievement scores for subjects in each of these categories with respect to reinforcement

TABLE 1
Reinforcement Preference with Respect to Delay in Relation to n Achievement Scores, Aspirations, and Acquiescence

Reinforcement Preference: N DelR[a]	n Achievement N	n Achievement M*	n Achievement SD	n Achievement Distribution of Scores[b] −5 to −3	−2 to −1	0	+1 to +2	+5 to +2	Aspirations[c] Occupational	Achievement Trait	Personal Trait	Acquiescence Yes	Acquiescence No
Consistently Delayed:													
3	37	.92	2.35	1	12	6	7	11	18	4	14	25	12
Inconsistent:													
2	18	1.11	2.32	0	4	4	6	4	8	2	7	12	6
1	27	0 −.74		8	4	6	8	1	4	5	17	21	6
Consistently Immediate:													
0	30	−.70	2.62	11	6	3	5	5	9	0	17	27	3
Totals:	112			20	26	19	26	21	39	11	55	85	27

[a] N of delayed reward choices made by subject.
[b] Subject's total score for the five TAT cards: N of subjects in each category of distribution.
[c] N of subjects giving Occupational aspirations, Achievement Trait aspirations, and Personal Trait aspirations; seven subjects failed to state any aspirations.

* t of 3 DelR versus 0 DelR on mean n Achievement = 2.61, $p < .01$; t of 3 DelR + 2 DelR versus 1 DelR + 0 DelR on mean n Achievement = 3.78, $p < .001$.

preference. As anticipated, the mean n Achievement score of Consistent DelR subjects as compared to Consistent ImR subjects is significantly higher ($t = 2.61$; $p < .01$). (One-tailed tests of significance are used throughout this paper.) The hypothesized relationship between preference for ImR as opposed to DelR and n Achievement is thus strongly supported. Similarly, if subjects are dichotomized into "High DelR" (2 or 3 DelR responses, $M = .98$; $SD = 2.22$), and compared on mean n Achievement with "Low DelR" (0 or 1 DelR response, $M = -.41$; $SD = 2.46$), the resulting t is 3.78 ($df = 110$; $p < .001$). Clearly, subjects showing greater preference for DelR have significantly higher n Achievement scores than subjects with lesser preference for DelR. Of secondary interest is the fact that the mean n Achievement scores of subjects in the Inconsistent R category are between those of the Consistent DelR and Consistent ImR groups. The difference in means between the Consistent DelR group and the Inconsistent R group reaches significance ($p < .05$), but the difference in means between the latter and the Consistent ImR group does not reach an acceptable level. If the data are analyzed in correlational terms, a point biserial correlation of .31 ($p < .01$) is obtained from the correlation of n Achievement scores with Consistent DelR or Consistent ImR choice. A Pearson correlation between the number of DelR choices (0–3) and n Achievement scores yields an r of .27 ($p < .005$).

The data for the relationship between aspirations and reinforcement preference patterns with respect to delay are presented in Table 1. A chi square comparison of subjects giving 3, 2, 1, and 0 DelR choices with the number of responses given by these groups in each of the three aspiration categories cannot be made meaningfully since this results in an excess of expected frequencies that are less than 5. Combining categories, subjects giving 2 or 3 DelR choices ("High DelR") were compared with subjects giving 0 or 1 DelR choices ("Low DelR") in regard to the number of responses in each of the three categories of aspirations. This comparison results in a chi square of 7.49 ($df = 2$; $p < .05$). Subjects with "High" DelR preference tend to give more Occupational and fewer Personal Trait responses than subjects with "Low" DelR preference. Chi square analyses of High-Low DelR in relation to number of Occupational aspiration responses versus number of all other aspiration responses, or in relation to a combination of the Occupational category and the Achievement Trait category as opposed to the Personal Trait category, both show a significant relationship of the same nature ($p < .02$, chi squares corrected for continuity).

Acquiescence and Reinforcement Preference

The acquiescence data for yeasaying or naysaying in an ambiguous situation are related to the reinforcement preference patterns in Table 1. Consistent DelR subjects gave 25 yes and 12 no responses; consistent ImR subjects gave 27 yes and 3 no responses. Application of the chi square test to these data results in an uncorrected chi square of 4.80 ($df = 1$; $p < .05$). Similarly, a dichotomization into "High DelR" as opposed to "Low DelR" to compare number of yes or no responses, results in an uncorrected chi square of 4.33 ($df = 1$; $p < .05$).[2] As anticipated, subjects high in preference for DelR gave relatively more no and fewer yes responses than did subjects low in preference for DelR.

The primary relevance of these data is that they serve as an empirical link between the patterns isolated by Couch and Keniston (1960) to distinguish yeasayers and naysayers and the present distinction between subjects consistently preferring DelR or ImR. Clearly the patterns have strong conceptual overlap empirically supported by the present findings.

Social Responsibility in Relation to the Other Measures

As regards the SRS, the relationship between preference for DelR and social responsibility reported earlier (Mischel, 1961) is replicated. A Pearson correlation of .28 ($p < .005$) is obtained between number of DelR choices (0–3) and SRS scores. Using t tests, significant differences between means ($p < .01$) are obtained when "High DelR" subjects (3 and 2 DelR choices) are compared with "Low DelR" subjects (1 and 0 DelR choices). The means and SDs of the former are 31.25 and 4.28, and of the latter 29.05 and 3.70. A secondary finding of considerable interest is a strong relationship between SRS and n Achievement ($r = .40$, $p < .001$ with TAT measure; $r = .33$, $p < .001$ with aspiration measure). This appears to be one of the very few instances in which a significant positive correlation is obtained between n Achievement and a *questionnaire* measure. Theoretically, although not specifically predicted, it seems extremely plausible that social responsibility and achievement motivation should be interrelated. Operationally, it is encouraging that at least in this cultural setting, questionnaire data do appear correlated with scores based on fantasy material.

An Overview

Summarizing the results, preference for DelR, n Achievement measured by two different but intercorrelated methods (TAT and open-ended aspirations), and SRS scores, are all significantly and positively interrelated. The

---

[2] If extreme caution is used and the decision is made to apply the Yates correction for continuity on all 2×2 contingency tables, although all expected frequencies in each cell do exceed 5, the comparison of Consistent DelR with Consistent ImR subjects on acquiescence results in a chi square of 3.59; the comparison of the "High" versus "Low" preference for DelR dichotomy with acquiescence results in a chi square of 3.51. A chi square of 3.84 is required for $p < .05$ and of 2.71 for $p < .10$.

intercorrelations were low to moderate, ranging from $r = .26$ to $r = .41$. The acquiescence measure is not significantly associated with social responsibility scores ($r = .06$, $p < .20$), although, as discussed above, low significant relationships do seem to hold between naysaying and preference for DelR and between naysaying and Occupational (as opposed to all other) aspirations. Finally, partial correlations were computed between preference for DelR and n Achievement, holding SRS constant, and between preference for DelR and SRS, holding n Achievement constant. In both cases, low but positive and still significant correlations result ($r = .18$ and .19, respectively, $p < .05$). This finding suggests that the major measures used to delineate the cluster of correlates associated with preference for DelR as opposed to ImR, while themselves significantly intercorrelated, still appear to tap different aspects of the constellation.

The main import of the over-all findings is that they relate reinforcement preference to other more thoroughly explored variables. When the present findings are taken collectively with those obtained on other previously reported samples, a network of meaningful correlates becomes apparent. These are interpreted as providing considerable evidence that an obviously crucial but relatively unstudied dimension of behavior, the ability to delay the relatively trivial but immediately available for the sake of larger but later outcomes, can be explored usefully with relatively simple direct measures of choice preference. The correlates of these choice preferences are becoming increasingly clear, although controlled studies of antecedents are still lacking.

The simple preference patterns with respect to delay elicited thus far provide only an early model and a prelude to more complex and subtler batteries. In such batteries, delay preference patterns systematically sampling a variety of value and need areas could be tapped, and the valences of particular intervening work and fantasy activities (in addition to the simple waiting period over a time interval used at present) could be elicited. The ultimate aim would be the construction of predictive individual topographies for complex choices on the dimension of delay, and the measurement of individual time lines.

14. ACHIEVEMENT MOTIVATION TRAINING FOR UNDERACHIEVING HIGH-SCHOOL BOYS

David A. Kolb

The failure of socializing agencies to provide the kind of experiences that promote the acquisition of motives relevant to academic achievement may be a reason why some children such as the academically disadvantaged are not successful in school. Formal instructional programs may be one means to compensate for these deficiencies. If so, then it is necessary to know what variables are involved and how to measure their effects on behavior.

The empirical study of procedures to implement changes in these highly complex processes have tended to be discouraging to the social scientist for theoretical and pragmatic reasons. Motives are, presumably, outgrowths of a long history of experience and so are believed to be enduring characteristics that are highly resistant to change. Thus, any program directed toward modification of this aspect of personality seemed to be an impractically extensive effort or doomed to failure.

However, when Kolb conducted his interesting study many events had already taken place to make it a congenial time for implementing such a program on an experimental basis. Much was known from surveys, interviews, and case studies about the etiology of such social motives as affiliation and achievement. Systematic investigations on learning by imitation were yielding new insights into the variables that affect a model's effectiveness. Some theorists were suggesting that raising expectations about a

SOURCE. Abridged and adapted from David A. Kolb, "Achievement Motivation Training for Underachieving High School Boys," *Journal of Personality and Social Psychology*, 1965, Vol. 2, pp. 783–792. (With permission of the author and the publisher, the American Psychological Association.)

person would favorably influence behavioral outcomes. Finally, a study in counseling strongly suggested that achievement motivations could be modified on a practical basis and with a corresponding change in academic performance.

Kolb's program employed a composite of techniques implied by these events. Underachieving boys in the lower- and middle-socioeconomic strata were taught the nature of the achievement motive and the instrumental behaviors necessary for its implementation. They were taught the character of realistic risk-taking, what changes in behavior to expect and what reactions to expect from other people as a result of these changes. Expectations were developed that achievement motivation and achievement in school would be influenced favorably. Since a number of procedures were built into the overall program it was not possible to isolate the differential effects of specific factors. Their identification remains a potentially fruitful topic for further research.

The present study tests the effect of a training program designed to increase concern for academic achievement in a group of underachieving high-school boys. The content of the training program derives from the research on achievement motivation carried on by McClelland and his associates (Atkinson, 1958; McClelland, 1961; McClelland et al., 1953).

The training techniques used in this program stem from four different experimental backgrounds.

1. *Identification*: The identification models of Kagan (1958) and Hill (1960) maintain that learning takes place through emulation of effective role models, this learning being reinforced through vicarious affective experience. Goldberg (1959) has found that identification with a positive role model seems to be associated with academic improvement in underachieving boys.

2. *Expectation*: There is a growing body of research which indicates that the expectations held by the experimenter and subject (Orne, 1962; Rosenthal, 1963) or the therapist and patient (Goldstein, 1962) can measurably affect the outcome of the experiment or therapy. In this study the research team model developed by Schwitzgebel and Slack (1960) was adapted. Schwitzgebel (1962) has found the research team model useful in reducing juvenile delinquency.

3. *Ideomotor response*: Perhaps the most sophisticated modern statement of this theory is George Kelly's (1955) role construct theory. He maintains that behavior is determined in large measure by the way a person construes the world. Burris' (1958) study suggests that teaching underachievers achievement constructs and encouraging them to think in achievement terms can lead to better performance in school. In the current study the technique is to implant the idea of achievement by teaching the students

the n Achievement scoring system and to observe the results in action, that is, academic performance.

4. *Games*: Games provide a well-defined psychologically safe situation where men can try out new ways of thinking and behaving. In this study the game concept was used in two ways: in actual games designed to teach achievement skills (e.g., Litwin & Ciarlo, 1961) and as an analytic device in counseling to aid in understanding real-life problems (Leary, 1961a).

METHOD

Setting

The Achievement Motivation Training Program (AMTP) was carried out as part of a summer school for underachieving high-school boys held at Brown University. The summer school was designed to give stimulating instruction using outstanding teachers and exciting subject matter.

The project was 6 weeks long, beginning in late June and ending in the first week of August. The schedule was a 5-day week of classes in history, English, and mathematics, with weekend recreation at various parks and beaches in the area. The boys lived together on three floors of a college dormitory on the campus and ate in the college dining hall.

Subjects

Fifty-seven boys drawn mainly from public and private schools in New England were enrolled in the project. Eight of these boys (four control and one experimental) withdrew from the program. Their data were not included in the final analyses. Two general classes of students were recruited: boys from homes where sufficient interest, parental background, and finances favored college entrance and boys from homes where these were lacking.

A breakdown by social class based on occupation (Warner, Meeker, & Eells, 1949) shows 14 boys in Class 1, 11 in Class 2, 11 in Class 3, 5 in Class 4, 6 in Class 5, 2 in Class 6, and 1 in Class 7. The mean IQ score (WISC) of the boys was 126 (range: 109–149) and their mean school grade average was D to D+ (range: F–C+). The average year in school was 9.0 (range: 7–11) and their average age was 14 years (range: 12–16). Stanford Achievement Test scores showed them to be at an average grade level of 10.9 (range: 8.8–12.7).

Experimental Design

Twenty of the 57 students were randomly assigned to the fourth floor of the dormitory. This group received the AMTP in addition to their regular summer school schedule. The remaining 37 students received only the regular summer school program.

Subjects were tested in the following manner.

Pretesting. On the second day of the summer school, 57 subjects were given the following tests: the Test of Insight, scored for n Achievement according to the published scoring manuals (Atkinson, 1958); the Stanford Achievement Test; the Taylor Manifest Anxiety (*MA*) scale; and the Mandler-Sarason Test Anxiety Scale (TAS). In addition the following data were collected for each subject: age, year in school, IQ (WISC), 1961 school grade average, and parents' socioeconomic status based on father's occupation (Warner et al., 1949).

August 1961 posttest. The same tests were administered to the subjects on the next-to-last day of the project. In addition all subjects received grades in each of the three subjects taught in the summer school. AMTP members were ranked on their participation in the AMTP and assessed in moderate risk-taking ability using the Litwin-Ciarlo (1961) Business Game.

January 1962 follow-up. The midyear school grades were collected for all boys who completed the project.

April 1962 follow-up. At this time 33 of the summer-school participants were selected on the basis of proximity to Brown University to return for a testing session. Twenty-seven boys returned (experimentals = 10, controls = 17) and were given the Test of Insight, Form A.

January 1963 follow-up. School grades were collected for the Spring 1962 semester. Unfortunately these were available for only 37 boys (experimentals = 12, controls = 25).

Experimental Condition: The Achievement Motivation Training Program

The experimenter lived in the dormitory with the AMTP boys and served as their counselor. The experimenter behaved in a manner consistent with the behavior of a person with high n Achievement, so that the subjects would have a visible high n Achievement role model to imitate. The overall procedure changed from the use of external rules and discipline to internal control and personal responsibility.

Initially the boys met with the experimenter in a classroom twice a week for 1 hour. As the weeks progressed this meeting time was changed to better fit the summer-school schedule and meet the needs of the boys. The program is briefly described below.

First session. The first session was concerned with negotiating a contract. The aim was to involve the students in the hypothesis that the course would improve academic performance and achievement motivation thereby creating in them the expectation that the course would work.

After negotiating the contract, the characteristics of a person with high achievement motivation were described. Subjects were told that the person with high n Achievement has three major characteristics: he likes and chooses to take personal responsibility for his actions, he takes moderate risks, and he likes and attempts to obtain knowledge of the results of his actions (Atkinson, 1958; McClelland, 1961; McClelland et al., 1953).

Second session. The entire second session was spent playing the race game. The boys were asked to keep in mind as they competed with one another, the characteristics of the achieving personality in relation to the race, for example, (*a*) personal responsibility—How involved am I in the race? Do I care if I win or not? (*b*) moderate risk taking—How much of the time did I take too much of a risk? How often was I too cautious? (*c*) using knowledge of results—How well did I use my practice trials to judge my ability?

Third session. This session began with an introduction to the process of assessing motivation by analysis of thought (Atkinson, 1958).

Further discussion centered around future orientation, delay of gratification, ability to control impulses, and time orientation.

Fourth session. This session marked the beginning of the shift from structured lecture meetings to a program oriented more toward the individual. In essence the session was a renegotiation of the contract.

The last half of the session was spent discussing how thought influences action and the relationship of achievement thinking to achievement behaviors.

Fifth session. This session was devoted to a group discussion on the analysis of Test of Insight stories. Example stories from the protocols of control students were read to the class and discussed. Following this discussion the students were offered help in scoring their protocols for n Achievement.

Sixth session. A major theme that occurs over and over in the Insight Tests is a conflict between achievement and affiliation goals (see Parsons, 1959). The session was focused on this conflict and on learning to take realistic risks.

Informal sessions. Beginning on Thursday of the fifth week, the group began meeting every evening on the lawn on an informal basis. Attendance at these sessions was not required and subjects could come and go as they pleased. The boys wanted this arrangement so they could discuss how the techniques they had learned could be applied to specific problems in their lives. These discussions were intense and seemed to be of considerable benefit to those who attended.

Individual counseling sessions. Counseling on an individual basis was done informally. The problems discussed in individual sessions were usually concerned with the application of principles talked about in class to the life of the boy. These ranged from using the principles of moderate risk taking to play a better tennis game, to setting realistic goals in study tasks, to staying out of arguments at home.

Litwin-Ciarlo Business Game. This training device is designed to train a person to take moderate risks and use knowledge of results, and to assess his capacity to do so.

RESULTS

As described in the section on method, the boys in the project were of two types—boys from homes where interest, parental background, and

TABLE 1
Change in n Achievement by Social Class

	M Change		
Testing Interval	Experimental Group	Control Group	p[a]
High social class (1 and 2)			
Pretest to August posttest	8.4 (n = 9)	—0.3 (n = 9)	<.05
Pretest to April follow-up	5.7 (n = 7)	—5.8 (n = 5)	<.025
Low social class (3 through 7)			
Pretest to August posttest	5.0 (n = 9)	— .6 (n = 20)	<.01
Pretest to April follow-up	0.3 (n = 3)	—3.2 (n = 12)	<.10

[a] Mann-Whitney *U* test, one-tailed probability.

finances favored college entrance (i.e., high SES boys) and boys from homes where these were lacking (low SES boys). Because of these differences, all of the change comparisons were made by social class (high SES = Classes 1 and 2, low SES = Classes 3–7). In both lower- and upper-class groups, experimental subjects increase significantly more than control subjects in n Achievement score.

While Mann-Whitney *U* tests indicated no significant differential changes in Stanford Achievement Test scores, *MA* scale, TAS, or summer-school grades, there were differential changes in school grades in both the January 1962 and January 1963 follow-up periods. These effects are reported in Tables 2 and 3 for the high SES and low SES groups, respectively.

The total grade average of high SES experimentals improved significantly

TABLE 2

Change in School Grades: High Social Class Boys

	M Change		
School Subjects	Experimental Group	Control Group	p^a
Pretest to January 1962 follow-up			
Total grade average	9.5 ($n = 10$)	1.8 ($n = 13$)	<.005
English	9.4 ($n = 10$)	0.7 ($n = 13$)	<.01
Science	0.5 ($n = 3$)	4.4 ($n = 8$)	
Foreign language	10.5 ($n = 8$)	10.0 ($n = 3$)	
Mathematics	13.0 ($n = 10$)	−12.0 ($n = 11$)	<.01
History/civics	7.2 ($n = 4$)	4.6 ($n = 7$)	
Pretest to January 1963 follow-up			
Total grade average	11.9 ($n = 6$)	1.9 ($n = 11$)	<.05
English	9.5 ($n = 6$)	3.7 ($n = 11$)	
Science	8.8 ($n = 5$)	7.1 ($n = 8$)	
Foreign language	9.8 ($n = 5$)	− 2.0 ($n = 8$)	
Mathematics	11.2 ($n = 6$)	3.0 ($n = 10$)	
History/civics	6.0 ($n = 4$)	5.2 ($n = 6$)	

[a] Mann-Whitney U test, one-tailed probability.

more than controls in the January 1962 follow-up and in the January 1963 follow-up. In addition, high SES experimentals improved significantly more than controls in English and mathematics in 1962. No subject areas were significant in the 1963 follow-up.

The trend reported for high SES experimentals was reversed for low SES experimentals. In most cases they improved less than control subjects although these improvements only approached significance in science and mathematics in the 1963 follow-up. Low SES subjects showed no significant differential changes in total grade average in either follow-up period.

In Figure 1 the total grade averages are plotted for high SES and low SES experimentals and controls for the initial pretest and the two follow-up peri-

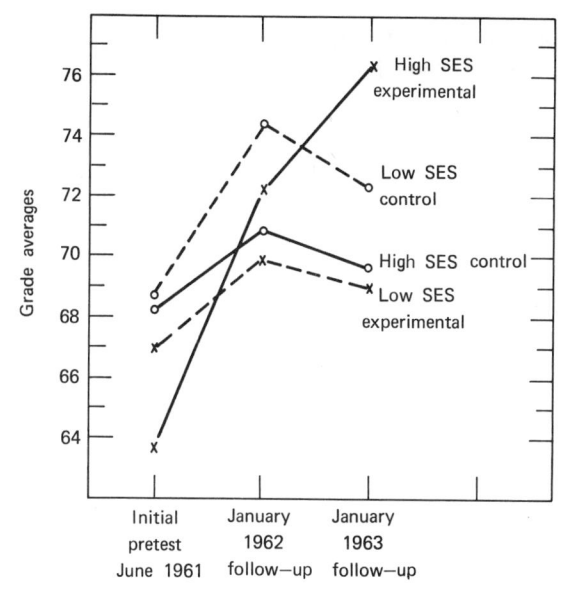

FIGURE 1. School grade average in pretest and follow-up periods.

ods. The high SES experimental group is the only group to show an improvement in grade average in the 1963 follow-up. This group shows a 12-point increase in grade average in the 1963 follow-up, moving from a D— to a C average.

Similar change comparisons were made with the data divided into high MA and low MA, high TAS and low TAS, high IQ and low IQ, but no significant differences were found.

Analysis of Change within the Experimental Group

To analyze patterns of change within the experimental group, seven variables were intercorrelated: three predictor variables—social class, initial n Achievement score, and WISC IQ score; three participation variables—ranking on course participation by the counselor, a moderate risk-taking score from the Business Game, and the change in n Achievement score from the pretest to the August posttest; and the criterion variable—change in school grades. Changes in grades for 18 boys in the January 1962 follow-up were used since using 1963 changes would too much reduce the already small sample.

None of the three predictor variables showed significant correlations with change in school grades although when SES was divided into high and low groups as was done for control group comparisons, a median test showed that high SES boys tended to improve more than low SES boys ($\chi^2 = 7.29$,

$p < .01$). None of the predictor variables was significantly related to participation variables, although there was a weak relationship between IQ and Business Game and IQ and n Achievement change.

Two of the participation variables can be seen as measures of how well the boys learned major themes of the course. The Business Game score gives an indication of the boy's ability to take moderate risks and use the results of his previous experience (i.e., feedback) at the end of the course. This score correlated .63 with change in school grades. The change in n Achievement score gives an indication of how well the boy learned to think like a person with high need for achievement. This score correlated .42 with change in grades. The multiple correlation coefficient of Business Game score and change in n Achievement with change in school grades was .68 ($p < .025$, one-tailed). The third participation variable, the participation ranking by the counselor, did not correlate significantly with the criterion, although it did with change in n Achievement.

DISCUSSION

The fact that improvement in experimental group grades differs significantly from control group improvement in the 1963 but not the 1962 follow-up seems to be based mainly on a decrease in the control group improvement score in 1963. This would suggest that while the summer school alone gave some boost to the grades, there is a tendency for this effect to decay over time, while the addition of the AMTP to the summer program seems to promote a more permanent and perhaps increasing improvement in school grade average. This effect is seen most strikingly when the data are analyzed by social class (see Figure 1).

The significant differences in subject areas, especially when controls improve more than experimentals, are difficult to explain with the data available.

The strong differential effect that social class had on change in grades requires some examination. The fact that only high social class experimental boys seemed to benefit significantly from the AMTP might be explained in two ways.

One might reason that the course was designed to appeal more to boys from the upper classes where education is valued more than to lower-class boys (Kahl, 1952). The course was, in fact, pitched at a rather intellectual level and expounded high educational values—Harvard, research, and good grades. But if this argument were so, one would expect social class to be positively correlated with the participation variables—course participation ranking, Business Game score, and change in n Achievement. This was not the case. In addition, *both* high and low SES experimentals increased significantly more than controls in n Achievement score.

The alternative explanation is not based on the differential reaction of high and low SES boys to the AMTP but on the different environments to which they returned. An underachieving upper-class boy finds himself in sharp dissonance with his subculture. There is constant pressure for him to achieve and do well in school. The underachiever from the lower classes is not pushed by such strong values on achievement and hence he is more likely to be in harmony with his subculture. Hence when the boys returned home after learning new techniques for achieving, the high SES boys used these techniques to alleviate the tensions their failure to achieve had created. Although we would have to assume that the low SES boy also felt some of these tensions (his parents did care enough to send him to the summer school), the aspirations that the subculture holds for the boy are not so high (Kahl, 1952) and thus he need not improve his performance as much to bring himself in harmony with his subculture.

The experimental group's improvement over controls in school grades lends encouraging support to the hypothesis that teaching underachieving boys the characteristics of the person with high achievement motivation can lead to better academic performance. The hypothesis is further supported by the high correlation of change in n Achievement and Business Game score with improvement in school grades in the experimental group.

This experiment, however, does not allow any conclusions about what techniques produced the experimental group's improved academic performance. The improvements could theoretically be a result of any or all of the following: the experimenter's particular personality (identification theory), learning n Achievement thought categories (ideomotor response theory and n Achievement theory), learning to take moderate risks and use feedback (n Achievement theory), learning to take personal responsibility for actions (n Achievement theory), and expectations of improvement created by participation in a research project and by the research team contract (expectation theory). Further research should attempt to measure and/or isolate the differential effects of these factors.

15. SOCIAL NORMS IN TEENAGE BOYS' PEER GROUPS

Barry Sugarman

The teenage peer group, which is a relatively more structured and formal organization than the preadolescent gang it supersedes, provides its members with opportunities for participating in interesting activities and for applying social techniques learned in the home and school. In it the boy or girl can congregate with others who have similar interests, values, intellectual ability, and energy. This combination of factors makes the peer group a cohesive social situation with the potential of regulating the behavior of its members through the imposition of sanctions—reward for "good" behavior and punishment for "bad" behavior. Thus, for example, peers within a clique of boys in the lower socioeconomic class may reject a boy who performs well in school. By these means, the peer group can be an important socializing agent, whose influence will be limited mainly by whether a member desires acceptance, and, if so, how much he is accepted into the group or clique. Accordingly, it can function to modify the adolescent's existing attitudes either by strengthening those attitudes congenial to, or weakening those in conflict with, the values of the group. Similarly, it can function to develop new attitudes that coincide with its norms.

Much of the research on peer groups has been oriented toward influences affecting acceptance of a boy or girl into a group. The present study by Sugarman, however, examines effects in the opposite direction

SOURCE. Abridged and adapted from Barry Sugarman, "Social Norms in Teenage Boys' Peer Groups: A Study of Their Implications for Achievement and Conduct in Four London Schools," *Human Relations*, 1968, Vol. 21, pp. 41–58. (With permission of the author and the publisher, Tavistock Publications [1959] Ltd.)

in its concern with the effect of the peer group on school achievement. Sugarman investigated, in some detail, how informal peer groups are formed in addition to investigating the values and norms they impose on their members. Several clearly identifiable cliques were classified on the basis of sociometric data, teacher ratings, and academic records according to the value placed on academic achievement (underachievers or overachievers) and conformity to school norms (good conduct or poor conduct). The individual's level of striving and achievement was found to correspond to the composition of the group. This study also showed that both intergroup comparisons of group members with nonmembers, which focus on leadership and popularity differences, provide complementary data for further understanding of the effects of group membership on individual behavior.

This study explores two related questions, both fundamental to small group theory: how social groups are formed spontaneously among teenage boys at school and how the boys' behaviour is affected by their membership in these groups.

The question of group influence is the more complex of the two and may, broadly speaking, be approached in either of two ways. One approach starts from the premise that among people who interact recurrently certain norms develop and tend to influence members' behaviour (Homans, 1950). Whereas this approach focusses attention mainly on differences between groups with different norms, the other approach emphasizes rather the difference between being a member of some group and not being a member. Thus according to Havighurst and Neugarten (1957, p. 127) "Many a boy or girl drops out of school at the first opportunity, not for lack of academic ability, or for failure to meet the school's requirements, but for failure to gain acceptance into the peer group."

Some support for both approaches comes from a study by Wilson (1963) of high schools in the socially distinct areas of Berkeley, California. He finds that college aspirants tend to be more popular and are less often isolates than non-college aspirants in *all* schools, and, significantly, that this pattern is more strongly marked in the schools drawing their pupils from the areas with highest social class composition (p. 228).

Along similar lines, James S. Coleman, in *The Adolescent Society* (1961), develops an argument which rests on two major propositions: (1) that the degree to which the peer group rewards academic achievement affects the degree to which pupils are committed to academic values; and (2) that the more strongly pupils are committed to academic values, the higher will be their level of academic attainment. Although he has shown a connection between status among peers and values, Coleman has shown neither that peer group status is related to academic attainment *when IQ is held constant* nor that the strength of commitment to academic values is related to actual academic attainment (Sugarman, 1966; 1967). In earlier papers this writer has reported data that show an association between commitment to academic values and achievement and several studies can be cited in support of the hypothesis that the values rewarded in the peer group affect the level of members' striving and/or achievement.

Hallworth (1953) studied the natural history of sociometric groups in eleven school classes in one grammar school. Over time he found that they became larger and better integrated, patterned essentially the same way on three different sociometric criteria. Each group had some common values and norms which were recognized by the members and which were reflected in differences between groups in rates of absenteeism, in school marks, and in dropout rates.

Cartwright and Robertson (1961) report a study conducted with a small number of older students attending a short business course. They found evidence to support their hypotheses that within the spontaneously formed friendship cliques there were norms and values relating to level of achievement, that they would differ between groups, and that the achievement levels of students would vary accordingly, independently of preexisting individual differences.

The study we shall now report was designed to explore further the way in which informal peer groups form at school and the kinds of norms and values operating in them.

METHOD

Subjects

Data were obtained in the course of a survey of 540 fourth-form boys in four London secondary schools. All four sample schools (comprising one grammar, two secondary modern and one comprehensive) had a distinctly larger proportion of their pupils from non-manual homes than the national average (especially the grammar school). All four were boys-only schools.

Procedure

In the four schools the entire fourth year class was surveyed by questionnaire which the investigator administered in person. Within this group, a sample of eighty boys was interviewed.

On the questionnaire pupils were asked, "At school which other pupils do you usually go around with?" The answers of the different pupils were collated on charts where it was recorded which pupils named which others as associates. Three pupils were prescribed as the minimum number for a group and to qualify they should have at least two mutually confirmed relationships and one unconfirmed among themselves. This triad was taken as the working basis for larger groups. Any extra member required not less than one confirmed and one unconfirmed link between himself and two established members of the group.

Reliability

The subsamples of pupils who were later interviewed were asked to name their regular school associates and these answers were compared with their answers to the similar item on the questionnaire, which they had completed about three months previously. For sixty-eight respondents this comparison can be made. They named a total of 279 associates in their interviews and 269 on their questionnaires. The names that were common to both lists number 174. That is to say, pupils confirmed 65 of those whom they had named as associates after an interval of three months. The proportion of pupils who gave identical lists of names on both occasions was .23 and the proportion giving lists that differed only in the addition or omission of one name was .41. The proportion of questionnaire names that were repeated in the interview was .68 for peer group members and .57 for nonmembers. The proportion of interview names that also appeared on the questionnaire was .78 for peer group members and .46 for others.

DEFINITION OF PEER GROUPS

This procedure results in identifying 66 peer groups which include 230 pupils out of a total of 540 (57 per cent). The next step is to classify these peer groups in terms of their members' academic achievement and conduct.

To measure academic achievement the boys of each school were stratified by IQ as measured at the age of eleven and then each IQ group was divided into roughly equal thirds on the basis of attainment as assessed by the school. The top third will be called "overachievers," the middle third "middle-achievers" and the lower third "underachievers." These terms refer to achievement *relative* to what might be expected on the basis of their IQ scores and are intended to carry no implication other than this.

The conduct of pupils or their conformity to school norms was assessed by teachers specifically for this study. All were provided with an identical rating scheme and asked to base their rating on what they know of pupils' conduct from other teachers as well as their observations.

On the basis of the IQ and conduct data four types of peer groups were defined (see Table 1). Type 1 (high achievement and good conduct) peer groups are those where the proportion of underachievers is below .30 and where the proportion with poor conduct records is below .40. If a group

TABLE 1
Categorization of Peer Groups

Peer Group	Achievement	Conduct	No. of Peer Groups	No. of Pupils
Type 1	Good	Good	24	99
Type 2	Good	Bad	17	73
Type 3	Bad	Good	9	61
Type 4	Bad	Bad	12	63
No Peer Group	—	—	—	231
Missing Data			4	13
Totals			66	540

chi square $= p > .05$ for Type 1
chi square $= p < .001$ for Type 2

exceeds both of these minima, it is a Type 4 (low achievement and poor conduct) group. Otherwise it is intermediate, either Type 2 (high achievement and poor conduct) or Type 3 (low achievement and good conduct).

These four types of peer groups are defined on the basis of the characteristics of their members as individuals, rather than on the basis of group structure or process. The present concern was to determine the extent to which the one kind of difference is associated with the other, especially with regard to evidence related to differences in normative pressures.

RESULTS

Peer group patterns were identified by examining differences in behavior and attitude between pupils who are members of different types of peer groups and those who are members of none. Among Type 1 only 43 come from homes of low intellectual quality while among Type 4 there are 90 with such backgrounds.[1] Therefore, in order to restrain the effect of home background somewhat while we examine the difference between members of different types of peer groups, we shall make the comparison separately for boys of high and low quality of intellectual home background.

The most striking finding is that boys *from homes of low intellectual quality who belong to Type 1 groups on the whole score more highly for their adjustment to school* (favorable attitude and planning to stay longer) *than the aggregate of all boys from homes of high intellectual quality*, more

[1] The intellectual quality of home background was assessed on the basis of boys' answers to questions about the newspapers read by their parents, the number of books in the house and whether their parents take them out to such events as plays, concerts, art exhibitions or encourage them to go alone.

highly than boys from high-quality homes who do not belong to any cliques, and almost as highly as those from high-quality homes who belong to Type 1 groups like them.

The difference between the two sets of Type 1 boys (from different backgrounds) is very small, averaging between five and six percentage points, while the difference between the aggregate proportions for all boys from high and low quality backgrounds is considerably greater, averaging around 15 or 16 percentage points. Interdependent with this fact is another: Type 1 boys from high quality homes are less sharply differentiated from the aggregate of all who have similar backgrounds than are Type 1 boys from low quality homes. In terms of percentage points the differences for high quality backgrounds average 12 and those from low quality backgrounds average 23. This may mean one of two things: either that these peer groups in these schools function to level up their members' behavior and attitudes in terms of the official values and goals of the schools; or that acceptance into Type 1 peer groups generally requires relatively high scores on those attitudes that are expected by teachers and that tend to correlate with a good adjustment to school.

Thus, there is a moderate relationship between peer group affiliations and the behavior and attitudes of boys, particularly when they are deviating from the modal behavior of those from a similar background. On the whole, though, these boys tend to mix with others from similar backgrounds. (This is true whether we look at father's occupation or the intellectual quality of the home.) Accordingly, if peer groups have any effect in and of themselves then for most of these boys their participation in school peer groups will tend to reinforce the influence of their homes.

Norms and Values

For all peer groups members we know the number of votes they received as "someone to sit next to in class for a whole term" (popularity), as a "leader for some group activity." The following data are therefore based not on the whole sample of 540 but only on the 296 pupils who belonged to the 62 peer groups for which there are sufficient data.

The logic of this analysis is that if (say) high-achievers have higher sociometric scores in Group A than they do in Group B, we take this to mean that Group A has a value system in which academic achievement (or some closely related attribute) ranks more highly than it does in the value system of Group B, implying that it is more highly rewarded with the esteem or deference of one's associates. This is asserted by definition, i.e., this is how the term *value system* is being used here.

The association between popularity and achievement was first considered. Our hypothesis requires that it should be stronger within Type 1 and 2 groups (relatively high-achievers) than among Types 3 and 4 (relatively low-achievers). In *all* four types a positive association between achievement and popularity is found and, contrary to hypothesis, it is a lot stronger in Types 3 and 4 than it is in Types 1 and 2. The only respect in which the hypothesis stands up is that the strength of the relationship is greater in Type 1 than in Type 4.

Concerning the relationship between votes as leader and achievement, our hypotheses are the same. Both hypotheses are supported: Type 1 has a stronger relationship than Type 4. The relationship between leadership votes and achievement is stronger in Types 1 and 2 combined than it is in Types 3 and 4 combined. However, it must not be overlooked that, in these schools and by these criteria, there is *no inversion* of values in Type 4 groups.

By the leadership criterion then we have some support, though not so strong as it might be, for the hypothesis that in these different types of groups there is a difference in the valuation of academic achievement.

Concerning the association between conduct ratings and popularity, our hypothesis states that the strength of this relationship should be greater in Types 1 and 3 (relatively good conduct) than it is in Types 2 and 4 (relatively poor conduct). In fact, high popularity is associated with relatively good conduct ratings in all four types and the relationship is far stronger in the two poor conduct groups (2 and 4) than in the good conduct groups, which is the reverse of our hypothesis. Why should this be?

Here we can only speculate, but since all conduct ratings in groups 2 and 4 are low, it is possible that the boys with the lowest ratings of all in these groups are socially maladjusted and not only unable to conform to the standards of their teachers but even to those of their peers. So they are not popular in groups 1 and 3, however, the average level of conduct is quite good and those who are rated better than the rest by teachers are likely to be considered by their peers as dull and hence somewhat less popular.

Over all groups there is a very slight association between poor conduct ratings and receiving higher numbers of leadership votes. Although this relationship is very weak, it is interesting that it is in the *opposite direction* to the one between popularity and conduct. Our hypothesis is modified accordingly to state that in Types 1 and 3 poor conduct is less closely associated with high leadership votes than it is in Types 2 and 4. In fact, the reverse is true. Poor conduct is actually more strongly related to high leadership votes in the two relatively good conduct groups (Types 1 and 3) than it is in the other two.

Taking these two sets of findings that relate to conduct together, we see a clear difference between the principles on which these boys choose their friends and their leaders. It seems from these data that boys who get into trouble with teachers are apt to be chosen as leaders (in *all* groups especially those characterized by good conduct ratings) but they are not desired as seat-mates or class companions. This may imply a restriction as to the esteem accorded them or it may just represent prudence on the part of fellow-pupils who enjoy having them in the class to liven things up and respect them for their nerve, but prefer not to have them as seat-mates to get them personally into trouble.

In any event, it is clear that on both leadership and popularity criteria we must reject any hypothesis that conduct-related values or norms (as defined) operate in these groups. In order to lend a little more strength to these conclusions we will briefly repeat the same kind of analysis with two further variables: the strength of verbal *affirmation of middle-class values*, which has been found to correlate with differential academic achievement (Sugarman, 1966),[2] and the degree of *involvement in youth culture*, which correlates with differential conduct in school (Sugarman, 1967).[3]

To measure value orientations a questionnaire was used. Pupils responded "agree", "disagree", or "don't know" to a list of statements, some phrased so as to affirm one of the supposed middle-class values of future orientation, activism and individualism, and some in the opposite direction. Thus, to score highly on future orientation, pupils would have to disagree with statements such as "There is no sense in worrying about the future so long as you are doing all right now" and agree to statements such as "You have to give up having a good time now to do well later on." To score highly on activism they would have to reject statements like "One must learn to take life as it is without always trying to improve things." To get high scores for the third value, individualism, they would have to reject statements like "It is best to be like everyone else and not stand out from the rest" and endorse others like "Nowadays you have to look out for yourself before helping your parents."

We hypothesize a closer association between values scores and popularity in Type 1 and 2 groups (high-achievers) than in Types 3 and 4. At least, we hypothesize a closer relationship in Type 1 than in Type 4. In fact both hypotheses are fulfilled. The corresponding hypotheses involving values and leadership votes, however, are altogether rejected.

Type 1 groups stand out. In these groups there is a marked association between high scores on middle-class values and popularity, and in these groups *alone*. On the popularity criterion, therefore, we may conclude that these groups have values relating to pupils' standing on these middle-class values.

---

[2] Affirmation of middle-class values is also associated with conduct ratings, though not so strongly as achievement. Coefficients of contingency: values and achievement $C = .21$ $(p < .001)$; values and conduct $C = .15 = (p < .02)$.

[3] Involvement in youth culture is also associated with achievement, though not nearly so strongly as conduct. Coefficients of contingency: youth culture and conduct $C = .36$ $(p < .001)$; youth culture and achievement .18 $(p < .001)$.

This finding tends to support the one concerning achievement, though in the case of the latter it was the leadership, rather than the popularity criterion which upheld the hypothesis.

The analysis was repeated for the degree of pupils' involvement in youth culture. This variable was measured on the basis of pupils' reports of their own behaviour: whether they considered themselves regular listeners to pop music radio stations, wearers of teenage fashions, keen dancers, or frequenters of coffee bars, how much they smoked and whether they went out with girls. We find no vestige of support for the hypothesis that between these peer group types there are differences in the value assigned to youth culture involvement. Since involvement in youth culture is closely related to conduct ratings, this confirms the previous evidence on the basis of which we rejected the hypothesis that conduct-related values operate in these peer groups.

DISCUSSION

We have examined some differences in the way sociometric choices are patterned in different types of peer groups, in order to draw inferences about differences in the value systems of these groups.[4] Our findings give a limited amount of support for the view that the peer group to which a pupil belongs at school may affect his level of academic achievement. In some peer groups the value system favours academic achievement and middle-class values, as indicated by the greater sociometric preference for members who have these characteristics. However, the evidence is far from being consistent or unequivocal.

On the whole it seems that the content of pupil peer group culture, at least that part of it which is susceptible to study by these kinds of methods, is very little concerned with how far pupils' behaviour measures up to or falls short of official school norms either with respect to performance or with respect to conduct. Mainly the cultures of these congeniality groups centre around activities which are essentially recreational or distractions from official classroom activities. Each group has its own customary activities. The norms which did come to light in this part of the enquiry are mostly focussed on these activities.

This is not inconsistent with the fact that most boys want to have good

---

[4] Some readers may regret the absence of the familiar tests of significance from this data analysis, so it should be pointed out that the problem under consideration differs from the more common research problems in a special way. It concerns, not the difference between two proportions, but the difference between the extent of such differences in different types of peer group. As such, it is hard to see how standard significance tests could be employed.

marks, even very unacademic boys, nor with the fact that there is rivalry among some members of some peer groups over marks. In the latter case, the response to one who gets higher marks than the others is less likely to be admiration than jealousy or mockery. Nor is it inconsistent with the fact that members of some peer groups define themselves as being more or less academically oriented than specific out-groupers.

Leaving aside now the difficult question of differences between peer groups of different types, we can demonstrate certain differences between pupils who belong to any peer group (regardless of its type) and those who belong to none,[5] although the interpretation of what these differences reflect presents a problem.

Peer group members as a whole are rather more likely to be over-achievers than are nonmembers (.34 compared to .28) and less likely to be under-achievers (.27 compared to .38). This difference could well be due to the differences in IQ and home background between peer group members and nonmembers in this particular sample. As we noted earlier, it is not a representative sample since pupils of middle-class background are overrepresented. Thus, the relationship may be the outcome of preexisting factors which affect peer group membership rather than membership *per se*. Hence we must discount this association until it has been replicated in more representative samples. In the case of conduct ratings the comparison of members and nonmembers goes in the opposite direction so it cannot be dismissed in the same way. Among peer group members of all types .42 have poor conduct ratings compared to .37 of nonmembers.

A pupil who belongs to a solidarity peer group can feel that his friends stand behind him while the teacher holds him up to ridicule, hence its effect on him as punishment or deterrent is very much reduced. Similarly, I would suggest that the timidity that restrains some pupils from talking out in class operates less strongly in the case of peer group members. Not only can they count on their friends to laugh at their jokes but they can feel that they have their moral support. While the importance of these processes varies between peer groups of the different types, I suggest that it operates to some extent in all of them.

CONCLUSION

The study of teenage peer groups presents many problems, especially when one tries to assess the effect of group membership on individuals' behaviour.

---

[5] Nonmembers should not be equated with isolates. Nonmembers include boys who have one special friend, those who are peripheral members of a group, those who have access to two or even more groups, as well as true isolates.

This study shows this well enough at least. In the introduction we outlined two approaches to this kind of analysis: intergroup conparisons, focussing on normative differences and the comparison of group members as a whole with nonmembers. Both approaches were found useful here and no grounds emerged for rejecting one in favour of the other. However, both lines of analysis led us deep into the realms of interesting speculation and, in so doing, suggest some potentially fruitful areas for further investigation.

16. THE SOCIAL CONTEXT OF AMBITION

Ralph H. Turner

Whatever its definition, ambition is typically cast as a form of striving behavior, but the explanation of its origin differs in emphasis according to the interests of the investigator. Most people probably view ambition simply as a matter of overcoming a series of hurdles on the way to success. For them, ambition is a trait. Either one has ambition or he doesn't. Kurt Lewin, the field-theorist, was concerned in his studies of the level-of-aspiration with the effects of prior experience on ambition defined as the setting of increasingly challenging goals. Success was related to the setting of realistically higher goals and failure to the setting of unrealistically high or low goals. McClelland viewed ambition in terms of the achievement motive, defined as competition against a standard of excellence. Its origins were traced to democratic, but gently demanding, family climates that promote self-confidence and a desire for mastery.

A theory of ambition must also consider the effects of different social contexts on the nature and nurture of ambition. Turner, in an intensive questionnaire study of several hundred high school juniors and seniors, examines ambition within the framework of the theoretical marginal man who, as a member of two groups, is confronted with two sets of incompatible demands. To enjoy the advantages of one means relinquishing the privileges of the other. He is marginal because of his inability to make a choice between them.

High school pupils with *mobility-ambition* have the status of the mar-

SOURCE. Adapted and abridged from Ralph H. Turner, *The Social Context of Ambition*, 1964, Chapter 8, pp. 207–225. (With permission of the author and the publisher, Chandler Publishing Co., San Francisco, California.)

ginal man. They must forsake the rituals, values, and ties of their strata (socioeconomic class) of origin for those of their strata of destination. Pupils with *eminence ambition* are assumed to experience little conflict in this respect since they strive to move upward within an occupation or by entering a different occupation without leaving their stratum of origin. Each is shown to be associated with distinctive personality patterns. Of particular interest is Turner's examination of the influence of the social setting on the important socialization mechanisms during a major transition period in the life cycle when pupils are separating from their peer groups and are about to embark on different careers.

This discussion stresses the evidence regarding mobility as a marginality-inducing experience and its relationship to ambition-oriented behavior. The marginal-man hypothesis asserts a causal linkage between situation, experience, and personality. The situation is extensive involvement in two societies or subsocieties whose relationship is such that loyal membership in one means disloyalty to the other and acceptance of the values of one constitutes violation of the values of the other. The experience is the inability to choose between groups, with involvements in the area of personal loyalties impeding choice in the realm of values, and vice versa. The personality consequences are less clearly specified, but consist generally of personal conflict and lack of self-confidence and of heightened objectivity, relativity, and often creativity.

For the upwardly mobile experience to be that of marginality, social strata must be characterized by severe cleavage in friendship and interpersonal loyalty and by incompatible subcultures. The contrasting possible relationships between social strata are class consciousness and value contradiction, or prestige identification and value discrepancy. Within the schools, the presence of mechanisms to facilitate the transition in class identity and the operation of a youth culture obscuring differences in background would mitigate the tendencies toward marginality brought on by value contradiction and class consciousness.

Our evidence deals only with the youth group and cannot tell us about the characteristics of the adult society in which the students live. But among the youth, prestige identification appears to exceed class consciousness, and value discrepancy is more characteristic than value contradiction. The problems of moving between strata should consequently be less intense than those envisaged by the theory of the marginal man. It was not possible to show that youth culture played a special part, though it may do so in middle-level neighborhoods. But anticipatory socialization and social cleavage by ambition suggest that there are mechanisms facilitating the transition for the mobile person.

We found no evidence either that the mobile person was more relativistic or uncertain in his choice of values, or that he took the values of the stratum of his destination more seriously than did persons born in the stratum. In other respects the symptoms and experiences of marginality were not explored.

The mobile person may be marginal, but the attitudes of his high school peers will neither insure nor prevent his marginality. While the impact of family background is not erased, class differences are not sharp and transitions in values are frequently made at this stage in life. Whether transitions in actual social affiliations are being made with great frequency we do not know, but we do know that they are with respect to friendship desirability. On the whole, it appears that the high school peer situation is one in which the discontinuities which normally lead to marginality are moderated.

THE NATURE OF AMBITION

In speaking of marginality we have treated ambition as all of one kind. Sociologists, by their stress on rates of mobility as the measure of democracy, often seem to adopt a view that there is only one kind of success—movement up the socioeconomic ladder. But it is clear that people are ambitious for very different accomplishments. In this investigation we have attempted to take some simple differentiations of ambition into account.

Social strata are broad groupings of people who are only relatively more homogeneous than the entire population. By almost any desideratum, the strata overlap greatly. Likewise, there is a wide range within each stratum. Consequently, a person who is ambitious to improve himself has the option of doing so within his occupational bracket or by entering a different type of occupation. In societies in which the range of value attainable within any given stratum is large, the measure of interclass mobility is only a very partial measure of the individual's success in improving himself.

To allow for ambition which does not find expression in interclass mobility, we employed a question dealing with eminence. We found eminence ambition to be almost unrelated to mobility ambition, and to be prevalent at all levels. In values we found that the boy with high eminence ambition showed the same commitment to secular success as the boy with mobility ambitions, except when success was opposed to the tender values of family and kindness. There was also a bare suggestion that he might have a more "enlightened" or secondary-group attitude toward his social responsibilities.

In an unreported small-scale study of university men students we found little relationship between objective mobility and (a) willingness to sacrifice personal convenience to attain success and (b) the degree to which students set improvement over parental achievement as their standard of success.

Clearly, there is need to recognize another dimension of ambition and to measure more adequately what was only approximately indicated by our measure of eminence ambition. There is need for an entire body of theory dealing with the choice of this kind of ambition and with the social experience and personality of pursuing it.

Among those whose ambition directs them toward interstratum mobility there are again differences. We explored only one of these differences, but found distinctions in value constellations and even a possible social cleavage. We employed educational and material ambition as the very approximate indexes respectively of types of ambitions stressing the improvement in material goods and comforts that everyone wants, and the achievement of a genteel or cultured style of life which many would not want. No greater degree of anticipatory socialization characterized either type. But a somewhat stronger development of some of the traditional middle-class values (or entrepreneurial values) characterized the latter, and a strong theme of institutional repudiation marked the former.

The mobility experiences of persons with these divergent emphases in ambition will probably be different, and what they expect to encounter in completing their mobility prepares them differently for the movement between social strata.

AMBITION AND STRATIFICATION

In order to interpret the data related to these issues, it is necessary to suggest approaches and propositions dealing with the realm of stratification on a much wider scale than the specific problems of the investigation. Three of these areas deserve special mention.

STRATIFICATION OF DESTINATION

The basic model of "class man" in stratification research is the established adult male. He has a station in society which is both based upon and contributive to his occupation and his position in the economic system on a broader scale. When women and persons too young to have earned comprehensive stations of their own are studied, it is customary to identify their class positions by their family connection. Thus the wife is known by her husband's position, and the child by his father's. From two standpoints this treatment of the child is theoretically justified. It is justified insofar as the impact of life situation is felt through the family. The mutuality of the family means that resources, opportunities, and obstacles are shared by family members. It is also justified as the process of socialization takes place through the family. Children learn the values and perspectives of their parents and consequently acquire a class outlook to the extent that their own parents have such a set of attitudes.

But to the extent that they share in life situations other than their families' and experience socialization which does not come through the family, some of the effects of family background may be lessened. Reciprocally, as people react to them less according to their family and family-linked characteristics, the social consequences of background are lessened. It is customary then to think of a progressive neutralization of the impact of class position. Accordingly, class factors and nonclass factors are sometimes weighed against one another in this context.

It is only appropriate to speak of the class position of an eighteen-year-old boy as that of his father on the basis of the assumed continuities with the past that we have just mentioned. But if it is proper to speak of a person's class position by reference to something in his past rather than in his present, may it not be equally justifiable to speak of his class position by reference to his future? Indeed, which reference for stratification is more appropriate must depend upon the time orientation which a person himself holds and which dominates the society or subsociety in which he interacts. It may be argued that the past refers to actual experience and the future to hopes which in many cases will not be realized.

Future-oriented components in stratification are not uncommon throughout society. The occupation "with a future" conveys more prestige than an occupation without a future, even though the objective facts at the moment do not justify the difference in standing. In all probability, societies and regions differ in the extent to which stratification of destination is a component of the total stratification.

Defining stratification exclusively according to origin runs the danger of underestimating the importance and prospects of stratification in a future-oriented society such as high school youth. Some of the classic "middle-class" values were uncorrelated with stratification of origin, but were correlated with stratification of destination. Social cleavage with respect to desired friendships was absent when related to stratification of origin, but appeared when related to stratification of destination. There is good reason to suppose that the cleavage and value differentiation are portents of the nature of the adult stratification into which the students are moving. The stratification of destination may provide a better clue to stratification in the larger society than the stratification of origin.

VALUES AND SOCIAL STRATIFICATION

Values are inferences we make from behavior, and when we characterize the behavior of a class of people, we usually do so on the basis of conspicuous representatives of the class. On both counts, there are problems for the theory of "social-class values." The most conspicuous members of higher strata are the eminently successful, and the most conspicuous members of lower strata are the unsuccessful and the deviant and delinquent. The behavioral contrasts between strata are likely to approach caricatures unless corrections can be made for conspicuousness and ease of class identification. Inferring values from behavior encounters the further problems of deciding how directly or indirectly the value has been applied in the situation, the extent to which the effective value is a specific choice or a general value in a hierarchy, and how effectively compartmentalized the values are. Only with trepidation can assertions be made about "social-class values."

The first impression from our data is that the relationships between stratification and values are remarkably small. There is a temptation, then, to suppose that the items did not pinpoint the appropriate value issues, to ascribe the results entirely to selective drop-out of students, or to wonder whether Los Angeles is notably more amorphous than other cities that have been studied. But two lines of further observation mitigate the impression of unusual findings. First, a careful re-examination of some of the prior studies of class differences in values shows that relationships found by others have often been quite modest. Frequently, only significance measures are reported so that the low degree of relationship is not called to the attention of the reader. Often indexes composed of several items conceal the fact that some of the items are not themselves related to stratification. Second, recent studies of childrearing patterns have revealed much less impressive class differences than were heretofore supposed to exist, and Miller and Swanson have supplied a rationale for the lessening of class-value differences through the emergence of a new middle class. Perhaps the conviction of sharp value differences is unwarranted by the evidence available. The emergence of serious stratification study during the Depression years and in communities in which lower-class and recent peasant origin were inseparable may have instituted biases which now need to be re-examined.

One principle, though inadequately tested in these data, may supply an important key in the understanding of class-value differences. It is proposed that groups differ not only in the values they endorse, but also in the relevance they see in situations. In particular, there is a difference between accepting a value and translating it into a goal in one's own behavior. One may believe sincerely in the value of artistic beauty, but hesitate to attempt to paint for oneself. Hence, we hypothesized that strata would differ more in the values they accepted as goals for their own behavior than in the values which they would endorse in less personal contexts. With data of limited adequacy, there was fairly impressive support for this view in case of stratification of origin among males.

It is the nature of stratification of destination that the ultimate situation in which the values are to be expressed has not yet been experienced intimately. Hence, the situational pressures cannot operate in the way that they can in the stratification of origin or of the contemporary situation. What seems to happen instead is that boys bring their values into line with their goals. The very future-orientation which accounts for the stratification of destination seems also to make personal goals the pivotal point in the formation of more impersonal values. Orientations to the past, and perhaps also to the present, are less active stances. As such they can tolerate the discrepancies between values and personal goals. But the highly active stance of future-orientation leads to adjustment of values in the abstract to greater correspondence with the goals being sought.

WOMEN IN STRATIFICATION

Stratification studies often treat the family as a unit, accepting the husband or wife indiscriminately as an informant regarding class values and styles of life. In explorations of ambition women are often treated in the same fashion as men, as if educational and occupational ambition meant the same thing to them as to men. While we have placed major emphasis on men students, we have also attempted to explore when possible the unique features of the woman's relationship to stratification. Our limited efforts have been productive enough to warrant the judgment that stratification should be more extensively studied from the standpoint of the woman.

The observation of most general interest in this connection is that most of the same values which differentiate strata also differentiate men from women. For the most part the masculine values are the high-strata values, and the relationships are perhaps even clearer for sex than for stratification. The association may be an artifact of our choice of values, concentrated disproportionately in the realms of individualism and secular success. But even if the relationship does not apply to other areas of values, the finding suggests that each family unit incorporates some heterogeneity in class values through its division into male and female roles. The assumption that socialization to class attitudes takes place in a value-homogeneous family microcosm comes under questioning. A more complex process of transmission must be in operation, if the family does transmit class values.

The further observation that some of the values adopted by ambitious girls, but not associated with high background among girls, are values linked to high background among boys is a related finding. Somehow the ambitious girl acquires in certain respects a less feminine constellation of values than other girls. Possibly in some respects she identifies with boys from high backgrounds and takes over some of their values.

There is apparently a complex interplay between class values and masculine-feminine values in relation to class position and ambition. The boy is exposed to some heterogeneity within the home, but through role identification he is able to acquire a set of values which fit his sex, even though his mother carries a set of values which are appropriate for a male of lower standing. Perhaps because ambition is so characteristically masculine, ambitious girls take on some values from across the sex line.

While ambitious women do adopt some masculine values, they also exhibit a special set of values which fits the peculiarities of their sex role. The values of deferred gratification in the ambitious male and individuality in the ambitious female appear to express the peculiarities of their roles. Deferred gratification in some sense epitomizes the active posture, the planning, controlling attitude toward events. If the male is to control later and more important events, he must accumulate his resources now. By contrast, individuality, when divorced from other aspects of individualism, epitomizes the passive posture in self-advancement. The ambitious female makes herself conspicuous, so that she will have a wide rather than narrow range of choice in the marriage market.

This function of individuality is underlined by the difference between women who stress material ambition disproportionately and those who stress educational ambition. The latter apparently take a more active orientation toward ambition, expecting to advance to some extent by their own accomplishment, while the former probably include more of the girls who expect to advance by being chosen. It is the girls who have high material ambitions without proportionately high educational ambitions who stand out most clearly for their endorsement of individuality values. Individuality values are also related to high background among girls, but not so comprehensively as they are to ambition.

A further consequence of the feminine role is the apparently different emphasis in ambition upon the scale of living and the specific occupation of the husband. Our data are not sharply enough directed toward this problem to force a specific interpretation upon us. But examination of the comparative intensity of ambition in various directions renders one interpretation plausible. The male investment is likely to be in a specific occupation; it may be called a career-orientation. Investment of the self in career reaches the point that he does not readily turn from one occupation to another for the sake of tangible advantage. The woman's orientation is toward the *products* of occupational activity, rather than toward the husband's career itself. The product is not merely material, though many girls who are willing to set very low occupational standards nevertheless set their material standards considerably higher. The girls include a severe standard of eminence striving in the ambitions they set for their future husbands. There are probably elements of dignity and pride in effort and accomplishment which they expect along with material reward, without, however, being equally restrictive about the occupation itself.

Ambition is both formed and realized within the family. Somehow or other, these divergent views of success and the divergent values attached to ambition in male and female must come into a working relationship within the family of procreation. Our data indicate that very few girls plan to escape these problems through avoiding entirely the homemaker role. As the distinctive perspectives are brought into the family, their interplay in turn must constitute an element in the socialization experience of the next generation.

A final hypothesis regarding male and female roles in social stratification may be constructed from the findings regarding values and sociometric choice. Women appear to be less weaned from their strata of origin than men are at this stage in life. They are oriented toward the future, and they do reveal anticipatory socialization. But they appear in certain respects to have gone less far than boys in giving up the anchorage to their strata of origin. One scrap of suggestive evidence is their failure to conform to the value-relevancy hypothesis. Men differ less according to background in the values that determine whom they admire than in the values that determine their personal goals. They have gone further in erasing the traces of background in the set of values they employ impersonally than the constraints of their life situations will allow them to do with respect to their personal goals. The girls, however, continue to accept in more impersonal contexts the class-of-origin-linked values which shape their personal goals. Stated another way, the girls continue to believe in the values which their backgrounds have forced on them while the men do not.

We attempted to use the reputation of a student in his schoolwork as a device to separate the impact of the official school social system from the indigenous peer system in accounting for the structure of social preference. Among the boys, the association between socioeconomic background and student leadership *may* have been principally a consequence of the correlation between scholastic reputation and background. Both boys and girls from higher backgrounds were likely to be reputed as *wheels*. The peer system accommodates itself to the official school system to the extent of according some preference to the outstanding student. Among boys this accommodation to the official school system might be enough to account for the slight preponderance of high background among *wheels*. Among girls, however, student leadership is related to background apart from the impact of the scholastic system. Stratification of origin is a significant variable in the indigenous peer social system for girls, but not for boys.

The foregoing observation refers to the choices received as *wheels* rather than to the choices given. It is not that the girls are more class-of-origin-conscious in their selection of *wheels*; it is rather that a girl's peer status as a *wheel* is more likely to be a function of her background independently of scholastic reputation. The data, then, say something about the determinants of the girl's role in the high-school social system. If the high-school girl clings more seriously to the values of her stratum of orientation than the high-school boy, it may be because the peer system is more likely to take her origin into account in the status it accords her. The connection is, of course, wholly speculative in relation to present data. But it represents one more aspect of stratification in which sex differentiation might be profitably examined.

CHAPTER 4

Growing Responsiveness to Socially Administered Rewards

The social scientists often speak of the use of language as distinguishing man from the lower organisms. It would not be far from wrong if the extensive dependence of socialized man on social reinforcers was also considered as another of man's distinctive characteristics. Although socially dependent behavior may be found in other organisms as low in the phylogenetic scale as ants and bees, individual reactions to the stimuli provided by others of their kind are hardly comparable, except by analogy, to those described in this chapter.

People do respond strongly to gestures, words, or other symbolic forms of praise or reproof from others. Such stimuli may cover the entire range from the affectionate smile or hug the mother offers her infant, the father's prideful hand on the shoulder of his son, and the matron's raising of a quizzical eyebrow, to the slight variation in intonation of the spoken word. In general, one tends to behave in ways that will enhance the probability of receiving positive social reinforcers in the form of signs of approval from his friends and colleagues and that will decrease the probability of being the recipient of their disapproval. Thus, it is not at all surprising that parents and teachers employ social reinforcers, almost to the exclusion of all other kinds of reinforcement, for changing and maintaining the behaviors of their children and pupils. But all too often these reinforcers are used to the extent that their effectiveness seems to be taken for granted, and without much thought as to their supposed effect. The reader will see below that the latter notion is invalid in view of the growing body of experimental evidence.

It will undoubtedly be illuminating to many readers that intensive efforts at systematic investigations, aimed at understanding the precise effects of social reinforcement on children's behavior, were initiated as late as the last half of the 1950's. However, scattered experimental evidence regarding verbal praise and blame was to be found at least since Hurlock's (1925) study. Perhaps there was little research on responsiveness to social rewards before the fifties for the same reason that parents use social rewards, that is, because their effectiveness seemed so apparent as not to be an interesting topic to researchers. On the other hand, it may not have been until that period that theory and research techniques had advanced to the point that systematic study of social reinforcement was made possible.

In any event, the situation has changed with remarkable rapidity. The evidence to date has shown that differential responsiveness to social rewards is related to *environmental variables* such as membership in a social class or ethnic group; to the *characteristics of the person* such as his age, intelligence, or sex as well as characteristics due to his history of social reinforcement and social interaction; to the *kind of tasks* he performs whether involving motor, cognitive, or social skills; to the *kind of social reinforcement* employed, that is, whether it is approval only or corrective feedback; and, to the *characteristics of the reinforcing agent*. Considering social reinforcers as a dependent variable, research interest has been directed toward learning how the variables listed above affect responsiveness to the social stimuli that are often the consequences of a child's behavior; considering social reinforcers as independent variables, the concern of researchers has been with understanding how such reinforcements can be used to modify other behaviors. Some comments on the issues involved in these two orientations will provide a means of integrating the findings of the research papers in this chapter and may suggest hypotheses for further investigation. As with all relatively new areas of investigation there are many potential explanations, the evidence for which may be at times conflicting or nonexistent, thereby making further research all the more necessary.

The environmental variables considered to be important are illustrated by membership in a socioeconomic class and institutionalization. For example, the performance of noninstitutionalized children in response to social reinforcers has been compared with the performance of institutionalized children; the performance of children from the lower-socioeconomic stratum has been compared with children from the middle-socioeconomic stratum. In both circumstances the environment is assumed to impose different demands and opportunities for social interaction on the individual. Membership in one social class makes one set of demands compared to demands made by membership in another social class; a noninstitutionalized child has different, or more, opportunities for social interaction than does an institutionalized one. Incongruency between a child's familial social class and the social class of the setting in which he must work, learn, and play creates different expectations regarding the achievement of social rewards, or punishments, and consequently different levels of responsiveness, than when the two are congruent.

In a study presented below, Rosenhan hypothesizes that the lower-class child, coming from a large family, has received little social reinforcement. Furthermore, the values of the lower class are such that few of the experiences that prepare him for school have been provided, and may, indeed, conflict with his adjustment to school. The home setting of the middle class child, on the other hand, has provided him with experiences that enhance the acquisition of values associated with school. In addition, he has had many encounters with school-like tasks and materials. Upon entering school the middle-class child will feel relatively comfortable in the setting and will not overrespond to the teacher's demands. The lower-class child, it is hypothesized, may be alienated due to the discrepancies between his values or expectations and those of the school and teachers. Experiencing anxiety in the unfamiliar setting, he would be more than delighted, probably elated, with signs of approval and, conversely, overly disturbed by signs of disapproval compared to the child from a middle-class home. It is also possible that signs of approval or disapproval administered in one socioeconomic class mean quite different things to members of another class, thereby modifying the quality of responsiveness. Although his findings support the alienation position, Rosenhan's paper is especially valuable for his critical examination of his findings in terms of several alternative theoretical positions.

In a somewhat different manner, the institutional environment can also affect responsiveness to social rewards when it isolates the child from nurturant and supportive interaction with adults. Stevenson and Fahel's study clearly demonstrated, with mentally retarded children, a main effect associated with institutionalization. One theory suggests that the immediate effects of separation from home and family on the child is an intensification of anxiety over social deprivation caused by the relative absence of attentive adults and other family members. Thus, institutionalized children are hypothesized to be especially motivated to achieve social contact with another person. And, as shown by the findings of these researchers, the performance of both normal and retarded institutionalized children is facilitated by social reinforcement more than is the performance of noninstitutionalized children.

There are several plausible "theories" suggesting reasons why responsiveness to social reinforcers increases after periods of isolation. One of these explanations, the social-deprivation hypothesis, is based on notions very similar to those found in traditional behavior theory: A period in which the child is removed from all contact with people is said to result in a state of deprivation, with a complementary increase in the need for social reinforcement. The child's performance is presumed to be facilitated more by social reinforcers than by tangible reinforcers, and to be facilitated more after a period of isolation than after a period of deprivation. The anxiety-arousal theory, on the other hand, suggests that the child's anxiety is aroused when he is placed in a room by himself for any length of time. Any condition which promotes his security or otherwise reduces anxiety would facilitate his performance. Certainly, social contact and praise would be among such events.

The stimulus-deprivation hypothesis is similar to the social-deprivation hypothesis except that it is more general. This explanation suggests that isolation for any period of time typically removes the child from normal stimulation, and so he will be more responsive to any form of reinforcement. By this reasoning one would expect children to be less responsive to social reinforcers if stimulation was provided during the isolation period than if no provision for stimulation was made. The results from such experimentation have not clearly supported this hypothesis; children seem to respond more favorably to social than to tangible reinforcers in either condition.

At the present time, the social-deprivation and anxiety hypotheses appear to be among the major competing explanations for the effects of isolation on responsiveness to social rewards. The investigators concerned with this issue have turned to the laboratory to examine the value of these alternative positions. In the present selection of articles such studies are represented by Lewis' investigation in which the lengths of deprivation periods were varied in a parametric study. He assumed that if the social-deprivation hypothesis was tenable, the length of the deprivation period would be linearly related to the effectiveness of social reinforcement. In the actual experiment, children were taken to a room where they remained for a period of 3, 6, 9, or 12 minutes. Then a simple task was performed by the child immediately after isolation. Responsiveness to social rewards was found to increase as a function of isolation, much as it does for institutionalized children. But the unique feature of the finding was that the relationship between performance and the length of the isolation period was a parabolic, not a linear one, that is, greater facilitation was found after the three- and twelve-minute periods than after the six- and nine-minute periods of isolation. However, these results can be explained equally well by either the social-deprivation or anxiety-reduction hypothesis, and indicate the considerable difficulty in separating the relative effects of social deprivation, stimulus deprivation, motivational arousal, and similar hypothesized events that seem to be inextricably entwined with anxiety. Nevertheless, the empirical demonstration of isolation effects on receptivity to social reinforcers is clearly a replicable one.

The effectiveness of social reinforcers is further modified by the child's socialization experiences. One who has a history of little reinforcement can be expected to react quite differently to praise, or blame, than one who is continually reinforced. Children younger than five years of age seem to be more receptive to M-and-M's, token, trinkets, pennies, and other tangible rewards. Children older than 12 years of age, for example, are as responsive, if not more so, to informative feedback as they are to mere approval. Mental age, too, can be an important variable related to history of experience. As shown in Stevenson and Fahel's study an extremely retarded child may experience isolation effects even though he remains with the family and is not institutionalized. In such instances isolation may be considered to be *derived* rather than *imposed*, in the sense that it is caused by the child's inability to maintain optimal levels of social interaction. Accordingly, he is alone even though he is among others. Because he is "socially different" he must adapt to those around him thereby increasing his sensitivity to their demands and approval.

Conversely, the characteristics of the reinforcing agent will clearly alter the effects of his social value and consequently of the social reinforcers he uses. Perhaps one of the most consistent findings in this area is the cross-sex effect. Reinforcers administered by a male experimenter appear to be more effective for girls than those administered by a female experimenter, and reinforcers administered by females are more effective for boys than those administered by a male experimenter. Familiarity with the reinforcing agent might also be hypothesized to affect his effectiveness, but the effects of this variable, too, can be modified. Thus, negative reaction tendencies will be developed toward punitive adults, whether parents or strangers, and positive reaction tendencies will be developed toward adults or peers. As shown in McCoy and Zigler's study in Chapter 2, their respective roles of punitive and reinforcing persons as effective reinforcing agents will be decreased or increased accordingly.

The notion that people are most responsive to a rewarding person than to a nonrewarding one was investigated in the study by Hartup and Coates, which was particularly interesting because it dealt with the especially important social behavior of altruism. Children with histories of frequent peer reinforcement imitated altruistic behavior from rewarding models, probably because of their greater incentive value, to a greater extent than they did from unrewarding ones. For children with a history of infrequent reinforcement, both rewarding and nonrewarding peers were effective. However, the nonrewarding peer was more efficacious than the rewarding one, probably because the former creates anxiety which can be reduced by imitation while the latter reduces incentive to imitate. The studies in this area suggest the strong interaction of the child's socialization history and the characteristics of others, who act as reinforcing agents, on responsiveness to social rewards.

The above summary briefly describes some points of progress made in the *analysis* of social reinforcement processes. Of equal concern to educators are the potentials of these processes for changing behavior and the pitfalls that might be encountered in *applications* to practical situations. It is more than likely that whatever new principles are found in practical educational settings, or whatever principles are validly used in those settings, will make as much of a contribution to this area of knowledge as those principles identified in the laboratory. Some related questions are as follows: Will the principles identified in the laboratory be sufficiently powerful, or can they be sufficiently controlled, to influence behavior against the array of variables operating in a practical setting? Can these principles be used to influence complex social processes such as cooperation, conformity, or aggression? Can children be influenced to become more responsive to one kind of social reinforcer than to another?

Considerable ingenuity will be required in translating a laboratory procedure, such as the administration of verbal approval to a captive subject involved in a marble-dropping task, to the complex activities that take place in a classroom where the child may be engaged in a multiplicity of activities. If such practices are to be effective, the principles on which they are based must be relatively well established, or their effects succumb to other uncontrolled or unidentified, but more potent variables. Fortunately, two representative studies have been identified for presentation in this chapter which indicate that modification of behavior by capitalizing on responsiveness to social rewards is far from being a fragile effect. Nevertheless, to be effective, precise operational definition was required before the change of behavior in natural settings was attempted. In other words, it was necessary for the reinforcing agent to know exactly the nature of the behavior to be changed and what stimuli he provided that led to the desired changes.

The pragmatic applications are illustrated in the studies by Scott, Burton, and Yarrow, and by Allen, Hart, Buell, Harris, and Wolf. In both studies a child's behavior was modified in a natural, nursery school setting. Both investigations took place over a period of several days rather than the very brief periods typically used in laboratory studies.

In the research by Scott et al., a child's negative social acts toward his peers was found to be reinforced by his responsiveness to adults and by their responsiveness to him. (Parenthetically, it should be noted that the topic of children's responses as social reinforcers for adults has not been a part of the systematic investigations in this area but would appear to be a fruitful area for further study.) This observation was then used by an experimenter in the classroom, to reduce the frequency of the child's aggressive acts and to increase the frequency of his positive social behaviors. The validity of the procedure was established by returning to whatever reinforcement schedules were regularly imposed by the teacher, and then, once again, reinstating the experimental procedures before terminating the study. Predicted changes in behavioral tendencies of the subject coincided with the changes in treatments.

In the study by Allen et al., the regular teachers in the classroom were instructed in the use of attentive responses and other social reinforcers for increasing the attractiveness of peer interaction to a child who tended to isolate herself from other children. The frequency of the child's social interaction was increased by reinforcing her participation as a member of a group project rather than as an individual.

At the present time the complexity and importance of the entire process of social reinforcement is fully recognized by researchers. But even after the passage of more than a decade, research has yielded only the most rudimentary understandings as shown also in reviews by Hartup (1965) and Stevenson (1965). For many years to come, unraveling the variables that are intertwined with responsiveness to social rewards will be a challenging and rewarding task, though not an easy one, for investigators both in the laboratory and in the more pragmatic settings. Yet the fascinating articles presented in this chapter indicate that progress is being made even at the moment, not only in the analysis of the process, but also in its practical applications. This is fortunate since a fuller understanding of the socialization process than is now available must depend, in large part, on knowledge about the way social reinforcement functions to affect behavioral trends.

17. EFFECTS OF SOCIAL CLASS AND RACE ON RESPONSIVENESS TO APPROVAL AND DISAPPROVAL

David L. Rosenhan

Although many of the effects of rewards and punishments, as behavioral consequences, are generally predictable, a given consequence is not equally effective in all environmental contexts. There is now considerable evidence, for example, that changes in the absolute size of a reward, administered to an individual during a training period, produces corresponding changes in his performance. However, a more interesting finding, and one especially relevant to the present study, suggests that a change from a small reward to a large reward *elevates*, and a change from a large to a small reward depresses the effect normally obtained by the exclusive use of a reward of one or the other magnitude.

In this article, it is demonstrated that such relative changes in reward value can also be accomplished by characteristics of the naturalistic contexts in which social interactions normally occur. Rosenhan hypothesizes that *alienation* may be one source of such influence. He suggests that, in some circumstances, the lower-class child feels separated from the middle-class environment because of his lack of direct or vicarious contact with its institutions. Thus, when he is among people from the middle class, as he is in the school setting, he is especially sensitive to their demands and evaluations. In a sense, this extra degree of sensitivity increases the positive affective value of approval and the negative value of disapproval administered by a middle-class teacher. As a consequence, the lower-class

SOURCE. Adapted and abridged from David L. Rosenhan, "Effects of Social Class and Race on Responsiveness to Approval and Disapproval," *Journal of Personality and Social Psychology*, 1966, Vol. 4, pp. 253–259. (With permission of the author and the publisher, the American Psychological Association.)

child's responsiveness to evaluative comments will tend to be more exaggerated than that of the middle-class child. On the other hand, the middle-class child seems to employ a productive problem-solving strategy in which he depends more on his own resources than on feedback from an external source.

This study is interesting not only for its findings, which support the alienation hypothesis, but also for its provocative interpretations. Rosenhan's alternative explanations of his results are based on differential child-rearing practices in lower- and middle-class homes, anxiety, and class versus color. They provide a rich source of hypotheses for further investigation.

Recent concern with the academic failure of the culturally deprived or the culturally different has yielded a number of hypotheses regarding the potential sources of this failure (cf. Passow, 1963; Riessman, 1962). Since the term culturally deprived implies primarily lower-class children, and particularly those who are nonwhite, these hypotheses have sought to explain the failures of these children in terms of characteristics that are presumed to be possessed primarily by the lower class. Thus, their relatively impoverished status is seen as relevant to their academic failure. So, too, their transient status in the community, their unstable parental identifications, their negative self-images, the degree to which they are encouraged to achieve—all these and others are seen as potential sources for the academic performance discrepancies between young children from the lower and middle classes.

The present study takes a social class interaction position (cf. Clark, 1963; Rosenhan, 1965). It examines the notion that the lower-class child may be more alienated than the middle-class child in a middle-class school system. Taking alienation to mean a lack of relationship with one's environment (English & English, 1958) and particularly an inability to comprehend environmental expectancies, the argument runs as follows: For the middle-class child, the middle-class school may be seen as an extension of his middle-class home. Often, long before he has entered first grade, he anticipates going to school and has learned something about school from his parents. Commonly enough, he has been introduced to some of the materials that he will subsequently encounter in school. Moreover, he is reasonably familiar with middle-class institutions and is comfortable with middle-class people. Thus, for this child, the school is a comfortable situation with which he often has prior familiarity. For the lower-class child, however, the situation may be quite different. In his environment, attending school may not be an especially high-status activity. He has probably received little if any of the vicarious and anticipatory reinforcement that the middle-class child receives prior to going to school. Indeed, what with the larger family that he tends to come from and the greater need for both of his parents to be employed, the school may have subtly acquired negative reinforcing properties in the sense that it may be viewed as a repository in order to permit the parents greater freedom. From whatever source, then, it is conceivable that the lower-class child experiences greater alienation in middle-class institutions and with middle-class people than does the middle-class child.

In the present study we examine one hypothesis derivable from the above proposition: If lower-class children are more alienated in a middle-class institution, they should be more responsive to praise than middle-class children would be. By the same token, the performance of lower-class children should be more disrupted by disapproval than that of their middle-class peers. In general, the relationship of a lower-class child to middle-class institutions can be viewed in much the same way that a Westerner might experience, say, an Oriental wedding. Feeling quite unfamiliar with the rites and rituals he would be more delighted than an Oriental would be by a remark that approved of his behavior. On the other hand, having done something that evoked disapproval, he would be more disturbed by the criticism than would one who was relatively more at home at such ceremonies.

In order to test the hypothesis, a middle-class male experimenter verbally reinforced the performance of first-grade lower- and middle-class subjects in a binary-choice game. Half of the subjects were given positive reinforcement when they made the correct response. No reinforcement was offered for incorrect responses. The remaining subjects were given negative reinforcement for incorrect responses, with no reinforcement given for correct responses.

It has been suggested (Riessman, 1962) that the Negro lower-class child suffers an especial handicap in that his color leads him to acquire a negative-identity image more rapidly and more deeply than the white child. We examine this hypothesis in this experiment by considering separately the effects of disapproval and approval on white and Negro lower-class children. (Negro middle-class children were not available for this study.) If both the alienation and the negative-identity hypotheses are correct, then Negro children should be more positively affected by approval than white children and more negatively affected by disapproval.

METHOD

Subjects

Subjects were 72 first-grade boys who were drawn from two public schools of mixed socioeconomic class. Socioeconomic class was determined on the basis of parental occupation (Warner, Meeker, & Eells, 1949, p. 140). Subjects were randomly assigned to the approval and disapproval conditions. Twenty-four subjects were middle- and 48 were lower-class children. Of the lower-class children, half were Negro and half were white. A comparable Negro middle-class sample could not be obtained. Table 1 describes the composition of the groups.

A middle-class white male experimenter conducted the study. He was told that the experiment dealt with the effects of approval and disapproval on probability learning, but was not aware of the social class hypotheses. Nor did he realize that the subjects had been presorted on the basis of social class and race.

Apparatus

A black metal box, measuring 7 $\times$ 12 $\times$ 7 inches, served as the binary-choice apparatus. Mounted on the lower right and left corners of the panel was a toggle-type automatic-return switch which the subject manipulated. The subject's responses activated either of two lights on the experimenter's clipboard indicating which lever the subject had depressed. The experimenter then responded accordingly. The subject was seated before a low table on which was the binary-choice game. The experimenter instructed the child in the use of the switches and, for the approval condition, told him that "each time you press the right button, I will say 'right.'" For the disapproval condition, the instructions were reversed, namely, "each time you press the wrong button, I will say 'wrong.'" The instructions were repeated several times.

Prior to the training trials, the subject was administered four practice trials, for which the first and last trials were correct (i.e., they were reinforced for the approval condition; for the disapproval condition the second and third practice trials were negatively reinforced).

When it was clear that the subject understood the instructions, he was administered 160 training trials. A reinforcement ratio of 70 : 30 to the left and right levers, respectively, was employed. That is, for the approval condition the left lever was positively reinforced 70% of the time, and the right lever 30% of the time. For the disapproval condition the reinforcement ratio was reversed—70% of the right and 30% of the left lever presses were negatively reinforced. Reinforcements were randomized in blocks of 20 trials. Thus, the response behavior demanded—pressing the left lever—was the same for both the approval and disapproval conditions and constituted the dependent variable for this study.

RESULTS

Three analyses of variance were applied to the mean performance data shown in Table 1. The first analysis considered the effects of approval and disapproval on lower-class children. It examined whether Negro and white boys responded differentially to these reinforcers. As will be seen in Table 2, no race differences emerged either as main effects or in interaction with other variables. The effects of reinforcers were such that lower-class children were much more responsive to approval than to disapproval.

The trials' main effect in this as in the subsequent analysis indicates that

TABLE 1

Composition of the Sample and Performance of the Subjects ($N = 12$ in Each Group)

Subject Group	CA[a] M	CA[a] Range	Socioeconomic Class M	Socioeconomic Class Range	Responses to Left Lever (Percentage of 160 Trials) M	Responses to Left Lever (Percentage of 160 Trials) Range
Middle-class white						
Approval	6:1	5:10–6:6	1.4	1–3	60	04
Disapproval	6:2	5:11–6:4	1.4	1–3	62	03
Lower-class white						
Approval	6:2	5:10–6:7	5.8	5–7	64	06
Disapproval	6:3	5:9–6:8	6.0	5–7	55	04
Lower-class Negro						
Approval	6:3	5:11–6:10	6.4	6–7	63	09
Disapproval	6:1	5:9–6:11	6.0	5–7	55	04

[a] At time of testing.

TABLE 2

Summary of the Analyses of Variance for the Color and Class Comparisons

Source	df	I Lower Class: White Versus Negro Subjects MS	I F	II White Subjects: Lower Versus Middle Class MS	II F	III Lower-Class Negro Versus Middle-Class White MS	III F
Between subjects	1	1.5052	.06	16.9216	1.27	28.5208	1.30
Groups (A)	1	577.5469	22.05[a]	97.7552	7.32[a]	102.0833	4.65[b]
Reinforcers (B)	1	.0469	.00	194.0052	14.53[a]	200.0833	9.12[a]
A × B	44	26.1928		13.3509		21.9461	
Error b							
Within subjects							
Trials (C)	3	313.4219	125.39	179.8108	158.26[a]	133.1875	71.94[a]
A × C	3	3.8108	1.52	38.6302	34.00[a]	19.4097	10.48[a]
B × C	3	13.3524	5.34[a]	4.5469	4.00[a]	1.3889	.75
A × B × C	3	1.0191	.41	6.4358	5.66[a]	2.3889	1.29
Error (w)	132	2.4995		1.1362		1.8513	

[a] $p < .05$.
[b] $p < .01$.

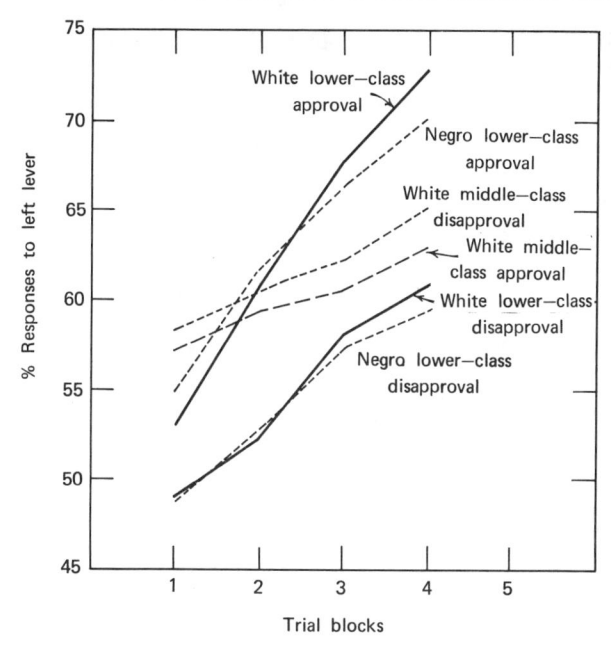

Growing Responsiveness to Socially Administered Rewards 201

FIGURE 1. Mean performance of subjects by experimental group and blocks of 40 trials.

the tendency to respond to the left lever increased over the four blocks of trials. The subject's performance began at or near the 50% level and increased as he gained more experience with the reinforcement contingencies. The interaction between trials and the reinforcer valence demonstrated that the subject's tendency to respond to the left lever rose under approval conditions but remained relatively stable (and low) under conditions of disapproval. Figure 1 presents the data across trials for these lower-class subjects and for the middle-class subjects.

The second analysis of variance (Table 2) examined the responsiveness of lower- and middle-class white children to approval and disapproval. Again, the main effects of the reinforcement dimension were significant. However, they interacted with social class such that compared to middle-class boys, the performance of lower-class boys was facilitated by approval and retarded by disapproval.

Looking now to the between-blocks-of-trials analysis, we find that the main effects of trials are marked: The subjects' performances improve over trials. The Trials × Social Class interaction is seen in Figure 1, where the early performance of lower-class subjects in the approval condition is below that of middle-class subjects in either condition. Terminal performance of lower-class subjects under approval is, however, higher than that of any other group.

Approximately similar results obtained from the third analysis which considered the effects of approval and disapproval on lower-class Negroes and middle-class whites (Table 2). While the overall effect of approval was greater than that of disapproval, lower-class Negroes performed better with approval and worse with disapproval than did middle-class whites. And while the performance of all groups improved over the four blocks of trials, the amount of improvement for Negroes in the approval condition (whose initial performance was below that of the middle-class boys in either condition) was substantially greater than it was for middle-class whites.

DISCUSSION

It is clear from these data that identical reinforcers—approval or disapproval—have differential effects according to the social class of the subject. Taking performance to mean the number of times the subjects pressed the left lever, the performance of lower-class subjects was substantially improved under conditions of approval relative to middle-class subjects. Under conditions of disapproval, however, lower-class boys performed more poorly than their middle-class peers.

The data are consistent with the view that lower-class children, at least on entry into middle-class institutions and with middle-class people, are unfamiliar with their surroundings and therefore experience a greater sense of alienation than do middle-class boys. This presumed sense of alienation leaves them especially sensitive to external social reinforcers that convey approval or disapproval of their behavior. Unable, as it were, to assure themselves that they are legitimate members of the environment in which they find themselves, they rely more heavily than middle-class children on external indexes of the quality of their performance.

At the same time we have an instance where alienation is not necessarily deleterious to performance. If learning is viewed as the tendency to respond to the more reinforced lever, then for lower-class children, approval facilitated learning. And while the paradigm is limited to a brief experimental event and to a small sample of performance, the data are sufficiently encouraging to speculate that the longer term effects of middle-class approval might produce a generally elevated performance in lower-class children. Long-term disapproval, on the other hand, might have relatively enduring opposite effects, reducing the performance of lower-class children far below what it might be under other conditions.

Alternative Interpretations of These Findings

Differential child-rearing practices in lower- and middle-class homes: The effect of reinforcer adaptation and variability. Sears, Maccoby, and Levin (1957) have shown that social classes differ in their methods of child rearing. Specifically, lower-class parents are more prone to employ physical punishment with their children while middle-class parents use verbal persuasions and penalties. It is conceivable that by the time the middle-class child is 6 years old, he has become relatively adapted to (satiated on?) verbal reinforcers such that neither approval nor disapproval affect him deeply or differentially. For lower-class children, however, who are relatively less adapted to verbal methods of behavior control, approval and disapproval have more potent effects.

If there is some difficulty with this interpretation, it rests with the strong effects of disapproval on lower-class children. For while lower-class parents tend to utilize physical means of punishment, they do not use such means exclusively. Presumably it is combined with verbal disapproval such that lower-class children ought to have become adapted to both kinds of disapproval, or perhaps to disapproval in general. Their performance in the disapproval condition, relative to middle-class children, indicates clearly that this is not the case, weakening thereby a child-rearing interpretation of these data or requiring a more complex model.

Anxiety. The data are clearly interpretable within an anxiety framework; namely, lower-class children are more anxious in a middle-class setting than are middle-class children. Thus, for lower-class children, approval reduces anxiety while disapproval heightens it. Since middle-class children, on the other hand, are presumed to be quite secure in this setting, neither approval nor disapproval affects them strongly.

Such an interpretation is not inconsistent with an alienation view of lower-class children's behavior in that these children may be anxious because they are alienated. Offered by itself, of course, an anxiety interpretation gives no clue as to why lower-class children should be more anxious. And since no independent measures of anxiety were obtained it was felt that the alienation interpretation offered was the more appropriate one at this time.

Class versus Color

While there is considerable evidence that young children are perceptive of and sensitive to racial differences, these differences do not appear to affect their responsiveness to verbal reinforcement. Ordinarily, one might have expected Negro lower-class children to experience most alienation with a middle-class white experimenter, by virtue of the combined effects of both class and color differences. Thus, their responsiveness to both approval and disapproval should have been heightened relative to lower-class white children. Since this did not occur it can be argued that, at least for very young boys, social class differences rather than color differences are the critical variables that determine responsiveness in reinforcement situations. It should be noted that a similar failure to obtain differences between Negro and white lower-class children, this time in a simple conditioning task, occurred previously (Rosenhan & Greenwald, 1965).

18. THE EFFECT OF SOCIAL REINFORCEMENT ON THE PERFORMANCE OF INSTITUTIONALIZED AND NONINSTITUTIONALIZED NORMAL AND RETARDED CHILDREN

Harold W. Stevenson & Leila S. Fahel

After a year or two in those institutions that provide only routine attention by a number of adults, there is an appreciable decrease in the child's IQ and other developmental indices. These effects are clearly similar to those observed in comparisons of children from educationally disadvantaged environments with those from more advantaged backgrounds. Thus, the origins of developmental deficiencies are not rooted in the fact of institutionalization *per se*, but are attributable to whatever factors are associated with institutionalization and which are shared in common with the isolated mountain community, the ghetto, or the barrio. As with most other environments, institutions can, and do, vary. They differ in the provisions they make for contact with a mother surrogate, for social stimulation, and for the development of social skills.

Although the effects of these variables on the child's cognitive development, as reflected in his IQ, are readily apparent and quite generally accepted, the effect on his social development and motivation has recently gained renewed attention from investigators. In this study, Stevenson and Fahel show that the mere social presence of an adult may be an especially salient stimulus for institutionalized children whose performance, as a consequence, improves more than does the performance of noninstitutionalized children. Nevertheless, these results are severely complicated by the find-

source. Adapted and abridged from Harold W. Stevenson and Leila S. Fahel, "The Effect of Social Reinforcement on the Performance of Institutionalized and Noninstitutionalized Normal and Feebleminded Children," *Journal of Personality*, 1961, Vol. 29, pp. 136–147. (With permission of the senior author and the publisher, the Duke University Press.)

ing that noninstitutionalized retarded children responded more favorably to verbal support and encouragement than did the institutionalized children.

These differential saliencies of social stimuli for the two groups are examined by Stevenson and Fahel in terms of *imposed* environmental factors, such as social deprivation that might exist in institutions, and *derived* social deprivation, such as that which might occur for a noninstitutionalized retarded child whose relative incapacity leads to a state of deprivation because he is unable to maintain a high level of social interaction.

Though the use of institutionalized children as subjects is a convenient means for examining effects of certain variables on behavior that would be otherwise impossible, for ethical reasons, to investigate experimentally these investigators emphasize a number of caveats that must be observed if one is to make valid inferences. Especially important are the necessity for institutionalization controls, for considering children's possible reactions to overly simple tasks, and for considering frustration as well as social deprivation influences on responsiveness to social stimuli.

In a recent study by Zigler, Hodgden, and Stevenson (1958), two hypotheses were advanced concerning the role of social reinforcement in modifying children's performance. It was hypothesized that (a) adult attention and adult approval are more effective as reinforcers for the responses of institutionalized feebleminded children than of noninstitutionalized normal children, and (b) supportive comments made by E during the course of S's performance are more reinforcing than unresponsive attention from E. The first hypothesis was based on the assumption that institutionalized children tend to be deprived of adult contact and approval and therefore have a higher motivation to secure such contact and approval than do normal children.

The results of the study provided some support for these hypotheses. The fact that institutionalization was confounded with intellectual retardation in the feebleminded group, however, makes it impossible to determine whether the differences in performance were attributable to the effects of social deprivation accompanying institutionalization or to other characteristics differentiating normal and retarded children.

The purpose of the present experiment is to clarify the interpretation of the earlier study and to provide further information about the operation of social reinforcement. Institutionalized and noninstitutionalized normal and feebleminded children were tested in a task similar to that used in the previous study. In addition to the variables of institutionalization, type of Ss, and social reinforcement, the variable of task complexity was introduced in order to determine whether the number of alternatives for response significantly influences performance.

METHOD

Subjects

The Ss consisted of 112 normal children and 112 feebleminded children, selected so that the average CA of each group would be comparable. Half of each group was living at home and half in an institution.

The noninstitutionalized normal (N-NI) children were obtained from a public elementary school in a suburb of Austin, Texas. A school was chosen with classes of children with average intelligence and of average socioeconomic level. All children in each class visited were included as Ss. The noninstitutionalized feebleminded (FM-NI) children were obtained from classes of retarded children in the Austin, Texas, public schools. Names were selected from the central files of the school system of children of the familial type of mental deficiency who had no gross motor, sensory, or emotional disturbances.

The institutionalized normal (N-I) children were in residence at a state orphanage. All children at the school who were of the appropriate CA levels were included in the study. The institutionalized feebleminded (FM-I) children resided at state schools for the retarded. Again, only familial Ss with no gross motor, sensory, or emotional disturbances were used. No institutionalized children with IQ's below 40 were included.

Data concerning the characteristics of the Ss in each group are presented in Table 1. The major difficulty encountered in obtaining Ss was that of finding the institutionalized feebleminded children who met the criteria for selection, and the sample obtained is of a slightly higher average CA than the other groups.

Apparatus

The apparatus consisted of a specially built, 30 × 30 in. table. Centered and 8 in. from the front of the table were two 8 × 10 in. sunken bins. The

TABLE 1

Mean CA, MA, and Length of Institutionalization of Ss in Years

Group	N	CA M	CA SD	MA M	MA SD	Length Inst. M	Length Inst. SD
N-NI	56	8.8	1.1	8.8[a]	1.4		
N-I	56	9.4	1.6	8.7[b]	2.1	2.4	1.6
FM-NI	56	9.3	1.5	6.4	1.6		
FM-I	56	10.2	1.5	5.9	1.2	2.0	1.5

[a] Based on 48 Ss.
[b] Based on 43 Ss.

left bin extended 5 in. below the table and was used for the storage of marbles. The right bin extended 14½ in. below the surface of the table and was used for inserting marbles. An upright panel, 4 in. high and extending across the table, was placed 12 in. from the rear of the table. The panel made E's recording inconspicuous to S.

The right bin was equipped with two interchangeable Masonite plates which fit tightly over the opening to the bin. Centered on one plate was a hole ⅝ in. in diameter. On the second plate were six holes ⅝ in. in diameter, placed randomly about the surface. The sides of the right bin were contoured so that a marble rolled down the sides of the bin into an aperture. Extending below, and connected to the aperture, was a small section of pipe. A photoelectric cell was mounted so that as a marble rolled down the pipe the beam of the photoelectric cell was broken and an electric counter was activated. In the left bin were 2200 marbles, with an equal number of green, orange, blue, and turquoise.

Procedure

The Ss were tested individually. The E introduced herself (all Ss were tested by the same female E, a graduate student in psychology) and engaged S in friendly conversation as she brought S to the experimental room. The non-institutionalized Ss were obtained from the classroom and the institutionalized Ss from a waiting room where they had been called from classes, from work, or from their dormitories. After spending several minutes gaining rapport with S, E introduced the game.

The S was told, "We're going to play a game now. I think it will be fun. This is called the marble game. See all these marbles here. And see this hole (these holes). Now you pick up the marbles one at a time and put them in the hole (in any of the holes). Let's see how many marbles you can put in. Pick them up one at a time (and you can put them in any holes you want to) and I'll tell you when to stop." The E demonstrated how the marbles were put in the holes at the appropriate point in the instructions.

The first minute of the game was used to establish a baseline rate of response for each S. During this minute E played the role of an attentive but nonreinforcing observer of S's performance. The E observed S in an interested but undemonstrative manner, and took notes on S's number of responses and manner of responding.

For half the Ss, those in the neutral condition, E maintained the observer role for the remaining five minutes of the game. No verbal support was given, and E was careful to avoid nodding, smiling, or giving other types of nonverbal support. For the other half of the Ss, those in the reward condition, E began to be responsive to S's performance after the first minute. Twice a minute and as S was responding, E made supportive statements about S's performance and did not avoid smiling and nodding if S glanced at E. Five statements were used: "You're doing very well." "That's very good." "You know how to play this game very well." "That's fine," and "You're really good at this game." These were made in a predetermined random order. At the conclusion of the game all Ss were told they had done very well.

Half of the Ss played the game with the single-hole plate ("simple" task) and half with the six-hole plate ("complex" task). As a result four subgroups for each of the four categories of S were formed: simple task-reward (S-R), complex task-reward (C-R), simple task-neutral (S-N), and complex task-neutral (C-N). Fourteen Ss from each of the four categories of Ss were assigned at random to each subgroup. The design therefore included a total of 16 subgroups of 14 Ss each.

RESULTS

The primary measure used in the analysis of the results was the mean difference score obtained by subtracting the number of marbles inserted during the first minute of the game from the number inserted on each successive minute. Because of the correlation between the obtained scores and their variances, a logarithmic transformation of the data was performed for the purpose of statistical analysis.

A $2 \times 2 \times 2 \times 2$ analysis of variance of the transformed scores was performed, with entries for Type of Subject (S), Institutionalization (I), Type of Task (T), and Reinforcement condition (R). The only significant main effect was that associated with Institutionalization, $(F = 6.47, df = 1, 208, p < .05)$. The F's obtained for Type of Subject and Reinforcement Condition were less than 1.00 and the F associated with Type of Task was 2.16 $(p > .05)$. The significant double interactions were $I \times S$ $(F = 17.27, df = 1, 208, p < .001)$, and $I \times T$ $(F = 8.63, df = 1, 208, p < .01)$. The significant triple interactions were $I \times S \times R$ $(F = 7.19, df = 1, p < .01)$ and $I \times T \times R$ $(F = 5.76, df = 1, 208, p < .05)$. All other interaction terms yielded F's of less than 1.00, except the triple interaction, $I \times S \times T$, for which the F was 3.60, which is significant between the .05 and .10 levels.

The average increment of response per minute of the game is presented for each of the subgroups in Fig. 1. It is clear that the main contribution to the significant difference between the performance of institutionalized and noninstitutionalized Ss is derived from the high level of response by the institutionalized Ss in the neutral condition of the complex task.

In general, there is some support for the hypothesis that institutionalized children have a greater motivation for social interaction with an attentive adult than do noninstitutionalized children. The hypothesis that social rein-

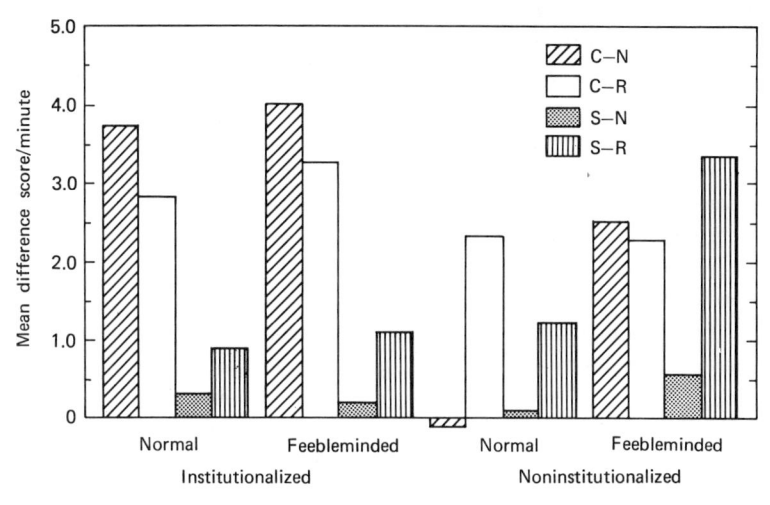

FIGURE 1. The mean difference score per minute of the game obtained by the four groups of Ss tested in the complex and simple tasks under neutral and reward conditions.

forcement is generally more effective as a reinforcing agent than adult attention was not supported. There are several qualifications that must be made to a general statement about the effect of institutionalization upon performance, however, and a discussion of the interaction terms will help to clarify what these are.

The significant $I \times T$ interaction indicates that performance was differentiated by the type of task, depending upon whether or not S was institutionalized. Performance was higher in the complex task for both the normal and feebleminded institutionalized Ss, but the difference between performance in the two types of tasks was less marked for the noninstitutionalized Ss. The significant $I \times S$ interaction indicates that among noninstitutionalized children, performance differed depending upon whether or not S was feebleminded. The difference in the average increment in response was greater for the two types of normal Ss.

The significant $I \times T \times R$ interaction indicates that the reinforcement conditions produced different effects on performance in the simple and complex task for the institutionalized Ss than they did for the noninstitutionalized Ss. For the institutionalized Ss, the reward resulted in a greater increment in performance, while for the complex task, the neutral condition resulted in the greater increment. For the noninstitutionalized Ss, the reward condition resulted in the greater increment in both the complex and simple tasks.

Concerning the significant $I \times S \times R$ interaction, for the institutionalized

Ss, the neutral condition resulted in a greater increment than the reward condition for the normal Ss, while the reward condition resulted in a greater increment for the feebleminded Ss. The difference between the average increment in response in the reward and neutral conditions for the noninstitutionalized Ss was 1.77 for the normal Ss, while it was 1.26 for the feebleminded Ss, the reward condition resulting in the greater increment in both cases. The reward and neutral condition therefore produced a greater difference in performance between the two types of noninstitutionalized Ss than between the two types of institutionalized Ss.

In order to determine whether the initial response rates of Ss in the subgroups were comparable, an analysis of variance was performed of the number of marbles inserted during the first minute of the game in each subgroup. The only comparison which was significant was that for Type of Subject ($F = 48.36$, $df = 1, 208$, $p < .001$). During the first minute the feebleminded Ss inserted an average of 19.6 marbles, and the normal Ss, 26.7 marbles.

All intercorrelations of the various measures related to Ss and their performance were computed. Significant positive correlations were found between CA and response rate and MA and response rate during the first minute of the game for all groups except the normal, noninstitutionalized Ss (see Table 2). Since CA and MA were highly intercorrelated, the partial

TABLE 2

Correlations Between Various Measures and S's Response Rate During First Minute of Game

| | Group | | | |
Measure	N-I	FM-I	N-NI	FM-NI
CA	.66[b]	.32[a]	.01	.46[b]
MA	.61[b]	.46[b]	.08	.62[b]
MA	.18	.34[a]	.09	.48[b]
Mean diff. score	−.31[a]	−.41[b]	−.40[b]	−.34[a]
Total number responses	.94[b]	.88[b]	.92[b]	.91[b]

[a] $p < .05$.
[b] $p < .01$.

correlations were computed between MA and initial response rate with CA held constant. The partial r's for the feebleminded groups were significant, indicating that performance during the first minute is related to mental age in the feebleminded, but not in the normal Ss.

In order to determine what the level of response and pattern of response in the various conditions would be for younger children with mental ages near those of the feebleminded Ss, 56 normal preschool children were tested in the four experimental conditions. The mean CA of this group was 4.25 years, and the mean MA was 5.44 years.

The rate of response during the first minute was 12.4 marbles, which is much lower than that obtained for the older normal Ss. The mean increments in response were similar in the complex task to those obtained for the older noninstitutionalized normal Ss. The mean increment in the neutral condition was .53 marbles, and 1.98 in the reward condition. Performance in the simple task, however, differed from that of the other groups for there was a mean decrement in the reward condition (—.40 marbles) and an increment (.96 marbles) in the neutral condition. The correlation between MA and initial response rate was .33 ($p < .05$), and the correlation between CA and initial response rate was .19 ($p > .05$). The partial correlation between MA and initial response rate with CA held constant was .42 ($p < .01$). This tendency for initial response rate to correlate with MA is the only way in which the performance of the young normal Ss and the feebleminded Ss was comparable. The pattern of response found in either subgroup of feebleminded Ss cannot, therefore, be attributed to their level of intelligence.

DISCUSSION

The study indicates that children's performance in a simple game in the presence of an adult is significantly influenced by whether or not the children live in an institutional environment. The other variables investigated exerted significant effects on response only in interaction with each other. Supportive comments made by E during the course of the game did not have a greater influence on the children's general level of performance than did E's presence in a neutral, attentive role.

The most important implication of these findings for studies of personality and social behavior of feebleminded children is that the effect on performance of institutionalization as well as of retardation must be considered before an attempt is made to interpret the behavior of feebleminded children. Kounin (1941), for example, concluded that the greater perseverative behavior manifested by institutionalized feebleminded children compared to noninstitutionalized normal children was due to a more rigid personality structure accompanying retardation. Such an interpretation is inappropriate since the important control of having a group of institutionalized normal children was lacking in Kounin's study.

The results of the experiment differ from those of Zigler et al. (1958), who found a significantly greater difference between a reward and a neutral condition in the performance of their feebleminded than in the performance of their normal Ss. The significant triple interactions in the present study indicate that the reinforcement conditions did have differential effects on performance, but only as they interacted with other variables. The tendency, however, was for the difference in performance between the two reinforcement conditions to be greater for the noninstitutionalized than for the institutionalized Ss. A similar tendency for social reinforcement to produce greater differences in the performance of noninstitutionalized compared to institutionalized children was found in another recent study (Stevenson & Cruse, 1961). Unfortunately, the tasks and the experimental conditions differed in the three studies, making it difficult to determine the basis of the discrepant findings.

One of the problems encountered in interpreting the present results is to account for the high level of performance of the institutionalized children in the neutral condition of the complex task. It may be that social deprivation resulting from institutionalization increases motivation for adult interaction to such a degree that in certain situations contact and attention from an adult have as great an effect on short-term performance as do an adult's supportive comments. On the other hand, it is possible that motivation to secure adult approval is actually increased when E remains unresponsive to S's performance. The failure of highly motivated Ss to obtain some sort of positive response from E may produce a frustration effect of the type suggested by Amsel and Roussel (1952), which would result in a higher level of motivation. Such an effect would persist until S's expectations for reinforcement were extinguished, which would presumably take longer than the six minutes of the present game. Such an account would not, of course, explain why the neutral condition should fail to produce a high level of performance in the simple task, unless it is also assumed that the task was so repetitive and dull that it was obvious to Ss that they were succeeding and they did not expect to receive confirmation of this from E.

The results indicate that there were differences in performance between the normal and feebleminded children. The slower rate of response of the feebleminded Ss during the first minute of the game is in line with the general finding that retardation is accompanied by poor motor performance. The smaller difference in performance between the institutionalized and noninstitutionalized feebleminded groups than between the comparable normal groups poses a problem for interpretation. It is possible that noninstitutionalized feebleminded children experience greater social deprivation than noninstitutionalized normal children because of an inability of the former group to maintain a high level of social interaction with other persons. If this were the case, a smaller difference in performance between the two feebleminded groups would be expected.

19. SOCIAL ISOLATION: A PARAMETRIC STUDY OF ITS EFFECT ON SOCIAL REINFORCEMENT

Michael Lewis

Social isolation is clearly among the determinants of increasing responsiveness to social reinforcers, at least for the typical child who is accustomed to the presence of others. For such children, a short period of isolation, during which they are deprived of social contact, heightens their receptivity to social reinforcers when performing cognitive, motor, or social learning tasks. The principal alternative explanations of this effect suggest, on the one hand, that isolation leads to an increase in *social drive* with a corresponding increase in the need for social reinforcement, and, on the other, that isolation induces a specific *anxiety* over loss of social contact which can be reduced by social reinforcement.

These explanations share in common the possibility that social isolation, at the least, induces some state of need or motivation although there may be some question of the nature of the motivational state. Accordingly, Lewis hypothesizes in this study that variations in the amount of deprivation should be monotonically related to increases in responsiveness to social reinforcement as reflected in the child's performance on a binary-choice problem. However, the results of his interesting experiment indicated that the shortest and longest periods of isolation produced greater increases in apparent need for social reinforcement than did the periods of intermediate lengths. A tentative description of the sequence of events experienced by the child provided a partial explanation of these findings, as follows:

SOURCE. Adapted and abridged from Michael Lewis, "Social Isolation: A Parametric Study of Its Effect on Social Reinforcement," *Journal of Experimental Child Psychology*, 1965, Vol. 2, pp. 205–218. (With permission of the author and the publisher, the Academic Press.)

the initial period of deprivation immediately affects the child's sensitivity to, or awareness of, the novel state of isolation; subsequently, his attention is redirected or rechanneled to exploration of his surroundings; and, finally, after exploration ceases there is a reinstatement of concern about being alone and about the return of the experimenter.

The study supports the hypothesis that isolation affects responsiveness to social reinforcers, but the relationship is not a linear one. Furthermore, the results can be explained equally well by either an anxiety or social-drive theory. Thus, it can be seen that while isolation in an empty room may induce a social need, it might conceivably also arouse anxiety in a young child taken there by a relative stranger. Similarly, while social reinforcement reduces a social need, in principle it can also reduce anxiety. Other studies will be necessary to determine the precise locus of the effects of social deprivation. This may be difficult to accomplish unless innovative experimental operations are devised to separate, more clearly than has been the case up to the present, the distinctions between social drive and anxiety.

Renewed interest in social isolation, especially its effect on social reinforcement, has resulted in a series of studies which demonstrate that a minimal amount of social isolation is capable of producing marked effects on a simple conditioning or learning task (Gewirtz and Baer, 1958a,b; Lewis and Richman, 1964). All of these investigations show that when the reinforcement for the correct response is social approval, Ss who experience a previous period of social isolation display faster conditioning or learning than Ss who have no such isolation experience. It has also been demonstrated that following a social isolation experience, social reinforcement, rather than another type of reinforcement, is particularly effective in producing faster conditioning or learning (Dorwart, Ezerman, Lewis and Rosenhan, 1965; Erickson, 1962; Lewis, Wall and Aronfreed, 1963). The results of all these experiments appear to indicate that an increased need for reinforcement can be produced by subjecting Ss to periods of social isolation. The work of Walters and his associates (Walters and Ray, 1960; Walters and Karal, 1960) and that of Gewirtz and Baer (1958a,b) employs relatively long periods of isolation (20 minutes), while the work of Lewis with young children (Lewis et al., 1963; Lewis and Richman, 1964; Dorwart et al., 1965) indicates that brief periods (3 minutes) also can produce this phenomenon.

The interpretation in all of these isolation experiments has been that the need for social reinforcement increases as a result of the social isolation procedures. This was based on the implicit assumption that the increased rate of conditioning (learning) reflected an increased effectiveness of value of the reinforcing stimulus. Lewis and Richman (1964) increased the power of this assumption by demonstrating not only differential rates of learning but also differential strategies. Thus, the isolation group showed a strategy associated with maximal reinforcement, while the non-isolated group showed a strategy associated with problem solving.

The causes of this increased need for social reinforcement, however, are not clear. Gewirtz and Baer maintain that deprivation of the social drive produces the increased need for reinforcement. Walters and his associates assert that deprivation causes a nonspecific state of arousal or drive that needs no specific type of reinforcement such as social approval. Lewis and Richman (1964), however, interpreted this phenomenon as resulting from a specific anxiety; namely, anxiety over loss of social reinforcement. This position obtains support from a series of experiments which tested the effect of social and non-social reinforcers following periods of isolation (see Erickson, 1962; Dorwart et al., 1965; Lewis et al., 1963). These studies all demonstrate that social reinforcement (i.e., adults delivering praise for a particular response) is more effective in eliciting increases in a desired response than is non-social reinforcement (a light). The failure of the non-social reinforcement cannot be accounted for by Ss' unawareness of the relationship between the response and the reinforcement (see Walters and Parke, 1965). In the Lewis et al. (1963) and the Dorwart et al. (1965) experiments, four practice trials accompanied the information that: "See, you guessed the correct side and you made the light go on." S's were instructed and given practice trials to insure that they understood explicitly the relationship between the response and the non-social reinforcement. The results of both of these studies, as well as those found by Erickson (1962), indicate that the need produced by the isolation experience is best reduced by social, rather than non-social, reinforcement. Thus, if anxiety is the motivating state, it is a specific kind of anxiety; that is, an anxiety over the loss of social reinforcement.

Also implied in the isolation experiments is the belief that the need for social reinforcement can be varied by the preceding amount of deprivation or social isolation experience. This last implication, however, has never previously been tested. It is the purpose of this paper to report such a test. Stated more formally, this study was designed to test the effect of five different deprivation or social isolation periods on S's need for social reinforcement.

METHOD

Subjects. One hundred fifty third-grade children, 72 boys and 78 girls, from a public elementary school were randomly divided into five experimental conditions (see Table 1). To maximize the effect of isolation and

TABLE 1
Distribution of Subjects by Social Isolation Periods and Sex

Subjects	Minutes Isolated				
	0	3	6	9	12
Female (78)	16	16	15	15	16
Male (72)	15	15	14	13	15

subsequent social reinforcement, young children were used as subjects (see Lewis et al., 1963 and Dorwart et al., 1965). However, because of the prolonged periods of isolation, the youngest grades were not chosen. Third graders seemed to optimize both the isolation effects as well as the emotional strain of being left alone for relatively long periods of time.

Apparatus. The learning task consisted of a deck of 30 cards. On each card was a picture of either a dog or a cat in the ratio of 70 : 30, such that there were 21 cats to 9 dogs. This task is a shorter version of a two-choice probability learning problem used by Lewis and Richman (1964).

Procedure. The social isolation experience preceded the administration of the learning task. Each child was taken to an empty room by a female E and told to sit down and wait for her return. E then left the room and waited either three, six, nine, or twelve minutes before returning. After the appropriate time, E returned to the room and explained the task that the child was about to perform. In the case of the 0-minute condition or control group, upon instructing the child to sit down, E immediately explained the task to the subject.

In a pleasant manner, E showed S a drawing of a dog and a drawing of a cat and asked S to identify them. S was then instructed that the game consisted of his trying to guess which picture, a cat or a dog, would appear on the next card. The deck of cards was face down, and after S made his choice, he was shown the correct event. The card was then removed from S's sight. All Ss were reinforced for each correct response by E's saying warmly either, "Good," "Right," "Very good," or "Fine." Incorrect responses were not reinforced. E recorded S's responses to the 30 cards on a check list placed at one side of the table.

It was predicted that social isolation would produce a need for social reinforcement. As in the case of the earlier isolation experiments, this increased need for social approval would be reflected in S's performance; the greater the need, the more likely S would be to guess the more frequently reinforced event (in this case, cat).

RESULTS

Table 2 presents for both sexes the mean per cent of responses to the most reinforced event (cat) over each block of five trials for each isolation

TABLE 2
Mean Percentage of Response to Cat

Isolation Conditions	\multicolumn{6}{c}{Blocks of 5 Trials}
	1	2	3	4	5	6
\multicolumn{7}{c}{Girls}
0 minutes	41.25	48.75	51.25	51.25	56.25	46.25
3	41.25	53.75	43.75	53.75	57.50	60.00
6	46.67	44.00	53.30	50.67	54.67	58.67
9	45.33	45.33	56.00	52.00	52.00	54.67
12	52.50	57.50	55.00	58.75	51.25	52.50
\multicolumn{7}{c}{Boys}
0 minutes	45.33	48.00	44.00	50.67	54.67	52.00
3	42.67	50.67	57.33	53.33	56.00	50.67
6	38.57	45.71	50.00	50.00	58.57	51.43
9	41.53	52.31	50.77	53.85	49.23	60.00
12	46.67	52.00	54.67	60.00	58.67	53.33

condition. An analysis of variance was performed for each sex separately in order to test the effect of isolation conditions, trial, and any interaction between them. Significant trial effects were observed for both sexes ($F = 3.76$, $p < 0.01$ for girls; $F = 5.05$, $p < 0.001$ for boys). While there were no significant interaction or condition effects for either sex, the condition effect tended toward significance for boys. Because of the limited number of trials presented to each child, a trial analysis, concerned with stable learning curves (asymptotic behavior) could not be performed. However, it has been shown that total number of responses to the most reinforced event over all trials, is a sufficiently sensitive measure of reinforcement effectiveness (see Lewis and Richman, 1964).

Figure 1 presents the mean percentage of responses to cat across all 30 trials for each sex and social isolation group. With all the isolation groups pooled for each sex, a Mann-Whitney U test (Siegel, 1956) revealed that social isolation produced a significantly greater need for social approval than did the control, or non-isolated group ($U = 101$, $p < 0.01$ for girls; $U = 109$, $p < 0.01$ for boys).

The effect of each isolation condition was considered next. Each isolation condition was compared to the control group by use of the Mann-Whitney U test. The results revealed that for boys, only the 3- and 12-minute conditions produced a significant difference ($U = 73$, 0.05, $> p < 0.10$; $U = 69$, $p < 0.05$, respectively). While the 3-minute isolation condition for the girls did tend to produce a difference in the need for social approval, only the 12-minute condition provided a significant difference ($U = 67$, $p < 0.05$).

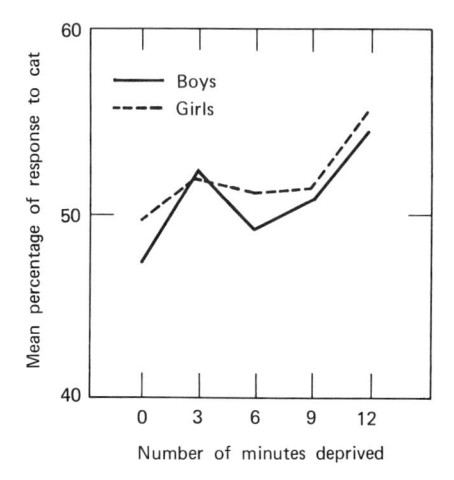

FIGURE 1. Mean percentage of responses to cat across all trials by sex and social isolation group.

Because the trial data indicated that there might have been an initial cat bias for some conditions, which would favor a response of cat even without isolation, the data for the first three trials were analyzed. The data revealed no significant sex difference in the proportion of children choosing cat. Second, there were no significant differences between the isolation conditions for either sex. Thus the effect of an initial cat bias as an explanation of the results must be rejected.

A least square regression analysis was performed in order to determine the function that would best fit the data of Figure 1. It was hypothesized that a quadratic, specifically a parabola, would best fit the data. The independent variable, of five discrete time periods, was transformed into the scores at the times preceding 12 minutes of time 12 (t_{12}). That is, the scores at time t became a function of the scores at t_1, t_2, etc., and the dependent variable became the score at time t_{12}. The parabolic relationship among the scores was tested by computing a linear multiple regression on the first differences. The multiple correlation coefficient r equaled 0.60. Another multiple regression was performed to insure that the parabolic function best fitted the data. To test if a linear function was the best fit, the transformed data were tested by running a linear multiple regression analysis. The multiple correlation coefficient in this case was $r = 0.50$. Thus, the parabolic function accounts for more of the variance than does the linear function and together with the other data support the notion that the 3- and 12-minute groups were responding differently than the 6- and 9-minute groups.

The school had previously assigned the children to one of three classes

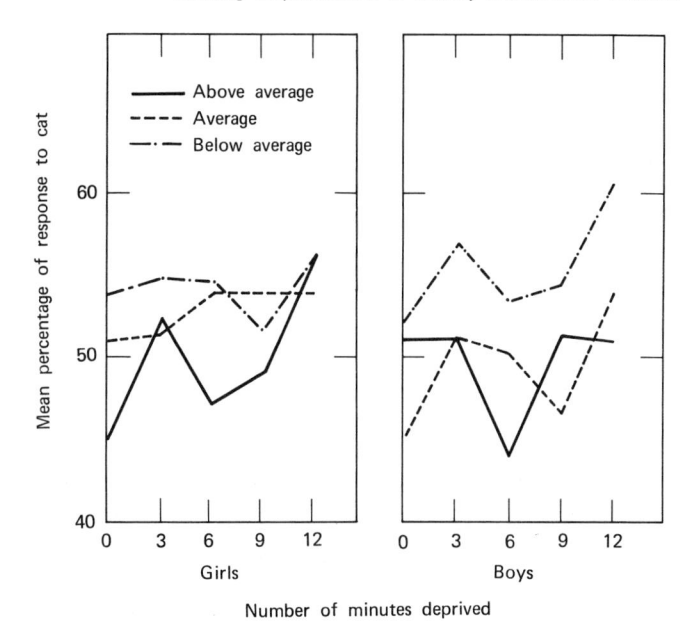

FIGURE 2. Mean percentage of responses to cat across all trials by social isolation group, sex, and intelligence level.

representing an approximation of their intelligence level. Analyses performed for each sex by separating each of the five groups into these three predetermined classes yielded no significant sex difference for each of the three intelligence levels, although the boys, in general, had higher scores than the girls. Combining sex, a Kruskal-Wallis one-way analysis of variance test (Siegel, 1956) indicated that these three groups were not drawn from the same population ($p < 0.01$).

Figure 2 presents the mean percentage of responses to cat across all 30 trials for each social isolation group, sex, and intelligence level. Because of the small number of subjects in each cell (approximately 5), an analysis of variance was not considered. However, inspection of these data indicates several important effects.

First, the data clearly indicate that, across all conditions of isolation, and for both boys and girls, the below-average group chose cat significantly more (received more social reinforcement) than did the above-average group ($p < 0.01$ for both sexes via the Mann-Whitney U test).

The second point to note is the intelligence level by isolation interaction. Considering the girls, it is only the above-average intelligence group which showed the isolation effect. Using the Mann-Whitney U test, the difference between each of the 3- and 12-minute conditions and the control (zero isolation) condition was significant ($p < 0.08$ and $p < 0.001$, respectively). For the boys, it was the below-average and average intelligence groups that showed the isolation effect: Only the 12-minute condition was significant (by Mann-Whitney U test, $p < 0.03$), for the average group, while both the 3- and 12-minute conditions were significant (by Mann-Whitney U test, $p < 0.08$, $p < 0.06$, respectively) for the below-average group. For the above-average intelligence group, there was no significant difference for any of the isolation conditions when compared to the control condition.

DISCUSSION

Because the present design systematically varied the length of the deprivation period, it afforded an opportunity to explore the effect of increased amounts of social deprivation or isolation on the need for social reinforcement as measured in this task. The results tend to indicate that monotonic increases in isolation do not result in monotonic increases in the need for social reinforcement. The results point to a parabolic relationship between the isolation conditions. That is, it is the short and long periods of isolation that are most effective in producing what is felt to be increases in the need for social reinforcement. In a further analysis for each of the sexes, it was the 3- and 12-minute periods of isolation, rather than the 6- and 9-minute periods, that produced increased need for social reinforcement. Although the effect of the 3-minute condition was not strong, the present results confirm the findings of earlier studies which indicated the effectiveness of brief periods (3 minutes) of isolation in producing the need for social reinforcement (Dorwart et al., 1965; Lewis and Richman, 1964). It is clear, however, that for both sexes the 6- and 9-minute isolation conditions failed to produce an increased need for social approval.

At present, the explanation of these findings can be only speculative. It is suggested that during the initial minutes of isolation, the child was quite anxious, anticipating when and what was going to occur when the unfamiliar person (female E) returned. As time passed, competing responses such as interest in the environment increased and visual exploration occurred. It is to be noted that the experiment was conducted in a room totally unfamiliar to the child. Except for two chairs and a table, it was a small, empty room adjoining the principal's office. The room was previously used as a storage room. As time continued to pass, the child, having visually explored the room, again began to become anxious about why he was brought there and when the experimenter was going to return. It is proposed, therefore, that there was an initial anxiety caused by the isolation, which waned with the onset of exploration, only to return again once the exploration had ceased.

The present results add little direct information to the social drive-anxiety controversy. The data could equally fit both explanations of the increased effectiveness of social reinforcement following isolation, and not until a direct measure of anxiety can be devised can this controversy be resolved.

There are surprisingly few sex differences when intelligence level is not considered. The data do indicate that the girls receive more reinforcement than did the boys. That boys in both the control (zero) and the isolation conditions failed to obtain more reinforcement (failed to show greater performance levels) from a female experimenter is inconsistent with Stevenson's results (1961). He showed that the approval of a female E increased the rate of marble dropping for male Ss more than for female Ss, while the approval of a male E increased the performance level of female Ss more than for male Ss.

The difference in results between experiments can be explained by differential task complexity. In Stevenson's experiment, it would appear that the children were minimally interested in the relatively simple task; and therefore, E's reinforcement was of central importance. In the more complex task used in the present experiment, variables other than E's reinforcement become important. It might be argued, for example, that the boys were more interested in solving the problem, thus explaining the scarcity of correct or reinforced guesses (see Lewis, 1965; Lewis and Richman, 1964), while the girls were more interested in approval. The differential results of the zero isolation condition make it impossible to argue that girls were more affected by their social isolation, and thus explain the failure to replicate Stevenson's findings. Thus, not only is there an interaction between the sex of the experimenter and the sex of the subject (see Stevenson, 1961), but there also appears to be a further interaction between task complexity, sex of experimenter, and sex of subject.

Several papers (Crandall, Solomon and Kellaway, 1961; Jones and Liverant, 1960; Kessen and Kessen, 1961; Lewis, 1963, 1965; Stevenson and Weir, 1959; Stevenson and Zigler, 1958) have demonstrated that duller and younger children perform better than do brighter and older ones. In a recent paper, Lewis (1965) argued that bright children attempt to solve the binary-choice problem, whereas dull children tend to seek reinforcement. This differential approach to the task is also reflected by age differences; the older children seek the solution to the problem, while the younger children seek the reinforcement. Because there can be no solution to this problem (due to the stochastic nature of the program), problem-solving behavior results in a lower performance score (less reinforcement) than does the reinforcement-seeking behavior. Thus, the present data are consistent with the notion that increased intelligence level results in lower binary-choice performance.

20. IMITATION OF A PEER AS A FUNCTION OF REINFORCEMENT FROM THE PEER GROUP AND REWARDINGNESS OF THE MODEL

Willard W. Hartup & Brian Coates

Although a child's behavior can be influenced by the administration of rewards or aversive stimuli, his behavior will also be influenced by the behavioral example of another person. A wide range of response patterns can be acquired through emulation of a model—from speaking a language to the acquisition of hostility, aggression, fear, assertiveness, or, as shown in this article, altruism, a little-studied but important social behavior. The psychologist's task is to identify the events that account for variation in the extent of learning that occurs by imitation.

Hartup and Coates have approached this problem from Mowrer's theoretical position that the rewardingness of a model enhances the secondary reinforcing properties of his imitated acts, thereby encouraging imitation of his behavior. The observation remains that rewardingness does not induce imitation equally for all subjects. Situational and individual differences, including sex differences, personality characteristics, and the kind of behavior imitated, are suggested as variables potentially capable of modifying a subject's responsiveness to a rewarding model.

The investigators in this study were especially interested with the effects of subject's prior history of receiving rewards from persons like himself on his imitation of the behavior (donating earned trinkets to a stranger). Friendly, supportive, and nurturant peers were found to increase the incentive value of imitation, that is, of matching the altruistic behavior,

SOURCE. Adapted and abridged from Willard W. Hartup and Brian Coates, "Imitation of a Peer as a Function of Reinforcement from the Peer Group and Rewardingness of the Model," *Child Development*, 1967, Vol. 38, pp. 1003–1016. (With permission of the authors and the publisher, the Society for Research in Child Development.)

for subjects who perceived themselves as similar to the model. In such instances, rewardingness of the model functions to increase an already existent perceived similarity between him and the subject. The secondary reinforcement value of matching the model's behavior is thereby enhanced for the subject. Conversely, children who had been previously reinforced only on infrequent occasions, were more influenced by nonrewarding than by rewarding models. Such children, characterized by a prior history of nonreinforcement, are believed to experience anxiety in the presence of a nonrewarding model and, accordingly, defensively emulate his behavior. Thus, an important feature of this study is the dualistic nature of the explanation proposed to account for the differential imitation of rewarding and nonrewarding models by children with different socialization histories.

Considerable research has been generated by the hypothesis that rewarding models are imitated to a greater extent than nonrewarding models. The formulation developed by Mowrer (1950; 1960) is particularly specific concerning the mechanisms underlying imitation. Mowrer suggested that rewards given to S by a model increase the secondary reinforcing value (for S) of behaviors manifested by the model. When S reproduces these behaviors, the proprioceptive feedback from the imitative acts is presumed, as a consequence of stimulus generalization, to be secondarily reinforcing. This secondary reinforcement predisposes S to reproduce the behavior of the model. Although Mowrer originally provided this theory as an explanation for the imitation of verbal behavior, the theory has since been extended to account for all imitative acts (Mowrer, 1960; Sears, 1957).

Many of the findings from research within this general framework support the secondary reinforcement theory of imitation. Simultaneously, they suggest that situational and individual differences modify the effect of reward from the model on imitation. Sex of S, personality characteristics, and type of response being imitated are examples of such modifiers. But what antecedents are responsible for these interaction effects? What, for example, are the antecedents of sex differences in the impact of rewarding models on imitation? Differences in the socialization history of boys and girls are probably responsible, but which?

The main purpose of this experiment was to study one likely source of variation in the effect of the model's rewardingness on imitation—S's general history of reinforcement from persons resembling the model. The study was based on the hypothesis that the effects of exposure to a rewarding model, as compared to a nonrewarding model, depend on the nature of S's previous experience with people who are like the model. Peers were selected as the class of models to be used. Nursery school children were believed to be appropriate Ss because, even in nursery school groups, the range of reward frequencies exchanged among them is large.

The study was guided by the dimensional prediction stated above. Directional predictions were partially formulated prior to the experiment. For example, it was expected that rewarding peer models would produce more imitation than nonrewarding models for children with a history of frequent reinforcement from their peers. The results for children with histories of infrequent peer reinforcement were more difficult to predict because low frequencies of reinforcement from peers are often characteristic of children who are actively rejected or who are fearful in social situations. Solely on the basis of Mowrer's hypothesis, it would be expected that the rewarding-model effect would be diminished for such Ss. To the extent that such Ss are socially anxious, however, it is possible that nonrewarding peers may exert greater imitative influence than peers who, in the past, have been sources of reassurance and support.

The behaviors modeled in the experiment consisted of an altruistic response plus a group of verbal and motoric actions "incidental" to the altruistic act. Since the study involved peers as models and altruistic behavior as the major dependent variable, it accomplishes two secondary purposes: (a) it contributes to the slowly growing literature concerning the influence of peer models on the socialization of the child (e.g., Bandura & Kupers, 1964; Clark, 1965; Grosser, Polansky, & Lippitt, 1951; Hicks, 1965), and (b) it adds to the sparse evidence concerning imitation as a determinant of altruism (Rosenhan & White, 1967).

METHOD

Subjects

The pool from which Ss were drawn consisted of 64 children enrolled in four groups at the Laboratory Nursery School of the University of Minnesota. These Ss ranged in age from 3–9 through 5–4, with a mean age of 4–6.

Experimental Design

The experimental design consisted of the following groups:

Frequent reinforcement from peers (FR):
  Rewarding peer model (RM) ($N = 12$)
  Nonrewarding peer model (NRM) ($N = 12$)
Infrequent reinforcement from peers (IR):
  Rewarding peer model (RM) ($N = 12$)
  Nonrewarding peer model (NRM) ($N = 12$)
No model (control) ($N = 8$)

Assignment of Subjects

The initial step in the assignment of Ss was the measurement of reinforcement frequencies occurring in the nursery school peer group. For this purpose, observations were conducted extending over a 5-week period.[1] Briefly, the observations produced 12 3-minute samples of each child's behavior, recorded in running account form by observers stationed in the nursery school. These records contained information concerning the child's activity, persons in his vicinity, and accounts of the interaction occurring between the child and other persons.

The 3-minute protocols were then rated by two judges. The records were screened for instances in which the child dispensed or received "generalized social reinforcers" (Skinner, 1953). Four types of positive social reinforcers were tabulated: (a) attention and approval (e.g., attending, offering praise, smiling and laughing, offering guidance or suggestions); (b) affection and personal acceptance (both physical and verbal); (c) submission (e.g., passive acceptance of another child's demands, sharing, compromise); (d) tokens (tangible objects).

A total of 161 protocols were rated by both raters. The ratio of agreements concerning the occurrence of social reinforcement divided by agreements plus disagreements was .77.

The children were divided into two groups: those above the median, for their own nursery school class, in number of reinforcements received (frequent reinforcement group) and those below (infrequent reinforcement group).[2] The mean number of reinforcers received from peers in the FR group was 24.9, while the mean for the IR group was 9.0.

The children in each of the two reinforcement groups were then randomly assigned to model conditions: rewarding peer model (RM) or nonrewarding peer model (NRM). The observational records for each S assigned to group RM were searched for the name of the like-sex peer who had given S the most frequent reinforcement during the observations. This peer was designated as S's model. The RM Ss had received a mean of 5.4 reinforcements from their models during the 36 minutes of observation. Next, a list was prepared for each S in group NRM consisting of all like-sex children in the

---

[1] A detailed description of the observational procedure can be found in Charlesworth and Hartup (1967).

[2] The extent to which the total number of positive reinforcements received serves as an index of total social interaction is not known. It was possible to compute correlations between receipt of positive and receipt of negative reinforcements for Ss in two of the preschool groups. These correlations were .43 ($p < .10$) and .51 ($p < .05$). Incidents of nonreinforcing contacts among peers were numerous but were not tabulated.

class who had never been observed to furnish S with reinforcement. One child, randomly selected from this list, was designated as S's model. The mean reinforcements given to the NRM Ss by their models had, of course, been zero.

The final preliminary step consisted of establishing a testing sequence permitting all the available children to serve as Ss. Some children participated only as Ss; others, who were designated as models, participated first as Ss, then were trained and served as models during subsequent sessions (not more than two for any child).

One boy and one girl from each preschool class were required to start the testing by serving as "first" models. These children were randomly selected. If this selection did not make it possible to test all of the children in that preschool class in sequence, substitute first models were picked. Those children designated as first models completed the experimental task prior to being trained as models. This group of eight children (two from each preschool class) thus comprised a no-model control group (C).

Procedure

No-Model Condition. The S was brought to a laboratory room which contained three hats (maroon, green, and yellow) hung on pegs, three feathers (white, yellow, and orange) placed on a chair, three pencils (black, brown, and green) also hung on pegs, and a table containing a stack of dittoed mazes (simple one-turn puzzles) and three bowls. One bowl, placed in front of the child, was a receptacle for trinkets released by a dispensing device. The other bowls were placed to S's left and right (counterbalanced across Ss); one was designated as belonging to a preschool child (not known to S) whose picture was attached, the other was designated as S's bowl. The following instructions were given:

We have a game for you today. It is a puzzle game and these are the puzzles. (E displays puzzles.) The way you play this game is to draw a line from one flower to another flower, like this. (E demonstrates.) Now you can do some. (S was helped to complete two or three of the puzzles.) There is one other thing that I want to tell you about the game. Whenever you are doing a good job on the puzzle, some little cats will come out of the machine back there. They will come down this chute and fall into this bowl. Whenever some cats come down the chute I want you to put them in one of these other bowls. Either put them over here in Alec's bowl (Kathy's for female Ss) or over here in your bowl. Alec is another boy in the nursery school. Now remember, whenever you are doing a good job on the puzzle, some little cats will come out of the machine into this bowl here and you are to put them in one of these two bowls, either in Alec's bowl or your bowl, your bowl or Alec's bowl. Do you understand? I have to do some work so I will sit in here. Nothing further was said concerning whether S could keep the trinkets in his bowl at the conclusion of the session. The E then went into an adjoining room, left the door ajar, and seated himself out of sight. S was told to proceed, and after each maze was completed six trinkets were ejected through the chute. The session consisted of ten mazes, each followed by the dispensing and allocation of six trinkets. If S failed to pick up the trinkets, E urged him to do so by saying, "Put the cats in the bowls; in Alec's bowl or your bowl, your bowl or Alec's bowl."

Model Conditions. (a) *Training the model.*—Each child designated as a model was brought to the laboratory several days after he had participated as S. He was reminded of the earlier session, given an opportunity to complete two mazes, and asked to help E by demonstrating the game for another child from his class. The E stressed that it was necessary to play the game in a particular way. First, M was told that he should go to the hats, pick out the green one (color alternated across Ss), attach the white feather (also alternated) to the hole in the hat, and put the hat on his head. Next, he was told to select the black pencil (color also alternated), to seat himself at the table, and begin work on the puzzles. Then M was instructed to pick up the six trinkets ejected after each maze, place them in a row on the table, and to pick them up one at a time, placing all but the last one in Alec's (or Kathy's) bowl. The M was also instructed to repeat the words "One for Alec" each time a trinket was placed in "Alec's bowl." The E stressed that only the last trinket should be placed in M's own bowl. This procedure was practiced, with E coaching and sometimes demonstrating, until M was able to perform the task with consistent accuracy. The M accompanied E to the nursery school for the purpose of inviting S to play the game.

(b) *Experimental session.*—When the children arrived in the laboratory, E described the game using the instructions given above. He also explained that the children would take turns and that M would be first. The S was seated so as to face M at a 90° angle and was told that he should try not to bother M. The E entered the adjoining room, leaving the door partly open. Then M was told to proceed. If M failed to respond or engaged in distracting behavior, E prompted him from the other room. In no case, however, were mistakes in allocating trinkets corrected. Such mistakes were made by only two Ms whose Ss were subsequently excluded from the experiment.

After ten mazes, the children were told it was time for S to play the game. The M was invited to wait in the adjoining room with E, and the instructions were repeated briefly to S. When everyone had reached his appropriate spot, S was told to begin.

Response Measures

The following information was recorded by E (observing through a small one-way window): (a) whether or not S chose a hat, a feather, and/or a pencil and the colors of these objects; (b) whether or not S lined up the trinkets and whether the trinkets were placed in the bowls one at a time or in groups; (c) frequency with which S reproduced the verbalization of M; and (d) the particular bowl chosen for allocation of each trinket.

The response measures derived from these records included: (a) presence-absence of imitative hat, feather, and pencil choices; (b) presence-absence of "line up" behavior on each trial (ranging from 0 to 10 over entire session); (c) presence-absence of imitative verbalization (ranging from 0 to 6 on each trial); (d) number of trinkets placed in the "other's" bowl (ranging from 0 to 6 on each trial); (e) latency of the first nonaltruistic choice—the number of trinkets placed in "other's" bowl before placement of the first trinket in S's own bowl (ranging from 0 to 7 on each trial).

RESULTS

Intercorrelations among four of the dependent measures (giving to other, latency of giving to self, verbalization, and line up) were calculated. The correlations, which were computed only for Ss who observed a model, are all significantly positive, but five are relatively small, ranging from $r = .28$ to $r = .54$. The two altruism scores (frequency of "giving to other" and latency of "giving to self") are highly correlated ($r = .92$). This relation is artifactual. Consequently, "giving to other" was used alone as the altruism index in the data analysis.

Wherever possible, subsequent analyses were completed with scores divided into two five-trial blocks. Inspection revealed that the treatment effects varied over time.

Effect of Model

To assess the effects of observing a model on altruistic behavior, a one-way analysis of variance was conducted on the data for all five of the groups in the experiment. "Giving to other" scores were analyzed separately for the first and second blocks of five trials. The treatments effect was significant in all instances. For the first trial block, $F = 7.49$, $df = 4/51$, $p < .005$; second trial block, $F = 3.39$, $df = 4/51$, $p < .02$.

Contrasts between the amount of "giving to other" in group C and in each of the model groups (t tests) revealed significant differences for each contrast in both trial blocks. Thus, observation of the model produced significantly more altruism than occurred when no opportunity to observe a model was provided (see Table 1).

TABLE 1
Mean "Giving to Other" Scores in Blocks of Five Trials by Reinforcement Condition and Type of Peer Model

	Trial Block	
Group	1	2
Frequent reinforcement:		
Rewarding model	21.00	19.25
Nonrewarding model	13.42	13.83
Infrequent reinforcement:		
Rewarding model	17.50	17.08
Nonrewarding model	22.83	18.58
No model	5.63	3.75

Observing the model also affected the frequency of "incidental" behaviors. Statistical analysis was not performed, but it can be seen in Table 2 that no verbalization or "line up" behavior occurred in group C, although appreciable amounts were displayed by Ss who had observed a model.

TABLE 2
Mean Number of "Incidental" Behaviors According to Reinforcement Condition and Type of Peer Model

Group	Verbalization (Total)	Line-Up Responses (Total)
Frequent reinforcement:		
Rewarding model	36.83	4.50
Nonrewarding model	7.58	1.67
Infrequent reinforcement:		
Rewarding model	21.08	3.92
Nonrewarding model	18.00	3.92
No model	0.00	0.00

Effects of Peer Reinforcement and Rewardingness of Model

The "giving to other" scores for Ss who observed models were subjected to mixed-design analysis of variance. The between-Ss factors were reinforcement from peers (FR vs. IR) and type of peer model (RM vs. NRM). The within-Ss factor consisted of trial blocks (first vs. second five trials). Mean scores for each subgroup may be seen in Table 1.

The analysis revealed a significant effect of trial blocks ($F = 7.80$, $df = 1/44$, $p < .01$), indicating that fewer altruistic responses were made during the second block of five trials than during the first. In addition, the interaction between reinforcement from peers and type of model was significant ($F = 4.59$, $df = 1/44$, $p < .05$), as was the interaction between reinforcement from peers, type of model, and trial blocks ($F = 7.80$, $df = 1/44$, $p < .01$). Further analyses revealed that the treatments effects were confined principally to the first five trials. There was a significant interaction between reinforcement from peers and type of model in the data for the first five trials ($F = 8.44$, $df = 1/44$, $p < .01$), but not for the second. During the first trials, Ss who had received frequent reinforcement from their peers imitated a rewarding peer model more frequently than a nonrewarding model ($t = 3.17$, $p < .01$). On the other hand, Ss who were observed to receive infrequent peer reinforcement imitated a nonrewarding model more frequently than a rewarding model ($t = 2.61$, $p < .02$). Additional contrasts made on the data for the first five trials revealed: (a) among Ss who observed a rewarding model, those with a history of frequent peer reinforcement did not differ significantly from those with a history of infrequent reinforcement ($t = 1.41$, $p < .20$); (b) among those who observed a nonrewarding model, Ss who had received infrequent reinforcement from the peer group imitated significantly more than those who had received frequent peer reinforcement ($t = 4.88$, $p < .01$).

Analysis of imitative verbalization scores was conducted as described for the preceding measure. None of the interactions was significant. Rather, a significant main effect of type of model was obtained ($F = 5.39$, $df = 1/44$, $p < .02$). As can be seen from Table 2, Ss who observed a rewarding model reproduced the model's verbal behaviors more frequently than Ss who observed nonrewarding models. This trend is less clear for IR Ss than for FR Ss, and the interaction between reinforcement from peers and type of model approached significance ($F = 3.53$, $df = 1/44$, $p < .10$). With respect to other incidental behaviors, the experimental conditions failed to influence differentially the child's imitative behavior.

DISCUSSION

Effects of Model

Observation of altruistic models increased the frequency of altruistic behavior of the Ss, a finding which confirms the results of Rosenhan and White (1967). Can it be assumed that the behavior displayed by the model was construed by S as "altruism"? It is true that S was not told explicitly that he would be able to keep the trinkets in his own bowl and that those in the other child's bowl were to be given away. Nevertheless, in postsession interviews with ten Ss, all ten thought they could keep the trinkets in their own bowl, and seven thought the trinkets in the second bowl would be given to the child whose picture was attached to the bowl. Consequently, the assumption that the experiment involved imitative effects on altruism is tenable.

Among Ss who observed a model, those showing imitative altruism tended to imitate other components of the altruistic response sequence. The peer reinforcement history tended to have significant effects on behavior which was central in the altruistic response sequence (frequency of "giving to other"). The failure of the treatment effects to generalize to all incidental measures could simply have been a function of "response centrality" or that these behaviors occurred much less frequently than trinket sorting or verbalization.

Effects of Peer Reinforcement

The relation between rewardingness of the peer model and imitative altruism was positive when S was reinforced frequently by the peer group but negative when reinforcement was infrequent. It is known that peer reinforcement is correlated with social acceptance (e.g., Hartup, Glazer, & Charlesworth, 1967; Marshall & McCandless, 1957). Therefore, the four experimental groups were contrasted with respect to the social acceptance of the models, the acceptance of the Ss, and the friendliness existing between the models and their respective Ss. Data from a picture sociometric test indicated that, overall, status differences among the groups do not account for the observed differences in imitation.

It is concluded that the results support Mowrer's secondary reinforcement theory of imitation when S's history includes relatively frequent reinforcement from persons resembling the model. For infrequently reinforced Ss, the influence of model rewardingness did not diminish; rather, nonrewarding models proved to be more efficacious than rewarding ones.

One explanation for these results is based on the assumption that children who receive little reinforcement are also anxious when placed in contact with other children.

This argument implies a dual theory of peer imitation: (a) when reinforcement from peers is frequent, matching the behavior of a rewarding model has greater incentive value than matching a nonrewarding model (the Mowrer hypothesis); (b) when peer reinforcement is not frequent, a nonrewarding model sustains or increases anxiety, whereas the presence of a rewarding model reduces such motivation for imitation. From psychoanalytic theories of identification, it could be hypothesized that (a) nurturant models are emulated (anaclitic identification) when reinforcement from persons like the model has been frequent, and (b) when reinforcement has been infrequent, the model who elicits anxiety (or who does not behave in such a way as to reduce it) is defensively emulated. Thus, the present speculations contain interesting implications for predicting the conditions under which anaclitic and defensive identification operate.

The present study helps to clarify the influence of the model's rewardingness on imitation. The generality of the results needs to be assessed in further research and theoretical implications explored. It appears, however, that the child's socialization history contributes importantly to the effects on imitation of rewards from the model.

21. SOCIAL REINFORCEMENT UNDER NATURAL CONDITIONS

Phyllis M. Scott, Roger V. Burton, & Marian Radke Yarrow

The control of specific responses, through administration of carefully prescribed reinforcement contingencies, can be precise, but, because the responses are relatively simple, the application of these principles to practical situations often seems remote. However, by employing their knowledge about a nursery school child's responsiveness to social reinforcers, Scott, Burton, and Yarrow demonstrate that behavioral control of complex social interaction processes can also be implemented.

Unlike most laboratory investigations, this study extended over 28 contact days divided into four phases: A baseline was established, training of the new behavior was conducted, the baseline setting was resumed, and training was again reinstated. It was a particularly relevant study for this chapter because it explains how negative social behavior initially came under the control of social reinforcers administered by teachers and peers, and how the frequency of positive social acts in the child's behavior was increased by intervention in a natural setting.

The reader will find the general procedure especially interesting: Identify the operant; establish its operant level, that is, its baseline frequency of occurrence; note the discriminative stimuli that are the occasions for the elicitation of the behavior; identify the consequences that increase, and those that decrease, the frequency of the undesired behavior and, if different, of the desired behavior; apply the appropriate consequences

SOURCE. Adapted and abridged from Phyllis M. Scott, Roger V. Burton, and Marian Radke Yarrow, "Social Reinforcement Under Natural Conditions," *Child Development*, 1967, Vol. 38, pp. 53–63. (With permission of the authors and the publisher, the Society for Research in Child Development.)

when the desired behavior occurs and withhold consequences that accelerate the undesired behavior.

While these techniques were successfully employed by Scott, Burton, and Yarrow, they note in their report that behaviors changed in this way may extend beyond the child's capabilities and thereby could result in failure. Thus, the child may need help in developing new skills as well as in using substitute skills as a support. If such provisions are not made, the child may himself substitute other, often more undesirable, behaviors in place of the eliminated behaviors. Furthermore, the adult must exercise care that the rewarded behaviors do not jeopardize the child's esteem with his peers. If he is placed in conflict, the child may come to infer that behaviors reinforced by adults, or the social reinforcers used by them, lack validity for effective social interaction with one's peers.

The S of this experiment was a 4-year-old boy who experienced considerable difficulty in interaction with peers. An attempt was made to measure the effects on this child of reinforcement conditions in the regular nursery school environment compared with reinforcement conditions which were experimentally manipulated.

Information from observations, both impressionistic and directed, was used in selecting the S. While his behavior was within the normal range there was a relatively high frequency of unprovoked aggression. Positive approaches to other children seldom developed into sustained play sequences; these approaches were often of an immature, attention-seeking nature. Episodes in which S assumed the role of a lion were frequent. These approaches consistently gained the attention of peers who would sometimes chase S, squealing excitedly, or sometimes run for adult protection. Teachers allowed some play of this nature, but more often than not they intervened. Long, friendly conversations between S and teachers often followed these interventions.

EXPERIMENTAL DESIGN

The application of operant reinforcement principles to this situation would suggest that both teachers and peers might be consistently contributing to the maintenance of antisocial behavior. The experiment, therefore, aimed to test the effectiveness of adult attention as social reinforcement for modifying two classes of behavior. Rather than to modify a single, clearly circumscribed response, the aim was to demonstrate possible control over two complex classes of social behavior. Negative acts included physical assault, taking other's property, physical or verbal threats, aggressive derogatory remarks and demands. Positive acts included giving suggestions, sharing ideas on information, helping, showing concern or sympathy for others, and carrying on friendly conversation.

To assess any differential effect of natural versus experimental contingencies of adult attention on child behavior, an attempt was made in the present experiment to preserve intact the behavior of the regular teachers during the course of the study. Then the original conditions of reinforcement from these adults could be readily reinstated as a comparison with the experimentally manipulated reinforcement.

The experiment was carried out with two regular teachers and *E*, who had teaching experience. The regular teachers were told only that the study concerned the types of behavior to which adults paid attention. On some days, *E* would give special attention to *S* and assume responsibility concerning *S*'s behavior with his peers.

The experimental design included four periods:

1. *Baseline (5 days).*—The operant levels of the behaviors to be modified were established, and the existing adult reinforcements for *S*'s negative and positive interactions with peers were recorded. The regular teachers conducted activities as usual, and *E* interacted in a friendly way with all the children.

2. *Period 2 (13 days).*—The *E* stayed in close proximity to *S*. Reinforcements used during the experiment were mainly verbal, such as "Yes, that's right," or "That's fine," but also included smiling, nodding approval, increasing physical nearness, or showing added interest.

During this second period, change in the teachers' behavior did not involve modification of *differential* contingencies of their attention but was of a gross nature of relinquishing major responsibility for *S*'s interactions with other children. Contacts between teachers and *S* continued in other contexts than peer interactions. Thus, during this period, adult reinforcements contingent on *S*'s negative interactions with peers were not forthcoming from either the teachers or *E*. In occasional emergency situations, where the physical safety of other children might be jeopardized were *S* not restrained, *E* did take action but still avoided paying attention to *S*, concentrating on comforting the object of his attack. If further restraint seemed necessary, a teacher's help was quietly sought.

3. *Period 3 (6 days).*—The teachers resumed their usual responsibilities, and *E* returned to her baseline role.

4. *Final period (4 days).*—The conditions of period 2 were reinstated.

The length of experimental periods was governed by partial analysis of daily observations and by such practical conditions as the end of the school year.

DATA COLLECTION

Six tape-recorded observations, each of 12 minutes' duration, were made daily. These were spread over the morning at approximately half-hour intervals. The observer reported events in sequential fashion, attending to conditions preceding and following S's responses. On a given day, three observers worked in rotation, each being responsible for two periods of observation. Each observer coded her own observations from tapes. The coding system consisted of specific categories, such as "requests permission," "hits or pushes," "praises, shows approval." These categories were applied to the behavior of the S, peers, and adults.

In an attempt to keep the observers uninformed about the purpose of the experiment, each was given a daily assignment of which children she would observe and was not told which children were assigned to the other observers. On some days, a child other than the S was assigned.

A second set of data was collected by an informed observer (Scott) who was present during all of the observations. As bias arising from observer knowledge of the hypothesis being tested has been found to influence results in past research (Rosenthal, 1964), these two sets of data made it possible to check on the reliability of such observations.

RESULTS

Reliability

Reliabilities between the records of the informed and uninformed observers were computed on daily frequencies of positive and negative units of interaction with peers. The data show a high degree of correspondence. A correlation of $+.87$ was obtained for daily frequencies of positive units and $+.91$ for negative units. It is interesting to note that the uninformed observers were not aware of reporting the changes in behavior which the analysis revealed. Based on a sampling of 12 days over the course of the experiment, reliability was also computed on daily frequencies of reported adult reinforcements. A correlation of $+.95$ was obtained.

A second examination of these data assessed the possibility of bias from the informed observer's knowledge of the hypothesis being tested. A comparison based on the direction of difference on both classes of responses simultaneously, and an analysis of positive and negative response classes separately, showed the informed observer's records were more confirming of the experimental hypothesis.

The slopes of the lines fitted to the daily frequencies of the two classes of responses are essentially the same and parallel, except in the final period when there are dramatic differences in the slopes of both the positive and negative units, with the informed observer's slopes reflecting much more strongly the direction of the hypothesis.

These differences between informed and uninformed observers give no factual basis for judging veridicality of either record. Whether these discrepancies are due to bias or to greater sensitivity is a question of degree of change and do not alter any of the findings reported for this experiment.

Positive-Negative Emphasis in Interaction

The daily frequency of positive and negative units of interaction with peers, as shown in Figures 1 and 2, in general, changed in the direction one would expect from reinforcement principles. Positive interactions increased and negative interactions decreased in periods 2 and 4. In period 3 the frequency of negative acts rose steadily; the expected decrease in positive units did not occur, although the *rate* of increase dropped.

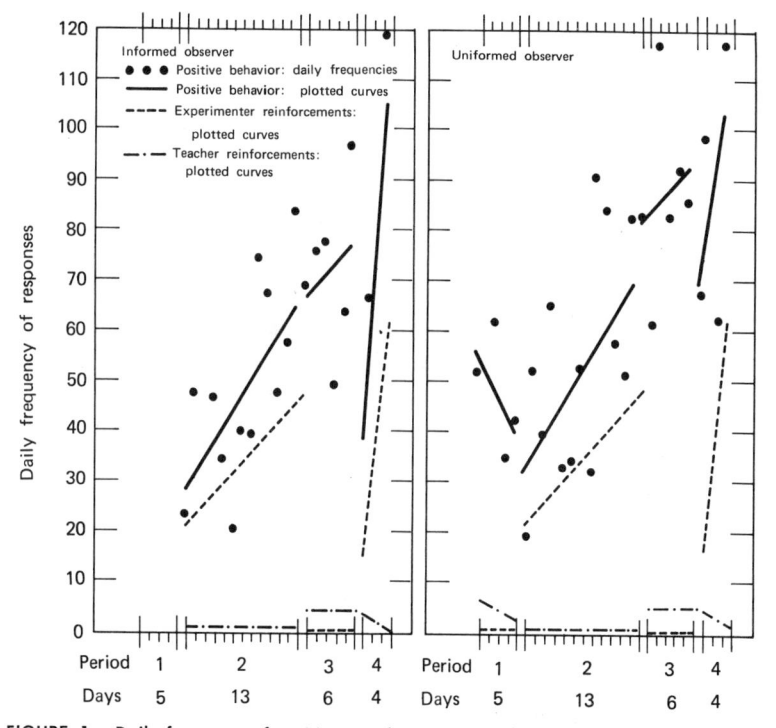

FIGURE 1. Daily frequency of positive social responses under varying conditions of adult reinforcement (reinforcement by teachers from uninformed observers' records; reinforcement by teacher-experimenter from informed observer's record, except in period 1 when only uninformed observers were recording).

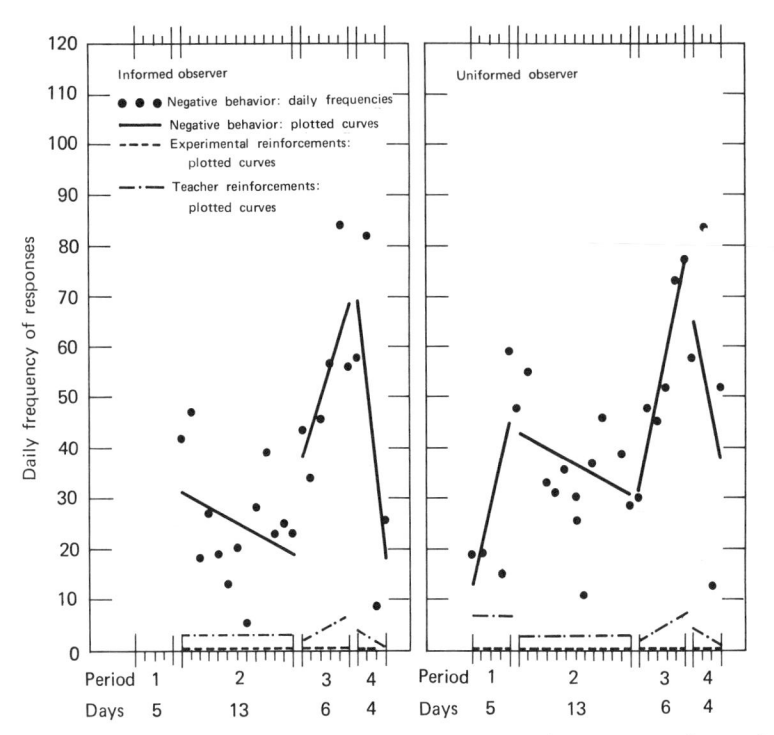

FIGURE 2. Daily frequency of negative social responses under varying conditions of adult reinforcement (see Fig. 1 for source of data on reinforcement).

The effect of experimental conditions can also be seen in the difference scores (Fig. 3): The changing ratio of positive to negative units showed an increased positive balance in periods 2 and 4 and an increased negative balance in period 3. These changes took place against a background of increasing interaction with peers, which reached both its highest average frequency and rate of increase during period 3, when both positive and negative responses occurred at a high rate.

Specific categories of positive and negative behavior with peers were also examined. In negative behavior, the most clear-cut change occurred in a decrease of physical assaults under conditions of extinction for negative acts (periods 2 and 4) and a rise during period 3 when reinforcement of negative behavior returned to the baseline rate. No clear evidence of change was found in less direct physical aggression, such as physical threats or struggles over objects. About half of the negative units fell into the categories of physical assault and verbal aggression.

In positive units, friendly nonpersuasive conversation rose with reinforce-

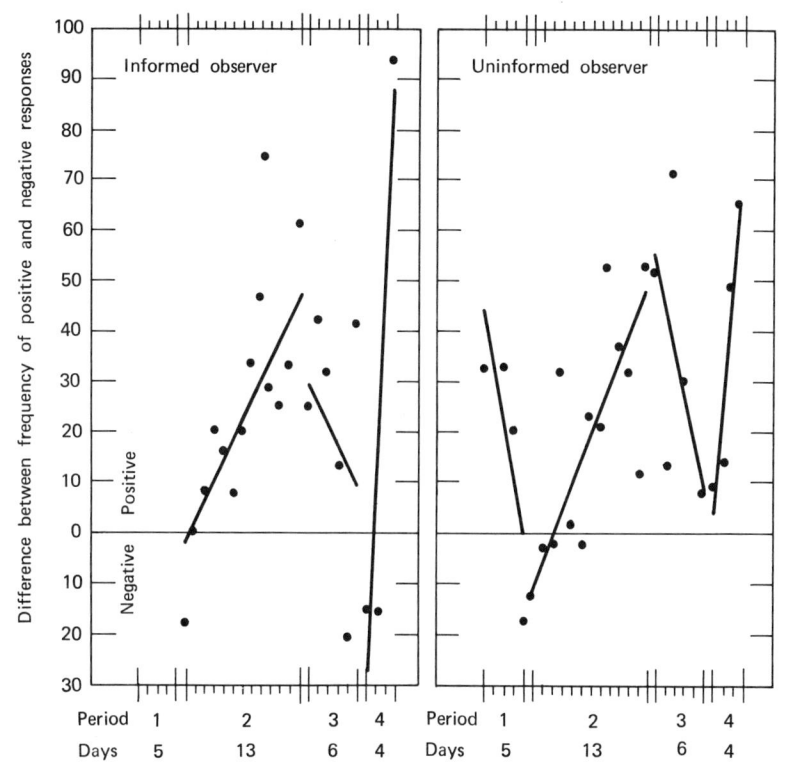

FIGURE 3. Difference scores between daily frequency of positive and negative social responses.

ment for positive behavior (periods 2 and 4) and decreased in period 3. Requests for permission and direction from peers increased over the experiment. About a third of the positive units fell in the category of friendly conversation.

None of the category groupings within either the negative or positive framework changed in an opposite direction to the expected one. The amount of change within a category was not related to the frequency of occurrence of that category.

Additional Analyses of Interaction

In a natural setting, additional effects might be hypothesized as occurring in the child's cognitive and affective responses, in the reinforcements coming from his peers, and in the changing stimulus properties of child and adult interactors.

An analysis was directed to the quality of change in S's response, other than the changing balance in his overall positive and negative interactions with peers. Actions clearly initiated by S showed that his manner of approach to peers changed in ways consistent with the pattern of change in the total positive and negative interaction units. Neither the relative frequencies of fleeting and sustained interaction sequences nor the daily mean length of these sequences showed any consistent changes associated with experimental conditions. However, several instances of intense unprovoked aggression, directed toward play materials and animals, occurred in period 4; these had not appeared in earlier observations. Several long sequences of fantasy play were also observed in which S made "poison ivy" and proceeded to pour this on the feet of adults. These episodes suggest that though the experimental conditions decreased overt expression of negative feelings, they may not have reduced the motivation for such hostile behavior.

To determine the nature of reinforcement coming from other children, the peer's act immediately following an act of the S was coded as (1) going along with, (2) showing opposition to, or (3) showing no response to S. There was no evidence that modifications of S's behavior were initially due to peer reinforcement. The curves of peers' positive reinforcements, in general, parallel the changes in S's behavior associated with experimental conditions. There are some interesting sex differences. Boys' responding is suggestive of an increasing discrimination. In the baseline period, they were equally likely to oppose or go along with S's negative behavior. In period 2, their reactions became increasingly appropriate: Their positive responses to negative behavior decreased, and their opposition to negative acts increased. At the same time, their positive responses to positive behavior increased.

During period 3 when the regular teachers again paid attention to negative acts, boys and girls continued to respond positively to S's positive acts. Boys in particular approached S more often, receiving a strongly positive response, and interaction occurred at a higher rate than at any other time. This increased attention from peers may account for the continuing rise in positive acts from S during this period, despite the withdrawal of adult reinforcement.

Girls' responses did not show any discriminative change. However, in period 3, an increase occurred in the girls' reacting (squealing, crying, fighting back) to S's negative behavior. This change may have contributed to the dramatically increasing frequency of S's negative acts in this period.

These exploratory analyses can only hint at some of the possible derivative effects for peer interactions of changes in the contingencies of adult attention to S.

Interpretation of Findings

The changing overall balance of positive and negative acts by the S is clearly in the direction expected from the application of operant conditioning principles. One additional interpretation might be that the teacher-experimenter inhibited negative responses, especially direct forms of aggression, by her being a constantly observing adult. If negative behavior were inhibited, S could then either decrease his interactions with other children or increase his positive forms of interaction. When the teacher-experimenter relinquished her responsibility for S during period 3, not having her always near could have disinhibited the negative responses.

Another interpretation is that already-formed discriminations established different stimulus functions for the regular teachers and E. When the regular teachers were in charge, negative behavior tended to receive attention; but with E, attention was contingent on positive behavior.

Both teachers and E were, however, present throughout the four periods. Also, the data in Figures 1 and 2 show that the daily frequencies of both the positive and negative acts produce curves showing an increase or decrease over the experimental periods in the directions expected by reinforcement theory. There is not a sudden differentiation between positive and negative acts at the beginning of period 2, and then a reversal of this at the beginning of period 3, nor do the data show that a plateau in either class of behavior was quickly reached during any of the four periods. These results indicate that neither of the alternative discrimination hypotheses is adequate to account for the findings. The most parsimonious interpretation is that the contingencies of adult attention during the different experimental periods were modifying the S's behavior over the whole period of this study.

Application of Reinforcement Principles

The setting of this experiment in a nursery school group drew attention to theoretical issues in operant conditioning not critical for short-term experiments but important at the point of application by a teacher or parent in the regular course of events.

One issue concerns the situational variability in the effectiveness of a reinforcer. In a nursery school group, one finds that quickly changing situations bring constantly changing combinations of reinforcement to which the child responds selectively. Awareness of this means that the adult must quickly assess the relative strengths of different reinforcers in each situation and try to control the immediate contingencies of those which appear to carry most weight. Successful application of reinforcement principles may depend on one's ability to control as much as possible the contingencies and extent of reinforcement from sources which vary from one moment to the next. Advance identification of these possible sources for a particular child is likely to increase the degree to which this type of control can be achieved.

In the present study, adult reinforcement of acceptable social behavior with peers brought S up against the limits of his physical skill in some social situations, thus exposing him to public failure. Limitations in S's social skills were also highlighted as a result of the general increase in interaction with peers. An increase in the frequency of asking permission and seeking orientation from peers accompanied the overall trend toward more interaction over the period of the experiment. This suggests the possibility of an increasing exposure of, as well as an increase in, the child's uncertainty in social contacts. One sees the potential danger of aversive situations which come about through the concentration on a single aspect of the child's behavior. Without some help in learning more adequate social and physical skills, discouraging experiences involving these skills could eventually outweigh the effectiveness of adult reinforcement, especially if satiation effects occurred. It might place the child in a conflicting situation which could have repercussions for adult-child affectional relationships and might result in learning that reinforcements from adults do not coincide with those from peers or self.

Reinforcement theory, then, can add substance to the somewhat mysterious teaching and learning process. It gives the teacher some principles with which she can use existing resources more efficiently. It does not, however, remove the need for sensitive assessment of an individual's experience in a particular situation, the need for information on his past experience, the problem of what to reinforce and when, or concern with the effects of such choices on all aspects of his development.

22. EFFECTS OF SOCIAL REINFORCEMENT ON ISOLATE BEHAVIOR OF A NURSERY SCHOOL CHILD

K. Eileen Allen, Betty Hart, Joan S. Buell, Florence R. Harris, & Montrose M. Wolf

A child's normal developmental pattern of increasing social interaction with his peers, and responsiveness to their approval, sometimes becomes redirected into the defensive pattern of isolating himself from them and seeking mainly the approval of adults. Where reasons for the rechanneled behavior remain elusive remedial measures often require prolonged cooperative efforts between specialized personnel, and parents or teachers. However, as was shown in the study by Scott, Burton, and Yarrow (1967), presented earlier in this chapter, well-meaning adults often inadvertently impose contingencies of reinforcement that encourage mildly deviant patterns of aggression, overdependence on adults, or withdrawal.

The previous study by Scott et al. examined systematic intervention by an experimenter in a natural setting to achieve a deceleration of aggressive behavior. The present study by Allen and her colleagues is a companion article in the sense that it attempts an acceleration of peer interaction in a natural setting by the teachers themselves. Both studies employed parallel procedures emphasizing *systematic* application of reinforcement principles for behavioral control. The authors are emphatic in their view that reinforcement contingencies cannot be established casually. Care must be exercised in determining what is reinforced if precise behavioral control is to be achieved. The reader will especially note, in a comparison of the two studies, that an analysis of the behavior during all stages of learning

SOURCE. Adapted and abridged from K. Eileen Allen, Betty Hart, Joan S. Buell, Florence R. Harris, and Montrose M. Wolf, "Effects of Social Reinforcement on Isolate Behavior of a Nursery School Child," *Child Development*, 1964, Vol. 35, pp. 511–518. (With permission of the authors and the publisher, the Society for Research in Child Development.)

was essential: baselines were established; stimuli to which the subjects were especially responsive were identified; change procedures were implemented; and the procedural effects were evaluated by reversal to the original situations and then by reinstatement of the initial behavioral change.

By pairing adult reinforcement in the form of attention, encouragement, and other supportive acts with ongoing group play, in which the subject was a participant, the teachers in the study reported below effectively increased the valence or secondary reinforcing value of the subject's peers. As a consequence, she became more responsive to them and participated as a confident member of the school group.

This report presents an application of reinforcement principles to guidance in a preschool. Teachers used systematic presentation of positive social reinforcement (adult attention) to help a child showing persistent and marked isolate behavior to achieve and maintain more play relationships with peers. Adult attention was defined as: a teacher's going to, talking to, smiling to, touching, offering and/or giving assistance to the child. Play relationships were defined as interactions between the subject and one or more children, such as conversing, looking or smiling toward each other, touching, helping, or working with each other on a project.

Reinforcement principles have been established in experiments with several subhuman species, and some applications have been made to human problems. Wolf, Risley, and Mees (1964) and Ferster and DeMyer (1961) have applied them to the treatment of autism in children; Brady and Lind (1961) to functional blindness; Ayllon and Michael (1959) and Ayllon and Haughton (1962) to psychotic behavior; Harris, Johnston, Kelley, and Wolf (1964) to regressed motor behavior of a preschool child; and Hart, Allen, Buell, Harris, and Wolf (1964) to operant crying. In each instance systematic improvement in behavior was achieved.

METHOD

Subject

Ann was 4.3 years old at the start of the study. She was enrolled at the Laboratory Preschool of the University of Washington in a group of eight boys and eight girls, homogeneous in terms of age (4 to 4.5 years), intelligence levels (higher than average), and family background (upper middle class).

During the first days of school, Ann interacted freely with adults but seldom initiated contact with children or responded to their attempts to play with her. She did not seem severely withdrawn or frightened; instead she revealed a varied repertoire of unusually well-developed physical and mental skills that drew the interested attention of adults but failed to gain the companionship of children. Teachers gave warm recognition to her skilled climbing, jumping, and riding; her creative use of paints and clay; her original songs and rhythmic interpretations of musical selections; her collections of nature objects; her perceptive and mature verbalizations; and her willing and thorough help-with-cleanup behaviors.

With passing days she complained at length about minute or invisible bumps and abrasions. She often spoke in breathy tones at levels so low that it was difficult to understand what she said. Her innumerable, bulky collections of rocks or leaves seemed to serve as "conversation pieces" valued only so long as they drew adult comments. She spent increasing time simply standing and looking. Frequently she retired to a make-believe bed in a packing box in the play yard to "sleep" for several minutes. Mild, tic-like behaviors such as picking her lower lip, pulling a strand of hair, or fingering her cheek were apparent.

After six weeks of school, a period considered ample for adjustment to the nursery school situation, the teachers made a formal inventory of Ann's behaviors and appraised the time she spent with children, with adults, and by herself. The evaluation revealed that Ann's behavior consisted of isolating herself from children and indulging in many varied techniques for gaining and prolonging the attention of adults. Close scrutiny further revealed that most of the adult attention given to her was contingent upon behaviors incompatible with play behavior with peers.

A plan was instituted to give Ann maximum adult attention contingent on play with another child, and minimum attention upon isolate behavior or upon interactions with an adult when alone. Approximately the same total amount of adult attention was to be available to Ann each day provided she met the criteria for obtaining such behavior from the teachers.

Effort was made to hold all variables other than adult social reinforcement constant throughout the study: no changes were to be made in the regular nursery school program or in supervisional assignments of the three teachers. Teachers were to continue to be physically present, as usual. The only change instituted was in the conditions under which they were to give Ann attention, and this was governed by the schedule of reinforcement in effect at a given phase of the study.

Recording

In order to make assessments of changes in Ann's behavior, objective data were obtained each morning by two observers, the same throughout the study. Each observer worked half the morning. To ascertain rater reliability, they recorded jointly for two mornings. Their records showed 81 and 91 per cent agreement.

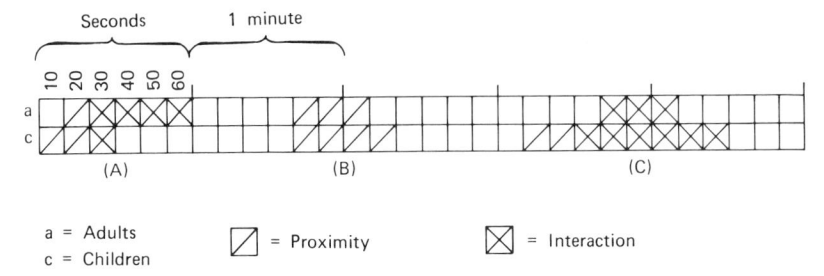

FIGURE 1. A sample line from a data sheet which accommodated 12 such lines (1 hour of recording), spaced. Proximity was defined as physical closeness to adult or child (within 3 feet). Interaction was defined as conversing, smiling or looking toward, touching, and/or helping an adult or a child. All interaction with adults was recorded in row a; interaction with children was recorded in row c. Notations were made every 10 seconds, by the observer, using a stop watch. Neither capital letters in parentheses nor time notations above the line appear on data sheets, but merely facilitate explanations in the text.

Proximity and interaction with adults and with children were recorded at 10-second intervals. A sample line from a data sheet is given in Figure 1. The sample shows 5 minutes of recorded behaviors. In the top row (a), the single strokes indicate four intervals of proximity to adults; the ×'s indicate seven intervals of interaction with adults. In the bottom row (c), single strokes indicate eight intervals of proximity to children; ×'s indicate seven intervals of interaction with children. Blank squares indicate intervals when Ann was neither in proximity to nor interacting with an adult (upper row) or a child (bottom row). A behavioral account might read as follows: Ann stood near a child when a teacher drew near (A). Ann talked to the child, and the teacher at once smiled at her and spoke to both children. Ann turned all her attention to the teacher, following her as she moved away. The teacher busied herself exclusively with some other children, and Ann turned and walked to a gravel area where she started to gather pebbles alone. She moved near some children and a teacher (B), where she stayed for half a minute without interacting with them. Shortly after the teacher left the group, Ann moved away, continuing to gather pebbles by herself. A child approached her (C) and joined her in picking up pebbles. They smiled at each other. A teacher at once came and talked to both children. The teacher left after half a minute. Ann continued to play with the child for 20 seconds. After the child left, Ann continued picking up pebbles alone.

Behavior during a daily scheduled group activity which averaged about 15 minutes was excluded from the data. During this part of the nursery school program the children were expected to sit in close proximity to each other and to the teacher.

Procedures

Before reinforcement procedures were initiated, an objective record was obtained of the actual amounts of time Ann was spending with children, adults, and alone.

After five days of baseline data had been secured, teachers were instructed to give attention to Ann whenever and only when she interacted with children. To begin with, any approximations to social interaction, such as standing near another child or playing beside another in the sandbox or at a table, were followed by teacher attention. As soon as Ann interacted with a child, an adult immediately gave her direct individual attention. A sample interaction was, "Ann, you are making dinner for the whole family." When she played alone, Ann was not given attention, and when she contacted an adult she was given minimum attention unless she was with another child.

It was immediately apparent that a direct approach to Ann tended to draw her away from the play with children and into interaction with the adult. Original procedures were amended as follows: the teacher made comments and directed other attending behaviors to Ann, not individually, but as a participant in the ongoing group play; whenever possible, the adult approached the group prepared to give Ann an appropriate material or toy to add to the joint play project. A sample amended operation was, "You three girls have a cozy house! Here are some more cups, Ann, for your tea party." Whenever Ann began to leave the group, the teacher turned away from her and became occupied with some other child or with equipment. This procedure, which extended over six days, seemed to bring Ann into interaction with other children more frequently and for longer periods.

In order to substantiate whether the behavior changes effected by the above procedures had indeed been produced by the application of reinforcement principles, procedures were reversed for five days. Solitary pursuits and contacts made solely with an adult were once more made discriminative stimuli for adult attention. Ann was disregarded by adults whenever she interacted with children, and given only an unavoidable minimum of attention when she, in the company of another child, contacted them.

After this reversal, the previous contingencies were reinstated. For the next nine days teachers again gave (a) a maximum of attention for all play with children, (b) no attention when Ann was alone, and (c) a minimum of attention when she contacted adults, unless she was with a child. When she began spending longer periods in continuous interaction with children, adult reinforcement of interaction was gradually made more intermittent until she received adult attention in an amount normal for the group.

Following the last day of systematic reinforcement of interaction, the observers recorded Ann's behaviors on four days spaced at irregular intervals during the last months of school.

RESULTS

The data on interactions with adults and with children are shown in Figure 2. Since the total observation time each morning varied slightly (average of 114 minutes, with a range from 100 to 130 minutes), each dot on the graph represents a percentage of a morning Ann spent in interaction (a) with adults and (b) with children. Open dots represent periods in which baseline and reversal procedures were carried out. Closed dots represent periods in which interactions with children were reinforced by the teachers. The percentages of interactions on a given day sometimes total more than 100 per cent, since Ann often interacted with both an adult and a child in the same 10-second interval (see C, Figure 1).

As can be seen in Figure 2, the baseline data collected over five days showed that Ann was spending little more than 10 per cent of the time interacting with children and 40 per cent with adults. For at least half the time

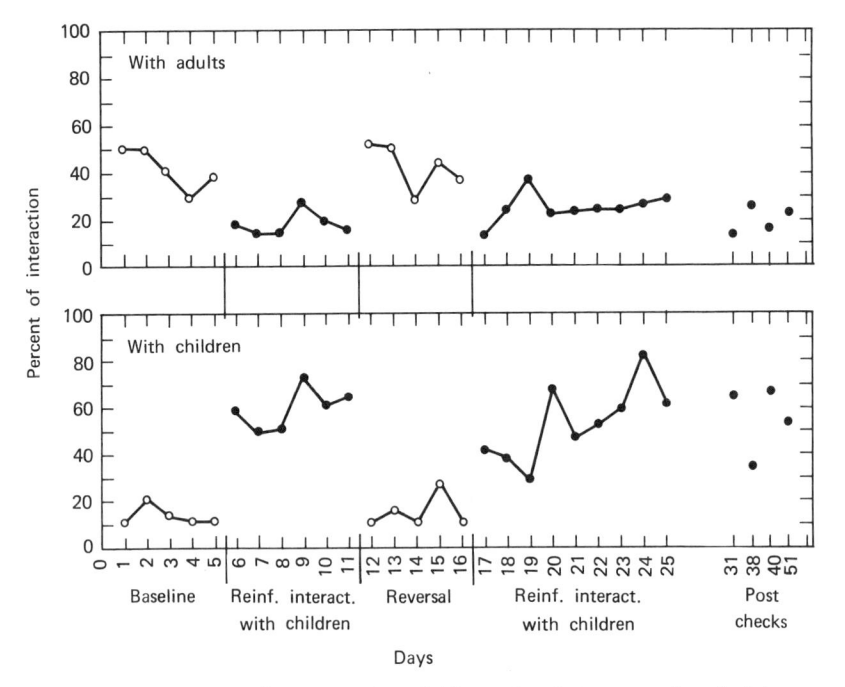

FIGURE 2. Percentages of time spent in social interaction during approximately 2 hours of each morning session.

she was essentially solitary. Analysis of the data indicated that her isolate behavior was being maintained and probably strengthened inadvertently by adult social reinforcement. Using traditional nursery school guidance techniques, the teachers responded warmly to Ann whenever she contacted them and remained in conversation with her for as long as she desired. When she stood about alone, they usually went to her and tried to get her into play with children. If they succeeded, they left shortly, to allow Ann to play freely with other children. All too frequently Ann was "out" again as soon as the teacher left, standing on the periphery, soliciting teacher attention, or playing alone.

On day 6, when Ann was first given teacher attention only when she was near children or interacting with them, an immediate change in her behavior took place. She spent almost 60 per cent of that morning first in approximations to interaction, and then in active play with children. Adult-child interaction, which was not followed by attention, dropped to less than 20 per cent. These levels of interactions varied little throughout the six-day period of continuous reinforcement of child-child interaction. Over the period, Ann spent increasing time in play with other children.

When procedures were reversed (12th day), Ann's previous patterns of behavior immediately reappeared. She spent the first few minutes after her arrival in close one-to-one interaction with a teacher, which was, of course, continuously reinforced. With this beginning, she spent the remainder of the morning much as she did during the baseline days. Over the five days of reversal she averaged less than 20 per cent of mornings in interaction with children and about 40 per cent in interaction with adults. She repeatedly ignored the contacts of other children and remained in some solitary activity where a teacher could attend to her. When she did enter play with children, she nearly always broke away after a few minutes to contact and remain with a teacher.

On the 17th day the final shift in contingencies was initiated and Ann was given adult attention only when she interacted with children. An immediate change in her behaviors again occurred. Less than 20 per cent of that morning was spent interacting with adults and 40 per cent interacting with children. Interaction with adults was for the most part adult-initiated, as when the teacher reinforced her play or gave routine instructions. Over the ensuing eight days of the study her interactions with adults stabilized at about 25 per cent of mornings; interactions with children rose to the previous level of about 60 per cent. During the last days of this reinforcement period, teachers gave increasingly intermittent (nonsystematic) attention for interaction with children. The schedule of nonreinforcement of adult contacts was similarly relaxed.

Six school days after the last day of reinforcement (25th day), the first post check of Ann's interactions with children and adults was made (Figure 2: 31st day, post checks). The data showed Ann to be spending more than 60 per cent of the morning in interaction with children, and only 12 per cent in interaction with adults. Further checks taken on the 13th, 15th, and 26th days subsequent to the last reinforcement day (25th day) indicated that Ann was maintaining an average interaction rate with other children of about 54 per cent per morning. Interaction with adults on these days averaged about 18 per cent per morning. On day 38, Ann's mother was present during school hours. Her presence seemed to influence Ann's behavior in the direction of less interaction with children, although the rate was higher than during either the baseline or the reversal periods.

DISCUSSION

Within the first half hour of the first morning of reinforcing interaction with children, Ann seemed to react to the contingencies for getting teacher attention. The immediate change may be attributed to the fact that she already had a repertory of skills readily adapted to play with peers. Similar studies in progress show that the development of adequate play behavior is not always so rapid as in Ann's case. Other children who tend to be off to themselves have taken several weeks to achieve similar levels of social play. During the six days of increasing interaction with children, other changes were noticed. Her speech rose in volume, tempo, and pitch, and complaints about abrasions and bumps dropped out entirely. She appeared to enjoy her play contacts, and the other children responded well to her.

When baseline procedures were again instituted, it immediately became apparent from the decrease in percentage that Ann's play with children was not yet so reinforcing as interaction with adults. Concurrently, her speech again became slow, drawling, and frequently almost inaudible. She again sought adult attention for various minor ills.

During the final period of reinforcing interaction with children, the inappropriate vocal and complaining behaviors quickly disappeared. At times Ann even took and held a strong, give-and-take role in play with five or six other children. Occasionally she defended herself vigorously. In general, her behavior indicated she had become a happy, confident member of the school group.

During the final period of the study teachers had further evidence of the care they must continue to exercise in judging how and under what circumstances to give adult social reinforcement to Ann: on the 19th day (see Figure 2) the children, with the help of a teacher, were making Easter baskets and dyeing eggs. Ann was in almost continuous proximity to both children and the teacher. But most of her interaction was with the adult, as can be seen from the sharp rise in child-adult interaction on this day. This tendency for Ann to gravitate readily to exclusive interaction with the reinforcing adult had been noted early in the study. Teachers had been trained to give attention and approval to Ann as a member of the group by commenting to the group on her contribution, offering some item which Ann could add to the group's play, or approving of the group activity as a unit. Such close pairing of adult reinforcement with children seemed effective in increasing the positive reinforcement values of Ann's peers.

Systematic application of reinforcement principles as a nursery school guidance technique seems to be an important advance toward more effective analysis and use of the existing knowledge about child behavior and development. Guidance measures such as "Encourage him to play with other children" are familiar to every parent and teacher. They imply that adults are to give attention to the child. Reinforcement principles offer a clear, objective guide for precisely discriminating occasions for giving and for withholding adult attention, a positive reinforcer for most young children. The only aspect of reinforcement principles that seems relatively new in nursery school guidance can be subsumed under the word *systematic*.

It seems noteworthy that this study was conducted by teachers in the course of their regular professional work with children. As they helped a child needing special guidance, they examined a guidance technique. Such a combination of the functions of research and service seems both practical and desirable.

CHAPTER 5

Imitation and Identification— Semi-Autonomous Steps Toward Maturity

One of the basic problems in any theory of behavior is to account for the initial occurrence of a new behavioral pattern. Trial-and-error orientations indicate that a new response occurs accidentally or by chance and then is strengthened by reinforcement. Some stimulus-response theories describe the extension of simple reflexes, as units of behavior, into chains, and then into larger sequences or structures. Piaget's developmental theory employs the process of accommodation which means that the child deliberately learns to use new adaptive behaviors in conjunction with his developing schemas, that is, his newly emergent motor patterns of internalized thought processes.

Another kind of learning has become an integral part of developmental psychology and has been studied extensively, in its brief history, by psychologists with special interest in social learning. For them, *imitation* is an important means by which social behaviors are acquired and new behaviors entered into one's behavioral repertoire. These responses are learned directly by *matching* or copying the specific behaviors, used by another person, referred to as a model. A parent, a respected adult, peers, movie stars, or even symbolic figures represented in the communications of the mass media are potential models with whom the child can and does identify.

Nearly every form of learning important to education can be acquired, at least in part, by some variant of imitative learning. Demonstration is a most frequently used teaching method for transmitting new perceptual motor skills. As a result of using this procedure, a teacher expects the learner to acquire at least some part of the response by observation, and to adopt the new behavior as part of his behavioral repertoire. Cognitive learning, too, is clearly influenced by the example of others. For example, teachers assign biographical material with the intent that the pupil will profit by knowing behaviors instrumental for the success of eminent men and by avoiding the mistakes of the past. As a final illustration, one has but to observe a child emulating the gestures and mannerisms of his father during the mutual experiencing of a distasteful event to realize that attitudes, biases, and prejudices can be strongly rooted through imitation. In these illustrations the terms "emulation," "demonstration," and "learning-by-example," imply that learning by imitation is an interactive process.

There is nothing in these definitions that indicates imitation will result in socially-approved patterns. Anxiety as well as self-confidence can be learned. Attitudes related to delinquency as well as to community-mindedness may be acquired. The model's potential influence in these examples is apparent. Once the learner assimilates a behavior, whatever its characteristics, as his own, conduct and standards have gone through the first steps toward becoming autonomous.

There are several theories of imitation that explicate different facets of this form of learning. In one, the view is expressed that an imitated response is learned when and if it is reinforced, either directly or vicariously. Whether all such learning can be accounted for by reinforcement is open to question. There are anecdotal accounts of children who are punished for the same tendencies found in other members of the family. Upon analysis to determine which of the two competing tendencies are learned, the process of learning by example rather than by reinforcement appears to be the dominant influence.

The question sometimes arises as to the extent to which imitative behavior represents the imitater's identification with the model being imitated. Sanford (1955) for example, notes that identification is present when a person responds to the behavior of another by initiating in reality or fantasy similar behavior in himself. There can be no doubt that some imitative behavior may be interpreted in terms of identification, but from a learning-theory point of view other possibilities exist. In his discussion, reported in this chapter, Kagan makes the point that motives and reinforcements involved in imitative behavior can also explain similarities in the behavior of two people. Kagan presents a differential of imitative behavior in terms of identification, imitation learning, and prohibition learning.

Mowrer's (1950) theory places the role of reward in observational learning in a different perspective. According to this view, any of the actual or generalized behaviors of a rewarding model are associated with positive reinforcement and thereby acquire secondary reinforcing properties for the observer. An interesting point of this position is that these behaviors, when reproduced by the child, can be employed by him for self-reinforcement.

Once the response is acquired, success in its use will also elicit reinforcement from external sources, thereby helping to maintain the response at full strength.

A particularly lucid account of a theory, within the instrumental learning framework, by Gewirtz and Stingle is included in the articles for this chapter. Its assumptions are that imitation itself is a learned process. Thus, a parent may imitate a child thereby eliciting further imitative behavior from the child. The cycle is completed when the child's behavior is then reinforced by the parent through smiling, physical expressions of affection, or additional imitation. The initial matching-to-sample behavior becomes extended or generalized, by encompassing other behaviors until the "matching-response" class of behaviors, that is, imitation, is acquired as a generalized response pattern.

As in Mowrer's theory, imitative behavior is then maintained by reinforcement from a variety of sources including extrinsic reinforcement, vicarious reinforcement, and sensory-feedback as postulated by Mowrer. Since such reinforcement occurs on an intermittent schedule, the behavior is highly resistant to extinction. These authors recognize that the appropriateness of the imitative responses varies for different models and from occasion to occasion. Accordingly, they hypothesize the behavior is dependent on stimulus control of discriminative cues provided by the model or the setting. These notions have been extended to numerous other concerns in social development such as imitation in the absence of a model, and identification, wherein the child acquires values, motives, and ideals from observing the behavior of another person. Most importantly, imitation and identification have been placed within a learning framework. This organization of ideas facilitates further analysis, investigation, and modification of constructs employed in descriptions of imitation processes by capitalizing on their relationships to variables already described in an extant body of knowledge.

Aside from the role of reinforcement in imitation and observational learning, theories of imitation have been concerned with the determinants of effective models. The role of models in transmitting new patterns of behavior such as aggression, altruism, hostility, and the like is apparent in a number of papers in this book. As Bandura (1962) and Gewirtz and Baer suggest, *models produce cues* which function to elicit specific imitative responses, but they also elicit other responses in the same response class that were not precisely used initially by the model. In addition, the expression of responses by the model that are typically negatively reinforced for the observer may, as a result, have an inhibitory, or disinhibitory effect on the anxiety of the observer. As a consequence, the frequency or intensity of the observer's use of the response will be modified.

It is apparent that models differ in their relative efficiency or capacity for promoting the acceptance of their behaviors. Aggressive models tend to be imitated more by children than are nonaggressive models. Film-mediated models, whether human or cartoon characters, were found to be as effective as real-life models in transmitting aggressive behavior. Nurturant adult models influenced child-observers more than did the adult who behaved "coolly" toward them. Whether or not the model is reinforced also makes a difference. It shall not be necessary to discuss further the well-known distinctions between primary and secondary reinforcers at this point. However, the research on imitation has added the construct of *vicarious reinforcement* to the other kinds of reinforcements. It refers to reinforcements received by the model, and experienced only indirectly by the observer. This empathic experience can affect the imitative behavior of the observer. Conclusions from several studies indicate that *direct* reinforcement, that is, reinforcement dispensed by one person directly to another, affects the subject's *learning* or *acquisition* of a new response. Vicarious reinforcement, on the other hand, energizes the elicitation of an existing, learned, behavior pattern; that is, vicarious reinforcement affects *performance* but not *learning*. Accordingly, vicariously experienced punishment will inhibit the performance of a response even though the observer has learned the response and might typically use it in a given situation.

A number of the model's characteristics have been found to interact with the sex of the observer to further modify the outcomes of observational learning. For example, an attentive model facilitates imitation, but more so for girls than for boys. Similarly, aggression by a male model is imitated more than aggression by a female model. In other studies aggression viewed on television over a period of time (Eron, 1963) influenced boys' behavior but not girls'.

A model's behavior is not transmitted without some mediating influence. Thus, it would be reasonable to hypothesize that some degree of empathy or similarity between the model and the observer is a facilitating influence on transmission of new behaviors. In learning sex-typed behavior, for example, the model is the parent of the same sex. Observational learning does require that the person is capable of reproducing the behavior or that it can be stored in memory for reproduction at a later time. Similarity is one way of assuring that behaviors of another can be approximated following observation. Thus, the observer who views himself as similar to the model probably has good reason for doing so. The study by Rosekrans, presented below, found that observers who perceived themselves as similar to the model did, indeed, employ more of the model's behaviors in later situations than of the model perceived as dissimilar.

The study by Bandura, Ross, and Ross, also presented below, compares somewhat abstract characteristics of the model on his effectiveness in transmitting new behaviors. The alternative hypotheses examined in their study suggest that observers imitate the model whose status is envied, the model who has power, or the model who rewards. These qualities were translated into experimental operations in a setting paralleling that of the nuclear family. The model with power won, "hands down"; the child-observers identified with the controller of the rewards rather than with the rewarding adult or with the receiver of the rewards.

The importance of peers and of the peer group both as a model for identification and as a reinforcer of conformity and imitative behavior is usually assumed in school practice as well as in the psychological literature. But, in this area generalizations have to be made with caution since factors such as chronological age, experience, and special conditions may present a context in which the expected behavior either does not appear or in which it goes in the opposite direction. The article by Costanzo and Shaw indicates that in early childhood the individual seems relatively unaware of peer standards and pressures to conform. On the other hand, with the advent of puberty the dependence of the child on his peers for patterns of behavior become much greater with attendant pressures to conform and to imitate. However, in late adolescence and in maturity the pressures become less and the individual is not as likely to display imitative behavior. In these later years the pressures tend to be more subtle and, with the appearance of alternatives, probably less threatening.

In Epstein's study the finding, with certain exceptions, that following a period of social isolation, commitment to further isolation reduces a child's motivation for social reinforcement offers at least a limited suggestion for teachers who, proceeding with proper safeguards, are seeking to inculcate certain adult approved objectives that may run counter to behaviors receiving peer acceptance.

Imitation, then, is usually an influential process in promoting change in social behavior. Children and people *do* learn from models. As the child matures these new behaviors become internalized as parts of their own behavioral repertoires. We have shown that a variety of such behaviors presumably can be acquired in this way, including cognitive and motor skills, emotional tendencies, and values. And we have shown that, through vicarious reinforcement, models also have the effect of energizing behavior, and through the discriminative cues they provide, of indicating to the observer when it is appropriate, or inappropriate to use a behavior already learned. Aside from the vast opportunities for further research on this exciting topic, there are many pragmatic implications. The parent's role, as a model in child-rearing practices, does influence the transmission of such social behaviors as are involved in sex-typing. In some families, parents deliberately emphasize patterns of behavior for their children that correspond to the acceptable cultural role definitions for boys or girls. In other families, children acquire these social behaviors by accidental or fortuitous circumstances, and, in more unfortunate cases the child might acquire behaviors which are in opposition to those roles. Schools, as well as families, can undoubtedly capitalize much more than they now do on what is known about imitative processes. More attention to the models for the career-oriented girl, for the politically-minded boy, for the child who will eventually go into the trades or the professions would seem to be essential if education is to accomplish its objectives of being an institution for the kind of preparation required in order for the pupil to make a career and contribute to the solution of societal problems.

23. THE CONCEPT OF IDENTIFICATION

Jerome Kagan

In the literature of psychology two kinds of papers are particularly helpful to the teacher seeking information about the behavior of children. One, represented by most of the articles included in this book, is a research study in which an investigator either tests one or more hypotheses, compiles descriptive normative data, or seeks to find correlations existing among various behavior or demographic variables. The other is the presentation or explication of a theoretical position. This last may be the simple unsupported presentation of a theory, or it may have the added feature of citations from the literature which, in the author's opinion, appear to lend support to his position. The reader must understand that theoretical presentations are only assumptive, and while they may follow logically from what is known of behavior and may possess considerable face validity, they are only tentative statements. Such theories must sooner or later be subjected to confirmatory research specifically designed to test the theory. A teacher, in the absence of direct confirmatory research, may regard them only as working hypotheses, and while she may find their application useful in her everyday work, she should keep in mind their tentative nature and realize that research may subject them to refutation.

Kagan's discussion of the concept of identification which follows is a theoretical formulation related to the findings and discussions of others. But, in its present form it is assumptive. His discussion does have implications for teachers, but direct confirmation is not reported in his article. He

SOURCE. Adapted from Jerome Kagan, "The Concept of Identification," *Psychological Review*, 1958, Vol. 65, pp. 296–305. (With permission of the author and the publisher, The American Psychological Association.)

takes the position that behavioral similarities existing between an individual and a model do not necessarily indicate identification since limitation and prohibition learning may involve motives and reinforcements capable of explaining the behavioral similarities that may exist between two people. He differentiates imitation behavior according to whether it is based on identification, imitation learning, or prohibition learning. In general, he attempts an analysis of identification and places it within a learning theory structure.

In an analysis of the concept of identification Sanford suggested that the term be applied to situations in which "an individual may be observed to respond to the behavior of other people or objects by initiating in fantasy or reality the same behavior himself . . . the individual strives to behave in a way that is exactly like that of the object" (1955, p. 109). Sanford further suggested that the motive for this imitative behavior was a threat to the person's self esteem. By limiting the term "identification" to those imitative behavioral sequences in which the motivation for the act was anxiety over self esteem, Sanford emphasized two points: (a) mere similarity in overt behavior between a subject and a model was not necessarily a measure of identification, and (b) the motive for the imitative behavior was one of the defining characteristics of an identificatory response.

The various behavioral phenomena which have been labeled "identification" differ in their manifest properties and motivations. The following four classes of behavior have been described as related to the process of identification because they all can lead to similarities in behavior between a subject and a model.

Imitation Learning

This term refers to the initiation and practice of certain responses (gestures, attitudes, speech patterns, dress, etc.) which are not subject to prohibition by the social environment and which are assumed to be the result of an attempt to imitate a model. The behavior has been labeled either "matched-dependent behavior" or "copying" by Miller and Dollard (1941). Miller and Dollard posit that initially the imitative act occurs by chance and the act can only be reinforced if some drive is reduced following the execution of the response. According to this view only direct reward from the social environment, like praise or affection, can strengthen the person's tendency to imitate a model. Mowrer (1950) distinguishes between developmental and defensive identification. In the former process, the person imitates or reproduces the behavior of a model in order to "reproduce bits of the beloved and longed-for parent" (1950, p. 615). Mowrer suggests that most imitation of a model is the result of the desire to reproduce responses which have acquired secondary reward value through association with a nurturant and affectionate model. Thus, Mowrer emphasizes the self-rewarding aspect of certain imitative acts as opposed to Miller and Dollard's emphasis on direct reward from the social environment.

Prohibition Learning

This term refers to the adoption and practice of the prohibitions of the parents and parent substitutes. The acquisition of these prohibitions bears some relation to the process of superego development as described by psychoanalytic theory. Several investigators have suggested that a major motivation for the acquisition of some prohibition is anxiety over anticipated loss of love. Sanford (1955) labeled this process "introjection" and suggested that the learning and maintenance of this class of behavior might be explained without use of the concept of identification.

Identification with the Aggressor

This phrase refers to the adoption of behaviors which are similar to those of an aggressive or threatening model. The motivation for this "imitation" is assumed to be anxiety over anticipated aggression or domination by the threatening model. It is difficult to explain this behavior as a product of either prohibition or imitation learning, since the motive and reinforcement do not seem related to anxiety over anticipated loss of love or desire for a direct, social reward like praise or affection. Anna Freud (1937) has labeled this phenomenon "identification with the aggressor," Mowrer (1950) has called this process "defensive identification" (as distinct from developmental identification), and Sanford has suggested that the term "identification proper" be restricted to this class of behavior.

Vicarious Affective Experience

This phrase refers to the experience of positive or negative affect on the part of a person as a result of an event which has occurred to a model. Salient examples of this phenomenon are (a) a child's elation or depression at learning that his parent is a success or failure, or (b) a mother's elation following the success of her child in school. This phenomenon of vicarious, affective experience has been attributed to a person's identification with a model, but this affective response has been difficult to explain and often neglected by psychologists investigating the identification process. These four phenomena (imitation learning, prohibition learning, identification with the aggressor, and vicarious affective experience) appear to be mediated by different motives and rewards.

In different contexts, social scientists have used the term "identification" to refer to three different sets of variables: (a) the process of identification;

(b) individual differences in the content of the behaviors, motives, and attitudes acquired as a result of the identification process; and (c) the differential effect of various models that are used during the identification process. This paper recognizes the relevance of the model and content dimensions but is primarily concerned with the process of identification, and will attempt to analyze this process in behavioral terms. It is suggested that the process remains the same regardless of the models used or the specific behavioral content that is acquired as a result of an identification.

Definition

Identification is defined as an acquired, cognitive response within a person (S). The content of this response is that some of the attributes, motives, characteristics, and affective states of a model (M) are part of S's psychological organization. The major implication of this definition is that the S may react to events occurring to M as if they occurred to him. The thesis of this paper is that the motivation to command or experience desired goal states of a model is salient in the development and maintenance of an identification.

The Acquisition and Maintenance of an Identification

Although identification has been defined as a cognitive response, it is not implied that the content of the response is available to consciousness or easily verbalized. Thus the terms "cognitive response," "belief," "wish," or "assumption" will be used in this text to include cognitive processes not always available through verbal report. Identification is not viewed as an all-or-none process. Identification is a response that can vary in strength and there will be differences in the degree to which an S believes that the characteristics of a model, whether assets or liabilities, belong to him. In addition, the S may become identified, to differing degrees, with a variety of models. The motives and reinforcements that are involved in the acquisition and maintenance of this cognitive response are elaborated in the following assumptions.

Assumption 1

Initially, the S perceives that the M possesses or commands goals and satisfactions that the S desires. This perception leads to a wish to possess these desired goal states.

Assumption 2

The wish to command the goal states of the M leads to the desire to possess the characteristics of the M because S believes that if he were similar to the M he would command the desired goals. That is, the S assumes that the more similarity there is between the S and M the more likely S is to possess or command the desired goal states of the M.

Assumption 3

The identification response (i.e., "some of the characteristics of the model are mine") is reinforced each time S perceives or is told that he is similar to the M. One type of reinforcement for the identification response occurs when an S is told directly that he and the M are similar in temperament or appearance. It is suggested that a second type of reinforcement for this cognitive response is S's own perception of similarity to the M.

Assumption 4

In order for the identification belief to be maintained, the S must not only perceive similarity between the S and M but he also must experience some of the desired, affective goal states of the M.

The Acquisition of Behavior Similar to a Model: The Motives for Imitation, Identification, and Prohibition Learning

Since perceptions of similarity between the S and M reinforce the identification response, the S may imitate the M during the acquisition phase of an identification in order to increase the degree of similarity. It is acknowledged that the social environment rewards imitative behaviors with affection and praise, and these direct, social reinforcements may strengthen the tendency to imitate adults independently of any identification motives. However, it is suggested, along with Sears et al., that direct, social reinforcement of imitative behavior cannot account for all of the imitative responses that the S initiates. A four-year-old child may simulate adult behaviors when the child is alone or in situations where the parents discourage or punish the imitative response. However, despite the punishment or absence of social reward for some imitative behaviors, the behavior continues to be practiced. Sears et al. call this behavior "role practice" and assume that it is motivated by the "desire to reproduce pleasant experiences" (Sears, 1957, p. 370). Consider the three-year-old girl who plays the role of mother alone in her room. It is hypothesized that a potential reinforcement for this behavior is the creation, in fantasy, of perceptual similarity between the behaviors of the S and M. This perception strengthens S's identification with the M and allows S to share vicariously some of the positive goal states which M commands.

A somewhat different phenomenon is the behavior called "identification with the aggressor" by A. Freud or "defensive identification" by Mowrer. Anna Freud describes a girl who was afraid of ghosts and suddenly began to make peculiar gestures as she ran in the dark. She told her brother, "there is no need to be afraid, you just have to pretend that you're the ghost who might meet you" (Freud, 1937, p. 119). The present theory assumes that the child desired the threatening power of the feared object and this motive elicited the imitative behavior. The fantasied perception of similarity to the feared model gave S a vicarious feeling of power and reduced her anxiety over attack. It is suggested that "identification with the aggressor" does not differ from other identification responses with respect to the basic mechanism of acquisition but does involve a specific motive and goal state. Identification with the aggressor involves a specific relationship between the S and M in which S fears the M. Thus, S desires the aggressive power or threat value of the M in order to reduce his own anxiety over anticipated attack. It may be misleading to classify "identification with the aggressor" as qualitatively different from other identificatory behavior merely because the motive and goal differ from those involved in other identifications.

A third motive which can lead to behavioral similarity between an S and M is anxiety over anticipated loss of love or nurturance. It is suggested that many social prohibitions which the M practices are learned by the S in situations in which this anxiety motivates the acquisition and maintenance of the response. The reinforcement for the learned prohibition is continued acceptance and a consequent reduction in anxiety over rejection.

At a more speculative level, it is suggested that the behaviors which have been called "self actualizing" (Goldstein, 1939) could be motivated and reinforced by a desire for perceptual similarity to an M and be an indication of early identification tendencies.

Two Goals Motivating Identification: Mastery and Love

It has been assumed that S's desire to command certain goal states motivates his identification with a model. It is suggested, for the child especially, that two important goal states that the S desires to command are (a) a feeling of power or mastery over the environment and (b) love and affection. Attainment of these goals should lead to diminution in anxiety over helplessness or loneliness. The young child perceives that he is not able to gratify all of his needs while the parental model is perceived as more capable of dealing with the environment. This discrepancy between the S's perception of his own relative helplessness and the power that he perceives M to possess motivates the wish to have M's power and the search for perceptions of similarity between himself and the M.

A second goal state which may motivate identification is the desire for nurturance and affection. In addition to Freud's classical hypothesis that the child identified with the same-sex parent in order to receive vicariously the affection of the opposite-sex parent, there are situations in which nonparental models command sources of affection. The relation between siblings is such a situation, and the younger child may identify with an older sibling if the former perceives that the latter commands parental affection. The research of Koch (1956) indirectly supports this hypothesis. She reported that school-age boys with older sisters tended to develop more feminine attributes than boys with older brothers. On the other hand, girls with older brothers tend to be more masculine than girls with older sisters.

Factors Influencing the Strength of Identification

The strength of the identification habit, following a basic behavioral law, should be a function of the strength of the motive and the quality and frequency of the reinforcement (Hull, 1943). It would be predicted, therefore, that the most intense identification would occur when the S had strong needs for love and power, felt incapable of gratifying these motives through his own skills, and perceived similarity between himself and an M who commanded these goals. Utilizing this hypothesis, two generalized predictions can be made concerning the strength of identification for different ages and models.

1. The strength of identification tendencies should decrease with age because, in general, the individual's ability to gratify his needs for mastery and love through his own behavior, rather than through a vicarious mechanism, should increase with development. Thus, the identifications of a young child should be more intense than the identifications of older individuals.

2. An identification with an M with whom S was in direct contact should be stronger than with an M with whom S was not in contact, assuming that the motivation for identification was constant and the models were perceived as equally potent. This statement is based on the assumption that the reinforcements of perceived similarity are stronger when S perceives the affects and attributes of the M directly as opposed to instances in which he is merely told that he is similar to the M. Thus, degree of identification with a father with whom S was in contact should be greater than with an imagined fantasy father whom S had never seen. Only very indirect evidence is available to support this prediction. However, reports by P. S. Sears (1946) and Sears et al. (1946) suggest that absence of the father from the home tends to decrease the degree of "masculine" doll play in preschool boys while this experience has little effect on the doll play of girls. The results are open to alternative interpretations but are not inconsistent with the present hypothesis.

SUMMARY

This paper has attempted to analyze the concept of identification and place the concept within a learning-theory framework. Identification was defined as an acquired, cognitive response. The content of this response was that some of the characteristics of a model belonged to the individual and the individual behaved as if some of the characteristics and affective states of the model belonged to him. Identification was not viewed as an all-or-none process. An identification can vary in strength and the individual can identify, to differing degrees, with a variety of models. The motive for the acquisition and maintenance of the identification response was a desire for the positive goal states commanded by the model, and mastery of the environment and love-nurturance were suggested as two important goals. The reinforcement for the acquisition of the identification was perceived similarity in attributes between the person and the model. Thus, the person may strive to imitate aspects of the model's behavior in order to create perceptual similarity between himself and the model. Once the identification was established, the individual behaved as if the goal states of the model belonged to him and the positive affect derived from this vicarious sharing of desired goal states helped to maintain the identification.

It was suggested that the usual emphasis on similarities in overt behavior between an individual and a model is not the best measure of identification, since the motives and reinforcements involved in imitation and prohibition learning could also explain similarities in behavior between two people. A differentiation of imitative behavior based on imitation learning, prohibition learning, and identification was attempted.

24. LEARNING OF GENERALIZED IMITATION AS THE BASIS FOR IDENTIFICATION

Jacob L. Gewirtz & Karen G. Stingle

It was only natural that research directed toward identification of the variables which make a difference in who is imitated by whom, in the responses which are imitated, and in the amount of imitation that occurs, should be accompanied by an interest in the process of imitation, that is, in the variables that affect if, when, and how imitation takes place. Many investigators previously have suggested that imitation, as a class of behavior, is acquired without specific training. However, Gewirtz and Stingle present an alternative model in which the primary mechanism is one of instrumental learning, briefly described as follows: The child selects from a wide array of available responses, already in his behavioral repertoire, the one that *matches* the cues provided by the model. The matching, or "copying," behavior is reinforced by some external source. The range of matching-to-sample behaviors that occur and the variety of settings in which they occur serve to increase the generalizability of the behaviors. Thus, the relevant features of the process are that the discriminative cues produced by the model are common to all settings and the responses which they evoke belong to the generalized class of imitative behavior functionally defined by reinforcing agents including vicarious reinforcement. Once established, imitation is maintained on an intermittent schedule of reinforcement. These basic ideas are used to explain why the observer comes to focus on a single, or a few models; why the imitated behavior can occur

SOURCE. Adapted and abridged from Jacob L. Gewirtz and Karen G. Stingle, "Learning of Generalized Imitation as the Basis for Identification," *Psychological Review*, 1968, Vol. 75, pp. 374–397. (With permission of the authors and the publisher, the American Psychological Association.)

in the absence of a model; and why imitated behavior occurs in situations where extrinsic reinforcement is unavailable.

The concept of generalized imitation is extended to identification processes in which values, motives, and ideals of another person are acquired. The authors suggest, for example, that dependence-attachment to the model, in the present framework, is an abstraction that indexes the discriminative and reinforcing value to the observer of cues provided by the model. Relating identification to learning processes facilitates its modification through established laws of behavior, and its adaptability to further investigation.

After the response of another (a "model") has been witnessed, the observer will often exhibit a response resembling that of the model. This response class, termed *imitation*, does not consist of a specific set of responses classifiable by content or by similarity alone. Rather, a behavior is termed imitative if it is matched to the cues provided by the model's response and is similar to his behavior, but is not emitted because of common stimulus antecedents or environmental constraints. The term *generalized imitation* can be used when many different responses of a model are copied in diverse situations, often in the absence of extrinsic reinforcement. In contrast, the term *identification* has usually referred to a person's taking on abstract psychological characteristics of a model like those termed motives, attitudes, values, roles, or affective states, rather than specific behavior patterns.

Our interest in generalized imitation stems from the awareness that much of the child's early learning is accomplished through that process. It has also evolved in reaction to the widely held view that this tendency to imitate as well as to identify is acquired *without* specific instrumental training (e.g., Aronfreed, 1967, 1968; Bandura, 1962, 1968; Sears, 1957). As an alternative to that position, we suggest that a simple instrumental learning model, with imitation representing one type of acquired stimulus control over responses, can encompass the complex behavior outcomes ordered under that concept and perhaps also many grouped under the heading of observational learning. This paradigm emphasizes intermittent extrinsic reinforcement of an instrumental response class containing a potentially unlimited number of responses, varied in content and matched to response-provided cues from many models (but which may be focused on one model), and often occurring in situations where the model is absent or where there is no extrinsic reinforcement for imitation. In the remaining portion of the paper, we consider the phenomena generally grouped under the rubric of identification and propose that they can be reduced to the simple conception of generalized imitation, and that this reduction can facilitate a research approach to identification.

IMITATION

An experiment by Baer, Peterson, and Sherman (1965) provides a dramatic demonstration of imitation learning with implications for practical application, as well as a useful point of departure for the conceptualization of imitation which shall be proposed. By physically assisting the child to make the desired imitative responses initially and reinforcing each such response immediately, Baer et al. taught several imitative responses to retarded children whose behavior repertoires had been observed closely for a period and did not appear to include imitation. After training on a few such responses, each S could then imitate new modeled responses, and eventually response chains, without assistance. Further, the rate of a generalized imitative response that was never directly reinforced, but had been maintained when interspersed with reinforced imitative responses, declined when reinforcement was withdrawn from the imitative behaviors that were previously reinforced.

A Simple Mechanism for the Acquisition and Maintenance of Generalized Imitation

In this context, a simple mechanism for the acquisition and maintenance of generalized imitation will be detailed. The first imitative responses must occur by chance, through direct physical assistance, or through direct training (with shaping or fading procedures applied by a reinforcing agent to occurring responses). When such responses occur, they are strengthened and maintained by direct extrinsic reinforcement from environmental agents. After several imitative responses become established in this manner, a class of diverse but *functionally equivalent* behaviors is acquired and is maintained by extrinsic reinforcement on an intermittent schedule. Differences in response content of the imitative behaviors are thought to play a minimal role as long as the responses are members of the imitative response class as defined functionally *by reinforcing agents*.

In addition to an emphasis on the environmental stimuli (from the model's responses and discriminative settings) that cue the occurrence of imitative responses, we emphasize also those stimuli that maintain (reinforce) them as essential in the process. Thus, the term imitation implies for us just one type of stimulus control over responses. As with any functional response class under some kind of stimulus control, the response class has no special intrinsic value independent of the stimulus conditions that control it.

An analogy to the functional class of generalized imitation is provided by the matching-to-sample conditional-discrimination learning paradigm (Cumming and Berryman, 1965; Lashley, 1938). The S is required on each trial to respond to the stimulus, in an array of comparison stimuli, that is the same as (or similar to) a conditional or standard stimulus. Thus, in the conditional-discrimination (as in the imitative) context, the significance of the discriminative stimulus varies across trials, changing relative to the conditional stimulus that preceded it. In such contexts, the conditional stimulus (like a model's response) comes to function as a differential cue or selector of discriminations rather than as a simple cue for individual responses. Through extrinsic reinforcement of the class of matching responses (i.e., those made to each matching comparison stimulus), S acquires the relevant matching-response class. This behavior then governs his responses to a wide range of stimuli differing in content. On each trial, S's response to the comparison stimulus that matches the conditional-standard stimulus (the "sample"), from the finite number in the array, is analogous to his selecting from a large set of alternatives (i.e., from his own repertoire) the response that matches the cues provided by the model's response. As reinforced matching responses in the functional imitative class are diverse, and under intermittent reinforcement, discrimination between matched behaviors that are reinforced and those that are not is unlikely to occur, and some copying responses that are never directly reinforced will therefore persist unless they are specifically punished or are incompatible with stronger responses in the child's repertoire. On this basis, new matching responses will continue to enter the functional imitation class in the child's repertoire.

Life Conditions for Learning Generalized Imitation

Conditions in life settings make our analysis particularly appropriate in accounting for the rapid acquisition of topographically accurate imitative behavior sequences that typically occurs. There is an abundance of extrinsic reinforcement occasions and efficient shaping processes during all stages of the child's development, particularly for response classes like imitation. These reinforcers come from a variety of sources, on an intermittent schedule overall, and for diverse imitative behaviors. Thus, generalized imitation will be acquired relatively early in the child's socialization, maintained at high strength, and relatively resistant to change. Although, as a learned social behavior, imitation should be reversible, its extinction would rarely occur, since strict elimination of reinforcement for such pervasive response classes is unlikely to be implemented in complex life settings.

Parents often deliberately set out to teach the child to imitate, using direct tuition, shaping, and fading of the sort employed by Baer et al. (1965, 1967) or Lovaas et al. (1966). The child's imitation can be highly reinforcing *to* parents or models (when contingent on their behaviors). Sometimes a parent may himself imitate the child, either as a spontaneous response or as a step in the process of teaching him to imitate. Among other effects, this may facilitate the child's discrimination of the degree of similarity between his and the model's responses, and can constitute steps in a shaping procedure wherein the child's response it matched to the model's with increasing closeness through successive approximations. This procedure very likely plays an important role in the child's language learning (Gewirtz, 1969).

Behaviors of the child that are in the direction of increasing competence and are thus reinforced by socializing agents are almost invariably behaviors the child has observed older models perform (e.g., walking, talking, writing), and his performance of those behaviors is frequently reinforced in the presence of models who are exhibiting them. In a sense, these behaviors are also imitative. Thus, reinforcement for progress toward increasing competence can at the same time be reinforcement for generalized imitation. As the child is subjected increasingly to the socialization process with age, the behaviors for which he is reinforced will change with his growing capacities. The agents reinforcing him will also vary and increase in number, each reinforcing on a different schedule and for different behaviors. In the face of this continual change, one thing remains constant for the child: The imitative response class continues to be reinforced at a high rate throughout his development.

Like other social behaviors, the appropriateness of imitative responses varies from one situation to another. Thus, the imitative behavioral unit usually includes a *discriminative occasion* indicating that an imitative response is likely to be reinforced. Reinforceable occasions may be preceded by an explicit verbal cue, like Baer, Peterson, and Sherman's "Susy, do this," or by a less explicit cue indicating that imitation is appropriate. The imitator learns to discriminate those cue stimuli from cues indicating that noncopying, complementary interactive responses—for instance, dependence—are appropriate. For example, based on differential reinforcement of the child's behaviors in the past, the model's *being oriented toward* the child (physically or otherwise), or his *not being occupied* in some ongoing activity, may acquire discriminative stimulus value for the child's emitting *complementary* interaction responses and for suppressing copying responses, which would be clearly inappropriate. Imitative behaviors are more likely to be reinforced when the model is busily engaged in a *solitary* activity and can more readily reinforce the child's parallel behaviors (like imitation) than his approach or interactive behaviors, as the model can then continue his activity without long interruption. If the child is frequently reinforced for making disruptive dependency initiations in this situation, he may not learn to discriminate that such behaviors are inappropriate and may interrupt the model at will, thus in extreme cases becoming what could be termed "spoiled." It is possible that such children do not learn to imitate to as great an extent as children whose models discourage interruptions of the model's task. It is also likely that at the same time they do not acquire autonomous task-oriented behavior patterns independent of frequent reinforcement from their socializing agents.

There remains a considerable need for a detailed analysis of the discriminative cues that indicate to the child, in specific and more general cases, when it is appropriate to imitate (i.e., when imitation is likely to be reinforced) and which model it is most appropriate to imitate when alternative models are available. An analysis from our intentionally simple approach would attend only in passing to developmental changes in imitative behaviors and learning that occur in typical life settings.

Focused versus Nonfocused Generalized Imitation

The generalized-imitation paradigm as we have used it up to now has been relatively *non*focused with regard to the model imitated, summarizing imitation of diverse responses of *many* models. Yet a selective or focused imitation pattern can result from a combination of relatively frequent contact with one model and frequent reinforcement (from the model and others) when the child imitates a variety of the behaviors of that model. (This distinction is analogous to that made by Gewirtz (1961, 1969) between nonfocused dependence and focused attachment.) That model's behaviors will therefore acquire discriminative value for the child, indicating that his imitation of them has an even higher probability of being reinforced than does imitation in general.

Children of both sexes typically interact more with their mothers than with their fathers, but it is assumed the boy comes to imitate his father and the girl her mother because of differential reinforcement for copying each of them. The child will discriminate which single model it is usually most appropriate to imitate, on the basis of being differentially reinforced for such imitation; and because of frequent chances to observe that model, the child will imitate an extensive range of his behaviors. More will be said on this issue when we consider sex typing.

Generalized Imitation Extended

We will now see how the generalized-imitation concept can account for related behavioral phenomena that will be relevant to our analysis of identification. These include imitation of the model's behavior in his absence, imitation of a large portion of a model's behavior role in play settings, and wide-ranging similarities in abstract values or attitudes.

Imitation in the model's absence. Delayed imitation, including imitation of the model's behavior in his absence, can be regarded as a simple variant of the generalized-imitation paradigm. All imitative behaviors occur *after* the model's performance that provides the relevant cue has terminated and often while the child is not even looking at the model. In that sense they are always performed in the *absence* of the model. The delay between the model's performance and the imitative behavior may be further lengthened through shaping techniques, implemented either deliberately or in an unplanned way by reinforcing agents. Immediate direct reinforcement for delayed imitation in the model's absence may frequently be provided by agents other than the model, and sometimes in the form of statements like "you are acting just like your father" or "like a big boy." In addition, the agent may indicate explicitly that what is being reinforced is not only performance of the response, but its performance in the model's absence.

Imitation of the model in play. Imitation of large segments of a model's behavior role in play situations where the model is not present may also be facilitated by ecological factors. Props given to the child can be appropriate to the model's role, as in the case of toy kitchen utensils being made available to a young girl. Reinforcement can be provided through the reciprocal role play of other children, or through occasional direct reinforcement from the model or other adult witnesses. These toys may serve a dual purpose, in that they can also provide a sanctioned discriminable context for the child's imitation of a model's behaviors in his absence when these behaviors might be hazardous or inappropriate in their usual context.

Generalized imitation of values. The generalized-imitation concept can also be extended readily to account for wide-ranging similarities in abstract values (attitudes, life styles, or motives). For example, often a child will act as the model might in a situation even if he has not actually witnessed the model in that situation, or he will strive for the same goals as the model.

An example of a model's value is "tidy housekeeping." A mother's behavior may exemplify that value, and her daughter either may be extrinsically reinforced for nonimitative tidying responses or may exhibit these responses through simple generalized imitation (with or without extrinsic reinforcement), as we have been emphasizing. An important assumption for extending our analysis is that a daughter generally reinforced for acting like her mother may come to discriminate the common elements of responses exhibited by the model in a class of related stimulus contexts (such as housekeeping). She might also inductively arrive at a statement like, "Mom keeps a tidy house." The child's value is based on her discrimination of such a functional class of the model's responses (some would term it a "concept"). It would then apply to situations in which the child, as generalized imitator, may not actually have seen the model perform. Although some of the daughter's responses may be quite different in topography from those of her mother (because of changed climatic conditions, technological and socioeconomic levels, etc.), they will produce the same outcome: a tidy house. Once the value has been acquired in this manner, the mother is likely to reinforce the resulting responses, and the value will be maintained. As is true of all learned behaviors, however, the permanence of a value will depend on the continuation of the same reinforcement matrix for the class of responses implying that value, and thus it is potentially subject to change.

In the next section we will argue that a substantial proportion of the phenomena grouped under the concept of identification may be ordered by the concept of generalized imitation and these extensions.

IDENTIFICATION

The child's acquisition of the motives, values, ideals, roles, and conscience of an important other person (the model), particularly of his parents and especially the same-sex parent, has been termed identification. The term has been used variously to refer to the process by which these characteristics are acquired, to the person's desire to possess the characteristics of the model and his belief that he does, and to the resulting similarity of behavior patterns of child and model. Several of these usages are often found in the same analysis. The identification term has also been used often as if it were a unitary concept that involves a single, incompletely specified complex paradigm with demographically defined independent variables (e.g., gender of S in an intact nuclear family) and no consensually valid dependent variable.

Psychoanalytic theory provided the earliest framework for the approach to the phenomena of identification, and much of identification theory still relies on those early attempts. While Freud dealt with identification in a scattered way through half a century of his writing, and there were apparent variations in his approach, he seems to have employed the term in at least two ways: as a *process* and as the behavior-similarity *outcome* of that process. Thus, Freud (1933) regarded identification as the process by which "one ego becomes like another one, which results in the first ego behaving . . . in certain respects in the same way as the second; it imitates it, and as it were takes it into itself [p. 90]." And, in one of his writings, Freud's (1920) index of the outcome of identification was imitation of the model's behaviors. When assumed to result from complete instrumental dependence upon and an emotional tie to the model (typically the parent), identification has been termed "anaclitic" in Freud's approach and by Sears (1957; Sears et al., 1965) and "developmental" by Mowrer (1950); while "aggressive" or "defensive" identification (Freud, 1937; Mowrer, 1950) is assumed to result from fear of punishment from the model, with the child avoiding punishment by becoming like the model. The child's superego, the locus of self-observation, conscience, and ideals, has been assumed to be based largely on this latter type of identification and to be built upon the model of the parents' superego rather than on their actual behavior.

Although many would agree that the child can learn to imitate a range of behaviors on the basis of simple trial-and-error learning (as involved in generalized imitation), imitation has typically been treated in the literature as somehow distinct from identification. Thus, despite an early instance where Freud (1920) used imitation to index identification, the typical psychoanalytic view appears to be that the relatively precise matching to the model's overt behavior in imitation is a transient, surface, even symptomatic process, whereas the wider-ranging, less precise behavioral matching in identification results from a more fundamental or dynamic underlying process.

Kohlberg (1963) has proposed that identification differs from imitation on three counts: (a) Identification is a "motivated disposition" because of the intrinsic reinforcing properties of perceived similarity to the model; (b) similarity between the behaviors of S and the model often occurs in the absence of the model; and (c) many aspects of the model's behavior are reproduced. These factors appear to have been the bases for many theorists' considering identification as a "higher-order" process than generalized imitation. (More recently, Kohlberg, 1966, has proposed that attachment follows [generalized] imitation, and that the combination of those two factors leads to identification, but it is not clear what are the roles of the above three criteria in his recent approach.)

It has been suggested within the learning-theory tradition that identification may be an abstraction for diverse imitative habits (Miller and Dollard, 1941; Seward, 1945). Bandura (1962) and Bandura and Walters (1963) have noted that observational learning is often termed imitation in behavior-theory approaches to personality development and identification in more traditional personality theories, with no substantial differences between the two usages. In our similar view, often the only reason that generalized-imitation learning is assumed inadequate to account for identification phenomena is that factors like a motivation to be like, an emotional attachment to, or envy of the model that are assumed relevant for identification are just not considered at all relevant to generalized imitation, and, indeed, some even appear to think of them as outside the sphere of simple learning.

Generalized Imitation as the Basis for Identification

It often appears that the only real distinction in use between identification and imitation may be that the identification process is typically defined in a less precise, more complex, and more inclusive way than is imitation. Further, a large number of loosely related and often overlapping terms at varying levels of conceptual analysis, like introjection, incorporation, internalization, modeling, role copying, and sex typing, all of which lead to similarities between the model's and the identifier's behavior patterns, are included under identification. This situation has further complicated the concept of identification and appears to have implied, as an artifact, a larger number of seemingly distinct processes than is warranted. Therefore, the reduction of these terms to a common level of analysis in basic paradigms open to a learning analysis may show that apparent differences between them are attributable to segments of the behavior stream emphasized, particular stimuli evoking the responses, available functional reinforcers, or methods of assessment, factors that do not ordinarily justify separate paradigms. Such a reduction can be implemented by regarding identification concepts as based on the simpler generalized-imitation paradigm, with behavioral similarity as the outcome.

For example, *introjection* is often defined as the act of incorporating a value system in its entirety, with identification as its result (Fuchs, 1937). Thus, while introjection appears to refer to the acquisition process and identification to its result, those terms may only reflect emphasis on different stages in the behavior process by which generalized imitation is learned and maintained, with introjection pointing to a somewhat earlier phase of the learning than does identification. The use of two different terms therefore seems to emphasize arbitrarily what may for most purposes be a trivial distinction.

Similarly, *sex typing* usually connotes identification with models of the same sex as the child, and has itself been broken down further into sex-role identification, sex-role preference, and sex-role adoption (Lynn, 1959). Thus, it refers to the shaping of the child's behaviors to match behaviors specifically appropriate to his sex category. These behaviors are usually assumed to be acquired through observation of a model or a class of models. So defined, they can be regarded as the result of generalized imitation, with the gender of the model serving as a discriminative stimulus for a higher frequency of extrinsic (immediate or delayed) reinforcement for imitation. Kohlberg (1966) has reported that a shift from generalized imitation of the mother to imitation of the father typically occurs in boys between ages 4 and 7, which he interpreted as reflecting changes in boys' conceptualization of age and sex roles. The approach being advanced in this paper is open to such possibilities, but we would conceive them as resulting from a systematic shift in the discriminative conditions under which imitative behaviors are reinforced. Mischel (1966) has reviewed a number of other results of sex-typing studies done to date and interpreted them from a learning approach very much like ours.

The salient issues for our analysis must be operational, such as whether or not discriminative stimuli for imitation are present and whether or not functional extrinsic reinforcers follow imitative responses. In addition to reducing demographic variables to a more useful level of analysis, such factors can provide the basis for distinguishing among possibly diverse paradigms. By attending to the actual stimuli, responses, and the sequential details of their interaction, this level of analysis makes possible a flexible, individual-oriented approach to identification phenomena. This approach provides greater precision and flexibility in detailing the history of the individual child in question in terms of what similarity behaviors have been acquired and how they are evoked and maintained. But equally important, it can also highlight the conditions responsible for a failure to acquire particular identification behaviors and the conditions that may facilitate, extinguish, or otherwise modify such behaviors. Reversibility or change in identification-behavior patterns is almost never assumed or tested, yet is a perfectly reasonable corollary of the conception of learning, in representative life settings as in the laboratory.

The present approach, then, regards the development of identification behaviors as due to extrinsic reinforcement of the child's imitation of his parent's (or model's) behaviors. The degree to which a child is identified with a particular model is thus grossly determined by the value to the child of the reinforcers contingent upon his imitation of that person's behavior. His identification will also be a function of the amount of exposure to other potential models and reinforcement for imitating them, the frequency of reinforcement for original, nonimitative behaviors, and the value of the reinforcers provided for each of these behavior classes. Identification with the model at the level of abstract values may require finer discriminations by the child but, as we have already shown, should follow the same principles as simpler imitation.

The advantages of this functional approach are evident when one looks at such work as that by Lovaas (1967) with schizophrenic children. Besides teaching the children to imitate vocalizations and to converse, as was described earlier, Lovaas reinforced non-verbal imitation in order to teach behaviors in the areas of personal hygiene, games, drawing, and affectionate behavior, with the intention of eventually shifting the control of these behaviors (by fading procedures) away from the model to control by more appropriate or general stimuli. Noting that the behaviors learned by these children were neither as representative nor did they occur in as wide a range of settings as those covered by such terms as identification, Lovaas nevertheless implied that bringing about this more extensive imitation is not incompatible with the procedures he had been using and may primarily involve increasing the reinforcing value of stimuli from the model and others. Thus, besides permitting a more precise evaluation of the factors involved in the children's failure to identify, this approach suggests specific areas of attack to remedy the deficiencies.

Relationships of Other Identification Issues to the Learning Model

The role of reinforcement in identification. A basic assumption in our approach is that the child comes to copy diverse responses performed by his parent-models because he is consistently reinforced directly for that class of behaviors, perhaps even more consistently than for behaviors that he initiates on his own. The class of copying responses is highly likely to culminate in extrinsic reinforcers in a variety of settings and from many sources, both social and nonsocial. We assume that many imitative behaviors may occur without direct reinforcement, but only *after* the response class has initially been established in the child's behavioral repertoire by direct reinforcement and only if it is still being directly reinforced at least occasionally.

Regardless of how often the model is rewarded in the presence of the child, we do not conceive of the child's imitating him (identifying) unless the child himself is at least occasionally rewarded for it. Likewise, the adult's withholding of reinforcement from the child can be effective only if in other situations or for other behaviors such reinforcement is not withheld. In the terms of our analysis, the model would make the withheld resources available to the child contingent upon various classes of behavior, one of which is likely to be imitation. What seems too little appreciated by many theorists is the ability of intermittent, even infrequent, extrinsic reinforcement to maintain an extensive class of behaviors, many of which are *never* reinforced, as has been well established by the research of Baer et al. (1965, 1967) and Lovaas et al. (1966) and the context of behavioral technology from which these studies spring. At the same time, such research clearly demonstrates the necessity of at least occasional reinforcement in the acquisition and maintenance of a behavior.

The role of dependence-attachment in imitation-identification. Among the factors assumed necessary for or related to the child's identification with his parent-model, that is, his pervasive imitation of the model's behaviors, are nurturance or love from, or social-emotional dependence on, the parent, and a personal attachment, strong tie, emotional intensity, or warm relationship between the child and the parent. An alternative possibility is that imitative behaviors may precede the learning of specific attachments and, by increasing the child's responsiveness to others, may thus directly or indirectly contribute to attachment learning. In our view, these issues may be artifacts of the gross level of conceptual analysis from which both imitative-identificatory and dependence-attachment phenomena have been typically approached.

In life settings, social dependence-attachment behaviors and imitative-identificatory behaviors may be acquired concurrently or sequentially from identical or similar stimulus conditions, as both behavior classes are emitted in the presence of many of the same discriminative stimuli and are maintained by many of the same reinforcers provided by the parents. Indeed, the latter behaviors may be considered a subset of the former, insofar as they are a means by which the child can obtain social stimuli from the parent (model). As changes in the social stimuli (and their efficacy) provided by the parents may be reflected in both imitative-identificatory and dependence-attachment behaviors, the acquisition of these two processes is not likely to be independent. Nevertheless, in our view, dependence-attachment is not necessary for the learning of generalized imitation; they are two separate response systems that can be represented by distinct paradigms, and are interdependent only in their use of some of the same stimulus elements for their acquisition and maintenance. Since a large number of imitative behaviors are maintained by social discriminative and reinforcing stimuli, the correlation between the strengths of imitative and attachment behaviors may be high, but this should not be taken to indicate that attachment is a precondition for generalized imitation, or vice versa.

Thus, from our approach the existence or strength of a dependence or attachment, the quality of a relationship, or the degree to which nurturance and affection were received earlier are gross abstractions. Nurturance summarizes the social stimulus conditions provided to the child earlier, and dependence-attachment summarizes the efficacy for the child of social stimuli from a person or a class of persons. Such broad concepts will to some degree predict the effectiveness of social stimuli from the parent in functioning as discriminative stimuli and generalized reinforcers for the child's responses, including his imitative-identification ones. However, they will inevitably be nonspecific about the details of these contingencies. Further, there is no reason to expect that the person to whom the child is most strongly attached —that is, from whom discriminative and reinforcing stimuli (e.g., approval) should be most effective for his behaviors—will necessarily be the model for the child's behaviors. However, through differential reinforcement that person may determine who the model will be, as in the case of the mother who reinforces her young son for acting as his father does.

The role of fear in identification. For heuristic simplicity, in this analysis we have avoided the use of concepts like "fear of rejection," "fear of punishment," or "anxiety" often used in identification theories, for example, as the assumed basis for defensive identification (Freud, 1937; Mowrer, 1950). We regard the paradigms for those concepts as compatible with ours for the acquisition and maintenance of generalized imitation, except that they may imply different classes of reinforcers, for example, removal or avoidance of a noxious stimulus. Self-critical responses and others labeled "guilt" or "resistance to temptation" reflecting "internalized controls" or "conscience" can undoubtedly be reinforced by such consequences, but they can also be acquired through the direct positive reinforcement processes we have emphasized.

CONCLUSION

In this paper, we have used only basic instrumental conditioning and S-R chaining concepts to order many of the assumed complexities of generalized imitation. We have proposed that the phenomena usually grouped under the rubric of identification can also be reduced, under a discriminated-operant learning model, to this more parsimonious conception of generalized imitation and its direct extensions. We have not advocated this approach for the sake of reduction per se, but rather to bring these phenomena to a level at which they will be dealt with more productively than they have been so far. Since identification phenomena involve systematic changes in behavior effected by recurring environmental conditions, a learning analysis is appropriate, and its use makes immediately available a wealth of knowledge about the functioning of stimuli and responses. Under a systematic learning approach to identification phenomena, the relevant behaviors are potentially subject to acquisition, discrimination, facilitation, extinction, and other modifications, according to well-established laws of behavior. The study of such modifications would be in contrast to the typical approach to identification, in which the effects are for the most part assumed to be long term, and reversibility or change in the process is never tested and almost never even assumed.

25. IMITATION IN CHILDREN AS A FUNCTION OF PERCEIVED SIMILARITY TO A SOCIAL MODEL AND VICARIOUS REINFORCEMENT

Mary A. Rosekrans

Learning by imitation has both cognitive and affective properties. In the first place the imitator must perceive, observe, and interpret the behaviors and role patterns of the model. To employ these behaviors as part of his own behavior they must be rehearsed and recalled for later use. Second, the observer vicariously experiences whatever consequences are achieved by the model's behavior. Such outcomes characteristically have a pleasant or unpleasant feeling tone which, as indicators of the potential effects of the behavior, depend on a degree of empathy with the model if they are to be interpreted accurately. The successful adoption of a given behavior therefore depends on what is perceived and how it is interpreted by the observer. If the effects of the imitated behavior are unpredictable the imitator will learn not to depend on imitation or will turn to another model. For these reasons many psychologists have hypothesized that one learns to imitate a model with attributes similar to oneself. Obviously, the behaviors of such models will be readily understood, realistically interpreted, and capable of attainment by the observer. In support of these hypotheses the typical finding suggests that the observer attends to and recalls more of the behavior of a model who shares his personality traits than of one who does not. It can also be expected that learning by imitation will be enhanced if the child identifies with the person in the tutorial role.

This study by Rosekrans investigates the effects on imitation of a model's

SOURCE. Adapted and abridged from Mary A. Rosekrans, "Imitation in Children as a Function of Perceived Similarity to a Social Model and Vicarious Reinforcement," *Journal of Personality and Social Psychology*, 1967, Vol. 7, pp. 307–315. (With permission of the author and the publisher, the American Psychological Association.)

behavior, of different consequences for performing given instrumental acts by a model who is presented as similar or dissimilar to the observer. She found that a model perceived as similar to the observer was clearly more efficacious in transmitting his behaviors than one perceived as dissimilar. Unlike the findings of previous studies, however, the findings regarding consequences were tenuous. Rosekrans explains that delay of a consequence until the end of a sequence of instrumental acts may have reinforced (or punished) only the last act in a sequence rather than the entire sequence as she initially supposed it might, thereby suggesting another variable that may affect imitation. This article also provides a unique method for inducing similarity of a model to observer by reference to interests, abilities, and group membership of both.

Previous research has shown that one determinant of matching behavior is the degree to which the subject perceives himself as similar to the model. It has been hypothesized, for example, that the perception of similarities existing between persons leads to perceiving or creating still further similarities. Stotland and his associates have tested this hypothesis using several different procedures. Stotland and Patchen (1961) found that perceived similarity to a model in background and personal characteristics produced a shift in attitudes of prejudice and authoritarianism toward those of the model. In a similar study (Burnstein, Stotland, & Zander, 1961), it was found that sixth-, seventh-, and eighth-grade boys adopted more of the sea-diving preferences of a deep-sea diver portrayed as being similar to them in background and other characteristics than of a deep-sea diver described as dissimilar.

Although the foregoing studies dealt primarily with the modification of opinions and preferences in adult subjects, the results suggest the hypothesis that perceived similarity to a social model should also influence the extent to which instrumental behaviors are imitated by children. The first purpose of the present study was to test this hypothesis.

Among other factors that influence imitation are the observed consequences of the model's responses, for example, reward and punishment. The effects of such consequences to the model are undoubtedly complex, but may be due to the fact that the observer empathically experiences pleasantness or unpleasantness from the observation of pleasant or unpleasant consequences of the behavior of others (Berger, 1962). With respect to the empathic phenomenon, Aronfreed (1965) has hypothesized that the affective response of an observer can parallel the affective state of a model only to the extent that their respective past experiences share common elements. According to this reasoning, then, high similarity to a social model should enhance the effects of the response consequences to the model, relative to low similarity.

A second purpose of the present study was to assess the effect of manipulations in perceived similarity to a social model on the potency of the response consequences to the model. An interaction between perceived similarity conditions and response consequences was predicted, with high similarity, relative to low similarity, enhancing the effects on imitative behavior of reward and punishment to the model.

Preadolescent boys observed a male model perform behaviors which culminated in either reward, punishment, or no consequences. Half of the boys in each group observed a model who was portrayed as being similar to themselves, and the remainder observed a model portrayed as being dissimilar to themselves. Interpersonal similarity was operationalized in terms of background, group membership, skills, and interests. A seventh group of boys observed no model.

A final purpose of the study was to determine the effects of similarity to a model on indexes of imitative learning as differentiated from imitative performance. In order to investigate this problem, two groups, in addition to those above, observed either a similar or a dissimilar model receive no consequences for performing the behaviors. Instead of being given an opportunity to perform imitative responses spontaneously (as they were in the groups described above), subjects in these two groups were asked to reproduce the model's behavior as accurately as possible. The effects of similarity on spontaneous rehearsal and under elicited conditions could then be compared.

It was assumed that the number of different imitative responses produced under elicited (recall) conditions would serve as a relatively accurate index of learning. A significant effect of similarity under elicited conditions, as well as on spontaneous rehearsal of imitative responses, would indicate that similarity to the model had an effect on imitative learning. If similarity produced a difference in the spontaneous rehearsal of imitative responses, but no difference due to similarity was found under elicited conditions, it would suggest that performance but not learning was influenced by similarity to the model.

METHOD

Subjects

The subjects were 90 boy scouts, aged 11 through 14, randomly assigned to 9 subgroups of 10 subjects each. These particular subjects were used because boy scouts is a major reference group for young boys. Mutual membership in the organization could, therefore, serve as one component in the induction of similarity to a model. The experimental sessions were conducted at the troop meetingplace during individual appointments. Thus, the salience of membership in the organization and in the particular troop was maximized.

Procedure

The six steps in the procedure for subjects in the eight experimental conditions requiring observation of a model occurred in the order given below. The same procedure was followed for subjects in the no-model condition with the exception of the induction procedure, the administration of the first and second Perceived Similarity Test (PST), and the film presentation of the model.

Introduction and completion of personal information sheet. Upon entering the experimental room the subject was asked to fill out a personal information sheet. The subject was then told that the experimenter was interested in finding out how well boys his age could "plan things out," and that this could be done by having the subject figure out a problem in a war strategy game. The objective of the game was to move the advancing army along the roads leading to the enemy and to surround the enemy for the most strategic attack. The subject was told that the experimenter would show him a movie of another boy playing the same game to give him an idea of how someone else went about this kind of task.

Induction procedure. The experimenter explained that she could tell the subject something about the boy in the film, since he had also filled out a personal information sheet. In order to induce a feeling of high similarity to the model (high similarity group), the experimenter showed the subject a picture of the model dressed in a boy scout uniform and described him as having many characteristics and interests in common with the subject.

In order to induce a feeling of low similarity to the model (low similarity group), the experimenter showed the subject a picture of the model dressed in street clothes and described him as being different in all respects from the subject.

First PST. After the induction of either high or low similarity, the experimenter administered the PST to provide a measure of perceived similarity to the model as induced by the experimenter's description of the model and the picture of the model.

Film presentation of model. The subjects assigned to modeling conditions observed a film of a 12½-year-old boy playing the war-strategy game. At the beginning of the film an adult male experimenter was shown pointing out the game and specifying rules and objectives. The model then performed a sequence of verbal and motoric actions, some of which involved strategy and style of maneuvering the pieces and some of which involved breaking the rules of the game. Subjects in the high similarity group observed a film in which the model was dressed in a boy scout uniform, and subjects in the low similarity group observed a film in which the model was dressed in street clothes. The male experimenter was shown remaining in the room while the model performed, but appeared to be busy with some paper work.

Three alternative endings were prepared for the film. One showed the experimenter praising the model, one showed the experimenter criticizing the model, and one involved "no consequences," that is, neither praise nor criticism.

Test for imitation: Spontaneous rehearsal of imitative responses. After the exposure session, the experimenter explained that the subject could play the game by himself and that she could determine how well he did by the arrangement of the pieces when he finished the game. The experimenter set a minute timer and told the subject that he had 7 minutes to play the game. The subject was told that when the timer rang he should knock on the door so that the experimenter would know that he had finished. The subject was observed for the 7-minute session through one-way glass from an adjoining room.

Test for imitation: Elicitation of imitative responses. After the exposure session, each subject in the two elicitation subgroups (no-consequences-elicited condition) was told that the experimenter had made a mistake and showed the wrong film and that she did not want him to see how that boy played the game. The experimenter then explained that she could not use the game to test the subject's planning ability, but that instead she wanted to test his memory. The subject was then asked to play the game and do everything the same way as it was done by the boy in the film. The subject's behavior was recorded by an observer in the same room.

Second PST. At the end of the experimental session another form of the PST was administered to provide a measure of how well the effectiveness of the manipulation held up after exposure to the film including the response consequences to the model.

Response Measures

Spontaneous rehearsal. The 7-minute observation session was divided into 5-second intervals by means of an electric interval timer, yielding a total of 84 intervals. For each interval the actions of the subject were recorded and scored in one of the following categories: (a) imitation, (b) partial imitation, (c) nonimitation. The verbal behavior of the subject was also recorded and scored as imitative or nonimitative.

From these observational records, the following response measures were derived:

1. Frequency of imitative behavior (the number of intervals in which imitative behavior occurred) and frequency of partially imitative behavior (the number of intervals in which partially imitative behavior occurred).

2. The number of *different* types of imitative responses. It was possible for the subject to perform as many as eight different imitative responses during the rehearsal session.

3. Replication of the model's strategy in placing the seven pieces at the end of the game.

Elicited. The response measures for subjects in the no-consequences-elicited condition were obtained by simply recording the number of different imitative or partially imitative behaviors each subject could perform or describe verbally, yielding a range from 0 to 8. Replication of the model's strategy in placing the pieces at the end of the game was also scored, yielding a range of scores from 0 to 7.

Reliability. Assessment of observer reliability was based on simultaneous observation by two observers. Within each response category the number of agreements was divided by the number of agreements plus disagreements. The average reliability ratio was .90, with a range from .82 to .98.

Perceived similarity scores. The difference between the subject's rating of himself and his rating of the model yielded D scores ranging from 0 to 6 for each item.

RESULTS

A repeated-measures analysis of variance performed on the average of the two D scores indicated induction of high versus low similarity had a significant effect on perceived similarity to the model ($F = 210.42$, $df = 1/64$, $p < .001$). The subjects in the high similarity group perceived themselves as significantly more similar to the model ($\bar{x} = .71$) than did the subjects in the low similarity group ($\bar{x} = 2.20$).

Neither the main effect of response consequences to the model nor the interactions of response consequences with other variables were statistically significant. These findings indicate that the subject's perception of similarity to the model, as induced by the experimental manipulation, was not altered by the model's response consequences observed in the film. All subjects perceived themselves as less similar to the model on the second administration of the PST than on the first ($F = 9.57$, $df = 1/64$, $p < .01$).

All comparisons between the no-model condition and the low similarity condition, on all measures described below, indicated highly significant ($p < .001$) differences between the two groups via the t-test. These data indicate each of the behavioral indexes was affected by observation of the model.

Rehearsal of Imitative Responses

The means and standard deviations for the total imitation scores are presented in Table 1. An analysis of variance was performed including the following factors: similarity condition (high versus low) and response con-

TABLE 1

Means and Standard Deviations for Total Imitation Score

	Total Imitation Score	
Group	$\bar{X}$	SD
High similarity		
Model rewarded	15.90	3.78
Model punished	16.75	2.44
No consequences	18.75	6.79
Low similarity		
Model rewarded	12.10	6.53
Model punished	10.10	4.62
No consequences	14.10	4.61
No model	1.90	2.61

sequences (model rewarded, model punished, no consequences). The only significant effect found was that due to the similarity condition ($F = 12.38$, $df = 1/54$, $p < .01$). Subjects in the high similarity group produced significantly more imitative behavior than subjects in the low similarity group.

Number of Different Imitative Responses

The means and standard deviations for the number of different imitative responses may be seen in Table 2.

The results of an analysis of variance of the number of different imitative responses yielded a significant main effect of similarity condition ($F = 4.08$, $df = 1/54$, $p < .05$). The size of the behavior repertoire acquired from the model by subjects in the high similarity group was significantly greater than that acquired by subjects in the low similarity group. Neither the interaction between similarity condition and response consequences nor the main effect of response consequences was significant.

Imitation of position of pieces (position replication score). The means and standard deviations for the position replication score (extent to which the subject reproduced the arrangement of pieces at the end of the game) are shown in Table 2.

The analysis of variance of the position replication scores revealed an interaction of borderline significance between similarity condition and response consequences ($F = 3.44$, $df = 1/54$, $p < .10$). A 2 × 2 analysis of variance (excluding the no-consequences condition) performed on this measure also yielded an interaction of borderline significance between similarity condition and response consequences ($F = 2.48$, $df = 1/36$, $p < .10$). Orthogonal contrasts performed on the cell means revealed a significant difference between the model-rewarded and model-punished conditions for the high

TABLE 2

Means and Standard Deviations for Number of Different Imitative Responses and Position-Replication Score

	Score			
	No. Different Imitative Responses		Position Replication	
Group	$\bar{X}$	SD	$\bar{X}$	SD
High similarity				
Model rewarded	3.50	.97	3.50	1.43
Model punished	2.90	.24	2.50	.92
No consequences	3.00	.77	3.40	.80
No consequences–elicited	5.80	1.07	4.60	1.35
Low similarity				
Model rewarded	2.45	1.10	3.00	.63
Model punished	2.35	1.40	3.10	1.04
No consequences	2.95	1.06	2.30	.90
No consequences–elicited	4.85	.97	3.60	.78
No model	.80	.64	1.80	1.29

similarity group ($F = 4.63$, $df = 1/54$, $p < .05$), but not for the low similarity group.

Effects of Perceived Similarity on Elicitation of Imitative Responses

The effect of perceived similarity on the learning of imitative responses was assessed by comparisons involving no-consequences subgroups only. Subjects who were given the opportunity to rehearse imitative responses spontaneously were compared to subjects from whom imitative responses were elicited. Only the main effect of rehearsal versus elicitation was found to be significant ($F = 52.10$, $df = 1/36$, $p < .001$). A greater number of imitative responses was apparently learned than was performed spontaneously. The interaction was not significant. However, since differences between cells had been predicted, they were tested by means of orthogonal contrasts. The results revealed a significant difference between the high and low similarity groups in the elicitation condition ($F = 4.48$, $df = 1/36$, $p < .05$). Subjects in the high similarity group were able to recall a greater number of imitative responses than subjects in the low similarity group. No significant difference was found, however, between the high and low similarity groups in the rehearsal condition. The results of a two-way analysis of variance performed on the position replication scores (imitation of position of pieces at the end of the game) also revealed a significant main effect of a rehearsal versus elicitation. The model's placement of pieces was replicated more accurately in the elicitation condition than in the rehearsal condition ($F = 15.65$, $df = 1/36$, $p < .01$). A significant main effect of similarity condition was also yielded by this analysis ($F = 9.56$, $df = 1/36$, $p < .01$). Significantly more imitation of the model's strategy in placing the pieces occurred in the high similarity condition than in the low similarity condition.

DISCUSSION

The evidence confirms the hypothesis that the efficacy of a social model in transmitting imitative behaviors is increased when the observer perceives himself as similar, rather than dissimilar, to the model. Both the frequency of imitation and the size of the behavior repertoire were greater when the observer perceived himself as similar, rather than dissimilar, to the model in interests and skills, background, and group membership.

These findings are in accord with the results of previous studies which have dealt with the modification of opinions and preferences in adult subjects (Burnstein et al., 1961; Stotland & Patchen, 1961; Stotland et al., 1962). The present research demonstrates that perceived similarity to a social model influences the extent to which instrumental activities are imitated by children. The results support Stotland's theory of generalizing similarities; that is, the subject's perception of similarities existing between himself and another person leads him to the perception or creation of other similarities between them.

What explanations can be offered for the tenuous findings concerning the effects of response consequences to the model? The most plausible answer involves the timing of the reward and punishment used in this study. In the film, the adult had his back turned to the model and appeared to be busy with paper work while the model performed. The positive or negative reactions to the model's performance were expressed only after the model had completed the game and when the adult paid particular attention to the end product, that is, the position of pieces. It was assumed that the reward and punishment would generalize to the whole sequence of behavior. It is probable, however, that when the adult administered his criticism or approval a contingency was established between response consequences and the position of pieces at the end—a contingency not established with respect to behavior occurring earlier in the sequence. With respect to this interpretation, it is notable that the only suggestion that the response-consequences effects were enhanced by perceived similarity was found in the analysis of the position replication scores (imitation of the position of pieces at the end of the game).

The fact that perceived similarity affects imitative learning (as well as performance) is clearer than the manner in which this effect occurs. One possibility is that attentiveness to the model is increased by high perceived similarity and thus facilitates learning of the model's responses. Kagan (1967), for example, has recently reported that more attention is given to models who possess personality attributes that are similar to the subject than to models who are not similar to the subject. Kagan has suggested that similar models elicit greater attentional involvement than dissimilar models because the condition of similarity violates the commonly held expectancy that one does *not* share basic personality traits with most of the strangers that one meets.

It should be noted that perceived similarity may not have been the only factor underlying the effects obtained in the present study. The induction of similarity in some subjects and dissimilarity in others may have generated contrasting positive and negative feelings toward the model. It is possible, then, that differences in perceived similarity combined with different attitudes toward the model to produce the findings reported.

The present study, however, helps to demonstrate the role of perceived similarity as a determinant of imitation. In particular, the study clarifies the effects of similarity as induced by reference to interests, abilities, and group membership toward which attitudes are generally positive. Perceived similarity in negative or socially disapproved characteristics may affect imitation in quite different ways from similarity in positively valued characteristics. Therefore, future research should concern effects on imitation of perceived similarity in negative as well as positive characteristics.

26. A COMPARATIVE TEST OF THE STATUS ENVY, SOCIAL POWER, AND SECONDARY REINFORCEMENT THEORIES OF IDENTIFICATORY LEARNING

Albert Bandura, Dorothea Ross, & Sheila A. Ross

The literature on social development contains three interesting and contrasting theories of imitation and identificatory learning: status envy, secondary reinforcement, and power. The *status envy* theory argues that a child will imitate, in fantasy or overtly, the behaviors of an envied model who is perceived as controlling the attainment of such resources as affection, attention, food, and care, more capably than he does. The *secondary reinforcement* theory has been described in conjunction with papers in Chapter 4. It assumes that the behaviors of a rewarding model, that is, one who provides gratification of needs, acquire secondary reinforcing properties through repeated association with rewards. Imitating behaviors that have thus become positively valenced is a way of administering rewards to oneself. The *power* theory explains it is the model with influence, the model who is seen to control the behaviors of others by dispensation of rewards who is most imitated. His attractiveness is enhanced further by continued association with rewards.

Bandura, Ross, and Ross, in this important contribution, compare the efficacy of these three theories for predicting which model will be imitated. Three-person groups, representing prototypes of the nuclear family, were employed in which one person was an adult controller who dispensed a collection of fabulous toys, another an adult consumer to whom the con-

SOURCE. Adapted and abridged from Albert Bandura, Dorothea Ross, and Sheila A. Ross, "A Comparative Test of the Status Envy, Social Power, and Secondary Reinforcement Theories of Identificatory Learning," *Journal of Personality and Social Psychology*, 1963, Vol. 67, pp. 527–534. (With permission of the authors and the publisher, the American Psychological Association.)

troller freely gave toys, praise, and attention, and the third was a child-subject who observed the transactions but was not an active participant. In a second treatment-condition the second adult was ignored and the child was the recipient or consumer of the rewards. In the experimental tasks that followed, the adults performed uniquely distinctive behaviors that could be separately imitated by the child when he, too, performed the tasks. The *status envy theory* predicts that the child would adopt the behaviors of the adult consumer with whom he unsuccessfully competes for the toys; the *power theory* predicts the child would imitate the role of the controller or dispenser of toys; and the *secondary reinforcement theory* predicts imitation of the adult who dispensed rewards directly to him.

The power theory was unequivocally supported, although the authors emphasize the importance of contextual manipulations in altering these relationships. Power exerted through negative reinforcement, and changes in the roles of the model as related to the sex of the observer have quite different effects on imitation. Power as represented in the role of the controller, may also influence imitation as much through status envy as through exertion of influence. These conceptual distinctions provide a fruitful area for further research.

In the experiment reported in this paper predictions were derived from three of the more prominent theories of learning by identification, and tested in three-person groups representing prototypes of the nuclear family. In one condition of the experiment an adult assumed the role of controller of resources and positive reinforcers. Another adult was the consumer or recipient of these resources, while the child, a participant observer in the triad, was essentially ignored. In a second treatment condition, one adult controlled the resources; the child, however, was the recipient of the positive reinforcers and the other adult was assigned a subordinate and powerless role. An adult male and female served as models in each of the triads. For half the boys and girls in each condition the male model controlled and dispensed the rewarding resources, simulating the husband dominant family; for the remaining children, the female model mediated the positive resources as in the wife dominant home. Following the experimental social interactions the two adult models exhibited divergent patterns of behavior in the presence of the child, and a measure was obtained of the degree to which the child subsequently patterned his behavior after that of the models.

According to the *status envy theory* of identification recently proposed by Whiting (1959, 1960), where a child competes unsuccessfully with an adult for affection, attention, food, and care, the child will envy the consumer adult and consequently identify with him. Whiting regards any forms of reward, material and social, as valued resources around which rivalry may develop. The status envy theory thus predicts that the highest degree of imitation by the child will occur in the experimental condition in which the rivalrous adult consumes the resources desired by the child, with the consumer adult serving as the primary object of imitation.

In contrast to the envy theory, other writers (Maccoby, 1959; Mussen & Distler, 1959; Parsons, 1955) assume that the controller, rather than the consumer, of resources is the main source of imitative behavior. The *power theory* of social influence has received considerable attention in experimental social psychology, though not generally in the context of identification theories.

Social power is typically defined as the ability of a person to influence the behavior of others by controlling or mediating their positive and negative reinforcements. The use of threat or coercion, in which the controller derives power from his ability to administer punishments, not only develops avoidance behavior toward the controller but also decreases his attractiveness and hence his effectiveness in altering the behavior of others beyond the immediate social influence setting (French, Morrison, & Levinger, 1960; Zipf, 1960). The use of reward power, in contrast, both fosters approach responses toward the power figure and increases his attractiveness or secondary reward value through the repeated association of his attributes with positive reinforcement. Attractiveness is assumed to extend the controller's power over a wide range of behavior (French & Raven, 1959).

In the present investigation power based upon the ability to dispense rewards was manipulated experimentally. In accordance with the social power theory of identification, but contrasting with the status envy hypothesis, one would predict that children will reproduce more of the behavior of the adult who controls positive reinforcers, than that of the powerless adult model, and that power inversions on the part of the male and female models will produce cross-sex imitation.

The *secondary reinforcement theory* of identification, which has been alluded to in the discussion of social power through attractiveness, has been elaborated in greatest detail by Mowrer (1950, 1958). According to this view, as a model mediates the child's biological and social rewards, the behavioral attributes of the model are paired repeatedly with positive reinforcement and thus acquire secondary reward value. On the basis of stimulus generalization, responses which match those of the model attain reinforcing value for the child in proportion to their similarity to those made by the model. Consequently, the child can administer positively conditioned reinforcers to himself simply by reproducing as closely as possible the model's positively valenced behavior. This theory predicts that the experimental condition in which the child was the recipient of positive reinforcements will yield the highest imitation scores with the model who dispensed the rewards serving as the primary source of imitative behavior.

METHOD

Subjects

The subjects were 36 boys and 36 girls enrolled in the Stanford University Nursery School. They ranged in age from 33 to 65 months, although the variability was relatively small with most of the ages falling around the mean of 51 months.

An adult male and female served as models in the triads so as to reproduce possible power structures encountered in different types of family constellations. A female experimenter conducted the study for all 72 children.

Design and Procedure

The subjects were assigned randomly to two experimental groups and one control group of 24 subjects each. Half the subjects in each group were males, and half were females.

High rewarding power was induced experimentally through the manipulation of material and social reinforcements, and the use of verbal structuring techniques. While accompanying the child to the experimental room, for example, the experimenter informed the child that the adult who assumed the role of controller owned the nursery school "surprise room," as well as a fabulous collection of play materials.

As soon as the experimenter and the child arrived in the experimental room, they sat down at a small table and played with the few Lincoln Logs and two small cars that were provided. A short time later the other adult appeared and announced that the controller also granted her permission to play in the room.

The controller then entered carrying two large toy boxes containing a variety of highly attractive masculine and feminine toys, a colorful juice dispensing fountain, and an ample supply of cookies. As soon as the controller appeared on the scene, the experimenter departed.

For children in the Adult Consumer condition, the adult who assumed the role of consumer requested permission to play with the articles and the controller replied that, since the child appeared to be occupied at his table, the consumer was free to use the play materials. This monopolistic move by the consumer adult left the child stranded at a table with two relatively uninteresting toys.

During the 20-minute play session, the controller was most helpful, supportive, and generous in dispensing social reinforcers in the form of praise, approval, and positive attention to the consumer, who, in turn, commented frequently on the controller's highly attractive resources so as to further enhance the controller's rewarding status. The consumer also verbalized considerable positive affect characteristic of a person experiencing positive reinforcements.

The procedure for the Child Consumer condition was identical with that described above except the child was the recipient of the material rewards and the social reinforcement. During the session the other adult sat at the opposite end of the room engrossed in a book, and was totally ignored by the controller.

For half the boys and girls in each treatment condition the male model controlled and dispensed the resources, simulating the husband dominant family; for the remaining children the female model mediated the positive resources as in the wife dominant home.

At the completion of the social interaction session the controller announced that he had a surprise game in his car that the three of them could play together. The controller then asked the other adult to fetch the experimenter to assist them with the game, and as soon as the adult departed, the controller removed the toys and assembled the imitation task apparatus.

Imitation Task

The imitation task was essentially the same two-choice discrimination problem utilized in an earlier experiment (Bandura & Huston, 1961), except the response repertoires exhibited by the models were considerably extended, and the procedure used in the acquisition trials was somewhat modified.

The discrimination problem was employed simply as a cover task that occupied the children's attention while at the same time permitted observation of the models as they performed divergent patterns of behavior during the discrimination trials in the absence of any set to attend to or learn the responses exhibited by the models.

Before commencing the trials, the controller invited the other participants to join him in selecting a "thinking cap" from hat racks containing two identical sets of four sailor caps, each of which had a different colored feather.

The models then went to the starting point, the child returned to his seat, and the experimenter loaded both boxes with sticker pictures for the models' trials.

During the execution of each trial, each model exhibited a different set of relatively novel verbal and motor responses that were totally irrelevant to the discrimination problem to which the child's attention was directed.

As soon as the experimenter gave the signal for the first trial, the controller remarked, "Forward march" and began marching slowly toward the designated box repeating, "March, march, march." When he reached the box he said, "Sock him," hit the doll aggressively off the box, opened the lid and yelled, "Bingo," as he reached down for the sticker. He then remarked, "Lickit-sticket," as he pressed on the picture sticker with his thumb in the upper-right quadrant of a 24 × 24 inch sheet of plain white paper that hung on the wall immediately behind the boxes. The controller terminated the trial by replacing the doll facing sideways on the container with the comment, "Look in the mirror," and made a final verbal response, "There."

The other model then took her turn and performed a different set of imitative acts but equated with the controller's responses in terms of number, types of response classes represented, structural properties, and interest value.

The two sets of responses were counterbalanced by having the models display each pattern with half the subjects in each of the three groups.

The models performed alternately for four trials. At the conclusion of the fourth trial the controller explained that he had to check some materials in his car and while he and the other model were away the child may take his turns. Before they departed, however, the experimenter administered a picture preference test in which the models were asked to select their preferred picture from six different stickers pasted on a 5 × 8 inch card, after which the child was presented a similar card containing an identical set of stickers and requested to indicate his preference.

At the beginning of each of the blocks of subjects' trials, the experimenter administered the picture preference test and the selection of stickers that matched the models' choices was recorded. In addition, on the eighth trial the models removed their hats and hung them in different locations in the room. If the child removed his hat during the session and placed it along side one or the other of the model's hats, this imitative act was also scored.

At the completion of the imitation phase of the experiment, the children were interviewed by the experimenter in order to determine whom they considered to be the controller of resources, and to assess their model preferences.

Children in the control group had no prior social interaction with the models but participated with them in the imitative learning phase of the study. The experimenter assumed complete charge of the procedures and treated the models as though they were naive subjects. This control group was included primarily to determine the models' relative effectiveness as modeling stimuli. In addition, the models alternated between subjects in the order in which they executed the trials so as to test for the possibility of a primacy or a recency of exposure effect on imitative behavior.

Imitation Scores

The imitation scores were obtained by summing the frequency of occurrence of the postural, verbal, and motor responses described in the preceding section, and the hat, color, and picture preferences that matched the selections of each of the two models.

The children's performances were scored by three raters who observed the experimental sessions through a one-way mirror from an adjoining observation room. In order to provide an estimate of interscorer reliability, the performances of 30% of the children were recorded simultaneously but independently by two observers. The raters were in perfect agreement on 95% of the specific imitative responses that they scored.

RESULTS

The control group data revealed that the two models were equally effective in eliciting imitative responses, the mean values being 17.83 and 20.46 for the male and female model, respectively; nor did the children display differential imitation of same-sex ($M = 22.30$) and opposite-sex ($M = 18.50$) models. Although children in the control group tended to imitate the second model ($M = 22.21$) to a somewhat greater extent than the one who performed first ($M = 16.08$) on each trial, suggesting a recency of exposure effect, the difference was not of statistically significant magnitude ($t = 1.60$).

Table 1 presents the mean imitation scores for children in each of the two

TABLE 1

Mean Number of Imitative Responses Performed by Subgroups of Children in the Experimental Triads

Subjects	Objects of Imitation			
	Male Controller	Female Consumer	Female Controller	Male Consumer
Girls	29.00	9.67	26.00	10.00
Boys	30.17	18.67	22.33	16.17
Total	29.59	14.17	24.17	13.09
	Controller	Ignored	Controller	Ignored
Girls	22.00	16.17	31.84	22.17
Boys	29.17	16.67	26.83	34.50
Total	25.59	16.42	29.34	28.34

experimental triads. A $2 \times 2 \times 2 \times 2$ mixed factorial analysis of variance was computed on these data in which the four factors in the design were sex of child, sex of the model who controlled the resources, adult versus child consumer, and the controller versus the other model as the source of imitative

TABLE 2

Summary of the Analysis of Variance of the Imitation Scores

Source	df	MS	F
Between subjects	47	310.17	
Sex of subjects (A)	1	283.59	<1
Sex of controller model (B)	1	128.34	<1
Adult versus child consumer (C)	1	518.01	1.61
A × B	1	23.01	<1
A × C	1	1.76	<1
B × C	1	742.59	2.31
A × B × C	1	21.10	<1
Error (b)	40	321.49	
Within subjects	48	113.24	
Controller versus other model (D)	1	2,025.84	40.61[c]
A × D	1	297.51	5.96[a]
B × D	1	237.51	4.76[a]
C × D	1	396.09	7.94[b]
A × B × D	1	256.76	5.15[c]
A × C × D	1	19.52	<1
B × C × D	1	23.02	<1
A × B × C × D	1	184.00	3.69
Error (w)	40	49.88	

[a] $p < .05$.
[b] $p < .01$.
[c] $p < .001$.

behavior. As shown in Table 2, the findings of this study clearly support the social power theory of imitation. In both experimental treatments, regardless of whether the rival adult or the children themselves were the recipients of the rewarding resources, the model who possessed rewarding power was imitated to a greater degree than was the rival or the ignored model ($F = 40.61$, $p < .001$). Nor did the condition combining resource ownership with direct reinforcement of the child yield the highest imitation of the model who controlled and dispensed the positive rewards. The latter finding is particularly surprising since an earlier experiment based on two-person groups (Bandura & Huston, 1961), demonstrated that pairing of model with positive reinforcement substantially enhanced the occurrence of imitative behavior. An examination of the remaining significant interaction effects together with the postexperimental interview data suggest a possible explanation for the discrepant results.

The differential in the controller-other model imitation was most pronounced when the male model was the controller of resources ($F = 4.76$, $p < .05$), particularly for boys. In fact, boys who were the recipients of rewarding resources mediated by the female model tended to favor the ignored male as their object of imitation. In the postexperiment interview a number of boys in this condition spontaneously expressed sympathy for the ignored male and mild criticism of the controller for not being more charitable with her bountiful resources.

As a partial check on whether this factor would tend to diminish the differential imitation of the two models, six children—three boys and three girls—participated in a modified Child Consumer treatment in which, halfway through the social interaction session, the ignored adult was informed that he too may have access to the playthings. He replied that he was quite content to read his book. This modified procedure, which removed the rivalry and the exclusion of the model, yielded four times as much imitation of the controller relative to the model who was ignored by choice.

The significant triple interaction effect indicates that the differential in the controller-other model imitation was greatest when the same-sex model mediated the positive reinforcers, and this effect was more pronounced for boys than for girls.

The data presented so far demonstrate that manipulation of rewarding power had produced differential imitation of the behavior exhibited by the two models. In order to assess whether the dispensing of positive reinforcers in the prior social interaction influenced the overall level of matching responses, the imitation scores in each of the three groups were summed across models and analyzed using a Sex $\times$ Treatment design.

The mean total imitative responses for children in the Child Consumer, Adult Consumer, and the Control group were 50.21, 40.58, and 37.88, respectively. Analysis of variance of these data reveals a significant treatment effect ($F = 3.37$, $.025 < p < .05$). Further comparisons of pairs of means by the t test, show that children in the child rewarded condition displayed significantly more imitative behavior than did children both in the Adult Consumer treatment ($t = 2.19$, $p < .05$), and those in the Control group ($t = 2.48$, $p < .02$). The Adult Consumer and Control groups, however, did not differ from each other in this respect ($t = .54$).

The model preference patterns were identical for children in the two experimental conditions and consequently, the data were combined for the statistical analysis. Of the 48 children, 32 selected the model who possessed rewarding power as the more attractive, while 16 preferred the noncontrolling adult. The greater attractiveness of the rewarding model was significant beyond the .05 level ($\chi^2 = 5.34$). The experimental triad in which boys were the recipients of positive reinforcers while the male model was ignored, and the female consumer-girl ignored subgroup, contributed the highest preference for the noncontrolling adult.

In addition to the experimental groups discussed in the preceding section, data are available for 9 children in the Adult Consumer condition, and for 11 children in the Child Consumer treatment who revealed, in their post-experiment interviews, that they had actually attributed rewarding power to the ignored or the consumer adult despite the elaborate experimental manipulations designed to establish differential power status. A number of these children were firmly convinced that only a male can possess resources and, therefore, the female dispensing the rewards was only an intermediary for the male model.

DISCUSSION

To the extent that the imitative behavior elicited in the present experiment may be considered an elementary prototype of identification within a nuclear family group, the data fail to support the interpretation of identificatory learning as the outcome of a rivalrous interaction between the child and the adult who occupies an envied status in respect to the consumption of highly desired resources. Children clearly identified with the source of rewarding power rather than with the competitor for these rewards. Moreover, power inversions on the part of the male and female models produced cross-sex imitation, particularly in girls. The differential readiness of boys and girls to imitate behavior exhibited by an opposite-sex model are consistent with findings reported by Brown (1956, 1958) that boys show a decided preference for the masculine role, whereas, ambivalence and masculine role preference are widespread among girls. These findings probably reflect both the differential cultural tolerance for cross-sex behavior displayed by males and females, and the privileged status and relatively greater positive reinforcement of masculine role behavior in our society.

Failure to develop sex appropriate behavior has received considerable attention in the clinical literature and has customarily been assumed to be established and maintained by psychosexual threat and anxiety reducing mechanisms. Our findings strongly suggest, however, that external social learning variables, such as the distribution of rewarding power within the family constellation, may be highly influential in the formation of inverted sex role behavior.

Theories of identificatory learning have generally assumed that within the family setting the child's initial identification is confined to his mother, and that during early childhood boys must turn from the mother as the primary model to the father as the main source of imitative behavior. However, throughout the course of development children are provided with ample opportunities to observe the behavior of both parents. The results of the present experiment reveal that when children are exposed to multiple models they may select one or more of them as the primary source of behavior, but rarely reproduce all the elements of a single model's repertoire or confine their imitation to that model. Although the children adopted many of the characteristics of the model who possessed rewarding power, they also reproduced some of the elements of behavior exhibited by the model who occupied the subordinate role. Consequently, the children were not simply junior-size replicas of one or the other model; rather, they exhibited a relatively novel pattern of behavior representing an amalgam of elements from both models. Moreover, the specific admixture of behavioral elements varied from child to child. These findings provide considerable evidence for the seemingly paradoxical conclusion that imitation can in fact produce innovation of social behavior, and that within the same family even same-sex siblings may exhibit quite different response patterns, owing to their having selected for imitation different elements of their parents' response repertoires.

27. CONFORMITY AS A FUNCTION OF AGE LEVEL

Philip R. Costanzo & Marvin E. Shaw

The relationship of chronological age to various aspects of children's behavior has been a popular subject for psychological research from considerably before the turn of the present century. Such studies are often concerned with tracing developmental changes with increasing age and with the endeavor to provide descriptive age-based norms. Results have been of considerable aid to teachers both in helping them to anticipate the behavior that can normally be expected of children in any given grade and in building appropriate curricula and extra-class activities. Such studies have had a further value in either confirming or calling into question popularly expected attributes and motivations of specific age groups. One caution, however, that teachers who read such research should bear in mind is that within any age range there is considerable variation, and results can only be expressed as tendencies or mean trends within the curve of normal distribution. For that reason findings cited in terms of immediately adjoining age groupings can not be regarded as definitive as they would be if two or more years separated the age groups being compared. A further caution in applying findings has to do with special attributes that may be possessed by sub-cultural or regional groups, attributes that may make them distinctly different as compared to the general cultural pattern.

In the present study Costanzo and Shaw have confirmed the hypothesis, with which they entered their study, that conformity increases until adolescence and decreases thereafter. Specifically, the results of their study

SOURCE. Adapted from Philip R. Costanzo and Marvin E. Shaw, "Conformity as a Function of Age Level," *Child Development*, 1966, Vol. 37, pp. 967–975. (With permission of the authors and the publisher, The Society for Research in Child Development.)

indicate that, with the sample used, conformity to pressure from peers is a nonlinear function of age. Subjects in the study were subjected to erroneous judgments in a simulated conformity situation. The design of the study included both sexes and four nonadjoining age groups. In generalizing from the results of the study the reader should remember that only 96 subjects were included and that these came principally from a laboratory school at the University of Florida. However, there is other research confirmation of the Costanzo and Shaw hypothesis which was originally derived from previous work accomplished by Piaget.

It is generally assumed that conformity behavior is the result of developmental processes (Berg & Bass, 1961). However, the nature and consequences of these developmental processes have not been fully explored, and the theories concerning the relation between ontogenetic level and conformity are often in disagreement. The stimulus for the present study is derived from the work of Piaget (1954). He proposed that social development progresses through an orderly sequence of stages. Implicit in his analysis of the way the child learns the "rules of the game" is the hypothesis that the relation between age and conformity to rules (norms) is curvilinear. That is, at an early age the child is uninfluenced by rules but gradually begins to follow them until at about age 11–12 the rules are internalized and utilized completely. After this stage, the individual begins to express individual modes of response by creating and codifying certain of his own rules. Since conformity is the act of behaving in accordance with social rules or norms, it follows that conformity behavior should increase with increasing age until the child reaches the stage at which rules are internalized, and decrease thereafter.

METHOD

Subjects

The subjects were 72 students from the P. K. Yonge Laboratory School at the University of Florida and 24 undergraduates at the same university. The admissions policies at the laboratory school virtually insure that subjects in different age groups are similar with respect to general intelligence and socioeconomic level. Half of the subjects were male and half were female.

Experimental Design

A 2 × 4 factorial design was utilized, involving sex and four age groups. Twenty-four subjects, 12 male and 12 female, were assigned to each age group. Group I subjects ranged in age from 7 to 9 years; Group II subjects ranged from 11 to 13 years; Group III subjects ranged from 15 to 17 years; and Group IV subjects ranged from 19 to 21 years.

Materials and Apparatus

The apparatus used was similar to that described by Crutchfield (1955). It consisted of five booths arranged in a semicircle. The center booth was occupied by the experimenter (E). It contained a Besseler opaque projector for projecting the stimuli on a screen in front of the booths, and master panels of lights and switches. The subjects (Ss) occupied the four side booths and faced the projection screen which was approximately 10 feet from each booth.

Each subject booth contained a panel of twenty lights arranged in four rows of five lights each, with five mercury switches placed below the fourth row of lights. Each of these switches, when turned on, activated the light immediately above it in the fourth row and a corresponding light on the master response panel in E's booth. The lights in the other three rows on the S's panel were controlled by master switches in E's booth, although the procedure was such that each S believed these lights reflected the responses of other Ss. In the present experiment, only three of the five lights in each row were utilized.

The stimulus materials were patterned after those used by Asch (1958). Twelve stimulus cards were prepared, each containing three comparison lines and a standard line. One of the three comparison lines was the same length as the standard, one was $1/4$-inch shorter than the standard, and the third was $1/4$-inch longer than the standard. The S's task was to choose the line which matched the standard in length.

Procedure

The experimental sessions were conducted in a room located at the school from which the Ss were drawn. Four Ss, all from a given age group and of the same sex, were run in each experimental session. The order in which the groups were run was random within the limits imposed by scheduling difficulties.

When Ss reported at the scheduled time, they were asked to select one of the four subject booths and be seated. The nature of the task and the manner of responding were explained in detail. The Ss were told that the order of responding would be random and that each S was to respond when E called out the number in his cubicle. Talking was prohibited. After the general instructions were given, E went to each booth and answered any questions that Ss posed concerning procedure. At this time, each person was assigned the number "4." When E was sure that everyone understood the instructions, five practice trials were administered to insure that Ss understood and were able to perform the task. Following the practice trials, each stimulus card was presented twice in a predetermined order. Erroneous responses were signaled by E for Ss 1, 2, and 3 on 16 of the 24 trials. The conformity score for each E was the number of times his response agreed with the erroneous responses on these 16 critical trials. Therefore, the score for any given subject could range from zero to 16.

At the end of the experimental session, each S was asked the following question: "Did you find that some of your answers were different from the others, and if so, what do you think the reason for this was?"

RESULTS

The results of pressure on conformity behavior under the various experimental conditions are presented graphically in Figure 1. The only significant effect was that produced by the age variable ($p < .001$). As can be seen in Figure 1, conformity was least for Group I (ages 7–9), increased to a maximum for Group II (ages 11–13), and decreased again for Group III (ages 15–17) and Group IV (ages 19–21). Females conformed more than males at all age levels, although differences were not statistically significant.

It is perhaps worth noting that conformity as a function of age was also examined for each age level. The pattern of conformity was essentially the same as that shown in Figure 1, although the curve was not as smooth. Maximum conformity occurred at age 12.

The responses to the postexperimental question indicated that all Ss perceived some discrepancy between their responses and those of the other Ss in the group. The reason given for these discrepancies were classified as either "internal" (that is, self-attributed reasons) or "external" (that is, other-attributed reasons). For example, "I must be going blind; I was wrong most

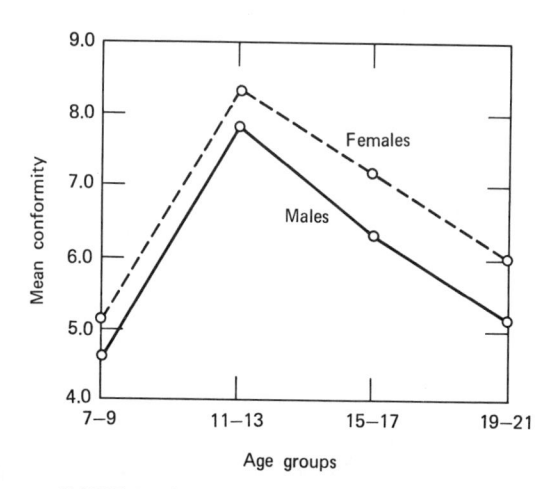

FIGURE 1. Mean conformity as a function of age.

of the time"; was classified as internal, whereas "I think the other guys were crazy" was classified as external. These classifications were made by four graduate students in psychology who showed 100 per cent agreement. Since the two classes are reciprocally related, only the internally attributing responses were considered: The 7–9 age group gave 6 internally attributing responses, the 11–13 age group gave 17, the 15–17 age group gave 13, and the 19–21 age group gave 11. The distributions of internal-external responses among age groups differed significantly ($\chi^2 = 10.44$, $p < .02$). This pattern corresponds closely to the pattern of conformity behavior suggesting that Ss who blame themselves when their behavior is discrepant from that of their peers are more likely to conform to group pressure than Ss who place the blame on others.

In order to test this suggestion more directly, a biserial r was computed between conformity and internal-external classification of subjects. This showed a highly significant relation ($r_b = .87$, $p < .01$). To clarify further the relations among age, blame attribution, and conformity, an index of correlation was computed between age and conformity. This yielded a value of .57 ($p < .01$), thus further supporting the results from the analysis of variance. The results indicate, therefore, that both the tendency to blame one's self and the tendency to conform to peers increase with age during the preadolescent period and decrease thereafter—at least through early adulthood.

DISCUSSION

The results of this study lend decisive support to the hypothesis that conformity to pressure from peers is a nonlinear function of age. The developmental function (see Fig. 1) representing the mean number of conforming responses in each of the composite age groups supports the hypothesis that, from the preadolescent to the adolescent period of development, the amount of conformity to external social pressure increases, whereas conformity decreases after adolescence and through early adulthood.

Essentially, it appears that the development of conforming behavior patterns runs parallel with the socialization process. That is, the child in his early development is probably not fully aware of the social pressure to conform to certain standards adopted by his peers. Thus the effect of a unanimously wrong majority is not extremely threatening to the younger child, and hence the lower percentage of conformity in the 7–9 age group in this experiment. On the other hand, with the onset of pubescence, the child becomes acutely aware of his social peers and relies upon them for many of his external behavior patterns (that is, ways of dress, "code" between buddies, clubs, "gang age," etc.). Therefore, the child at the pubescent stage displays much uncertainty with his own judgments and mirrors the behavior of his peers. By the postadolescent and early adulthood stages, the individual has learned that there are both situations which call for conformity and those which call for individual action. Thus, he becomes more confident about his own judgments despite the disagreement of a unanimous majority. However, since the individual in this postadolescent and young adult stage has experienced socialization, and since he has at some earlier time experienced the penalties of nonconformity, he does not attain the degree of individuality of judgment that is evident in the presocialization stage.

28. EFFECTS OF COMMITMENT TO SOCIAL ISOLATION ON CHILDREN'S IMITATIVE BEHAVIOR

Ralph Epstein

Various theories have been advanced not only to account for personal behavior in social situations, but also to make possible probabilistic statements about an individual's future behavior when he is confronted by certain specified conditions. Some of the theories are directly aimed at interpersonal transactions while others are more general in nature and have been extended by persons other than their original propounders to explain aspects of specific personal interactions. All of these theories possess heuristic value and, if they are well conceived, suggest research possibilities. For educators, however, such theories together with related research are of possible applicational use in their teaching and guidance functions. The article by Epstein presented below represents a theory-based research study that has applicational transfer value for those who work with children. Of particular interest are the manipulation and reinforcement techniques used in gathering data.

In his study Epstein endeavored to confirm aspects of Festinger's (1957) theory of cognitive dissonance as it relates to children's imitative behavior in a social isolation situation. The theory predicts that, following social isolation, commitment to further deprivation as a result of choice results in dissonance, but that the dissonance may be lessened by decreased social motivation as evidenced by poor conditioning to social approval. Epstein's research confirms the theory's prediction, although greater differences

SOURCE. Adapted from Ralph Epstein, "Effects of Commitment to Social Isolation on Children's Imitative Behavior," *Journal of Personality and Social Psychology*, 1968, Vol. 9, pp. 90–95. (With permission of the author and the publisher, The American Psychological Association.)

between high and low approval-need children might have been expected than Epstein found to be the case with his subjects. Epstein notes in his discussion, ". . . when a person voluntarily chooses to commit himself to behavior which has negative consequences for the satisfaction of a relevant motive, the resulting inconsistency may be attenuated by reducing the strength of that motive." Teachers should consider the implications of this statement for conflicts between peer-group and school objectives.

It is generally recognized that social reinforcement constitutes a major means for effecting behavioral change in children (Stevenson, 1965). For this reason, considerable research has focused on a significant antecedent of social reinforcement effectiveness, namely, the availability of social reinforcers. Although the results of this research have been somewhat inconsistent, the facilitative effects of social isolation upon the effectiveness of social approval have been demonstrated (Erickson, 1962; Gewirtz & Baer, 1958a, 1958b; Walters & Ray, 1960). A major limitation of this research is suggested by Zimbardo's (1966) observation that most studies of human motivation are based on a "cognitionless" model of man which fails to consider the individual's cognitions regarding situations of deprivation or aversive stimulation. A consideration of cognitive variables in motivation leads to a reevaluation of the traditional assumption that instrumental and consummatory behaviors are directly related to the magnitude of deprivation or to the physical intensity of drive-arousing stimuli. Thus, the goal of this study was to ascertain the conditions under which isolation relates to social responsiveness by focusing on those cognitive, mediational variables which influence the child's perception of the experimental situation.

The nature of these variables is suggested by Festinger's (1957) theory of cognitive dissonance. It is assumed that dissonance results from obverse cognitions; that is, the belief that one is motivated to obtain social reinforcement due to earlier isolation is inconsistent with the cognition that one is committed to further deprivation. A major means for reducing this dissonance is by reducing the strength of the motive for social reinforcement so that deprivation is made more consistent with the commitment behavior. This reduction should result in a decrement in those instrumental behaviors, for example, conditioning, which are associated with the social motive. Dissonance theory also assumes that the greater the proportion of cognitions inconsistent with commitment, the greater the dissonance and consequent effects on the social motive and the instrumental behaviors related to that motive. One relevant cognition might be subjects' need for approval; that is, commitment to further isolation should produce more dissonance and subsequent dissonance-reducing behavior for high than low need for approval children. These theoretical formulations suggest the hypotheses that subsequent to social isolation: (a) high-dissonant subjects (those who have committed themselves to further isolation) should reduce their motivation for social reinforcement and, therefore, condition less than low-dissonant subjects; and (b) these effects should be more marked among high than low need for approval children.

METHOD

Subjects

The initial sample consisted of 60 girls who comprised the third and fourth grades at a Detroit elementary school. This school serves children whose socioeconomic background, as determined by residential area, is predominantly low middle class.

Measure of Need for Social Approval

Need for social approval was inferred from Crandall, Crandall, and Katkovsky's (1965) Children's Social Desirability (*CSD*) Questionnaire, a scale adapted from the Marlowe-Crowne Social Desirability scale (Crowne & Marlowe, 1960). The direct-question form of the *CSD* presents the child with 47 yes-no items which can only be answered in a socially desirable way by dissembling. Some items ask the child if he always behaves in some particular fashion which is normatively prescribed, whereas other items ask whether he engages in disapproved acts. The score refers to the total number of items on which the child maintains that he has an undeviating socially desirable attitude. The split-half reliability of this scale, corrected by the Spearman-Brown prophecy formula, ranges from .82 to .95, and the test-retest reliability for a 1-month period is .90. It is apparent that highly satisfactory reliability has been demonstrated.

Experimental Design

The *CSD* scale was group administered to 60 children. The 20 highest and 20 lowest scorers were assigned to four experimental conditions based on a 2×2 factorial design: need for approval, high versus low, and choice for further deprivation: high versus low. Thus, 10 subjects were employed in each of the experimental conditions. The dependent variable consisted of the degree of imitative learning resulting from a schedule of consistent reinforcement administered subsequent to the choice condition. The dissonance and reinforcement procedures were administered by a female experimenter.

Behavioral Situation

A behavioral task was employed which enabled (a) the subject to imitate the experimenter's judgments of the relative loudness of paired pure tones,

(b) the experimenter to reinforce imitative responses with social approval, for example, "fine," "good." The subject's attention was focused on two metal response panels. One panel faced the subject and the other faced the experimenter. Each panel contained two response keys marked 1 or 2 and two electric bulbs, blue and red. Subjects were told that the purpose of the study was to determine how well children and adults distinguish the relative loudness of tape-recorded pairs of pure tones. Subjects were told to press Key Number 1 if the first member of a pair of sounds appeared louder than the second and to press Key Number 2 if the second seemed louder. The subject observed that Keys 1 and 2 lit up the blue and red bulbs on the experimenter's panel, thereby enabling her to record the subject's judgments. The subject then observed how the blue and red bulbs on her panel could be similarly activated by the keys on the experimenter's panel. In order to insure the experimenter's role as a model for imitation, a rigged coin toss was used prior to the operant phase to insure that the experimenter would have the first turn. Since discriminable differences between judged sounds might limit imitative learning, each pair of sounds consisted of identical pure tones. In order to avoid monotony, the loudness of paired sounds was varied on every fourth trial. Furthermore, the experimenter's choice of the "louder" sound was determined randomly prior to the experiment, and this random order was maintained for all subjects.

Operant Level

An operant series consisting of one block of 12 trials was administered to the subjects. Each trial required the subject to communicate her judgments regarding the relative loudness of two successive sounds. During this period, the experimenter pressed Key 1 or 2 on a random basis. Subjects' imitative and nonimitative responses were recorded by the experimenter without contingent reinforcement.

Manipulation of Deprivation

Subsequent to the operant period, the experimenter adjusted a fraudulent control panel so that the subject would assume erroneously that (a) the correctness of her auditory judgments could be evaluated electronically by the control panel, and (b) this evaluation would be communicated by the panel to the experimenter via a flashing white light located on the experimenter's response panel. The experimenter indicated that the subject would be informed of the correctness of her responses in a suitable manner. These instructions provided the experimenter with a basis for reinforcing the subject's imitative responses. Unknown to the subject, the white light on the experimenter's panel was controlled by a hidden calibrated variable resistor.

In order to induce social isolation, the experimenter pointed out that the white light was malfunctioning, and this problem required the experimenter's absence so that she could obtain the appropriate equipment for fixing the light. In this manner, subjects were deprived of her presence for 15 minutes. Since social deprivation effects may be confounded by sensory deprivation (Hill & Stevenson, 1964), an attempt to minimize sensory deprivation was made by providing subjects with simple, interesting games during the isolation period.

Manipulation of Dissonance

At the end of the 15-minute period of deprivation, the experimenter returned to the subject and informed her that there would be an additional delay. For the high-dissonance group, the experimenter stated, "You have been patient. However, I have to leave for another few minutes. You may continue to remain here until I return or you may go back to your class if you wish. The choice is up to you." For the low-dissonance group, the experimenter interpolated, "Please remain here until I come back. Don't return to your class," after the sentence, "However, I have to leave for another few minutes."

Reinforcement

The experimenter returned to the experimental room about 2 minutes after the dissonance-inducing instructions. Thus, all subjects were isolated for a period of 17 minutes. The experimenter then gave the impression of repairing the white light on the panel. After announcing that this light was repaired, the experimenter briefly repeated the instructions relevant to communicating auditory judgments via lever pressing. The experimenter administered five reinforcement blocks (60 trials) in which subjects' imitative judgments were rewarded with social approval. In order to convince the subject that the correctness of her judgments was communicated to the experimenter via the control panel, the subject was permitted to observe the white light for two blocks of trials. Effectiveness of reinforcement was measured by the difference in frequency of imitative responses between the operant and fifth reinforcement blocks.

Postexperimental Questionnaire

In order to facilitate frank self-reports, the following measures were administered by an experimenter other than one who had administered the previous procedures. The effectiveness of the dissonance-inducing procedure was evaluated by requesting subjects to respond to, "Did you have any choice regarding remaining in the room?" by circling yes or no alternatives. Since the reduction of dissonance might involve the subjective distortion of the duration of social isolation, subjects rated the amount of time spent alone on a 6-point scale ranging from 5 to 30 minutes. Dissonance might also be reduced by attributing specific attitudes to the experimenter. Thus, subjects rated the experimenter on the following 5-point bipolar semantic differential scales: kind-unkind, good-bad, fair-unfair, pleasant-unpleasant, friendly-unfriendly. Also, subjects rated their own feelings during isolation on the following dimensions: calm versus nervous, afraid versus unafraid, bad versus good. Finally subjects rated their preference for social approval on a 4-point scale ranging from "not at all" to "very much."

DISCUSSION

The results support the hypothesis that, subsequent to a period of social isolation, commitment to further isolation reduces a child's motivation for social reinforcement. This commitment is inferred from the child's acceptance of a choice for further isolation and affects conditionability to social approval. Thus, statements regarding the effects of isolation upon children's responsiveness to social influence are likely to be unreliable unless the child's awareness of his voluntary commitment to isolation is taken into account.

Although the postexperimental choice scale indicated that differential levels of volition were successfully induced, the effectiveness of this procedure may be questioned insofar as no subjects dropped out of the study. A number of situational variables may have mitigated against a self-selection process. The novelty, interest value of the experiment, and the status of having been selected as a subject were probably more rewarding than returning to the mundane activities of the classroom. Another significant empirical issue with reference to the choice variable is that the results on the postexperimental choice scale may reflect the veridicality of subjects' perceptions of the choice manipulation rather than the effectiveness of the desired effects of the manipulation, dissonance arousal. This issue suggests the necessity for developing more refined and direct evaluations of the purported effects of inconsistency by utilizing phenomenological or physiological measures (Singer, 1966). The possibility that such evaluations may contribute to further theoretical exploration of the role of choice in dissonance research is indicated by subjects' postexperimental ratings of their affect. Whereas high need for approval subjects reported somewhat more negative affect than lows under the high-choice condition, low need for approval subjects reported significantly more negative affect under low-choice conditions. Insofar as the latter subjects may have a stronger need and preference for autonomy (Crandall, 1966), their functioning in a situation providing minimal independence or choice probably aroused discomfort. These findings suggest a major oversimplification in dissonance research (Zimbardo, 1966), which fails to consider that, for certain subjects, no choice may lead to more discomfort than choice itself.

The clear results with reference to the choice variable should not becloud the theoretical complexities of the volitional variable. For example, insofar as high and low choice may have been associated with a permissive and authoritarian atmosphere, respectively, the greater conditioning in the latter condition may have resulted from subjects' view of the experimenter as preferring compliant behavior. This sensitivity regarding conforming to the experimenter's demands may be related to the experimental instructions which implied that the subject's judgments would be compared with those of an adult. Although this formulation cannot be ruled out entirely, its implausibility is indicated by the fact that high-choice subjects appeared more compliant or conditionable than low-choice subjects in the early reinforcement blocks (see Table 1).

TABLE 1

Mean Frequency of Imitative Responses for Operant (Block 1) and Conditioning Trials[a]

Experimental Groups	I	II	III	IV	V	VI
High need for approval						
Deprivation—High choice	7.5	9.2	9.2	9.1	9.6	9.6
	(2.55)	(1.75)	(1.07)	(1.58)	(1.56)	(1.11)
Deprivation—Low choice	7.0	9.2	8.7	9.4	9.8	10.7
	(1.67)	(1.47)	(2.24)	(1.85)	(1.83)	(1.61)
Low need for approval						
Deprivation—High choice	7.2	8.8	9.5	9.5	9.9	9.5
	(2.32)	(1.40)	(2.25)	(1.43)	(1.30)	(1.36)
Deprivation—Low choice	6.6	8.5	9.2	9.9	9.2	10.3
	(2.34)	(2.25)	(1.40)	(2.26)	(2.04)	(1.36)

[a] Standard deviations are enclosed in parentheses.

Another formulation of these findings could be derived from the internal-external control dimension (Rotter, 1966). It is conceivable that low choice may have induced a feeling that one is not causally related to the environment (external control), whereas high choice may have led to the belief that events are contingent on one's behavior. Insofar as externality may be manifested by a passive, submissive orientation to one's environment, greater conditionability would occur in the low-choice condition. These speculative statements point to the need for future study of those correlates of high, low choice which may account for the effects of this volitional variable.

The results of this study support the assumption that when a person voluntarily chooses to commit himself to behavior which has negative consequences for the satisfaction of a relevant motive, the resulting inconsistency may be attenuated by reducing the strength of that motive. However, these results raise a number of interesting theoretical questions regarding the motivational substrate of consistency striving behavior. For example, it is possible that the decreased social responsiveness resulting from the choice condition may have resulted from a denial or suppression of a motive for reinforcement rather than a basic reduction in the motive itself. Clarification of this issue may be achieved by eliciting fantasy responses to projective stimuli which vary in terms of their relevance to reinforcement motivation. The role of denial would be implicated by significantly more drive-related responses to the neutral than drive-related stimuli. Furthermore, further research would be desirable in evaluating the generalizability of current knowledge of motivational processes such as drive states to dissonance phenomena. Thus, the relevance of the "drive" construct to conceptualizing consistency striving behavior may be tested by determining whether the presence of irrelevant drives (e.g., hunger or anxiety) contributes to (a) the level of arousal stemming from commitment to further deprivation, and (b) the subsequent intensification of dissonance-reducing behavior.

The negative findings regarding need for approval suggest that this motive may not be manifested in approval-seeking behavior due to its association with avoidant tendencies resulting from a low expectancy for approval. The role of these avoidant, defensive tendencies is implicated by the finding that high need for approval subjects reported a weaker preference for the experimenter's approval than low need for approval subjects. This formulation is consistent with Crandall's (1966) report that high-*CSD* girls were withdrawn, unable to seek affection or help, and unsociable.

CHAPTER 6

Role-Playing, Role-Taking, and Role-Commitments

Man as compared to other living organisms has many gifts, but chief of these is an evolved neurological apparatus enabling him to think and to express his thoughts in a complex spoken language. This ability makes it possible for him in his thoughts and in his written records to transcend the barriers of time and space. No other member of the animal kingdom has this knowledge of the past of his own species, and equally, none has his speculative view of the future. Hence it is not surprising that one of man's great preoccupations across the centuries has been the problem of his own nature, leading to the question, "Who and what am I?" Although this question is of interest to all, any systematic attempt to answer it was for many centuries almost solely the province of theology and philosophy. In the modern era, psychology also assumed the task, bringing to it a new outlook, a new body of related knowledge, and a repertory of research techniques designed to unlock some of the secrets of human behavior. One grouping of psychologists in particular have tried to look at man in terms of his concept of self and have tried to examine the implications of an individual's concept of self for his intrapersonal as well as his social behavior. The six articles reported in this chapter are examples of the kind of research that is presently being accomplished in analyzing the nature of self, its manner of development during ontogenesis, and its exemplifications in everyday behavior. Obviously, the results of such research have substantial implications for an understanding of children's behavior and for dealing with and guiding that behavior in the school context.

The reader should be warned, however, that these are still early days in psychologists' examination of the nature of self and self-engendered behavior. The problem of definition has been particularly difficult and self as a construct still remains largely in the metaphysical domain. Yet, progress is being made, particularly in the area of developmental descriptions and in the area of certain behavioral events that seem to researchers self-manifesting. Among such self-manifesting behaviors are those of the roles that individuals assume in their social transactions. Research efforts are being made not only to describe the various roles that persons assume in specific situations, but also to describe how these roles are learned and how they normatively develop with increasing chronological age. In particular, the family is seen as a source for the learning of many of the roles that persons assume. Sex typing and sex modeling as role-evolving are frequently the focus of research efforts. Most of the studies reported in this chapter deal with the acquirement of sex roles and with the family as a context for role learning. Of course such studies can furnish only a partial and very indirect answer to the prior question, "What is the nature of the self?" But, as was indicated earlier, they look at what may be defined as self-manifesting behavior and hence give us behavioral data that may take us one step further in our attempts to define and analyze the nature and meaning of self.

Long and her associates, relating their work to previous studies accomplished by themselves and others, have investigated developmental changes in self-concept in boys and girls from the sixth through the twelfth grades. For their study they selected seven components of self, ordinarily manifested in relation to significant other persons, and tested these components by the administration of a Self-Social Symbols Tasks Test. The components included (1) self-esteem, as seen by an individual's self-rating in comparison to others; (2) dependency, as measured by a person's perception of himself as a group member as contrasted to his perception of self as a separate entity; (3) power of self, as seen in relation to certain authority figures; (4) centrality, as measured by an individual's focusing of attention upon himself as contrasted to his focus of attention on others; (5) complexity, as measured by differentiation of the self-concept; (6) individuation, as seen by the degree to which an individual differentiates himself from his peers; and (7) personal and group identification, as measured by social distance and social inclusiveness. Findings relate to the relative significance of various other persons in a child's environment, particularly the high position accorded the father in contrast to the teacher or the principal. It was the feeling of the investigators that a continued high position of the father during adolescence is a favorable self-concept sign, whereas a higher position (as compared to the father) for the less closely identified teacher or principal may well indicate a derogation of self. A particularly salient finding had to do with the considerable sex differences to be found in the development of self-patterns and the differences to be expected of boys and girls of the same age in their approaches to interpersonal relationships.

In a study such as that of Long, Ziller, and Henderson, a great deal depends upon the validity and reliability of the measuring instrument used as well as upon the acceptability of the definition of the construct being tested. In this study the instrument is quite ingenious and the reader should be interested in the nature of the tasks used to measure each component. The question of whether the seven components are adequate for a view of the self—or indeed, whether some of the components have any place in a measure of self—is perhaps moot. But, as self-concept studies are presently designed, the one by Long et al. is particularly well conceived and designed.

In contrast to the Long et al. study, which considered largely the self-perception of an individual as he compared himself to others, the study by Bryan and Test deals with the kind of behavior actually exhibited by an individual in a series of situations. In this case the behavior was that of altruism and, as such, is more of the order of an attribute usually included in tests of personality. Self-concept theorists have not as yet really made clear to what extent tests of personality have a place in self-concept research, but altruism, with its combination of selflessness and its reference of self to others, would appear to be a personal style of behavior having implications for an individual's concept of self. Bryan and Test report that even an attribute as closely self-related as altruism is at least partly learned through the influence of a model, and that the presence of a helping model significantly increases subsequent altruistic behaviors. From this study teachers could at least tentatively accept the hypothesis of the importance of their own personal example in their relationships with children as a way of promoting desired behavior in a child. For example, one way of breeding generosity in children is to be generous in one's relationships with them. Obviously, however, generosity is only one factor to be considered in an interpersonal transaction and the Bryan and Test finding can not be considered a panacea completely solving the problem of the inculcation of value-based behavior.

Maccoby's study on role-taking and its consequences for social learning offers general support for the Bryan and Test finding. Maccoby makes the point that a child's acquisition of the repertoire of actions that characterize him as a person come through his covert practice of the actions of significant adults. She warns, however, that not all aspects of adult behavior are acquired equally well through covert role practice and that it must be realized that some acquired behaviors will remain latent until the child perceives a situation in which their use seem to him to be appropriate. For example, if the child perceives a given behavior as specifically characteristic of an adult role, then it will tend to appear in his behavior only when he himself becomes an adult or when he perceives himself as assuming an adult role. Maccoby also points to the importance of the specific social interaction context in which a given behavior might be acquired. For example, if the modeling adult exercises considerable power over the child, then there is a greater probability that the child will covertly rehearse the adult's actions than would be true if the adult were to be perceived by the child as relatively powerless. Further, Maccoby notes that frequency of interaction is a positive element promoting aspects of modeling behavior in the child. Maccoby's discussion was based on child-parent interaction, but it is reasonable to assume that her statements may also be applied to teacher-child interaction. Their implication for school practice is that the teacher would do well not to abdicate her responsible discipline prerogatives in dealing with children. Too frequently social pressures or mistaken ideas of a teacher's role in the learning process have led teachers to assume egalitarian or nonleadership stances entirely out of keeping with their responsibilities in dealing with children. Maccoby's point about frequency of interaction should also be of interest to teachers because it offers support for a more personalized approach in which there is considerable teacher-pupil interaction. Increasing enrollments, particularly at the high school level, have often led to teaching techniques that serve to decrease the frequency of the personalized interactions that a teacher has with her pupils.

There has been considerable discussion in the recent literature about the relative importance of various significant adults in a child's life. There has been a consensus that the most influential adults where a child's social learnings are concerned are his parents, and, of these, the mother is often seen as most important. A number of studies, however, have pointed to the primacy of the father's influence where certain behaviors are concerned and, in particular, to his influence upon his son where sex-role modeling is concerned. Johnson, in her study of sex-role learning in the nuclear family, points to the primacy of the father in sex role learning. It is her position that adequate identification with the father is necessary for girls as well as for boys if adequate sex-role learning is to take place. It would appear that feminine women and masculine men are most likely to identify with their fathers. The reader should, of course, be careful of overgeneralizing on the basis of studies such as Johnson's. Minuchin, in the study reported in this chapter, notes that differing philosophies of child-rearing and education are influential in the formation of sex-role attitudes and reactions. Certainly, all fathers and all mothers do not follow the same child-rearing practices, nor do they offer the same models to their sons and daughters. The culture is changing and certain subsections within the culture are adopting new behaviors and attitudes to the point that many child-rearing generalizations have to be more subcultural provisional than was previously the case. Hence, the question arises as to which subcultural classifications are worthy of consideration in analyzing child-rearing practices and parental modeling behavior. For some time sociological variables such as socioeconomic class position have been considered particularly profitable subcultural variables to include in studying child-rearing practice differences, and they still have a place. However, new dimensions, more psychological in nature, are proving even more effective. In her study using an essentially homogeneous middle-class sample, Minuchin made comparisons of families whose outlook was essentially "traditional" with those whose outlook was essentially "modern." Children from "modern" backgrounds, particularly girls, tend to display less sex-typical reactions than is true of those from "traditional" backgrounds. The "traditional" families tended to produce a greater pattern of male-type aggression in boys and greater family orientation and dependence in girls. Minuchin reports specific differences in the relative influence of the school and of the home, each appearing to have its own area of primacy.

Hetherington, confining her study to boys, considered the influence of the father in sex-typed behavior in relation to the child's stage of development. Her finding is that the father's influence is most important early in a boy's development. Absence of the father from the home after age 5 seems to have little effect on the sex-typed behaviors of boys, but boys who have lost their fathers early, before identification can be assumed to have been completed, show considerable deviation in sex-typed traits. Hetherington's study offers further evidence confirming the existence of critical periods in such psychosocial aspects of behavior as role modeling.

29. DEVELOPMENTAL CHANGES IN THE SELF-CONCEPT DURING ADOLESCENCE

Barbara H. Long, Robert C. Ziller, & Edmund H. Henderson

The study of self and of self-concept has a long history in psychological theory and research extending back to the closing years of the last century. As an area of study the concept of a self has presented many difficulties, not only in definition and theoretical analysis, but also in formulating significant supporting research and in designing instruments and approaches for data collection. Obviously, there have been many disagreements among those interested in self-concept, but at the same time there are some areas in which a general consensus can be found. Among these last is the belief that the period of adolescence is a most crucial time in the development of an individual's self-concept. It is during adolescence that the adolescent tests his self-concept against reality, modifies it, and finally moves toward the realization of a stable and mature self picture.

In the article which follows, Long and her associates have added to our knowledge of the sequence of the development of a self-concept during adolescence. While their data were obtained by cross-sectional rather than longitudinal methods, it appears that the results they report may be taken to indicate what happens to a person's self-concept and his behavioral exemplifications of it as he proceeds through the years of his adolescence. In performing their study the authors have made two assumptions. They are (1) that both contemporaneous and future behavior stem from an individual's self-view of himself in relation to others, and (2) that self-view

SOURCE. Adapted from Barbara H. Long, Robert C. Ziller and Edmund H. Henderson, "Developmental Changes in the Self-Concept during Adolescence," *The School Review*, 1968, Vol. 76, pp. 210–230. (With permission of the authors and the publisher, University of Chicago Press.)

varies as a function of both developmental and environmental change. The authors' findings describe age-related differential perceptions of self-other relations during adolescence. Sex differences and parent-other relationships are considered.

The years of adolescence are a period in which numerous personal and social changes occur. Physically, adult size and secondary sex characteristics are acquired; the individual also attains sexual maturity. Socially, the adolescent gradually advances in status and is exposed to a greater range of social conditions than in childhood (Sherif, 1966). Relationships with peers of both sexes are increasingly an important concern. In transition from the role of a child in the parental family to that of an adult in a new family unit, the adolescent may be thought of as between groups—as a marginal man (Lewin, 1936) with attending problems in self-identity (Erikson, 1959).

In view of these changes and ambiguities in roles with their attendant shifts and uncertainties in social expectancies, it is hypothesized that the adolescent's view of self in relation to others will also change over time in these years. Changes in perception of power and value for the self may accompany changes in size and status. New patterns of identification with parents, teachers, and peers may demand an altered conception of the self and social world.

This study has explored these general hypotheses, making use of a nonverbal method. Previous studies of the self-concept during adolescence have been numerous. Both Strang (1957) and Jersild (1952), for example, collected and analyzed self-descriptions from large samples of adolescents. Other studies have related the self-concept during this period to delinquency (Reckless, Dinitz, Kay, 1957), physical maturity (Mussen, Jones, 1957), school achievement (Shaw, Edson, Beil, 1960) and to ethnic and socioeconomic background (Rosenberg, 1964). One limitation of these studies is that the measures of the self-concept are in many cases global or verbal. While it is of interest to have an estimate of some over-all rating, such as "self-evaluation" or "self-acceptance," the self-concept appears to be complex enough to merit more molecular analysis (Wylie, 1961). Likewise, verbal measures are highly susceptible to the effects of social desirability, verbal ability and fluency, and conscious manipulation.

The present study, in which a non-verbal method has been used, is an extension of a previous study (Long, Henderson, Ziller, 1967) which investigated developmental changes in the self-concept during middle childhood. For the present study, a longer, more extensive form of the Self-Social Symbols Tasks was developed. This form was largely derived from earlier tests, which had been used in a program of research that has applied this method to a variety of problems and populations.

In this method, a subject, working in a test booklet, selects and arranges symbols to represent himself in relation to salient other people. The assumption is made that individuals are able to communicate various aspects of their self-social system symbolically and that certain symbolic patterns have common meaning. It is assumed, for example, that physical distance in the test may represent psychological distance in the person's life space. Hierarchies of power, or dimensions of importance or value, are also assumed to be reflected in specific symbolic patterns, as are degrees of self-centrality, self-complexity, and self-differentiation from peers. The validity of these assumptions is supported by a variety of findings related to the construct validity of particular items in the test.

In the present form of the test, attention is focused upon seven components of the self—usually in relation to salient other people. These components are assumed to be part of an integrated system and represent dimensions upon which the self as a social object may be described.

METHOD

Self-Social Symbols Tasks. The Self-Social Symbols Tasks provide measures of (1) esteem relative to selected groups of other persons; (2) dependency upon a group consisting of parents, teachers, and friends; (3) power in relation to selected authority figures; (4) centrality of self relative to friend; (5) complexity of self; (6) individuation of the self in relation to peers; and (7) identification as measured by closeness to mother, father, teacher, and friend, and by number of others included in the self-group. Each of these measures is represented in the test by from two to ten items, with scores summed across items to derive total scores. All measures have been found to be independent of I.Q. Brief theoretical and operational definitions, along with a summary of evidence for construct validity, are presented below.

Esteem. Self-esteem is defined as the value or importance attributed to self in comparison with others. In the six items measuring esteem, the subject places the self and five specified other persons (e.g., your father, a successful person, your friend, etc.) in a row of circles. Positions to the left are assumed to represent greater importance. This assumption is supported by a finding by Morgan (1944) that the stimulus to the extreme left in a row of stimuli is ranked as more important than those appearing further to the right.

In another study, American children placed the "smartest" child to the left, the "dumb" and "bad" child to the right to a significant degree ($p = .001$). Further evidence of validity was provided by a sample of forty-eight children who placed themselves further left among a group of peers than among a group of adults ($p = .02$).

Dependency. Dependency of the self upon others is assumed to be the degree to which the person conceives of himself as a part of a group of others, as opposed to a conception of the self as a separate entity. In the six items measuring dependency, the subject draws a circle to represent the self within or without a group consisting of parents, teachers, and friends. Placement of the self within the group is assumed to express greater social dependency. This assumption is supported by a finding that children placing the self within the group preferred to pursue more group activities than did those placing the self outside the group ($p = .01$).

Power. Power of self in relation to certain authority figures is assumed to be a conception of the self as superior, equal, or inferior to the other person. In these six items, the subject selects a circle to represent the other person (e.g., father, teacher, principal, etc.) which is either above, even with, or below the self. A higher position for other person is assumed to represent less power for the self. This assumption is supported by the finding that children placed a friend lower than they placed teacher (in a separate item) ($p = .01$ in each of several samples).

Centrality. Centrality of the self is assumed to reflect the focusing of attention upon the self, rather than the other—that is, an inward rather than an outward orientation. In the six centrality items, the subject draws a circle to represent the self and one to represent a friend within a large circle, labeling each appropriately. The placement of the self closer than the other to the center of the circle is assumed to represent greater self-centrality, perhaps partly because the circle nearest the center is ordinarily the one drawn first. Supporting the validity of these assumptions are the findings that both adult neuropsychiatric patients and emotionally disturbed children placed the self more often in the central position ($p = .05$ and .001, respectively) than did normal controls, as did sociometric isolates in comparison with sociometric stars ($p = .005$), and children who had moved frequently from community to community as compared with those who had lived in but a single community ($p = .01$).

Complexity. Complexity of the self is assumed to be the degree of differentiation of the self-concept. In the ten complexity items, arrays of three figures varying in complexity, which were derived from the work of Glanzer and Clark (1963, 1965) are presented to the subject. He selects one of the figures to represent the self, with a higher score associated with more complex figures. This item is relatively new. One recent finding is that, among a sample of high-achieving fifth graders, the "good" readers (on the basis of the Iowa Tests of Basic Skills) represented the self as more complex than did the "poor" readers ($p = .001$).

Individuation. Individuation is defined as the degree to which the individual differentiates himself from his peers. The extremes of this dimension are considered to be "like" and "different from" others. In the ten individuation items, the subject chooses a circle to represent the self which is either the same or different from those representing peers. The choice of a "different" circle is assumed to express a greater degree of individuation. This assumption is supported by the finding that a sample of twins represented the self more often as the "same" than did non-twins of the same age, sex, and class in school ($p = .05$). Children who had moved frequently represented the self more often as "different" than did those who had lived in a single community ($p = .05$). In a sample of elementary school children (grades 1–6), boys were found to be more individuated than girls ($p = .001$).

Identification. Identification is defined as the conception of the self in a "we" category with the other person or persons (Glanzer, Clark, 1965). This construct is measured by two kinds of items. In the first of these, a letter representing another person (father, mother, friend, or teacher) is placed to the extreme right or extreme left in a row of circles. The subject selects one of the other circles to represent the self. Physical distance is assumed to represent psychological distance, with greater identification associated with less distance. This assumption is supported by the finding that among a group of disadvantaged first-grade children, those separated from their natural fathers placed the self significantly further from father than did those living with father ($p = .02$).

The second measure of identification, termed "group identification," is assumed to reflect the social inclusiveness of the individual. In these four items the subject arranges arrays of ten people including the self into groups. The number of persons in the self group is assumed to reflect degree of identification with others. This measure has been found to differentiate both adult neuropsychiatric patients and emotionally disturbed children from their normal controls, with the deviant group in each case placing fewer persons with the self ($p = .05$ and $.001$, respectively).

Subjects and design. In the present study, the Self-Social Symbols Tasks were administered to 420 students (thirty boys and thirty girls of proper age for grade in each grade, grades 6–12) in four schools in Queen Anne's County, Maryland. The subjects were white, varied widely in socioeconomic class and academic ability and achievement, and lived in a rural area on the eastern shore of Maryland. Their ages ranged from eleven to eighteen.

Analyses of variance in relation to grade and sex were carried out for each measure on the test, with the exception of identification with particular other—here distributions were not normal, and non-parametric statistics were employed. Reliability was estimated by split-half coefficients corrected for length. The reliability coefficients ranged from $+.58$ to $+.95$ with a median of $+.82$ for the twelve measures. Intercorrelations of all twelve measures were carried out with a sample of five boys and five girls from each grade, seventy in all.

RESULTS

The intercorrelations revealed that the twelve measures were independent with the following exceptions:

1. Identification with father, mother, teacher, and friend were positively related ($+.26$ to $+.43$);
2. High dependency was related to greater identification with friend ($+.38$);
3. Greater identification with mother was related to higher esteem ($+.30$);
4. Greater power of self was related to less identification with teacher ($-.29$).

Analyses of variance upon the measures of esteem, dependency, group identification, power, complexity, and centrality revealed significant effects for grade or sex for esteem, dependency, and group identification. Self-esteem increased with grade level ($p = .05$), continuing a trend found in elementary school. Dependency, again continuing a trend, increased until the ninth grade and declined thereafter ($p = .01$). The sex by grade interaction for dependency was also significant ($p = .05$)—girls, as compared with boys, had lower scores in junior high and higher scores in senior high. In the items measuring group identification, boys placed more other persons in the self group ($p = .001$).

With the measures of identification with father, mother, teacher, and friend, distributions departed widely from normal—in three of the measures, approximately half of the responses consisted of the minimum score. Therefore, non-parametric statistics were used with these data.

Each score was first categorized as indicating placement of the self next to the other person on both items, or not. Frequency tables for the sex by grade matrix were then compiled. Chi squares were first computed for these data for sex, combining across grades, and for grade, combining the sexes. Here only one significant effect was found—boys were found to identify significantly more than girls with father (boys 59 per cent, girls 49 per cent; $\chi^2 = 4.6$; $p = .05$).

Because trends suggested a sex by grade interaction in several of these measures, it was decided to pool the data into two categories for grade (older-younger) for each measure for each sex.

With the data arranged in this way, a number of significant effects were found. (1) Younger girls (grades 6–8) identified less with mother than did the older girls (grades 9–12) ($p = .001$), and less than boys of the same grades ($p = .05$). Older boys identified less with mother than older girls ($p = .05$). (2) Among the girls, identification with friend was greater in the higher grades (10–12) ($p = .05$). An opposite tendency was found among the boys ($p = .10$), so that boys, in comparison with girls, had higher scores in the lower grades ($p = .10$) and lower scores in the higher grades ($p = .05$). (3) Younger girls (grades 6–9) identified less with father than older girls ($p = .05$) and than younger boys ($p = .005$).

In addition, when the twelfth-grade boys were compared to those younger, they were found to be significantly less identified with teacher (10 per cent vs. 29 per cent; $\chi^2 = 5.1$; $p = .025$) and with father (40 per cent vs. 62 per cent; $\chi^2 = 5.8$; $p = .025$).

DISCUSSION

When attempting to integrate these varied findings into meaningful patterns of self-other orientations, one notes first the differences between the sexes. One such difference not anticipated was the inclusion of more other persons in the self-group by the boys. A possible explanation for this effect involves the assumption that larger self-groupings are indicative of greater acceptance of others. The male adolescent may be more acceptant because his social contacts and mobility are less restricted. Supervision of adolescent girls in this culture tends to be more stringent than that of boys, and class distinctions are enforced more sharply for girls. The present results suggest that the greater freedom of boys may lead to a greater social inclusiveness—a perception of the self as a part of a larger and more varied group than is the case for girls.

A second difference between the sexes is the greater identification of the boys with father. This relationship was also found among kindergarten and first-grade children (Long, Henderson, 1968) and among the second, third, and fourth grades of elementary school (Long, Henderson, Ziller, 1967). In the fifth and sixth grades in the latter study and in the twelfth grade of the present study, however, girls placed the self closer to father than did boys. The over-all pattern of identification with father in relation to age and sex thus appears to be relatively complex.

Combining the data from this study with those of the earlier study of elementary school children, one finds that for the boys there is an increase in identification with father until the fourth grade (where 90 per cent of the sample placed the self next to father). After this comes a gradual decline until the sixth grade, after which a more or less level period occurs (at about 60 per cent) until the twelfth grade, where a further decline is seen (to 40 per cent). During the adolescent years, then, the boy appears to have a perception of self in relation to father which is relatively stable and fairly close. Such a perception would seem beneficial in that the boy's self-identification as a male would be supported. The relatively sharp break away from father found in the twelfth grade may indicate that the boy is reacting to his imminent departure from his parental family. A similar movement away from teacher is found at this time. That the physical separation is preceded by a perceptual separation may indicate a kind of anticipatory socialization which may ease the transition to the adult role.

It should be noted that the withdrawal of the twelfth-grade boys from father and teacher is accompanied by a relatively high self-esteem. It is possible that this positive self-regard facilitates the move toward greater separation of self from others.

For the measures of dependency and those of identification with mother and friend (and, to a certain extent, identification with father), similar grade by sex interactions were found. In each case, the junior high boys and the senior high girls were found to place the self closer to others. The appearance of similar patterns in four separate measures lends support to the validity of the relationship and suggests the need for a single interpretation of these results. When responses to these measures are viewed in conjunction with those made by the younger children of the earlier study, it is seen that there is a relatively sharp movement away from others for girls at about the time of puberty. This change appears to be dramatic because heretofore the girl has generally been close to others, particularly her mother.

In addition to those findings differentiating the sexes, there are a number common to both sexes. One of the most striking of these is the higher position accorded father in the power items, in contrast to teacher or principal. In addition, father is placed increasingly higher as a function of increased grade, particularly by the boys. This decline in power for the self relative to father seems paradoxical in later adolescence, when adult size and greater independence are ordinarily acquired.

One possible explanation is that this item may reflect the adolescent's feelings of respect for the person, rather than his power per se. This interpretation would seem a reasonable explanation for the increasing power of father over the years, since respect for the parent may increase in spite of a growing independence from his authority.

In addition, a greater respect accorded father in contrast to teacher or principal, may be related to the adolescent's closer identification with him. It has been suggested that in early childhood an identification with a powerful parent makes it possible for the child to share the parent's higher status. This psychological effect may continue in adolescence. If so, a higher position for the father would tend to reflect favorably upon the self-concept of the adolescent, whereas a higher position for teacher or principal, where close identifications are not involved, may indicate a derogation of the self.

The greater egalitarianism in relation to teacher found in the senior high years would seem to indicate a greater acceptance of the teacher, and the dying out of a certain amount of junior high rebelliousness. It may be argued that perhaps the most rebellious adolescents have left school by the senior high grades. The present study attempted to control for this effect by including only students of the proper age for grade (under the assumption that those who will later drop out will have failed one or more years by the junior high grades). Whatever the reasons for the greater egalitarianism, however, it would seem to provide a good basis for a democratic learning situation in the senior high years.

The findings of greater dependency (until grade 9) and increased esteem (until grade 12) over the adolescent years continue trends found among the elementary-aged children. These trends which extend from grade 2 to grade 9 or 12, respectively, demonstrate continuities in development in contrast to the striking discontinuities found among the girls in the identification and dependency measures. The increase in dependency over the years may reflect an increased socialization or social interest for the older child and adolescent. The decline in dependency after grade 9, on the other hand, may be another example of anticipatory socialization in preparation for the independence of early adulthood.

The increase in esteem with age appears to represent an integration into self-conceptions of the increased status of the older child and adolescent. An increase in self-evaluation with the increase in physical size and maturity and educational level may be an important aspect of the development of the self-concept, a development which permits and facilitates that transition from child to adult. When one considers that a high self-esteem is dissonant with failure, then one might predict both higher aspirations and lower tolerance for failure in later adolescence. An understanding of these motivational patterns might facilitate the development of educational programs for this age group.

In conclusion, the findings of this study appear to provide certain insights into differential perceptions of self-other relationships during adolescence: (1) the greater stability and inclusiveness of the boys' relationships with others; (2) withdrawal from others of girls in early adolescence and their subsequent return; (3) the higher position accorded father in comparison with teacher and principal; (4) the increased tendency with age to place father in a higher position and teacher in a more egalitarian position; (5) the increase in dependency during early adolescence followed by a decrease in later adolescence; (6) an increase in self-esteem with age. Although limited to a specific sample and by a cross-sectional method, the study also appears to demonstrate the complex and dynamic nature of patterns of development of the self-concept during adolescence.

30. MODELS AND HELPING: NATURALISTIC STUDIES IN AIDING BEHAVIOR

James H. Bryan & Mary Ann Test

Altruism may be defined as concern for the welfare of others as opposed to exclusive concern for oneself. Operationally, altruism is manifested by the willingness of one individual to help another even though the person to be helped is unknown to the helper, and even though the helping behavior is inconvenient or difficult. The extent to which altruism characterizes human behavior as well as the origins of its occurrence in any individual have often been subjects for research and speculation, although many of the questions about altruism are still unanswered. Among the questions still needing answers are: (1) To what extent and under what conditions are individuals prompted to help each other when helping behavior involves personal inconvenience and extra effort; (2) Are there some persons who conceive of themselves as playing an altruistic role; (3) What kind of person is most apt to display altruistic behavior; (4) Is it in fact possible for an individual to adopt an altruistic role unless some self-satisfaction elements are involved?

Bryan and Test have endeavored to answer some of the questions about altruistic or helping behavior in the series of four experiments they describe. Three of the experiments were addressed to the effects of altruistic models upon helping and one dealt with the amount of helping behavior elicited by a standard situation. Their results across all experiments were quite consistent. The presence of a helping model significantly increases

SOURCE. Adapted from James H. Bryan and Mary Ann Test, "Models and Helping: Naturalistic Studies in Aiding Behavior," *Journal of Personality and Social Psychology*, 1967, Vol. 6, pp. 400–407. (With permission of the authors and the publisher, The American Psychological Association.)

helping behavior, although interpersonal attributes appear to be a relevant variable in at least some kind of helping situations.

Bryan and Test's research still leave most of the questions about altruism unanswered, but in their study we learn of the importance of imitative behavior in human affairs and we are once more reminded of the importance of individual differences and specific situational variables.

Recently, concern has been evidenced regarding the determinants and correlates of altruistic behavior, those acts wherein individuals share or sacrifice a presumed positive reinforcer for no apparent social or material gain. Studies addressed to these behaviors have explored both individual differences in the tendency to be altruistic and the situational determinants of such responses. Gore and Rotter (1963) found that students at a southern Negro college were more likely to volunteer for a social protest movement if they perceived sources of reinforcement as internally rather than externally guided. Subjects high on internal control were more likely to volunteer as freedom riders, marchers, or petition signers than subjects who perceived others as primary agents of reinforcement. Experimental evidence has been generated supporting the often-made assumption that guilt may serve as a stimulus to altruistic activity. Darlington and Macker (1966) found that subjects led to believe that they had harmed another through incompetent performances on the experimental tasks (three paper-and-pencil tests) were more willing than control subjects to donate blood to a local hospital. Midlarsky and Bryan (1967) found that children exposed to treatment conditions designed to produce empathy were more willing to donate M&M candies than subjects given control conditions, while Handlon and Gross (1959), Ugurel-Semin (1952), Wright (1942), and Midlarsky and Bryan have found sharing to be positively correlated with age among school-age children. Lastly, Berkowitz and Friedman (1967) have demonstrated that adolescents of the working class and the bureaucratic middle class are less affected in their helping behaviors by interpersonal attraction than adolescents of the entrepreneur middle class.

Three hypotheses have emerged regarding the situational determinants of self-sacrificing behaviors. One suggests that individuals behave in an altruistic fashion because of compliance to a norm of reciprocity. That is, individuals are aware of the social debts and credits established between them, and expect that ultimately the mutual exchange of goods and services will balance (Gouldner, 1960). Berkowitz and Daniels (1964) have suggested that individuals might show a generalization of such obligatory feelings and thus aid others who had not previously assisted them.

A second hypothesis was put forth by Berkowitz and his colleagues (Berkowitz, 1966; Berkowitz & Daniels, 1963; Berkowitz, Klanderman, &

Harris, 1964; Daniels & Berkowitz, 1963) who have postulated the social responsibility norm. They have contended that dependency on others evokes helping responses even under conditions where the possibility of external rewards for the helper are remote. Using supervisor's ratings of an unknown and absent other to produce dependency, and a box-construction task as the dependent variable, considerable support has been generated for the suggestion that dependency increases helping.

A third major determinant of helping may be the presence of helping (or nonhelping) models. While attention to the effects of models has generally been directed toward antisocial behaviors (cf. Bandura & Walters, 1963; Freed, Chandler, Mouton, & Blake, 1955; Lefkowitz, Blake, & Mouton, 1955), some recent evidence suggests that observation of self-sacrificing models may lead to subsequent succorant behavior by children. For example, Rosenhan and White (1967) have demonstrated that children are more likely to donate highly valued gift certificates to residents of a fictitious orphanage if they have seen an adult do so.

The present series of experiments was designed to test the effects of models in natural settings on subject samples other than college or high school students, and in contexts other than a school room or university setting. The first three experiments reported are concerned with the impact of observing helping models upon subsequent helping behaviors, while the fourth is addressed to the influence of interpersonal attraction upon donation behavior.

EXPERIMENT I: LADY IN DISTRESS: A FLAT TIRE STUDY

Few studies have been concerned with the effects of models upon *adults*, and fewer still with the impact of *prosocial* models upon them (Wheeler, 1966). Those that have been concerned with such behaviors have invariably employed college students as subjects. For example, Rosenbaum and Blake (1955) and Rosenbaum (1956) have found that college students exposed to a model who volunteered, upon the personal request of the experimenter, to participate in an experiment would be more likely to consent than subjects not exposed to such a model or than subjects who observed a model refuse to cooperate. Pressures toward conformity in these experiments were great, however, as the request was made directly by the experimenter and in the presence of a large number of other students.

Test and Bryan (1966) found that the observation of helping models significantly increased the subsequent offers of aid by observers. However, in that study, subjects were given the task of solving arithmetic problems and then rating their difficulty, a task ordinarily requiring autonomous efforts. Furthermore, the experiment was conducted within a university setting, a context where independence of thought is often stressed. The effects of the model may have been simply to increase the subjects' faith that assisting others was allowed. While questionnaire data of the study did not support this interpretation, such effects could not be ruled out entirely. Thus, it is possible that the model impact was simply a propriety-defining activity which reduced the inhibitions associated with such helping behavior.

In general, then, investigations of modeling that employ adults as subjects and that demand self-sacrifice on the part of subjects are limited in number, exploit strong pressures toward conformity, and rely upon college students as subjects. The present experiment was designed to assess the impact of models upon subsequent spontaneous offers of help in other than a university setting.

Method

The standard condition consisted of an undergraduate female stationed by a 1964 Ford Mustang (control car) with a flat left-rear tire. An inflated tire was leaned upon the left side of the auto. The girl, the flat tire, and the inflated tire were conspicuous to the passing traffic.

In the model condition, a 1965 Oldsmobile was located approximately $\frac{1}{4}$ mile from the control car. The car was raised by jack under the left rear bumper, and a girl was watching a male changing the flat tire.

In the no-model condition, the model was absent; thus, only the control car was visible to the passing traffic.

The cars were located in a predominantly residential section in Los Angeles, California. They were placed in such a manner that no intersection separated the model from the control car. No turnoffs were thus available to the passing traffic. Further, opposite flows of traffic were divided by a separator such that the first U turn available to the traffic going in the opposite direction of the control car would be after exposure to the model condition.

The experiment was conducted on two successive Saturdays between the hours of 1:45 and 5:50 P.M. Each treatment condition lasted for the time required for 1000 vehicles to pass the control car. While private automobiles and trucks, motorscooters, and motorcycles were tallied as vehicles, commercial trucks, taxis, and buses were not. Vehicle count was made by a fourth member of the experiment who stood approximately 100 feet from the control car hidden from the passing motorists. On the first Saturday, the model condition was run first and lasted from 1:45 to 3:15 P.M. In order to exploit changing traffic patterns and to keep the time intervals equal across treatment conditions, the control car was moved several blocks and placed on the opposite side of the street for the no-model condition. The time of the no-model treatment was 4:00 to 5:00 P.M. On the following Saturday, counterbalancing the order and the location of treatment conditions was accomplished. That is, the no-model condition was run initially and the control car was placed in the same location that it had been placed on the previous Saturday during the model condition. The time of the no-model condition was 2:00 to 3:30 P.M. For the model condition, the control car was placed in that locale where it had been previously during the no-model condition. The time of the model condition was 4:30 to 5:30 P.M.

Individuals who had stopped to offer help were told by the young lady that she had already phoned an auto club and that help was imminent. Those who nonetheless insisted on helping her were told the nature of the experiment.

Results

The dependent variable was the number of cars that stopped and from which at least one individual offered help to the stooge by the control car. Of the 4000 passing vehicles, 93 stopped. With the model car absent, 35 vehicles stopped; with the model present, 58 halted. The difference between the conditions was statistically significant ($\chi^2 = 5.53$, corrected for continuity, $df = 1$, $p < .02$, two-tailed). Virtually all offers of aid were from men rather than women drivers.

The time of day had little impact upon the offering of aid. Fifty vehicles stopped during the early part of the afternoon; 43 during the later hours. Likewise, differences in help offers were not great between successive Saturdays, as 45 offers of aid were made on the first Saturday, 48 on the second Saturday.

The results of the present study support the hypothesis that helping behaviors can be significantly increased through the observation of others' helpfulness. However, other plausible hypotheses exist which may account for the findings. It is possible to account for the differences in treatment effects by differences in sympathy arousal. That is, in the model condition, the motorist observed a woman who had had some difficulty. Such observations may have elicited sympathy and may have served as a reminder to the driver of his own social responsibilities.

Another explanation of the findings revolves around traffic slowdown. It is possible that the imposition of the model condition served to reduce traffic speed, thus making subsequent stopping to help a less hazardous undertaking. While the time taken for 1000 autos to pass the control car was virtually identical in the model and no-model condition and thus not supportive of such an explanation, the "slowdown" hypothesis cannot be eliminated. Assuming the model effect to be real, one might still argue that it was not a norm of helping that was facilitated by the model, but rather that inhibitions against picking up helpless young ladies were reduced. That is, within the model condition, the passing motorists may have observed a tempted other and thus felt less constrained themselves regarding similar efforts. Indeed, the insistence of some people to help in spite of the imminent arrival of other aiders suggested the operation of motives other than simply helping. Indeed, while the authors did not index the frequency of pick-up attempts, it was clear that a rather large number were evidenced.

Because of the number of alternative explanations, the evidence supporting the hypothesis that the observation of helpers per se will increase subsequent aiding is weak. Experiment II was designed to test further the prediction that the perception of another's altruistic activity would elicit similar behavior on the part of the observer.

EXPERIMENT II: COINS IN THE KETTLE

The investigation was conducted on December 14th between the hours of 10:00 A.M. and 5:00 P.M. The subjects were shoppers at a large department store in Princeton, New Jersey. Observations made on the previous day indicated that the shoppers were overwhelmingly Caucasian females.

A Salvation Army kettle was placed on the sidewalk in front of the main entrance to the store. Two females, both in experimenter's employ, alternatively manned the kettle for periods of 25 minutes. One solicitor was a Negro, the other a Caucasian. Each wore a Salvation Army cape and hat. Although allowed to ring the Salvation Army bell, they were not permitted to make any verbal plea or to maintain eye contact with the passing shoppers, except to thank any contributor for his donation.

The model condition (M) was produced as follows: Once every minute on the minute, a male dressed as a white-collar worker would approach the kettle from within the store and contribute 5 cents. As the model donated, he started a stopwatch and walked from the kettle toward a parking lot as if searching for someone. He then returned to the store. The following 20-second period constituted the duration of the treatment condition.

Following a subsequent lapse of 20 seconds, the next 20-second period defined the no-model condition (NM). Within any one minute, therefore, both M and NM treatments occurred. There were 365 occasions of each treatment.

It should be noted that it was possible that some subjects in the NM condition observed the contribution of the model or a donor affected by the model. If that hypothesis is correct, however, the effects of such incidents would be to reduce rather than enhance the differences between treatments.

Results

The dependent variable was the number of people who independently donated to the Salvation Army. People obviously acquainted, as for example, man and wife, were construed as one potential donating unit. In such conditions, if both members of a couple contributed, they were counted as a single donor.

Since there were no differences in model effects for the Negro or Caucasian solicitor, data obtained from each were combined. The total number of contributors under the NM condition was 43; under the M condition, 69. Assuming that the chance distribution of donations would be equal across the two conditions, a chi-square analysis was performed. The chi-square equaled 6.01 ($p < .01$).

In spite of precautions concerning the elimination of correlated observations within a treatment condition, it was possible for subjects in any one observational period to influence one another. Such influence may have been mediated through acquaintances not eliminated by our procedures or the observations of others as well as the model donating. A more conservative analysis of the data, insuring independent observation, was therefore made. Instead of comparing treatments by analyzing the number of donors, the analysis used, as the dependent variable, the number of observation periods in which there was a contribution, that is, those periods in which more than one donation occurred were scored identically to those in which only a single contribution was received. Occasions of donations equaled 60 in the M treatment, 43 in the NM condition. The chi-square equaled 2.89 ($p < .05$).

The results of Experiment II further support the hypothesis that observation of altruistic activity will increase such behavior among observers. But the matter is not yet entirely clear, for when the observer saw the model donate he saw two things: first, the actual donation, and second, the polite and potentially reinforcing interaction that occurred between the donor and solicitor. Conceivably, the observation of an altruistic model, per se, who was not socially reinforced for his behavior, would have little or no effect on an observer. The third experiment was designed to examine this possibility.

EXPERIMENT III: COINS IN THE KETTLE II

The experiment was conducted at a Trenton, New Jersey, shopping center from the hours of 10:00 A.M. to 5:00 P.M. Again, the majority of the patrons were Caucasian females. It is likely, however, that these shoppers were of a lower socioeconomic status than those in the Princeton group.

Salvation Army kettles were placed before the main entrance of a large department store (Kettle 1) and a large food center (Kettle 2). The kettles were separated by more than 200 yards. During the first 120 observations (10:00 A.M. to 12:00 P.M.), two male college students, employed by the Salvation Army and wearing its uniform, manned the kettles. The site of the experiment was Kettle 1, except on those occasions where the worker took his "coffee break." At those times, data collection was centered at Kettle 2. An equal number of M and NM conditions were run at each site, although approximately two-thirds of the observational time was spent at Kettle 1. During the remaining 240 observational periods (1:00 P.M. to 5:00 P.M.) the same male worker and his spouse alternately manned Kettle 1. The wife was stationed by the kettle for 136 minutes, the male for 104 minutes. The experiment was conducted only at Kettle 1 during the afternoon period.

Solicitors were told to make no verbal appeals for donations or responses to the model upon his contribution. While they were not informed of the hypothesis underlying the experiment, they may well have deduced it. The model was the same as in Experiment II, and again was dressed as a white-collar worker.

The imposition of the treatment conditions were identical to those described in Experiment I with the following exceptions. Since the kettle was more visible at this site than at the previous one, 30-second rather than 20-second periods were used for each treatment. To simplify the procedures, no waiting periods between treatments occurred. Additionally, after donating, the model would return to the parking lot. There were a total of 360 occasions of each of the M and NM conditions.

Results

The criteria defining a donor were identical to those outlined in Experiment I. Under the M condition, 84 donors were tallied; under the NM treatment, 56. The chi-square value was 4.86 ($p < .025$).

Since it was possible that one donor might have seen a donor other than the model receive social approval from the solicitor, the more conservative comparison of the treatments as outlined in Experiment II was made. That is, treatments were compared by noting the number of observational periods in which any donation occurred. Therefore, those donors who may have been influenced by a contributor receiving the solicitor's thanks were excluded. Of the 360 observational periods under the M condition, there were 75 in which some donation was made. Of the 360 periods, 51 were marked by contributions. Chi-square yielded a value of 5.09 ($p < .025$).

EXPERIMENT IV: ETHNOCENTRISM AND DONATION BEHAVIOR

While Experiment III was conducted to eliminate the solicitor's explicit social approval as a mechanism underlying donation behavior, it is possible that the model's impact was due to the information communicated to the observer regarding the consequence of donations. Work by Bandura, Ross, and Ross (1963), for example, found that children observing a model rewarded for aggression would be more aggressive than children who had observed a model being punished for such behavior. Additionally, considerable data have been gathered within the university laboratory suggesting that interpersonal attraction may greatly influence the helping response. Berkowitz and Friedman (1967), Daniels and Berkowitz (1963), and Goranson and Berkowitz (1966) have suggested that positive affect increases the probability of low payoff helping behavior.

The present experiment was designed to assess the impact of the solicitor's race upon the donation behavior of shoppers. It was assumed that a Negro solicitor would be held in less esteem by Caucasian shoppers than a solicitor of their same race, and that such attitudes would affect contributions. While the applicability of the "consequence to the model" hypothesis in accounting for the model's effect was not tested directly, the study assesses the importance of interpersonal attraction in eliciting charitable behavior.

Method

The experiment was conducted on December 2 and 3 between the hours of 10 A.M. and 6 P.M. at the Trenton area site. The subjects were Caucasian shoppers at a large department store. Three thousand seven hundred and three shoppers were observed; 2,154 females and 1,549 males. In order to reduce the possibility of including the same subject in the experiment on more than one occasion, tallies were made only of existing shoppers.

Two Salvation Army kettles were placed at two store exits, their location being separated by approximately 75 yards. Two female solicitors, a Negro and a Caucasian, manned the kettles. Both were in their early twenties, wore the uniform of the Salvation Army, and were in the employ of the experimenter. Each was instructed to make no verbal appeals for donations and to avoid eye contact with the shoppers. After a period of 25 minutes, the girls rotated kettle assignments, and during the last 10 minutes of the hour were allowed to take a coffee break. Hence, during a single hour, each solicitor manned both kettles. Each solicitor manned each kettle on seven occasions per day. Thus, each solicitor was observed for a total of 28 observational periods; 14 on each day (seven on each kettle) over a period of two days.

Two observers, each assigned to a particular kettle, tallied the number and sex of the exiting shoppers and contributors during each of the 25-minute periods. In addition, records were kept of the amount of money donated within any period, although it was impossible on this measure to separate those donations made by incoming from outgoing customers.

Results

The dependent variable was the percentage of donors contributing to the kettle within an observational period. That is, observational periods were assigned a percentage donor score. Shoppers within an observational period were treated as a single group, with differences between groups on percentage donor score forming the critical comparisons. The total N of the study was then the 56 observational periods, rather than the 3,703 shoppers. Since the mean group size for the Negro solicitor was 70.32 and for the Caucasian 61.93 (standard deviations equal to 53.33 and 42.98, respectively), it was assumed that the percentage score was relatively stable.

The effects of race, kettle location, and day and their interactions were analyzed by analysis of variance.

As can be seen from Table 1, both the main effect of race and of day were

TABLE 1

Analysis of Variance of Percentage Donor Scores

	df	MS	F
Race (A)	1	38.778	4.84[a]
Day (B)	1	98.315	12.28[b]
Kettle (C)	1	.018	
A × B	1	1.511	
A × C	1	11.340	
B × C	1	1.031	
A × B × C	1	3.206	
Error	48	8.009	

[a] $p < .05$ (2-tailed).
[b] $p < .01$ (2-tailed).

significant. As predicted, the Negro solicitor elicited a statistically significant lower percentage of donors than did the Caucasian. For the Negro solicitor, the average percentage donor score for observational periods was 2.22 ($SD = 2.36$), while for the Caucasian solicitor the average percentage donor score was 3.89 ($SD = 3.60$). Additionally, Saturday shoppers were by and large less generous than Friday customers. The average percentage donor score of the group was 1.73 ($SD = 1.97$) for the Saturday shopper, and 4.38 for the Friday shopper ($SD = 3.52$).

A second dependent variable was the amount of money donated during each time period. No significant differences were found for race, day, or kettle location.

The present investigation does support, albeit equivocally, the notion that interpersonal attraction may affect donations even when the solicitors are not the eventual recipients of such contributions. While it is possible that race differences simply fail to remind observers of their social responsibilities, it is also feasible that the subjects wanted to avoid interpersonal contact with a minority group member. If this is true, then it is interesting to note that interpersonal attraction may play an important role even in those situations where personal anonymity is high and escape from unpleasant situations easy.

DISCUSSION

The results of the first three experiments clearly replicate those of Test and Bryan and extend the findings over a variety of subject populations, settings, and tasks. The results hold for college students, motorists, and shoppers; in the university laboratory, city streets, and shopping centers; and when helping is indexed by aiding others solve arithmetic problems, changing flat tires, or donating money to the Salvation Army. The findings then are quite consistent: the presence of helping models significantly increases subsequent altruistic behavior.

Generosity appears to breed generosity. Subjects seem less inclined to act quickly in emergency situations when in the presence of other potential helpers. Whether faced with a medical emergency (a simulated epileptic seizure) or a dangerous natural event (simulated fire), the rapidity with which students sought to aid was reduced by the presence of others. These findings have been interpreted in three ways: as reflecting the subjects' willingness to diffuse responsibility (others will aid); as reflecting their diffusion of blame (others didn't aid either); or as reflecting conformity to the nonpanicked stooges. It is clear that the results of the first three experiments in the present series do not follow that which might be predicted by the diffusion concepts. A giving model apparently does not lend credibility to the belief that others than the self will make the necessary sacrifices. The helping other did not strengthen the observer's willingness to diffuse his social obligations, but rather stimulated greater social responsibility. In light of these results, the delayed reaction exhibited by the subjects tested by Darley and Latané might be best attributable to conformity behavior. As they have suggested, subjects faced with a unique and stressful situation may have been either reassured by the presence of calm others or fearful of acting stupidly or cowardly. Additionally, it is possible that diffusion of responsibility is only associated with anxiety-inducing situations. The current data fail to indicate that such diffusion occurs in nonstressful situations which demand fulfillment of social obligations.

While it appears clear that the behavior of the motorists and shoppers was not dictated by a variety of situational and social pressures usually associated with the study of modeling in adults or experiment in academic settings (Orne, 1962), the mechanisms underlying the effects are not obvious. While the presence of the model in the flat-tire study may have reminded the motorists as to the social responsibility norm, a hypothesis does not appear reasonable in accounting for the results in the coins-in-the-kettle series. The bell-ringing Salvation Army worker, with kettle and self placed squarely in the pathway of the oncoming pedestrian, would seem to be reminder enough of one's obligation toward charity. A priori, it would not appear necessary to superimpose upon that scene the donating other for purposes of cognitive cueing (Wheeler, 1966).

One hypothesis to account for the model effect is that the observer is given more information regarding the consequences of such donation behavior. Experiment IV suggested that solicitor status or personal attraction might operate on donation behaviors even under conditions of personal anonymity and few social constraints. It is possible that the model serves to communicate to the potential donor relevant information concerning the consequences of his act. That is, the model may demonstrate that an approach to the solicitor does not involve an unwanted interpersonal interaction (e.g., lectures on religion).

A second hypothesis to account for the data pertains to the shame-provoking capacities of the model. It is reasonable to assume that most people feel that they are, by and large, benevolent and charitable. Furthermore, it is likely that such a self-image is rarely challenged: first because charitable acts are not frequently required; second, at least in the street scenes employed in the current series of studies, solicitations are made in the context of many nongiving others. That is, a multitude of negative models —of noncharitable others—surround the solicitations in the current series of studies. Indeed, the contexts are such that most people are not helping; many more cars pass than stop to offer aid to the lady in distress; and there are many more people who refuse to put coins in the kettle than those who do. However, the witnessing of a donor, an individual who not only recognizes his social responsibility but in fact acts upon it, may produce a greater challenge to the good-self image of the observer. Acts rather than thoughts may be required of the observer in order to maintain the self-image of benevolence and charity. If such is the case, then the model characteristics most effective in producing prosocial behavior by socialized adults would be those directed toward shame or guilt production (e.g., donations from the poor), rather than those reflecting potential reinforcement power (e.g., donations from the high status).

Whatever the mechanism underlying the model effect, it does appear quite clear that prosocial behavior can be elicited through the observation of benign others.

31. ROLE-TAKING IN CHILDHOOD AND ITS CONSEQUENCES FOR SOCIAL LEARNING

Eleanor E. Maccoby

How, from his earliest days, does a child gradually acquire the repertoire of actions that characterize him as a person and enable him to assume the various roles appropriate to his environment? In her theoretical discussion Maccoby maintains that such actions are acquired as he practices covertly the actions displayed by the adults with whom he most frequently associates and who have control over the resources of which he is most in need. However, such actions are situation related and will only make their appearance when an appropriate occasion arises. For example, if an action is a part of adult role behavior then it will remain latent in the child until a situation occurs in which he can appropriately play the adult role when he himself becomes adult or when in play he assumes the role of an adult.

Of course, not all aspects of parental behavior are equally well acquired by the child through covert role-practice. Maccoby contends that motor skills are less efficiently learned by this means than is verbal behavior and that responses of others may be learned without learning the cues that guided the responses. She also notes that as the child builds his repertoire of actions, reactions toward self are learned as well as adultlike social actions directed toward others.

In presenting her theoretical position, Maccoby proposes two hypotheses. Her first hypothesis states that the greater the frequency of interaction with another person the greater the probability that the individual will learn what he has to do to promote harmony in the interaction as, through an-

SOURCE. Adapted from Eleanor E. Maccoby, "Role-Taking in Childhood and Its Consequences for Social Learning," *Child Development*, 1959, Vol. 30, pp. 239–252. (With permission of the author and the publisher, Society for Research in Child Development.)

ticipation he learns the content of the other's behavior. The second hypothesis proposes that the greater the amount of power that one individual exercises over another, the greater the probability that the person against whom the power is applied will rehearse the power figure's actions in his absence.

Let us assume that a large part of what a young child learns is acquired through the process of instrumental learning. This process involves selection of some of the child's overt actions via reward, and the elimination of others either through nonreward or through punishment. I wish to propose that concurrently the young child is acquiring a repertoire of behavior through a different process: that of practicing covertly the characteristic actions of other people with whom he interacts.

Since reproducing other people's actions has been labeled "imitation," and imitation has been described as a product of instrumental learning, [cf. Miller and Dollard (1957)], it may be well to begin with a detailed description of the kind of imitation I am talking about, and to consider whether it does indeed follow the principles of instrumental learning.

Let us draw on some of the ingenious and marvelously detailed descriptions of imitation in the first year of life reported by Piaget (1951). In describing the behavior of one of his infant daughters, Piaget notes that at first she seemed to react to voices without any apparent effort to imitate specific sounds. Here is a report when the infant was 1 month and 25 days old:

> She was watching me while I said "a, ha, ha, ra" etc. I noticed certain movements of her mouth, movements not of suction but of vocalization. She succeeded once or twice in producing some rather vague sounds, and although there was no imitation in the strict sense, there was obviously vocal contagion (1951, p. 10).

Genuine imitation began at about 3 months of age. Piaget describes the sequence as follows:

> I noted a differentiation in the sounds of her laughter. I imitated them. She reacted by reproducing them quite clearly, but only when she had uttered them immediately before (1951, p. 10).

Piaget uses the term "circular reaction" to describe this kind of imitation, and indeed we are reminded immediately of Holt's circular reflex principle. Piaget specifically disavows the interpretation that simple conditioning is the explanation of what he has observed. He says:

> If we consider first of all the circular reaction, how are we to explain the fact that perception "combines" with a movement and acquires

a motor power, which is not inherent in it? It cannot be a question of passive association, otherwise the child's activity would be the plaything of the most haphazard occurrences (1951, p. 17).

If we were to rephrase the problem in language more familiar to American psychologists, the question would be "How are we to explain the fact that a perceived stimulus (such as the sound 'ba') comes to elicit a response which it did not formerly elicit?" The stimulus is the action of another person, and the response is a similar, or almost identical, response. Piaget's disavowal notwithstanding, I believe his descriptions are consonant with the interpretation that simple conditioning (or what he calls "passive association") is indeed occurring. We note that in order for imitation of a sound to occur the child must first have made it spontaneously. According to the circular reflex principle, the child's utterance stimulates his ear at the same moment that the motor activity required to produce the sound is occurring; thus, by the Guthrian principle of association by contiguity, the auditory stimulus comes to have the power to elicit this particular response of the vocal apparatus, and we have the conditions laid down for repetitive babbling: that is, the child's hearing his own voice saying "ba" will stimulate him to say "ba" again. If someone else makes a sound similar enough to "ba," the child will also be stimulated to say this syllable, and we have imitation. It should be evident at once that it should be easier to establish imitation of speech sounds than of bodily movements and especially of facial expressions. For the child always stimulates his own ear when he vocalizes, and the stimulus is much the same as that which occurs when others vocalize the same phoneme in his presence. But he makes certain movements without seeing them (as for example, when he smiles). True, he has the motor feedback from his response. But the feeling of his facial muscles moving is quite a different stimulus from the sight of someone else's mouth smiling. There is no reason why the sight of someone else wrinkling his nose, for example, should stimulate the child to do the same, since this stimulus is not ordinarily present when he wrinkles his own nose. Piaget gives us some descriptions bearing on this point. He had been trying for some time to get one of his infant daughters to imitate various hand movements that he made. When the child was nearly seven months old, he would slowly open and close his hand in front of her, and she would not imitate this movement. Then he reports the following when the child was 8½ months old:

> I observed that she alternately opened and closed her right hand, watching it with great attention as if this movement, as an isolated schema, was new for her. I made no experiment at that point, but the same evening I showed her my hand as I opened and closed it rhythmically. She thereupon imitated the movement, rather

awkwardly but quite distinctly. She was lying on her stomach and not looking at her hand, but there was a clear correlation between her movements and mine (1951, p. 23).

Here we have a situation in which, once the child makes a movement that she can see, the sight of her own movement seems to become an adequate stimulus for eliciting the movement. Only after this learning has occurred can the sight of someone *else* making the movement elicit the response. Similarly, Piaget reports trying to produce imitation of a kind of clapping movement, and being unable to get the response until he observed the child (now 6 months old) spontaneously bringing her hands together and moving them apart, at which point he moved his hands in front of her in just the way her own hands had previously moved, and she imitated him. Piaget's own conclusion is that an infant of this age can imitate any hand movement that he can make spontaneously, but cannot imitate new movements.

What about movements that the child cannot see, such as facial expressions? Piaget found it much more difficult to obtain imitation of such movements. Even though the child spontaneously put out its tongue, or wrinkled its nose, for example, it would not perform these actions when someone else did them. What proved to be necessary was what Piaget called "training in imitation"; that is, he had to wait till the child made the movement spontaneously, then at once make the response himself to establish a connection between the stimulus of his facial movement and the child's matched response. In other words, he had to imitate the child, before the child could imitate him, when the movement was one the child could not see himself make. Presumably, a child could learn to imitate such movements also by watching his own face in a mirror.

While it is likely that Piaget showed pleasure when the child imitated successfully, so that there would be some reward for the child and some basis for instrumental learning, the first occurrence of the imitative response can be explained on the basis of simple association by contiguity. Let us then conclude that contiguity is a *sufficient* condition for the simple kind of imitation described above.

Where does all this lead us, as far as understanding role-taking is concerned? Are the concepts of imitation and role-taking synonymous? I think not. I would like to posit that all role-taking is imitation, but not all imitation is role-taking. Where does the distinction lie? *Role* behavior, as it is commonly defined, is behavior characteristic of a *position*. The role behavior associated with a given position is the behavior which others expect an incumbent of that position to display. Let me give an example of what could be considered clearly role behavior. Mrs. A came to visit Mrs. B, and Mrs. A brought with her her young baby whom Mrs. B had not seen before.

During the visit, the baby lay on a blanket on the living room floor. After a time, it began to cry, and its mother, Mrs. A, picked it up and changed its diaper. A week later, a very similar scene was enacted in the same setting. Mrs. B adopted a baby; Mrs. A, her good friend, rushed over to see it, this time leaving her own baby at home. The newly-adopted baby lay on a blanket on the living room floor, and after a time, began to cry. This time Mrs. B, not Mrs. A, picked up the baby, soothed it, and changed it. Why was Mrs. B's action different? The stimulus situation was the same—an unfamiliar baby crying, and another woman present who could have taken care of it. Her behavior was different because she now occupied a different *position*, the position of *"mother,"* toward which she and others had very well-formed views about the behavior appropriate to the position. Her action then was *role* behavior because the behavior was not elicited except when she occupied the appropriate position. It will be seen that we need the concept of "role" in psychology for much the same reason that we need the concept "drive"—in both cases, the problem is that a given stimulus situation sometimes leads to a given response, and at other times does not. We employ the concept "drive" to designate the conditions under which a previously-learned response will be performed (e.g., the hungry animal will run to the food box when hungry and will not do so when satiated, although external conditions remain constant). At least one set of operations which make a difference in the response to a given stimulus situation are those of deprivation, and these are the antecedent operations which we relate to the concept "drive." The antecedent operations which can be related to *role* are not so clear. In the case of role behavior, the controlling condition which will determine whether previously-learned behavior is performed appears to be a categorical label, applied by others or by the person himself. This categorizing of oneself and others and the performance of the actions appropriate to one's category seems to work quite smoothly in many instances. For example, a man and a woman who are strangers to one another approach a revolving door; custom dictates that the woman shall step forward and the man back, and a collision is avoided when each person performs the action appropriate to his sex role.

Let us return to the problem of role-taking in children. A child's imitation of someone with whom he interacts may properly be called "taking the role of another" only if the action imitated is inappropriate for a child, and is appropriate instead for the occupants of some other position or status. Here is an example: A 2-year-old had a toilet accident. She looked sternly at her mother and said, "I'm 'prised at you!" in the tone of voice ordinarily used by her mother. Another 2-year-old in a similar predicament said to her uncle, who was taking care of her, "Naughty girl! You must come and tell mommy!" Here we have children making statements appropriate to the disciplinary function of a mother. The child is, then, at this moment, playing the mother role. We assume that much similar role-playing occurs covertly and overtly during solitary play when no adult is present to reinforce it. A possible explanation of these bits of role-taking behavior is, I think, that the stimulus situation makes the child think of what the mother would say in such a situation; that the auditory image of the mother's phrase being said is sufficient on the basis of the circular reflex principle to get the child to say the phrase, either aloud or covertly. Please note an assumption implicit in this explanation. It is that, whenever we hear someone else saying something to us, *we learn it*, provided the necessary response units are already in our repertoire.[1] This means that the child will not be able to call to mind the mother's scolding phrase until he has mastered the words that make it up, just as we are not likely to remember and rehearse the phrases that are spoken to us in a foreign language. Inaccurate learning of a set of phrases may occur when the hearer does not possess the necessary response units. For example, a first-grade child being taught the salute to the flag learned, "One country, in the miserable, with liberty and justice for all," not possessing the response-unit "indivisible." We would expect that the features of a mother's behavior that a young child learns would be a quite oversimplified version of the original because of the limitations in the child's response repertoire. But, if a child does already have command of the response units, then he can rehearse the phrases that he hears and will be in a position to employ them when an appropriate situation occurs. I do not intend to imply that all phrases spoken in a child's presence are equally well learned, nor equally likely to be employed by him at a future date. I will try to specify later what some of the conditions may be that govern the degree of learning.

When a young child does imitate actions that are appropriate only for adults, he is likely to meet with a negative reaction from his parents. If a little girl tries to use her mother's lipstick, she will be told that she's only a little girl, and that lipstick is for grown women. A child who has been spanked may try to "spank" his parent on an occasion that seems to him to call for it, but this response is not likely to be maintained long, at least overtly, in view of the fact that most parents do not allow their children to be overtly aggressive toward adults. Thus, a child will soon learn that while certain items of grown-up behavior, such as tying one's own shoes, are appropriate for a child to perform as soon as he has mastered the manual skills involved, other items of behavior are not appropriate for a child. These are usually labeled according to the age and sex role to which

---

[1] The reader will note that a contiguity theory of learning is implied, although drives that can be aroused and reduced in fantasy (e.g., aggression) could presumably serve as the basis for reinforcement of covert responses.

they do belong, and the child is often explicitly taught that certain activities which are denied him now (such as driving a car) he will be allowed to perform when he is older. Let us use the term "adult role behavior" for the actions that are appropriate for the adults with whom the child interacts, but which the child may not, or cannot (because of physical limitations) perform in turn. Adult role behavior characteristically includes disciplinary actions directed toward a child who does something disapproved; controlling actions designed to protect a child from danger or protect other people and precious possession from damage *by* the child; and a variety of nurturant actions, such as feeding the child, comforting him when hurt, putting on an extra blanket when he is cold, etc.

During the early phases of a child's development, his own actions are most intimately bound up with the adult-role actions of his caretakers. Every one of the child's needs can be satisfied only through the mediating action of a caretaker. He cannot get his own food, walk where he wants to go, reach something he wants on a shelf, or dress himself; part of the sequence of actions he performs to satisfy any of these wants must be to elicit the necessary cooperative behavior from his caretaker; then he must orient himself to perform efficiently the reciprocal actions which the caretaker requires from him. For example, the following characteristic behavior was observed in a 2-year-old: He would always go to the right-hand side of his high chair when ready for a meal, holding himself in a characteristic position ready to be picked up. When he had been lifted into the chair, he would duck his head sideways, for the tray to be swung over his head; then he would lift his chin for the bib to be put under it, then bow his head down on the tray so the bib could be tied around the back of his neck. He was obviously prepared for a particular sequence of actions by his mother. He was utterly confused and upset when a new baby-sitter tried to lift him up from the *left* side of the high chair, and tried to put his bib on before swinging the tray into place. The little boy and his mother had learned what might be described as two halves of the same habit. Until she was asked about it, the mother was quite unaware that she always performed her part of the habit in a stereotyped way; but actually the interaction of these two people was made smooth and effortless by virtue of the fact that the behavior of each was highly predictable by the other. I wish to postulate that, in the course of an often-repeated intimate interaction sequence like this one, each person not only is oriented toward what the other person will do but actually anticipates it to the extent of reproducing some elements of the other person's action covertly. Thus, the child who says, "I'm 'prised at you," when he has been naughty is anticipating the phrase his mother will say, and rehearsing it.

We are now able to specify what some of the conditions are which determine how thoroughly we incorporate into our own behavior repertoire the actions of other people with whom we interact. The first hypothesis is that the more frequently we interact with another person (and the more our own actions are interdependent with his) the more we must learn to anticipate what he will do if the interaction is to be harmonious; and, in anticipating him, we learn the content of his behavior. This hypothesis would predict that the worker and the first-line supervisor would learn each other's behavior more thoroughly than would two people who were *two* levels apart in a hierarchy. This rule applies to the learning that occurs when both members of the diad are present and serving as stimuli to one another. But we may also assume that a certain amount of spontaneous rehearsal of the other person's actions occurs when he is *not* present. Consider, for example, the case of a small child who falls down in the back yard and cuts his knee. While he runs to the house, crying for his mother, he thinks of his mother bandaging his knee, before she is actually there doing it. We are accustomed to dealing with expectations in S-R learning theory by labeling them as "r_G"—the anticipatory goal response. But note that "r_G" is a consummatory action—the child's own action; in the example just given "r_G" would consist of anticipatory elements of the process of *being bandaged*; in addition, I am now saying, there is an anticipatory response which includes at least some elements of the response of the other person; in this case, the child is practicing an anticipatory response of *bandaging*, as well as that of *being bandaged*.

I have said that the frequency with which we practice elements of another person's responses is a function of the frequency with which we interact with that person, and the intimacy with which our actions must be coordinated with his. But we suggest there is a more important condition governing the frequency of covert practice of another's responses, and this condition has to do with the power relationships between the two people concerned. Our second hypothesis is this: the more power another individual exercises over ego, the more ego will rehearse alter's actions in the absence of alter. John W. M. Whiting has used the phrase "control of resources" to describe more fully what kind of exercise of power will bring about covert practice of the role of another. A resource is something ego wants. According to Whiting's hypothesis, if the resource is mediated by alter, so that ego cannot satisfy his need except through a mediating action of alter's, then ego will more fully learn alter's characteristic behavior. Why should this be so? Presumably, because there will be numerous occasions upon which the arousal of a need in ego will provide the occasion for him to think about an action of alter's. Suppose a child is hungry; if he lives in a household where he is allowed to go to the refrigerator and get the ingredients for a sandwich, he will not engage in any covert role practice. If he is not allowed to do this, but must ask his mother, then, when he becomes hungry, he will think about asking his mother for a sandwich and will imagine a number of things she might say in response, "It's too soon before dinner," or, "If you've finished cleaning your room, you may have it." He may decide not to ask her for the sandwich after all, but meanwhile he will have practiced some of her characteristic responses, and added an increment to the habit strength of these responses in his own repertoire. If most things that an individual wants are not under his control but under the control of others, then presumably much of the vicarious trial-and-error that he engages in must involve his trying out various approaches to getting the help or avoiding the censure of others, and imagining the probable responses to these approaches. In our view the process of learning through role-playing the actions of others encompasses instances of "identification with the aggressor." Our position says that a child should covertly rehearse both the rewarding and the punishing actions characteristic of his parents, for both are highly relevant to him in guiding his plans about future actions.

Let us reiterate that we are *not* saying that the mind is like a tape recorder, automatically recording and retaining for future use all the phrases and actions that other people emit in ego's presence. We are saying that the learning process is highly selective, and that a law of frequency applies. That is, the probability of ego's using a particular phrase that he has heard someone else use may be very low or very high, depending in part upon the number of times he has rehearsed this phrase to himself. Furthermore, the conditions which will cause him to rehearse it are predictable.

The relations of status to role-taking should now be clear. Our first hypothesis was that whenever two people interact frequently, especially if the actions are mutually dependent in some way, both participants will learn something about the actions of the other. This would mean that the mother does some role-playing of her child's behavior, as well as vice versa. But the second hypothesis was that fantasy role-playing when the other person was not present was a function of power; according to this hypothesis, the worker should think about the behavior of his boss much more than the boss should imagine the behavior of his employees. And within the family, the young child must be almost wholly oriented toward the actions of his parents, since the parents mediate all resources for him, while the parents have much less reason to role-play the child in fantasy when he is not present. As a matter of fact, it is probable that learning by role-playing occurs more frequently in early childhood than at any other time of life, since the young child is almost completely dependent upon others; as the child grows older, he can fulfill more of his own needs without the mediation of another person, at which time his learning should be more of the direct instrumental kind.

Adult role behavior was defined earlier as behavior not deemed appropriate for children. Let us consider the fate of the adult-role actions learned by the child through fantasy role-playing. The child does not have an opportunity to practice these actions overtly. There may be a number of reasons why he cannot practice them. A major reason is that the appropriate stimulus situation does not arise. No one is directing child-like actions toward him that would call for a reciprocal adult-like response. Secondly, a child cannot practice some adult-role actions overtly because of physical limitations (e.g., he is too small to lift another 2-year-old into a high-chair). And finally, if an opportunity did arise to perform an adult-role act and the child was physically capable of doing so, he might still be prevented by his adult caretaker on the grounds that the behavior is not appropriate for his age. So overt practice does not occur, but we assume that *covert* practice continues to occur so long as the child is in a dependent position in which the resources he needs are mediated by others. Now what about behavior that has been practiced covertly *only*, without opportunity for overt practice? Can such actions be said to have habit strength in the same way that conventional overt responses do? I think yes, but of course only those elements of a response that *can* be practiced covertly would acquire habit strength. There is little motor feedback from a covert response. For the acquisition of motor skills, feedback is of great importance, especially in the coordination of discrete motor elements. Therefore, it would appear that covert role-playing would be an inefficient way to learn motor skills. An example of this fact is seen in the case of an army inductee, who listens to his sergeant barking orders for close-order drill; the inductee mutters the orders to himself as the sergeant gives them, and can soon say them covertly in perfect cadence; but when he is required to lead the squad and actually deliver the orders in a loud voice he finds himself out of breath and is soon hopelessly out of rhythm. His covert practice never included co-ordinating his breathing with shouting the orders aloud. It would follow from this, for example, that a young child that has frequently had its diapers changed would acquire a tendency to try to change a crying baby, but would not learn how to fold a diaper, nor how to put one on so as not to be stuck with a pin in the process. But while covert practice may be inefficient for the acquisition of a motor skill, it should be perfectly adequate for the acquisition of *verbal* response tendencies.

Perhaps a more important limitation on the kind of learning that can occur via covert role-practice has to do with the perceptions of stimuli to which alter is responding. So far, I have implied that being able to reproduce some element of the responses characteristic of another person would constitute playing the role of that other person. I have also pointed out that very young children (under 2) can do this. Yet we have been told by Piaget and others that very young children are egocentric—that they can't put themselves in the place of someone else. Piaget has illustrated this fact in a number of ways. First there is his "brothers test," when he asks a child how many brothers he himself has, and then how many brothers one of his brothers has (Piaget, 1928). A child can report accurately about how many brothers he himself has at a fairly early age, but it is not until middle childhood that most boys realize that they must count themselves as one of their sibling's brothers. As another example, Piaget recounts the difficulty young children have imagining how an object would look to someone standing in a different place than the place where the child himself is standing. An example of this particular kind of egocentrism was observed in a young child who was quite capable of using parental words and phrases in play with dolls. This child was capable, then, in one sense, of playing the role of another person. Yet the following incident occurred: The child liked her milk to be quite cold; she took a sip from a glass of milk, and said, "Mommy, it's too warm." Her mother said, "No, it isn't dear, I just took it out of the refrigerator." The child held up the glass for her mother to see, and then ostentatiously took another sip of it, saying triumphantly to her mother, "See? It *is* warm!" She evidently believed that when she tasted something, her mother tasted it, too. The realization that other people are not experiencing the same stimuli that we are comes slowly; a young child, talking to someone on the telephone, will hold up an object for the person at the other end of the line to see, not realizing that the other person is in an entirely different visual environment.

We see, then, that while a young child may be able to reproduce the response of another person, this does not mean that he can put himself in another's place in the empathic sense. He may be making quite a different stimulus-response connection than his model is making. That is, he may connect his model's response (as represented in his own fantasy) to whatever set of stimuli are impinging upon himself at the moment, because he is not yet capable of discriminating his own cues from those stimulating others. Thus, for example, if a mother is cleaning out a closet and comes upon a garment with moth-holes and says, "Oh! How awful!" the small child playing in the room may practice this remark in relation to whatever he himself was looking at, and may learn nothing whatever about the evil qualities of moth-holes.

What does all this mean in relation to the kind of behavior that may be learned by covert role-playing? First, it means that a child may learn to respond to a different cue than that which elicited the mother's response; perhaps more importantly, he may *fail* to learn to respond to the cues that were actuating the mother's behavior. Let us give an example that illustrates why this failure may be important. Recently we were interviewing some children between the ages of 11 and 16 concerning their concepts of which kinds of behavior were adult-like and which child-like, and concerning their observations of children assuming adult roles. A high-school girl, when asked what she had observed about 12-year-olds acting as baby-sitters, said,

"Personally, I wouldn't trust them." When asked why, she said, "They're still in the 'soft' stage." Further exploration revealed that according to her observation, a very young baby-sitter feels sentimental over little children, but would fail to respond to cues of danger. A young sitter could not tell, for example, when a 2-year-old was about to dash into the street, or about to fall, and consequently could not act the caretaking role effectively despite the greatest feelings of solicitude for the child. I wish to suggest that this situation results from the young sitter's having learned only certain aspects of her mother's behavior in earlier years when she was herself a child receiving maternal care. She could hear, and practice, her mother's statements toward herself as a child; she could even practice her mother's protective actions; but she did not necessarily notice the cues that set off these actions in her mother. She had no practice, for example, in seeing that a particular facial expression in a child presaged a dangerous action that would call for an instant maternal response. A child has no training in responding to this kind of cue because he cannot see his own face. Instead, he *does* have training in the cue elements that are internal. Suppose, for example, that a child has certain internal feelings when he is about to mark on a wall. He can feel his own arm reaching out for the pencil, etc. This impulse will serve as a cue to remind him of the things his mother will probably say if he does it—he hears, in his mind's ear, the scolding phrase, "You naughty boy, give me that pencil this instant!," thus practicing this phrase and increasing the probability that he will one day say it himself in an appropriate situation. But, in the future, what cue will cause him to say it? We know that organisms do learn to respond to cues to which a model has responded. Church (1957), in an experiment with rats, trained follower rats to make the same turns in a maze as the leader rats made. The leaders were following previously learned visual cues. After a number of runs, the follower rats were put in the maze alone, and were able to make some use of the visual cues the leaders has previously been following. In a similar vein, in studying the material that movie-viewers learned from a movie, Maccoby and Wilson (1957) found that if there were two leading characters, and the viewer chose one of them as the person who became for him the principal protagonist of the story, he remembered later somewhat more of the cues relevant for his chosen hero's actions than those relevant for the actions of the other leading character. But we are suggesting that this learning will occur primarily with respect to those cues which stimulate both the observer and the person he identifies with in the same way and at the same time.

I am also suggesting that a child will learn to produce the adult-role response more dependably to *internal* cues than to external ones. Thus, in the case of the 12-year-old baby-sitter, we would expect that if the sitter *herself* were tempted to run into the street, or felt *herself* endangered by an oncoming car, then she would make a protective gesture toward her young charge. We see this clearly in the case of a very young child; if he says to his doll, "You naughty doll, you wet your pants," the experienced mother will urge the child himself to go to the bathroom. She rightly assumes that the child's disciplinary remark toward the doll was elicited by the cues of the child's own impending deviation.

This brings up a central point, having to do with the development of attitudes toward the self. If a child learns the adult-role behavior characteristic of his parents, he may be expected to manifest the behavior in two sets of circumstances: when another person performs child-like actions toward him (e.g., when another child is hurt and needs solace, or when another child breaks a rule and needs discipline), or when he himself performs these child-like actions or has the impulse to do so. Suppose a child has parents who characteristically react by withdrawing their love from him when he does something they disapprove of. If he learns their characteristic mode of response to the deviation of another person, we would expect him to react to another child who breaks a rule by refusing to play with the other child. But, in addition, when he himself deviates, he will respond to his own impulse by withdrawing love from himself—a phenomenon we more commonly refer to as a loss of self-esteem. Thus, the parents' attitudes toward the child, and the parents' techniques of dealing with the child, will be reflected in the child's self-attitudes as well as in his attitudes and behavior toward others. We should not regard the trait of extrapunitiveness and that of intropunitiveness as being opposite ends of a scale. Rather, if a child has punitive parents, we would expect that, if the conditions are such that the child has engaged in a good deal of covert practice of the parents' actions, he will in the future be punitive toward others who deviate, and will be likewise punitive toward himself if he transgresses.

We must guard against having a theory that predicts more homogeneity between generations than actually exists. So far, I may have implied that most children will behave just as their parents do. Let us point out some specific reservations about such a generalization. First of all, parents are not the only people who control resources the child wants. There are usually a succession of important figures who perform this function. First, the mother assumes primary importance with respect to the issues of early childhood; feeding, toilet training, and dependency. The father may play a more important role with respect to the control of aggression, especially for sons, and later controls one of the most important resources of all: information about skills the boy wants to acquire. Teachers play an important part, as do older brothers and sisters, and finally of course, the individual's spouse. We would expect that the growing individual would add behavior items to his repertoire from each of these people with whom he interacts. It would also follow that for most people the behavior they show when a young child asks them for food will be like that of their mothers, while their behavior in response to other kinds of instigations may have been learned through interaction with different agents. Thus, we are not talking about "identification" with any *single* individual in the child's life history, and no child should be a mirror image of any single adult.

Another factor which limits the similarity between a child's actions and those of his parents is instrumental learning. The action tendencies learned through covert role-playing may be in conflict with the action tendencies learned through the reward and punishment of overt actions. Consider, for example, the case of a boy who lives in a neighborhood where there is only one other child his age. The other child pushes him around mercilessly until one day he chances to push back hard, and the other child stops harassing him. He will learn aggression as a successful instrumental response to the attack of another person. Suppose his mother is the kind of person who responds to attack by withdrawal; the child will have learned this tendency, too, through covertly practicing her behavior. It is difficult to predict what will be the outcome of these conflicting action tendencies; perhaps, the child will be more aggressive than his mother, but less so than the success of his overt aggressive behavior would lead one to expect; or perhaps the child will begin to discriminate a set of situations where aggression is appropriate from a set where withdrawal is appropriate. In any case, he will not be precisely like his mother with respect to this area of behavior. As a matter of fact, we might expect that there would often be some conflict involved in the overt expression of behavior learned through role-playing the parent of the opposite sex. Particularly for boys, the rewards for masculine behavior and the disapproval of feminine behavior are such that the strictly feminine items of behavior that he has learned through role-playing his mother will never become manifest, but will be latent all his life.

Some children have much more opportunity than others to practice overtly, as they are growing up, the adult-role actions they have learned through interaction with their parents. Some children, for example, are allowed to discipline their younger siblings, others are not. If a child does have opportunity for overt practice of adult-role actions, we should expect that the tendencies learned through covert role-playing of the parents would be either strengthened or weakened, depending upon the response of others to the child's adult-like behavior. If he tries to boss other children and they ostracize him for it, his tendency to imitate a dominant parent would be weakened. We hypothesize that a child's adult-like action will be most similar to that of his parents on the first occasion when the action becomes overt. After this, the events which follow the response will often cause divergence of the child's response tendencies from that of his parents.

32. SEX ROLE LEARNING IN THE NUCLEAR FAMILY

Miriam M. Johnson

This article proposes a theoretical position on sex role learning supported by an analysis of a selected portion of the available research literature. It differs from most papers reported in this book in that it is neither a report of personal research performed by the author nor a nontheoretically based review of the literature. Studies are selected by the author to confirm her point of view and to illustrate the points she is making. Articles such as this, if they are carefully thought out, make a valuable contribution not only in presenting an integrated theoretical viewpoint, but also because they are apt to stimulate further discussion and research. A theory has no real validity until it has been confirmed by adequate research, and although Johnson's position has been derived from previous research findings it can not stand as a confirmed theory in the form presented in this paper. Even though the evidence relevant to her hypothesis is generally supportive, sooner or later the theory must stand a crucial post-test of the hypotheses of which it is composed. All of this does not detract from Johnson's genuine accomplishment of having derived a plausible theory. It simply places the article in perspective and advises the reader of necessary next steps if the theory is to find acceptance. As Johnson notes, "A new idea for which there is some strong evidence . . . does not necessarily lead anywhere unless there is a systematic attempt to assess the relation to and implications for a larger body of theory."

The position of this paper is that adequate identification with the father

SOURCE. From Miriam M. Johnson, "Sex Role Learning in the Nuclear Family," *Child Development*, 1963, Vol. 34, pp. 319–333. (With permission of the author and the publisher, Society for Research in Child Development.)

is necessary for sex role learning for both boys and girls. Sex role learning is viewed as the internalization of a reciprocal role relationship in which the father assumes the major parental role.

THEORETICAL PROPOSAL

Basically, our major proposition is a simple one: we suggest that it is identification with the *father*, in the sense of internalizing a reciprocal role relationship with the father, which is crucial for producing appropriate sex role orientations in *both* males and females. In order to see how women might learn their sex role by identifying with the cross-sex parent, it is necessary to define identification, following Parsons (1958, 1955), as the internalization, not of a total personality or of personality traits, but of a reciprocal role relationship that is functional at a particular period in the child's development. As Parsons puts it:

> Only in a very qualified sense can one say that an infant learns to be like his mother. Rather, he learns to play a social role *in interaction* with her; his behavior—hence his motivation—is organized according to a generalized pattern of norms which define shared and internalized meanings of the acts occurring on both sides (1958, p. 328).

If one takes this view of identification, it becomes possible to postulate, as Parsons does, that the development of personality in the child involves his making a series of successive identifications with increasingly specialized and differentiated social roles. We assume, following both Parsons (1958, 1955) and Mowrer (1950), that both boys and girls identify initially with the mother but that this identification is not sex typed. The possibility we are suggesting is that it is the next identification, with the father, coming after the stage of infantile dependency on the mother, which is crucial for appropriate sex role learning in females as well as in males. Obviously, if girls are to become feminine and boys masculine, the nature of this reciprocal role relationship with the father must be different for each sex. We shall cite evidence later to show that the father does differentiate his role toward opposite sexed children whereas the mother does not.

It is generally assumed, once the Oedipal stage is reached and beyond, that the father takes a less demanding and more "appreciative" attitude toward his daughter than toward his son, playing husband to the girl and mentor to the boy. What has not been generally accepted, however, although the empirical evidence for this too definitely exists, is that the mother does not make a distinction symmetrical to the father's. Although the mother does share common cultural values with the father about what is appropriate masculine and feminine behavior, and may assign tasks, for instance, on a sex typed basis, there is considerable evidence that she does not make a basic differentiation in her attitude toward male and female children. She neither plays wife to her son nor does she urge her daughter to "buck up and get in there and be a woman," rather she thinks of both sexes as "children" whom she treats in the light of her general nurturant and supportive role in the family.

Our theoretical reasons for expecting the father to differentiate his role along the aforementioned lines, while the mother does not, rest on certain considerations about the nature of masculinity and femininity. We think that the crux of this multifaceted differentiation is best captured by Parsons' instrumental—expressive distinction. The expressive role player is oriented toward the relationships among the actors within a system. He is primarily oriented to the attitudes and feelings of these actors toward himself and toward each other. The instrumental role player, by contrast, is oriented toward actively securing a favorable relation between the system and its environment. If we take the family as a whole as the relevant system, the mother is the expressive leader, responsible for the care of individual family members; the father is the instrumental leader, primarily responsible for providing for his family as a unit in the environment.

Motivational Requirements for Expressive and Instrumental Action

Expressiveness is characterized by an orientation toward "pleasing" in the specific sense of receiving rewarding responses from others by virtue of giving them rewarding responses.[1] For example, by being solicitous, appealing and "understanding," a woman seeks to get a pleasurable response by giving pleasure. Theoretically, then, it seems appropriate that expressiveness, a direct sensitivity and responsiveness to the attitudes of others, should be learned through reciprocal interaction with an expressive partner in a relatively permissive context of mutual gratification.

An instrumental role player, almost by definition, cannot be *primarily* oriented to the positive and negative emotional reactions of others to him in the immediate interactional situation because his orientation involves a disciplined pursuit of goals that transcend this situation. In short, he is disposed to view the interaction as a means to an end. He must resist pressures to become affectively involved in the immediate situation itself. Certainly as Bales (1953, p. 161) suggests, one major attitudinal requisite of instrumental

---

[1] When applying the expressive—instrumental distinction to a concrete situation it is necessary to state the interactive system with which one is concerned. A mother may find it necessary to displease one family member (e.g., punish a child who refuses to share) in the interest of harmonious relations in the family as a whole. The proper classification of this act depends on which interactive system one focuses upon.

action would seem to be the ability "to take" the hostile reactions from others which such action is likely to generate. It seems highly unlikely that one could be masculine with the unself-conscious, self-sustaining determination required by instrumentality in order to "please" or be loved. As Arnold Green argues in his classic article, "The Middle Class Male Child and Neurosis" (1946), the male child when made too dependent upon parental love cannot function adequately and aggressively in his peer relations even though his parents expect it of him. Bronfenbrenner's findings in a exploratory study of 400 tenth grade students have led him to the same conclusion. He suggests that:

> . . . love-oriented socialization techniques . . . while fostering the internalization of adult standards and the development of socialized behavior, may also have the effect of undermining capacities for initiative and independence particularly in boys (1961, p. 78).

Propitiation and accommodation in order to get love and masculinity in the sense we define it would seem to be incompatible motivational systems. It would therefore seem more appropriate that an instrumental orientation be inculcated by one who bases his demands, not on love, but on objective punishment or deprivation. This view finds recent empirical confirmation in the studies of child-rearing reported by Sears, Maccoby, and Levin (1957) and by Miller and Swanson (1960). Both studies report "love oriented" techniques seem to produce guilt while physical punishment, threats, and withdrawal of tangible privileges are likely to produce outward aggression in the child.

Male socialization, we think, requires a distinctive "push" into instrumentality that female socialization does not require. A recognition of the difference in the kinds of reinforcement required for the two roles is even reflected in our everyday speech. One never says to a girl "screw up your courage and act like a woman," neither do the women's branches of the armed services promise that their discipline will "make a woman out of you." To males one says "try to be a man," to females one simply says, "be a woman."

Mechanisms of Internalization

It seems fairly clear that the mechanism we have deduced to be appropriate to instrumental learning is closely akin to Freud's "castration fear" or, more generally, fear of overt aggression. On the other hand, the mechanism we think appropriate to expressive learning (love reciprocity) is not quite the same thing as Freud's "anaclitic identification" or fear of loss of love. We think that there are actually three mechanisms which operate, only two of which, fear of aggression and love reciprocity, are specifically relevant to sex role learning. It would seem that "fear of loss of love" is the mechanism most appropriate to the initial, asexual (although expressive) identification made by children of both sexes with the mother. In this first identification children learn to get love rewards from the mother by pleasing her, by being "good" children. It seems likely that it is in this asexual love relationship with the mother, where the child is in a situation of maximum dependency on the rule giver, that the primary superego is formed. It has always appeared unlikely that the presence or absence of conscience should be a sex-linked characteristic. If superego formation, induced by fear of loss of mother's love, *preceded* sex role identification, however, this disturbing conclusion need not arise.

The mechanisms which we think appropriate to the learning of specifically masculine and feminine orientations, then, do not directly involve "fear of loss of love." For the boy "fear of overt punishment" and positively a desire for "respect" would seem to be conducive to an instrumental orientation, and for the girl "love reciprocity" would produce mature expressiveness. In this "love reciprocity" relationship the girl is motivated by the positive desire to get love by giving love which we think is the defining attribute of femininity.

The Father's Role

To argue that the mechanisms for learning masculine and feminine orientations must be fundamentally different does not directly support the conclusion that it is the father who manipulates these mechanisms for both sexes. This conclusion does seem justified, however, if we take into account the proposition that both sexes in order to "grow up" must become emancipated from their infantile love-dependency relationship with the mother. The father as the instrumental leader of the family as a whole represents the outside world to his children. It would seem strikingly appropriate from a psychological standpoint that the parental figure representing independence be the parent responsible for sex role learning, because it seems clear that sex role internalization should take place in a context of at least relative emancipation from infantile dependency.

It should be made explicit that we think the mother does play a part in her children's sex role learning. She does it, however, we suggest, in her role as mother in the family rather than by differentiating her role in the mother-daughter and mother-son subsystems of the family. If she loves her husband and defines him to the children as a worthy person, then this should enormously facilitate the success of the father in emancipating the children from the mother and in determining their sex relevant orientations. In line with this, Helper (1955) reports that males and females are more likely to describe themselves as similar to the father if the mother approves of him as a model.

Expressive Components in Both Sexes

In their early exclusive attachment to the mother, we think that both males and females learn expressive behavior. The task of the girl, then, is to shift her expressive attachment from the mother to a more mature expressive attachment to an adult male. The task of the boy is to shift his expressive attachment to an adult female and also to learn an entirely different orientation, instrumentalness, to be capable of acting effectively upon the nonfamilial environment.

A closely related conclusion is that the masculine personality has two components while the feminine personality basically has only one. The male must be instrumental but also capable of expressiveness, while the female need only be expressive.

TABLE 1

Correspondence Between M-F Personality and Two Parental Roles

		Sources of Male and Female Personality Types	
		Mother's Attitude	Father's Attitude
Personality components of	Males	expressive	instrumental
	Females	expressive	expressive

In very gross terms we think the male-female personality distinction may be expressed as seen in Table 1 which shows the correspondence between the masculine and feminine personality and the two parental roles.

In summary then we have argued theoretically for the following view of identification processes: The mother is predominantly expressive toward children of both sexes and uses, intentionally or not, "love oriented" techniques of control on both. It is in this first identification of both male and female children with the mother in a love-dependency relationship that the basic superego is laid down. Sex role differentiation then follows the initial mother identification and results from the identification of both sexes with the father in differentiated role relationships. The father adds the specifically feminine element to the female's initial expressiveness by rewarding her, by his appreciative attitude, not simply for being "good" but for being "attractive." With his son as with his daughter the father is solidary, but with his son he is also demanding, thus giving the extra push that instrumentalness requires.

EMPIRICAL EVIDENCE

There is no way now to present anything like a crucial test of these theoretical propositions; however, a careful review of the literature, both sociological and psychological, reveals that the empirical findings relevant to our major hypotheses are generally quite consistent with them. Crucial to the argument is the hypothesis that the father differentiates his role toward opposite sexed children whereas the mother does not. Let us begin by considering the evidence on this.

Studies Concerning Parental Attitudes and Roles Toward Male and Female Children

Using a sample of 10- to 14-year-old children in a rural Illinois community, Brodbeck (1954) investigated the question of the separate influence of parents on the moral standards of their children. On the basis of comparisons made between the subjects' responses to identical items from a Parent Description Test and a Personal Values Test he concludes that:

> . . . the major way in which conscience remains sex typed throughout the adolescent years is in terms of the greater influence of the father on the boy's moral views than he has on the girl's. The mother's influence throughout this period does not seem to be differentially sex typed at all, but instead, she seems to have equal amounts of influence on children of both sexes (1954, p. 223).

Here we see evidence of the nonsex typed influence of the mother as well as the differentiated effect of the father. These data also fit the idea that male instrumentality involves new standards, a plus factor, different from the expressiveness learned from the mother by both sexes.

Evelyn Goodenough (1957), in a study involving intensive interviews with upper status parents and nursery school children concerning their conceptions of masculinity and femininity, reports that the mothers are not nearly so concerned with appropriate sex typing in their children as the fathers (1957, p. 311). In addition, she finds the father to be actively and personally involved in sex typing while the mother is aware of it but does not actively implement it. She concludes, admitting some surprise:

> It almost seems as if sex-typing goes on in boys independent of maternal influence, and goes on in girls with very little effort from the mother to exclude masculine influence (1957, p. 312).

An unanticipated finding reported by Pauline Sears (1951) in connection with a study of aggression expressed in a standardized doll play situation by nursery school children from unbroken homes supports yet another facet of this same phenomenon. She reports that:

> These preschool-aged boys express more aggression toward the father doll than toward any other, while the girls depict the father as receiving the least aggression of any of the dolls. There is therefore a highly reliable sex difference on the *father* doll as object of aggression. There is no such difference, however, in the amount of aggression shown by boys and girls toward the mother doll (1951, pp. 11–12).

This finding is quite consistent with the idea that the father is more demanding toward boys than girls and hence generates more aggression toward himself from boys, whereas the mother makes no sex relevant differentiation in her demandingness. Sears herself suggests that "the frustrating value of the mother may be less sex-linked than that of the father" (1951, p. 13), but she does not pursue the implications of this further.

A recent exploratory study by Bronfenbrenner on approximately 200 tenth grade students concerning the relation of parental behavior to the development of "leadership" and "responsibility" in adolescents yields findings exactly in keeping with our hypothesis. In discussing sex differences in parental behavior, he reports as follows:

> ... generally speaking it is the father who is especially likely to treat children of the two sexes differently.... Girls receive more affection, attention and praise than boys—especially from their fathers—whereas boys are subjected to greater pressure and discipline, again mainly from their fathers (1961, p. 249).

He also finds that "... it is primarily fathers whose absence, affection and especially, authority have differential *effects* on both sexes" (p. 255) especially with respect to "responsibility." His analysis of the relation of parental behavior to adolescent behavior is of considerable interest from our standpoint, but its relevance to our problem is somewhat obscured by the fact that he is concerned with his subjects' "leadership" and "responsibility" rather than with their masculinity and femininity.

Several other studies, for example, by Tasch (1952) and Aberle and Naegele (1952), which unfortunately do not take *both* parents systematically into account, report evidence that fathers seem to be concerned about implementing performance relevant characteristics in their sons while they show less concern about and more appreciation for their daughters. The many studies done which involve only mothers, however, do not find such differences in their attitudes and behavior toward opposite sexed children. A study on child-rearing practices by Sears, Maccoby, and Levin (1957) which is based on a large sample of mothers of kindergarten aged children is a case in point. In their chapter on sex differences they report that "a good many mothers did not have very strong attitudes about differentiating the roles of boys and girls" (1957, p. 406) and that "There were surprisingly few dimensions on which the sexes were differently treated" (1957, pp. 401–402). They found that aggression was the area of child behavior in which the greatest sex distinctions were made by parents; however, even though the mothers had differential *values* about the desirability of aggression as between girls and boys, they did not implement these values in their own behavior (1957, p. 253).

With regard to discipline in general they find that:

> The task of disciplining girls of kindergarten age was primarily in the hand of their mothers. For boys the father took a larger role in discipline when both parents were at home (1957, p. 406).

In 1960, the author, using 105 female and 131 male students in various sociology classes as subjects, was able to show this phenomenon of father differentiating, mother not, from a still different standpoint. As a crude measure of the instrumental-expressive dimension, we used five potency scales from Osgood's semantic differential on the assumption that low potency ratings (soft, lenient, light, weak, yielding) are indicative of a more expressive role. The subjects rated themselves ("To me I seem") and their parents' attitude toward them ("With me my mother seems," "With me my father seems") in terms of these five, seven-point potency scales. We were able to show that potency words do differentiate between males and females since males' self-ratings were significantly higher than females' self-ratings on the potency factor and both males and females rated their mother as being lower in potency than their father. While there was no difference between male and female ratings of their mothers on the potency factor, males rated their fathers higher on this factor than females did. (The null hypothesis of no difference was rejected at the .01 level using the Mann-Whitney U Test.) We interpret this to mean that males and females perceive the mother to be equally expressive toward them while females perceive their father to be more expressive toward them than males perceive him to be.

Identification with the Father and Adjustment

In spite of the accumulation of empirical studies dealing with identification, their findings have added up to very little, often being noncomparable and apparently contradictory. One major difficulty with these studies, we think, is that in many instances identification is assumed to take place with total personality characteristics or traits rather than with those aspects of a personality appropriate to a particular role relationship. An important empirical confirmation of the untenableness of the view that sex role identification takes place with the parent's total sex role comes from a study by Angrilli (1960). He measured the M-F characteristics of 30 middle class nursery school boys and their parents using several different instruments and reports as follows:

> No significant relationship was found to exist between the boys and their parents on any individual instrument or combination of instruments. . . . Boys showing high masculine identification may have parents showing high sexual identification to the same extent that they have parents showing low sexual identification. The same is true of boys showing low sexual identification (1960, p. 334).

In the studies on which we shall report, identification has not been defined as trait similarity, but instead these studies in one way or another measure "felt identification," "assumed identification," or "solidarity" with the parent. The apparent logic of the "symmetry" assumption that women *must* identify with their mothers in order to be feminine and that men must identify with their fathers to be masculine has been so pervasive that there are remarkably few identification studies which have taken both parents in relation to each sex systematically into account. Those studies which have done so, however, have yielded "unexpected" results. While in general the assumption that normal men "identify" with their fathers has not been contradicted by the data, the data indicate that normal women also seem to identify in important respects with their fathers. As we shall see, these findings about females have been interpreted in such a way as to leave the "symmetry" assumption essentially unchallenged, however.

Several studies on inferred identification have been done using the semantic differential. The results of these studies are summarized by Osgood (1957):

> The parental identification picture we get as a whole is one in which young men fit the expected pattern fairly well—normal men identifying more with their fathers than their mothers, more with both parents than do neurotic men, and seeing their fathers as nearer the ideal. But this is not the case with the women subjects in these studies. Young women seem to identify as much with their fathers as their mothers, the distinction between normal and neurotic women is not so clear (1957, p. 254).

Gray (1959) studied the relation of perceived similarity to parents and indices of personal and social adjustment in a group of laboratory school children in the fifth through the eighth grade. She concludes:

> Boys who perceive themselves as more like their fathers than their

mothers are perceived more favorably by their peers. With girls, to the extent that a relationship exists, it is in the direction of girls who see themselves as more like their mothers being seen less favorably by their peers (1959, p. 104).

In connection with his study of parental influence on the self-conceptions of high school students, Helper (1955) found that in boys a relatively high degree of self-concept modeling after the father is associated with high adjustment, while with girls a high degree of self-concept modeling after the mother is not associated with adjustment. Thus, all three of the above studies indicate that perceived similarity to the mother is for females either negatively related or not related to indices of personal adjustment.

Perhaps the clearest support for our hypothesis that feminine women and masculine men identify with their fathers comes from a study by Sopchak (1952) on male and female college students in which degree of identification is defined as the similarity among the subject's responses when he took the MMPI as himself, as he thought his father would respond, and as he thought his mother would respond. He finds that for both men and women failure to identify with the father was more closely associated with trends toward abnormality than failure to identify with the mother (1952, p. 165). Most significant of all from our standpoint is his finding that the relation between abnormality in women and lack of identification with the father is *strongest* with respect to the M-F scale of the MMPI, a clear reversal of common sense expectations.

> Women who possess tendencies toward abnormality show a lack of identification with their fathers which is significant at the .01 level in the case of the masculinity scale only.... This finding is difficult to interpret since it indicates that *"masculine" women identify less with their fathers than feminine women* (1952, p. 164, italics mine).

Sopchak's finding that general adjustment in women, to some extent, and femininity, to a marked extent, is related to identification with the father provides an important empirical basis for questioning the usual explanation for Osgood's (1957), Helper's (1955), and Gray's (1959) findings cited above. The usual logic (explicit with both Osgood and Gray) runs like this: When women identify with their fathers, it must mean they are masculine, and, when it turns out these women are well adjusted, it must be because women have to be masculine to be well adjusted in this "masculine" culture. Sopchak's data, however, do not substantiate this interpretation, since they indicate that women who identify with their fathers are feminine and that adjustment is consequently related to being feminine and being identified with the father.

Type of Relationship with Father and Degree of Femininity in Women and Masculinity in Men

The above studies, which have taken both sexes and both parents into account, all suggest that felt or assumed similarity to or preference for the father is important for adjustment in both sexes. We turn now to two studies, one on females only and one on males only, that yield evidence that feminine women do have fathers who interact with them in an expressive manner and that masculine men have fathers who are solidary with them but who are also demanding.

The author in her dissertation study, "Instrumental and Expressive Components in the Personalities of Women" (1955), ranked a random sample of 200 seniors in a women's college in the South on an instrumental—expressive scale based on their responses to a series of role conflict questions. On the basis of another questionnaire given to this group concerning their parents' attitudes toward them (only girls from unbroken homes are considered), we found that the more expressive girls had fathers who would be more disturbed than their mothers "at the thought of (their) growing up and living away from home." This relation reaches statistical significance when restricted to those cases where both parents are described as being "strongly" and "almost equally" doting (1955, p. 171). We also found a marked though nonsignificant trend for expressive girls to be more likely than instrumental girls to answer "father" in response to the question, "Which parent do you feel is most closely attached to you?" (p. 175).

A more detailed study was made of a group of sophomores from unbroken homes taking Introductory Sociology who were ranked either "extremely instrumental" or "extremely expressive." The expressive women described their fathers as being very attentive and protective in their behavior toward them. For example, one expressive girl said, "He brings me little tokens to make me happy," and another said, "He always waits up for me at night, no matter how late I'm going to be" (p. 137). The least expressive women, on the other hand, had fathers whom they tended to describe by such terms as "distant," "cold," and "critical." For example, one of these girls says, "Father, although I know he does, does not seem to care what I do. Often it is as though I did not even exist." Another says, "My father is not a person who shows his feelings" (p. 179).

Although these data, derived from content analysis of descriptive material, are not as systematic as we would have liked, they do strongly suggest that those girls who were least feminine had fathers who were not solidary with them, while the most feminine girls had a solidary relationship with the father in which he was highly expressive. On the other hand, we found that the descriptions of their mothers given by the girls were not related to the latter's sex role orientation (p. 139).

A recent study of kindergarten boys done by Mussen and Distler (1959) comes to the same conclusion with respect to the significance of the mother for sex role learning. They found that the high and low masculinity groups as measured by the It Scale for Children were not significantly different on any of the variables related to their mothers but were significantly different on variables related to their fathers. The authors find that the fathers of high masculinity boys are depicted in doll play by the boys as both high on "nurturance" *and* on "punishment." This finding is exactly in line with the view that masculinity depends on an effective solidarity with the father who is at the same time demanding.

A Summary Study

Using a sample of "only children" in nursery school, Emmerich (1959) designed a study to test the hypothesis that the child would be more likely to identify with attitudes associated with the same sexed parent's sex role than with those associated with the opposite sexed parent's sex role. The great advantage of this study from our standpoint is that it attempts to measure parental attitudes toward and expectations for the child in a role relationship rather than to measure traits characteristic of the parent's total personality. The degree of similarity between the child's conception of a parent's "nurturance" and "control" attitudes (presumably toward him) as assessed in the structured doll play interview and his own nurturance-control attitude was used as an index of the child's identification with the parent.

This procedure yielded precisely the same asymmetry that the other identification studies found, that is, the tendency to select the same sexed parent's attitude as a model turned out to be statistically significant in the case of boys but not for girls. He also finds that, while boys discriminate between parental roles on the nurturance-control dimension, girls do not do so to a significant extent.

In attempting to explain this, Emmerich speculates briefly on the possibility that "parents tend to differ more in their nurturance-control attitudes toward their sons than toward their daughters" (1959, p. 284), but he rejects this on the basis of a questionnaire given to the parents. In spite of a table (p. 283) which clearly indicates that it is the nurturance-control attitude of the *father* with respect to which the sexes differ most (girls giving him a much more nurturant score than boys), he does not entertain this as an explanation.

To us, these data clearly show that girls fail to see a sharp distinction between their parents on the nurturance-control dimension because fathers are more nurturant toward girls than toward boys. Thus, the father would be perceived as being almost as nurturant as the mother. Boys would make a sharp distinction between the parents because the father is more controlling toward them than the mother whose degree of nurturance-control is roughly the same toward both sexes.

33. SEX-ROLE CONCEPTS AND SEX TYPING IN CHILDHOOD AS A FUNCTION OF SCHOOL AND HOME ENVIRONMENTS

Patricia P. Minuchin

Changing times bring new ways and social scientists find it necessary from time to time to reexamine old concepts to learn if previously accepted generalizations still hold their validity in the presence of new conditions. Sometimes, also, advances in techniques of data collection and analysis or in the perception of the importance of new variables lead research workers to make new generalizations or to modify or abandon old ones. In the article which follows Minuchin has taken cognizance of changes in people's attitudes toward male-female sex roles and of the tendency to apply more permissive limits to what is seen as constituting sex-appropriate behavior. In accord with an increasing tendency to question the all-pervasive influence of certain contextual variables, Minuchin has tried to discover to what extent children in similar familial and socioeconomic backgrounds are developing different sex-role concepts and sex-typing as a result of both the home and the non-home environmental factors to which they are exposed. This approach is in marked contrast to some previous studies which have tended to assume that socioeconomic status will take precedence as a determining variable over interpersonal transactions. The reader, however, should not assume that psychologists in their research have not taken cognizance of interpersonal parent-child interactions. They have, as

SOURCE. Adapted from Patricia Minuchin, "Sex-Role Concepts and Sex Typing in Childhood as a Function of School and Home Environments," *Child Development*, 1965, Vol. 36, pp. 1033–1048. (With permission of the author and the publisher, Society for Research in Child Development.) The study described in this paper was undertaken by the Bank Street College of Education and supported by the NIMH (Grant M-1075) and the U.S. Office of Education (Cooperative Research Project 1401).

the approach of the preceding article by Johnson shows. But studies such as Johnson's have not analyzed data in terms of socioeconomic and other physical context variables.

Minuchin's findings indicate that sex-roles and sex-appropriate behavior are indeed both context related and interpersonal-transaction related, but that the latter takes precedence over the former. Children from middle class schools and homes that stressed traditional socialization standards displayed the behavioral characteristics and attitudes traditionally expected of their sex. Such individuals were firmly attached to their sex roles, including family orientation for girls and aggressive expression for boys. On the other hand, middle class children from "modern" homes stressing permissiveness and individualized development tended on the whole to depart markedly from conventional expectations. All of the children in the study are from middle class homes whose main variation has to do with modern as compared to traditional child rearing practices. An important aspect of Minuchin's study is the finding of crucial within class differences. Here we have a further study indicating the inadvisability of generalizing contextual influence from a single category of variables such as socioeconomic status. The reader will be interested to know that Minuchin and colleagues have published a book on this study—*The Psychological Impact of School Experience*. N.Y.: Basic Books, 1969.

This century has seen a broadening in the range of prevailing attitudes toward social sex roles for men and women and sex-appropriate behavior for boys and girls. Increasingly flexible attitudes have grown up and now coexist with more conventional and sex-typed conceptions. Though there has been little specific attention paid to the change as it affects American schools, social scientists have described and discussed this change in the American culture and family (Bronfenbrenner, 1958; 1961; Miller and Swanson, 1958; Parsons, 1942; Riesman, 1958; Sanford, 1958; Sears, Maccoby, & Levin, 1957). They have described an increasing similarity in parents' relations with boys and girls. They have also noted a lessening of dichotomous, sex-typed expectations on the part of parents concerning the interests, abilities, and personality characteristics of their sons and daughters.

These trends are stronger in some sections of the culture than in others. They are more characteristic of the middle than the lower class and more prevalent among the well educated (Bronfenbrenner, 1961; Parsons, 1942; Rabban, 1950; Sanford, 1958). They also vary, obviously, within the educated middle class; some families and schools have been more responsive to these trends, intellectually and psychologically, than others. Where changing attitudes toward sex roles and sex typing have taken root—usually as part of a generalized move away from the traditional—children have been growing up in subcultures different from those with equivalent class characteristics but more traditional orientations. Children who belong to these families or attend schools of similar orientation experience sex-role standards that are less specific, dichotomous, and imperative than those described as traditionally typical of American culture.

It is a primary research task, at this point, to examine the nature of the effects on children—to determine whether children of otherwise comparable backgrounds are developing different sex-role concepts and sex typing in behavior as a function of differences in attitudes and models offered by their schools and homes. This paper presents data bearing on this question.

The material to be presented is drawn from a study that had multiple purposes and a broad scope. It was designed to assess the effects of different educational and home environments on the psychological development of children (Biber, Zimiles, Minuchin, & Shapiro, 1962; Minuchin, Shapiro, Dinnerstein, & Biber, 1961). The different environments were defined in terms of their relatively traditional or modern philosophies and practices. Psychological development was broadly defined and included cognitive functioning, interpersonal attitudes, and aspects of self-image. Material relevant to sex-role concepts and sex-typical reactions constituted a part of the data obtained on the children's development.

The research design involved the study of four urban elementary schools as social institutions, the observation of children in fourth-grade classrooms of these schools, six individual sessions with 105 children from these classrooms, and interviews with mothers of the children selected for study. Since this paper will concentrate on comparing sex-role concepts and sex-typical reactions of children from traditional and modern backgrounds, the description of procedures and methods will be limited to facts essential to an understanding of the findings to be presented.

BACKGROUND AND PROCEDURES

Selection of Schools

Four schools from a large metropolitan area were selected as the study settings, after consultation with local school officials, visits to the schools, and interviews with their principals. They were selected for their variability on a modern-traditional continuum of values, goals, and methods, combined with their equivalence on other basic dimensions: socioeconomic background of the parent population, stability of administration and viewpoint, reputation as good schools, and willingness to cooperate in the research. The differences in modern or traditional viewpoints of the schools constituted the major independent variable of the study.

The "traditional" viewpoint (in school or home) is defined in this study as stressing the socialization of the child, through known and standardized methods, toward established and generalized standards. The schools selected as relatively traditional, therefore, were those that stressed the teaching and mastery of a definite and established body of facts, the competitive and comparative evaluation of achievement, and the maintenance of a distant and inflexible authority role on the part of adults. Relatively fixed conceptions of sex-appropriate roles and behavior were considered part of this constellation.

The "modern" viewpoint is defined in this study as fostering the individual development of the child, through more varied methods and toward more complex and individually relevant standards. By definition, the modern environment incorporates more of the accumulating knowledge of personality formation, child development, motivation, and learning into its methods and goals. The schools selected as modern were those that stressed intellectual exploration and involvement, the shaping of curriculum to basic developmental trends, the individualized evaluation of mastery, and flexible, close relationships between teachers and children. Relatively open conceptions of sex-appropriate roles and behavior were considered part of this constellation.

Two schools (Adams and Browning) were selected as traditional, two (Conrad and Dickens) as modern. Subsequent detailed study of the four schools confirmed the original categorization. Three schools are part of the public school system, but Conrad, the most modern, is an independent school.

Subjects

The sample consists of 105 children, 57 boys and 48 girls, drawn from fourth-grade classrooms in the four schools. Children whose families did not meet the socioeconomic criteria were eliminated from the research. The study children were white, middle-class, urban nine-year-olds, who had been attending their schools since the earliest grades. Fifty-two subjects attended traditional schools and 53 attended modern schools.

Children in all schools except the modern private school came from homes that varied in modern-traditional orientation. For these schools the home and school viewpoints were not correlated. Children in the modern private school, however, tended to come from homes that varied less and were predominantly modern in orientation.

Categorization of Families

Socioeconomic and educational characteristics. A Socio-Economic-Cultural Index (SEC), comprised of family income, parents' education, and the social status of parents' occupations, was applied to all families whose children were considered for inclusion in the study. The SEC Index served as a means for eliminating families with too low a status to match the private-school families and as a means for comparing families that met the selection criteria. Though there is a range among the selected families, the entire sample can be categorized as middle middle class or upper middle class. Income and occupational status tend to be high. Most parents are college graduates.

Modern and traditional orientations. The basic distinctions between modern and traditional families are the same, ideologically, as those for the schools, but, in keeping with the different functions and relationships within the family, the definition is different in detail.

Traditional families are defined as those that stress the social acceptability of the child's behavior and his adaptation to the expectations and standards of his society. In these families adults exercise authority as a fixed prerogative of the adult role. Modern families are defined as those that stress the individual child's needs and rate of growth. They attempt to balance demands for socialization with provision for impulse gratification and individual expression, and they exercise authority in a relatively functional and flexible way.

Ratings of the Modern-Traditional Orientation (MTO) of the families were based on questionnaires and interviews conducted with the mothers of the study children. The questionnaire was concerned with the mother's values and attitudes on child-rearing and education. The interview centered on the mother's attitudes, her actual enactment of her parental role, and her views about education. The composite MTO rating was based on scores considered relevant to the modern-traditional dimension. These were questionnaire and interview scores of modern-traditional ideology and interview ratings on the following measures: enactment of authority role, emphasis on standards of behavior and achievement, encouragement of child's individual interests. The composite MTO rating is along a 7-point scale from most traditional to most modern.

In view of the fact that sex-role attitudes are known to vary with education and socioeconomic status, it is of some importance to describe the relationship, in this sample, between socioeconomic variables and the modern-traditional orientations of the families. There is no correlation between the educational level of the parents and the MTO rating ($r = .09$), probably because the educational level is generally high and the range relatively small. There is no correlation between the SEC Index and the MTO rating for the total sample ($r = .15$) or for the parents of boys ($r = -.09$). There is a significant correlation, however, for the families of girls between higher socioeconomic status and modern orientation ($r = .39$; $p < .01$). While not highly correlated, these factors are not totally independent for parents of girls, even in this sample of relatively restricted range.

In the presentation of findings, correlations with the SEC Index will be included wherever they are at significant levels.

Testing Procedures

The techniques were administered to the children in six individual sessions. They included interviews, intelligence tests, problem-solving tasks, projective techniques, and several miscellaneous tasks. Material for this paper has been drawn from the interview, the Stick Figure Scale (a self-sealing technique), a play session, and the Children's Picture Story Test. Description and scoring of the tests will be indicated in the subsections below.

Protocols were masked for name, school and sex before scoring. Data were analyzed for school and sex differences through analysis of variance.

RESULTS

The material will be presented in two sections, representing two categories of data: social sex-role attitudes, and sex typing in play and fantasy. It was predicted that the traditionally educated and reared children would hold more conventional sex-role attitudes and demonstrate more conventional sex typing than children from more modern backgrounds.

Social Sex-Role Attitudes

Techniques. The children were asked about their sex-role preferences and opinions through two techniques, each calling for consciously held opinions expressed directly to the interviewing adult.

Interview.—In a direct interview question, the child was asked whether it was "best to be a boy or girl."

Stick Figure Scale.—In this technique, based on the work of Mary Engel (Engel and Raine, 1963), the child was presented with ten items, for each of which two stick figures were drawn at opposite sides of the page. The interviewer described the figures in terms of contrasting qualities along some dimension of self-description. The child was then asked which one was more like himself and requested to draw himself in. Of the ten items two are relevant to this paper:

Item A

Here's a boy [girl for girl Ss] who thinks boys have the most fun and the best life.

Here's a boy [girl for girl Ss] who thinks girls have the most fun and the best life.

Responses were coded along a 3-point scale: opposite sex, middle choice, own sex. "Middle" choices were those responses where the child drew himself in the middle, usually with some comment that both have fun, each has advantages, he cannot choose because he has never been a girl, etc. These were considered more open, less committed responses than the "own-sex" choice.

Item B

For boys:

Here's a boy who likes the kind of girl who's a good athlete, strong, likes to play games.

Here's a boy who likes the kind of girl who's sort of sweet, shy, and likes to dress up.

For girls:

Here's a girl who likes the kind of boy who's a good athlete, strong, likes to play games.

Here's a girl who likes the kind of boy who is smart, likes to make things and reads a lot.

It was considered that general cultural stereotypes favor the strong athletic boy and the sweet, reticent, clothes-conscious girl. Responses were coded along a 3-point scale, from less to more stereotyped.

Findings. The interview question yielded a strong group trend and little range of response: 85 per cent of the children chose their own sex as best. Of the remaining children, five—all girls—chose the opposite sex, and these girls came from varied school and home backgrounds.

Item A of the Stick Figure Scale (SFS), though it also showed a clear group trend toward own-sex choices, drew a greater range of response. Sixty-one per cent unequivocally chose their own sex, with boys tending to this choice more than girls ($F = 5.24$; $p < .05$). Of the remaining children, 28 made middle choices and 12, 9 of whom were girls, chose the opposite sex. Children who chose the opposite sex were scattered through the schools and through the range of modern and traditional homes. It seems likely that individual factors were stronger than consistent styles of modern or traditional influence in bringing out this kind of articulate and direct protest.

A comparison of own-sex choices with middle choices, however, yielded a significant connection between the response and the modern or traditional orientations of both schools and homes (see Tables 1 and 2).

Table 1 indicates that traditional school children more consistently chose their own sex as having "the most fun and the best life." Modern school children were more likely to make a middle choice, the difference being carried primarily by the girls. As Table 2 indicates, the relation between the responses and home orientation is in the same direction. The correlations are of a low order, but in the case of the total group, significant. A low order but significant correlation also obtained for girls between own-sex choices and a lower family SEC Index ($r = -.24$; $p < .05$), though not for boys or for the total group.

In relation to both home and school, an unequivocal commitment to the

TABLE 1
Choice of "Best Sex" by Modern and Traditional School Children[a] (Stick Figure Scale)

Item A	No. Traditional School Children (Browning + Adams)	No. Modern School Children (Dickens + Conrad)	Total
Own-sex choice	34	28	62
Boys	19	19	
Girls	15	9	
Middle choice	8	20	28
Boys	5	9	
Girls	3	11	
Total	42	48	90

[a] χ^2 (traditional vs. modern) $= 4.34$; $p < .05$.

TABLE 2
Correlations between Modern-Traditional Orientation of Home and Children's Responses Concerning "Best Sex" and Preferred Qualities in Opposite Sex (Stick Figure Scale)

Stick Figure Scale	Boys	Girls	Total
Item A:			
Own-sex choice	$+.18$[a]	$+.21$	$+.20$**
N	(52)	(38)	(90)
Item B:			
Preference sex-typed qualities opposite sex	$+.21$*	$-.26$	$+.05$
N	(53)[b]	(48)	(101)

[a] Product-moment correlations. Positive correlations signify relationship between described choice and more traditional home orientation.

[b] Discrepancies in N's, on tables, reflect instances where children did not receive tests, respond to certain items, etc.

* Significant at $p < .10$.
** Significant at $p < .05$.

advantages of their own sex tended to be characteristic of children from traditional backgrounds. More open responses were more characteristic of children from modern backgrounds. Overt commitment to the advantages of the opposite sex, however, was not characteristic of either group.

In Item B of the SFS, there was a significant association between modern-traditional school background and the extent to which responses reflected cultural stereotypes. Table 3 presents the means of boys and girls from the

TABLE 3

Preference for Culturally Sex-Typed Qualities in the Opposite Sex: Means of Modern and Traditional School Children (Stick Figure Scale, Item B)

	Traditional School Children						Modern School Children					
	Browning		Adams		B. + A.		Dickens		Conrad		D. + C.	
	N	Means	N	Means	N	Means	N	Means	N	Means	N	Means
Boys	9	1.89	17	2.12	26	2.04	11	1.55	16	1.19	27	1.33
Girls	8	2.50	16	2.38	24	2.42	12	1.92	12	2.25	24	2.08
Total	17	2.18	33	2.24	50	2.22[a]	23	1.74	28	1.64	51	1.69[a]

[a] $t = 3.46$; $p < .01$.

modern and traditional schools and indicates a significant difference in the expected direction.

The relation between responses to Item B and home background is more complex, as indicated in Table 2, at least for the girls. While the preference among girls for strong, athletic young males is associated with more traditional school backgrounds, it is apparently associated with less traditional home backgrounds, as suggested by a low but significant correlation. To illuminate this finding, it might be necessary to explore the particular qualities of these girls' fathers. It should be noted that no relation obtains between girls' responses to this item and the SEC Index of the family ($r = .06$).

Among the boys, the findings from both school and home comparisons are consistent. The boys from traditional backgrounds showed some interest in the sweet and nicely presented girl, while boys from modern schools and homes tended to choose "pals" and reject the decorative girl. No boy from Conrad, the modern private school, reversed this pattern.

Interview discussion about reasons for best-sex choices tended to corroborate the implications drawn from the findings. Only traditionally schooled boys talked of female lives as dull and uninteresting, only traditionally schooled girls projected female advantages in terms of attractiveness, clothes, and the protection and deference accorded adult women. It might be noted, however, that when girls from the most modern background defended their preference for being girls, they tended to describe the disadvantages of the opposite sex rather than offering positive reasons for preferring their own sex role. It seems possible that these girls had neither incorporated cultural stereotypes of their own role nor, at this age at least, developed alternative images that were clear and specific.

The data tapping conscious, directly expressed attitudes about sex-role advantages and social sex images can be summarized as follows:

1. There is a group trend toward stated preference for one's own sex and

toward conventional role imagery, but this trend is more consistently characteristic of children from traditional backgrounds. More open attitudes are associated, as predicted, with more modern backgrounds.

2. An open stance toward sex-role preferences is more characteristic of the girls than the boys. It is particularly characteristic of the girls from schools and homes with modern orientations and from families of higher socioeconomic status.

3. A clearly stated preference for opposite sex roles is rare in this sample and not systematically related to either modern or traditional backgrounds.

4. Both school and home orientation appear to influence these attitudes.

Sex Typing in Play and Fantasy

The idea that certain interests, fantasies, and personality reactions are typical of a particular sex tends to be well documented and accepted. It is generally expected, for instance, that aggression will be typical of boys, dependency and family orientation typical of girls (Kagan, 1964). These differences are considered a partial function of intrinsic factors, but they are generally attributed in large measure to cultural expectations and reinforcements. The modern homes and schools of this study were less bound by conventional cultural expectations than the traditional. They considered a wider range of expression and exploratory behavior acceptable and normal for both boys and girls. It might thus be expected that the play and fantasy concerns of children from modern subcultures would be less consistently sex typed. Projective data were therefore examined for the relation between modern-traditional environments and sex typing in play and fantasy, with particular attention to themes of aggression, dependency, and family orientation.

Techniques. Relevant data were drawn from two projective techniques.

Children's Picture Story Test.—The CPST is a story-telling test, similar to the TAT, consisting of 12 pictures selected for relevance to the age level.

Play session.—A session of approximately 1½ hours in which the child selected from a wide array of miniature toys (people, animals, vehicles, etc.) to play out and verbalize dramatic stories.

Protocols were rated on the following variables:

1. Sex-typed play (play): a rating of the extent to which the child's play was exclusively concerned with content considered typical for the sex (rating 1–2).

2. Aggressive-destructive thema (play): a rating of the incidence of aggressive-destructive themes (war scenes, battles with animals, fire, etc.) in the play session (rating 0–3).

3. Primacy of family life (play): a rating of the extent to which play was centered on family figures and themes (rating 1–3).

4. Incidence of parent figures (CPST): a count of the presence of parent figures in the stories (range 1–10).

5. Projection of benevolent adult behavior (CPST): a rating of the projected emphasis on socializing, disapproving aspects of adult behavior with children as opposed to nurturing, affectionate aspects (rating 1–4; high rating indicates greater projected benevolence).

Findings. There was a general tendency in the group to play out themes easily identified as "typical" for the sex. Boys played out stories of combat, of adventure and action, of boys as central characters. Girls played out stories of family life and interaction, of girls as central characters. There was much play that was not clearly typical for the child's sex, however. Children played out themes considered characteristic of the opposite sex, or developed play involving life sagas, farms and animals, trips, circus performances, city scenes, varying characters, etc., in ways that might characterize their own sex, the opposite sex, or neither.

The incidence of sex-typed play was significantly higher among boys than girls (see Table 4). Two-thirds of the boys played out exclusively sex-typed themes, while most of the girls included themes in their play that were not clearly typical for their sex. This quality of play was most evident among the girls from Conrad, the most modern school. There were no general differences, however, between modern and traditional school groups on the measure of sex-typed play.

As seen in Table 5, there is a significant correlation, for girls, between family orientation and sex-typed play. Wider ranging play is associated with more modern families. No correlation obtains between sex-typed play and the SEC Index. In a separate analysis of 47 children who came from the most clearly traditional or modern families (rated 1, 2, 6, or 7 on the MTO Scale), the general trend was further sharpened (Minuchin and Shapiro, 1964). Girls from clearly modern families were significantly less sex typed in their play than either girls from clearly traditional families or boys from either group (all at $p < .01$).

On the measure of aggressive-destructive thema, there were strong sex differences. Boys tended to play out aggressive themes more than girls (see Table 4). There was considerable variability among the boys, however, and this variability was related to background factors. More aggressive play appeared among the boys of the traditional schools, less among boys of the modern schools, though differences were not statistically significant. Boys and girls of all schools were significantly different from each other in the extent of aggressive play, but the distinction was least evident in Conrad, the most modern school.

For the total group, but especially among boys, there was a low but signifi-

TABLE 4

Sex-Typed Play, Aggressive-Destructive Thema, and Orientation toward Family and Family Figures in Projective Material: Means of Modern and Traditional School Boys and Girls[a]

Projective Variables	Traditional School Children			Modern School Children			Statistical Comparisons
	Browning	Adams	B. + A.	Dickens	Conrad	D. + C.	
Play							
Sex-typed play:							B > G: $F = 9.12$***
Boys	1.70	1.67	1.68	1.67	1.82	1.76	Conrad: B > G: $t = 3.52$***
Girls	1.63	1.38	1.46	1.58	1.25	1.42	
Total	1.67	1.53	1.58	1.62	1.59	1.61	
Aggressive-destructive thema:							B > G: $F = 46.44$***
Boys	2.20	1.89	2.00	1.67	1.50	1.57	B. + A. boys > D. + C. boys: $t = 1.10$ N.S.
Girls	0.25	0.56	0.46	0.42	0.58	0.50	Browning: B > G: $t = 4.53$***
Total	1.33	1.26	1.29	1.04	1.11	1.08	Adams: B > G: $t = 4.16$***
							Dickens: B > G: $t = 2.98$***
							Conrad: B > G: $t = 2.36$*
Primacy of family life:							G > B: $F = 46.16$***
Boys	0.80	0.72	0.75	0.42	0.63	0.54	Browning: G > B: $t = 4.15$***
Girls	2.50	1.75	2.00	2.33	1.17	1.75	Adams: G > B: $t = 3.03$***
Total	1.56	1.21	1.33	1.38	0.86	1.10	Dickens: G > B: $t = 5.97$***
							Conrad: N.S.

TABLE 4 (Continued)

	Traditional School Children			Modern School Children			Statistical Comparisons
Projective Variables	Browning	Adams	B. + A.	Dickens	Conrad	D. + C.	
Children's Picture Story Test							
Incidence of parent figures:							
Boys	5.00	5.18	5.11	4.17	4.35	4.28	Dickens: G > B: $t = 2.24$*
Girls	5.75	4.33	4.83	5.58	4.58	5.08	
Total	5.33	4.78	4.98	4.88	4.45	4.64	
Projection of benevolent adults:							
Boys	1.30	1.18	1.22	1.58	1.38	1.46	G > B: $F = 23.96$***
Girls	2.38	1.93	2.09	2.75	1.55	2.17	Browning: G > B: $t = 3.21$***
Total	1.78	1.52	1.61	2.17	1.44	1.78	Adams: G > B: $t = 2.68$**
							Dickens: G > B: $t = 3.44$***
							Conrad: N.S.

[a] Total sample of 105, with occasional missing cases. See Table 3 for approximate N's.
* Significant at $p < .05$.
** Significant at $p < .02$.
*** Significant at $p < .01$.

TABLE 5

Correlations between Modern-Traditional Home Backgrounds and Children's Scores on Sex-Typed Play, Aggressive-Destructive Thema, and Orientation toward Family and Family Figures

Projective Variables	Boys	Girls	Total
Play:			
Sex-typed play	+.05[a]	+.32**	+.15
Aggressive-destructive thema	+.22*	+.10	+.19**
Primacy of family life	−.05	+.26*	+.03
CPST:			
Incidence of parent figures	+.11	+.33***	+.21**
Projection of benevolent adults	−.06	+.29**	+.09

[a] Product-moment correlations. Positive correlations signify relationship between high score and more traditional home background.
 * Significant at $p < .05$.
 ** Significant at $p < .02$.
 *** Significant at $p < .01$.

cant correlation between aggressive-destructive thema and traditional family orientation. The study of the 47 children from clearly modern or traditional families strengthened this trend. Boys from clearly traditional families were significantly more aggressive in their play than boys from modern families (at $p < .05$) and much more aggressive than girls from clearly traditional families (at $p < .01$). Boys and girls from modern families were not significantly different from each other.

In general, the direction of association on the measure of aggressive-destructive thema is consistent. It suggests that boys from modern backgrounds are less aggressive in their expressed fantasies than boys from traditional backgrounds. It suggests also that the discrepancy between boy and girl aggressive reactions is less extreme among children of the modern subcultures than among those of the traditional.

On the three remaining measures, there were consistent general sex differences. The girls of the sample tended far more than the boys to play out family drama, to make up stories involving parents, and to project adults who were benevolent and nurturing in their attitudes toward children (Table 4). Variations among the girls were great but did not follow lines of modern-traditional difference in school experience. The girls from Conrad, as might be expected, were least oriented toward such themes and were most like the boys, but the strongest orientation toward such themes appeared among the girls of one traditional and one modern school (Browning and Dickens).

There were significant correlations for girls, however, between all three measures and home orientation (see Table 5). Primacy of family life in play themes correlated both with traditional family orientation ($r = .26; p < .05$) and a lower SEC Index ($r = .25; p < .05$). The other two measures did not correlate with the SEC Index but did correlate with family orientation. Traditional family orientation was associated with a high incidence of parent figures in CPST stories and greater projection of benevolent adults. The tendency to project benevolent adult figures in the CPST stories was in contrast to the group trend, which emphasized adult-child conflicts. It seems likely that these girls used the fantasy situation to project their dependent need of protective adults. The study of the 47 children from clearly modern and traditional families bore out the particular family oriented position of girls from traditional homes, as contrasted with the boys and with girls from modern homes.

The data on sex typing in play and fantasy can be summarized as follows:

1. There is a substantial group trend toward sex-typical reactions and concerns, but this trend is more characteristic of children from traditional backgrounds. Less sex-typical reactions are associated, as predicted, with more modern backgrounds. The direction of association is consistent on all measures, though the order of magnitude is not generally high.

2. Girls from modern backgrounds are particularly apt to depart from sex-typed expectations.

3. In areas where sex-typed expectations are particularly strong for one sex (aggression in boys, family orientation and dependence in girls), variability of reaction within that sex is relatively great. Higher aggression in boys and stronger family orientation and dependence in girls are associated with more traditional backgrounds.

4. The influence of family orientation is more evident, in these projective data, than that of the school.

DISCUSSION

The data reported here suggest a consistent connection between modern-traditional background factors and the social sex-role attitudes or sex-typed behavior of children. Previous research in this area has established a connection between children's attitudes and other variables, such as sex membership and socioeconomic family status. Open role commitment and lesser sex typing have been found to be more characteristic of girls than boys and more characteristic of upper middle- than lower middle-class children (Brown, 1956; Emmerich, 1959; Rabban, 1950). The present study corroborates the finding that girls are less sex typed and more flexible in role commitment than boys. It also offers partial support for the relevance of socioeconomic factors, albeit tenuously in this relatively homogeneous sample. Primarily, however, this study suggests that psychological dimensions—differing philosophies of child-rearing and education—are influential in the formation of sex-role attitudes and reactions.

Seen in terms of group patterns, the reactions of the children in this study would be considered typical for boys and girls of this age. They stated a preference for their own sex membership and role and tended to play along sex-typed lines. Boys expressed more aggressive fantasies than girls; girls showed a stronger home and family orientation than boys. As predicted, however, it was mostly children from modern subcultures who departed from conventional expectations and group patterns. These children came from families and schools where socialization toward generalized cultural standards was not the touchstone of child-rearing and education and where expectations for boys and girls were not so dichotomous as in traditional environments.

That this relation was clearer for girls is of particular interest, and not unexpected. Roles for both men and women have been changing, but the most obvious and dramatic changes, certainly, have involved women. The contrast between traditionally accepted standards for female behavior and the modern vision of individual expression and development makes for sharp differences in the experience of girls from different backgrounds. This is particularly true if female adults holding "modern" viewpoints are themselves models for exploratory and complex role integrations. The girls from modern backgrounds, exposed perhaps to both modern attitudes and complex models, exhibited the more open attitudes toward social sex roles. They showed a greater and less sex-typed range of reactions than would conventionally be expected and were relatively free of predetermined stereotypes. At the same time, they were somewhat unclear about the specifics of their own role. Hartley (1964) has noted that we know more about how upper middle-class girls do *not* define their sex roles than about the details of how they *do* define them. The problem may lie not only in a research lag, as she suggests. It may lie also in the complexity of the image that girls from middle-class, modern-oriented backgrounds are attempting to form and integrate.

The relative influence of families and schools is difficult to assess in this study, partly for methodological reasons and partly because they are actually interwoven in the child's experience. There is nonetheless some psychological plausibility to the suggested pattern of findings. The families seem more systematically influential at a level of inner fantasy and personality organization. The schools seem influential at attitudinal levels, where children may be affected not only by direct attitudes toward social sex-role development but by attitudes toward the formation of thought and opinion and the value of exploratory reactions rather than rapid, conventional responses.

In addition to further exploration of the relative roles of home and school, two lines of research seem indicated. One involves elaboration of the background variables contributing to different sex-role attitudes and reactions. It is self-evident that child development in complex areas must be affected not only by specific teachings but by a constellation of general factors, such as authority structure, methods of socialization, attitudes toward individual growth. Such constellations are difficult to describe and measure, and their influence is seldom demonstrated. The establishment of a relation between general modern-traditional attitudes, as defined in this study, and sex-role reactions of children is interesting and important at its own level. To account in greater part for the children's reactions, however, it would clearly be necessary to integrate these findings with research on other factors: the influence of peer-group attitudes, the influence of parents and teachers as identification figures, of sibling structure in the family, of parental sex-role preferences, etc.

The second line of research involves the relation between sex-typed reactions and the process of maturation toward a resolved sex identity. It does not seem valid to assume, though psychological research has sometimes done so, that all departures from sex-typical behavior indicate faulty identification and a poor prognosis for normal, integrated development. Modern homes and schools have, in fact, followed different reasoning. They have assumed that the loosening of stereotypes in social roles and the provision of opportunity to develop in keeping with individual propensities would result in more integrated development and more resolved identity. Research would need to evaluate the course of development for children from modern and traditional backgrounds, assessing sex-role resolution as these children move into stages of adolescence and maturity.

34. EFFECTS OF PARENTAL ABSENCE ON SEX-TYPED BEHAVIORS IN NEGRO AND WHITE PREADOLESCENT MALES

E. Mavis Hetherington

Behavioral scientists and other professional workers at every level have long recognized that the family is the most important component of the culture in determining a child's level of adjustment and future behavior. Certainly there is ample research evidence to support their belief. Yet, despite the large amount of research already accomplished on the family the complexity of family internal and external relationships is such that much yet needs to be done. Hetherington has considered in her study the consequences of father absence on preadolescent boys' sex-role preferences, aggression, dependency and recreational outlets. In doing so she has analyzed her data for Negro-white comparisons.

A young child spends the greatest proportion of his time within the family circle, and it is there that he learns the roles he must play. His family defines his status, initiates his socialization experiences and directs them throughout the first two decades of his life. It gives as well as withholds opportunity, and can become a place of refuge as well as a prison. In all of these matters the parents, of course, play a major role. Thus it is of particular importance in gaining an understanding of child development to know something of the dynamics of personal interaction within the family. One aspect of interaction has to do with the relative influence of the various members of the family unit under a variety of different conditions.

SOURCE. Adapted from E. Mavis Hetherington, "Effects of Parental Absence on Sex-Typed Behaviors in Negro and White Preadolescent Males," *Journal of Personality and Social Psychology,* 1966, Vol. 4, pp. 87–91. (With permission of the author and the publisher, The American Psychological Association.)

Hetherington's results give us insight into crucial aspects of early masculine identification.

This study investigated the effects of father absence on the development of sex-role preferences, dependency, aggression, and recreational activities of Negro and white preadolescent boys. All children had mothers but no father substitutes present in the home and no contact with the fathers subsequent to separation.

In previous studies of the effects of father absence on the development of children, total and final absence of the father usually had not occurred. The father was either temporarily away due to war (Bach, 1946; Sears, Pintler, & Sears, 1946) or to occupational demands (Lynn & Sawrey, 1959; Tiller, 1958). An exception to this is the McCord, McCord, and Thurber (1962) study of boys from broken homes. These studies frequently indicated disruption of masculine identification in boys whose fathers were absent. Boys with fathers absent from the home tended to be less aggressive in doll-play situations (Sears et al., 1946), had father fantasies more similar to those of girls (Bach, 1946), and were more dependent (Stolz et al., 1954; Tiller, 1958) than boys whose fathers were living in the home. In contrast to these findings McCord et al. found no differences in dependency between boys from homes in which the father was absent and those in which the father was present and found the former group was more aggressive. The Lynn and Sawrey study also indicated that boys deprived of regular contact with their fathers made stronger strivings toward masculine identification shown by preference for a father versus a mother doll in a Structured Doll Play Test, and manifested an unstable compensatory masculinity. They found no differences between boys whose fathers were absent and those whose fathers were present in ratings of dependency in the doll-play situation and attribute this to a "compensatory masculine reluctance to express dependency [p. 261]."

It might be expected that if boys with absent fathers in contrast to those with a father present manifest compensatory masculinity they would score high on behaviors associated with masculinity such as independence, aggression, masculine sex-role preferences, and participation in activities involving force and competition. Moss and Kagan (1961) suggested that for boys, participation and skill in sports is closely involved with maintenance of sex-role identification. However, if father absence results in a direct expression of a failure to establish masculine identification, boys without fathers would be rated low on the previous variables.

The age at which separation from the father occurs could differentially affect the form of disrupted identification in boys. Early separation may result in greater disruption of sex-typed behaviors than would later separation when identification is well under way or completed. Early separation might result directly in less masculine sex-role behaviors since identification with the father has never developed. In contrast later separation may have little effect on these behaviors or result in exaggerating masculine behavior in an attempt to sustain the already established masculine identification with the major role model, the father, absent.

It might also be expected that the effects of father absence would interact with the race of the family. It has frequently been suggested that the Negro family structure is basically matriarchal (Karon, 1958). Maternal dominance has been demonstrated to have a disruptive effect on sex typing in boys (Hetherington, 1965; Mussen & Distler, 1959). In such mother-dominated families, absence of the father might be expected to have a less disruptive effect on sex-typed behavior of boys than it would in a father-dominant family.

Kardiner and Ovesey (1951) suggest that Negroes have strong inhibited aggressive needs which are displaced and expressed in competitive sports. It would therefore be predicted that Negroes would be rated lower in overt social aggression than would white boys, but would show a marked preference for aggressive, competitive activities.

METHOD

Subjects were 32 Negro and 32 white first-born boys between the ages of 9 and 12, who were attending a recreation center in a lower-class urban area. Sixteen of the boys in each group were from homes in which both parents were present, and 16 from homes in which the father was absent. In half of the father-absent homes for Negro and white families, separation had occurred at age 4 or earlier, and in half, after age 6. Father separation as caused by desertion, divorce, death, and illegitimacy. No father substitutes lived in the home. There were no significant differences in causes of father separation between groups, although illegitimacy was a cause only in the early groups.

Forty-nine of the subjects were only children, seven subjects had a younger male sibling, and eight subjects had a younger female sibling. These subjects were distributed approximately evenly across groups, although there was a slightly larger proportion of only children in the group of children whose fathers left early than in the groups whose fathers were present or had left the home after age 6.

Procedure

Two male recreation directors who had known the subjects for at least 6 months rated them on 7-point scales measuring dependence on adults, dependence on peers, independence, aggression, and on an activities test. The scales ranged from 1, very rarely and without persistence, to 7, very often and very persistently. Interrater reliabilities ranged from .85 to .94. All subjects were also individually administered the It Scale for Children (ITSC; Brown, 1956).

Measures

Scales for dependence and independence were based upon those used by Beller (1957). The aggression scale was based on that of Sears, Whiting, Nowlis, and Sears (1953). Behaviors involved in each scale were more fully elaborated as in Beller (1957), but used behaviors appropriate to the age group of the present study. A total rating for each of these three scales was obtained.

Rating Scale for Dependence on Adults was comprised of ratings of:

1. How often does the boy seek physical contact with adults?
2. How often does the boy seek to be near adults?
3. How often does the boy seek recognition (any form of praise and punishment) from adults?
4. How often does the boy seek attention from adults?

Rating Scale for Dependence on Peers was composed of the same items as dependence on adults oriented toward children.

Rating Scale for Independence involved the following four of Beller's autonomous achievement striving scales:

1. How often does the boy derive satisfaction from his work?
2. How often does the boy take the initiative in carrying out his own activity?
3. How often does the boy attempt to overcome obstacles in the environment?
4. How often does the boy complete an activity?

Rating Scale for Aggression involved the following items:

1. How often does the boy act to necessitate correction, scolding, or reminding?
2. How often does the boy ask for special privileges?
3. How often does the boy attack other children or their property to show envy?
4. How often does the boy threaten adults?
5. How often does the boy threaten other children?
6. How often does the boy destroy the property of the Center or of other children?
7. How often does the boy derogate others?

8. How often does the boy quarrel with other children?
9. How often does the boy display undirected aggression?
10. How often does the boy attack other children physically?
11. How often does the child exhibit display aggressive attacks?

The Activities Test was comprised of ratings on a 7-point scale ranging from 1, very rarely participates in this activity, to 7, very often and persistently participates in the activity. Five activities in each of four categories were rated. In standardizing the Activities Test three recreation directors were asked to sort a group of 48 activities into the following four categories. Only those on which the three judges agreed were retained.

1. Physical skill involving contact—boxing, wrestling, football, basketball, battle ball.
2. Physical skill not involving contact—foot racing, bowling, horseshoes, table tennis, darts.
3. Nonphysical competitive games—dominoes, checkers, scrabble, monopoly, cards.
4. Nonphysical, noncompetitive games—reading, watching television, building things, working on puzzles, collecting things.

Total ratings for each of the four types of activities were obtained.

The ITSC (Brown, 1956) is a test of sex-role preference which presents the child with an ambiguous figure (It) and asks the child to select from a group of toys and objects those that "It" prefers. A high score indicates masculine preference.

RESULTS

Separate two-way analyses of variance involving race and father status (early absent, late absent, and present) were calculated for each scale. When significant F ratios were obtained, t tests between means were calculated. Table 1 presents the means for all groups on all variables.

The analysis of variance of total dependence on adults yielded no significant differences; however, the analysis of dependence on peers yielded a significant F ratio ($F = 10.18$, $p < .005$) for father status. Subsequent t tests indicated that both early-separated and late-separated boys were significantly more dependent on peers than were the boys with fathers living in the home ($t = 2.23$, $p < .05$; $t = 2.90$, $p < .005$).

No significant differences were found between groups on total independence scores.

The analysis of total aggression scores indicated a significant effect of father status ($F = 10.39$, $p < .005$) on aggressive behavior. Both boys who were deprived of their fathers after age 6 and boys whose fathers are present

TABLE 1

Means for Father Separation Early, Father Separation Late, and Father Present, Negro and White Boys

	Father Present		Early		Late	
	White	Negro	White	Negro	White	Negro
Dependency on adults	15.69	15.19	14.25	14.00	12.75	13.00
Dependency on peers	15.31	15.50	17.62	18.25	18.25	19.12
Independence	15.75	15.69	18.25	15.37	15.25	18.25
Aggression	39.87	47.06	32.00	30.75	51.00	52.12
ITSC	67.56	70.69	53.50	55.00	65.12	73.25
Physical contact	20.62	23.62	14.87	18.87	21.50	21.87
Physical noncontact	21.06	18.75	15.37	17.50	21.12	17.00
Nonphysical, competitive	21.44	20.81	16.87	18.62	20.12	17.62
Nonphysical, noncompetitive	17.69	16.62	24.25	22.37	21.37	19.12

manifested more aggression than boys who were deprived of their fathers at an early age ($t = 3.20$, $p < .005$; $t = 2.21$, $p < .05$, respectively).

The results of the ITSC also yielded a significant effect for father status ($F = 4.966$, $p < .025$). Boys experiencing late separation from the father and boys from unbroken homes have more masculine sex-role preferences than early-separated boys ($t = 2.32$, $p < .05$; $t = 3.14$, $p < .005$).

The Activities Test indicates that early-separated boys play fewer physical games involving contact than do either late-separated boys or boys with fathers living in the home ($t = 2.06$, $p < .05$; $t = 2.60$, $p < .025$). Negro boys tend to play more games of this type than do white boys ($t = 2.22$, $p = .05$). It should be noted that this is the only significant racial difference found in the entire study. No significant effects were obtained in the analysis of physical activities involving no contact or in nonphysical competitive activities. However, a significant effect ($F = 8.236$, $p < .005$) for father status was found in nonphysical, noncompetitive activities. Early-separated boys spend more time in these activities than do boys living with both parents.

It seemed possible that the obtained differences between early- and late-separated boys were a result of the total time elapsed since the father left the home, rather than the developmental stage at which separation occurred. The early-separated children may have had more time for a loss of cathexis on masculine behaviors. In order to investigate this possibility, an attempt was made to compare subjects in the early- and late-separation groups who had been deprived of their fathers for 6 years. The resulting Ns in each group were too small to permit an adequate analysis of the scores ($N = 4$ in early separated, $N = 3$ in late separated); however, the results appeared to parallel those of the total early- and late-separated groups.

394   SOCIAL DEVELOPMENT: READINGS IN EDUCATIONAL RESEARCH

The small sample size and predominance of only children did not permit a satisfactory analysis of the effects of family size and sex of sibling on the behavior studied.

Table 2 presents the intercorrelations among all variables studied for all subjects.

TABLE 2

Correlations among All Variables for All Subjects

	1	2	3	4	5	6	7	8	9
1. Dependence on adults	1.00	.02	−.25**	.06	.04	.04	.06	.11	−.06
2. Dependence on peers		1.00	−.10	.06	.04	−.02	.03	−.26	.10
3. Independence			1.00	.05	.02	−.01	.11	.17	−.17
4. Aggression				1.00	.21*	.40****	.22*	−.01	−.33***
5. ITSC					1.00	.38***	.02	.09	−.29***
6. Physical contact						1.00	.13	.03	−.59****
7. Physical noncontact							1.00	.17	−.16
8. Nonphysical, competition								1.00	−.23
9. Nonphysical, noncompetition									1.00

Note.—Numbered variables in columns correspond to those in rows.
 * $p = .10$.
 ** $p = .05$.
 *** $p = .01$.
 **** $p = .001$.

Dependence on adults but not on peers is negatively related to independence. Masculine sex-role preferences, aggressive behavior, and participation in physical activities cluster together. Conversely, it appears that boys who enjoy nonphysical, noncompetitive activities are low in masculine sex-role preferences, aggression, and in participation in activities involving physical contact or nonphysical competition.

DISCUSSION

The results of the study indicate that absence of the father after age 5 has little effect on the sex-typed behaviors of boys. These boys in most respects do not differ from boys who have their fathers present. They are similar in their independence, dependence on adults, aggression, and sex-role preferences. In preferences for activities involving physical force or competition which might permit socially accepted expression of compensatory masculinity we again find no differences. An increased dependence on the adult all-male staff of the recreation center might have been expected if the boys lacking fathers were seeking attention from other adult males as father substitutes. This did not occur. It appears that any frustrated dependency needs which loss of a father might have produced do not generalize to other adult males. In fact there was a trend for boys with no fathers to be less dependent on adults ($F = 2.56$, $p < .10$). The greater dependence on peers of boys who have lost their fathers early or late is difficult to explain. It may be that loss or lack of a father results in a mistrust of adults with a consequence compensatory increase in dependence on peers. This general pattern of relations was reported by Freud and Burlingham (1944) in their studies of children separated from their parents by World War II. These children showed strong ties to their peers but few emotional ties to adult caretakers in institutions.

Boys who lost their fathers early, before identification can be assumed to have been completed, showed considerable deviation in sex-typed traits. They are less aggressive and show more feminine sex-role preferences than the other boys. They also participate less in physical games involving contact and more in nonphysical, noncompetitive activities. This preference for the latter type of activity could be considered an avoidance of activities involving the appropriate masculine behaviors of competition and aggressive play. An alternative explanation might be that it is a manifestation of social withdrawal since the activities in that category tend to be ones which involve a minimum of social interaction. It is difficult to accept this interpretation in view of the high dependency on peers ratings obtained by these boys. One could speculate that these boys make unsuccessful dependent overtures to peers, are rebuffed, and remain socially isolated.

The results suggest that adequate masculine identification has occurred by age 6 and that the identification can be maintained in the absence of the father. If the father leaves in the first 4 years before identification has been established long-lasting disruption in sex-typed behavior may result.

The predictions concerning racial differences were only partially confirmed. Differences between Negro and white boys in overt aggression which would be expected if Negroes inhibit direct expression of aggression were not obtained. However, the predicted high participation of Negroes in competitive activities involving contact was found. On the basis of this study it must be concluded that the behavior of Negro and white boys observed in the setting of a recreation center appears very similar.

CHAPTER 7

Learning to Understand and to Live with Others

The founding fathers of the United States, building on the American colonial people's conviction that there should be recognized certain inherent and inalienable rights of man, incorporated into the Declaration of Independence and the Bill of Rights certain statements affirming their faith in the essential political equality of man and the ideal of a classless society. These documents affirmed political rights and extended political protections, but did not deal with the social implications of the laws they provided—although some of the founders (Jefferson, in particular), in advocating the protective apparatus of the Supreme Court, seemed well aware of the likelihood and desirability of eventually including social implications in the laws of the land. Today interpersonal social rights, indeed, have been incorporated into explicitly stated law and judicial interpretation. But constitutions, their supporting statutes, and evolved precedents can be legal formalities—even fictions insofar as their actual effective implementations are concerned. However, in the everyday interpersonal relationships of people, laws cease to be fictions and become the facts of daily living. For the real implementation of the ultimate social equality extension of our democracy we must look to the attitudes, the feelings, and the knowledges that our citizens, both children and adult, have about each other. And these are matters of learning, of modeling, and of direct personal transaction. As a people we need to know a great deal about each other, including the nature and meaning of our prejudices and their bases in fact if our democracy is to reach full fruition. Fortunately, America is dedicated to the concept of universal education and our schools since World War I are indeed gradually becoming schools for all the children of all the people.

Children initially learn to understand the world as it is presented to them, and presentation and inculcation are the tools of education. Thus, schools through their educational programs, their attitudes, and the examples they model are in a position to do much to make possible desirable democratic social changes. Next to parents, and in some aspects even before parents, teachers have the greatest responsibility and the greatest opportunity to participate in democratic social learning for children.

But in order to proceed most efficiently in working with prejudice and social behavior teachers need to know as much about these matters as they possibly can. A major source of knowledge about prejudice and social behavior of children has been the research accomplished in psychology and the other behavioral and social sciences. Some of the studies have been descriptive, relating merely the extant situation as it obtains among various demographic and subcultural groupings. Others have been concerned with the process of learning during socialization, and still others have been concerned with the dynamics of interpersonal relationships. The findings of these studies should be of interest to everyone concerned with the education of children in a democracy, particularly if they are engaged as professionals in those teachings designed to lead to democratic behavior. The six articles included in this chapter are examples of research in children's social understandings. The results of each study have specific relevance for children's socialization and provide teachers information about the normative base of understanding and outlook they can assume among at least some of the groupings of children placed in their charge.

At about what age do awareness of group differentiations, psychological needs arising out of group memberships and social prejudices develop in children? Do the beginnings of such development occur in adolescene or do they come as early as middle childhood or, perhaps, even in early childhood? The answer has important implications for the kinds of social learnings that schools should attempt to introduce at various points in the curriculum. Most persons would tend to assume that these learnings are hardly an issue in the earlier years of childhood, but the study by Radke, Trager, and Davis indicates that these learnings do begin in the early years and that awareness, interests, and fears and securities related to group factors can not be deferred beyond the preschool and early school years if the personal-social needs of children coming of age in a democracy are to be met. In their study, using as subjects first and second graders, Radke and her associates examined the origin and nature of children's social concepts as they apply to racial and religious groups. Of particular concern to the investigators were children's awareness of social values, conflicts, and differences in status. In their answers to questions children in the study reacted to Negro, white, Catholic, Protestant, and Jewish groupings although not all of these groupings were equally familiar to all of the children. Findings include not only the early childhood origins of cultural content and attitudes relating to racial and religious groups but also the pertinence as models of adult attitudes. The group appears to be important in early childhood as a context for a child to learn not only his own personal role and attitudes but also for him to learn the expectancies that he should have about others' roles and attitudes toward himself and the subcultural group of which he is a member. Minority status can have a negative effect upon a child in child-group transactions if the group is not accepting of his status. The educational implication of this study beyond curriculum placement of social learning experiences is that the child-group itself may be used by the teacher as a desirable means of providing social learnings and, conversely, that without educational guidance the child-group may become the source of a whole array of undesirable social learnings.

Teachers who learn from studies such as that of Radke et al. that the child-group can be used for purposes of social learning at a given age level need further information on methods and techniques designed to further their social learning objectives under specified conditions. A number of available research studies do provide some indication of possible techniques, although the main topic of many such studies is not specifically addressed to the location and testing of techniques. An example of a study providing technique information is the one performed by King. King's study was designed to investigate spatiotemporal relationships resulting from friendly and unfriendly interactions among a group of kindergarten children. It was found that the ratio of unfriendly acts to the total number of acts made by one child to another during a free play situation was highly related to the mean distance maintained by the recipient of the unfriendly acts from the aggressor. King reported that when two children were playing some distance apart because of previous unfriendly interchanges, a means of bringing them at least spatially more closely together was effected by placing a prized toy or some other desired stimulus object in juxtaposition to the recipient of the unfriendly acts. The resulting approach behavior of the child farthest from the desired stimulus object would give the teacher an opportunity to take action designed to promote a more friendly level of interaction between the two.

When a teacher has to deal with two populations differing on some obvious variable such as race it is helpful for her to know not only to what extent the two are different or similar on other less obvious variables but also, where differences do occur, something of the reason for their occurrence. Studies comparing Negro and white children have reported important overall differences in racial self-identification, racial recognition ability, and racial preference. But, in view of the existence of individual differences it is reasonable to ask to what extent overall patterns conceal individuals and groups who deviate from the pattern. Morland's study is an example of an attempt to look for such intragroup differences. Using as his sample members of both races in nursery and day care centers in Virginia and Massachusetts, he reexamined the question of differences in race awareness from the point of view of region as well as race. His sample was divided into northern Negro, northern white, southern Negro, and southern white. His general finding was that American Negro and white children of preschool age differ in racial awareness even across regional areas. However, some regional differences in magnitude exist. Differences between white and Negro children are accentuated in the southern setting; but, interestingly enough, in examining cross-racial preferences Morland found that southern Negroes were more likely to prefer whites than northern Negroes. A further confirmation of this tendency occurs in a study by Epstein and Komorita, who reported that Negro children (Circa 1966) tend to identify with various aspects of the general white culture rather than with their own minority racial group. Their sample consisted of fifth-grade Negro boys and girls of predominantly working class parents. They found, in agreement with previous studies, that there is a well-defined tendency among Negro children to adopt the prevailing prejudices of the white majority. However, individual propensities and up-bringing appear to be important in determining the extent to which a child's rejection and acceptance stance will be directed toward or against his own race as well as toward races and groups other than his own. With a child of any race, parents' child-rearing practices can become a crucial issue. One problem faced by the Negro in his analysis of white attitudes is that he can only make assumptions, and these assumptions may be opposed to reality. For example, Epstein and Komorita note that the Negro child's frequent pattern of low self-esteem is based less on socioeconomic than on racial factors, suggesting that the Negro's perception of dark skin color as the basis for the white person's hostility may be discrepant from the basis employed by many whites, namely the Negro's low socioeconomic status. It is in such areas of misunderstanding that school social learning programs including members of both races may offer real help.

The final paper by Stein, Hardyck, and Smith provides an optimistic note for educators wishing to build programs designed to promote understanding and communication between the two races. They report that when teenagers are forced to evaluate stimulus individuals in terms of their beliefs, then belief congruence is more important than race. However, when the belief component was not made explicit the teenagers tended to react on racial bases, making stereotyped assumptions about the belief systems of others. It would appear that schools that permit children of different races to encounter each under such favorable perceptions of belief congruence as equal-status contacts are in a position to do a great deal to reduce racial prejudice.

35. SOCIAL PERCEPTION AND THE ATTITUDES OF CHILDREN

Marian Radke,[1] Helen G. Trager, & Hadassah Davis

Traditionally, school curricular objectives emphasized the attainment of information and skills. Relatively little attention was paid to attitudes and values, the assumption being that the attainment of knowledge resulted in the possession of desired values. Research has indicated that such is not the case and over the past few decades there has been increasing interest in the non-subject matter outcomes of the school experience. Today, with pressures engendered by an increasing population and a new recognition of the problems and rights of minority groups there is an even greater reason for schools to concern themselves with teaching for social values. But instructional techniques aimed at the domain of interpersonal transactions require a great deal of knowledge and skill on the part of teachers, including acquaintance with the nature and origins of the behaviors they are trying to inculcate. Research on the social perception and attitudes of children such as that accomplished by Radke and her associates can serve the valuable function of helping teachers attain a better understanding of the behaviors with which they are concerned in their instructional programs.

Using as its target area attitudes toward racial and religious groups the

SOURCE. Adapted and abridged from Marian Radke, Helen G. Trager, and Hadassah Davis, "Social Perception and Attitudes of Children," *Genetic Psychology Monographs*, 1949, Vol. 40, pp. 327–447 as presented in R. G. Kuhlen and G. G. Thompson (Eds.) *Psychological Studies of Human Development*, New York: Appleton-Century-Crofts, 1970. (With permission of Drs. Radke Yarrow and Trager and the publishers, The Journal Press and Appleton-Century-Crofts.)

[1] Now Marian Radke Yarrow.

study reported below is concerned with the nature and origin of children's social concepts and with their awareness of social values, conflicts, and differences in status. Results are presented in terms of attitude development theory and the effects upon the individual of membership in a group. Two hundred fifty children enrolled in kindergarten and in the first and second grades were used as subjects in the study. Data were gathered by means of interviews and a picture Social Episodes Test.

SUMMARY OF FINDINGS

1. Cultural Content and Attitudes Relating to Racial and Religious Groups Are Learned Early in Childhood

Almost all the children studied show some differentiation of their social environment in group terms. At a minimum this differentiation involves an association of group labels with some fragment of personal experience ("Catholic is St. Anne's school") or with hearsay ("Colored is bad"). At the other extreme of differentiation, some children describe group characteristics and customs in detail; they describe status positions and group conflicts; they express their own feelings toward the groups and see social relations among different persons modified by such various considerations as:

> White don't like colored, but maybe they know the boy (and will let him play).
>
> They (children in picture) are saying, "I don't like these people I hate them and they are too fresh." I don't say that to hurt other people's feelings. I play with them.

The groups studied (Negro, white, Catholic, Protestant, Jewish) are not equally familiar to the children. While none of the subjects fails to recognize Negro and white differences, many are unable to supply content for one or more of the religious groups. "Catholic" is unknown to 19 per cent of the white children and 53 per cent of the Negro children; "Protestant" is unknown to 61 per cent of the white children and 87 per cent of the Negro children; and "Jewish" is unknown to 21 per cent of the white children and 59 per cent of the Negro children.

Group differentiations are made at various levels of understanding: (a) The group label is only a thing, something to do, an institution, but without clear reference to people (Catholic is "beads"; Jewish is "pickles"; Protestant is "sing songs"). (b) Group labels represent classifications of people along clearly or vaguely defined dimensions ("Jewish is people" or "Catholic, Jew, any kind of people, Protestants"). (c) Group labels stand for transitory conditions or behavior which make one a certain kind of person or give one a certain kind of experience ("When he gets dirty he turns into a colored boy"), ("You are Catholic when you go to Catholic school"). (d) Group labels represent classifications of people about whom evaluations are made ("They are saying the Catholic people are no good. Some people just hate Catholic people").

Varying shades of hostility and friendliness are expressed toward each of the groups. Group differences are recognized as signals for various kinds of "appropriate" social behavior. The group receiving the greatest amount of hostility and rejection is Negro. Responses toward Negro correspond to adult culture patterns: (a) segregation of white and Negro ("White and colored can't play together"); (b) racial hostility ("I don't like nigger kids"); and (c) stereotypes of Negro character ("tough," "dirty," "kill whites").

The white children ascribe aggression to both races. When it is aggression in the sense of exclusion and rejection, it is more frequently seen as expressed by whites; when it is physical aggression it is more frequently attributed to Negroes. The Negro children have learned the same culture patterns of rejection by the white group and hostility between the races. The effects of this awareness upon self-concepts are discussed below.

Regarding the religious groups, expressions of aggression are more frequent against Jewish than against Catholic and Protestant. The nature of the aggressions against each religious group again follows cultural prescriptions, and, more evidently than in the case of Negro and white, follows the peculiar patterns of the immediate neighborhoods (see 2 below).

Based on responses to questions, "Is this little boy glad he is_____ (Negro, white, Catholic, Protestant, Jewish)?" and "Why?" the relative acceptance of each group compared with every other group was obtained. The results are, in general, in line with the status positions of these groups in American culture. The groups, in ascending order of acceptance, are Negro least accepted, Jewish next, and Catholic and Protestant next, about equal. (It is hazardous to interpret too literally the results on "Protestant," since it is an unfamiliar term to many children.) The order of acceptance is the same when responses of children who do not belong to the group in question and responses of children who are members of the group in question are considered separately.

2. The Social Learning Concerning Racial and Religious Groups Reflects the Particular Cultural Context in Which the Child Lives

Local neighborhood patterns and family group memberships are among the important subcultural differences which influence the responses. In a neighborhood in which tensions exist between Italian Catholics and Jews, the children show a heightened awareness of these groups. They tend to classify people with reference to these groups; thus, if told "These children are

Jewish," a probable continuation by the child is "These others are Italian." They express competitive and hostile attitudes toward one or the other group. In another neighborhood, in which Protestant and Catholic religions are an issue, the children are more aware of Protestant than in any other neighborhood, and the in- and out-groups in their story themes are frequently Protestant and Catholic. "Jewish" is a more remote out-group, often classified as "not American." Similar, though less striking, local variations appear in the children from other neighborhoods. There is much less neighborhood variation in responses on Negro than on religious groups.

3. The Child Learns the Adults' Attitudes Toward Groups

Adult values and interpretations of the social world play a considerably more prominent role than do interpersonal experiences of the child with members of any one of the groups. The role of the adult as intermediary can be inferred from the children's references to parents' admonitions ("Sometimes other people's mothers don't like Protestants to play with Catholics"); to adult accounts of experience ("A colored man gave my father [taxi-driver] a dollar tip"); to religious teachings which "justify" attitudes ("They put God on the cross and that's why they [children in the picture] don't like them," "I learned about colored and white in Sunday School"); and to generalizations which are probably formulated by adults ("If you're kind you play with everybody").

Many of the statements which express the child's own reactions to a group are of the kind, "It is bad to play with _____" or "I don't like _____." They are rarely of the kind in which personal experience alone leads to a negative reaction, such as the hypothetical response, "I played with a Negro boy; he was mean to me, and therefore, I don't like Negroes." There are numerous responses which show that prohibitions or expectations set up by adults either prevent personal experience which is available in the child's environment and by which the child could form his own opinions ("If she's white she's allowed to play in people's yards") or which predispose him to negatively affected perceptions of his experience ("Well, my mother said that sometimes colored people beat up white children").

4. The Extent of the Learning about Groups and the Degree of Crystallization of Attitudes Increase with the Age of the Child

Increases in social learning correlated with age are in the direction of greater *awareness* of group conflicts, patterns of exclusion, and forms of stereotyping and derogation; and in the direction of greater *acceptance* of prejudiced attitudes. There is no age trend (between kindergarten and second grade) in the accuracy of information about groups. There are as many misconceptions and distortions of facts among the older children as among the younger.

The following changes with age indicate increasing crystallization of attitudes. (a) Where picture interpretations are made in racial or religious terms rationalizations are given for the behavior projected. (b) The attitudes expressed by the child toward a given group tend to be the same each time that group appears. (c) A philosophy of behavior toward persons or groups is expressed. (d) The group label and its "meaning" become attached to people rather than to symbols or institutions or behavior. (e) The child shows personal involvement in responding to the pictures, sometimes through identifying himself with the child pictured, sometimes in showing emotional reactions to groups other than his own.

5. When Allowed to Discuss the Topic, Children Show Considerable Interest in Cultural Differences. Combined with This Interest Is an Awareness of the "Verboten" Nature of the Topic

In initial reactions to the interview topic there is, invariably, a reserve, an uneasiness, or an effort to avoid the mention of race and religion. This is most evident in reactions to Negro and white, especially by Negro children.

After a permissive situation has been established, the children's responses indicate their many ideas, curiosities, and also some preoccupations about racial and religious differences. It is apparent, too, the topics are discussed by the children among themselves.

6. Group Membership Is One Aspect of the Self-Concept of Children

Many of the children interviewed indicate a sense of own group membership. This is most frequent in regard to racial belonging. The child identifies himself with one race, usually with a preference for one or the other race implied or expressed.

Self-awareness of religious group belonging is less frequently apparent. Jewish children show greater awareness than either Catholic or Protestant children. Negro children very rarely identify themselves in religious terms. There is confusion, too, for some children who are uncertain as to whether they are Protestant or Catholic. Only a very few children who volunteer their religious group identify themselves incorrectly.

It should be noted that nonmembership in a group may be sensed by the child with as much import for his self-picture as membership in a group ("I'm glad I'm not Catholic," and a Negro girl referring to Negro-child in picture, "She wishes she was white").

7. Group Membership Is Related to the Child's Needs for Acceptance

From the findings discussed above, certain effects of group membership upon the child's feelings of acceptance and rejection are inferred: (a) Group-belonging is seen by the children as one determinant of acceptance in play groups. The most marked influence in this regard is with racial membership. (b) Group-belonging is linked with conflicts which the child anticipates will occur in his social relations with his peers. (c) Some children find security in belonging to a group which they perceive as most desired ("I'm glad I am a white boy. Some colored people say, 'I wish I was a white boy and [the children] would like to play with me.'" "They wishes they was American like us."). (d) Concepts of groups which give an inherent "badness" or "goodness" to members of these groups contribute an abasing or enhancing quality to the child's self-image.

8. Negative Self-Feelings and Personal Conflict Concerning Group-Belonging Arise Frequently in Minority Children

Many children experience serious ego-threats as a result of group prejudices. Negro children reveal most vividly and most often the feelings of insecurity resulting from anticipated rejection or insult from the white children. The same phenomenon appears among the Jewish children. On occasion, Catholic and Protestant children show an anxious concern over an anti-Catholic or anti-Protestant remark which has been the topic of competitive discussion among their playmates. Experiences of social conflict by some of the minority group children have given rise to ambivalent feelings toward their own group,—expressions of self-hatred at an early age.

9. The Effect of Group Membership upon the Self-Concept Varies with the Role of the Particular Group in Society. This May Be to Increase or to Decrease the Importance of the Group Membership for the Individual

The frequency with which children identify themselves by group membership and the function of the identification varies with the group and neighborhood to which the children belong. The importance which identification assumes is appreciably greater (as evidenced by the kind and amount of content offered in the interview) for children belonging to minority groups or to groups involved in local community conflicts, than for children whose group is not greatly involved in cultural tensions. The role of group variables for the individual child cannot be predicted solely on the basis of cultural forces, but factors of intrafamily relations and personality modify attitudes, intensify or diminish cultural conflicts experienced by the child.

CONCLUSIONS

The findings of this study challenge a number of familiar assumptions and practices concerning children. It has been assumed that awareness of group differentiations, psychological needs arising out of group memberships and social prejudices do not develop until later childhood and the teen age. The data demonstrate the falsity and danger in this assumption. Some of the implications for the formal and informal education of children are clear. If the personal-social needs of children in our culture are to be met, their awareness, interests, fears and securities related to group factors must be dealt with. This cannot be postponed until adolescence, but must be begun in preschool and early school years.

Research on children's concepts of the world has explored with great thoroughness children's abilities to comprehend time, space, physical phenomena, etc. Research on methods of teaching these facts is extensive. But children's concepts of anthropology and sociology have not had the benefit of the same amount of research effort. For the most part, the concepts are allowed to "just grow" without the benefit of planned teaching and without regard to the gross and damaging misconceptions which develop. Surely these social concepts are not more difficult, and surely they are not less important in personal development than concepts in arithmetic, geography, physiology, etc.

To proceed as if group differences did not exist is to ignore the cultural context in which children live, for society does not ignore differences; family customs and values and names and languages all reflect group-derived variations. A rule of silence about differences not only fails to help the child to achieve a better understanding of group factors, but the silence may also be perceived by him as tacit agreement with societal prejudices.

There is much evidence to indicate that children's perceptions of groups develop out of adult values and the status quo; that is to say, that many of the children have opportunity for only the kind of learning about groups which involves stereotypes and rejection, especially of groups not present in the child's environment.

The training needed is of the kind which faces cultural diversities in the form and in the situations in which the child experiences them (as the child differs from his playmates, as he observes rituals, customs, characteristics for which he knows no explanation); and which provides him with information and attitudes and social techniques required for adjustment in a culturally diverse world.

36. INTERPERSONAL RELATIONS IN PRESCHOOL CHILDREN AND AVERAGE APPROACH DISTANCE

M. G. King

In the more applied fields of psychology, the question is often asked, "To what extent can research with animals have any relevance for human behavior?" There are various answers to this question, but one of the most plausible is that animal research can sometimes provide leads that suggest research possibilities with human subjects. Unfortunately such transpositions do not occur as often as they might, but enough have occurred to confirm the validity of the answer. The dominance behavior research reported by King in the article that follows is a case in point. Following research involving pecking behavior among chicks in which subordinate flock members maintained characteristic within flock distances under specified circumstances, King studied friendly and unfriendly actions on the part of informal groups of kindergarten children at play and found that such actions were related to the spatiotemporal relationships existing among the children. Specifically, during a free-play situation the ratio of unfriendly acts to the total repertoire of acts performed by one child in relation to another was substantially related to the mean distance from each other maintained by the two children in an oblong sand pit. Placing a prized toy close to one of the two children usually resulted in the mean distance being much closer to the composite goal.

Following on from Murchison's series of experiments on "social physics" (1935, 1935), King (1965) showed that subordinate members in flocks of

SOURCE. Adapted from M. G. King, "Interpersonal Relations in Preschool Children and Average Approach Distance," *Journal of Genetic Psychology*, 1966, Vol. 109, pp. 109–116. (With permission of the author and the publisher, The Journal Press.)

fowl maintained characteristic distances from more dominant members and that these average approach distances were related to the frequency of noxious stimulation that the subordinate members received from the more dominant members. King went on to show that these characteristic approach distances reduced to zero when a food source was juxtaposed with the more dominant member.

A subsequent study by King (1966) related the behavior pattern outlined above to approach and avoidance tendencies. In particular the situation represented by a more dominant S to a subordinate S was shown to fit Miller's approach-avoidance conflict paradigm (1959).

The present study was carried out for two main reasons. First, it was hypothesized that if responses between young children could be limited to simple approach and avoidance tendencies, then results comparable to those obtained by King (1965) might also be obtained at the human level. The second reason derived from the different type of dominance relationship prevailing in children's groups. In most strains of domestic fowl, the dominance relationship fits what Allee (1952) calls "peck right": i.e., the more dominant of each pair noxiously stimulates the less dominant, but the latter rarely, if ever, retaliates. This type of relationship is contrasted with a "peck-dominance" relationship: i.e., both the more and the less dominant of each pair may noxiously stimulate each other, but the former usually wins out.

Apart from the question of whether or not approach distances may be demonstrated in preschool children, the existence of a "peck-dominance" type of relationship poses some interesting questions, that do not arise with the "peck-right" relationships.

Accordingly, the present project was designed to probe some of these questions. Since the subordinate in a "peck-dominance" relationship may noxiously stimulate the dominant, does the dominant maintain some characteristic distance to the subordinate? On the other hand, since the subordinate may noxiously stimulate the dominant S, would this make it more likely for the subordinate to approach closer to the dominant?

METHOD

Subjects

From a kindergarten center with 180 children between 3 and 5 years in chronological age, a sample of 36 Ss was drawn at random and allocated without replacement to triads. The following restrictions were placed on the formation of the triads: (a) each triad contained children of the same sex, (b) chronological ages within triads differed by no more than six months, and (c) all Ss had attended the kindergarten center for at least six months prior to experimentation. Six of the experimental triads were composed of males and six of females.

Procedure

This was the same for each experimental triad and consisted of (a) Stage 1: appraisal of friendly and unfriendly acts made by each member to each other member during free play, and (b) Stage 2: subsequent determination of average approach distances between pairs of children making up each triad.

(a) *Stage 1*. Each experimental triad was observed for 30 minutes in free play in an observation room. This was a small room wired for sound and fitted with a one-way screen. In it a small table was placed centrally with three chairs around it. For the groups of boys three toy automobiles were provided, while the girls each had a doll.

During the free-play session, interactions were observed by three experimenters, who were either graduate students or staff members of the Department of Psychology, University of Queensland. If any S directed what was judged to be a friendly act or vocalization toward another member, this was scored as a positive point for the S making the act; if the act or vocalization was judged as unfriendly the performer received a negative point.

At the conclusion of each observation session, each E had recorded the number of friendly and unfriendly acts made by each S to each of the other two members of the triad.

(b) *Stage 2*. Approach distances were measured between pairs of Ss in a sandpit, 20 feet long, four feet, six inches wide and with sides six feet high. The walls of the sandpit were decorated with cartoon figures. Sand was spread evenly on the floor to a depth of about six inches and was levelled after each testing. A movie camera, geared to fire once every 30 seconds, was mounted over the center of the sandpit at a height of 25 feet.

Ss were taken two at a time from the observation room to the sandpit, while the third remained with the teacher. One S was privately instructed to remain at one end, while the other S was free to move anywhere in the sandpit. In order that responses might be confined to simple approach and avoidance tendencies between Ss in the test situation, communication had to be restricted in the alleyway. In a pilot group, the following instructions proved effective (but two triads in the experimental groups had to be rejected because of extensive communication). Let S_1, S_2, and S_3 represent the members of a triad (the subscript is not meant to designate position in a hierarchy). Consider the pair S_1 and S_2 where S_1 designates the collaborator. S_1 was placed at one end of the sandpit and told:

> We are going to play a game on S_2. If you stay right up this end I

will give you a lolly (i.e., a sweet or candy) at the end of the game, but you must keep it a secret from S_2. Here is a bucket and spade—now you can build some sand castles."

Simultaneously, a second E placed S_2 at the opposite end of the sandpit and said, "Here is a bucket and spade—now you can build some sand castles." At this juncture Es withdrew and the camera started. After seven minutes, E returned and placed a rocking horse at the collaborator's end of the alleyway and said, "S_1 and S_2, look what I've got for you to play with." E again withdrew and filming continued for a further three minutes. S_1 and S_2 were then taken from the sandpit.

Subsequently S_2 and S_3 were filmed, using the same procedure as outlined for S_1 and S_2, but with S_2 acting as collaborator. For the filming of S_1 (collaborator) and S_3, the ends were reversed to counter any tendency S_3 might have acquired on the previous trial.

For other triads the sequence S_1-S_2, S_1-S_3, S_2-S_3, and S_1-S_2, S_1-S_2, S_2-S_3 (where the first of each pair denotes the collaborator) were also randomly used. Other possible sequences could not be employed, since they require the use of an S subsequent to sophistication as a collaborator.

RESULTS

During the free-play session, each E judged the frequency of friendly and unfriendly acts made by each S to each other S in the triad. It was found that observers disagreed on the frequency of acts but agreed on the ratio of friendly and unfriendly acts. Disagreement over the frequencies probably resulted from the fact that observers had to sample acts as they occurred rapidly in many of the groups.

In view of this, the interaction ratio for each S to each other S was calculated. For example, the interaction ratio (I.R.) of S_1 to S_2 was the ratio of unfriendly acts to the sum of friendly and unfriendly acts made by S_1 to S_2: interaction ratio equals frequency of unfriendly acts divided by total number of acts. For S_1, then, each observer had estimated two I.R.s, S_1-S_2 and S_1-S_3, and this applied to each member of each triad.

Comparison of corresponding I.R.s for each observer showed that Es agreed highly; Kendall's "W" coefficient was calculated to check on the reliability of observers' estimates of each I.R. In the experimental triads, the "Coefficient of Concordance" was significant at the 1 per cent level of confidence for eight of the groups and at the 5 per cent level for the remaining two triads. In view of this, the mean value of all observers' estimates of each I.R. was taken. For example, assume that Observer 1 estimated the I.R. of S_1 to S_2 to be x_1, Observer 2 estimated x_2, and Observer 3 estimated x_3; then the mean I.R. of S_1 to S_2 was the mean of x_1, x_2 and x_3.

In Table 1 mean I.R.s are given. The left-hand score is the I.R. of the collaborator to the S. The score next to that on the right is the complementary I.R. of that S to the particular collaborator.

Distances between each pair of Ss in the sandpit were obtained by reading off the distances between Ss' heads on enlarged negatives. Since the camera fired every 30 seconds, mean distance is given by the following formula:

$$\text{Mean Distance} = \frac{\sum_{i=1}^{N} D_i}{N},$$

where D_i = physical distance between collaborator and S on frame i, and N = number of frames taken.

On the right-hand side of Table 1, two mean distances are given for each pair tested—the extreme right-hand score being the distance maintained after the rocking horse was introduced into the alleyway. The score next to that on the left is the distance maintained by S before the rocking horse was introduced.

DISCUSSION

Several important relationships emerge from Table 1 and these are presented as *tau* coefficients (Siegel, 1956). Since both I.R.s and mean distances occur within subgroups, the treatment follows a method outlined by Torgerson (1958) wherein *tau* coefficients for subgroups are pooled and the overall significance determined.

In the first place, there appears to be very little relationship, taken over all subgroups, between the I.R. of collaborator to S and the complementary I.R. of S to collaborator. The pooled *tau* between these two sets of I.R.s was —.04, $p > .05$. This lack of statistical relationship does not coordinate with either an aggression-aggression or an aggression-suppression hypothesis between pairs of children interacting in triads. However, there does appear to be considerable variation between subgroups in this respect, which calls for further investigation.

The correlation was determined between (a) the I.R. of collaborator to S (in the observation room), and (b) the corresponding mean distance maintained by S from the collaborator (in the sandpit). This relationship indicates whether the interactions occurring between members in children's groups influence the spatio-temporal relationships outside the group situation. The value of the pooled *tau* was .74, $p < .01$.

Further, the correlation was determined between (a) the I.R. of S to the collaborator (in the observation room), and (b) the corresponding mean distance maintained by S from the collaborator (in the sandpit). The value of the pooled *tau* was .11, $p > .05$.

These correlations indicate that the I.R. of collaborator to S, as compared to the I.R. of S to collaborator, played a much larger part in the determinancy of the mean distance of S as was suggested in the research hypothesis.

TABLE 1

Mean Interaction Ratios of Collaborators and Subjects in Each Triad and the Corresponding Mean Distances Observed in the Sandpit Before and After Introduction of the Rocking Horse

Triad	I.R. Collab. to S	I.R. S to Collab.	Mean Distance in Feet without Horse	Mean Distance in Feet with Horse
1	.17	.00	2.3	2.1
	.44	.50	7.8	1.5
	.50	.29	11.7	3.7
2	.19	.21	6.7	4.3
	.26	.25	9.3	1.8
	.33	.00	7.3	5.0
3	.94	.56	17.8	18.2
	.84	.58	16.0	7.1
	.76	.65	13.2	2.6
4	.31	.30	11.6	6.8
	.50	.50	camera failed	5.7
	.50	.50	8.3	camera failed
5	.04	.05	2.0	3.7
	.00	.29	2.9	12.2
	.22	.47	3.8	3.4
6	.43	.21	15.9	12.5
	.34	.27	8.3	3.2
	.38	.37	12.9	2.8
7	.67	.30	8.6	4.8
	.83	.67	10.2	5.8
	.81	.55	8.1	1.8
8	.43	.40	16.9	3.5
	.37	.50	13.3	1.3
	.36	.44	11.1	3.3
9	.43	.27	3.8	4.6
	.21	.80	4.1	6.3
	.58	.38	17.1	3.8
10	.00	.00	2.6	2.9
	.74	.36	10.9	3.1
	.50	.56	7.0	3.8

Further, it would seem that the I.R. of S to the collaborator played a relatively minor part and was not nearly as important as the I.R. of the collaborator to S.

Table 1 shows that the I.R.s of some collaborators were equal to or lower than the complementary I.R.s of the S, which brings out certain features of the "peck-dominance" type of relationship. However, in view of the error of measurement involved in taking the mean interaction ratio, a collaborator is only regarded as dominant over S if his I.R. to the S is .1 greater than that of S to the collaborator. Using this convention, in 13 of the pair relationships the collaborator was clearly dominant over his S in terms of a "peck-dominance" relationship. In the remaining 17 cases the collaborator was not dominant over S. Thus a comparison can be made between collaborators whose I.R.s were distinctly greater than those of their Ss and those whose I.R.s were not. Taken over all cases, the relationship between I.R. of collaborator to S on the one hand, and mean distance maintained by S on the other, appears to be rectilinear. However, where the collaborator was not clearly dominant over S—i.e., for cases where the collaborator's I.R. was approximately equal to or less than that of S—the regression shows a curvilinear trend. But this may be artifactual, as there are no instances in Table 1 of I.R.s greater than .5 where a collaborator is not clearly dominant over S. Clearly, further studies need to be carried out to include high dominant collaborators with high dominant subjects, as information on this is lacking in the present study.

In the second part of this experiment, a rocking horse was juxtaposed with the collaborator in the alleyway. This was intended to parallel an earlier study by King (1965) in which characteristic distances maintained by subordinate from dominant fowls were shown to reduce to zero when a food source was juxtaposed with the dominant S in a test alleyway. In the present study it is possible to compare mean distances before and after the introduction of the rocking horse. Correlations were calculated between (a) the I.R. of collaborator to S (in the observation room), and (b) the mean distance of S to collaborator and rocking horse (in the sandpit). The pooled *tau* was .14, $p > .05$. The correlation was also calculated between (a) the I.R. of S to collaborator (in the observation room), and (b) the mean distance of S to collaborator and rocking horse (in the alleyway). The pooled *tau* was $-.33$, $.01 < p < .05$.

Consider these correlations in relation to Table 1; the differences in correlation must arise from changes in mean distances as the same I.R.s are considered in both cases. Table 1 shows that for most Ss juxtaposition of the rocking horse had the effect of reducing mean distances: i.e., it generally brought the locus of S closer to the composite goal. In the study by King (1965), juxtaposition of a food trough with the dominant fowl invariably reduced minimal distances to zero. For most Ss this is consonant with the present results, in as much as most mean distances reduced. However, as Table 1 indicates, the reduction in distances was not as consistent or drastic as shown by King.

Introduction of the rocking horse was associated with two important changes in the level of correlation. In the first place, the pooled *tau* between I.R. of collaborator to S and mean distance fell from .74, $p < .01$ to .14, $p > .05$. Consequently the pooled *tau* between I.R. of S to collaborator and mean distance rose from .11, $p > .05$ to $-.33$, $.01 < p < .05$, a significant change in the opposite direction. In this connection Table 1 reveals a general tendency for Ss to approach much closer to the composite goal after the introduction of the rocking horse. But four Ss moved in the opposite direction, while four other Ss were hardly influenced by the second treatment. Examination of the I.R.s for these discrepant Ss revealed that such effects cannot be ascribed to cases where the I.R. of collaborator to S was high and the corresponding I.R. of S to collaborator was low.

It appears that the significant negative correlation between I.R. of S to collaborator and mean distance ($tau = -.33$) arose from a tendency on the part of low dominant Ss to approach closer to the composite goal than would be predicted. It is suggested that such effects arise from the greater likelihood of deprivation encountered by low dominant Ss in competitive situations.

SUMMARY

An experiment was designed to investigate the effect that friendly and unfriendly interactions occurring in small groups of kindergarten children had on their spatio-temporal relationships. In particular the ratio of unfriendly acts to the total number of acts made by an S to another S during free play was strongly related to the mean distance maintained by the second S from the first. The mean distances, however, were found to reduce in most cases when a prized toy was juxtaposed with the first S.

37. A COMPARISON OF RACE AWARENESS IN NORTHERN AND SOUTHERN CHILDREN

J. Kenneth Morland

Many teachers in America have had relatively little experience teaching children of a race other than their own. Yet, as the day of the segregated school passes into history, more and more teachers will find themselves facing children about whose background and attitudinal structure they know relatively little, and that little may well be overlaid by their own prejudices or misinformation about individuals of races other than their own. Research studies that they may have encountered during their training as teachers deal mostly with samples composed of white children, and psychological generalizations made from these samples seldom take racial differences into account. More studies involving Negro subjects and more racial comparisons are now appearing in the literature but their proportion to solely white subject studies still remains small. A further complication, mentioned by Morland in his study, is the growing reluctance of many schools (often sanctioned by law) to allow racial identification or comparisons to be made. However commendable such an attitude may be, it still interferes with teachers acquiring information that might make them more effective in their dealings with children of another race. The following are fair questions for a teacher to ask. To what extent do psychological generalizations apply to both Negro and white children and to what extent do they not? Further, where generalizations do not apply, what is the reason for the differences? Morland's comparison of northern and southern Negro and white preschool children on race awareness is an example of a

SOURCE. Adapted from J. Kenneth Morland, "A Comparison of Race Awareness in Northern and Southern Children," *American Journal of Orthopsychiatry*, 1966, Vol. 36, pp. 22-31. (With permission of the author and the publisher, American Orthopsychiatric Association.)

study that can supply needed information. His study not only points to the existence of specific differences but also supplies a lead in his northern-southern comparisons suggesting the environmental basis of these differences. In general he found that Negro children tended to prefer and identify with the opposite race, while white children tended to prefer their own race. Preferences, however, were accentuated among southern subjects. Morland's study offers a further confirmation of the following study by Epstein and Komorita, and suggests a possible adjustment problem as integration proceeds.

Studies of race awareness in American children have shown that significant differences exist between Negroes and whites in racial recognition ability, racial preference and racial self-identification. However it is not clear from these studies whether children vary in race awareness by region as well as by race. A basic goal of the study reported in this paper is to try to clarify this question of regional variation by comparing children reared in a southern city under conditions of rigid racial segregation offically and traditionally supported with children reared in a northern city under less segregated conditions and where there is official disapproval of racial discrimination.

SUBJECTS

The subjects were 164 children of preschool age in Lynchburg, Virginia, and Boston, Massachusetts. These two cities offered a contrast in regional environment so far as the organizing of race relations is concerned. All of the Lynchburg children were in racially segregated nursery schools and day-care centers. The Boston children had current or recent association with children of the other race, most from interracial nursery or playground groups. Furthermore, Lynchburg has had state and local policies of racial segregation until changed recently by federal rulings. Such changes have yet to have any effect on the nursery schools and day-care centers attended by the subjects, and indeed only token integration has taken place in other areas of community life. In contrast, the state of Massachusetts has an official commission to prevent discrimination. Data on the Boston children were gathered during the summer of 1961 and those on the Lynchburg children during 1962 and 1964.

The subjects were divided into four regional-racial groupings, designated as northern Negro, northern white, southern Negro, and southern white. Forty-one children matched by age and by sex were placed in each grouping. Previous research had shown that race, age, and possibly sex were significantly related to race awareness and therefor had to be controlled before valid regional comparisons could be made. Although no precise control of socioeconomic level was made, children of parents of varying occupations, ranging from professional and managerial to domestic and laboring, were included in each of the four groupings. Also, subjects were not matched on intelligence test scores, although none of the children tested had been found by their teachers to be mentally retarded.

Since the children studied were not selected randomly from the total population of preschool children but rather were those available in certain nursery schools, day-care centers and playground groups, there is no claim that they form a representative sample in the two cities.

DATA-COLLECTION TECHNIQUES

The measuring instrument consisted of a set of six 8-by-10 black and white pictures about which questions were asked. The pictures were obtained through professional photographers and were selected by a panel of Negro and white judges who agreed that those in the pictures were readily identifiable by race and were reasonably comparable in expression and dress. The set of pictures underwent two revisions following pretesting. Included in the version of the test employed in this research were pictures of children of both races and both sexes engaged in preschool activities, and adults of both races and both sexes. The six pictures depicted the following: five white boys and girls sitting at a table drawing pictures; five Negro boys and girls sitting at a table drawing pictures; four men, two Negro and two white, holding cokes and looking at a book; six women, three Negro and three white, sitting at a table and drinking tea; six girls, three white and three Negro, playing at a set of swings; four boys, two Negro and two white, playing on a "go-around."

Interviews were held separately and privately with each subject and lasted five to six minutes on the average. The children treated the interview as a picture game and frequently asked to look at the pictures again on subsequent days. Interviewing was done by senior sociology majors who had had a course in research methods and who were trained for the project and supervised by the author. While all of the interviewing reported in this paper was done by whites, pretesting in which Negroes interviewed Negro subjects showed no significant differences in the responses by race of the interviewer.

The pictures and the interview were designed to measure four aspects of race awareness: racial acceptance, racial preference, racial self-identification and racial recognition ability.

RACIAL ACCEPTANCE

To find out how willing the subjects were to accept Negroes and whites as playmates, each was given three chances to say if he would like to play with

Negro children and with white children in the pictures. He was asked if he would like to play with individuals of both sexes and with children as a group. Race or color was not mentioned in these questions. The interviewer pointed to a picture and asked the subject, "Would you like to play with this child (or these children)?" Following his response, the subject was asked, "Why?" or "Why not?" The responses of a subject were scored as "Acceptance" if he indicated a majority of times that he would like to play with the members of the race in question, "Nonacceptance" if he said most frequently he would not like to play with them for any reason other than racial, and "Rejection" if he said most often he did not want to play with them because of their race or color. Almost all of the children of both races accepted the white children as playmates. While a large majority in each grouping accepted the Negro children in the pictures, the percentages were somewhat smaller than for acceptance of whites. However, only southern whites were significantly lower in their acceptance of Negroes than in their acceptance of whites. Southern whites were significantly lower than southern Negroes in accepting Negroes, and they alone rejected children because of their race, with almost 10 per cent rejecting Negroes for racial reasons.

RACIAL PREFERENCE

Three of the questions called for an indication of a preference between Negro and white children in the picture. Each subject was asked if he would rather play with a group of Negro or a group of white children, with a white or a Negro boy, and with a Negro or a white girl. Again the interviewer did not mention race or color in these questions, but pointed to the picture and asked, "Would you rather play with this child (these children) or with that one (those)?" Responses were scored as "Prefer Own Race," "Prefer Other Race," or "Preference Not Clear," depending on the subject's most frequent response. The responses revealed that a majority of subjects in each of the four groupings preferred whites. Southern Negro subjects were least likely and southern white most likely to prefer members of their own race. It is to be noted that preference for one race, however, did not mean rejection of the other race, for the great majority in the four groupings accepted members of both races when no choice was required, as has already been seen.

RACIAL SELF-IDENTIFICATION

Three measures were made of the subject's racial self-identification. One measure was based on the response to a question asking which of the children in the picture composed of Negroes and whites of his own sex the subject looked most like. Once again the interviewer pointed to the picture and did not use racial terms. It was found that white subjects were more likely to say they looked like one of the white children than the Negro subjects were to say that they looked like one of the Negro children.

A second question dealing with self-identification asked which of the children in the picture of Negroes and whites of the subject's sex he would rather be. Without mentioning race or color, the interviewer pointed to the picture and asked, "Which child would you rather be?" A significant difference was found between the responses of Negro and white subjects regardless of the region. More than three-fourths of both northern and southern whites responded that they would rather be one of the white children in the pictures, while only about one-half of the Negro children stated that they would rather be one of the Negro children. In other words, whites were more likely to identify with a child of their race than Negroes were to identify with a child of their race.

The third measure of racial self-identification sought to find out whether the subjects would identify their mothers as one of the Negro or one of the white women in the picture of six women. The subject was shown this picture and asked, "Which one looks most like your mother?" White subjects were more likely than Negro subjects to identify their mothers with one of the women of their own race. While there were significant differences between the races in each region, identification with whites was more likely among the Lynchburg than among the Boston children. More than nine out of ten southern white subjects stated that their mothers looked most like one of the white women, while fewer than three out of ten southern Negro subjects stated that their mothers looked most like one of the Negro women.

RACIAL RECOGNITION ABILITY

A final measure reported in this paper concerns the ability of the subjects to designate correctly the race of those in the pictures. After questions regarding acceptance, preference and self-identification had been asked, the pictures were shown again, and for each one the subject was asked, "Do you see a white person in this picture?" If the child said he did, he then was asked to point to the white person. For the same picture the child next was asked, "Do you see a colored person in this picture?"[1] Again, if the child replied affirmatively, he was asked to point to the colored person. This gave 12 chances, two for each of the six pictures, for the subject to identify Negro and white children and adults of both sexes. If the respondent an-

---

[1] The term "colored" was used because pretesting had shown that children both in Lynchburg and in Boston were more familiar with this designation of the races than they were with the term "Negro."

swered correctly for all 12, or if he missed only one, he was scored "High." If he missed more than one, he was scored "Low." The responses showed that southern white subjects had significantly higher ability to make racial distinctions than any of the other groupings. Although almost three-fourths of the southern whites scored high, less than one-half of those in the other three groupings scored high. Further analysis of recognition ability by age indicated that proportionately more southern whites than subjects in other groupings scored high in each age category. However, the greatest differences were found at the ages of four and five, particularly at age four.

CONCLUSIONS

In general the research on the Boston and Lynchburg children supported previous findings that American Negro and white children of preschool age differ in race awareness, and that these differences between Negro and white hold across regional lines. Thus northern and southern Negro subjects differed significantly on only one of the seven measures, namely racial preference. Northern and southern whites differed significantly on only two, racial recognition ability and identification of mother. In contrast southern whites differed significantly from southern Negroes on six of the seven measures, while northern whites differed significantly from northern Negroes on four. The direction of the differences was that the white subjects in both regions tended to prefer and identify with members of their own race, while Negro subjects in the two regions tended to prefer and to identify with members of the other race. This can be interpreted to mean that regardless of the region the overall effect of American society on very young children has been to influence them to develop a bias for whites. In other words, American society as it now operates teaches that racial differences are very important and that being white is preferable to being Negro. Under such conditions young Negro children probably unconsciously learn to prefer and identify with the dominant race.

There are some regional variations, however, for the differences between white and Negro appear to be accentuated in the southern subjects. In the measure of racial preference in which there was a significant difference between northern and southern Negro subjects, southern Negroes were more likely to prefer whites. In the two differences between the white groupings, southern whites were more likely than northern whites to identify their mothers as white and to have high racial recognition.

These regional variations, while not extensive, can be logically accounted for by the sociocultural explanation of the development of the perception of race. The segregated southern system can be assumed to place an even greater importance on being white than does the less segregated northern system. Thus the southern white subjects were somewhat more likely than the northern whites to acquire a bias for whites and to develop racial recognition ability earlier. The southern Negro subjects, on the other hand, were more likely than the northern Negro to prefer the dominant race. This comparison suggests that the southern children may have a greater problem of adjustment as the nation moves toward the elimination of overt forms of racial discrimination. The southern white subjects evidenced such strong racial bias that reactions toward Negroes as persons, on a basis of equality, will probably not be easy. For the southern Negro subjects the realization of their correct racial membership and their actual low position in the social order can be traumatic. Such an assumption is in accord with findings from studies of personality traits in Negroes which have indicated that the southern caste system has a more detrimental effect on Negroes than has the northern system.

The results of this study on race awareness in young children suggest that as the sociocultural milieu in America changes, such awareness will change. There is little question that the structure of race relations throughout the United States is being altered by state and federal legislation, court rulings and the insistence of racial minorities on equal treatment. The elimination of forced racial segregation and the opening of educational and occupational opportunities according to ability will make for more association on the basis of equality between the races. Also, as mass media begin to include all races in advertisements, dramatic performances and the like on the same basis, a new image of Negroes in American society should emerge. It would be instructive to repeat the measurements of this study in another 10 years or so to see if racial preference, self-identification and recognition ability have changed along with the expected changes in the organization of race relations.

The results of studies of race awareness in young children also suggest certain kinds of teaching that might have an effect on racial attitudes. The American social system implies that race is of fundamental importance in judging the worth of a person. In spite of changes taking place, this situation probably will continue for some time. However, scientific studies indicate that race in and of itself is not related to the intelligence, character, or creativity of the individual. Furthermore, cross-cultural studies show that the unity of a people lies in the sharing of values, ideals, and norms rather than in racial similarity. As American children begin to move more freely across racial lines, accurate information about race and race differences should enable them to move more easily than if they are burdened with notions of racial superiority and inferiority. Controlled experiments on the effect of accurate information on racial attitudes are needed to guide the development of teaching in this area. The author is convinced from his own experience that teaching of facts about race can affect the attitudes and behavior of Negro and white college students. However, systematic research is required before the effectiveness of such teaching can clearly be determined. We are reminded from other research that information alone is not a sufficient condition to change attitudes (although the author is convinced that in the case of racial attitudes it is a necessary condition). If attitudes are to be affected, behavior itself also must be changed. In their experiment with young children in Philadelphia, Trager and Yarrow concluded that democratic attitudes must be specifically taught and practiced if they are to be learned. If such teaching and practice are combined with the changes already taking place in the larger sociocultural milieu, it can be expected that American children will be less likely to develop racial biases that handicap them in a democratic society.

38. PREJUDICE AMONG NEGRO CHILDREN AS RELATED TO PARENTAL ETHNOCENTRISM AND PUNITIVENESS

Ralph Epstein & S. S. Komorita

No one can doubt the all-pervasive importance of parental behavior and attitudes upon the behavior and attitudes of their children and, although parents are not the only influences in moulding the immediate and subsequent behavior of children, a long series of research studies have indicated that we must look first to parents as the leading factor in moulding children's behavior. Children spend more time in the home than they do elsewhere and, from infancy on, parents act as models to be imitated. In a real sense as a young person goes forth into the community, whether in school or elsewhere, he is identified by his family and often finds acceptance or rejection in much the same terms that his parents do. Numerous studies have identified and described many of the variables of parental behavior crucial in the development of a child's personality and his attitudinal structure. Epstein and Komorita have chosen to study parental punitiveness and children's perceptions of the parents' social attitudes as they are related to social distance attitudes. They used a sample of 120 Negro fifth-graders of both sexes. The experimental situation consisted of presenting a fictitious group as middle or working class and as Negro or white. The measure of parental punitiveness used was designed to secure an estimate of a child's perception of his parent's punitiveness when faced with aggression. Findings indicated that Negro children appear to possess strong self-rejecting attitudes that the authors feel mirror prevailing white majority preju-

SOURCE. Adapted from Ralph Epstein and S. S. Komorita, "Prejudice among Negro Children as Related to Parental Ethnocentrism and Punitiveness," *Journal of Personality and Social Psychology*, 1966, Vol. 4, pp. 643–647. (With permission of the authors and the publisher, The American Psychological Association.)

dices and that the children's expressed social distance toward own and other racial groups represent a generalized predisposition or misanthropic attitudes learned in the home. Such attitudes provide a nonfacilitative base that teachers should take into account when they are trying to inculcate self-esteem and acceptance of other racial groups.

The scapegoat hypothesis has dominated contemporary research literature on the origins of childhood ethnocentrism. This hypothesis maintains that severe discipline directed towards aggression may increase the instigation to aggress, and that anticipation of punishment for aggression directed towards the ingroup results in displacement from the original sources of frustration to outgroups. In order to clarify contradictory results related to this hypothesis (Masling, 1954; Miller & Bugelski, 1948; Stagner & Congdon, 1955), the authors conducted a series of investigations designed to evaluate the influence of two major variables upon displacement: child-rearing practices and stimulus characteristics of outgroups (Epstein & Komorita, 1965b, 1966). Although these studies demonstrated the significance of both variables, the results failed to support the displacement hypothesis. With regard to child-rearing practices, our earlier results suggested that moderate rather than severe discipline appears most conducive to the development of ethnocentric attitudes. Later findings replicated this result and suggested that both moderate discipline and high parental ethnocentrism were most conducive to the formation of childhood prejudice. These results were conceptualized in terms of identification theory (Sears, Maccoby, & Levin, 1957). It was proposed that a major consequence of moderate discipline is to orient the child towards obtaining parental approval and to reduce doubt regarding approval by internalizing parental attitudes. With regard to perceived characteristics of outgroups, working-class status greatly accentuated prejudice towards the Negro as compared with the white group. Middle-class status served to minimize differential attitudes as a function of ethnic affiliation.

The purpose of the present study was to replicate these provocative findings on a nonwhite population, namely, Negro children. Although the sparsity of systematic research on the ethnic attitudes of minority groups is striking, the available research consistently suggests that members of such groups adopt the ethnic attitudes of the majority culture (Hartley, 1946). Evidence for feelings of self-derogation and rejection among Negro children was provided in studies by Clark (1963), Radke and Trager (1950), and Stevenson and Stewart (1958). Although the prevalence of anti-Negro attitudes among Negro children has received some support, the correlates of these attitudes have remained unexplored.

It is hypothesized in this study that the development of prejudicial attitudes among Negro children is a function of those social learning conditions previously reported by the authors as conducive to the development of similar attitudes in white children, namely, parental ethnocentrism and moderate parental punitiveness. A first-order interaction between these variables is predicted whereby high parental ethnocentrism and moderate discipline will be associated with prejudice in the Negro child.

METHOD

Subjects

The sample consisted of 120 Negro boys and girls who comprised the fifth grade in an elementary school in Detroit, Michigan. This school serves children whose socioeconomic background, as determined by residential area, is working class.

Measure of Parental Punitiveness

The Parental Punitiveness Scale (PPS) was developed by the authors to measure children's perceptions of parental punitiveness towards aggression. A detailed description of the development of this scale is reported elsewhere (Epstein & Komorita, 1965a). Briefly, the scale consists of 45 items which measure parental punitiveness towards physical, verbal, and indirect aggression in each of five major situations: aggression towards parents, teachers, siblings, peers, and inanimate objects. The scale is scorable separately for fathers' and mothers' responses to aggression. However, since the correlation coefficient between fathers' and mothers' versions was found to be .60, the two scores were pooled to yield a single average punitiveness score. The split-half reliability of this average punitive score, with the Spearman-Brown correction, was .81.

Experimental Conditions

Three independent variables were used: (a) parental punitiveness towards aggression—high, medium, and low as determined by scores on the PPS, (b) race of target group—Negro versus white, and (c) socioeconomic class of target group—working versus middle class. Thus, a $3 \times 2 \times 2$ factorial design was employed with 10 subjects in each of the 12 experimental conditions.

The basic purpose of the experimental conditions was to create specific cognitions regarding a fictitious group, the "Piraneans." A fictitious group was used to minimize subjects' awareness of the purpose of the study and thereby facilitate nondefensive responding. Accordingly, subjects were presented slides which depicted Piraneans as either middle or working class, and Negro or white. Race of Piraneans was varied by presenting slides of four Negro or white children, two boys and two girls each, who were representative of the subjects' age range. Socioeconomic class was varied by presenting slides depicting residence and working place of Piraneans. For example, the "working-class" slides depicted scenes of a ramshackle house, deteriorated slum streets, and street construction, whereas the "middle-class" slides depicted a new split-level home, suburban streets, and a modern office building.

Prior to the group administration of the slides, the following instructions were given: "There is a group of people whom most of you have never seen. As a matter of fact, you have probably never heard of this group. They are called Piraneans. Would you like to see some slides of the Piraneans?" After viewing the slides, subjects completed a 7-item social distance scale with regard to Piraneans. These items ranged from "would you want to marry these people when you grow up?" (minimal) to "would you want these people to visit your country?" (maximal). Each item could be answered by checking one of four alternatives ranging from "very much yes" to "very much no."

In order to minimize the potentially confounding factors of differential clarity and brightness, the slides were matched as closely as possible in terms of these variables. The "low socioeconomic" slides were based on scenes within Detroit slums, whereas the "middle socioeconomic" slides were based on photos of suburban areas. Postexperimental interviews with a sample of subjects indicated that very few were able to state the specific locale of the slides, although several subjects believed that the photos were taken within the United States.

In order to determine the children's attitudes towards nonfictional groups, ratings of the following groups were obtained after the experimental sessions: Chinese, German, French, Catholic, Italian, Mexican, Negro, Japanese, Jewish, and Russian. Social distance scores for each of these groups were then pooled to obtain a measure of generalized social distance. Three weeks later, subjects were requested to indicate how they thought their *parents* would rate these same groups on the social distance scales. Thus, a measure of the parents' social distance attitudes, as perceived by the child, was obtained as well.

RESULTS

For the purpose of intergroup comparisons, Table 1 summarizes the means and standard deviations of the social distance scores for the 12 experimental groups.

An analysis of variance of these scores indicated that the main effects for parental punitiveness and social class were not significant. However, the main effect for race was significant at the .05 level ($F = 4.61$, $df = 1.108$), indi-

TABLE 1
Means and Standard Deviations of Piranean Social Distance Scores for Experimental Groups

Parental Punitiveness	Negro Working Class	Negro Middle Class	White Working Class	White Middle Class	X̄ SD
High	17.7 (6.07)	16.2 (5.46)	12.7 (2.93)	12.6 (5.29)	14.80
Medium	16.4 (4.92)	14.8 (3.66)	15.8 (7.18)	12.9 (5.75)	14.98
Low	14.1 (4.28)	14.6 (1.62)	11.5 (2.69)	15.7 (7.48)	13.98
Mean social distance	Negro: 15.63 Working class: 14.70		White: 13.53 Middle class: 14.47		

Note.—Standard deviations are enclosed in parentheses.

cating that subjects manifested greater social distance towards the Negro ($\bar{X} = 15.63$) than white Piraneans ($\bar{X} = 13.53$). None of the interactions were significant.

In order to delineate further the antecedents of social distance, the subjects' Piranean social distance scores for each experimental condition were correlated with (a) subjects' generalized social distance attitudes towards the nonfictional groups (omitting Negro in the summation score), and (b) parental social distance, as measured by children's reports of parental attitudes towards the nonfictional groups. The correlation coefficients are shown in Table 2.

The correlations in Table 2 are consistently positive as well as substantially significant, and with 28 degrees of freedom all of these correlations with parental social distance attitudes are significant at the .01 or .05 level. It is apparent that a highly significant proportion of the variance of children's social distance towards a fictitious group can be accounted for by their perception of parental prejudice. Furthermore, Table 2 indicates that social distance towards a fictitious group is highly correlated with the child's generalized social distance. Furthermore, the significant role of a generalized response set towards acceptance or rejection of other groups upon self-acceptance in Negro children is indicated by a correlation of .46 between subjects' social ratings of Negro and their generalized social distance ratings. This correlation, based on $df = 118$, is significant at the .01 level.

With regard to children's generalized social distance attitudes as a dependent variable, the correlation between children's and perceived parental

TABLE 2

Correlation Coefficients between Children's Social Distance towards Piraneans and Children's and Parental Generalized Social Distance[a]

Piranean Conditions	Generalized Social Distance — Children	Generalized Social Distance — Parental
White		
Middle class	.62**	.46**
Working class	.65**	.51**
Negro		
Middle class	.49**	.40*
Working class	.75**	.67**

[a] Sample size was 30 for experimental groups combined over three levels of PPS.
* $p < .05$.
** $p < .01$.

social distance attitudes was .73, and with $df = 118$ this is significant at the .01 level. The correlation between children's generalized social distance and perceived parental punitiveness was only .12. However, since earlier research suggested that this relationship is nonlinear and that there might be an interaction between parental punitiveness and parental social distance attitudes upon children's prejudice, the data were cast into a 3×3 factorial design with 3 levels of parental punitiveness and parental generalized social distance. The 9 cell frequencies ranged from 10 to 18, and an unweighted-means analysis of variance resulted in a significant main effect for parental social distance ($F = 39.42$, $df = 2, 111$, $p < .001$). This result reflects the previously reported positive relationship between parental and children's generalized social distance. In order to evaluate the influence of parental attitudes upon subjects' attitudes towards their own ethnic group, a correlation between parental and subjects' social distance attitudes towards Negro was computed. The resulting correlation of .62, based on $df = 118$, is significant at the .01 level. These findings suggest that the Negro child's social distance attitudes towards both other minority groups as well as his own are influenced by parental attitudes. Further research is necessary to evaluate the alternative possibility that prejudiced children may attribute prejudicial attitudes to their parents.

The main effect for parental punitiveness, as well as the interaction between punitiveness and ethnocentrism, failed to achieve significance at the .05 level. However, it is interesting to note that the differences between means reflect a trend which is consistent with earlier findings (Epstein & Komorita, 1966); that is, given a high level of parental ethnocentrism, moderately disciplined children manifested stronger social distance attitudes ($\overline{X} = 203.82$) than weakly ($\overline{X} = 187.47$) or severely disciplined (181.50) children. On the other hand, differential social distance as a function of discipline level was minimal for both low and moderate parental social distance groups.

DISCUSSION

A primary finding in this study is that among Negro children social distance attitudes are directed towards a fictitious group depicted as having the same racial characteristics as the subjects. These results are consistent with previous investigations (Clark, 1963; Hartley, 1946), which indicated that Negro elementary school children, residing in a northern urban community, adopted the prevailing prejudices of the white majority.

Furthermore, the correlational data suggest that social distance attitudes towards one's own groups, for example, Negro, as well as towards fictitional groups, for example, Piraneans, are significantly related to a generalized personality predisposition or response set which involves the rejection of people in general. Thus, prejudice towards a specific group may be viewed as a manifestation of a generalized misanthropy which encompasses multiple groups (Hartley, 1946). This conclusion is related to a major controversy within the area of intergroup relations, namely, the development of in- and outgroup distinctions in the development of ethnic attitudes. It has been assumed that a strong identification with the ingroup is conducive to the development of hostile attitudes towards the outgroup (Adorno, Frenkel-Brunswik, Levinson, & Sanford, 1950). Also, the perception of outgroups as threatening and the subsequent arousal of hostility towards such groups may intensify altruistic attitudes towards members of the ingroup (Campbell, 1965). However, our finding of a significant relationship between social distance towards Negroes and generalized social distance attitudes across groups is consistent with the alternative position, elaborated by Buss (1961), that prejudicial or self-rejecting attitudes reflect a generalized hostile predisposition or set of habits which may be elicited by both in- and outgroups.

Insofar as the significant relationship between parents' generalized social distance and subjects' generalized social distance attitude is based on correlational data, assumption regarding the direction of causality should be viewed as tentative. However, these findings are consistent with a social learning theory which focuses on the role of imitative processes in the development of ethnic attitudes. This conceptualization is consonant with recent investigations which demonstrated that children's prejudices may reflect parental attitudes. For example, Anisfeld, Munoz, and Lambert (1963) reported a strong relationship between the ethnocentric attitudes of Jewish children and those of their parents. Mosher and Scodel (1960) reported a similar relationship in a middle-class Protestant population.

Although previous research (Epstein, 1966; Epstein & Komorita, 1965b) suggested that among white subjects, social distance attitudes towards Negroes are determined to a large extent by the group's perceived inferior social status, the current research suggests that the Negro child's low self-esteem is based less on socioeconomic than on racial factors. This suggests that the Negro's perception of dark skin color as the basis for the white person's hostility may be discrepant from the basis employed by many whites, namely, the Negro's social status. These discrepant perceptions may be attributed to the possibility that the more concrete quality of the concept, skin color, relative to socioeconomic status may facilitate the acceptance of the former concept by the working-class Negro child as the basis for his rejection. In addition, relating the majority group's hostility to one's skin color is consistent with an external orientation in which negative reinforcements are attributed to chance, fate, and other events beyond personal control (Lefcourt & Ladwig, 1965).

39. RACE AND BELIEF: AN OPEN AND SHUT CASE

David D. Stein, Jane Allyn Hardyck, & M. Brewster Smith

In a democratic society the problem of prejudice and personal inflexibility can become a very serious one, whether the prejudice is directed toward race, religion, or any of the other matters of concern to a people committed to the principles of democracy. It behooves such a people to become familiar with the nature and etiology of prejudice so that they may be in a better position to guard against its effects whether in their personal lives or in the life of their nation. Of all of the agencies of society standing in the front lines in the war against prejudice, the home and the schools occupy an eminent position and bear a grave responsibility for the direction that the nation eventually takes. Yet the area of prejudice is a difficult one complicated by problems of affect and of personal aspiration. Much is being done to understand prejudice, and teachers and parents should be avid consumers of new information and theory relating to prejudiced behavior. One of the well known positions is that of Rokeach who contends that prejudice stems from perceived dissimilarities in belief systems. Various writers, among them Triandes, have taken issue with Rokeach's contention and have advanced alternative hypotheses. Thus, the consumer is placed in the position of asking the quite fair question, "Is Rokeach's stand well taken and can it stand further objective research examination?" Stein and his associates have endeavored to test Rokeach's contention. They used as subjects forty-four white ninth-graders who responded to a social-distance

SOURCE. Adapted from David D. Stein, Jane Allyn Hardyck and M. Brewster Smith, "Race and Belief: An Open and Shut Case," *Journal of Personality and Social Psychology*, 1965, Vol. 4, pp. 281–289. (With permission of the authors and the publisher, The American Psychological Association.)

scale designed to measure their belief similarity to designated white and Negro "stimulus teenagers." The subjects were also asked to indicate their level of friendliness toward each of the stimulus persons. Results provided general support for at least part of the Rokeach theory. Given information on values, belief similarity was responsible for much more variance than was race effect. However, in the absence of such information a strong race effect was present. Curricular implications for such a finding are worth considering.

One of the many ideas presented in *The Open and Closed Mind* (Rokeach, 1960) is that prejudice may be in large part the result of perceived dissimilarity of belief systems. That is, Rokeach, Smith, and Evans (1960) contend that the prejudiced person does not reject a person of another race, religion, or nationality because of his ethnic membership per se, but rather because he perceives that the other differs from him in important beliefs and values. He reports a study in which the stimulus individuals were white or Negro in one group; in the other they were Jewish or gentile. Racial and religious attitudes and general beliefs of the stimulus individuals were also varied. In this situation, it was found that the friendship preferences expressed were determined primarily on the basis of congruence in beliefs rather than on racial or religious grounds.

Triandis (1961) took issue with this position, stating that:

"People do not exclude other people from their neighborhood, for instance, because the other people have different belief systems, but they do exclude them because they are Negroes" [p. 186].

He has reported results contrary to Rokeach's contention regarding the primacy of belief congruence over race as a determinant of prejudice. Since he objected to Rokeach's use of the single criterion of friendship as the measure of prejudice, he employed a social distance scale of 15 items. For his manipulation of belief congruence, he used "same philosophy" or "different philosophy" as determined by the subjects' most and least preferred of Morris' (1956) "13 ways to live." Stimulus individuals in the study were varied in race, religion, and occupational status as well as in philosophy. He obtained a "race effect" that accounted for about four times as much variance, in terms of the percentage of the total sum of squares, as any of the other three effects singly, although all four main effects were highly significant.

Rokeach (1961) replied with the objection that the long and involved passages of Morris' "ways to live" could not be equated with belief systems as he defined them; the "ways to live" were too vague and were not salient to the subjects. He concluded that the results of Triandis' study were therefore irrelevant to the point at issue. In a more recent study, Byrne and Wong

(1962) essentially supported Rokeach's position, employing personal feelings of friendliness and willingness to work together in an experiment as dependent variables.

The present study was designed with the intent of reconciling these disparate findings. It seemed reasonable to assume that there might be some truth in each position, and that the large differences between the results obtained by Rokeach et al. and by Byrne and Wong, on the one hand, and by Triandis, on the other, followed primarily from the methods used.

In the design of the present study, our first concern was that of making our "stimulus individuals" appear real to our subjects. In Rokeach's studies, pairs of individuals, described in very sketchy fashion, were presented in such a way that it was rather obvious to the subject that a choice was to be made between race and belief. In Triandis' study, there was less of a suggestion of choice, but the descriptions were equally sketchy and the measure of belief was, indeed, very vague. Our intent has been, following an improved procedure devised by Byrne (1961), to present to our subjects, as nearly as is possible on paper, realistic stimulus individuals. In this study, as in Byrne and Wong (1962), stimulus individuals were varied in race and in the similarity of their beliefs to those previously expressed by the subjects. This procedure makes it possible to elicit absolute rather than comparative judgments so as to minimize self-consciously ideological resposes. As our dependent variables, we employed both a measure of friendly feelings and a social distance scale, on which responses to each individual item could be separately analyzed.

METHOD

The sample consisted of 23 male and 21 female white teen-agers in two ninth grade classes of a California high school. The subjects, all of whom were 14 years of age, came mainly from working class homes in a nonmetropolitan industrial community. They participated in the study during their advisory periods.

At the beginning of the period, the experimenter introduced himself as "a research worker from the University of California" and handed out a mimeographed booklet to each student, by name. The instructions were printed on the front page of the booklet and read as follows:

> As you remember, a few months ago we asked you to answer some
> questions concerning your interests and attitudes about yourself,
> your friends, and certain groups of teenagers. You may also recall that
> there were some questions asking you to give first impressions about
> people when you knew only a few things about them, such as the

person's religion or type of job. We are very much interested in how people form these impressions.

In fact, we would like to know how you would feel about some teenagers who took the same questionnaires as you did, but in other parts of the country. Therefore, we have taken some of their answers and presented them on the following pages.

We want you to look at the descriptions of *four* teenage boys [girls] and then answer some questions about how you feel toward them. The four teenagers will be called: TEENAGER I, II, III, and IV. If you have any questions, please raise your hand and the research worker will help you. Be sure to read everything carefully.[1]

As the instructions indicate, 2 months prior to this study the students had filled out the pretest version of a questionnaire being developed for a large-scale study of teen-age attitudes towards minority groups. A value scale on the pretest questionnaire had asked the students, "Do you think teenagers in general *ought* to . . ." about each of 25 items. Five response alternatives were provided, ranging from "Strongly feel they should" to "Strongly feel they shouldn't." The students' own responses to these items on the pretest provided the basis for the manipulation of belief congruence in the present study.

For each of the subjects, two "stimulus teen-agers" were constructed who were like him in values, and two were constructed who were unlike him, following a procedure similar to that used by Byrne (1961). One "like" stimulus teen-ager was made up whose responses were identical with those given by the subject. In order to avoid raising the suspicions of the subjects, the other "like" teen-ager was made to differ slightly from the first by moving the responses to six items, chosen at random, one step on the 5-point scale. Each "unlike" teen-ager was created by choosing at random three of the items the subject had answered "Strongly feel they should" and changing them to "feel they shouldn't." Three more modest alterations were made as well, depending on the subject's original pretest response pattern.

Besides the information on how the stimulus teen-agers had "answered" the value items, the subjects were given the sex, grade and program in school, last year's grades, and race of the teen-ager. For half the subjects, this additional information preceded that on values throughout the booklet, and for the other half, the value scale information was presented first. The sex and grade in school were always the same as that of the subject, the program in school was college preparatory, and grades were "about a B average." Only race was varied. Thus, by combining like and unlike responses on the

[1] Male subjects answered questions about boys; female subjects answered questions about girls. Wording throughout the questionnaire was adapted to the sex of the subject.

value scale with "Negro" and "white," four stimulus teen-agers were created. These will be referred to as white-like, white-unlike, Negro-like, and Negro-unlike. These four were presented in eight different orders, the only restriction on ordering being that like and unlike teen-agers were alternated.

As the subject opened his booklet, he was confronted with the description of one of the four stimulus teen-agers, called Teenager I. The subject read this first description, at his own speed, and then turned to the next pair of pages and answered three questions. One of these served as a check on the manipulation of belief congruence, and the other two were measures of friendliness and social distance towards the stimulus teen-ager. The questions will be discussed in more detail under Results. The subject then went on to read the description of Teenagers II, III, and IV and in turn to answer the questions about them. When he had finished, usually in 20–25 minutes, he turned over his booklet and waited for the rest of the class to complete their booklets.

RESULTS AND DISCUSSION

Check on the Manipulation of Belief Congruence

One question answered by the subjects about each of the four stimulus teen-agers was the following:

How much like you would you say Teenager X is?
0 _____ as much like me as any teenager I can think of
1 _____ very much like me
2 _____ a little like me
3 _____ a little unlike me
4 _____ very much unlike me
5 _____ as much unlike me as any teenager I can think of

The subjects' responses to this question served as a check on the manipulation of similarity between the subject and the stimulus teen-agers. Mean responses to this question, for each of the four stimulus teen-agers, may be found in Table 1. It is clear that the white-like (1.63) and Negro-like (1.91) teen-agers are seen as more like the subjects than are the white-unlike (2.76) and Negro-unlike (3.27) teen-agers. The mean of responses to both like teen-agers combined (3.56) differs from the mean of responses to both unlike teen-agers (6.05) at well beyond the .001 level ($t = 6.99$). All individual like-unlike comparisons also yield t values significant at beyond the .001 level (p values reported henceforth are all two-tailed). From these data we may conclude that the manipulation of similarity or dissimilarity between the subjects and the stimulus teen-agers has been successful.

TABLE 1

Mean Response to Stimulus Teen-agers

		Stimulus Teen-ager			
Question	N	White-like	White-unlike	Negro-like	Negro-unlike
1. "How friendly"[a]	42	.59	1.69	.83	1.86
2. Social distance scale total score[b]	44	9.84	5.90	7.81	5.54
2A. Individual items on social distance scale[c]					
Invite home to dinner	44	.82	.36	.39	.20
Go to party to which this person was invited	44	1.00	.80	.93	.70
Go to same school	44	1.00	.91	1.00	.91
Have as member of social group	44	.91	.32	.82	.48
Have as speaking acquaintance	44	.91	.59	.91	.59
Live in same apartment house with this person and his (her) family	44	.89	.45	.43	.27
Eat lunch at school with	44	.93	.57	.84	.57
Sit next to in class	44	.98	.70	.93	.73
Close personal friend	44	.80	.27	.59	.32
Work on committee with	44	.93	.68	.91	.73
Date my sister (brother)	44	.68	.25	.09	.05
3. "How much like you?"[a]	43	1.63	2.76	1.91	3.27

[a] For these questions, a low score signifies greater friendliness and perceived similarity, respectively.

[b] Scoring: 1 for "yes," 0 for "no"; 11 points possible.

[c] Scores run from 0 to 1. A mean of 1.0 signifies endorsement of the item by everyone.

"Friendliness" Question

The first question the subject answered about each stimulus teen-ager was the following:

If you met this teenager for the first time, what would your immediate reaction be?

I think I would feel:
    0 _____ quite friendly
    1 _____ a little friendly
    2 _____ nothing either way
    3 _____ a little unfriendly
    4 _____ quite unfriendly

This question was intended to be a nearly pure measure of "affect"; that is, a measure of the subject's overall reaction to each stimulus teen-ager. The mean responses with respect to each of the teen-agers are given in Row

1 of Table 1. Subjects would feel most friendly towards the white-like teen-ager (.59), followed by the Negro-like (.83), white-unlike (1.69), and Negro-unlike (1.86) teen-agers. An analysis of variance using McNemar's (1955, p. 330) Case XIV mixed model reveals that belief congruence accounts for a much larger part of the variance of responses than does race, although the effects for both race and belief are significant. (F for the belief effect $= 37.72$, $p < .001$; F for the race effect $= 5.21$, $p < .05$.) This result, of course, is consistent with Rokeach's theory.

This question was also asked, in a somewhat different format, on the "pretest" questionnaire mentioned earlier. At that time subjects were asked to respond to a list of many different individuals, of which one was "A Negro teen-ager." Of the subjects in the present experiment, 35 answered this item on the pretest. An interesting finding emerges when we compare responses to "A Negro teen-ager," with no other information, with responses to Negro-like and Negro-unlike in the present study.

A rather obvious expectation is that the mean of responses to "A Negro teen-ager" should fall between the means for Negro-like and Negro-unlike. This is the case. Means for those subjects present on both occasions ($N = 35$) are given in Table 2. (They are .91, 1.34, and 1.80 for Negro-like, Negro teen-ager, and Negro-unlike, respectively.) Subjects feel significantly more friendly towards the Negro-like teen-ager than towards the Negro teen-ager ($t = 2.08$, $p < .05$) and significantly more friendly towards the Negro teen-ager than towards the Negro-unlike teen-ager ($t = 2.88$, $p < .01$).

One should also expect that subjects' responses to the Negro teen-ager should correlate moderately both with responses to Negro-like and Negro-

TABLE 2

Analysis of Responses on the "Friendliness" Scale towards Various Stimulus Teen-agers ($N = 35$)

Stimulus Teen-ager	M[a]	σ^2	Comparison	Correlation	t between Means	t between Variances
Negro-like	.91	.48	Negro-like versus Negro teen-ager	.15	2.08*	2.31*
Negro teen-ager[b]	1.34	.99	Negro teen-ager versus Negro-unlike	.62***	2.88**	<1
Negro-unlike	1.80	1.13	Negro-like versus Negro-unlike	.29	4.68***	3.01**

[a] A low score indicates greater friendliness towards the stimulus teen-ager.
[b] From pretest questionnaire.
* $p < .05$.
** $p < .01$.
*** $p < .001$.

unlike. This should be the case unless, for some reason, subjects have an expectation that Negro teen-agers in general are either like them or unlike them. Again referring to Table 2, we note that the correlation between Negro-like and Negro teen-ager is .15 and the correlation between Negro-like and Negro-unlike is .29. Neither of these correlations is large enough to be considered significantly different from zero. (The CR for the correlation of .29 reaches the .09 level of significance.) The correlation between Negro teen-ager and Negro-unlike, however, is .62, significant at beyond the .001 level, and also significantly different from the other two correlations, at the .01 and .05 levels, respectively.

These differences would seem to demonstrate an important point: namely, when our white subjects are given no information at all about a Negro teen-ager, they apparently assume that he is different from them in values and react towards him accordingly. It should be noted here, referring again to Table 2, that the variance of responses to the Negro-like teen-ager is significantly smaller than the variance of the other two distributions. Some caution must be exercised in the interpretation of the differences between the correlations for this reason. Our data from the question "How much like you would you say Teenager X is?" add further information, however. On that question, the subjects perceived the Negro stimulus teen-agers to be significantly less like them than were the white teen-agers, even when given the same information about both. The mean of responses to Negro-like and Negro-unlike teen-agers combined was 5.33, while the mean for like and unlike white teen-agers was 4.44 (t for this difference is 3.29, $p < .01$). That is, with belief similarity held constant, the subjects perceived that the white stimulus teen-agers were more like them, given *identical* information about the whites and Negroes. These results parallel findings reported by Byrne and Wong (1962, p. 247, Table 1), in which white subjects attributed greater similarity of attitudes to unknown whites than to unknown Negroes. Our data further indicate the expectation held by the subjects that a Negro teen-ager, simply by virtue of his being a Negro, will be different from them. It seems likely that their propensity to react negatively towards the Negro is based on this expectation, or, equally compatible with the obtained relationship, for persons sharing the anti-Negro prejudices endemic in American society, the sheer fact that a person is Negro marks him as significantly "different," however similar he may be in other respects.

Social Distance Scale

Our major measure of reactions to the four stimulus teen-agers was the following "teen-age social distance scale":

Everyone has his own preferences about the people he wants to associate with. There are probably some people with whom you would be willing to be very good friends, and others whom you would just as soon not ever be with. We would like you to tell us how close a relationship you think you would be willing to have with TEENAGER X. Check the blank under "yes" for each statement you agree with, and the blank under "no" for each statement you disagree with for TEENAGER X. Guess if you aren't really sure.

I think I would be willing:

Yes   No
___   ___   to invite this person home to dinner
___   ___   to go to a party to which this person was invited
___   ___   to go to the same school with this person
___   ___   to have this person as a member of my social group or club
___   ___   to have this person as one of my speaking acquaintances
___   ___   to live in the same apartment house with this person and his family
___   ___   to eat lunch with this person in school
___   ___   to sit next to this person in class
___   ___   to have this person as a close personal friend
___   ___   to work on a committee at school with this person
___   ___   to have this person date my sister [brother]

This social distance scale, which was devised for the pretest questionnaire, was patterned after that of Triandis. Items were changed, omitted, and added to make the scale suitable for teen-age subjects; for example, no negative items were used, on the assumption that they would not discriminate between the subjects. Total scores on the scale were obtained by simply summing responses to the 11 items, each scored "1" for "yes" and "0" for "no."

Responses to the social distance scale were analyzed in two ways. First, an analysis of variance of the total scores was computed. As in the analysis of the "friendliness" question, belief accounts for by far the largest amount of the variance, although effects for both race and belief are highly significant. (F for race $= 7.20$, $p < .02$; F for belief $= 48.51$, $p < .001$.) Then, t tests for both race and belief effects were calculated for each of the 11 items. That is, each subject's responses to the two Negro stimulus teen-agers were combined, and his responses to the two white stimulus teen-agers were combined. The t between the means of these scores evaluates the race effect. The belief effect was tested similarly, by combining responses to the two like teen-agers and comparing the mean of these scores with the mean of the summed responses to the two unlike teen-agers.

The t-test analysis adds more specific information concerning the areas in which race and belief effects are strongest. It is clear that belief has a very strong effect on all 11 items. All but one of the differences between responses to like and unlike teen-agers are significant at beyond the .001 level; the difference on the item concerning "Go to the same school" is significant at the .02 level. The race effect, however, appears to be specific to three items: "Invite him home to dinner," "Live in the same apartment house," and "Have him date my sister [brother]." These 3 items on which the race effect is significant at beyond the .001 level seem to be "sensitive areas," ones in which there is widespread resistance, in American society, to Negro-white contacts. Rokeach (Rokeach et al., 1960) has stated that his theory applies "insofar as psychological processes are involved . . . [p. 135]." As an example of institutionalized racial prejudice outside the framework of his theory he later states "the southern white bigot would not want his daughter to marry the 'good' Negro any more than the 'bad' one [p. 165]." In Rokeach's sense, the present "sensitive" items would seem to fall in the latter category. Clearly, an empirical definition of institutional prejudice in terms of an obtained "race effect" would be circular and meaningless. For purposes of future research, we would suggest two criteria for situations that may be expected to produce a "race effect": intimacy of contact and presence of others—in this case parents—who are the enforcers of social norms. At present, all we can state from our empirical finding is that a belief effect is strong on all the items, whereas a race effect occurs on items that appear to involve publicly visible relationships that are "sensitive" or controversial by prevailing cultural standards.

One further set of data is available, from the pretest, which provides an important comparison with the results of the social distance scale in the present study. On the pretest, subjects were asked to respond, on the same "teen-ager social distance scale," to stimulus teen-agers who resembled quite closely the stimulus individuals used by Triandis. "Same or different philosophy" and "same or different religion" which he used as variables were omitted. Our stimulus teen-agers were all stated to be Christians, and varied only in race, white versus Negro, and in status. For the status variable, program in school and grades were varied. The teen-agers were thus described as either "in the college preparatory program getting Bs" or "in the vocational program getting failing grades." Again, there were four stimulus teen-agers: white, low status; white, high status; Negro, low status; and Negro, high status.

The results of the analysis of variance of total scores on the social distance scale, in response to these four stimulus teen-agers show a very large race effect ($F = 45.50$, $p < .001$), about twice as large as a smaller, but still highly significant status effect ($F = 28.52$, $p < .001$), in terms of percentage of variance explained. These results, obtained on 37 of the 44 subjects used in the later study, resemble quite closely those obtained by Triandis. When belief is not a variable, as in these data, or when the belief effect is weakened by the ambiguity of the information provided, as in Triandis' data, both race and status account for appreciable portions of the variance, with race being by far the more important variable.

The explanation for all of these data, it would seem, is to be found in a very simple fact. Individuals make judgments about others on the basis of all of the relevant information they possess. If little information is provided, and a judgment is demanded, it is made on the basis of inferences from past experiences or information obtained from others. That first impressions are seldom accurate is due to the fact that very little information is available, and the person must be judged on the basis of some known group membership. The correlations presented earlier, between responses to Negro-like, Negro teen-ager, and Negro-unlike, seem to indicate that the inference made by most subjects about a Negro teen-ager, in the absence of other information, is that he is *unlike* them.

If the foregoing interpretation is correct, the very large race effects obtained by Triandis and also demonstrated in the pretest data are easily accounted for. The subjects are forced to guess at the belief systems of the stimulus individuals, and their guess is that the Negro is unlike them. Our subjects in this situation respond with a very large "race effect." When essentially the same subjects were provided, in the later study, with actual information about the belief systems of the stimulus individuals, they no longer had to guess, and they responded primarily, though not exclusively, in terms of the information about belief congruence with which they had been provided.

CONCLUSIONS

The data presented strongly support Rokeach's theory that the variable of belief congruence accounts for a major portion of the variance in prejudice, if it does not tell the "whole truth" about it. The teen-age subjects in this study, when given extensive information concerning the belief systems of stimulus teen-agers, react primarily in terms of similarity of beliefs and only very secondarily in terms of race. This was the case in an analysis of total scores on a social distance scale, and in an analysis of "friendliness" responses. Strong "race effects" were obtained on "sensitive" items on the social distance scale, perhaps reflecting institutionalized areas of prejudice, and on total social distance scores when information concerning belief systems was not provided.

Not only do our results support Rokeach's contention regarding the primacy of belief congruence, but they also account for the discrepancy between the findings reported by Rokeach et al. (1960) and by Byrne and Wong (1962), on the one hand, and those reported by Triandis (1961), on the other. When subjects are forced to evaluate stimulus individuals in terms of their beliefs, then belief congruence is more important than race. But when the belief component is not provided, spelled out in considerable detail, subjects will react in racial terms on the basis of assumptions concerning the belief systems of others, and of emotional or institutionalized factors. The practical implications of these results are obvious. If people of different races encounter one another under conditions favoring the perception of belief congruence (as, for example, in equal-status contacts), then racial prejudice should be substantially reduced.

CHAPTER 8

Acquiring Culturally-Approved Controls over Aggressive Behavior

Aggression as it is usually defined represents behavior in which an individual verbally or physically attacks some other person or object in his environment, although the individual may in some cases direct his aggression against himself. An attempt to destroy or appropriate possessions of another, to attack another's character or person, or an attempt to destroy one's self or one's own possessions represents aggressive behavior. Various forms of problem behavior including antisocial attitudes, alienation, and delinquency may also represent aggressive behavior. Aggression may also take the form of a generalized adverse reaction to the environment without being specifically directed against any one person or object. Thus, aggression is a negative or socially maladjustive act. Certainly its presence in a social transaction is essentially nonadjustive, usually leading to repercussions unfortunate or at least uncomfortable for all concerned. Aggression is often the behavior manifested by a discipline problem child in school. A person displaying aggression tends to have difficulty in controlling his own temper and is often overtly or covertly fearful of the effects his aggression may arouse.

Aggression needs, of course, a specific object such as a minority group, a teacher, another child, a policeman, or some object against which it can be directed although in its more generalized forms the objects or persons may be multiple. Aggression, particularly on the part of a person fearful of the consequences, may be covert or may be displaced in that it is directed against a "safe" person actually uninvolved. The consequences of aggression are often circular in that aggression tends to be responded to by aggression.

It is generally accepted that aggression is the result of frustration occurring because an individual's goals are blocked, the amount and strength of the aggression being a direct function of the amount of the frustration. In fact, aggression has been defined (the frustration-aggression hypothesis) as any behavior resulting from frustration. Although withdrawal behavior may also result from frustration, the frustration-aggression hypothesis posits that withdrawal is a second-order of behavior that occurs only when a series of aggressions have been tried without attaining a blocked goal or when the consequences of aggression have become so unendurable or so feared that the aggressor seeks recourse to withdrawal behavior.

Aggression may in some cases assume a relatively positive and socially approved form if it is manifested by ambition, hard work to prove a point, or a vigorous competitive spirit. Ordinarily such socially approved strivings are not conceived as aggression and in most cases they are not, but sometimes the individual's manner of handling these strivings or his reasons for assuming them make it evident that aggression is actually causing the behavior. However, the articles in this chapter adopt the more common standard definition of aggression as socially undesirable, personally maladaptive behavior.

It is, of course, true that during the course of a lifetime every individual suffers a great many frustrations, most quite minor in nature with occasional ones of major importance. And correspondingly, it can be expected that everyone expresses aggression from time to time. Unfortunately, aggression tends to be cumulative in its effects. An individual attaining his ends by aggressive behavior or one who grows into the habit of aggression tends to repeat the behavior found to work.

Thus, frustration and its consequent aggression may be seen as normal aspects of the developmental process. They become really serious only when their expression assumes too great a magnitude, when it gets out of control, or when an individual begins to display aggression in an increasingly broad range of situations with increasing frequency. Aggression also becomes serious when the individual develops it as a pattern and refuses to consider substitute attempts or more culturally approved means to attain goals. For some persons, hostility becomes a way of life to the point that aggression is displayed even when goals are attained, leading to a kind of "dog-in-manger" attitude. Because of this, it becomes necessary to begin to educate persons at a very early age to learn to handle their aggressions and to redirect them along more socially approved lines. If this education fails, the product is an individual who increasingly has little place in social transactions of any kind. Consequently, every school should give thought to the problem of teaching children to acquire culturally approved controls over aggression as well as to the problem of dealing with aggression when it occurs among children placed in its charge. Ideally, teachers and administrators should consider the extent to which the educational programs they espouse in their schools actually cause frustration in children and incite them to aggression.

The six articles about children presented in this chapter consider the nature of aggression, causal factors, contexts in which aggression occurs, and means of controlling and redirecting aggression into culturally approved channels. In the first of these articles, Bandura and Walters formulate a theory of the development of aggression based on the frustration-aggression hypothesis. As they conceive it, aggression begins in infancy but is confined to various forms of motor or vocal discharge representing forms of protest rather than actual aggression. Following this, a form of instrumental aggression occurs that is primarily a means of obtaining something that is desired or of getting rid of something that is unpleasant. During this period of development the child is experiencing some forms of parent imposed restraint as he tries to express aggression. Later still, as speech develops and as socialization proceeds, the child begins to express his aggressions by more sophisticated and more subtle means. Over the whole span of time various learnings involving aggression are taking place and, throughout, the primary persons to be dealt with are the parents who become the recipients of the aggression. Thus the parents are seen as the major factors in learnings involving aggression and by the time the child enters school and has to deal with teachers and peers some specific patterns of aggression are already quite well formulated, making some children quite aggression-prone and some much less so. It was Bandura and Walters' belief that by examining the child-parent relationships of a group of aggression-prone adolescents as compared to a nonaggressive group they would find significant differences between the groups in the ways they dealt with their parents and in the ways their parents dealt with them. In the line of reasoning advanced by Bandura and Walters, the implication for schools is that a child enters school with a well-set repertory of aggressive behaviors learned through his interactions with his parents and that these behaviors will be exhibited in outside-of-home social relationships. Since each child is operating from a previously acquired base, teachers can not assume that an educational program designed to promote acceptable social behavior will be equally effective for all, nor can they ignore individual differences in aggression-proneness learned during the years before the child entered school.

In a day when the communication media emphasize and even condone aggressive behavior, the question is often asked as to the extent to which such aggression-laden input begets aggression in viewers, listeners, or readers. One argument even runs that such exposure drains off tendency to aggression by providing a vicarious outlet. Geen and Berkowitz investigated some aspects of individual's tendency to express aggression after exposure to aggression. It would appear, extending Geen and Berkowitz's results, that tendency to express aggression following exposure is highly related to the emotional state of the recipient. If he has recently been subjected to aggression in his personal life or if for one reason or another he is aggression-prone then he is much more apt to express aggression following exposure to aggression via a communication medium than would be true of an individual who is neither aggression prone nor the recent recipient of aggression. Geen and Berkowitz's study has various implications for school practice. In view of their general results one might, for example, wonder about the effect of witnessing the application of punitive teacher behavior upon aggression-prone children or upon those who have themselves recently been subjected to discipline.

The study by Eron and his associates reported in this chapter also examines causal effects of aggression, and their findings should be cross referenced by the reader with those of Geen and Berkowitz and of Bandura and Walters. Studying the relation of home discipline upon a child's tendency to display aggression in school, Eron et al. note the presence of a significant relationship. Children do, through their display of aggressive behavior in school, seem to reflect the various degrees of punishment they receive at home. A child's socioeconomic status as well as his sex should, however, be taken into consideration by a teacher in building expectations both of the level of punishment the child is apt to have encountered at home as well as the level of aggression he is apt to display in school. Here once again we see the importance of considering a child's home background and the nature of the parent's child-rearing practices in making any assessment of the child. Visiting teacher programs, often mistakenly regarded as a frill, are essential if teachers are to have information that will make them maximally effective in dealing with children in school. One particularly interesting finding of the Eron study is that mothers who use a medium level of punishment tend to have sons who are less aggression prone than is true of those who use either a low or a high level of punishment. In all probability medium punishment is more likely to be seen by the child as reasonable and perhaps justified whereas severe punishment may be interpreted as rejection. Lack of punishment could also be interpreted by a child as rejection although it is equally possible that it may be interpreted as condoning aggression—the giving, in effect, of a license to aggress. It is quite probable that the same situation obtains for teacher administered discipline.

The study by Lewin, Lippitt, and White is often cited as a classical example of the investigation of the comparative effects of the "social" climates created by democratic, authoritarian, and *laissez-faire* procedures in dealing with groups of children engaged upon some adult directed task requiring group as well as individual effort. In general, as the children in the Lewin study go about their task, authoritarian procedures lead to increasing levels of aggression toward each other together with an attitude toward the leader either of submission or of persistent demands for attention. The reactions of the democratic group were more spontaneous, more fact-minded, and more friendly. The aggressive tendencies promoted by the authoritarian group tended to seek a scapegoat, after which the group became more friendly, only, after a time, to again resume the scapegoating behavior. The *laissez-faire* groups also exhibited a high level of aggression but of a somewhat different order than that characterizing the authoritarian group climate. Changing climates, as from authoritarianism to democracy, did change individual and group attitudes and behavior although the investigators do note the importance of personality factors in considering the total effects of group climate upon any given individual. The implications of this study for classroom instructional procedures is obvious although teachers' expectations of the overall probability of the success of any group guidance procedure should be tempered by the existence of background factors such as those discussed in the other five studies reported in this chapter.

In a further study of means of reducing aggressive tendencies, using a sample of children ranging in age from 3 through 7, Gordon and Smith find that the arousal of the affiliation motive in children furnishes a useful means of reducing situational aggression although this technique appears to be more successful with younger than with older children. An extension of this study to include adolescents would be of particular interest. Here again we find an example of the early origins of aggression with a clear indication of the advisability of imposing culturally acceptable controls as early in the child's developmental and educational experience as possible. First-grade teachers should be particularly concerned in including group socializations in their instructional and recreational programs for children. The study by Brown and Elliott, also concerned with means of reducing aggression makes the point that ignoring aggressive responses and attending cooperative ones tends to reduce the former and increase the latter, although greater success was obtained with verbal aggression than with physical aggression, possibly because teachers find it especially difficult to ignore physical aggression. The Brown and Elliott study was confined to nursery school children and results might be different with older children, particularly insofar as their previous socialization experiences had formed the basis of learnings less easily dealt with and as the objectives of the upper school would not permit as much modification as would be possible in the nursery school.

The studies on children's aggressive behavior presented in this chapter furnish concrete suggestions helpful to teachers in dealing with aggressive behavior. However, it should be remembered that all general statements have to be conditioned by the fact of individual differences and findings sometimes indicate mutually opposed approaches. For example, Brown and

Elliott's finding about the advantages of ignoring aggression have to be balanced against the Eron et al. finding that little or no parental punishment leads to increased aggression while moderate punishment appears to be aggression reducing. The answer is, of course, that behavioral variables interact and programs based upon concentration upon a single variable at the expense of all others may be easy to implement but will not, in the long run, be as effective as a multivariate approach. In any event, in formulating educational programs and desired teacher-pupil transactions teachers should be aware of the importance of a child's home background, stage of development, and previous general socialization experiences.

40. ADOLESCENT AGGRESSION

Albert Bandura & Richard H. Walters

What is the nature of aggression? This question may best be answered by observing the behaviors exhibited by persons of aggressive tendency in comparison to the behaviors of nonaggressive persons, and from these comparisons to derive explanatory hypotheses. In their study on adolescent aggression Bandura and Walters have studied the behaviors of a group of aggression-prone adolescent boys and compared them with the behaviors of a group of nonaggressive adolescent boys. Measures of behavior included ratings of direct physical, direct verbal, and indirect aggression. Separate ratings were made of aggression toward parents, aggression toward teachers, and aggression toward peers. Aggression toward parents was rated from interviews with both parents and their sons, while aggression toward teachers was measured only by interviews with the boys included in the study. Data were analyzed in terms of parental handling of aggression, boys' reactions as expressed in interviews, and boys' answers to a thematic test. In their discussion Bandura and Walters propose a theory of the development of aggression, and from the theory they propose a number of hypotheses which they test in their study. Teachers who read this study should gain a better insight into the dynamics of aggression as it operates in adolescent boys. They may also gain some insight into the behavior of parents and teachers when confronted with the aggressive act.

The hypotheses which will be presented here are largely derived from the frustration-aggression theory systematically expounded first by Dollard et al.

SOURCE. Abridgement of Chapter 3, "Aggression," from Albert Bandura and Richard H. Walters, *Adolescent Aggression*, New York: Ronald Press, 1959. (With permission of Dr. Bandura and the publisher, Ronald Press.)

(1939). This theory states that aggression is a learned response to frustrating situations, though not the only response to frustration, and that aggressive behavior is reinforced insofar as it proves successful in overcoming frustrations that prevent the satisfaction of biological drives or learned motives. The writers have previously noted that a sample of aggressive boys had experienced more frustration of their dependency needs than had a control group of boys. These frustrations, however, can account only for the boys' potentiality for displaying aggression; they cannot, alone, account for the amount and kind of aggression that the boys actually displayed. The present discussion is concerned with the extent to which parents permitted and encouraged their sons to display aggression and with the way in which they handled aggressive behavior when it occurred. In part, it is aimed at exploring further the differences between a group of aggressive boys and their nonaggressive controls.

A THEORY OF THE DEVELOPMENT OF AGGRESSION

Frustration may be defined as the occurrence of conditions that prevent or delay the attainment of a goal-response. Most of the early frustrations that an infant encounters are due to delay in the satisfaction of his bodily needs and result from his helplessness and inability to care for himself.

When a child is hungry or otherwise in discomfort, it can do nothing except emit motor or vocal responses which appear initially to be completely nonpurposive in character. The crying, restlessness, and flailing of limbs seen in infants seem in fact to be the precursors of later verbal and physical responses that would unhesitatingly be classed as aggressive. The conditions for the development of aggression are thus present for every infant; frustrations are inevitable, and, although infants differ in the frequency and strength of their responses to frustration, all at some time respond by some form of motor or vocal discharge.

As yet, however, the child's responses lack the distinctive characteristics of aggressive acts. It is only when the child has learned to attack persons or objects in his environment in such a way as to injure or damage them that he can be described as aggressing. This transition from a protest response to an aggressive one is possible only when the child has acquired a certain degree of motor control. Since earlier motor discharges have frequently elicited the mother's attention and so have been followed by the removal of discomfort, it is not surprising that the slightly older child will, when frustrated, lash out, flail its limbs, beat on objects, or respond in similarly aggressive ways. At first, however, one may doubt whether there is always or necessarily present any *intent* to hurt or destroy. The aggressive behavior appears to be wholly instrumental, a means of obtaining something that is desired or of getting rid of something that is unpleasant. Only when the child has learned that signs of pain, distress, or injury in another person are frequently followed by the removal of frustrations for himself, so that he now seeks to produce such signs, can one speak of an intent to hurt. Aggressive behavior is under these circumstances still, however, primarily instrumental in character.

At the same time as aggression is being learned, efforts are being made to bring it under control. Socialization of aggression is relatively severe in North American society (Whiting and Child, 1953), and most parents make some attempt to limit their children's aggressive displays through restraint or punishment. When frustrated, the young child quickly resorts to physical violence. As the process of socialization takes effect, he learns to substitute the more readily tolerated verbal means of aggression for physical ones (Goodenough, 1931). Even direct verbal expressions of anger nevertheless meet disapproval, and the child eventually learns more or less subtle forms of expressing aggression that do not involve a direct attack on the instigator. Most adults rarely engage in direct acts of physical violence, and even their verbal attacks tend to be softened or camouflaged to some extent. Very often, indeed, they may display no open aggression, but instead their hostile feelings are expressed in thoughts and fantasies (Lindzey, 1950; Nowlis, 1953; Wright, 1954). This process whereby a more tolerated form of aggression is substituted for a less tolerated one represents a kind of response displacement.

Another form of displacement simultaneously takes place under the pressure of anxiety about possible punishment or disapproval. The primary socializing agents are, of course, the parents, and they are undoubtedly in a position to be the most effective ones. Not only can they impose physical restraint or punishment on the child, but they have a very potent weapon in their ability to threaten the child with withdrawal of their affection and approval. Consequently, aggressive impulses first aroused against the parents, who must frustrate in order to train and control the child, tend to be displaced to other persons and even to nonhuman objects. For example, a child who has been thwarted by his parents may physically attack another child or pet, or damage a toy or household furniture. A similar process of displacement has been demonstrated in studies in which children who were frustrated by adults showed aggression toward peers (Lewin, Lippitt, and White, 1939). This second form of displacement, whereby aggressive acts are diverted from the original instigators to other objects, may be referred to as object displacement.

The process of socializing aggression thus involves training the child to react to frustration in ways that are relatively acceptable. Training is, of course, never completely successful; occasionally, almost every adult responds in an impulsively aggressive manner. The majority, however, learn to avoid for the most part the kinds of aggressive acts that might bring serious consequences for themselves or for the objects of their aggression.

HYPOTHESES

On the basis of the principle of generalization, it was predicted that the aggressive group of boys would display more direct aggression than would their controls, whether this aggression was expressed toward parents, toward teachers, or toward peers, and that they would express more hostility toward them during the interviews. It was also predicted that the aggressive group would show less anxiety concerning aggression.

There seemed two definite possibilities concerning the absolute amount of indirect aggression that the two groups of boys might show. It might be that the aggressive boys would display more aggression of all kinds, whether this aggression were direct or indirect in character. On the other hand, it seemed possible that, because of their readiness to express aggression in more direct ways, the aggressive boys would have less need to resort to indirect forms and consequently would express no more indirect aggression than would the control boys.

When a child develops a consistently aggressive pattern of behavior, one may suspect that in some way his aggression has been encouraged and reinforced. In order for reinforcement to be provided, aggression must be allowed to occur. Probably, the surest way to prevent a child from learning the efficacy of aggressive patterns of behavior is to make every effort to control aggression from the start by not allowing it to occur. Consequently, it was predicted that the parents of the aggressive boys would be more permissive of aggression than would the parents of the control boys. Supportive evidence for this prediction came from the Harvard study of Sears, Maccoby, and Levin (1957), which revealed a small, but significant, correlation between a mother's permissiveness for aggression toward herself and the amount of aggression her child displayed in the home.

When children are aggressive outside the home, the parents are frequently not at hand and consequently cannot intervene. Their attitudes toward such aggressive behavior may, however, be a strong influence in determining to what extent it occurs. For example, parents who are themselves aggressive may both instigate and reinforce their children's aggression through encouraging and condoning a combative, aggressive attitude toward others. However, even parents who display little overt aggression may directly or indirectly encourage aggression in their children. In fact, Johnson and Szurek (1952) have provided evidence that some parents keep their own antisocial impulses under control, yet at the same time subtly instigate and condone their children's antisocial acts and thereby obtain vicarious gratification of their own repressed antisocial impulses. On the basis of these considerations, it was predicted that the parents of the aggressive boys would encourage aggressive behavior more actively than would the control parents.

MEASURES

In order to study the process of displacement, it was decided not to make any over-all rating of aggression but to create scales for the separate rating of direct physical, direct verbal, and indirect aggression. Moreover, separate ratings were made of aggression toward parents, aggression toward teachers, and aggression toward peers. Thus there were nine main scales for the assessment of aggressive behavior. Ratings of aggression toward parents were made both from the parent and from the adolescent interviews; aggression toward teachers and peers was assessed from the adolescent interviews only.

The scale measuring *physical aggression* took account only of direct physical attacks, such as fighting, striking with the fists or with weapons, or throwing objects calculated to produce bodily injury. Under direct *verbal aggression* was included any form of attack which involved a face-to-face interaction and an undisguised expression of attack or defiance. For example, in this category were included not only name-calling or saying derogatory things to another person but also refusals to obey adults or hurtful criticism, provided these were openly expressed to the person whom it was intended to injure. Under *indirect aggression* were included less direct displays of verbal aggression, such as defamation, refusing favors in order to frustrate the petitioner (a not infrequent technique, it was discovered, of expressing dislike), and inciting others to aggression. Less direct forms of aggression that were expressed in actions rather than in words—for example, deliberately spurning or walking away from another person in order to show distaste for his company and all instances, such as door-slamming and throwing objects to the ground, in which aggression was displaced to nonhuman objects —were also categorized as indirect aggression.

Further estimates of the boys' aggression were obtained through scales which measured the boys' *hostility*. These estimates were based on the extent to which, during their interviews, the boys made disparaging remarks about their parents, teachers, and peers, respectively.

In addition to a measure of the extent to which aggressive behavior was manifested, an attempt was made to gauge the degree to which anxiety concerning aggression was present. It was assumed that with high anxiety there would be a relatively greater amount of indirect, than of direct, aggression so that, if aggression were expressed at all, its form would be more likely to be indirect than direct. Thus a scale measuring *directness of aggression*, which took no account of the absolute amount of aggression, was introduced. If a boy manifests little aggression, this may be because he is exposed to few frustrations or because aggressive responses are inhibited. If whatever aggression he expresses occurs in a direct form, there is a strong possibility that the former explanation holds. In this case he would obtain a high rating on the directness of aggression scale. If, on the other hand, a boy expresses much or little aggression, but all of it in indirect forms, it may reasonably be supposed that some inhibition is occurring. In this case he would obtain a low rating on the directness of aggression scale. Ratings were made of the directness of aggression toward parents, toward teachers, and toward peers.

Three aspects of the parents' handling of the boys' aggressive behavior were measured. Ratings were made of the parents' *permissiveness for aggression* toward themselves, toward siblings, toward peers, and toward adults other than the parents. Parallel ratings were also made of the parents' *punitiveness for aggression*. In addition, a single rating was made of the parents' *encouragement of the boys' aggression* outside the home.

RESULTS FROM PARENT INTERVIEWS

Boys' Aggression Against the Parents

Most parents declared that their sons had never displayed any physical aggression against them. Their reaction to the question: "Has he ever struck you?" tended to be one of surprise or dismay, as though an event of this kind were inconceivable. A few mothers of the aggressive boys, however, reported an occasional isolated act of striking or pushing, and this resulted in a small, but nevertheless significant, difference between the groups of mothers in the extent to which they reported physical aggression toward themselves.

On the other hand, none of the fathers of the aggressive boys reported a physical attack, whereas one control father reported very frequent sparring with his son. Since the raters had been instructed to rate material at its face value, this latter father secured a very high rating for the amount of physical aggression he reported. It was clear, however, from listening to the interview that this father was jocularly referring to playful sparring without intent to hurt, injure, or annoy. In effect, then, no father reported the occurrence of any hostile physical attack upon himself.

Judging from the parents' reports, most boys, both aggressive and control, had answered their parents back or shouted at them, but very few had sworn or used abusive language. Thus the data from the parent interviews did not reveal any difference between the two groups of boys in the amount of verbal aggression that they showed toward their parents.

Most of the boys' aggression was, according to their parents, quite indirect in nature. The boys most frequently displayed their anger by sulking, slamming doors, walking out of the house, or retiring to another room where on rare occasions they might stamp around, throw objects, or otherwise behave in a noisy manner. From the parent data it appeared that the aggressive boys showed more indirect aggression toward their fathers than did the control boys, but that the two groups of boys did not differ in the amount of indirect aggression that they showed toward their mothers.

Parental Handling of Aggression

The prediction that the parents of the aggressive boys would be more permissive of aggression was only partially confirmed. The mothers of the aggressive boys were significantly more permissive of aggression toward themselves than were the mothers of the control boys. The groups of fathers, however, did not differ significantly in this respect.

Most parents tended to be intolerant of aggression toward themselves. This was particularly true of the fathers, most of whom would tolerate only the more indirect forms of aggression.

The control fathers were, in general, equally unwilling to tolerate aggression from their sons but were usually more understanding and kindly in their way of responding to it.

The mothers in both groups characteristically took a more permissive attitude about aggression toward themselves than did their husbands. A good many of the mothers were prepared to let their sons "blow off steam." However, the control mothers seemed to place definite limits on the amount and kind of aggression they would allow and typically would tolerate little or no aggression of an interpersonal kind.

In contrast, some of the mothers of the aggressive boys would permit aggression to occur and sometimes do nothing to prevent its recurrence.

Some of the mothers in both groups felt none too competent to handle their sons' outbursts of aggression. While the mothers of the aggressive boys were in this case inclined to express an attitude of helpless resignation, the control mothers usually took some steps to prevent the recurrence of aggression.

No differences were found between the groups of mothers or the groups of fathers in their punitiveness for aggression toward themselves. Nor were there any differences of note between the groups of parents in their handling of aggressions toward peers or toward siblings. In general, parents were rated somewhat low in permissiveness for aggression toward peers and toward siblings, but very few were found to be highly punitive. Somewhat more drastic measures were likely to be taken when a boy had been aggressive toward one of his siblings than if he had aggressed against a peer who was not a member of the family, but even so punishment was very rarely severe.

The majority of parents were less permissive of aggression toward adults outside the immediate family than they were of any other form of aggression. Both the parent groups were rated very low on this permissiveness scale, and there was very little difference between the mean ratings of the parent groups. The greater strictness in this connection is precisely what might be expected, for it is a boy's aggression toward adults outside the family that is most likely both to bring serious trouble on himself and to bring the parents into disrepute. A parent whose son is insolent or defiant toward teachers or toward neighbors runs a strong risk of being looked upon as an unsuccessful parent.

It is not surprising, therefore, that the two groups of parents differed quite markedly in their punitiveness for aggression toward other adults. The mothers of the aggressive boys were, on the average, considerably more punitive than the mothers of the control boys, and while the difference between the groups of fathers was not quite as marked, it was nevertheless significant. As far as the mothers were concerned, the findings, taken as a whole, were thus somewhat similar to those of Sears, Maccoby, and Levin (1957); the aggressive boys had mothers who were both more permissive of aggression toward themselves and more punitive of aggression toward other adults than were the mothers of the relatively nonaggressive control boys.

Sometimes, although a father actually denied any encouragement of aggression, it seemed likely from his enjoyment of aggression that encouragement had in fact occurred.

Most control fathers wanted their sons to assert themselves in socially acceptable ways and, if necessary, to defend themselves against aggression. However, they usually discouraged physical aggression and under no circumstances would they allow their sons to provoke other children.

Some of the fathers of the aggressive boys encouraged their sons to show aggression against adults, as well as against other children, although in more subtle ways. They would demand that their sons should stand up for their own rights against adults, would side with the boys against their teachers, and would criticize the school in a way that might justify their sons' aggression against school authorities.

The control fathers almost invariably discouraged any hostile aggression toward adults. A number of them told their sons never to be impolite or resistant, but simply to let their parents know, if they felt that they were being unjustly treated by adults. If problems arose in the school, most control fathers would explain to their sons the difficulties that the teachers had to face and would simply advise their sons to work harder.

The mothers of the aggressive boys not only were more permissive of aggression toward themselves than were the control mothers, but they also more actively encouraged aggression outside the home. In fact, some of the mothers of the aggressive boys made as strong demands for aggression as did any of the aggressive boys' fathers.

Some of the mothers, while not blatantly encouraging aggression, showed a pervasive tendency to support and condone their sons' aggressiveness.

Most control mothers, in contrast, avoided encouraging any aggression of a socially unacceptable nature. They demanded only that their sons should be firm in maintaining their standards and principles and not be too easily influenced by others.

Most control mothers viewed hostile aggression as a sign of weakness and urged their sons to try to see the point of view of other persons rather than to oppose them.

It seemed that, in the aggressive boys' families, one or other of the parents almost invariably encouraged aggression. Indeed, when the ratings of mothers and fathers were combined to provide an estimate of the total amount of encouragement to aggress that the boys had received from their parents, a highly significant difference between the two groups of parents emerged.

There was no case in which a control parent instigated or condoned a boy's aggression toward the other parent. On the other hand, a few parents of aggressive boys subtly instigated, and quite clearly condoned, their sons' aggression toward their marital partners.

RESULTS FROM BOYS' INTERVIEWS

In accordance with predictions, the aggressive boys displayed significantly more physical, verbal, and indirect aggression and more hostility toward their teachers than did the control boys. In addition, they showed significantly less guilt after an aggressive act had been committed.

All the control boys appeared to have a generally positive attitude toward school authorities. They typically avoided open clashes with their teachers and tried to resolve any disharmony either by talking things over with them or by working harder in order to win the teachers' approval.

The hypotheses concerning aggression toward peers also stood up well to statistical tests. The aggressive boys reported more physical aggression toward peers and expressed this aggression more directly than did the control boys. They also expressed considerably more hostile feelings toward peers. The two groups of boys, however, did not differ greatly in the amount of direct verbal aggression they displayed toward their peers. On the other hand, the control boys showed considerably more indirect aggression than did the aggressive boys.

Some of the aggressive boys took obvious pride in their skill at physical attack even when this took a form that most adolescents would deplore.

The data from the boys' interviews did not yield any differences between the aggressive and the control boys in the amount of overt aggression that they showed toward their parents, nor did they differ in the amount of hostility they felt toward their mothers. Though the aggressive boys felt more hostility toward their fathers than did the control boys, it was clear that the majority dared not express their aggression too directly.

The aggressive boys seemed to be somewhat less fearful of showing aggression toward their mothers, but they found the more indirect ways of expressing anger to be usually safer and sometimes equally effective.

Some evidence that aggression generalizes from one situation to another was provided by the consistently positive correlations that were found between aggression toward parents, toward teachers, and toward peers. These correlations are based on estimates of total aggression obtained by combining ratings of physical, direct verbal, and indirect aggression.

RESULTS FROM THEMATIC TEST

Although there were no consistent differences between the two groups of boys in the extent to which they displayed overt aggression toward their parents, it seemed possible that the aggressive boys might express more hostility toward their parents in fantasy productions. Some of the thematic test items were clearly capable of eliciting material that might reflect the boys' attitudes toward their parents. However, the items were for the most part too structured to allow the boys to introduce acts of aggression that were not already depicted within the items themselves. Consequently, it was decided to score the protocols simply for the number of times the boys in the stories were depicted as having *hostile thoughts and feelings* about their parents.

The aggressive boys gave significantly more responses indicating hostility toward the father than did the control boys. There was no difference, however, between the two groups of boys in the number of responses indicating hostility toward the mother. No significance should be attached to the fact that both groups of boys obtained a higher rating for hostile feelings toward the father than they did for hostile feelings toward the mother; this difference is largely due to the inclusion of a picture that depicted a boy in the act of raising his fist to his father.

When the aggressive boys gave a response that could be scored for hostility toward the father, they tended to express the hostility in a vehement and generalized manner.

In contrast, the control boys tended to depict the story-character's anger as a temporary response to frustration and they sometimes mentioned that the father might, in fact, have been frustrating the boy for his own good.

Had the stories been rated for the intensity of hostile responses, the difference between the groups would undoubtedly have been much greater.

41. NAME-MEDIATED AGGRESSIVE CUE PROPERTIES

Russell G. Geen & Leonard Berkowitz

American children are continually presented, on television, in the daily press, in the books they read, and in the sports they watch, with numerous models of aggression. It is believed by many that such exposure to aggressive activity provides a stimulus to aggression on the part of those who are exposed. A counterargument presents the position that a spectator exposure to aggression is in fact beneficial in that it tends to drain off aggressive tendencies as the watcher empathizes with the aggressor and in that way finds an outlet in fantasy rather than in real life. Both positions are plausible and one could build a logical case for either one. The difficulty is that a logical case can be misleading and may actually bear little relationship to what actually happens in the arena of interpersonal transactions. Such opposing positions can only be resolved by the collection of objective data. Unfortunately, relatively little research has been done despite the fact that interpersonal aggression is a major problem and educators and other professionals need to learn all that they can about the etiology of the aggressive act, particularly as they have to design optimum educational programs and answer questions directed at them by the public. The following study by Geen and Berkowitz examines what happens when a person witnesses aggression. It was found, as might be expected, that there is no simple answer. College students who watched a prize fight in which one of the opponents received a severe beating displayed aggressive behavior in an experiment which followed their watching of the film, but

SOURCE. Adapted from Russell Geen and Leonard Berkowitz, "Name-Mediated Aggressive Cue Properties," *Journal of Personality*, 1966, Vol. 34, pp. 456–465. (With permission of the authors and the publisher, Duke University Press.)

the nature and amount of the aggression was altered by certain contextual conditions, personal perceptions, and personal relationships. The experimental conditions used by the investigators should be of particular interest to the reader.

A growing body of evidence indicates that the observation of violence can increase subsequent tendencies to commit aggressive acts (Bandura, Ross, & Ross, 1963; Walters, Thomas, & Acker, 1962; Berkowitz, 1965). At the same time research has also shown that inhibitions against aggression are elicited if the observed aggression is regarded as wrong or improper (Berkowitz & Rawlings, 1963; Berkowitz, 1965). These empirical findings indicate that when a person observes aggression, he becomes instigated, or "primed," to aggress, but that insofar as he is cognizant of the social norm opposed to overt hostile behavior, he may also inhibit his aggressive responses.

But are the aggressive consequences of witnessed violence to be accounted for solely by the observation and the observer's inhibitions against aggression? Berkowitz (1962, 1964) has argued that neither the witnessing of hostility nor the disinhibition of aggressive tendencies can be considered sufficient conditions for a display of aggression by the observer. Briefly stated his analysis stipulates that observed violence serves mainly to arouse the observer's previously acquired aggressive habits—to set them in operation, but only in "low gear," so to speak. Before these habits can erupt into a manifestly aggressive act, certain elicitory cues must also be present in the environment. These cues are stimuli having some connection with either aggression-instigating situations in the observer's past or with the aggression which he has just seen. According to this line of reasoning, then, stimuli which impinge upon a person who has just witnessed violence and which are associated by him with the violence become for him cues for aggressive responses.

To support this argument, Berkowitz (1965) showed that provoked Ss who watched a boxing movie subsequently directed significantly more aggression toward their frustrater when he was labeled a "boxer" than when he was said to be a "speech major." The label-induced association between the anger instigator and the aggressive film may have given this person sufficient cue properties to enable him to elicit the attack response. However, other findings in this study also indicated that the "boxer" label may have heightened the frustrater's cue value for aggression independently of his association with the film. A subsequent study by Berkowitz and Geen (1966) sought to circumvent this problem by manipulating the degree of association between the instigator's first name and that of the actor in a boxing film, Kirk Douglas, who portrayed a fighter receiving a severe beating. The anger instigator, a paid confederate, was introduced to S either as "Kirk" or as "Bob," the latter name not being connected with the film. S then viewed the fight movie. Findings were consistent with both theory and the earlier study. Angered Ss directed significantly more aggressive responses to "Kirk" than toward "Bob" after seeing the fight movie. This difference was not found when a control film, an exciting track race, was viewed.

The present experiment was designed as an extension of the Berkowitz-Geen study. It sought to determine whether a frustrater having a name-mediated connection with a character in the observed aggressive scene (rather than with an actor in that scene) would evoke greater attacks upon him following the film than a frustrater having no such name-mediated association with the witnessed violence. Would there be the same results if the association was based upon the story characters instead of the people depicting these characters? In addition, the experiment asked if the aggression-eliciting association could be with any character in the film, or did it have to be with a specific person, such as either the aggressor or his victim. Conceivably, a person's cue value for eliciting aggressive responses might be increased if he were associated not with the observed violence generally, but with the recipient of that witnessed violence specifically.

METHOD

Subjects

Ss were 105 male undergraduates at the University of Wisconsin. All were enrolled in elementary psychology classes and participated in order to earn points toward their final course grade.

Design

Two independent variables formed a 3×2 factorial design, with 15 Ss in each of the six resulting treatment groups. The design provided that half of the Ss would see the boxing film and half the film of the track race. Before the movie was shown the anger-arousing confederate was introduced as a fellow S and was given either one of two names associated with the fight film or a control name. Since the victim of the beating in the fight movie was named Midge Kelly, the accomplice was introduced to one-third of the Ss as "Bob Kelly"; this condition therefore associated the confederate with the target of the observed aggression. The boxer who beat Midge Kelly was named Johnny Dunne, and the confederate was accordingly introduced to one-third of the Ss as "Bob Dunne." This condition consequently linked the confederate with the agent of the observed violence. Finally, the accomplice was presented to one-third of the Ss as "Bob Riley," a name having no connection with the boxing film. A seventh group of 15 Ss viewed the fight movie and was told that the confederate's name was "Kirk Anderson." This group represented a replication of the comparable condition in the Berkowitz and Geen (1966) design.

Procedure

Both S and the confederate were met at the laboratory by E, who asked their names. The confederate gave the name appropriate to the treatment condition. After informing S that the experiment involved the administration of a mild and nonharmful electric shock E gave S an opportunity to be excused from the experiment. E then showed both men the apparatus in the experimental room: a telegraph key used for shocking a person in the adjoining room, a terminal set of electrodes from which shocks could be received when sent from the adjoining room, and a motion picture projector and screen for use later in the experiment.

E then outlined the experiment as one designed to measure performance in a problem-solving task under conditions of stress and distraction. S was told that he would be given a difficult problem to solve while working under a five-minute time limit. His solution would then be judged by the other person, who would communicate his evaluation by giving S a number of electric shocks ranging from one to ten. These shocks were to be administered at the other person's discretion, with one shock indicating that he judged S's solution to be very good and ten indicating that he judged it to be very poor.

Explaining that absloute privacy and lack of distraction were necessary for S, E then sent the accomplice to the adjoining room. At this time S was given his problem, which was to devise a sales promotion campaign for a department store. Before leaving the room, E asked S to help him check the shock apparatus by waiting a few seconds for E to get to the adjoining room and then pressing the key before him eight or 10 times. By recording the average duration of these shocks, E obtained a base-line measurement which later could be compared to the average duration of shocks which S would give to the accomplice. S was instructed to begin writing his solution as soon as he had finished pressing the key. Five minutes later E returned, picked up S's written solution, and attached the electrodes to S's forearm. He then left the room, supposedly to carry the solution to the other person. One minute later, the accomplice administered seven shocks to S. All Ss in this experiment were thus led to become angry with the other person, the accomplice. After waiting 30 seconds, E returned to S, asked him how many shocks he had received, and administered a short questionnaire. This consisted of four 14-point self-report scales on which S was asked to indicate his mood at that moment. The four scales were anchored by diametric adjectives: HAPPY-SAD, ANGRY-NOT ANGRY, RELAXED-EXCITED, and STRONG-WEAK.

While S filled out these scales, E recalled the confederate to the experimental room. When S had completed the questionnaire, E explained that since the experiment had been designed to measure distraction as well as stress, he would show a film of approximately seven-minutes' duration which had been chosen because it would probably hold the attention of Ss. S and the accomplice were asked to "sit back and enjoy the movie." Half of the Ss viewed a boxing film (a fight scene from the movie *Champion*); the other half saw a film of the 1954 mile race between Roger Bannister and John Landy. Ss in the "Kirk Anderson" condition saw the fight scene. The boxing movie was introduced by E with the "justified aggression" synopsis of the story; according to this summary the victim of the witnessed aggression is a scoundrel who deserves to be beaten. This synopsis had been found in earlier research (Berkowitz & Rawlings, 1963; Berkowitz, 1965) to lower inhibitions against aggressing. Furthermore, for the people in the *Kelly, Dunne* or *Kirk Anderson* groups, if S also was to be shown the fight film, E casually but pointedly remarked that the accomplice happened to have the same name as one of the people to be seen in the film. This was done to make sure that S grasped the connection between the confederate and the aggressive scene.

At the conclusion of the film, E again sent the accomplice from the room with instructions to work on a solution to the second problem. This problem was to devise a sales promotion campaign for an automobile service station. The type of business enterprise was changed from the first to the second problem so that S would not feel that the accomplice had simply copied his ideas. S was told that in five minutes he would be given the other man's written solution and that he would then give this person from one to 10 shocks as an evaluation of his work. After five minutes, S was handed a written solution to the second problem supposedly the other person's work but actually previously constructed to be standard for all conditions. E then went to the adjoining room and recorded the number and total duration of shocks given by S.

After 30 seconds E returned to the experimental room and administered the final questionnaire. This consisted of four questions asking S to rate (1) how much he would like to serve in another experiment with the accomplice, (2) how much he would like to know the accomplice better, (3) how much he would like to have the accomplice for a friend, and (4) how much he would like to have the accomplice for a roommate, if he were looking for a roommate. For each question a 14-point scale was provided, anchored at each end by the statements VERY MUCH and NOT AT ALL. No significant differences were obtained on any of these items, and nothing more will be said about these experimental results.

When the questionnaire was completed, E introduced S to the accomplice, explained the deception, and asked S to refrain from discussing the experiment until the end of the semester.

RESULTS

Effectiveness of the Experimental Manipulations

Since the experiment depended upon S's thinking of the accomplice in terms of his experimentally given name, each S was asked to give the "other subject's" name before being told the nature of the experiment. All Ss gave the name correctly. The experimental conditions also required that Ss recognize that they had been given seven shocks. All Ss correctly reported seven. There were no reliable differences among treatments in Ss' responses on any of the four scales measuring their experienced emotional states after receiving the shocks.

Number and Duration of Shocks Given by S

The primary measure of aggression in this experiment was the number of shocks administered by each S. The mean number of shocks given in each condition is shown in Table 1. It can be seen that our theoretical expectations are upheld. The results of the 3×2 factorial part of the experiment were analyzed by the analysis of variance. Results of the analysis are given in Table 2.

TABLE 1

Mean Number of Shocks Given to Accomplice

Accomplice's Name	Boxing Film	Track Film
Kelly	5.40_a	3.60_b
Dunne	4.15_b	3.87_b
Riley	4.40_b	4.00_b
Kirk Anderson	5.27	

Note.—Cells having a subscript in common are not significantly different (at the .05 level) by Duncan Multiple Range Test. There are 15 Ss in each condition.
Multiple comparisons by t test (two-tailed):
 Boxing Film—Kirk vs. Boxing Film—Kelly, $t = 0.30$; $df = 28$; n.s.
 Boxing Film—Kirk vs. Boxing Film—Dunne, $t = 2.59$; $df = 28$; $p = .02$.
 Boxing Film—Kirk vs. Boxing Film—Riley, $t = 2.01$; $df = 28$; $p = .07$.

It will be noted that Ss giving the greatest number of aggressive responses were those who watched the boxing film after having been provoked and who were then given the opportunity to attack a frustrater whose name associated him with the victim of the witnessed violence, i.e., "Bob Kelly." Even after witnessing the aggressive film Ss were no more disposed to attack a frustrater named "Bob Dunne" than they were to attack one named "Bob Riley." Mere association with the film, then, is not a sufficient condition for

TABLE 2

Analysis of Variance of Number of Shocks Given to Accomplice within the 3 × 2 Factorial Part of the Experiment

Source	df	SS	M	F	p
1. Film	1	15.2	15.2	10.11	<.01
2. Name	2	3.8	1.9	1.27	
3. 1 × 2	2	10.8	5.4	3.60	<.05
4. Pooled within	84	124.2	1.5		
5. Total	89				

a person's acquiring aggression-eliciting cue properties. The stimulus person apparently must have something in common with the "target" of the observed violence.

Results for Ss in the *Boxing Film-Kirk Anderson* condition were compared with those in the *Boxing Film-Kelly* condition by means of a *t* test. No significant difference between the two conditions was found ($t = 0.30$, $df = 28$). Ss who regarded the frustrater as "Kirk" thus gave him as many shocks as did those who thought of him as "Kelly," when both groups of Ss had seen the boxing film. This finding corroborates the results of the Berkowitz and Geen (1966) experiment. Ss in the *Boxing Film-Kirk Anderson* condition also gave a significantly greater number of shocks than did Ss in the *Boxing Film-Dunne* condition. The difference between the means of the two groups reached the .02 level of significance by a *t* test. The difference in the mean number of shocks given by Ss in the *Boxing Film-Kirk Anderson* and the mean number given by Ss in the *Boxing Film-Riley* condition barely fails to reach the .05 level of significance.

DISCUSSION

Generally, the findings of this experiment confirm and extend previous results. In line with earlier studies, evidence was presented which indicated that observed aggression by itself need not lead to overt aggression by the audience. The persons who are most likely to be attacked by someone who has recently witnessed violence are those people having appropriate aggression-eliciting cue properties. These cue properties seem to be derived from association with the victim, rather than the administrator, of the violence. Implicit in the foregoing reasoning, of course, is the assumption that the potential attacker has been adequately aroused so that he is ready to aggress and that his restraints against aggression are fairly weak.

The data also indicate that the connection between the available target and the victim in the film need not be direct but can be mediated through the name of the character or of the actor playing the role of the victim. A possible alternative explanation of the findings is that the label connecting the accomplice with the character "Johnny Dunne" gave rise to new inhibitions against aggression. Associating the accomplice with the man who carries out the proper punishment of the villain is, in effect, to connect him with the film's hero. This connection with a "good guy" may have invested the accomplice with stimulus properties which called forth responses of liking and positive affect in the period after the movie. Since we do not generally aggress against those whom we like, the resulting positive affect may have served to inhibit the number of electric shocks given in the *Boxing Film-Dunne* condition.

Because of the important position given to inhibitions in much of the current theorizing on aggression (Bandura & Walters, 1963; Berkowitz, 1962), this is a tempting alternative. The data obtained in this study, however, appear to argue against this explanation. If inhibitions were involved, then Dunne should have received less aggression than Riley, who would presumably arouse little or no inhibitions at all. While the results show a tendency in this direction (see Table 1), the difference between the number of shocks given to Dunne and the number given to Riley was not significant. Furthermore, the obtained differences can also be explained in terms of a stimulus generalization based upon the apparent "Irishness" of the names.

42. SOCIAL CLASS, PARENTAL PUNISHMENT FOR AGGRESSION, AND CHILD AGGRESSION

Leonard D. Eron, Leopold O. Walder, Romolo Toigo, & Monroe M. Lefkowitz

When a child displays an act of aggression teachers can assume the presence of some causal background and, although there are many possible causal sources, research on child-rearing has indicated the home as a particularly important source. Eron and his associates, using a sample of 451 third-grade children rated for aggression by their classmates, have examined various aspects of the family as a background for the inception of aggression. They found that: (1) as parents tended to punish for aggression at home there was a related tendency for their children to display aggression at school, (2) father's and mother's discipline is additive rather than interactive no matter which parent takes the major role in punishment, (3) boys' and, to a lesser extent, girls' aggression in school tends to increase with increases in their family's socioeconomic status, (4) there appears to be a significant interaction between parents' use of punishment and social class as predictors of children's aggression in school, (5) aggression against parents tends to receive punishment of equal severity no matter what the parents' socioeconomic status, (6) lower-class girls tend to be disciplined more severely for aggression against peers than is true of upper-class girls, and (7) there appear to be no class-related differences in either the physical or psychological punishment given children by their parents. Generalizations based on the findings of this study have to be limited since the subjects used were drawn from intact semirural families

SOURCE. Adapted from Leonard D. Eron, Leopold O. Walder, Romolo Toigo, and Monroe M. Lefkowitz, "Social Class, Parental Punishment for Aggression, and Child Aggression," *Child Development*, 1963, Vol. 34, pp. 849–867. (With permission of authors and the publisher, The Society for Research in Child Development.)

living in the southeastern section of New York State. However, other things being equal, the results of the study permit the reader to assume that either level of home punishment or parents' socioeconomic status are fairly good predictors of the likelihood of a child's display of aggression in school, with a combination of these two factors improving the level of prediction. However, children's aggressive behavior in school can not be assumed to stem from differential parental punishments from class to class. Obviously, additional confirming samples from other populations would strengthen the generality of the findings.

According to behavior theory (Child, 1954; Dollard, 1939), punishment for aggression should result in the learning of anxiety about its consequences and therefore have an inhibiting effect on the expression of aggression. Thus, it would be predicted that increased punishment for aggression will lead to reduced frequency of aggressive behavior, especially when the situations in which the behavior is punished and later evoked are similar. While carefully controlled laboratory studies with animals (Seward, 1946) and preschoolers (Hollenberg, 1951) and questionnaire studies of college students (Doob, 1939) have in general confirmed this view, survey studies of the child-rearing antecedents of aggressive behavior have on the whole yielded opposite findings. It has been monotonously reported in the latter studies (e.g., Bandura and Walters [1959]; Glueck and Glueck [1950]; Sears, Maccoby, and Levin [1957]) that increased punishment for aggression by socializing agents is related to increased aggression on the part of the child. These findings have been called into question because usually (except for Bandura and Walters' study with adolescents) the same informant is utilized in both antecedent and consequent measures (Eron et al., 1961). Indeed a seven-year follow-up study by Sears (1961) did show an inverse relation between punishment and aggression when he used different informants for these two measures.

Another regular finding is that children from lower class backgrounds tend to be more aggressive than children of upper class origins (Goldstein, 1955; McKee, 1955; Stolz, 1959). An allied finding is that punishment for aggression tends to be more severe among middle class children than lower class children (Davis, 1943), although this has been questioned by Maccoby and Gibbs (1954). In addition, psychological punishment has been reported as more characteristic of socialization practices of middle class parents and physical punishment of lower class parents (Allinsmith, 1960). However, no pattern of punishment can be the exclusive property of any one class and overlapping patterns of punishment no doubt exist from one social class to another (Littman, 1957). Is it the differential modes of punishment which supposedly exist in different classes which is the crucial factor in accounting for more aggression in one class than another or is there something else about social class which has to be invoked as an explanatory principle? For direct aggression, at least as experienced by children in their projective story completions, Allinsmith (1960) demonstrated that parental discipline in itself, independent of social class membership, was of overriding importance, while social class alone had no relation to direct expression of aggression in story completions. Do the same relations hold when aggressive behavior is measured by other than projective techniques?

In the present research it has been possible to study the aggressive behavior of a large sample of children of varied socioeconomic backgrounds and to relate this behavior to social class and punishment habits of mother and father and then to examine the interaction between social class and punishment in relation to aggressive behavior. It is emphasized that the aggression measure, the father data, and the mother data were all obtained independently from different informants.

PROCEDURE

Subjects

The subjects were 206 girls, 245 boys, each of their mothers, and each of their fathers. These children were drawn from the entire population of children enrolled in the third grade in the Spring of 1960 in a semirural county in New York's Hudson River Valley who were being studied in a larger investigation of the psychosocial antecedents of aggressive behavior. The current sample included every child in the larger pool ($N = 865$) who was from an intact family, who was in attendance at all three testing sessions conducted in the classroom a week apart, and whose mother and father both contributed scorable personal interviews (less 10 lost randomly in an IBM editing routine).

Measures

The aggression score for each child was derived from a peer-rating procedure in the form of a "Guess-Who" in which each child rated every other child in his class on a series of 10 items having to do with specific aggressive behaviors. The derivation, reliability, and validity of this instrument have been described elsewhere (Walder et al., 1961).

Parent measures were derived from a 286-item objective, precoded, personal interview, administered usually in the respondent's home but occasionally in the researcher's office. The mechanics of the interviewing procedure is described in more detail in Walder, Eron, Lefkowitz, and Toigo (1962). The punishment scale consisted of responses to 24 items. These had to do with the likely response of a parent to four kinds of aggressive behavior on the part of the child (two dealing with aggression toward the respondent and two with aggression toward other children). Two specific punishments from each of three levels of intensity were assigned to each of the four stems, giving 24 punishments in all. Each item received a weighted score (3 for high; 2 for medium; 1 for low intensity) if the respondent agreed that he would likely administer that punishment for the given behavior. The sum of the scores for all 24 items was the total punishment score used in the current analyses. The items were administered in block format, i.e., all six punishments for a given aggressive act were in a unit, although the four sets were randomized throughout the interview and the six punishments within each set were also randomized.

Occupation of father which was classified according to the Census Bureau classification of 10 categories of occupation was used as a measure of social class. Research has shown that the single occupational classification is as meaningful an index to social class as any combination of factors (Kohl, 1955; Lawson, 1960). The cutting points for the three status levels which were determined automatically by the computer so as to cut this sample into the closest approximation of equal thirds placed 0 and 1 classifications in the upper class; 2, 3, and 4 in the middle class; and 5 to 9 in the lower or working class.

RESULTS

Punishment

When punishment scores by mother, father, and mother plus father are categorized into three levels of intensity and the differences among the mean school aggression scores of the subjects whose parents fall into the three categories of punishment are evaluated by analysis of variance, it is apparent that there is a strong relation between punishment for aggression and the appearance of that behavior in school as rated by peers. Only for fathers of boys is the relation not significant, although the means for fathers of boys tend in the same direction as in the other comparisons, with the more severely punished children being rated more aggressive in school. The effect of mother's punishment seems more pronounced than that of father's punishment. When a two-way analysis of variance is done relating both mother's punishment and father's punishment in nine different combinations to school aggression as rated by peers, i.e., stratifying mother's punishment by father's punishment and vice versa, there remains a main effect only for mothers of boys. However, when boys' and girls' scores are added together, there is a main effect for both mother's and father's punishment and no interaction between these two. There is a steady increase in aggression score as you go from children of mothers and fathers who are both low punishers to mothers and fathers who are both high punishers. However, when mother is a moderate punisher, boys tend to be less aggressive than when mother is a minimal or severe punisher regardless of father's punishment (the interaction is not significant). Two additional factors are apparent. Boys get much higher scores than girls on the aggression measure and girls are punished less severely. This probably accounts for the increased strength of relation when boys and girls are pooled in one group.

Social Status

The simple randomized analyses of variance for father's occupational status, done separately for aggression scores of boys, girls, and total yielded a significant F for boys only ($p < .05$). However, the means for girls and for boys plus girls go in the same direction as those for boys alone, with children whose fathers have higher status jobs obtaining higher aggression scores than children of fathers with lower status jobs. It occurred to us that placing occupations 0, professional, technical and kindred workers, and 1, farmers and farm managers, into the upper status group might be giving undue weight to class 1 since there were indications that rural children in this study were rated as more aggressive than urban children (Toigo, 1962). However, the mean aggression scores for the two groups of boys (17.4 and 20.0, respectively, with 24 boys in each class) were not significantly different from each other ($t = .53$).

Social Status × Punishment

A two-way analysis of variance, comparing effects of father's punishment and occupational status on child's aggression, yielded interesting findings, especially for boys. When father's punishment is stratified for occupational level, there is a significant effect for his punishment on boy's aggression score; the main effect for occupational status becomes more significant than when there is no control for punishment; and there is a significant interaction between occupational status and punishment. It seems that high status boys who are severely punished for aggression are by far the most aggressive. Although girls show a main effect only for punishment, the high status girls who are severely punished are also the most aggressive of all girls. When all subjects are combined, the main effects of both occupational status and punishment, as well as the interaction between them, show up in even more striking manner.

However, when mother's severity of punishment is stratified by father's occupation, the only significant effects are for punishment, for both boys ($p < .005$) and girls ($p < .01$), essentially the same result as in the simple randomized design. There is no effect for occupational status and no interaction between occupational status and mother's punishment. The effect of mother's punishment is overriding. Social class does not contribute anything significant.

Since the effect of punishment is so clearly related to the social class position of the socializing agents, especially as measured by father's occupational status, it was considered desirable to see if there are actually different patterns of punishment for aggression from one status to another. There is a differing intensity of punishment for aggression according to occupational level for fathers of girls, so that lower status girls are punished more severely by their fathers for aggression than are upper status girls. The mean punishment scores by mothers of girls, according to father's occupation, are in the same direction, although there is no significant difference in score among the different occupational levels. There are also no significant differences for boys among mean punishment scores at each occupational level.

Since two of the aggressive stems for which differential punishments were tapped comprised aggression against the child's peers and the other two against his parents, the punishment score was similarly partitioned into punishment for aggression against peers and punishment for aggression against parents. Comparisons on mean score were made among the three occupational levels. There were no significant differences for occupational status when aggression against parents was considered. Parents of all occupational levels punish equally severely for this transgression. However, for aggression against the child's peers, there are important differences according to occupational status. Girls of high status are punished less severely by their parents for aggression against peers than are girls of low status (significant, $p < .005$ for fathers; same direction but not significant for mothers; but significant, $p < .005$, for mothers plus fathers). Boys of middle status mothers are less severely punished for aggression against other children than boys of either high or low status mothers. For fathers there is no difference in punishment intensity for boy's aggression against peers among occupational levels, although for mother and father combined there is such a difference with the middle status boys less severely punished than either the high or low status boys for aggression against other children.

To test the hypothesis that psychological and physical punishment were differentially applied according to social classes, the proportion of parents in each class who said they would respond to specific behaviors with a psychological or physical punishment were compared. Four questions were utilized for this analysis, two having to do with an aggressive act against another child and two with an aggressive act against the parent. Of the two acts against another child, one had a psychological punishment and one a physical punishment; similarly for the aggression against parent there was a psychological and physical punishment. In all cases the psychological and physical punishments were of similar intensity value (high punishment) as rated by judges in the aforementioned study. It is apparent that the relative frequency of use of psychological or physical punishment by parents is not a distinguishing characteristic of social status among these subjects.

DISCUSSION

It is apparent from the above results that punishment for aggression and social class as determined by father's occupation are both important factors in the child's aggression as rated by his peers in school. As for the first variable, the more these third grade children are punished for aggression by their parents, the more aggressive they tend to be as rated by their peers. This supports the finding of Sears, Maccoby, and Levin (1957) in their study of kindergarten children when both antecedent and consequent measures were obtained from the same informant (the mother). It is contrary to Sears' (1961) later finding when his subjects reached middle childhood (age 12) and rated themselves on aggressive attitude. At this age there was an inverse relation between these ratings and the punishment practices reported by the parents when the children were 5 years old. Sears ascribed this shift from a positive to a negative relation between aggression and related punishment to the supposition that, "during the intervening years, the inhibitory effect of the punishment had an opportunity to be influential; no longer was the punishment for aggression simply a goad to frustration—it reduced the tendency to express the punished forms of behavior" (p. 477). Apparently from our data by age 8 this shift has not yet occurred. Or else the difference in result may be accounted for by the different measurement operations of aggression in the three studies. Sears' earlier measure was ratings made by psychologists of verbatim accounts of mothers' punishment practices as given in individual recorded interviews. His later measure was self-rating of aggressive attitude. The measure used in the current study is of actual specific aggressive behaviors rated by the child's peers.

There is one interesting exception to the monotonous finding with our various samples of a positive relation between increasing punitiveness and increasing aggression, and that is the result with mothers of boys, where the relationship is apparently curvilinear. Those mothers who are in the medium punishment group have boys who are less aggressive than those with either low or high punishment. This result is one indication supporting behavior theory. Boys who are minimally punished at home for aggression tend to be more aggressive than those who are moderately punished for aggression. However, when they are maximally punished for this behavior, the instigating effect of the punishment (frustration) seems to overcome the inhibiting effect (anxiety) and the boys are very aggressive. However, this is not what would have been predicted from the conflict hypothesis

(McKee, 1949) which states that moderate punishment should lead to increased conflict between the tendency to aggression and anxiety inhibiting the expression of aggression, which in turn heightens the drive level and thus evokes increased aggressive behavior, and that very severe punishment should lead to generalized inhibition of aggressive behavior in many situations.

One interesting finding, when considering either mothers' or fathers' reports, is that the father is rarely credited with being the chief disciplinarian. Usually both parents or the mother alone take responsibility for the child's discipline. However, regardless of whether or not he is solely responsible for the child's discipline, father's punishment severity is related to aggression as rated by the child's peers. Possibly it is necessary to distinguish between delegated authority and absolute authority. Thus, even in those instances when the mother is seen as taking chief responsibility for child's discipline, there will be many cases where she is acting as a surrogate for the father. It is quite possible that for many mothers the capacity to discipline the children is derived from the moral authority of the father (as both she and her children perceive it). Hence, the father's style of discipline may be quite important in defining the limits of the mother's disciplinary activity, even though he may be physically out of the house most of the day. On the other hand, perhaps mother sets the patterns. This research design does not yield an answer.

Predictions improve when they are made from both punishment and father's occupation considered jointly. For example, father's punishment intensity by itself shows no significant relation to aggression of boys as rated by peers. However, when social class is controlled, a significant relation emerges. There is an interaction between social class and punishment, with boys of high status who are punished severely by their fathers being far and away the most aggressive. However, the effect of mother's punishment is not thus related to occupational status of the family. This may explain why Allinsmith (1960) found the effect of punishment to be independent of social class. She used only mothers' reports. Also, of course, the criterion measure of aggression is different. Allinsmith used a projective measure as reported in story endings made up by the subjects, and ours was a measure of reputation for aggression as rated by the subject's peers.

Our general finding that high status children are rated as more aggressive by their peers than low status children is contrary to most past results. The same is true for the finding that lower status girls are punished more severely for aggression against children than upper status girls and that children from all classes, both boys and girls, are punished equally severely for aggression towards parents. Much has been published by Davis (1941, 1943, 1948) suggesting that lower class parents encourage and reward aggression while middle class parents are less tolerant. Duvall (1946) writes that lower class children are much less likely to be punished for the overt expression of aggression, since in some neighborhoods it is necessary for the preservation of life. One of the few contrary findings is that of Maccoby and Gibbs (1954) who found middle class parents more permissive than lower class parents. They worked with nursery school children while the others worked with older groups of preadolescents. Maccoby and Gibbs explained the contradictory findings on the basis of this difference in age. Our data would indicate that even up to age 9 what differences do appear in socialization practices of parents of different classes are not in the direction of more leniency toward aggression on the part of lower class parents. In this respect, our findings, obtained in a semirural county, agree with those of Maccoby and Gibbs whose subjects were from a highly urban area. Lower class children tend to be less aggressive in school than upper class children and to be punished more severely, especially girls, for aggression against other children, while there is no difference among classes in punishment for aggression toward parents.

Further, we have no evidence that upper status parents use more psychological punishment and lower class parents more physical punishment. If anything, it would seem that upper class mothers use more physical punishment for aggression against other children and lower class fathers use more psychological punishment for aggression against both other children and themselves. The difference in these results from those of Allinsmith (1960) may perhaps be due to the difference in measurement operations. Allinsmith used ratings of recorded interviews, and the current measure is a simple count of "yes" responses to four questions having to do with the likelihood of a parent using a specific punishment for a specific behavior. Other reasons for differences include geographical and urban-rural differences in the samples.

However, all results reported here tend to suggest that some traditional notions about the differential distribution of socialization practices and child behaviors among various social classes may be in need of revision. It has been pointed out by Bronfenbrenner (1958) that the gap between social classes has been narrowing over the past quarter of a century with middle class parents becoming more permissive and lower class parents more conforming and restrictive. These data contribute additional evidence of the similarity in patterns of punishment at the present time among different social class levels. But this is not to say that social class membership is an unimportant influence on aggressive behavior of children since there is an interaction between social class and intensity of punishment, although no type of punishment is exclusively characteristic of any class. It may indeed strike the reader that we have substantiated some important class differences, e.g., lower class girls are punished more severely by parents for aggression against children than upper class girls and at the same time lower class girls are rated as less aggressive by their peers than are upper class girls (the latter is not significant). Also middle class boys are punished least for aggression against other children (not significant) and are rated as least aggressive by their peers. However, this does not tell us anything about the relation between punishment for aggression and aggressive behavior in individual boys and girls. The reader is referred to the controversy over the interpretation of ecological correlations which has appeared in the literature recently (Duncan, 1953; Lazarsfeld, 1961; Robinson, 1950). Our best information on the basis of the data presented here is that there is a positive relation between punishment for aggression by parents and the appearance of that behavior in school and that this relation is exaggerated by social class membership, with children of high status who are punished most severely being most aggressive as rated by their peers in school. Finally, it should be pointed out that our earlier assertions (Eron et al., 1961) in regard to the importance of obtaining parallel data from mothers and fathers independently about socialization practices have certainly been substantiated by these results.

43. PATTERNS OF AGGRESSIVE BEHAVIOR IN EXPERIMENTALLY CREATED "SOCIAL CLIMATES"

Kurt Lewin, Ronald Lippitt, & Ralph K. White

Lewin, Lippitt, and White's study of aggressive behavior in experimentally created "social climates" constitutes one of a series of experiments that have become classics in the experimental literature of psychology. Surely there are few studies that have been so often cited in so many places or that have provided as much insight into the dynamics both of group interpersonal relations and of group morale and productivity. There are many aspects to the study reported here, but essentially it is a comparison of the behavior and aggression tendencies of groups organized and conducted on the basis of democracy, authoritarianism, or *laissez-faire*. Obviously, teachers may organize and conduct their classes and their extra curricular groups in any one of these three manners, but after reading the results of the Lewin, Lippitt, and White study it is difficult to see how a teacher could justify the rejection of the democratic alternative except on the superficial basis of achieving momentary "order." Autocracy does achieve ostensible lack of aggression in the group situation, but such lack represents apathy rather than anything positive and simply means that aggressive outbursts are deferred and increased in other situations. Children dislike the autocrat and much prefer either the democratic or the *laissez-faire* leader and are willing to extend to him greater effort. In the autocratic situation children neither joke nor smile in the presence of the autocrat—they simply bide their time as they inhabit the dull grey world of oppression.

SOURCE. Adapted from Kurt Lewin, Ronald Lippitt, and Ralph K. White, "Patterns of Aggressive Behavior in Experimentally Created 'Social Climates,'" *Journal of Social Psychology*, S.P.S.S.I. Bulletin, 1939, Vol. 10, pp. 271–299. (With permission of Drs. Lippitt and White and the publisher, The Journal Press.)

The authors of this study base their research upon Lewin's topological theory of behavior and indicate that aggression can be interpreted in terms of four underlying factors: tension, restricted space of free movement, rigidity of group structure, and style of living as dictated by the culture. The study has been drastically abridged for this text—the reader may wish to read the original source for a more complete picture.

PROBLEMS AND METHODS

The present report is a preliminary summary on one phase of a series of experimental studies of group life which has as its aim a scientific approach to such questions as the following: What underlies such differing patterns of group behavior as rebellion against authority, persecution of a scapegoat, apathetic submissiveness to authoritarian domination, or attack upon an outgroup? How may differences in subgroup structure, group stratification, and potency of ego-centered and group-centered goals be utilized as criteria for predicting the social resultants of different group atmospheres? Is not democratic group life more pleasant, but authoritarianism more efficient?

In the first experiment Lippitt organized two clubs of 10-year-old children, who engaged in the activity of theatrical mask-making for a period of three months. The same adult leader, changing his philosophy of leadership, led one club in an authoritarian manner and the other club in accordance with democratic techniques, while detailed observations were made by four observers. This study, reported in detail elsewhere (Lippitt, 1939), suggested more hypotheses than answers and led to a second and more extensive series of experiments by White and Lippitt. Four new clubs of 10-year-old boys were organized, on a voluntary basis as before, the variety of club activities was extended, while four different adult leaders participated. To the variables of authoritarian and democratic procedure was added a third, *"laissez-faire"* or group life without adult participation. Also the behavior of each club was studied in different "social climates." Every six weeks each group had a new leader with a different technique of leadership, each club having three leaders during the course of the five months of the experimental series. The data on aggressive behavior summarized in this paper are drawn from both series of experiments. The contrasting methods of the leaders in creating the three types of group atmosphere are summarized in Table 1.

Observations of club behavior consisted of:

(a) A quantitative running account of the social interactions of the five children and the leader, in terms of symbols for directive, compliant, and objective (fact-minded) approaches and responses, including a category of purposeful refusal to respond to a social approach.

TABLE 1

Methods Used by Leaders in Creating Three Types of Group Atmosphere

Authoritarian	Democratic	Laissez-faire
1. All determination of policy by the leader.	1. All policies a matter of group discussion and decision, encouraged and assisted by the leader.	1. Complete freedom for group or individual decision, without any leader participation.
2. Techniques and activity steps dictated by the authority, one at a time, so that future steps were always uncertain to a large degree.	2. Activity perspective gained during first discussion period. General steps to group goal sketched, and where technical advice was needed the leader suggested two or three alternative procedures from which choice could be made.	2. Various materials supplied by the leader, who made it clear that he would supply information when asked. He took no other part in work discussions.
3. The leader usually dictated the particular work task and work companions of each member.	3. The members were free to work with whomever they chose, and the division of tasks was left up to the group.	3. Complete nonparticipation by leader.
4. The dominator was "personal" in his praise and criticism of the work of each member, but remained aloof from active group participation except when demonstrating. He was friendly or impersonal rather than openly hostile.	4. The leader was "objective" or "fact-minded" in his praise and criticism, and tried to be a regular group member in spirit without doing too much of the work.	4. Very infrequent comments on member activities unless questioned, and no attempt to participate or interfere with the course of events.

(b) A minute by minute group structure analysis giving a record of: activity subgroupings, the activity goals of each subgroup was initiated by the leader or spontaneously formed by the children, and ratings on degree of unity of each subgrouping.

(c) An interpretive running account of significant member actions, and changes in dynamics of the group as a whole.

(d) Continuous stenographic records of all conversation.

(e) An interpretive running account of inter-club relationships.

(f) An "impressionistic" write-up by the leader as to what he saw and felt from within the group atmosphere during each meeting.

(g) Comments by guest observers.

(h) Movie records of several segments of club life.

Extra-club information included:

(a) Interviews with each child by a friendly "non-club" person during each transition period (from one kind of group atmosphere and leader to another) and at the end of the experiment, concerning such items as comparison of present club leader with previous ones, with the teacher, and with parents; opinions on club activities; how the club could be run better; who were the best and poorest club members; what an ideal club leader would be like, etc.

(b) Interviews with the parents by the investigators, concentrating on kinds of discipline used in the home, status of the child in the family group (relations with siblings, etc.), personality ratings on the same scale used by the teachers, discussion of child's attitude toward the club, school, and other group activities.

(c) Talks with the teachers concerning the transfer to the schoolroom, of behavior patterns acquired in the club.

(d) Administration of a Rorschach test to each club member.

(e) Conversations with the children during two summer hikes arranged after the experiment was over.

RESULTS

Both psychological and sociological variables were utilized in analyzing the results of these experiments, but the present paper presents only certain data relevant to the dynamics of individual and group aggression.

We might first recall one or two of the most striking results of the first experiment (Lippitt, 1939). As the club meetings progressed the authoritarian club members developed a pattern of aggressive domination toward one another, and their relation to the leader was one of submission or of persistent demands for attention. The interactions in the democratic club were more spontaneous, more fact-minded, and friendly. Relations to the leader were free and on an "equality basis." Comparing the two groups on the one item of overt hostility the authoritarian group was surprisingly more aggressive, the ratio being 40 to 1. Comparing a constellation of "ego-involved" types of language behavior (e.g., hostile, resistant, demands for attention, hostile criticism, expression of competition) with a group of objective or "nonemotive" behaviors, it was found that in the authoritarian group 73 per cent of the analyzed language behavior was of the "ego-involved" type as compared to 31 per cent in the democratic club. Into the objective category went 69 per cent of the behavior of the democratic group as compared to 37 per cent of the language activities of the authoritarian group.

Acquiring Culturally-Approved Controls over Aggressive Behavior   483

A second type of data related to the dynamics of aggression as it existed in the first experiment. Twice during the course of the meetings of the authoritarian club the situation shifted from one of mutual aggression between all members to one of concentrated aggression toward one member by the other four. In both cases the lowered status of a scapegoat position was so acutely unpleasant that the member left the group, rationalizing his break from the club. After the emergence of both scapegoats, there was a rather brief rise in friendly cooperative behavior between the other members of the group.

The data on aggression averages in these three atmospheres indicate average amounts of aggression per 50-minute, five-member club meeting. They represent behavior records, as recorded by the interaction observer, and include all social actions, both verbal and physical, which he designated as "hostile" or "joking hostile." There appears to be a bimodal distribution of aggression averages in autocracy; four of the five autocracies had an extremely low level of aggression, and the fifth had an extremely high one.

The relative importance of the deliberately created social atmosphere, as compared with either the personality make-up of the group or the personality of the adult leader is an interesting outcome of the study. The same group usually changes markedly, and sometimes to an extreme degree, when it is

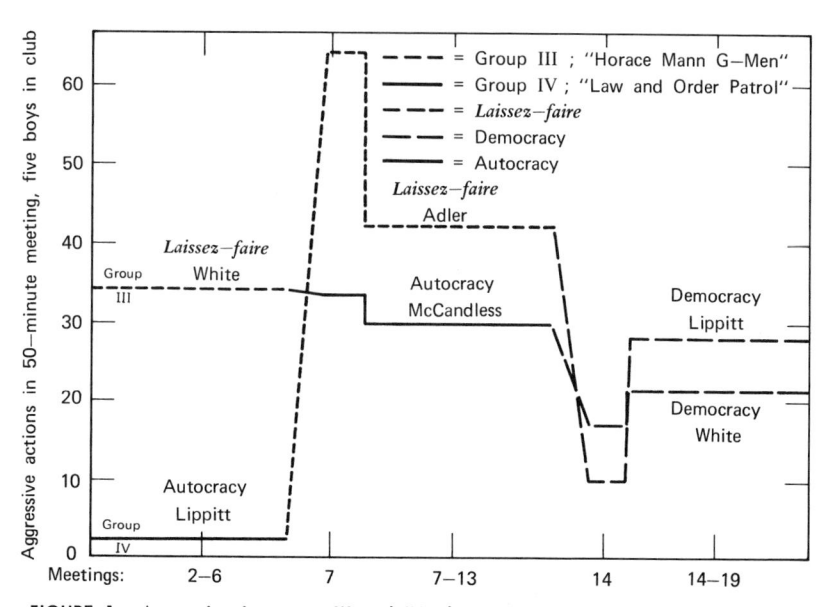

FIGURE 1. Aggression in groups III and IV. The same group in different atmospheres. Group IV shows changes to the levels typical for each atmosphere. It shows also the "release of tension" on the first day of freedom (7) after apathetic autocracy. Group III seemed resistant to change; it was relatively aggressive even in democracy.

changed to a new atmosphere under a different leader. There is usually a moderate amount of aggression in democracy and an abnormally small amount in autocracy, regardless of the personality of the leader and regardless of the personnel of the group itself.

Two of the *laissez-faire* atmospheres, shown in Figure 1, give very high levels of aggression although different groups and different leaders are involved. The most extreme change of behavior recorded in any group occurred when Group IV was changed from autocracy (in which it had shown the apathetic reaction) to *laissez-faire*. One of the autocratic groups (Figure 1) reacted apathetically, the other very aggressively. The aggressiveness of Group III may be due to the personalities of the boys, or to the fact that they had just previously "run wild" in *laissez-faire*.

The average number of aggressive actions per meeting in the different atmospheres was as follows:

Laissez-faire	38
Autocracy (aggressive reaction)	30
Democracy	20
Autocracy (apathetic reaction)	2

INTERPRETIVE COMMENTS

From the many theoretical problems involved we should like to discuss but one, namely, the problem of aggression and apathy. Even here we wish to show the complexity of the problem and its possible attack from a field theoretical point of view rather than to set forth a definite theory.

It is not easy to say what aggression is, that is, if one is not satisfied with mere verbal definition. One important aspect obviously is that one group or an individual within a group turns against another group (or individual). In case these groups are subgroups of one original group, it can be called aggression *within a group*, otherwise aggression *against an outgroup*.

Both kinds of aggression occurred in our experiments. All of these aggressions were spontaneous in character. In other words, it was not a situation where a group of people are ordered by a politically dominating power (like the state) to indulge in a certain type of directed activity called war. On the whole the aggression was the outcome of the momentary emotional situation, although in two cases the aggressions had definitely the character of a fight of one group against another group and showed a certain amount of co-operative organization within each group.

It is necessary to mention four points which seem to play dominant roles in the spontaneous aggressions: tension, the space of free movement, rigidity of group structure, and the style of living (culture).

1. Tension

An instance where tension was created by *annoying* experiences occurred when the group work was criticized by a stranger (janitor). There were two cases where fighting broke out immediately afterwards.

In the autocratic atmosphere the behavior of the leader probably annoyed the children considerably (to judge from the interviews reported above).

In addition, there were six times as many directing approaches to an individual by the leader in autocracy than in democracy. It is probably fair to assume that the bombardment with such frequent ascendant approaches is equivalent to higher *pressure* and that this pressure created a higher tension.

2. Narrow Space of Free Movement as a Source of Tension

On the whole, even more important than this single annoying experience was the general atmosphere of the situation. Experiments in individual psychology (Lewin, 1935) seemed to indicate that lack of space of free movement is equivalent to higher pressure; both conditions seem to create tension. This seemed particularly true if an originally larger space was narrowed down (one is reminded here of the physical tension created by decreasing volume, although one should not overstress the analogy).

Our experiments seemed to indicate that a similar relation between the narrow space of free movement and high tension holds also in regard to groups. The space of free movement in autocracy was smaller in relation to the activities permitted and the social status which could be reached. In *laissez-faire*, contrary to expectations, the space of free movement was not larger but smaller than in democracy, partly because of the lack of time perspective and partly because of the interference of the work of one individual with the activities of his fellows.

3. Aggression as the Effect of Tension

The annoying occurrences, the pressure applied by the leader, and the lack of space of free movement, are three basic facts which brought up a higher tension. Our experiments indicate that this higher tension might suffice to create aggression. This seems to be of theoretical importance; obviously some aggressive acts can be viewed mainly as a kind of "purposive" action (for instance, to destroy a danger), and one might ask whether or not this component is an essential part in the causation of any aggression. In our experiments, the two wars between the two outgroups can hardly be classified in this way. They seemed to be rather clear cases where aggression was "emotional expression" of an underlying tension.

4. Rigidity of Group Structure

However, to understand aggression one will have to realize that tension is only one of the factors which determine whether or not an aggressive action will take place. The building up of tension can be said to be equivalent to the creation of a certain type of need which might express itself in aggressive action. Tension sets up the driving force (Lewin, 1938) for the aggression (in the two situations with which we are dealing). However, whether these driving forces actually lead to aggression or to some other behavior, for instance that of leaving the group, depends on additional characteristics of the situation as a whole. One of these seems to be the rigidity of the social position of the person within the group.

Aggression within a group can be viewed as a process by which one part of the group sets itself in opposition to another part of the group, in this way breaking the unity of the group. Of course, this separation is only of a certain degree.

In other words, if M indicates a member or subgroup and Gr the whole group, an aggression involves a force acting on the subgroup in the direction away from the main group (f_{M-Gr}) or other part of the subgroup. From this it should follow theoretically that if a subgroup can easily locomote in the direction away from the group it will do so in case this force shows any significant strength. In other words, a strong tension and an actual aggression will be built up only in case there exist forces which hinder the subgroup from leaving the group.

In our experiment, autocracy provided a much more rigid social group than democracy. It was particularly difficult for the members of an autocracy to change their social status (Lewin, 1939). On the other hand in both groups the member did not like to leave the group as a whole because of the interest in the work project and the feeling of responsibility to the adult leader.

On the whole, then, the rigidity of the group will function as a restraining force (Lewin, 1938) against locomotion away from the group, or from the position within the group. Sufficient strength of this restraining force seems to be one of the conditions for the building up of a tension which is sufficiently high to lead to aggression.

It can be seen easily that the barriers limiting the space of free movement may have a similar function. We mentioned above, that a narrow space of free movement seems to be equivalent to pressure and, in this way, creates tension. At the same time, the barriers prevent locomotion, thus providing the restraining forces necessary for building up higher tension.

5. Style of Living (Culture)

Whether or not a given amount of tension and given restraining forces will cause a person to become aggressive depends finally upon the particular patterns of action which are customarily used in the culture in which he lives. The different styles of living can be viewed as different ways a given problem is usually solved. A person living in a culture where a show of dominance is "the thing to do" under certain conditions will hardly think of any other way in which the solution of this problem may be approached. Such social patterns are comparable to "habits." Indeed, individual habits as well as cultural patterns have dynamically the character of restraining forces against leaving the paths determined by these patterns. In addition, they determine the cognitive structure which a given situation is likely to have for a given individual.

For the problem of aggression, this cultural pattern, determined by the group in which an individual lives and by his past history, is of great importance. It determines under what conditions aggression will be, for the individual concerned, the "distinguished path" to the goal (Lewin, 1938). It determines, furthermore, how easily a situation will show for him a cognitive structure where aggression appears to be one possible path for his action.

The factors named are sufficient to warn against any "one-factor" theory of aggression. Here, as in regard to any other behavior, it is the specific constellation of the field as a whole that determines whether or not aggression will occur. In every case one has to consider both the driving and the restraining forces and the cognitive structure of the field. Such a field theoretical approach seems to be rather arduous. On the other hand, only in this way will one be able to understand for instance the paradox of behavior that autocracy may lead either to aggression or to apathy. It was stated that aggression is partly to be viewed as an emotional outbreak due to tension and that this tension, in turn, is due to pressure and restraining forces (lack of space of free movement). We have apathy when the pressure and the restraining forces from without are kept stronger than the forces within the person which lead to the emotional expression, and are due to the tension. Whether or not the forces from without or those from within are stronger depends upon the absolute amount of pressure and also on the "willingness" of the person to "accept" the pressure.

SUMMARY

1. In a first experiment, Lippitt compared one group of five 10-year-old children, under autocratic leadership, with a comparable group under demo-

cratic leadership. In a second experiment, Lippitt and White studied four comparable clubs of 10-year-old boys, each of which passed successively through three club periods in such a way that there were altogether five democratic periods, five autocratic periods, and two *"laissez-faire"* periods.

2. In the second experiment, the factor of personality differences in the boys was controlled by having each group pass through autocracy and then democracy, or vice versa. The factor of leader's personality was controlled by having each of four leaders play the role of autocrat and the role of democratic leader at least once.

3. In the first experiment, hostility was 30 times as frequent in the autocratic as in the democratic group. Aggression (including both "hostility" and "joking hostility") was 8 times as frequent. Much of this aggression was directed toward two successive scapegoats within the group; none of it was directed toward the autocrat.

4. In the second experiment, one of the five autocracies showed the same aggressive reaction as was found in the first experiment. In the other four autocracies, the boys showed an extremely nonaggressive, "apathetic" pattern of behavior.

5. Four types of evidence indicate that this lack of aggression was probably not caused by lack of frustration, but by the repressive influence of the autocrat: (a) outbursts of aggression on the days of transition to a freer atmosphere; (b) a sharp rise of aggression when the autocrat left the room; (c) other indications of generalized apathy, such as an absence of smiling and joking; and (d) the fact that 19 out of 20 boys liked their democratic leader better than their autocratic leader, and 7 out of 10 also liked their *"laissez-faire"* leader better.

6. A general interpretation of the above data on aggression can be made in terms of four underlying factors: tension, restricted space of free movement, rigidity of group structure, and style of living (culture).

44. CHILDREN'S AGGRESSION, PARENTAL ATTITUDES, AND THE EFFECTS OF AN AFFILIATION-AROUSING STORY

Jesse E. Gordon & Edward Smith

This study is somewhat unique because it combines findings about causal origins of aggression in children with specific findings about the reduction of aggression when it occurs. In their study, Gordon and Smith test the hypothesis that arousal of the affiliation motive in children tends to reduce their propensity to display aggression. They exposed two groups of children, one aged three to four and the other six to seven years of age, either to a neutral story or to one that could be assumed to arouse feelings of affiliation. Aggression was measured before and after the story exposures by means of doll play, a situation in which the experimenter's doll frustrated the subject's doll through an imagined story about the dolls recounted by the experimenter. Findings indicated that arousal of affiliation feelings actually did tend to reduce the aggressive reactions of the children used as subjects in the study.

Gordon and Smith also compared parents' attitudes on child rearing with the amount of aggression exhibited by their children. Results indicated the importance of physical punishment in the home as a promoter of children's outside aggression. Where girls were concerned, the greater the strictness of the mother in her child-rearing procedures the greater the likelihood of aggressive behavior in her daughter, particularly if the mother used physical punishment. In the case of boys, if the mother was

SOURCE. Adapted from Jesse E. Gordon and Edward Smith, "Children's Aggression, Parental Attitudes, and the Effects of an Affiliation-Arousing Story," *Journal of Personality and Social Psychology*, 1965, Vol. 6, pp. 654–659. (With permission of the authors and the publisher, The American Psychological Association.)

strict but did not use physical punishment her son was less apt to display aggressive behavior outside the home.

The results of this study provide evidence that teachers may use in discussing children's problem behavior with parents. They point, in addition, to the possibility of using the affiliative drive in working with children displaying aggressive behavior in school.

In a previous study (Gordon & Cohn, 1963) it was found that doll-play aggression in 4–5 year old children in a publicly supported nursery school could be reduced by reading the children a story designed to arouse affiliation motivation. The present study was designed to extend the earlier findings to different populations of children: 3–4 year olds in a more middle-class nursery school, and 6–7 year olds in a public elementary school.

The present investigation also examines the relationships among parental training practices, the aggression of their children in the doll play, and the children's responsiveness to the affiliation story. Our interest in parental attitudes of permissiveness for aggression, general strictness, and the use of physical punishment is based on previous work by Sears, Maccoby and Levin (1957), whose findings concerning these variables were inconsistent in some respects, and were based on maternal reports of their children rather than direct observation.

METHOD

Subjects

Subjects were 48 children, equally divided among males and females, young (3–4 years, in private nursery schools in Ann Arbor, Michigan) and old (6–7 years, in public elementary schools serving the same areas as the private nursery schools from which the young sample was obtained). Half of each group was assigned to the experimental (need affiliation arousal) group and half to the neutral group.

Procedures

Subjects were tested in their homes by one experimenter while another interviewed the mother and administered the questionnaires to her. The procedures for testing the children were as described by Gordon and Cohn (1963). These involved two structured doll interviews separated by the reading of the experimental or control story. In the original study, the story reading and second doll interview came about 1 week after the first interview. In the present study they were in the same session, with an interpolated task replacing the week interval. The interpolated task consisted of presenting to the child several dolls other than those used in the interviews, and asking the child to select one from the group in response to questions about his perceived self (Which one is like you?) and his admired goal (Which one would you like to be like?). This task was part of another study on identification.

In the doll interviews, subjects were given a doll for them to use in responding to the experimenter's doll, which frustrated the subject's doll through an imagined situation described by the experimenter (two children at a playground, with the experimenter's doll insulting and challenging the subject's doll). The subject's responses were recorded at the 12 points at which the subject was asked to respond. Each of the 12 responses was later rated as aggressive or not. The situations used in the first and second doll-play interviews (DP_1 and DP_2) were similar. The dolls used were rubber band puppets representing a whale and an alligator, manufactured by Creative Playthings, Incorporated.

The experimental story consisted of a short narration by the experimenter of a story in which a young dog searches for but cannot find any friends with whom to play. The control story was exactly the same as the experimental story in all wording except that the word "ball" was substituted for "friend," thus converting the story from one concerned with affiliation needs to a story about a dog looking for a ball with which to play. At the conclusion of the story, the subject was asked whether the dog would rather play with a pictured dog shown him by the experimenter, or with a pictured ball also presented. This choice allowed an independent check on the subject's understanding of the story theme.

Questionnaires

While the child was being tested in one room, another experimenter interviewed the mother and administered questionnaires in another room. One questionnaire was designed to measure general strictness. It consisted of 33 children's activities which might be considered obnoxious by the parent (for example, eating between meals, climbing on furniture, staying in the same room with company, etc.), with the instruction to check those activities which they did not permit their children to engage in. The second questionnaire was designed to measure permissiveness for aggression in particular. It consisted of 19 aggressive acts by children (spitting in anger, throwing toys, deliberately breaking objects, slapping other children), with instructions to the parent to indicate the age at which she would expect her child to not engage in such action any longer. This schedule was modeled after Winterbottom's measure for independence training attitudes (McClelland, Atkinson, Clark, & Lowell, 1953). In addition, the mother was asked to select from five alternative types of disciplinary actions, ranging from spanking to ignoring, which she would take if the child engaged in the aggressive action when he was a year older than the age at which the mother felt it should have been extinguished. A physical punishment score was obtained by counting the number of times that the mother selected "spanking" or "rough handling, shaking."

RESULTS

DP_1. There were no significant differences associated with the experimental condition, indicating that before the story-reading need affiliation arousal, the experimental and control groups were not different in aggression. There were also no significant differences associated with age, but boys expressed significantly more aggression than girls in the first doll play.

Because of sex differences in initial level of aggression, the experimental effects were evaluated through change scores from the first to the second doll play. In this analysis, there were no significant differences associated with sex, age, or experimental condition, but the interaction between age and experimental condition was significant. Analysis of this interaction revealed significant differences between the experimental and control conditions for the younger subjects but no difference for the older.

These results indicate that the experimental story was able to counteract the usual tendency for children to increase in aggression as a function of doll-play trials, but that this was only true for the younger nursery-school subjects. Although it is possible and reasonable that young subjects may be more responsive to affiliation arousals, because of their greater dependency, it is also possible that the story used was simply inappropriate for the older children, who are beyond the age at which simple stories about personified animals are convincing. It does not seem likely that possible social-class differences between children who attend nursery school and those in public elementary school would account for these results. If anything, the elementary school children would come from a somewhat lower socioeconomic level than the nursery children, but certainly no lower than the children of working mothers in the earlier study who behaved very much like the younger children in this study.

Parent Attitude Scales and Aggression

The measures of parental permissiveness and use of physical punishment were modestly but significantly intercorrelated.

The modest correlation between permissiveness for aggression and strictness, almost identical to the —.30 obtained by Sears et al. (1957), for the relationship between permissiveness for aggression and restrictiveness in other ways indicates that mothers do make discriminations between aggressive and other kinds of undesirable behaviors in their children.

The correlations between parental permissiveness and use of physical punishment are about the same for the two sexes, except for those between general strictness and physical punishment, where it is found that the more strict a girl's mother, the more likely she is to use physical punishment in controlling aggression while there is no evidence for such a tendency among mothers of boys. This is true even though the mother's standards for permissible aggression are about the same for the two sexes. Thus, while girls are not necessarily punished physically more than boys, their punishment is more closely tied to levels of maternal strictness.

The correlations between the parent scales and aggression as measured in DP_1 are presented in Table 1. The only significant correlation is with mater-

TABLE 1

Correlations between Parent Questionnaires and Children's Aggression

	Boys	Girls
Physical punishment and DP_1	.07	.03
Permissible aggression and DP_1	.19	−.29
General strictness and DP_1	−.50**	+.39*

* $p < .05$.
** $p < .01$.

nal strictness. The surprise is that the correlation is reversed in the two sexes. Sears et al. (1957) report "a slight tendency for mothers who had high restrictions to report that their children were low in aggression," but their data were not broken down by sex of child. It is possible that the sex differences in the punishment-strictness correlations may account for the differences between the sexes in the strictness-aggression correlations. If strict mothers of girls tend to use physical punishment more than do similar mothers of boys, then the sex differences in the strictness-aggression relationship might be the result of physical punishment. To test this possibility, the children were divided into high and low physically punished groups, and the correlations between strictness, permissiveness for aggression, and aggression within the two levels of physical punishment examined.

There is a strong tendency for parental permissiveness for aggression to be associated with low aggression in girls who are physically punished, but this relationship is not found in less physically punished girls, nor is it found at all among boys. On the other hand, our data show a strong relationship between maternal strictness and aggression, but it is different for the two sexes. The more strict a girl's mother, the more aggressive the daughter, if the mother uses physical punishment, but this is not found for girls not physically punished. On the other hand, for boys the more strict their mothers the less aggressive they are, especially if they are not physically punished.

These relationships lend some support to the hypothesis that children's imitation of parental aggression (physical punishment) depends to some extent on the sex of the child; the data are consistent with Sears' notion that girls imitate maternal aggression but they do not support the hypothesis that boys do also.

DISCUSSION

Parental Permissiveness: Practice Variable or Frustration-Source?

In comparing our findings with those of Sears et al. (1957), some striking similarities and differences appear. While Sears et al. found that parental permissiveness for aggression is associated with aggression, we find that the relationship depends on the use of physical punishment and sex of the child, and is reversed in girls from the one reported in their study. They interpreted their findings to mean that permissiveness for aggression allows a child to practice aggressive behavior, while punishment serves as an aggression-instigating frustration, and a model for the child to imitate. Our findings with respect to girls are more consistent with an interpretation of lack of permissiveness as a measure of the extent to which the mother produces aggression-instigating frustration, for the less the permissiveness, the greater was the girls' aggression. These differences between our data and Sears' may be a result of the differences in our measures of aggression. The present study used direct measures of the children's aggression, while Sears used maternal reports which may have been biased by mothers' needs to rationalize their own use of punishment, or by special sensitivities to aggression in mothers who punish extensively, or by defensive projections of the mothers' own aggression onto the children.

Although permissiveness for aggression and general strictness are correlated, unlike Sears et al. we find that general strictness is more highly related to children's aggression than is permissiveness for aggression. In the case of girls, the data further support the interpretation of the strictness-permissiveness dimension as one which functions as a potential source of frustration-instigating aggression, with aggression increasing with restrictiveness.

Punishment and Modeling

We find some logical support for the modeling function of maternal aggression. If we accept the proposition that parental restrictiveness provides a source of frustration and punishment provides a model for the child to imitate, then we should expect that the correlation between strictness and aggression should be greater in the highly punished girls than in the highly punished boys; this was found. Thus our data support the notion that the child's identification with the parents is an important variable in his responsiveness to their control techniques.

Parental Control Techniques and Child's Identification

The negative correlation between strictness and DP_1 aggression in the less physically punished boys is more difficult to interpret. It indicates that the more strict the mother, the less aggressive the boy, if the boy is not physically punished. One speculative possibility might be suggested: if the mother supports her restrictiveness with love-oriented techniques of discipline, rather than physical punishment, it puts the son in a difficult position. If he violates her standards, he loses her love. Boys, of course, are less likely to identify with their mothers than girls, and so do not imitate the mother's use of physical punishment, as indicated above. According to psychoanalytic theory, one function of identification is to free the child somewhat from dependence on the external source for affectional rewards by internalizing the parental rewards (Whiting & Child, 1953). If a mother withdraws love from her son, who does not identify strongly with her, then the son has no resource for replacing the loss. According to this theory, loss of maternal love to a boy is then a more serious threat than it might be to a girl, and is one which the boy is therefore less likely to risk. Thus the boys in our study respond to maternal strictness by inhibiting aggression, thereby lessening the threat of loss of love. While this account is admittedly speculative and goes beyond the data we have, there is some evidential support for it.

One source of support is the finding (Gordon & Smith, 1963) that girls are more closely identified with mothers who use physical punishment, while boys whose mothers do not use physical punishment are more closely identified with their fathers. That is, boys whose mothers are more likely to use love-oriented techniques of control do not identify with their mothers. Thus we have evidence that the non-physically-punished boys are less identified with their mothers than the physically punished girls.

Our findings also raise the interesting possibility that the same parental practices may have different effects on girls and boys. It is usually thought that if the sexes differ in aggressiveness, it must be because the parents differ in their treatment of boys and girls. Sears et al. (1957) had found that parental behaviors were different for the two sexes, but boys did not differ from girls on their measure of aggression. We found that the parents treated their sons and daughters in essentially similar ways, at least as far as scores on permissible aggression, general strictness, and physical punishment were concerned, but that the sexes did differ in aggression. Taken together, these results suggest that differences in aggression between boys and girls may not be a function of differences in parental training practices, but they may be a function of differences in the children's responsiveness to those practices.

Our data thus support Eron's (1963) conclusion that it is impossible to generalize from boys to girls in research on socialization, especially as far as aggression is concerned.

Affiliation-Aggression Conflict

Some comments concerning the affiliation arousal are in order. While our data confirm the earlier study which found that reading a story about loneliness to children could arouse motivations which conflict with aggression, they do so only with reference to the nursery-school children in the present study. Nevertheless, the change in the general strictness-aggression increase correlation in boys from —.70 in the control group to —.09 in the experimental group suggests that there were effects attributable to the story. These effects, interpreted as evidence for the ability of the story to inhibit aggression of boys with a high potential for disinhibition when in permissive situations, are thus seen to be selective with respect to personality characteristics of the audience members. To the findings of Himmelweit, Oppenheim, and Vance (1958) and Eron (1963) indicating that television viewing of aggressive themes is correlated with aggressive behavior in children, and the finding of Gordon and Cohn (1963) that story themes affect motivational states, we may now add the further suggestion that the effects of such themes are selective, depending on personality characteristics of the audience. One might draw the further conclusion, though this is more speculative, that the effects of the story themes depend on predispositional potentials toward the motivational state with which the theme is concerned.

45. CONTROL OF AGGRESSION IN A NURSERY SCHOOL CLASS

Paul Brown & Rogers Elliott

It sometimes seems that the display of aggressive behavior by the children who attend school is one of the most characteristic attributes of the American classroom. Such behavior is not only disruptive of the teaching function of the schools, but is also a complicating factor in the interpersonal relationships of teachers and pupils. For these reasons, teachers are often anxious to find out what they can do to alleviate the situation and redirect children's energies into more productive and less negative channels. Studies on normal children's aggression do not usually deal with the possibilities of intervention aimed at alleviation or redirection. The interest of their authors tends to be in the explication of the process of aggression, in normative descriptions of its occurrence, or in an examination of the etiology of the aggressive act. For example, among the studies reported in the present chapter is one by Eron and his associates indicating parental punishment practices and family status as causal factors in children's in-school aggressive behavior. Teachers reading such studies are apt to take the pessimistic stand that since aggression is caused by an outside-of-school factor there is really nothing they can do short of the traditional repressive fear-based disciplinary procedures. This is, of course, a misreading of the situation. While it may be true that some children bring a background to school increasing the probability that they will display aggression, studies reporting outside causal factors have not indicated that intervention will not supersede previous influences. They are simply

SOURCE. Adapted from Paul Brown and Rogers Elliott, "Control of Aggression in a Nursery School Class," *Journal of Experimental Child Psychology*, 1965, Vol. 2, pp. 103–107. (With permission of the authors and the publisher, Academic Press.)

silent on that aspect of aggressive behavior. The following is an example of a study that provides a specific suggestion for those teachers who wish to cope successfully with children's aggressive behavior. In their study Brown and Elliott demonstrated that the rate of emission of aggressive behavior in nursery school boys aged three and four could be successfully manipulated if the teacher in charge systematically ignored aggression and specifically paid attention to acts incompatible with aggression.

The aim of the present study was to add to the data of the field of social learning theory (Bandura and Walters, 1963). First, among the techniques of controlling operant social behavior, simple extinction (Williams, 1959), simple reinforcement (Azrin and Lindsley, 1956), or both of them in combination (Zimmerman and Zimmerman, 1962; Ayllon and Michael, 1960; Baer, Harris, and Wolf, 1963) have been employed frequently with children. Second, the use of explicit learning techniques has been shown effective in young nursery school subjects (Ss) in two recent papers (Baer et al., 1963; Homme, de Baca, Devine, Steinhorst, and Rickert, 1963). Finally, antisocial acts of the assertive-aggressive kind are known to have operant components which are extinguishable (Williams, 1959) and reinforcible (Cowan and Walters, 1963).

With the above as background, we took seriously the following:

> Theorizing and experimentation on the inhibition of aggression have focused exclusively on the inhibitory influence of anxiety or guilt, on the assumption that response inhibition is necessarily a consequence of pairing responses with some form of aversive stimulation. The development of aggression inhibition through the strengthening of incompatible positive responses, on the other hand, has been entirely ignored, despite the fact that the social control of aggression is probably achieved to a greater extent on this basis than by means of aversive stimulation (Bandura and Walters, 1963, p. 130).

We set out to control the aggressive behavior of all of the boys in an entire nursery school class, by using as techniques the removal of positive generalized reinforcement (attention) for aggressive acts, while giving attention to cooperative acts.

METHOD

Subjects

The subjects were the 27 males in the younger (3- to 4-year-old) of the two groups at the Hanover Nursery School. Observation and teachers' reports made it clear that the younger boys were more aggressive than any other age-sex subgroup.

Ratings

Aggressive responses were defined by enumeration of the categories of the scale devised by Walters, Pearce, and Dahms (1957). The scale has two major subcategories—physical aggression and verbal aggression. Each of these is subdivided into more concrete categories; e.g., under physical aggression are categories labeled "pushes, pulls, holds"; "hits, strikes"; "annoys, teases, interferes"; and there are similar specific descriptions (e.g., "disparages"; "threatens") under the verbal category.

The observations of the behavior were made by two raters, both undergraduates at Dartmouth. They were trained in the use of the scale, and given practice in observing the class during the free-play hour from 9:20 to 10:20 in the morning. Such observation was possible because the rater could stand in a large opening connecting the two spacious play areas. The rating scale had the categories of aggressive behavior as its rows, and 12 five-minute intervals as its columns. The raters simply checked any occurrence of a defined behavior in the appropriate cell.

One rater observed on Monday, Wednesday, and Friday mornings; the other observed on Tuesday and Thursday. On two of the four observed Wednesday sessions, both raters observed, so that interrater reliability could be estimated. At the conclusion of the study, the raters were interviewed to determine what changes, if any, they had observed in the behavior of teachers and children, and whether they had surmised the research hypothesis.

Procedure

The pre-treatment period was simply a one-week set of observations of aggressive responses by the younger boys, to furnish a reference response rate. Two weeks later the first treatment period was initiated by the teachers and the first author (see below) and it lasted for two weeks. Ratings were taken during the second week of this period. The teachers were then told that the experiment was over, and that they were no longer constrained in their behavior toward aggressive acts. Three weeks after this another set of ratings was taken to assess the durability of the treatment effect. Finally, two weeks after this follow-up observation, the treatment was reinstituted for two weeks, and, again, observations were made in the second of these weeks.

The teachers were the agents of treatment (along with the first author) and they were instructed verbally, with reference to a typed handout, which read in part as follows:

> There are many theories which try to explain aggression in young children. Probably most are partly true and perhaps the simplest is the best. One simple one is that many fights, etc. occur because they bring with them a great deal of fuss and attention from some adult.

If we remember that just 3 or 4 short years ago these children would have literally died if they were not able to command (usually by crying) attentive responses from some adult, we can see how just attending to a child could be rewarding. On the other hand, when a child is playing quietly most parents are thankful for the peace and leave well enough alone. Unfortunately, if attention and praise is really rewarding, the child is not rewarded when he should be. Thus, many parents unwittingly encourage aggressive, attention-getting behavior since this is the only way the child gets some form of reward. Of course this is an extreme example but it would be interesting to see if this matter of attention is really the issue, and the important issue especially in a setting where punishment of behavior is not a real option.

At the school I have noticed that whenever it has been possible cooperative and non-aggressive acts are attended to and praised by teachers. During the intervening week we would like to exaggerate this behavior and play down the attention given to aggressive acts. I hope to concentrate on the boys, but if a boy and girl are concerned that is perfectly all right.

Briefly, we will try to ignore aggression and reward cooperative and peaceful behavior. Of course if someone is using a hammer on another's head we would step in, but just to separate the two and leave. It will be difficult at first because we tend to watch and be quiet when nothing bad is happening, and now our attention will *as much as possible* be directed toward cooperative, or non-aggressive behavior. It would be good to let the most aggressive boys see that the others are getting the attention if it is possible. A pat on the head, "That's good Mike," "Hello Chris and Mark, how are you today?" "Look what Eric made," etc. may have more rewarding power than we think. On the other hand, it is just as important during this week to have no reprimands, no "Say you're sorry," "Aren't you sorry?" Not that these aren't useful ways of teaching proper behavior, but they will only cloud the effects of our other manner of treatment. It would be best not even to look at a shove or small fight if we are sure no harm is being done; as I mentioned before, if it is necessary we should just separate the children and leave.

RESULTS AND DISCUSSION

The Raters

The correlation between the raters of total aggressive responses checked in each of 24 five-minute periods was 0.97. This is higher than the average interrater correlation of 0.85 reported by Walters et al. (1957), but their raters were working with a one-minute, rather than a five-minute observation period.

TABLE 1

Average Number of Responses in the Various Rated Categories of Aggression

Times of Observation	Categories of Aggression		
	Physical	Verbal	Total
Pre-treatment	41.2	22.8	64.0
First treatment	26.0	17.4	43.4
Follow-up	37.8	13.8	51.6
Second treatment	21.0	4.6	25.6

When interviewed, one rater said that the only change he saw in the children was in the two "most troublesome" boys, who at the end (the fourth-rating period) seemed less troublesome. The other noticed no change in any of the children, even though his ratings described the changes shown in Table 1. One rater had noticed, again during the fourth-rating period, that the first author was being "especially complimentary" to one of the troublesome boys, and the other rater did not notice any change in the behavior of any adult.

Aggressive Responses

Table 1 presents the average daily number of physical, verbal, and overall aggressive responses in each of the four periods of observation. Analyses of variance of the daily scores as a function of treatments yielded F ratios ($df = 3, 16$) of 6.16 for physical aggression ($p < 0.01$), 5.71 for verbal aggression ($p < 0.01$), and 25.43 for overall aggression.

There seems little doubt that ignoring aggressive responses and attending cooperative ones had reliable and significant effects upon the behavior of the children.

Verbal aggression did not recover after the first treatment, while physical aggression did. Since we were rating children, not teachers, we offer the following speculation with only casual evidence. We believe the teachers find it harder to ignore fighting than to ignore verbal threats or insults. It is certainly true that the teachers (all females) found aggression in any form fairly difficult to ignore. During treatment periods, they would frequently look to the first author as if asking whether they should step in and stop a fight, and they often had the expression and behavior of conflict when aggressive, especially physically aggressive behavior occurred—i.e., they would often, almost automatically, move slightly toward the disturbance, then check themselves, then look at the first author. The more raucous scenes were tense, with the teachers waiting, alert and ready for the first bit of calm and cooperative behavior to appear and allow them to administer attention. The teachers, incidentally, were skeptical of the success of the method when it was first proposed, though they came ultimately to be convinced of it. What made its success dramatic to them was the effect upon two very aggressive boys, both of whom became friendly and cooperative to a degree not thought possible. The most aggressive boys tended to be reinforced for cooperative acts on a lower variable ratio than the others, because teachers were especially watchful of any sign of cooperation on their parts.

Conclusion

As Allen, Hart, Buell, Harris, and Wolf (1964) have pointed out recently, the principles involved in the present application of controlling techniques are simple. What makes this and other demonstrations of them successful in a real-life setting is systematic observation, systematic application, and systematic evaluation.

CHAPTER 9

Internalizing General Behavioral Controls

With the possible exception of the occasional "psychopathic personality," almost all civilized men and women possess "internal" controls that psychologically punish, or threaten to punish, them when they do, or consider doing, something "wrong" (a "bad" action, or even thought, as defined either by some sector of their culture or by their own individual and sometimes idiosyncratic standards). Although this assemblage of internal restraints has been variously interpreted down through the ages (e.g., psychologically inferred threats of punishment from spirits as communicated either directly, through personal interpreters, or by various natural signs), in more recent history it has generally been called *conscience*. Its functions are present in some form in all contemporary cultures, although cultural anthropologists may argue about its origins during socialization (as discussed so clearly in the paper included in this chapter by Ausubel).

Whatever may be the structure and dynamics of those psychological processes that encompass what modern man recognizes as the "voice of conscience," the social effects are real and appear to be an important dimension of becoming and remaining "civilized." The restraints of a personal conscience place a major *social responsibility* on the *individual*. The individual is forced to do something on his own about his own misconduct. As expressed in the King James' version of the *Holy Bible*:

> And if thy right eye offend thee, pluck it out, and cast it from thee: for it is profitable for thee that one of thy members should perish, and not that thy whole body should be cast into hell.

And if thy right hand offend thee, cut it off, and cast it from thee: for it is profitable for thee that one of thy members should perish, and not that thy whole body should be cast into hell. (St. Matthew 5:29, 30)

The individual is admonished to punish himself. And, indeed, he generally does—often far too harshly as judged by any social standards other than by his own masochistic demands.

In the paper by Sanford there is a suggestion of how man preserves the best of the past through the functioning of internal controls which he has acquired, and for which he has often been rewarded, simply because he has lived by the precepts and rules communicated to him by teachers, and other close associates. Can the average individual avoid being dominated and otherwise limited by being almost completely controlled by these internal controls which are based on teachings that are generally regarded as having served the best social interests of prior generations, but may no longer really be the most efficient or efficacious? Sanford presents an optimistic and well reasoned answer to such questions. Theoretically, he believes that it is possible for an individual to become involved in civic philanthropic affairs without sacrificing activities defining his creative individuality. In other words, he affirms the belief that internal controls need not be straightjackets of internally controlled personal responsibilities that are laced on once and for all in inexorable form by the experiences of childhood. Rather, these controls can, and should, serve as general guides. Sanford further believes that education, even with older individuals at the college and university level, can alter life philosophies and modify internal guides to behavior.

As the reader may have already noted, our understanding of the structure and dynamics of social development is blurred and in some instances completely obscured by the lack of fruitful theories and the absence of appropriate research methods or representative research settings in which investigations can be pursued. The paper by Boehm and Nass illustrates these problems, and gives some valuable hints to future investigators of variables that may be related to the development of conscience. Doubt is cast on the propaedeutic adequacy of Piaget's theory of moral judgment. This is not surprising when one considers that Piaget's theory of the development of moral judgment was formulated more than thirty-five years ago, and prior to what many psychologists regard as the years during which he had his most seminal ideas about psychological development. Boehm and Nass also pinpoint some of the methodological issues that must be resolved before high levels of replication of research findings can be expected in studies of the development of conscience. Certainly, these investigators show very clearly that the sociological concept of "social class" may not reflect enough heterogeneity in child-rearing antecedents to be very useful in studies of conscience development. Studies within extremely diverse cultures would appear to promise more progress toward explanation and prediction in this complex and important dimension of internalized controls.

Within Sigmund Freud's theorizing, the superego (that "reservoir" of parental precepts, threats, admonitions, and so on) played the dominant role as the mediator of those internalized controls that makes man's behavior generally civilized and human. Within recent years, however, theorists who have been most appreciative of Freud's magnificent insights into the psychological functioning of civilized *homo sapiens* have begun to de-emphasize the extreme supremacy of the superego and have given more emphasis to the ego functions of intellectual control, self-denials, delays of gratification, mental competence, and so on. White has been highly influential in this reconstruction of psychoanalytic theory. And, as pointed out in the paper by Grim, Kohlberg, and White, William James may have been correct in his belief that human intelligence is closely and substantially related to internalized controls of civilized (and even primitive) man's behavior and judgmental processes that are involved in the functions of conscience. The authors of this provocative report utilize a large number of research procedures that will be interesting, and hopefully useful, to some currently active investigators of this or related hypotheses about the development of internalized controls over human responses.

Many theorists believe that self-criticism is almost entirely, if not completely, learned through the experiences of early childhood. They further believe that self-criticism lies at the very heart of the acquisition of internalized controls that are generally designated as conscience in Western cultures. In his paper, Aronfreed presents a tightly-reasoned argument that self-criticism is a natural consequent of anticipatory anxiety and that social punishment is the prime precursor of anticipatory anxiety. It would be most encouraging and satisfying to very large numbers of American psychologists if intellectually satisfying and theoretically fruitful explanations for self-criticism and/or conscience could be developed within the general framework of neo-behaviorism. No other psychologist to date has tackled this assignment so vigorously and persistently as has Aronfreed. His valiant effort will be applauded by many contemporary psychologists.

Part and parcel of the concepts of the internalized controls that make up conscience are the responses of shame and guilt. In his paper, Ausubel challenges the proposition promulgated most widely in the writings of social anthropologists, such as Benedict and Mead, that there are "shame," as contrasted with "guilt," cultures—or vice versa. He reasons that internalized controls within all cultures are basically the same in social origins and effects; it is only the *modes of expressing* these internalized controls that differ from culture to culture. Ausubel warns all social scientists against the dangers of ethnocentrism in their theoretical formulations. This seems to be an especially timely warning as the generally affluent middle-class social scientist is doing his best to understand the variables that are most important in influencing the internalized controls of the economically (and culturally?) less privileged members of our society. Why do more of the latter show up in our penal institutions? Why do the latter suffer more extensively from certain debilitating forms of mental illness? Theories and research studies directed at providing answers to those and similar important questions cannot afford to be heavily influenced by what Ausubel calls ethnocentric biases if explanatory and predictive advances are to be realized.

All well-trained and experienced scientists are aware of the need for repeating (or "replicating") investigations before placing much confidence in the findings and related generalizations. There are many reasons for conducting such replications; however, the following possibilities for errors in generalizations are representative and among the most important: (1) there is always the possibility that the experimenter is unconsciously biased toward securing desired outcomes, (2) errors in recording and analyzing data are always present and are, unfortunately, sometimes very numerous and substantial, (3) there is always the possibility that very important variables are not properly controlled, or even recognized, (4) the prior history of the materials or organisms being studied may have profound influences on research outcomes.

Doland and Adelberg are concerned with the latter possibility for errors in generalization. They show that the internal controls for "sharing" within a nursery environment are significantly influenced by young children's home experiences. They further demonstrate that it is possible to alter this expression of behavior by laboratory conditions. The effects of such special socialization experiences on the acquisition of internal controls remains to be determined, as do so many other potentially important within-the-skin and outside-the-skin influences on the development of sharing behavior.

The existence of internalized controls over overt and covert responses among *homo sapiens* has been accepted for many centuries. The possibilities of influencing the scope and intensity of such internal controls have supported programs of character education for at least 3500 years. Some of the psychological variables involved in the development of conscience have been identified by social scientists during the last four or five decades, but all scientists recognize this progress as being only slightly above threshold level. The pedagogical procedures that may be most effective in influencing internalization as a means of guiding and controlling behavior are almost nonexistent. Much remains to be known in this realm of human development.

46. THE DEVELOPMENT OF SOCIAL RESPONSIBILITY

Nevitt Sanford

The following report is a detailed critical examination of the question of an individual's commitments to personal ideals, goals, and achievements as contrasted with his equally important loyalties to groups of individuals with whom he is closely affiliated. Some historical perspective on this personal and political issue is provided by the obvious loyalties of the majority of citizens in certain socialist countries (such as Poland and Russia) to the long-range purposes of their homelands. In contrast, a much greater emphasis is given in our own country to the many aspects of an individual's personal and social development. There is a strong and pervasive belief in America that what is best for the individual must also be best for the Republic.

As a part of his argument that even American individuals must accept a fair share of responsibility as well as concern for their own future, Sanford presents an outline and a brief sketch of a theory of social development that might well serve the need of most contemporary cultures. A most interesting part of this theory relates to Sanford's analysis of the adolescent's conflicts over his efforts to avoid alienation and at the same time escape from a social compulsion merely to do his civic duty. As the author wisely notes, the majority of college students resolve the conflicts, created by the widening horizons that hopefully emerge from their aca-

SOURCE. Adapted and abridged from Nevitt Sanford, "The Development of Social Responsibility," *American Journal of Orthopsychiatry*, 1967, Vol. 37, 22–29. (With permission of the author and the American Orthopsychiatric Association.)

This paper also appears as one of the chapters in Sanford's book, *Where Colleges Fail*. San Francisco: Jossey-Bass, 1968.

demic study, by eventually returning to more traditional value orientations after they graduate and return to their home communities. However, at least some find more creative and productive ways of integrating newly discovered insights into their daily functioning life philosophies. Sanford draws wisely and extensively upon his rich experience of observing and counseling college and university students in this report. He has been able to suggest several means for assisting young people to become socially involved and committed to helping to solve the social and moral-ethical problems of our time.

One of the first reviews of *The American College* (Sanford, 1962) appeared in a Polish newspaper. It approved of our general approach to the college as a social institution, but argued that the goal of college education is not individual development, but the improvement of society, and that the success of a particular institution could be judged only by the social contributions of its graduates. In reply to this criticism, I would say first that although we wrote mainly about personal development, we assumed, as did the Declaration of Independence, that fully developed individuals would naturally be concerned about the public welfare.

Some of the socialist countries, such as Poland and Russia, have shown that they know a great deal about how to win young people's devotion to the purposes of the state—a devotion sustained by the intense need of a relatively underdeveloped country to increase production and by the unanimity of parents, schools and government officials in telling young people what they should do and be. Responding to the obvious need, these young people are apparently able, at least in their teens, to feel that they are giving freely of themselves. There is no evidence that their unquestioning participation in socially useful group activity necessarily impairs future development of the personality. It seems obvious that the countries concerned could not run at all if the responsible adults did nothing but conform blindly to dictates from above.

Among the questions raised by this kind of society, however, is the degree to which it depends upon ethnocentrism, upon the categorical rejection of outgroups such as the "bourgeoisie" and "aggressor nations." Socialist nations, of course, have no monopoly on nationalistic "patriotism," for this can be found in some degree in any country and is generally encouraged by governments. In college, however, we seek to develop a higher order of social responsibility, which consists of loyalty to certain ideals that the individual understands, rather than to an aggregate of people whom he regards as being like himself. Naturally, loyalty to these ideals does not preclude opposition to others, but we should base our judgments upon principles, not upon the notion that other groups are categorically different and therefor irredeemably inferior. Such notions may help to sustain social effort within a nation, but they meanwhile increase the risk of war.

ACTIVISM AND APATHY IN TODAY'S STUDENTS

In contrast to ethnocentrism, social responsibility must be developed, not merely appealed to; during the 1950s our colleges were criticized widely for failure to develop it. In a discussion of several studies, Jacob contended that students were focused on a narrow, private sphere of interest—on how they and their families could benefit from society, but rarely on what they might do for it. In another interesting study, Gillespie and Allport (1955) compared the attitudes of our students to those of students in a dozen other countries. To an Egyptian villager, for example, an education meant the opportunity to do something for his people, while to our students it meant the promise of summers on Cape Cod. To describe this disinterest in public affairs, Reisman (1960) coined the word "privatism."

During this period, we were studying students at Vassar College, and we did find that, compared to earlier generations, these girls were intent on getting married and leading comfortable lives. What impressed us more, however, was that during college they were changing in what we considered to be favorable ways, and that as seniors they were relatively more restless and dissatisfied than earlier in their college careers. In general, they had become not only more accepting of themselves and of other people as individuals, but also less ethnocentric, authoritarian and conventional in their thinking. It seemed to us that the changes in such students promised well for their future, even though they were not expressing any great intentions at that time to go out and reform the world.

In writing about students during the fifties, my inclination was not to blame them for their conformity but to point instead to the state of affairs in the nation as a whole. With the Cold War in full swing, and the nation caught up in a surly, automatic anti-Communism, students were under great pressure to take their place in a society that, so they were told, already had developed as much as it was going to and that needed only a firm defense against its enemies. In those years there was little to inspire sensitive or idealistic young people. To the extent that students today are different we should credit the differences mainly to changes in outlook that pervade the whole society—changes such as the civil rights movement, the Peace Corps and the fresh accent on social welfare.

Even today, however, the proportion of students who are involved in social action is popularly overestimated. In a longitudinal study of student development at Berkeley and Stanford, Katz (1966) concluded that "activism" had attracted only about 15 per cent of the students. In 1961 the initial interview of the Student Development Study at Stanford included an item about interest in public affairs. After about two-thirds of the freshmen sample was interviewed, it was discovered that no one had indicated such an interest, so the item was dropped. Four years later, some of the same students were asked, "Which of the following experiences or activities have you engaged in during your college years?" Of the activities listed, six referred to political activity. Shown in Table 1, responses to these items would suggest that in 1965 most

TABLE 1

Percentage of Stanford and Berkeley Men and Women Engaging in Political and Social Service Activities*

	"Frequently"		"Occasionally"		"Never or Almost Never"	
	Stanford	Berkeley	Stanford	Berkeley	Stanford	Berkeley
	M W	M W	M W	M W	M W	M W
Civil rights activities in or near school	4 7	4 5	16 20	14 19	81 73	82 73
Civil rights activities in other states	1 1	0 0	4 3	0 1	95 94	99 97
National or community political activities	4 4	4 2	26 34	22 27	70 62	74 70
Campus political activities	8 8	7 4	23 26	21 24	69 66	78 71
Service activities off campus—work with unemployed, minorities, etc.	8 9	3 10	17 31	12 33	75 59	84 39
Student committees, etc.	15 22	7 14	38 42	23 29	47 34	70 57

* Based on responses in 1965 of approximately 500 senior Stanford men and women (about half of the graduating class) and approximately 600 senior Berkeley men and women (about one third of the graduating class)—all of whom had earlier taken part in a survey of freshmen.

of the seniors were apathetic about political issues. When these same students were asked to list the organizations and clubs that had been most important to them during their college years, very small proportions (never more than 10 per cent) listed groups for civil rights or for other political study or action.

The picture is much the same when students were asked about their future lives. The task was: "rank the following interests and activities according to the relative degree of importance you expect them to have in your life after graduation." In a list of 14 items which included "participation in activities directed toward national or international betterment," "participation as a citizen in the affairs of your community," and "helping other people," none of these three items was ranked in third place or higher by more than 11 per cent of the students.

Even the Free Speech Movement at Berkeley attracted only a minority of the total student population. In the fall of 1964, at the height of the controversy, Professor Somers (1965) of the Sociology Department questioned a representative sample of Berkeley students about their attitudes on the matter. He inferred that of 27,500 students about 30 per cent agreed with both the goals and the tactics of the "militants," another 30 per cent with the goals but not the tactics, and 22 per cent with neither (with the rest "undecided"). Even among students sympathetic to the cause, most usually sat on the sidelines. The largest demonstration drew about 6,000, or less than a fourth of the student population; and those who staged the Sproul Hall sit-in, presumably the most dedicated, numbered about 800. Somers points out that more than half of the militants were supported by their parents, some of whom were faculty members at nearby institutions.

Probably the 6,000 at Berkeley who demonstrated for free speech were not very different from the 5,000 who signed a petition in support of their professors during the loyalty oath controversy in early 1950. The "campus radicals" of the thirties were probably about as numerous, proportionately, as the "activists" of today—just numerous enough so that colleges such as Vassar were described by local citizens as "hot-beds of radicalism."

Along with a radical minority, our colleges have long been populated mainly by students who care little for politics and who generally reflect the conservative views of their parents. I remember that when we were in college, professors tried in vain to interest us in national affairs; but the events that concerned us occurred not in the larger world, but mostly on campus, on the football field, or perhaps midway between our college and the women's college across the lake.

THEORY OF SOCIAL DEVELOPMENT

In order to help students increase their sense of social responsibility, colleges need a theory of how that sense develops as children grow.

A child cannot develop except through interaction with other people. In particular he needs a family, and in time he develops attachments to them. In order to sustain these attachments, he has to carry out some obligations to the people around him. At first he is hardly to be differentiated from the group with which he lives, and he will love others in much the same way that others love him. He incorporates into his personality much of what is there in the social environment. If the social environment is loving, he tends to be loving, and his obligations to other people become closely tied to his obligations to himself. Gross failures in social responsibility, such as marked selfishness or aggressive self-seeking, are always tied to failures or distortions in these early familial and social relationships.

As an integral part of his need to be protected and loved, a child normally desires to give something to others, to give himself to causes or to enterprises in which he joins with others; and this becomes a basis of his good conscience and his self-respect. Chiefly as an outcome of struggle with his own antisocial impulses, the young person becomes more idealistic. In order to master his impulses, he strives for a kind of perfection and sets for himself high goals of moral achievement, which are accompanied by high expectations of other people. Meanwhile, the adolescent begins to shift his attachment from the family to groups outside the home. Often adolescents like to lose themselves in a group, to be fully accepted by it, uncritically loyal to it, and indiscriminately hostile to outgroups that seem to threaten it. At this stage, ideas of right and wrong are often based on the thinking of the group or of its real leaders. The individual likes to perform hard tasks in the interest of the group, and to be rewarded by it for what he does.

This unquestioning loyalty later may be generalized to larger social groups such as the nation, in which case we find the kind of nationalistic patriotism discussed earlier. But uncritical devotion to any group is a lower order of responsibility, for it does not require much ego or personal development or even much education or intelligence. Moreover, it is likely to be impermanent. It dissolves when the group dissolves, because it constantly has to be sustained by group influence.

By going through this stage and then growing out of it, an adolescent learns not only to work with others, but also to be wary of blind loyalty or the uncritical rejection of other groups. A youngster who misses this stage in high school ought to have a chance to go through it in college. I am thinking, for example, of an intellectual or aesthetic boy who never played with rough fellows, but came home instead to mother and his homework. When he arrives at college, this sort of boy usually rejects sports and other group activities, including everything that in our society has been a normal part of life among men, and goes on to become an intellectual or specialist so lacking in social feeling and techniques that he is alienated from the rest of society.

In order to avoid both alienation and the compulsion merely to "do one's duty," a person needs the experience of group loyalty followed by a chance to criticize the group and to compare it with others. In the latter stage, he will probably become disenchanted, as students often do, with his college, his community, his nation. He will complain about hypocrisy and phoniness and point readily to adults' failings. Meanwhile, his own values are challenged by exposure to other cultures and to new kinds of experience. After a few lectures on anthropology, especially on sexual customs, students often see that we have one way of doing things and others have another, and that between the two there is little to choose. "What is good for her," as the Vassar girls used to say, "might not be good for me."

Many students resolve the conflicts created by disenchantment and by their introduction to the relativity of values by returning to a traditional value orientation after they graduate from college. Others discover that there are group goals and purposes that can be accepted *after* they have been critically examined, and that the pursuit of these goals may serve a number of basic and persisting needs of the personality. Ideally they may find, in socially valuable work, satisfaction for a whole range of needs—both higher needs for good conscience and for self-respect and lesser needs for mastery, achievement, self-expression, or recognition. In a fully integrated personality socially responsible behavior can be a channel through which even childish needs can be expressed. One can, if he is sufficiently developed, find in group solidarity some of the same kind of wholeness that the child enjoys, only now it is on a totally different level because it is more conscious and therefore more susceptible to control, when this is needed.

From a developmental viewpoint, the task of the college is large. Freshmen are not very far along toward development of the kind of social responsibility of which I speak. Generally, they are still caught up in problems of authority, and are inclined, when the chips are down, to do what authority says rather than what they themselves have thought best. They are in a very poor position to take responsible action on the larger social front, often because they lack self-confidence and have an uncertain view of what they can do. They are also taken up with other problems.

In spite of this preoccupation with self, students at a liberal arts college do develop in the direction of mature social responsibility. In testing such as we have done at Vassar, Stanford, and Berkeley this development is reflected not by a prevalence of civics class slogans, but, for example, by a decline of ethnocentrism. When students are asked to respond to an attitude scale made up of items that state what a "good citizen" ought to do or that express approval of existing institutions, seniors actually obtain lower scores than they did as freshmen. In the Vassar research, we interpreted this change, with the help of other evidence, not as a decline in social consciousness, but as a growth in nonconformity. Knowing some of these seniors, we did not believe for a moment that their increasing skepticism or even cynicism concerning family, church, and state would lead them to neglect their civic responsibilities or to be unresponsive to human needs. What we found reassuring was the fact that these increasingly independent, critical and nonconforming young women were the same ones who showed the sharpest decline in ethnocentrism and authoritarianism. As their faith in institutions went down, their faith in themselves and in others generally went up.

Increasingly mature judgments about how society works (and ought to work) are seldom produced simply by "citizenship education." Although courses in government can awaken the critical spirit that may lead a student to his larger concerns, courses are regarded in general more as the subject of examinations than as a challenge to the way one lives. In order to strengthen social responsibility, the college must worry not only about its curriculum but about the values it lives by, the example it sets.

To change values fundamentally, we take a student from a community such as high school and help him to become a reasonably compatible member of a new community in which different values are expressed—values we hope the student eventually will assimilate. Newcomb (1943) demonstrated this process of acculturation at Bennington College, where the faculty and older students represented a consensus of values, which new students gradually came to accept. The same point has been vividly demonstrated at St. John's College in Annapolis, and at Reed College, where there are single, "monolithic," faculty-student cultures, and where students who choose (and are chosen) to stay have no alternative to participating in that culture.

At a minimum, assimilation of the values of a college culture may involve little more than a shift of adolescent loyalty to a new and larger group. Often there is merely an exchange of traditional values for prevailing ones. Conscience thus changes in content but not necessarily in structure nor in its connections with the rest of the personality. We noticed at Vassar that if, after sharing in the culture of the college a graduate married a man of similar outlook, she retained the social responsibility developed earlier. If, on the other hand, her marriage meant moving into a community with values quite different from Vassar's, the couple was more likely to fall back on values they had preferred before they went to college.

If a college is to encourage social responsibility, it must (as a minimum) run its own affairs according to values known to, and worthy of emulation by, its students. The extraordinary thing is how often this minimum requirement is lacking in colleges and universities today—perhaps especially in universities. In these large institutions, students seldom are confronted directly with models of the responsibility we would like them to develop; and among faculty members, they rarely are shown a sense of loyalty to the purposes of the whole institution.

Rarely are students told what the purpose of their education is, or that they should seek a purpose. Usually the message they get is, "You had better look after yourself." Most of the appeals and demands are addressed to self-interest, and most of the promised rewards are put in terms of self-satisfaction through success in some vocation or profession. Seldom are students told they should do something because they are going to be leaders of a society that expects important things of them.

Students have little chance even to feel that they are capable of giving anything to anybody else. In today's high-pressure system their problem is to survive, and if one is barely surviving, he naturally will have some difficulty in thinking of himself as a person who can lead others and give to others. For most students, being in college means capitulating to a kind of voluntary servitude, and it is quite a jump from that condition to one of socially responsible leadership.

To integrate social responsibility with the rest of the personality is the aim, and it is mainly through intellectual work and experience in college that this is to be accomplished. We cannot expect developing students to maintain a value orientation acquired merely through conformity with the ways of a college community, especially if such a community has few clear purposes that have anything to do with students. Nevertheless we should not regard such an acquisition lightly, for in some cases it still may be superior to the outlook with which the student arrived at college.

Our goal is to expand both the area of the intellectual and the area of motive and feeling, and then to bring the two together in a larger whole. To this end we try to mobilize the student's deeper needs and emotions in the interest of intellectual strivings, and at the same time we try to bring intellect to bear upon the issues he cares most deeply about. Once the student is aroused by social and political issues, he needs not only the support of a sympathetic group, but confidence in his own thought, judgment and decision-making—a confidence born only of practice. Instead of trying to avoid controversial issues, a college ought to promote analysis of them, including such conflicts of campus life as a student-administration struggle about rules or a faculty-trustees struggle about academic freedom.

I think again of the professor who tried to interest us in issues of the 1920's. In his course we were supposed to study contemporary Supreme Court cases which then would be presented in class. Although my friends and I did not have time to read many of the cases (and we sometimes used that class to prepare for the next one), our teacher managed somehow to convey to us the importance of his subject. We were impressed by the way that he refused to give up on us, by his assumption that sooner or later we would have to be interested in those great issues, and by his implied faith that we were, though still young and ignorant, the best hope of the nation.

Nowadays, of course, we dismiss from college young people who will not prepare their cases. In my day we did not have to worry about that possibility, for we had been given to understand that society was depending on us to take up many of its tasks. As a matter of fact, as soon as I was through with matters that really were pressing in college, I began to read material of the sort that our teacher offered, and I found it very interesting. What occurs to me now is that he should have used more concrete imagery to convey what the cases really meant. We did not have a clue, for example, about the meaning of labor relations, because we had no reliable images of labor, much less of its relations. Lacking any direct experience, we found the cases abstract and, aside from our persistent teacher, easy to ignore.

Many college students suffer not only from ignorance of the larger world, but also from a lack of opportunities to be of service. Fearful of appearing "soft" or unsophisticated, and required to compete successfully with others and find ways to "beat the system," they pass up chances to be helpful, thus generating a good measure of self-contempt. As this feeling toward the self builds up, some seek an opportunity to sacrifice themselves in some action of great significance. If they find no action of sufficient import, their unease increases. College students whom we think of as "uncommitted" or "alienated" often seem to be in this situation; they can even make a correct intellectual analysis of themselves and their trouble without its doing any good.

Possibly the only cure for self-contempt is an actual experience of being helpful, which often can best be had in some radically different setting. Although this experience sooner or later should be connected with or become a part of the student's intellectual life, I avoid suggesting that the only way to educate people to social responsibility is to involve them in social action right now. We know too little about the relationships between the patterns of college behavior and future performances in the world. Vassar women who became leaders in the community were not, in general, campus leaders, nor were they particularly active on the social front as students. In some cases students who are suppressed the most in college may even become radicals later on by striving for the freedom denied to them earlier. Furthermore, premature commitment to some patterns of social action can easily interfere with education.

In general, however, the development of full social responsibility requires experience in social action or in actions helpful to other people. A young person needs this experience in order to test the adequacy of his judgment, to familiarize himself with the limits of what he can do, and above all, to learn about the self-fulfillment that comes from being of service to others.

47. SOCIAL CLASS DIFFERENCES IN CONSCIENCE DEVELOPMENT

Leonore Boehm & Martin L. Nass

Leaders in human affairs are usually possessed of an extra measure of the spirit of adventure. They dare to speculate about what lies beyond the horizon, to describe the whole after having viewed only a few of the parts, to anticipate the probable course of events that have not yet occurred. Their creative imaginations and their sheer audacity permit them to hazard a guess about what is not yet known. But, because of the human frailties, these guesses are usually not completely accurate. Subsequent experience must provide the basis for necessary corrections and elaborations. However, the grand guess has done its work. It helps to instigate and guide the search, and thereby serves one of its unique contributions. As numerous philosophers of science have noted, a "bad" theory is better than no theory.

Piaget has been one of those daring adventurers in what some have started to call the growth sciences who has courageously guessed at much of the whole after having viewed only a very small part of the total picture. And it appears to many that his exceptional intellectual talents have permitted him to be "right" in his hunches a very high percentage of the time. But, as he himself acknowledges, his efforts constitute only a beginning. Much research and further theorizing are needed to unveil the most fruitful models for extending his prototheories.

The research reported in the following paper by Boehm and Nass tested and explored one small part of Piaget's theorizing about the development

SOURCE. Adapted and abridged from Leonore Boehm and Martin L. Nass, "Social Class Differences in Conscience Development," *Child Development*, 1962, Vol. 33, 565–574. (With permission of the authors and the Society for Research in Child Development.)

of moral judgment in children. The findings corroborate Piaget's general outline of developmental trends but cast doubt on some of his postulated correlates, such as the "morality of cooperation" being correlated with authority independence. This study also uncovers methodological problems that must be solved before further significant progress can be made via these and similar lines of investigation. It will be of interest to note that the present research was stimulated by a theory published thirty years prior to this reporting. This reflects something of the ubiquitous and persuasive effects of Piaget's theorizing on the conduct of contemporary research.

Piaget (1932), using the "clinical method," investigated the development of moral judgment in children. On the basis of these investigations, he concluded that there were two types of morality in the child. The first stage, referred to as morality of "constraint," exists until the age of 7 or 8 years. During this period adults are viewed as omnipotent, and obedience is automatic without reasoning or judgment. Punishment is regarded as a necessary retribution of justice to restore the status quo and is given in proportion to the size of the misdeed, independent of motive.

The more mature type of morality, which begins at about the age of 10, is the stage of "morality of cooperation" or reciprocity, highlighted by cooperation and mutual respect. Conscience has become more autonomous and the child evaluates intentions, rather than deeds alone. Punishment no longer needs to be "fair" and retributive. Piaget relates the emergence of this stage to the child's increased ability to differentiate between subject and object, to a more rational conception of authority, and thus to his liberation from the thought and will of others.

An intermediary stage in which the child internalizes rules without evaluating them was noted by Piaget in the 8- to 10-year-old group.

Piaget's work was extended by other investigators to include studies of variation in moral judgment as a function of (a) chronological age (Durkin, 1959a; Durkin, 1959b; Lerner, 1937; Medinnus, 1957; Morris, 1958), which indicated that more mature moral responses occurred with increasing age; (b) intelligence (Durkin, 1959a; Durkin, 1959b; MacRae, 1950), which resulted in contradictory findings; (c) social class and culture (Boehm, 1957; Dennis, 1943; Havighurst and Neugarten, 1955; Ugurel-Semin, 1952), in which the general trend was toward social class differences in moral judgment, but not of a consistent nature; (d) sex (Havighurst and Neugarten, 1955; Medinnus, 1957; Morris, 1958), which found girls to be more advanced than boys in the area of moral judgment. The existence of the two types of morality as described by Piaget has been questioned by Kohlberg (1958), MacRae (1950), and Caruso (1943).

In general, previous findings report age to be the only consistently operative factor in the development toward maturity of moral judgment.

The present investigation was designed to attempt a more systematic study of the influence of social class on children's responses to stories involving moral judgments.

METHOD

The Ss were 102 children aged 6 to 12 and in grades 1 through 6 of public elementary schools. Fifty-four of the group were of the upper lower socioeconomic class (referred to as working class); 48 were of the upper middle class. Parent occupation was used as the standard of evaluation, the lower group being occupational classes 4 through 7 and the upper middle class comprising classes 1 through 3. All of the children were of average intelligence (IQ 90 to 110) as measured whenever possible by the Pintner-Cunningham Intelligence Test administered in the first grade. The children were of white American born parents and included only those who had older siblings since previous research has found a more strongly developed conscience in only children and oldest children (Sears, Maccoby, and Levin, 1957). The groups contained an equal number of boys and girls. The children included in the study were without overt personality problems.

In addition to the above group the sampling was extended by Boehm to include a group of 58 intellectually gifted children in the public schools, 27 of working class background and 31 of upper middle class families. Since the responses of this group failed to show statistical differences from the original population, these data were combined with the average group.

TABLE 1
Comparison of Groups with Regard to Matching Variables*

	Number of Cases			Age (months)		IQ	
	Total	Boys	Girls	Mean	SD	Mean	SD
Working Class	81	32	49	106.8	20.1	111.7	17.7
Upper Middle Class	79	32	47	107.4	19.2	113.7	12.7

* With respect to the matching variables no significant differences appear between the groups.

Table 1 presents the composition of the groups. Thus, a total of 160 children were interviewed individually by the investigators using Piaget's "clinical method." Responses were recorded on tape and transcribed. The children were told that the study had nothing to do with their school work.

Each of the four stories told was designed to test a central hypothesis. The stories presented are as follows:

A. *Fight Story.* This story was employed to test the hypothesis that middle class children will concern themselves more with the underlying motive for a physically aggressive act than with the aggressive act itself, in contrast with working class children, who will still be primarily oriented to the amount of physical injury involved.

Two boys who were good friends got to school early one morning and had nothing to do. They decided to have a fun fight before school to see who was stronger. During the fight, Louis hit George's nose by accident and it began to bleed badly.

(The questions which follow are illustrative of the type used. In the course of his probing, the investigator may ask a large number of questions. The few here quoted are deemed sufficient to indicate the nature of the questions used.)

1. How do you think Louis felt about it?
2. Yes, Louis felt sorry (using the child's term) and wanted to do something to feel better. He thought that if he asked his teacher what to do, the teacher would tell him to write one hundred times, "I should not fight before school." He thought that some friends would tell him to give George one of his favorite toys, or to buy him a gift or to go to George and say that he is sorry, it was an accident. Whose advice do you think he followed?
3. Why?
4. Louis went to George to apologize (using the child's term). George told him to forget about it. He said, "You could have been hurt just as easily. The fight was just in fun." When do you think Louis felt better, when George said it was all right, when he wrote the pages for the teacher, or when he gave his toy to George?

B. *Cup Story.* This story was employed to test the hypothesis that working class children will concern themselves more with material values involved in the story than they will with underlying motives, the upper middle class group being more concerned with motivation.

1. A little boy named John (or girl named Mary depending upon the sex of the subject) is in his room. He is called to dinner. He goes into the dining room (kitchen) and opens the door. Behind the door is a chair with a tray with 15 cups on it. John had no way of knowing that it was there. He goes in, the door knocks against the tray, and all the 15 cups break.

   a. How do you think the mother felt about it?

2. A little boy named Henry (girl named Margaret) is at home alone. Just before his mother left the house she told him not to take any cookies. As soon as she leaves, he takes a chair, climbs up on it to get to the cooky jar. The cooky jar is too high for him to reach and while he stretches his arm he knocks over one cup that breaks.
   a. What do you think about the two boys?
   b. Why?
   c. Was one naughty, were both naughty (using child's term)?
   d. Should they be punished?
   e. Should one be punished more? Which one?

C. *Lost Story.* This story was employed to test the hypothesis that the groups will show no significant differences in their attitude toward lying.

1. A boy named Joe (girl named Alice) just moved into the neighborhood and didn't know the names of the streets very well. One day while he was playing, a man stopped him and asked where _____ Street was (street near child's school). Joe wasn't sure and answered, "I think it's there." It was not there. The man got lost and could not find the house he was looking for.

2. A boy named Mike (girl named Louise) knows the names of the streets very well. One day a man asked him where _____ Street was. Mike wanted to play a trick and said, "It's there," and showed him the wrong street. The man didn't get lost and was able to find his way again.
   a. What do you think of these two boys?
   b. Why?
   c. Is one of them naughtier than the other?

D. *Scout Story.* This story was employed to test the hypothesis that the groups will show no significant difference in a situation involving a choice between peers and authority.

A group of children X years old (the subject's own age) want to give a surprise birthday party for their scout leader. One boy has accepted the responsibility of decorating the room. He wonders whom he could ask for advice.

1. Whom do you think he might ask?
2. He thought of asking his teacher who knows a lot about English, social studies and math, but she doesn't know anything about art. He also thought of asking a boy in his class who is a good artist, knows a lot about decorating and even won prizes for it. Whom do you think he decided to ask?
3. He asked both and they gave him two different ideas. Whose advice do you think he followed?

4. He thought both ideas were equally good. Which one do you think he followed?
5. A friend heard about it and thought that the child's idea was better.
6. If he follows the friend's advice, how will he feel toward the teacher when she finds out he didn't follow her advice?

In addition to the above major hypotheses, the study hypothesized that girls' responses would indicate earlier maturity of moral evaluations than would boys' and that the child's sense of morality is dependent upon the specific situation and does not represent a common level in all situations.

Each child's transcribed protocol was scored independently by four judges. Identifying data were concealed. Responses were classified according to Piaget's three stages of morality (Piaget, 1932):

1. "Morality of constraint." There is automatic obedience to rules without reasoning or judgment. Adults are viewed as omnipotent. Punishment is seen as a necessary retribution of justice and is given in proportion to the size or the results of the misdeed, independent of motive. Intentions are of no concern to the child.

2. An intermediate stage in which the child internalizes rules without evaluating them or alternates in his responses to the situations.

3. "Morality of cooperation." This stage is highlighted by cooperation and mutual respect among peers. The child evaluates intentions rather than deeds or outcome alone. Moral behavior is engaged in for its own sake, not through fear of punishment.

RESULTS

Agreement among the judges on categorization of responses was unanimous in most instances. Only those interviews were used where at least three judges agreed. An example of one response follows:

Fight Story—(Female, aged 10–1, IQ 93, working class)
Q How do you think George felt about that?
A Well, I guess he felt sorry that he did it.
Q How do you think the other boy felt?
A He must have felt bad about it.
Q Whom do you think he asks, the teacher or the friend?
A I think the friend.
Q Why?
A Well, I don't think he would like to write five hundred times "I wouldn't like to fight."

Q What do you think would make George feel better?
A The toy.
Q What made him feel better, when George said it was all right, forget about it, or when he wrote down one hundred times "I shouldn't fight before school," or when he gives him the toy? Which makes him feel better?
A I think when he says he's sorry.
Q Why does that make him feel better?
A Well, he doesn't have to write five hundred times.

Scored "1" by all judges.

In the statistical analysis of the data it was found necessary, because of the small number of responses in the "1" and "2" categories of conscience level, to combine them and test them against "3." The results were then analyzed using a chi-square technique.

The percentages of responses by scoring category and the chi-square values for the several comparisons are presented in Table 2. The age break-

TABLE 2

Percentages of Responses in the Scoring Categories with Chi-Square Values*

Basis of Comparison	Fight Story 1	2	3	Cup Story 1	2	3	Lost Story 1	2	3	Scout Story 1	2	3
Working Class	38	10	52	28	34	38	12	20	68	11	25	64
Upper Middle Class	26	19	55	16	30	54	05	14	81	13	26	61
	$\chi^2 = .18$			$\chi^2 = 3.62$			$\chi^2 = 3.11$			$\chi^2 = .20$		
Boys	23	34	43	23	34	43	11	21	68	10	32	58
Girls	40	10	50	16	44	40	12	14	74	06	28	66
	$\chi^2 = .32$			$\chi^2 = .07$			$\chi^2 = .90$			$\chi^2 = 1.05$		
Below 9 Years	45	23	32	34	45	21	17	38	45	08	38	54
9 Years and Above	23	15	62	06	27	67	06	10	84	08	23	69
	$\chi^2 = 4.82$†			$\chi^2 = 35.27$‡			$\chi^2 = 13.13$†			$\chi^2 = 1.13$		

* All χ^2 data are based on the combination of scoring categories "1" and "2" tested against "3."
† Significant at the .05 level.
‡ Significant at the .01 level.

down for purposes of statistical analyses was to compare the "below 9" with "9 and above" levels because of insufficient numbers in each age group. This roughly divides the group in half.

The results indicate that age is the only variable which meets the test of statistical significance in three of the four stories. No other variables hold up statistically.

Viewing this finding with reference to the major hypotheses, one sees that two of the four are supported while two are refuted. That is, the lack of class difference in Scout Story and Lost Story supports the predictions. The responses to Cup Story show a trend in the predicted direction in which the working class group is more concerned with the actual material loss. In this case, however, the p value falls between the 10 and 5 per cent levels. With respect to the Fight Story no trend is evident since the responses of the groups are virtually identical. Thus, the expected social class differences are not supported by the data.

The comparison of the sexes reveals no statistical differences or trends and fails to show, as in previous studies (Havighurst and Neugarten, 1955; Medinnus, 1957; Morris, 1958), that girls are generally more advanced in their development of conscience than are boys.

Regarding age, the operation of developmental factors appears to a highly significant degree. Children below 9 years of age give significantly more immature responses to three of the four stories than do children of 9 and above. More complete age data are given in Table 3. The story for which

TABLE 3

Percentages of Children at Given Age Levels with Responses in the Three Scoring Categories

	Fight Story			Cup Story			Lost Story			Scout Story		
Age	1	2	3	1	2	3	1	2	3	1	2	3
6 Years	28	44	28	39	44	17	22	56	22	11	39	50
7 Years	47	24	29	29	53	18	13	31	56	6	44	50
8 Years	50	11	39	33	39	28	17	28	55	6	33	61
9 Years	12	35	53	0	29	71	6	12	82	0	16	84
10 Years	29	12	59	12	17	71	12	6	82	16	42	42
11 Years	27	0	73	6	40	54	0	13	87	6	13	71

no difference is noted is the Scout Story in which a uniformly higher level of response is found for all groups. The latter factor would tend to support the findings of Boehm (1957) who, using the same story, reports that American children are more advanced than their Swiss counterparts in the "peer-authority" situation and are emancipated from adult authority at an earlier age. This factor was recently commented upon by B. Inhelder in a personal communication. She indicates that Piaget's staff now finds that Swiss children develop more rapidly in this as well as other areas.

The age of 9 years seems to be a crucial turning point toward greater maturity: the majority of 9-year-old American children considered subjective more than objective responsibility, whereas in Piaget's investigation

(1932) only half of his 9-year-old subjects gave mature answers. Again, the time difference between the studies may be an important factor.

The hypothesis that the child's response is specific to the situation was tested by computing a Friedman two-way analysis of variance by ranks (Siegel, 1956). A χ_r^2 of 16.92 was obtained, with a corresponding p value of .001.

Chi-square tests dealing with possible sex differences within social class and class differences within sex were performed and failed to yield significant results. The one exception was in response to Cup Story, where the upper middle class boys showed a significantly greater concern with the motivation behind the material damage than did working class boys, who concerned themselves with the actual damage involved ($.05 > p > .02$). In Lost Story this same finding appears as a trend within boys ($.10 > p > .05$). No such differences appear in girls.

DISCUSSION

One of the hypotheses offered and confirmed by this study was that the stage of a given individual or group level of conscience development varies with the specific situation involved: It may be seen in Table 2 that the percentage of "immature" responses is shown to vary considerably with story, ranging within the upper middle class, for example, from a low of 5 per cent on Lost Story to a high of 26 per cent on Fight Story. These findings further emphasize the need for specificity with respect to the situation and the material involved when one deals with a discussion of children's moral evaluations. The differences in the same individual from story to story are at times much greater than group or class differences. Our results have not infrequently reflected the entire range of scoring category for individual children on the several stories, further underscoring the specific nature of the responses.

The results do not indicate that an increase in maturity of conscience is related to a decrease in authority dependence. A number of children who responded least maturely in Fight and Scout Story gave more mature responses in the other two series, neither of which presented a choice between peer and authority.

Turning to the individual stories, the lack of social class differences with respect to attitudes toward aggression, as manifested in the responses to Fight Story, runs counter to our hypothesis, which was drawn from the work of Davis and Havighurst (1947). The failure to confirm this hypothesis may be due to differences between our upper-lower class group and their lower-lower class group. Furthermore, our schools were not in slum areas but in mixed neighborhoods, so that our working class subjects were constantly exposed to middle class influences.

The greater differences which appear in response to Cup Story, although here too they fall short of statistical significance, reflect the working class group's stronger concern for material values. This concern may reflect a clear perception of the reality involved, for it is conceivable that a larger number of poor mothers than rich ones would in fact be more upset over the breakage of 15 cups than over one cup regardless of the reason, and "take it out" on the child. Nevertheless, according to Piaget's scheme, this approach does not reflect "moral relativity" but is an indication of immanent justice.

The failure of the responses to Lost and Scout Stories to differentiate between the two social class groups supports two of the study's original predictions, namely that the groups will show no significant differences with respect to their attitudes toward lying and toward ingratiation of authority or authority dependence. Both social class groups are willing to forgive "honest mistakes" regardless of the consequences but condemn a deliberate lie, even if it does no harm. Only a minor proportion of the group (12 per cent working class, 5 per cent upper middle class) felt otherwise. For the Scout Story these figures are 11 per cent and 13 per cent, respectively. Thus, our groups in these situations responded quite similarly, reflecting the common elements rather than the differences in American childrearing standards with respect to certain aspects of conscience. For example, the middle class concern for material damage in the Cup Story occurs more than twice as often as the working class concern about lying or ingratiation of authority.

The failure of significant sex differences to appear, either within the total group or within classes, runs counter to previous work in this area. Previous investigations in the area of conscience development (Morris, 1958; Piaget, 1932; Sears, Maccoby, and Levin, 1957; Ugurel-Semin, 1952) have found that girls tend to develop more rapidly than do boys. Why our groups fail to show this statistical differentiation is difficult to comprehend since this has rather been a pattern in previous studies. Our qualitative data, however, show that girls of 9 and below tend to score higher than boys, while boys above this age score as high or higher than girls.

In the middle class, the trend toward significance appears in the Fight Story, where girls show a more advanced level than do boys, who are at approximately the level of both working class boys and girls. This trend is an interesting one to note since it points out the working class's greater emphasis on responding to the act of aggression and perhaps a difference of childrearing in the middle class, where boys are taught more to "fight back" and girls to avoid such situations. Thus, the lack of aggressive responses in girls of the middle class may be a direct reflection of sex role differences, where such inhibition of aggression is not appropriate to the boy's role. This point can also be made for sex difference trends on the other stories, three of which involve a situation which can be broadly interpreted as containing elements of aggression.

In the Lost Story a reversal of this trend appeared. Middle class boys and girls reflect similar patterns, while a trend toward sex differences is noted in the working class, where girls show a more advanced pattern than do boys. The pattern of working class girls is similar to that of the middle class, and hence the group most inclined to support the individual playing the trick is the working class boys' group. The culprit is the one who caused the man to get lost.

With respect to age differences, the study's only clear-cut area of results is evident. The progressive nature of more mature moral evaluations, one of the basic components for the development of conscience, and the existence of the levels described by Piaget are fully substantiated. The fact that one of our stories failed to discriminate the below 9 from the 9 and above age group suggests that for the story in question our subjects had already made the shift at an earlier age. The basic developmental trends are apparent.

SUMMARY

A study was made of the effects of social class differences on conscience development. One hundred sixty children from working class and upper middle class backgrounds were interviewed, using Piaget's clinical method. Four stories were told each child, designed to measure his attitudes toward physical aggression, material values, lying, and ingratiation of authority and authority dependence. Responses were recorded and rated independently by four judges. It was found that:

1. None of the stories differentiated working class from middle class children at a statistically significant level, although a number of the predictions appeared as trends.

2. Although girls, when compared with boys, did not show the expected superiority of moral evaluations in the development of conscience according to statistical analysis, they showed a number of qualitative trends in this direction.

3. When divided into a "below 9-year-old" and a "9-year-old and above" group, significant developmental trends appeared.

4. It was found that "morality of cooperation" was not based on authority independence.

5. Tests of interaction were performed and nonsignificant trends were noted and discussed. The results were compared with those of Piaget and other investigators.

48. SOME RELATIONSHIPS BETWEEN CONSCIENCE AND ATTENTIONAL PROCESSES

Paul F. Grim, Lawrence Kohlberg, & Sheldon H. White

Serendipity defines that happy coincidence where an individual is searching for something very ordinary and expected, and during the process more or less accidentally stumbles across some highly extraordinary and unexpected phenomenon. Fleming's discovery of penicillin is an often cited example of serendipity. A few dirty agar dishes overlooked by an untidy laboratory assistant, an open window, and some wind-tossed spores set the stage. The dramatic and scientifically significant observation and subsequent action were supplied, however, by Fleming's noting that something unusual and extraordinary had transpired. This ability to take advantage of the unexpected and to change one's course is a signal hallmark of the creative scientist at work. He learns as he proceeds with his always tentative outline for next steps, and he is ever vigilant for anything new and promising.

The following study by Grim, Kohlberg, and White is an example of serendipity. "The evidence arose accidentally, through the chance meeting of investigators' conducting two different studies but using the same sixth-grade subjects. One study was concerned with attention and the other with moral behavior."

The resulting ego-strength, as contrasted with the usual superego-strength, interpretation of determinants of moral behavior is highly provocative, and should stimulate further important investigations along similar lines. The

SOURCE. Adapted and abridged from Paul F. Grim, Lawrence Kohlberg, and Sheldon H. White, "Some Relationships Between Conscience and Attentional Processes," *Journal of Personality and Social Psychology*, 1968, Vol. 8, 239–252. (With permission of the authors and the American Psychological Association.)

clever research procedures utilized in this study will be of interest to the reader, as will the productive use of factor analysis. The reader's attention is also called to the writers' acknowledgement that their hypothesis was anticipated in the writings of that greatest of all American psychologists, William James, who wrote, "The essential achievement of will is to attend to a difficult object and hold it fast before the mind." The present findings suggest that little moral behavior can be expected from individuals who cannot so attend and persevere.

Studies of moral conduct and ideology during this century have emphasized their fluctuation from one situation to another, perhaps in reaction to the too-ready popular acceptance of "honesty" and "character" as trait designations. The findings of the Hartshorne and May (1928, 1929, 1930) studies, in which children's cheating was found to be surprisingly widespread and sensitive to environmental circumstances, have been repeatedly cited as an indication that there are few continuously honest or dishonest children. Augmenting this argument have been the studies of class and culture which have repeatedly brought out the relativism of human morals.

Though all these studies have taught moral relativity, grounds remain for the position that there may be something to the notion of a moral trait. Burton's (1963) factor analysis of the Hartshorne and May data has suggested that those authors did, indeed, obtain some evidence for a weak "g" factor in cheating, a fact which Hartshorne and May (1928, p. 412) themselves recognized in their linkage of deception with "personal handicaps" such as relatively low IQ, poor resistance to suggestion, and emotional instability.

It would be of considerable interest to identify those characteristic individual mechanisms which are consistent across many situations and which would produce a moral trait. It has been suggested that individual differences in moral character depend on mechanisms of superego strength, good habits, or ego strength. The research evidence seems most consistent with an explanation based on ego strength; that is, there is substantial evidence relating indexes of moral character to ego-strength factors such as intelligence, anticipation of future events, control over fantasy, and self-esteem (Kohlberg, 1964).

The individual with high ego strength resists impulse and delays gratification. These capacities may have a wide significance for the individual, functioning in cognitive tasks as well as in moral conflict situations. The recent literature has suggested that cognitive operations which further attention to detail, planning, and inference are attained in part because the individual is able to resist the impulse toward less sophisticated solutions (Flavell & Draguns, 1957; Schilder, 1951; Werner, 1957; White, 1965a, 1965b). An analytic, field-independent cognitive style is correlated with delay of response and ratings of low impulsivity, though these correlations are somewhat sex specific (Kagan, Moss, & Sigel, 1963; Witkin, Dyk, Faterson, Goodenough, & Karp, 1962).

Such correlations between delay or restraint of action and analytic cognitive functioning suggest a "negative" definition of ego control, that is, one in which incorrect performance is inhibited. However, there must be an active component to ego control. The delayed response has a logic different from that of the impulse response, and the delay allows that logic to determine the individual's behavior.

It seems likely that delay permits stable, sustained, and decentered acts of attending to task stimuli. Analytic cognitive performance is correlated with frequent and decentered acts of attention (Gardner & Long, 1962). Low but significant correlations have been found between stability of simple reaction time (RT) and "awareness of growing behavior" and "awareness of adult emotional control," as well as between stability of RT and analytic performance on a perceptual task.

The present study examines evidence for interrelationships among psychomotor performance, psychophysiological recordings, teachers' ratings of moral behavior, and tests of cheating. The evidence arose accidentally, through the chance meeting of two studies using the same sixth-grade subjects, one study concerned with attention and the other with moral behavior.

The research on attention yielded 12 measures on each child, 4 based on RT variables and 8 derived from GSR measures obtained concomitant with RT performance. The research on morality yielded five measures, two based on teacher ratings and three based on experimental tests of cheating. This paper discusses factor analyses of these measures (plus age and IQ) for first-grade and sixth-grade samples of children.

The authors were and are intrigued by the unusual "stretch" of a relationship between two such different chapter headings in psychology as RT and moral behavior. The rather detailed analysis of these data is motivated not so much by a desire to draw final conclusions as by the desire to say all that can be said about the most likely beginning points for further analysis of this interesting relationship.

METHOD

The measure of attentiveness was derived from previous clinical research. Various studies, beginning with Huston, Shakow, and Riggs (1937), have shown marked differences between schizophrenics and normal controls in RT tasks in which successive trials mix short and long ready intervals. It has been assumed that a characteristic schizophrenic slowing of RT on trials with long ready intervals is caused by a loss of set, a wandering of attention, during the wait for the RT signal.

This kind of RT effect might also be characteristic of children, since in fact there is literature indicating a short attention span in younger children (Bott, 1928; Miles, 1933; Van Alstyne, 1932). Accordingly, a study was designed which compared first graders, sixth graders, and adults on an RT task and certain strategic psychophysiological measures.

Subjects

Subjects were 22 first-grade pupils, 22 sixth-grade pupils, and 22 adults. Both groups of children were drawn without selection from classrooms at the University of Chicago Laboratory School. (The adults, volunteers from a summer course at the University of Chicago Graduate School of Education, yielded data used in assessing developmental trends in Table 6, below, but were otherwise not involved in the comparisons discussed in this paper.) The median ages of the first-grade, sixth-grade, and adult groups were, respectively, 6, 12, and 31. Ages and IQs of the children were taken from school records.

Procedure

All subjects were given an RT procedure requiring release of a response key to illumination of a 3½-inch circular stimulus window. After practice trials, 20 trials were given in which ready intervals of 3, 5, 10, or 20 seconds were mixed in equal amounts. Exact descriptions are available elsewhere for apparatus (White, 1965b) and procedure (Grim, 1965).

RTs were obtained to hundredths of a second for each trial and were converted to log form. The transformed RT measures were then used to obtain three of the measures used in the present study:[1] RT *M*—mean RT for each subject over all trials; RT *SD*—standard deviation of RT measures over all

---

[1] An additional measure, RT slope, was also initially considered. This was a measure of the correlation between the length of the individual's RT and the length of the ready interval intervening between the preparatory signal and the reaction signal (Grim, 1967). Developmental increase in attentional stability is reflected in a decline in the correlation, that is, in a drop in the tendency for attention to wander (RT to increase) as the ready interval becomes longer. Selective correlations calculated prior to the factor analysis indicated that the measure was correlated with neither the other RT measures nor with the moral measures. The reason for this lack of correlation was probably due to the low reliability (in the split-half sense) of the measure as a measure of individual differences. The low reliability of the measure was due to the small number of observations employed in calculating slope for an individual with a resulting dilution of variance due to length of ready interval by the position effects involved in the RT 1st–4th measure and by the general variability reflected in the RT's measure. Accordingly, the measure was dropped from further analysis.

trials; RT 1st–4th—mean RT over a subject's first five trials minus mean RT over his last five trials.

A second set of measures was obtained in conjunction with GSR recordings. If a subject's attention tended to wander, it was thought likely that the longer the ready interval the more the eventual presentation of the RT signal would elicit a strong orienting reflex. Accordingly, continuous recording of GSRs was undertaken concurrently with the RT procedure using a Fels dermohmeter, Model 22A, driving a Stoelting galvanometer. Drops in skin resistance occurring 1–3 seconds after onset of the RT signal were tabulated and converted to log conductance change as a measure of specific reactions to stimuli (Grim, 1965; Grim & White, 1965). From these tabulations the following measures were derived: specifics M—mean log conductance change for each subject over all trials; specifics SD—standard deviation of log conductance change measures computed over all trials; specifics 1st–4th—mean log conductance change over a subject's first five trials minus the comparable mean over his last five trials.

Apart from these GSR drops in reaction to specific stimulus events, basal conductance level was felt to be of interest, since conductance has often been referred to as an index of arousal (Duffy, 1962). Accordingly, two measures of basal conductance were derived: basal M—basal skin resistance at the onset of each block of five trials, averaged; basal 1st–4th—skin resistance at the onset of the first-trial minus skin resistance at the onset of the last five trials.

A third GSR index was also taken into consideration. Any GSR record shows sporadic drops in skin resistance which are nonspecific, that is, not related in time to any specific stimulus given by the experimenter to the subject. Frequency counts of such nonspecifics have been related to impulsiveness (Lacey & Lacey, 1958; White & Grim, 1962) and to stress reaction (Silverman, Cohen, & Shmavonian, 1959). Accordingly, in the GSR records of these subjects all GSR deflections not specific to (not occurring within 1–3 seconds after) the RT stimulus and of at least a 200-ohm drop in resistance were counted as nonspecific responses. Three measures were derived from such counts: nonspecifics M—total number of nonspecifics over the entire experimental period per subject divided by minutes spent in procedure; nonspecifics SD—for each subject, standard deviation of nonspecifics counts for each minute of the procedure; nonspecifics 1st–4th—mean number of nonspecifics during the first five trials minus mean number during the last five trials.

Another attempt was made during the study to reach the orienting reflex in the way favored by Russian researchers (Sokolov, 1963), that is, as a simultaneous vasodilatation in the finger accompanied by vasoconstriction in the forehead. A specially designed photoplethysmographic system was used

(Grim & Anderson, 1965) which required the subject to hold his nonworking hand steady, while the heel of his hand rested on a table, the finger encased in a wooden stock. The incidence of complete orienting reflexes, finger and forehead, was too rare to be usable in statistical analyses, though finger vasoconstriction alone was related to ready interval. Most useful for the present analysis was a striking pattern of difficulty observed most frequently as the younger children complied with the task. Either through poor cooperation or through lack of motor steadiness, first graders repeatedly proved unable to hold their hands steady, and their pen records showed repeated bursts of movement artifacts.

Since there has been evidence relating variations in grip pressure to impulsive errors in children (Duffy, 1962) and fine finger tremor to poor adjustment (Jost, 1941), recordings of motor stability were included as measures in the overall analysis: movement—total number of bursts of movement artifact on the finger plethysmographic record for each subject.

Attention will now be turned to the measures of moral status through ratings and cheating tests. All subjects were rated on a "Scale of Moral Character" by their teachers. One teacher, who knew all the children quite well, was used for the first-grade ratings; for the sixth graders, two teachers were available to make ratings, and their ratings were averaged for a final value. The measures obtained from these ratings are described below.

Untrustworthiness. Each subject was assigned a number by the teacher(s) on a scale as follows: (0) completely trustworthy, can always be depended upon to do whatever he knows is right regardless of what he wants at the moment; (2) reliable, usually does what is right even with no one around to check on him; (4) conforming, follows rules mostly in order to keep out of trouble and/or to win approval; (6) unreliable, can only be depended upon to follow rules if someone is around to check, for example, might cheat if he thought he could get away with it; (8) untrustworthy, is always trying to get away with something.

Disobedience. Each subject was assigned a number by the teacher(s) on a scale as follows: (0) completely obedient, does whatever he is asked to do; (1) obedient, does whatever he is told unless he has a strong desire or reason for doing otherwise; (2) conforming, usually does what he is told; (3) unreliable, tries to get out of things; (4) disobedient, disobeys whenever he thinks he can get away with it.

Measures of Honesty

Two group tests of cheating, described more fully elsewhere (Krebs, 1967), were administered by a male experimenter. They were introduced as tests of mathematical spatial ability. The first test, the circle test, is an adaptation of Hartshorne and May's (1928, p. 62) peeping test, one of the Improbable

Achievement Tests. In this test, as used for the sixth grade, the children were asked to place numbers inside a series of 10 circles on a horizontal line with their eyes closed and repeat the performance on two more lines. The first-grade group was asked to put dots, not numbers, in the circle. Children were told to place their pencil on the first circle of the first line, to close their eyes, and on signal to put a number from 1 to 10 (or a dot) in each circle. The cheating score on this test was simply the number of correct responses, that is, the total numbers at least 50% within the circles. Insofar as high "cheating" scores might reflect some sort of task-ability and motivation variables as well as dishonesty, this would tend to artificially diminish rather than enhance the postulated correlations between honesty and attention.

The second test, the blocks test, is an adaptation of the Hartshorne and May (1928) Improbable Achievement Speed Tests. This test consisted of diagrams of seven piles of blocks. The children were supposed to discover how many blocks were touching each block that had an "x" on it and write the number next to the "x." The children were given a chance to practice on the first pile of blocks. The correct answers were given, and the experimenter answered any questions the children had about the procedure. The children were told to do as many of the remaining blocks as possible in a timed period. After 1 minute, 20 seconds the children were told to stop. The experimenter was called from the room by the second teacher who had been waiting outside the door. The experimenter remained outside the room with the teacher for a period of 2 minutes. He then reentered the room and collected the booklets. The "cheating" score for the second test was the total of numbers, accurate or not, that a child had put next to the "x's." The number of accurate responses was also scored for half of the total sample, but since the accuracy measure correlated highly with the total number score and had similar correlations to the other variables, this score was not calculated for the remaining subjects.

In addition to the two group tests of cheating, a verbal test of deceptiveness was used. This was an adaptation of Hartshorne and May's (1928) Lie Test. Items on the test are of the form, "Did you ever take anything (even a pin or a button) that belonged to someone else?" "Did you ever act greedily by taking more than your share of anything?" Both admission of sometimes performing "bad" acts done by everyone and denial of consistently performing "good" acts seldom actually done by the people are required for a high honesty score.

Almost all (30) of the Hartshorne and May items were used for the sixth-grade group, and 20 were used for the second-grade group. The phrasing of the second-grade items was shortened and simplified. To add some incentive to lie on this test, the children were told that while no one does all good things good students say they do more.

RESULTS

Table 1 presents the complete matrix of correlations between attention and morality measures found at the two ages. Correlations for the first-grade sample are presented above the main diagonal, those of the sixth grade, below the main diagonal.[2] There were 9 relatively independent measures of attention and 3 (Grade 2) or 4 (Grade 6) relatively independent measures of morality at each age, yielding a maximum possible number of 27 or 36 correlations between attention and morality measures at each age.[3] Table 1 indicates that for the sixth grade 10 of these possible 36 correlations are in the expected direction and significant beyond the .05 level (two-tailed probability). (It might be expected that 2 of 36 correlations would be positive and significant because of chance factors.) At the first-grade level, 8 of a possible 27 correlations are significant. Of more importance, most of the significant correlations are replicated at both ages, and some are of a high magnitude considering the low reliability of the measures involved. These major correlations between attention and morality measures are presented in Table 2.

The consistencies of pattern suggested by Table 2 are better considered in terms of a factor analysis of the correlation matrix presented in Table 1. The resulting unrotated principal component factors having an eigen-value greater than 1 are presented in Table 3.

The first unrotated factor in each grade deserves some note. The unrotated first factor best represents a notion of a general factor in a given domain because it is the single factor which is most like all of the test variables considered simultaneously. In these data the first factor represents 24% of the covariance among the variables in the older group and 20% of the covariance in the younger group. Inspection of the first factors in the two age levels indicates a great deal of similarity. This similarity is pictured in Table 4, which summarizes the first factors at the two ages in a form parallel to the summary of correlations in Table 1.

---

[2] Because of the small number of boys and girls at each grade, separate correlations for boys and girls are not reported. Such correlations were computed, however, and were quite similar for the two sex groups. Correlations between some of the major measures for boys and girls separately in a later study employing a large sample were reported by Krebs (1967).

[3] With the exception of two basal measures, the psychomotor and psychophysiological measures could be considered possible measures of attention. One measure, nonspecifics SD, had no independent variability, correlating .90 with nonspecifics M. The obedience rating had no independent variability, correlating .90 with the untrustworthiness measure. The blocks cheating test was not administered to the second grade.

TABLE 1
Correlations between Variables at Two Ages[a]

Variable	1	2	3	4	5	6	7	8	9	10
1. Age		−45**	−15	−11	45**	−10	—	−25	21	−34
2. IQ	04		−41**	−35	−08	01	—	−12	−40	−07
3. Untrustworthiness	−31	−06		94	16	−14	—	15	59**	41**
4. Disobedience	−23	−06	90**		12	−12	—	−01	59**	43**
5. Circles, cheating	−37	50**	26	21		34		08	25	43**
6. Lie Test	06	25	−11	−23	28		21	−11	−06	28
7. Blocks, cheating	−35	43**	23	26	64**	67**		—	—	—
8. RT M	−06	−18	74**	53**	24	03	21		−05	20
9. RT variability (SD)	−03	40	38	30	40	57**	55**	45**		43**
10. RT increase (4 − 1)	−15	30	50**	37	32	20	11	55**	66**	
11. Nonspecifics M	14	05	−02	13	15	42**	47**	−16	−01	−03
12. Nonspecifics SD	43**	22	08	17	−14	21	26	−09	11	16
13. Nonspecifics increase (4 − 1)	−16	26	26	18	55**	17	35	50**	28	30
14. Movement	−09	−29	43**	40	37	29	45**	00	21	15
15. Specifics M	−19	05	−18	−10	04	−10	−10	−32	−50**	00
16. Specifics SD	−43**	24	07	16	21	−03	20	−16	−34	−06
17. Specifics decrease (4 − 1)	−55**	29	16	22	−09	07	−04	−30	12	−01
18. Basal GSR	−20	03	−06	−14	03	−12	−28	16	−34	−13
19. Basal decrease (1 − 4)	00	12	−02	02	08	−16	13	07	−02	06

TABLE 1 (Continued)

Variable	11	12	13	14	15	16	17	18	19
1. Age	44**	41**	−05	−34	39	21	09	20	15
2. IQ	−30	−16	−10	−11	01	27	−42**	10	−30
3. Untrustworthiness	−12	−27	49**	41**	−25	−04	14	−25	−27
4. Disobedience	−16	−30	52**	27	−32	−06	10	−24	−21
5. Circles, cheating	22	12	47**	−61**	18	20	11	47**	21
6. Lie Test	−10	−15	−01	−25	17	24	42**	48**	23
7. Blocks, cheating	—	—	—	—	—	—	—	—	—
8. RT M	−07	−13	07	33	−18	−03	06	14	−43**
9. RT variability (SD)	−06	−16	42**	15	13	22	27	11	26
10. RT increase (4 − 1)	−29	−30	32	11	−18	05	−11	21	12
11. Nonspecifics M		90**	−26	24	−06	−35	−01	−19	−01
12. Nonspecifics SD	69**		−47**	10	−04	−43**	−09	−23	−01
13. Nonspecifics increase (4 − 1)	−03	−25		25	−04	23	09	25	−01
14. Movement	61**	28	19		−35	−21	−08	−20	−34
15. Specifics M	−08	−05	05	−39		77**	43**	29	34
16. Specifics SD	00	−02	18	−11	73**		28	50**	06
17. Specifics decrease (4 − 1)	11	04	−17	−04	05	47**		10	−03
18. Basal GSR	−01	−34	18	27	−04	−08	01		23
19. Basal decrease (1 − 4)	−15	−04	−17	−08	22	30	−06	−44**	

[a] First-grade (above diagonal) $N = 22$. Sixth-grade (below diagonal) $N = 22$.
** $p < .05$.

TABLE 2
Major Correlations between Attention and Morality Measures at Two Ages

Measure	6th Grade	1st Grade
Correlations replicated at both ages		
High untrustworthiness (disobedience)[a] and high RT variability (SD)	.38 (.30)	.59** (.59**)
High untrustworthiness (disobedience)[a] and increase of RT (4 — 1)	.50** (.37)	.41** (.43**)
High untrustworthiness (disobedience)[a] and increase of nonspecifics (4 — 1)	.25 (.37)	.49** (.52**)
High untrustworthiness (disobedience)[a] and high movement artifacts	.43** (.40)	.41** (.27)
High cheating, all tests,[b] and high RT variability (SD)	.61** (.61**)	(.16)
High cheating, all tests,[b] and RT increase (4 — 1)	.36 (.33)	(.44**)
High cheating, all tests,[b] and increase of nonspecifics (4 — 1)	.43** (.44**)	(.34)
Correlations found only at older age		
High untrustworthiness (disobedience)[a] and long RT $\overline{(X)}$	.74** (.53**)	.15 (.01)
High cheating, all tests,[b] and high nonspecifics $\overline{(X)}$	.42** (.36)	(.12)
High cheating, all tests,[b] and high movement artifacts	.47** (.46**)	(—.38)
Correlations found only at younger age		
High cheating, all tests,[b] and high basal GSR	—.13 (—.12)	(.48**)

[a] Correlations of disobedience ratings and the given variable are presented in parentheses.

[b] Correlations in parentheses indicate sums based on only the circles and Lie Test used at both ages.

** $p < .05$.

First Unrotated Factor: General Behavior Control

Table 4 indicates a central core of variables defining the first factor at both ages. The first factor appears to be a general behavior-control factor including both moral behavior and attentional stability measures. The highest loadings on the first factor at both ages are on the moral behavior ratings. In the sixth grade the experimental measures of morality are also highly loaded on the first factor, but not in the first grade.[4] In addition to the

---

[4] This is probably due to the lower reliability of the cheating tests for the first-grade sample. Three factors contributed to the lower representativeness of the test at the younger age. First, the tests were given to the first graders 10 months after the attention and the other morality measures were given. For the circles test the 10-month retest reliability at the seventh grade is .60 (Jones, 1936) and is probably considerably lower at the first-grade level. Second, only two tests instead of three were given to the younger children. Third, because the second-grade tests were only rough adaptations of tests originally devised for older children, they were probably not less reliable but less valid. The tests correlated better with an outside criterion (teachers' ratings) at Grade 6 than at Grade 1.

TABLE 3
Unrotated Factors at Two Ages

Variable	6th Grade F_1	F_2	F_3	F_4	F_5	F_6	F_7	5th Grade F_1	F_2	F_3	F_4	F_5	F_6
1. Age	−27	−69	16	05	−33	26	37	−22	43	−70	−11	−06	37
2. IQ	30	30	52	35	−24	−25	38	−28	04	74	18	01	36
3. Untrustworthiness	71	11	−50	−40	−06	−07	09	85	−33	−26	−10	−02	06
4. Disobedience	62	13	−37	−56	−05	−04	12	84	−30	−23	−03	−17	06
5. Circles, cheating	66	34	16	36	13	23	−04	28	58	−37	54	29	29
6. Lie Test	45	−21	61	30	09	−08	−18	09	54	13	22	37	−57
7. Blocks, cheating	74	09	50	08	07	18	−32	—	—	—	—	—	—
8. RT $\overline{X}$	67	−14	−60	03	−13	23	01	21	−30	14	−07	70	10
9. RT SD	76	21	08	28	−37	−38	−11	69	16	−41	−13	−24	−02
10. RT increase	63	05	−16	08	−38	−12	35	66	06	10	50	11	−19
11. Nonspecifics $\overline{X}$	31	−33	60	−40	42	15	10	−43	−19	−75	13	25	05
12. Nonspecifics SD	21	−41	54	−53	−13	04	38	−59	−20	−66	17	17	03
13. Nonspecifics, increase	52	25	−17	48	21	27	28	72	16	00	12	00	33
14. Movement	61	−33	−04	−28	53	23	−35	22	−67	−03	−25	18	−12
15. Specifics $\overline{X}$	−29	67	21	−12	−05	38	28	−13	74	−06	−50	−02	08
16. Specifics SD	01	84	26	−28	07	19	09	21	70	26	−42	08	29
17. Specifics decrease	07	46	21	−37	15	−72	−05	22	35	−24	−55	37	−40
18. Basal GSR	10	05	−28	30	74	−10	29	10	70	15	23	19	04
19. Basal decrease	01	30	09	−17	−56	−04	−35	−07	50	−20	22	−52	−43

TABLE 4
Major Variables Defining the Unrotated First Factors at Two Ages

Variable	Loading 6th Grade	Loading 1st Grade
Variables loaded on 1st factor at both ages		
3. Untrustworthiness	.71	.85
4. Disobedience	.62	.84
9. RT variability	.76	.69
10. Increase in RT (1st–4th)	.63	.66
13. Increase in nonspecifics (1st–4th)	.52	.72
Variables loaded on 1st factor only at 6th grade		
5. Cheating, circles	.66	.28
6. Cheating, Lie Test	.45	.09
7. Cheating, block test	.74	—
8. RTM	.67	.21
14. Movement artifacts	.61	.22
Variables nonloaded on the 1st factor at either age		
1. Age	−.22	−.27
2. IQ	.30	−.28
11. Non specifics M	.30	−.42
12. Nonspecifics variability	.20	−.59
15. Specifics M	−.30	−.13
16. Specifics variability	.01	.21
17. Specifics decrease	.07	.22
18. Basal GSR	−.10	.10
19. Basal decrease	−.01	−.07

Note.—A variable was considered to be loaded on a factor if the loadings would lead the single factor to generate correlations which would be significant at $p < .05$.

morality measures, the first factor picks up almost equally well the RT measures, movement artifacts, and nonspecifics change over time. These measures may define an instability of attentional focus.

Rotation Procedure

Consideration of the first unrotated factor provided a useful overview of the major consistencies in the data. To provide a more detailed analysis, orthogonal varimax rotations were carried out. The varimax procedure tends to maximize the replicability of factors from one subject population to another. Since the structure of a particular factor will change according to the number of other factors rotated, distinct rotations were carried out for each number of factors from three to seven. Inspection indicated that the first three factors were stable at each age regardless of the number of factors included in the rotation. Furthermore, the first three factors in one age group could be matched to the corresponding first three factors in the other age group, whereas later factors could not, suggesting that only the first three factors had a replicable functional meaning. Later-extracted factors essentially represented artifactual doublets or triplets of correlations resulting from use of the same raw scores to generate three variables (e.g., mean, standard deviation, and first to fourth increase in a given measure).

The first three rotated factors at each age level are presented in Table 5.

TABLE 5

First Three Rotated Factors at Two Ages

	Variable	6th Grade			1st Grade		
		F_1	F_2	F_3	F_1	F_2	F_3
1.	Age	−27	−19	18	04	13	65**
2.	IQ	−20	70**	01	−56**	06	−56**
3.	Untrustworthiness	94**	03	11	91**	−07	−06
4.	Disobedience	85**	−07	24	91**	−07	−11
5.	Circles, cheating	23	77**	01	21	88**	28
6.	Lie Test	−19	67**	44	−14	65**	−09
7.	Blocks, cheating	15	74**	47**	—	—	—
8.	RT $\bar{X}$	85**	19	−11	04	13	−02
9.	RT SD	43	68**	14	80**	09	05
10.	RT increase	56**	43	−04	48**	54**	−29
11.	Nonspecifics $\bar{X}$	−11	10	91**	−12	−03	91**
12.	Nonspecifics SD	−03	−05	81**	−28	−09	87**
13.	Nonspecifics increase	30	60**	−24	61**	35	−26
14.	Movement	46**	11	62**	28	−43	03
15.	Specifics $\bar{X}$	−28	−04	−21	−15	14	01
16.	Specifics SD	−07	11	−03	00	29	−37
17.	Specifics decrease	02	−02	19	21	12	16
18.	Basal GSR	−08	−03	−19	−12	69**	−17
19.	Basal decrease	06	03	−13	03	20	06

** Indicates a loading sufficient to generate significant ($p < .05$) correlations by the single factor.

First Rotated Factor: Task Conformity

After rotation the first factors at the two ages become quite similar, being defined by the morality teacher ratings and by the RT measures. At the sixth grade the factor picks up two psychomotor variables, RT mean and movement, not clearly present at Grade 1, while the nonspecific increase measure drops out. (The reasons for these differences between the first factors at the two ages are discussed below.) At both ages the first factor seems to be based on stable control, since it loads on both psychomotor measures of steadiness and on teachers' ratings of stable conformity to authoritative social expectations.

Second Rotated Factor: Inner Stability

The second rotated factor at both ages is most clearly defined by the experimental measures of dishonesty or cheating. The rotational procedures at Grade 6 have isolated these variables from the unrotated first factor, so separating rating and experimental measures of morality. At Grade 6, the next best definer of the factor after experimental honesty is IQ, in the direction of linking high intelligence to high cheating. For reasons highly specific to this sixth-grade laboratory-school group, high IQ positively correlated with both experimental dishonesty and experimental distractibility, correlations inconsistent with the findings of many other studies.[5] It might be suggested that the morality component of the second factor represents a more internalized disposition than the performance dispositions picked up by the first factor. Where the first factor seems related to the capacity of the child to exert restraint, the second factor seems more voluntaristic. The child who resists an opportunity to augment a test score by cheating must have both a willingness and capacity. The several loadings of psychomotor and psychophysiological measures on the second factor are not clearly interpretable. However, in later discussion, it is suggested that they may represent attentional stability as contrasted to the psychomotor efficiency variables loading on Factor 1. The name assigned to the factor, inner stability, is based on the cheating-test measures.

Third Rotated Factor: Restlessness

The third factor at each grade level is most clearly defined by two nonspecific measures (mean and standard deviation). In part, this factor is artifactual. The small number of nonspecifics in each minute used to generate a minute-to-minute variability measure leads to an artificially high correlation

---

[5] Hartshorne and May (1928) and Mutterer (1965) reported negative correlations between IQ and cheating using tests similar to ours with more representative populations. Krebs (1967) reported low negative correlations between IQ and attentional instability using measures similar to ours with a more representative population. Discussions with the teacher suggest that our peculiar finding was due to some artifacts of classroom grouping and atmosphere in a school of very bright, academic-background children. The classroom contained a group of somewhat oversophisticated and difficult children who perhaps refused to take conformity on either experimental attention or morality tasks with more than perfunctory seriousness. In any case, the finding does not derive from the fact that high scores on our cheating tests in fact reflect high ability to perform the tasks involved (counting blocks, etc.). Were the positive IQ-cheating correlation to be explained in this fashion, it should hold at our younger age level (Grade 1) and in other populations.

between the mean and variability measures. (The correlations between the mean and variability of nonspecifics were .90 at Grade 1 and .69 at Grade 6.) In addition, however, this factor picks up some cheating measures and movement artifacts in Grade 6. In Grade 1 it seems to represent a physiological maturation factor positively loaded on chronological age (and, because of inverse correlations between chronological age and IQ in first-grade placement, negatively loaded on IQ). This third factor, relating so directly to nonspecifics, does not seem worth detailed consideration. It does, however, suggest that nonspecifics are more clearly related to control factors in personality than are the other psychogalvanic measures used (i.e., Variables 14–19), but that this relationship only appears at the older age level. Insofar as it may have psychological meaning at Grade 6, it may be termed a restlessness factor. Several studies have shown positive correlations between the number of nonspecifics manifested by an individual, his impulsiveness in performance, and his tendency toward hyperkinesis (Kagan et al., 1963; Lacey & Lacey, 1958; White & Grim, 1962). Further support for this interpretation of the third factor arises from its linkage with movement artifacts. Duffy (1930, 1932a, 1932b) has reported that children who show fluctuations in grip pressure also tend to make errors of commission rather than omission; she has subsequently suggested (Duffy, 1962) that these grip fluctuations tap the characteristics of impulsiveness and hyperkinesis underlying the Laceys' nonspecifics measures. The interpretation also encompasses the fact that the third factor is more related to rated disobedience than to rated untrustworthiness, and that the cheating test on which it was most clearly loaded (the blocks) was one in which conformity required sitting still and doing nothing with an unfinished test.

Developmental Influences: An Analysis

It has been noted that certain psychomotor variables seem to come into significant relationships with moral control at Grade 6 which are not so related at Grade 1. These changing correlational patterns may be better understood by considering the extent to which individual differences in these variables may be considered due to "developmental" or ability factors as opposed to "personality" factors at the given ages. The data relevant to this issue are presented in Table 6.

Table 6 presents the means for the two age groups and for an adult sample (Grim, 1965, 1967). The variables are grouped under four headings—developmental variables, which increase continuously until adulthood; asymptotic development variables, which increase rapidly until sixth grade and only slightly thereafter; terminating development variables, increasing to Grade 6 but not thereafter; and nondevelopmental variables, which show no significant age change. It is apparent that the three psychomotor variables (mean RT,

TABLE 6
Means of Psychomotor and Moral Variables at Three Ages

	1st Grade		6th Grade		Adult	
Variable	M	Σ	M	Σ	M	Σ
Continuously developing variables						
9. RT variability (SD, 100 log sec.)	107.2	21.3	94.2*	33.8	57.5***	48.7
10. RT increase (4 — 1)	5.3	5.7	3.4	9.4	1.2**	7.4
Asymptotically developing variables						
8. RT M (100 log sec.)	180.8	9.3	162.6***	6.5	156.2***	6.9
14. Movement artifacts	17.7	16.4	4.0**	6.1	0.5**	1.7
12. Nonspecifics variability (SD)	2.9	.9	1.9**	.8	1.4*	.6
18. Basal GSR	64.0	25.4	89.1**	39.1	136.8	155.1
19. Basal increase (1 — 4)	1.8	21.3	—17.3**	21.6	—31.8	111.2
Terminating development variables						
11. Nonspecifics (per min.)	5.4	2.0	4.0**	1.9	4.0	2.1
17. Specifics decrease (1 — 4)	4.8	8.0	0.7	11.2	2.1	12.3
Nondevelopmental variables						
13. Nonspecifics increase (4 — 1)	1.8	3.4	— 2.8	8.9	— 1.0	17.3
15. Specifics M	27.0	15.0	22.8	17.8	28.4	18.0
16. Specifics variability (SD)	11.2	5.0	9.4	5.6	11.4	9.7
Uncertain						
3. Untrustworthiness	6.7	4.2	4.0**	3.3		
4. Disobedience	5.8	4.3	4.9	3.7		
5. Circles, cheating	18.1	5.1	13.2**	3.8		
6. Lie Test	14.6	3.2	14.5	4.3		

Note.—N = 22 at each level.

* Indicates a *t* test of the difference between the score at this age and that at the next earlier age is significant at $p < .10$.

** $p < .05$.

*** $p < .01$.

mean nonspecific, and movement) and the one psychophysiological variable (mean nonspecifics) which become associated with the moral variables at Grade 6 but were not at Grade 1 are of the asymptotic or terminating development variety. This suggests that at Grade 1 individual variability on the same measure primarily reflects the child's progress in developing psychomotor ability rather than what one might call "personality." For example, by Grade 6 all children have the psychomotor maturity to make short RTs; variations in mean RT may be primarily reflective of stability of attention rather than psychomotor ability. Thus, in Grade 1 mean RT shows some correlation with age variability ($r = .25$), while at Grade 6 it does not. Similarly, in Grade 1 mean RT is not correlated with stability of RT (r between mean and standard deviation $= .06$, between mean and increase $= .20$), while in Grade 6 it is (r

between mean and variability $= .45$, between mean and increase $= .54$).[6] This is presumably because young children show characteristically long RTs; the fastest reactions they give are regularly slower than those of older children or adults. By the time children reach the sixth grade, their fastest reactions are delivered with the same speed as those of adults. Now the interpretation of the performance of a slow-reacting child takes on a different meaning; his average slowness of RT is interpreted as mostly due to variation away from his optimum. Hence, RT M and variation become correlated, and, further, it becomes more and more likely that RT M will increasingly reflect an instability of attention. A similar interpretation holds for the movement response. At Grade 6 anyone can hold his finger still, so that variations in movement artifacts are due to inattention rather than sheer psychomotor inability. Individual variability in movement is correlated with age variation at Grade 1 ($r = -.34$), but not at Grade 6 ($r = -.09$). Accordingly, it is not surprising that movement relates more clearly to both morality and attention measures at Grade 6 than at Grade 1.

A grossly similar interpretation holds for mean nonspecifics. These are correlated with age at Grade 1 ($r = .44$), but not at Grade 6 ($r = .14$). Evidence on age specificity of nonspecifics as an indicator of impulsivity is discussed in White and Grim (1962).

While the psychomotor variables first correlating with moral control in Grade 6 are mainly asymptic, Table 6 indicates that the major psychomotor variables correlating with moral control at both ages are continuously developing variables. These variables are RT variability and RT increase. It should be noted that these variables are second-order measures of stability or consistency of performance rather than first-order measures of performance. It was claimed in the last paragraph that the asymptotic variables relating to morality at Grade 6 did so because they then began to be determined by the stability components now termed "continuously developing" rather than by the gross psychomotor maturation factors determining them at Grade 1. Hartshorne and May (1928, 1929, 1930) reported evidence suggesting a continuously developing factor of stability or consistency of cheating, distinct from the amount of cheating. While the amount of cheating did not decline from ages 10 to 14, the individual's standard deviation of cheating, a measure of inconsistency, did decline. In conjunction with the factor analysis, these considerations suggest a slowly developing factor of stability of attention and of ego control reflecting both personality and developmental differences among children. The present findings are consistent with a number of observational

[6] This age shift in relation between mean and stability measures is not due to artifacts of the RT measure. At Grade 6, mean RT is correlated with stability of nonspecifics (with nonspecifics increase $r = .50$) but it is not at Grade 1 ($r = .07$).

studies indicating regular trends of age development in attentional stability and duration throughout childhood (Bertrand, 1925; Bott, 1928; Moyer & Gilmer, 1955; Van Alstyne, 1932).

DISCUSSION

The finding of moderate to high correlations between measures of morality and measures of attention is one of a number of findings (Kohlberg, 1964) which indicate that individual differences in moral behavior are influenced by ego-control factors operating in a range of tasks far wider than those which usually seem to call into play distinctively moral rules or sanction. To the extent that moral behavior is influenced by factors which the authors have called "task conformity," "inner stability," and "restlessness," it is not a product of "conscience" or "superego" as those entities are usually assumed to operate. The present study, like others reviewed elsewhere (Kohlberg, 1964), indicates low to moderate correlations among experimental cheating measures ($r = .27-.66$); the three cheating tests correlate about as well with one another as they do with RT variability ($r = .40-.56$). In other words, if attention and ego factors are partialed out, the general correlations among cheating tests approach zero.

This conclusion may be more clearly stated in terms of the factor analyses which did not separate moral rating or tests as factors distinct from psychomotor and psychophysiological variables. Attentional variables load about equally with the honesty tests on all factors. Furthermore, the attention variables help to hold together or to give common meaning to the experimental and the rating measures of morality. While experimental and rating measures of morality are correlated to only a very low degree, the factor analysis suggests that they tap different, but related, aspects of common attentional dispositions. Factors 1 and 2 are broadly similar in terms of representing psychomotor or attentional stability, but the two factors differ in that one relates these variables to rated morality and the other to experimental measures of cheating. These findings suggest that honesty does not depend upon special moral personality factors (e.g., guilt, anticipation of punishment) called into play only when honesty is an issue to the subject, since it is doubtful that RT tasks evoke moral or honesty concerns.

The attention-morality correlations have been interpreted as reflecting primarily the influence of ego-attentional forces upon cheating, rather than as reflecting the influence of a general sociomoral trait of conscientiousness upon performance in experimental RT tasks. In large part the authors' interpretations of attention as the causally prior variable are based on the fact that attention appears to be a more situationally general variable than moral conformity. As an example, testers' ratings of stable attention to preschoolers in a Stanford-Binet situation were found to correlate in the high 60s with teachers' ratings of classroom attentiveness, and both correlated significantly with the experimental measure (RT variance) used in the present study (Krebs, 1967; Kohlberg & Jensen, 1966). In contrast, teacher ratings of morality correlated poorly and often nonsignificantly with one another and with experimental measures of honesty, and those experimental measures correlated poorly with one another (Hartshorne & May, 1928, 1929, 1930, findings of the present study). Associated with the greater generality of the attention variable is its clearer and earlier emergence as a test which is stable over time. Rank order of infants on EKG indexes of attentiveness has been found to predict significantly the rank order of the same children at age 2 on rated stability of attention in a free-play situation (Kagan, unpublished finding). Not only is there no evidence for the early emergence of an honesty trait, but even at age 12 the 10-month test-rated correlations on any given test are low, varying from .30 to .60 (Jones, 1936). Over longer periods of time, moral trait ratings are substantially lower (evidence reviewed in Kohlberg, 1964). It is likely that the greater generality and stability of attention measures is in turn related to the fact that attention variables show more clear and regular age-developmental trends than do moral variables. For these reasons, it appears more plausible, then, to center interpretation of the morality-attention factors around the more general, stable, and developmentally regular trait of attention than upon moral traits as such.

Why should a general attentional ability influence cheating behavior or resistance to temptation? Customarily, moral psychology has viewed cheating behavior as the quantitative resolution of a conflict between opposing needs or values, with the outcome being determined by the relative strength of internalized values not to cheat (fear of punishment, anticipation of guilt) and of the needs aroused by the incentive or reward attained by cheating in the situation. Attention does not seem to determine directly either set of needs. In fact, however, the temptation to cheat in the ordinary experimental situation is less an arousal of an intense drive than an interesting distracting stimulus. In experimental cheating situations the experimenter assigns a task and then creates an unusal opportunity to short-cut the task without surveillance. Cheating in these situations is usually either a short-cutting of a monotonous task or an attending to illicit novel and interesting cues in the task.[7] In other words, experimental honesty may reflect the ability to stick to boring tasks when more interesting and novel ways of doing the task (cheating) arise as distracting possibilities. In line with this interpretation is the finding that

---

[7] In our cheating situations, distractibility might be manifested by wondering, "What would happen if I opened my eyes?" "I wonder if other kids are opening their [requiring opening one's own] eyes," etc.

adolescents high on the present measures of distractibility and cheating are also higher on measures of divergent thinking, that is, on associating in terms of the novel and unusual (Libby, unpublished data). Also in line with this interpretation is the finding that high-distractible (high RT variable) children are more likely to report that they thought about cheating after temptation even if they did not cheat (Krebs, 1967). In other words, stable attention seems to promote honesty primarily by leading to a higher threshold to distracting thoughts of the opportunity to cheat.

The interpretation of the morality-psychomotor stability factors just advanced interprets these factors as representing a slowly developing cognitive-voluntary ability of sustained attention. There is another interpretation of these factors which is possible, however. In this interpretation the psychomotor-moral factors would represent inhibition of emotional or psychophysiological arousal rather than voluntary-ideational attention. In support of this second interpretation, it has been suggested that emotional arousal is reflected in frequency of nonspecifics. A significant positive correlation of .42 was found between cheating and frequency of nonspecifics in Grade 6, though not at Grade 1. Anxiety or arousal may also be associated with poor inhibition of motoric expression (fidgetiness or nervous movements). A significant positive correlation between movement artifacts and cheating was found at Grade 6 ($r = .48$) though not at Grade 1. Teachers' ratings of untrustworthiness related positively with movement at Grade 1 ($r = .41$) as well as at Grade 6 ($r = .40$).

While the findings just mentioned give some plausibility to an "emotional inhibition" interpretation of the first two factors, there are reasons for centering their interpretation upon ideational-volitional attention rather than emotional inhibition as such. In the first place, it should be noted that a tie-up between emotional lability and disobedience cheating would be theoretically quite ambiguous. In an emotional interpretation of moral behavior, moral action is the resultant of the balance between the two opposing emotional forces of temptation-arousal and anxiety-guilt. It is not clear why a general emotional inhibition factor should inhibit only motivation toward deviant, as opposed to conforming, behavior. Emotional inhibition in the RT situation does not represent inhibition of arousal by the temptation to cheat.

In the second place, present findings on basal skin resistance level are inconsistent with this interpretation. Low basal skin resistance is a traditional indicator of anxiety or arousal. At Grade 1, however, low skin resistance is significantly correlated ($r = .48$) with honesty, not cheating, while the two variables are uncorrelated at Grade 6.

In the third place, while some "arousal-emotionality" *level* measures do correlate with cheating, they do not correlate as consistently or as well with cheating as do the *stability* measures of the same variables. As an example, the stability measure of nonspecifics increase is a better definer of the factors at both ages than is the level measure of mean nonspecifics. If "emotionality" were the relevant factor, initially frequent nonspecifics should be as relevant as final nonspecifics to a control factor. What seems relevant is not emotionality but the wandering of attention, with an increase of nonspecifics representing increased attending to task-irrelevant internal or external stimuli.[8]

In the fourth place, an emotional interpretation seems questionable since the best definers of the control factors are not psychophysiological "emotional" measures, but voluntary psychomotor RT variables.

In the fifth place, an emotional stability or inhibition interpretation of the psychomotor-moral stability factor seems less plausible than an attentional interpretation because the variables which define it continue development until adulthood, suggesting a complex and cognitive type of development. If the factor were an emotional inhibition factor, its development would appear more likely to rest upon earlier developing maturational and socialization influences.

In the sixth place, the authors' attentional interpretation of the psychomotor-moral stability factor coincides with the findings with similar measures in schizophrenics as summarized and interpreted by Shakow (1962). Schizophrenics, who are defective in a number of the psychomotor and psychophysiological variables defining the authors' stability factor, cannot be characterized as generally emotionally overreactive (or even underreactive). Instead, they appear to be unable to maintain a set to discriminate between relevant and irrelevant stimuli in a task, that is, to maintain attention.

In stressing an attentional interpretation of these data, it is clear that the authors have drawn near to the older, introspective psychology of the moral will. The notion of will is introduced by common sense where action does not seem to be in line with minimizing tension (or with expression of the strongest of two conflicting impulses). According to James (1890): "If a brief definition of ideal or moral action were required, none better would fit the appearances than this: it is action in the line of the greatest resistance [p. 549]." James went on to account for moral will in terms of attentional processes:

> We reach the heart of volition when we ask by what process it is that the thought of any given object comes to prevail stable in the mind.

---

[8] The same may be said of the basal measures. While high initial basal correlates with high cheating at Grade 1, so does decrease in basal over time. In other words, a high terminal basal rate is related to high rather than low control or cheating, and relates negatively to increase in nonspecifics. Therefore, the correlation of nonspecifics increase to low moral control cannot well be attributed to an inability to emotionally adapt or habituate over time (reduce response) to the general task situation, but only as an increase in bored inattentiveness.

Attention with effort is all that any case of volition implies. The essential achievement of will is to *attend* to a difficult object and hold it fast before the mind.

This discussion has treated moral behavior as a product of the development of attention-will factors rather than as a product of internalized moral values as usually conceived. Evidence is offered elsewhere (Krebs, 1967; Kohlberg, 1968) suggesting that cognitive maturity of verbal moral values or judgment interacts with the attentional-volitional capacities discussed to determine cheating conduct. The formation of fully autonomous or internalized moral values prohibiting cheating is a late development. Children at Grade 1, and even at Grade 6, are typically able to advance few internalized reasons for not cheating, in contrast to college-aged subjects, who are more aware of values of equity, trust, and contract involved in cheating. The role of attention-will factors in controlling cheating appears to be maximal at the intermediate or conventional level of maturity of moral judgment, which is most frequent among Grade 6 subjects. Grade 6 children at a principled or autonomous level of moral judgment do not cheat, whether or not they are distractible. Grade 6 children who have not yet developed conventional moral values tend to cheat, whether or not they are distractible. (Indeed, they are more likely to cheat if not "distracted" into conforming.) Grade 6 children at the intermediate or conventional level tend to cheat only if they are distractible or readily tempted (Krebs, 1967). The heavy determination of moral behavior by nonmoral attentional factors found in the present study, then, is probably maximal at Grade 6 when moral values have been partially developed but have not become fully mature or autonomous.[9]

SUMMARY

22 1st-grade and 22 6th-grade children were administered measures of attention based on a reaction time (RT) task involving varying preparatory intervals with associated GSR measures, and experimental and teacher-rating measures of resistance to temptation (RTT) to cheating. In both groups sig-

---

[9] It is possible that lack of clear definition of the experimental honest-attention factor (Factor 2) at Grade 1 is due to this fact, that is, to the fact that the majority of the Grade 1 subjects are not yet at the conventional moral level with regard to cheating, rather than to the artifacts in our Grade 1 experimental honesty measure previously discussed. However, by Grade 2 a quite large proportion of our favored population is at the conventional level of moral judgment in the sense of valuing conformity to rules and authority somewhat independently of sanctions (Krebs, 1965). Accordingly, we have preferred an interpretation stressing the matching of factors at the two ages. In any case, the Grade 1 children have reached a sufficient degree of conventional moral orientation for the emergence of a general conformity factor, Factor 1.

nificant correlations were found between good performance on attention measures and RTT. The highest correlation (r's = .61, .59) was between high variability (SD) of RT and high cheating. Orthogonally rotated factor analyses indicated 3 similar factors at each grade. The 1st factor, task conformity, included psychomotor efficiency and teacher RTT rating variables. The 2nd factor, inner stability, included experimental RTT and psychomotor stability variables. The 3rd factor, restlessness, included nonspecific GSR and RTT rating variables. It is noteworthy that attention (psychomotor) and moral variables loaded on each factor rather than being separated by the factor analysis. The relations of the psychomotor to the moral variables at the 2 ages seemed to depend on the age developmental course of the former, relations being best when the variables represented attention rather than maturation of psychomotor skill. An ego-strength rather than a superego-strength interpretation of moral behavior is advanced to fit the findings. It is suggested that moral temptation distractors from task performance are psychologically related to the ordinary distractors of task performance. The interpretation advanced is James' (1890) notion that, "The essential achievement of will is to attend to a difficult object . . . [p. 549]."

49. THE ORIGIN OF SELF-CRITICISM

Justin Aronfreed

Should all the natural and especially contrived conditions for man's dream of a perfect utopia ever be known, high on the listing would surely be knowledge of detailed procedures that would permit the individual to internalize the demands and rules for living harmoniously with his fellow men. A concomitant and very probably a precursor of this development of conscience and ideals, which looms so large in the human ascent toward moral "maturity," is self-criticism. As pointed out in the following review by Aronfreed, self-criticism is often first seen in the very young preverbal child who slaps his own hand as he is reaching toward a forbidden object. It has often also been observed in older children who verbalize some variant of "I shouldn't be doing this" as they proceed to engage in parentally or societally forbidden actions. It is very commonly seen among older children (and adults!) after the execution of some forbidden act and the resulting self-recrimination, "I'm a very bad person for having done that."

Aronfreed sees the learning of self-criticism as complexly but closely associated with the individual's anticipatory anxiety. The motivating and signaling functions of social punishment are viewed as essential to the acquisition of self-criticism. This report is a forerunner of Aronfreed's later and more comprehensive discussion of moral development in his recent book. However, the guidelines to his more integrated theory are clearly anticipated in the following discussion.

SOURCE. Adapted and abridged from Justin Aronfreed, "The Origin of Self-Criticism," *Psychological Review*, 1964, Vol. 71, 193–218. (With permission of the author and the American Psychological Association.)

The reproduction of the punitive reactions of socializing agents is a readily observable phenomenon in the behavior of young children. Children often show punitive responses to their own actions, and they sometimes recreate their parents' disciplinary actions in exact motor detail. As language and cognition increasingly take the place of action, social punishment becomes most extensively and persistently reproduced in the form of verbal and evaluative responses. It is very common, for example, to see a young child react to its misdemeanors by saying aloud to itself: "You're a bad boy!" or "That was bad!" Such responses become more covert as the child's symbolic equipment expands. But people do continue beyond childhood to frequently direct toward themselves (and toward others) various components of the social punishment to which they have been previously exposed. These self-punitive reactions belong to a class of behavior whose social learning represents one important type of imitation or identification. They are also of considerable interest because they seem rather paradoxical when approached in terms of our conventional concepts of motivation and reinforcement.

The evaluative judgment of one's own actions has been traditionally regarded as the foundation of internalized conduct (Freud, 1936, Ch. 8; Hartshorne & May, 1928; Piaget, 1948; Sears, Maccoby, & Levin, 1957, Ch. 10). Many self-evaluative responses must be derived, of course, from social learning based on reward. But the tendency of children to independently replicate the punitive and prohibitive functions of socialization makes a distinct contribution, and one that is at least comparable with the effects of social reward, to the distant relationship that human behavior often bears to what would seem like more inherently preferred responses. This replicative effect of social punishment is clearly displayed in the internalized dispositions which lead people to impose upon themselves both restraint and unpleasant consequences of their own actions. In many contemporary psychological conceptions of internalization (Miller et al., 1960, Ch. 5; Sears et al., 1957, Ch. 10; Whiting & Child, 1953, Ch. 11), self-criticism is viewed as the mediator of other reactions to transgression, and also of control over the occurrence of transgression, when such responses can be elicited in the absence of direct external surveillance. It is, in fact, commonly assumed that the internalized consequences of social punishment require the operation of explicit standards or values which have been adopted from those of a model.

There is actually considerable evidence to question the assumption that the adoption of a model's values or standards is requisite to internalization. The casual observation of the first appearance of internalization in preverbal children makes it particularly obvious that internalized reactions to socially punished acts do not necessarily imply the presence of self-critical cognition.

Even when they do not yet have the equipment for social evaluation, young children frequently show signs of anxiety and anxiety-reducing maneuvers following a transgression that has not been apparently open to external observation. Some recent work with dogs (reported by R. L. Solomon in Mowrer, 1960b, pp. 399–404) also suggests that internalization does not require a highly developed cognitive base. Moreover, numerous studies have indicated that internalized responses to transgression show great variability, among both children and adults, in the nature and extent of the cognitive mediating processes on which they rest (Allinsmith, 1960; Aronfreed, 1960; Kohlberg, 1963; Whiting, 1959). Even self-corrective responses such as confession or reparation, have been found to occur frequently without evaluative standards being applied to a transgression (Aronfreed, 1961). Nevertheless, self-criticism surely deserves special attention among the internalized consequences of social punishment. In addition to its significance for the phenomenon of identification, it also provides verbal and cognitive signals through which other social responses can be mediated with a persistence and generalization that would be impossible if they were forced to depend only on the immediate stimuli of the transgression itself and of its external context.

ACQUISITION

Actions (and, sometimes, intentions or other intrinsic precursors of action) may be defined as transgressions to the extent that they have been followed, in the child's experience, by any form of social punishment. Social punishment includes, of course, not only the application of concrete noxious stimuli, as in physical punishment, but also withdrawal of affection and a wide variety of other kinds of aversive events. When an action is defined as a transgression, through its aversive social consequences for the child, its response-produced cues become signals for a conditioned drive state that can be given the general designation of anxiety. The anxiety may have, however, qualitative variations which reflect its cognitive context and possibly the nature of the original punishment. It is the invariant motivational source of the child's suppression of transgression, and also of a number of different responses to the occurrence of transgression, all of which share in common their instrumental value for reducing the anxiety. The instrumental status of these responses is derived from the attachment of anxiety attenuation to their discriminant stimulus properties, as a result of certain significant reinforcement contingencies which are present in the socialization process. The responses may be said to be internalized to the extent that the anxiety which motivates them has come to be directly elicited by transgression and independent of either external punishment or social cues which portend punishment. Such instrumental responses are quite variable with respect to the precise patterns of learning through which they become self-reinforcing for the child. Recent studies in the experimental induction of self-criticism and reparation suggest, for example, that these two reactions to transgression are different in the specific contingencies required for their acquisition and in their dependence on evaluative cognition (Aronfreed, 1963; Aronfreed, Cutick, & Fagen, 1963). They cannot be regarded as alternative expressions of a unitary evaluative and punitive agency such as "conscience" or "super-ego."

The anxiety-reducing value of some internalized responses to transgression, such as confession or reparation, may be acquired because the responses themselves originally received direct external reinforcement through the prevention or arrest of punishment (or through the removal of social cues which portended punishment). But other responses can produce cues to which anxiety reduction has become attached even when the responses have not occurred during the initial socialization process. The most prevalent instances of such responses are those in which the child reproduces components of its previous punishments. Under the ordinary circumstances of child rearing, many components of relatively brief social punishments are sufficiently close to the anxiety termination that follows them to take on substantial power as cues for the reduction of the anticipatory anxiety that has already become directly associated with transgression. The anxiety-reducing function of these components of punishment is central to an understanding of self-criticism. Quite aside from its cognitive requirements, self-criticism is a replication of the verbal medium of punishment. When a child's punishment incorporates verbal criticism—the application of verbal labels or standards to its behavior—the criticism, like any component of punishment, may attain the significance of a cue signaling the attenuation of the antecedent anxiety that occurs in the interval between transgression and punishment. Following subsequent transgressions, the child itself can make the critical response and thus provide itself with anxiety-reducing cues. The cue aspects of the self-critical response, initially presented in the punitive behavior of a model, thus acquire reinforcement value through their conjunction with anxiety reduction, without the response having to be first overtly emitted by the child and then externally reinforced. A component of punishment becomes preferred to the experience of anticipatory anxiety.

This description of the learning of self-criticism specifies that it is established as the consequence rather than the source of the negative effect that we experience following a transgression. The anxiety-reducing function of reproduced punishment is sometimes compellingly visible in young children who, even though they are unaware of being observed, may show evidence of acute discomfort when they misbehave and then apparent relief after they have criticized or punished themselves. The introspective perception that the self-critical response sometimes precedes unpleasant feelings may be phenomenologically misleading if it is used to judge the validity of the mechanism of acquisition set forth here. The response, once firmly acquired on an instrumental basis, may begin to occur directly to the cues of transgression with a latency shorter than that with which anxiety reaches substantial intensity. Its maintenance would continue to be dependent on anxiety reduction, however, since the response would tend to be repeated once the anxiety had attained sufficient strength. Recent studies (Brady, Schreiner, Geller, & Kling, 1954; Brush, Brush, & Solomon, 1955) emphasize the importance of distinguishing the position of anxiety in the acquisition of an aversive response from its position in the maintenance of the response, and Solomon and Wynne (1954) have analyzed this problem specifically in terms of latencies.

The learning of self-criticism embraces, then, two processes: (a) the attachment of anxiety to the response-produced cues of transgression through their repeated association with punishment; (b) an accrual of the intrinsic reinforcement value of the self-critical response through the inclusion of its cue properties within external punishment in such a way as to make them contiguous with the attenuation of anxiety. The use of two distinct processes to account for the establishment of aversive responses is not uncommon (Mowrer, 1960a, Ch. 3-7; Solomon & Brush, 1956). But the second process described here has certain features which are not ordinarily found in the experimental literature on aversive learning. The learning of an aversive response is typically effected by having the response first occur and then receive direct external reinforcement through avoidance of, or escape from, punishment. In contrast, self-criticism is representative of a class of responses whose acquisition of functional value does not require either that they occur overtly or that they have discriminable effects upon external reinforcing events. Instead, their value is accumulated as their cue properties are repeatedly presented independently, through the external social behavior of a model, in a temporal position that permits them to serve as signals for the reduction of an anticipatory state of anxiety. The child's subsequent emission of these responses therefore becomes immediately self-reinforcing upon their first occurrence. Support for such a conception is found in demonstrations that neutral stimuli may acquire either motivating or reinforcing properties, according to their temporal association with aversive states, while relevant instrumental responses are not being made by the organism (Gleitman, 1955; Montgomery & Galton, 1955; Solomon & Turner, 1962).

There are some convincing indications that direct instrumental learning can bring an organism to make responses which correspond to those of a model (Church, 1957; Darby & Riopelle, 1959; Miller & Dollard, 1941).

And Hill (1960) has recently specifically attempted to describe the learning of self-criticism by using punishment avoidance or escape as the external reinforcement of an initially overt response. But one would expect behavior that is established through direct social reinforcement, even when it happens to be similar to the behavior of a model, to have the kind of latitude usually permitted to responses whose instrumental consequences are originally externally defined. Social reinforcement is not ordinarily so selective as to be contingent on an extremely restricted form of response. Self-criticism, however, has the earmarks of the truly imitative response. It reproduces fairly precisely the stimulus properties of a model, and thus allows a strong presumption that its reinforcement is rather narrowly bound to those properties.

It also seems implausible for other reasons that direct external reinforcement makes any substantial contribution to the initial emergence of self-criticism. Of course, the overt verbalization of the response by young children, once it has been established, might result in the withholding of punishment or even in reward by their parents. But socializing agents can hardly consistently reinforce a response that is generally not apparent in behavior (indeed, they must often be administering punishment following self-criticism, whether it be implicit or overt). In view of the very limited opportunity for such a contingency that one sees in naturalistic child rearing, it would certainly seem a cumbersome and lengthy process to externally reinforce a tendency in the child to reconstruct a component of its previous punishment in order to avoid the delivery of punishment that is externally imminent.

Anyone who has observed the vigor and suddenness with which self-criticism characteristically becomes observable in young children cannot escape the inference that the response already has considerable strength at its first verbalization. This prepotency makes it necessary to go beyond the assertion that the stimulus properties of the response attain anxiety-reducing value without its overt occurrence. We must also assume that the critical label is implicitly emitted by the child during the original punishment learning. The response would then, before it became overt, have already been strengthened through the reinforcement value gradually attached to its intrinsic cue aspects. Given the cognitive capacity of children, the presence of the label in their response repertoire, and the possibly close connection between the receptive and productive functions of language, we might well expect their covert repetition of any label used by a socializing agent.

Finally, it should be noted that this conception of the learning of self-criticism touches upon an issue of more general significance. There are currently a number of inconsistent experimental findings on the question of whether stimuli can become positive reinforcers through their association with the termination of aversive states. The phenomenon has apparently been observed in some animal studies, under the appropriate conditions (Buchanan, 1958; Goodson & Brownstein, 1955; Montgomery & Galton, 1955), but other studies indicate primarily the difficulty of its demonstration in the laboratory (Littman & Wade, 1955; Mowrer & Aiken, 1954; Nefzger, 1957). Some of these experiments, however, do not really duplicate the conditions of social learning under which we could expect to observe such an effect. As Beck (1961) has recently pointed out, attempts to test the reinforcing properties of stimuli which have been contiguous with termination of anxiety or punishment may not be successful if they are carried out in situations in which neither anxiety nor pain is present. The acquisition of self-punitive responses does depend, of course, on the presence of anxiety during both socialization and subsequent occasions when the child itself can reproduce the components of punishment.

Naturalistic and Experimental Socialization

The view that self-criticism is acquired because it attenuates an aversive state does not require that the external criticism of socializing agents occur at a particular point in the course of punishment. What is crucial to the child's reproduction of punishment is the temporal position of its components with respect to onset and termination of anxiety, and not their position with respect to onset and termination of the punishment itself. The usual duration and intensity of social punishment to such that even a component at its onset might acquire some anxiety-reducing significance, provided only that there is sufficient time after the transgression for the arousal of anxiety. When children are quite young and under close parental control, punishment often follows fairly quickly upon transgression. But it does not follow so quickly as to prevent an interval of anticipatory anxiety, particularly since the anxiety comes to be elicited by the incipient precursors of transgression and not merely by its commitment. And, as children become older and more mobile, the interval between transgression and punishment tends to lengthen. Consequently, despite the great variability of parents in their timing and ordering of components of punishment, any component could assume some anxiety-reducing value.

To the extent, then, that parental punishment induces internalized anxiety and is administered in a verbal and cognitive medium, some acquisition of self-criticism by the child would seem inevitable. A close examination of the learning of self-criticism therefore requires artificial conditions under which the verbal components of social punishment are varied in their anxiety-reducing significance. The critical labels would presumably not become anxiety-reducing, for example, if they were to follow immediately upon the intrinsic cues of transgression (so that anticipatory anxiety would be negligible) and were consistently the first element in a punitive reaction of some duration. Conversely, one would expect the labels to have maximal anxiety-reducing value if they were always to occur at the termination of punishment. The acquisition of self-criticism under experimental conditions might also be facilitated if the onset of punishment (but not the critical labels) were close to the completion of transgression. Such a temporal contingency probably occurs quite often in the early phases of socialization, when the young child's behavioral limitations make it subject to fairly immediate punishment following forbidden behavior, and it may make a potent contribution to the anxiety that motivates self-punitive responses. Animal studies (Davitz, Mason, Mowrer, & Viek, 1957; Kamin, 1959) have indicated that short intervals between response-produced cues and the occurrence of punishment facilitate the acquisition of anxiety-reducing responses. These temporal variations do not occur with any consistency, of course, in the behavior of parents. But they can be brought under control in experimental situations.

An experimental induction of self-criticism ought further to be enhanced if the model's critical labels coincide with the termination of the response-produced cues associated with the transgression. In a naturalistic setting, parental punishment and criticism often interfere with an ongoing transgression, and thus eliminate its intrinsic cues and the anticipatory anxiety already attached to them. The child's reproduction of cue components of punishment might well be supported by this effect, since responses have been shown to have an advantage in learning when their stimulus properties coincide with the termination of a conditioned aversive stimulus (Brush et al., 1955; Church, Brush, & Solomon, 1956; Mowrer & Lamoreaux, 1942). A rapid acquisition of value by the critical labels of a socializing agent, when they coincide with termination of transgression, might also reflect the absence of any delay of the reinforcement represented in anxiety reduction. When the anxiety-reducing significance of a component of punishment becomes discriminable to a child, there is no delay between the parent's use of that component and the occurrence of anxiety reduction. Neutral stimuli have been shown to attain more powerful secondary reinforcing properties when there is a short interval between their presentation and the original reinforcement (Jenkins, 1950; Schoenfeld, Antonitis, & Bersh, 1950).

There is one other feature of naturalistic socialization whose effect upon the internalized consequences of punishment is difficult to assess, because it is relatively restricted in variation and inseparable from the total parent-child relationship. It is the parental nurturance and affection that serves as the background for punishment learning. Many psychologists have felt that the gratifications and rewards provided by parents are an essential ingredient of the child's adoption of their behavior and values in any form. Freud (1936, Ch. 8), for example, regarded the motivation to reproduce a loving and rewarding parental model as one of the major sources of identification. And other theorists (Bronfenbrenner, 1960; Miller et al., 1960, Ch. 5;

Sears et al., 1957, Ch. 10; Whiting & Child, 1953, Ch. 11) have attempted to extend this motivation to the internalization of social punishment.

The most detailed rationale for the generalized effects of nurturance upon internalization is found in the work of Sears et al. (1957, Ch. 10) and of Whiting and Child (1953, Ch. 11). The child is presumed to be broadly motivated to identify with its parents in order to reproduce the pleasurable experience associated with the stimulus aspects of their behavior. In making responses like those of the parents, particularly when they are absent or have withdrawn affection, the child provides itself with stimuli which have become powerful secondary reinforcers through their conjunction with parental rewards and gratifications. Thus, the child's application of the parents' critical evaluative responses to its own actions represents, according to this view, an instance of a more general tendency to reproduce many kinds of parental behavior. And when the child critically evaluates its own behavior, it experiences unpleasant feelings, just as when it was previously exposed to external criticism; that is, self-criticism is regarded as the original internalized source, rather than the consequence of the anxiety that follows a transgression.

MAINTENANCE

One of the remarkable characteristics of the internalized derivatives of social learning is their persistent maintenance in the absence of external surveillance and reinforcement. Aversive responses, in particular, can often be quite resistant to extinction (Miller, 1959; Solomon & Brush, 1956), and one would expect that self-criticism, a response that is even initially intrinsically reinforced, might easily become independent of its original conditions of learning. As has already been pointed out, the punishment and criticism of parents sometimes follow fairly rapidly upon occurrence of a response to which internalized anxiety is to be attached. Yet once the child's anxiety comes to precede its punishment, certain cue components of the punishment become associated with anxiety reduction. Correspondingly, in the experimental paradigm with labeling at termination of punishment, onset of punishment was immediately coincident with onset of the transgression signal, but the (external) presentation of the critical label directly coincided with the signal's termination. Such temporal relationships among the cues to which anxiety is attached, the occurrence of punishment, and the stimulus properties of aversive responses, appear to contribute as much to the maintenance of these responses as to their acquisition (Brush et al., 1955; Church et al., 1956).

Part of the relative insensitivity that self-criticism can show to changes in external conditions may be a function of the resistance to extinction of the intense anxiety attached to some transgressions (Bitterman & Holtzman,

1952; Solomon & Wynne, 1954). The actions around which parents hope to inculcate the most permanent and generalized internalization are those which they are likely to punish most severely. The failure of anxiety to disappear, when apparently deprived of its original support in the form of explicit punishment, may also follow from a kind of inconsistent reinforcement related to generalization of perceived punitive events. Children may perceive punitive implications even where punishment is not intended, because they can so easily assimilate both social and impersonal events to their experience of the wide spectrum of punitive capacities previously represented in the behavior of socializing agents. In the ecology of interaction between parents and children, inconsistency of perceived punishment would be inevitable. And even beyond childhood, the most infrequent application of real or perceived punishment would be sufficient to interfere with the extinction of internalized anxiety.

While internalized reactions to transgression do persist in the absence of predictable external punishment, their endurance when followed by punishment perhaps even more effectively shows that their reinforcement is not tied to external consequences. Children are often punished for their actions despite the intervening implicit or overt presence of self-criticism. The cue properties of their self-critical responses would, under these circumstances, precede external punishment. They would therefore no longer have quite the same signal value, with respect to onset and termination of anxiety, which they initially had as a component of punishment. The anxiety-reducing status of self-criticism could not be sustained under such conditions, if it actually remained dependent on the temporal relationship of the critical labels to the external events which originally marked anxiety reduction. Moreover, the continued experience of social punishment affords children many opportunities to observe that internalized anxiety can be terminated without their criticizing or punishing themselves, though not in a way that is equally under their control. It is possible, of course, that the irregular presence of punishment serves primarily to strengthen the anxiety that motivates self-criticism. A number of studies with animals have indicated that punishment of aversive responses heightens their resistance to extinction (Gwinn, 1949; Sidman, Herrnstein, & Conrad, 1957; Solomon & Wynne, 1954). But whatever the effects of external punishment upon the self-critical response, once it is established, it seems necessary to attribute its persistent maintenance to the anxiety-reduction attached to its intrinsically produced cues.

SOME FURTHER THEORETICAL IMPLICATIONS

Reproduction of Punishment

The experimental literature on punishment learning typically centers on the conditioning of anxiety (or "aversiveness") to the organism's own response cues, and the consequences of punishment are indexed in the suppression of the punished behavior (Dinsmoor, 1954; Estes, 1944; Miller, 1959; Mowrer & Viek, 1948). The inhibition of transgressions would be, of course, one of the derivatives of their definition through social punishment. But self-criticism provides a response for reducing the anxiety that follows the commission of a transgression. The response does not require reinforcement by avoidance or termination of external punishment, and it actually reproduces stimulus events which have been previously part of that punishment. We are confronted, then, with an anxiety-reducing response whose acquisition is contingent on the prior association of its stimulus properties with the presence rather than with the absence of punishment.

It is not really paradoxical that self-criticism can be acquired, and often permanently maintained, despite the fact that it reproduces punishment. Aversive responses have frequently been shown to be at least as sensitive to anxiety reduction as they are to punishment avoidance, when these two outcomes are partially separated, and sometimes they seem relatively impervious to their punitive consequences, (Gwinn, 1949; Sidman & Boren, 1957; Solomon & Wynne, 1954). It is possible, in fact, to interpret certain studies of both human and animal subjects (D'Amato & Gumenik, 1960; Farber, 1948; Maier, 1949) as indicating that, under high anticipatory anxiety and with no easily available avoidance response, subjects will move in the direction of external punishment because of its anxiety-attenuating significance. In a similar way, the anxiety that motivates self-criticism is initially dependent on the motivating properties of punishment, while the reinforcement of the response is dependent on its replication of the anxiety-reducing signal properties of punishment. Self-punitive responses are, therefore, clearly not to be regarded as having been originally learned as avoidance responses. Their self-reinforcing character is acquired on the basis of anxiety-reduction as the "primary reinforcement."

It is interesting to note that Freud (1936, Ch. 8) saw anxiety reduction as the function of children's adoption of the punitive or threatening behavior of a model, and that its role has also been previously suggested in concepts such as "identification with the aggressor" (A. Freud, 1946, Ch. 9) and "defensive identification" (Mowrer, 1950, Ch. 21). Certainly it is not difficult to perceive that the mechanism of reinforcement in the learning of self-criticism may serve as the general mechanism for what may be called identification through aversive learning—that is, for the acquisition of any response in which, without the benefit of external reinforcement, the individual directs toward himself the socially punitive behavior that he has previously experienced from without.

Further research on the anxiety-reducing properties of social punishment, and on their imitative reproduction, might well give attention to the intensity of punishment. There is no reason to assume that the punishment to be reproduced must be less "painful" than the antecedent anxiety. Nevertheless, when punishment is very severe, whatever decrement of anticipatory anxiety attaches to its cue properties could be overshadowed by the increment of aversive stimulation from its drive properties. Experimental socialization paradigms might be used to compare the conditions required for the learning of self-criticism with those required for the self-directed replication of nonverbal components of punishment, some of which would be more inherently unpleasant than a verbal label. Such paradigms might also be devised so as to suggest the theoretical extensions necessary to account for the child's learning to direct its reproduction of punishment toward others. They could further be used to examine other relationships of timing and magnitude among components of punishment. Presumably, any component of punishment could assume anxiety-reducing value, provided that it follows some minimal internalized anxiety. But the breadth of the phenomenon may be limited by the duration and relative severity of the remaining punishment that follows a given component. Verbal social responses which already have become mildly punitive to the child are often used by socializing agents as cues to signal more severe punishment if a transgression is completed or continued. It would be interesting to know whether such cues attain some anxiety-reducing value, despite their position as warning signals, because of their mediation of inhibitory responses which avoid the punishment. Finally, perhaps the most intriguing experimental translations of naturalistic socialization would be in the area of inconsistent punishment. Studies of the discriminative events within which punishment is inconsistent, and of the extent to which socializing agents provide consequences of transgression other than direct punishment, might reveal that inhibition, self-punishment, and other internalized reactions to transgression have common elements other than the anxiety that motivates them and the anxiety reduction that serves as their reinforcement.

Nurturance and the Internalized Consequences of Punishment

The internalization of punishment does not rest on a broader predisposition to reproduce the behavior of an otherwise nurturant or affectionate model. Nor does it appear, as some theorists have suggested (Kagan, 1958; Maccoby, 1959; Whiting, 1960), that self-criticism represents a generalized tendency to exercise control over the threatening punitive resources at the disposal of a socializing agent.

The contributions of punishment and anxiety to the learning of self-criticism should not be extrapolated, of course, to other kinds of imitative social learning, in which children do appear to provide their own reinforcement by reproducing those stimulus aspects of a model which have been directly associated with nurturance or reward. Persuasive theoretical cases have been made for the place of a reinforcement mechanism derived from reward in much of imitative behavior (Mowrer, 1950, Ch. 21; Mowrer, 1960b, Ch. 3; Sears et al., 1957, Ch. 10; Whiting & Child, 1953, Ch. 11); and there are empirical findings (Bandura & Huston, 1961; Mussen & Distler, 1959; Sears, 1953) which support the common observation that the warmth and affection of socializing agents foster the child's tendency to adopt a great variety of their responses. We can hardly be suprised, however, to find that the reproduction of social punishment cannot be subsumed under the consequences of a model's rewarding characteristics. Children sometimes reproduce behavioral pieces of the most entirely frightening figures which they encounter in both reality and fantasy. Similar phenomena in adults are described in Bettelheim's (1943) well-known report of life in a concentration camp, and are also seen by the sensitive observer under ordinary social circumstances. Conversely, there is no reason to expect the child's motivation to reproduce the behavior of a nurturant model to be so powerfully indiscriminate, even under the duress of withdrawal of affection, as to encompass the model's punishment. An account of the diversity of modeling responses usually taken as evidence of identification requires, then, an extension of learning processes derived from punishment as well as of those derived from reward.

The internalized consequences of social punishment would, nevertheless, not be totally indifferent to the nurturance and affection of socializing agents. Numerous descriptive surveys of internalized responses to transgression, whose rough indices of internalization have given much attention to self-criticism, indicate the absence of any consistently direct relationship between extent of internalization in the child and the amount of nurturance given by parents (Bronfenbrenner, 1961; Heinecke, 1953; Sears et al., 1957, Ch. 10; Whiting & Child, 1953, Ch. 11). There is evidence, however, that the usual effects of punishment upon internalization require a minimally nurturant context. The children of extreme parental groups, who are highly rejecting or punitive toward their offspring, appear to show poor internalization in their social behavior (Bandura & Walters, 1959; Nye, 1958; Sears et al., 1957, Ch. 10; Whiting & Child, 1953, Ch. 11). Loss of affection is probably a major element in the effectiveness of any form of social punishment administered by parents to their children. This element could be negligible, if parents have been so generally cold or punitive as to adapt the child to a high level of aversive stimulation in their presence. Their specific punishments might then not produce an increment of anxiety sufficient to independently attach itself to the child's own response cues, so that it could motivate self-criticism or other reactions to transgression even in the absence of external control. It seems even more probable that parents who are generally lacking in nurturance use unusually severe punishments. The intensity of ordinary social punishment permits its components to have some significance for attenuating anxiety and is not likely to disrupt the child's attention to this significance. Severe punishment, in contrast, may evoke competing responses, such as withdrawal or escape, which are more closely associated with anxiety reduction than is any aspect of the punishment itself.

The key role that has been assigned to self-criticism in many surveys of internalization also affords an opportunity to inferentially confirm the importance of the temporal relationships so vividly illustrated in the experimental paradigms. A number of investigators (Allinsmith, 1960; Aronfreed, 1961; MacKinnon, 1938; Sears et al., 1597, Ch. 10; Whiting & Child, 1953, Ch. 11) have found a rather limited positive association between the extent of children's internalization of responses to transgression and their parent's use of methods of punishment variously referred to as "love oriented," "psychological," or "induction" techniques. Withdrawal of affection has always been included among such techniques, and it often has been presumed to be their dominant common element. But the experimental findings reported by the author do not support the view that an explicit withdrawal of affection by a nurturant model induces a state of deprivation which is singularly effective in motivating a child's reproduction of the model's critical evaluative responses. The apparent discrepancy may be resolved by observing that, while loss of affection would enter into the child's experience of any form of punishment employed by its parents, their use of withdrawal of affection as the focus of their punishment might well incorporate certain features of administration and timing which are much less characteristic of other disciplinary techniques. These features are precisely those which have been artificially removed in the experimental nurturance paradigm, where the socializing agent's critical labels acquire little or no anxiety-reducing value because they are presented immediately upon the child's awareness of transgression, before substantial anxiety can be evoked.

Parents who focus on withdrawal of affection in their discipline may be those who are also most oriented toward inducing an internal governor of conduct in their children, in contrast to other parents who are more oriented toward sensitizing their children to the punitive external consequences of transgressions with which they are visibly confronted (Aronfreed, 1961; Bronfenbrenner, 1958). Accordingly, parents who emphasize withdrawal of affection may be more disposed to punish transgressions well beyond the point of their occurrence. And they may tend to maintain the cognitive and affective salience of their children's transgressions by reinstating affection only after some time has elapsed. It is the manner in which they use withdrawal of affection, then, that would induce in their children internalized anxiety of greater and more uncertain duration than that induced by other more direct and quickly terminated punishment. This more variable and prolonged period of anxiety would sustain a greater probability that the child would reproduce components of parental criticism or otherwise make its own anxiety-reducing responses, rather than wait upon external events. The fact that deprivation of affection does not require the physical presence of the parents (and is often effected by their absence) is also useful in understanding why it makes the child prone to produce anxiety-reducing stimuli through its own resources.

Cognitive Processes in Self-Evaluation

The treatment of self-criticism as an instrumental labeling response does not circumvent the importance of understanding the complex cognitive processes upon which self-evaluation is often based. We might consider, for example, whether reproducing the verbal components of social punishment is to be regarded as a moral response—or, to put it another way, whether it is to be taken as evidence of guilt. In the normative framework of our society, the term *moral* is commonly restricted to actions which follow from some degree of judgment exercised by the actor. The evaluative dimensions of such judgment are presumed to be ethical in nature, in the sense that they make articulate distinctions between right and wrong or good and bad. But many of the internalized derivatives of social reinforcement, including the application of either punitive or rewarding labels to one's own actions, may require only very rudimentary and tenuous cognitive support. Many other internalized responses reflect socially derived cognitive processes which are highly developed along evaluative dimensions which are not necessarily moral. This would surely be the case with the self-evaluation that attaches to success or failure in certain kinds of performance or control.

There are formidable problems associated with any attempt to define moral cognition in a way that escapes cultural relativism. It might be possible, however, to assign invariant properties to moral evaluation by reference to particular kinds of cognitive processes. Certainly the moral properties of an evaluative response would be determined by its cognitive dimensions. In western society at least, moral cognition appears to be characterized by reference to the consequences of an act for others, and, to a less definitive extent, by reference to the intention of the act.

It is suggested that the concept of guilt is too liberally employed when it is used to describe either the arousal of anxiety in the absence of external punishment or the presence of a self-critical labeling response that reduces the anxiety. The concept might be reserved more appropriately for an affective state with certain distinctive cognitive features. Both introspection and common usage suggest that the experience of guilt is compounded of the anxiety aroused by transgression and the evaluative perceptions which come through the filter of moral cognition. While this cognition can be normatively circumscribed for a given society and operationalized in verbal behavior, guilt must be viewed as an essentially phenomenological construct of variable substance.

50. RELATIONSHIPS BETWEEN SHAME AND GUILT IN THE SOCIALIZATION PROCESS

David P. Ausubel

The forces toward cultural ethnocentrism are exceedingly difficult to take into account and make allowance for when we attempt to describe and understand the structure and dynamics of various cultures and subcultures. Some of our attempts, as seen in retrospect, are almost as ludicrous as Alice's efforts to understand the Queen of Hearts during her excursions into Wonderland. We often misjudge when we attribute our own motivations and feelings to individuals reared under different social-cultural conditions, or when we postulate the existence of some antecedent new factor "X" to account for a puzzling consequent in another culture.

In the following report Ausubel takes a careful look at the criteria and the data that have led certain cultural anthropologists such as Benedict and Mead to differentiate between what they call *shame* and *guilt* cultures. This detailed analysis persuades Ausubel that individuals in a "shaming" culture, such as the Japanese or Navaho, are controlled by moral obligations, and experience feelings of guilt just as surely as are persons in our own and similar so-called "guilt" cultures. In Ausubel's judgment it is only the *modes of expression* that differ.

Whether or not the reader may be similarly persuaded to share Ausubel's conclusions, he will surely admire the cogency of his reasoning, which happily has implications for other cultural evaluations equally fraught with ethnocentric dangers. For example, is it possible for the white middle-class social scientist to divorce himself from his own cultural limitations

SOURCE. Adapted and abridged from David P. Ausubel, "Relationships Between Shame and Guilt in the Socialization Process," *Psychological Review*, 1955, Vol. 62, 378–390. (With permission of the author and the American Psychological Association.)

as he attempts to understand subcultures within the Black ghetto or in regions of white Appalachia? Maybe he can make some significant progress in the years ahead, but it will undoubtedly require intimate social exposure, assiduous and sustained effort, and considerable inspiration and ingenuity. It will certainly not take place over night (as we would all wish were possible) and it may require a series of corrective injunctions of the type illustrated in Ausubel's discussion.

Guilt is one of the most important psychological mechanisms through which an individual becomes socialized in the ways of his culture. It is also an important instrument for cultural survival since it constitutes a most efficient watchdog within each individual, serving to keep his behavior compatible with the moral values of the society in which he lives. Without the aid rendered by guilt feelings, child rearing would be a difficult matter indeed. If children felt no sense of accountability or moral obligation to curb their hedonistic and irresponsible impulses, to conform to accepted social norms, or to acquire self-control, the socializing process would be slow, arduous, and incomplete. Sheer physical force, threat of pain, deprivation, and punishment, or withholding of love and approval would be the only available methods—combined with constant surveillance—to exact conformity to cultural standards of acceptable behavior. And since it is plainly evident that the maintenance of perpetual vigilance is impractical, that fear alone is never an effective deterrent against antisocial behavior, and that the interests of personal expediency are not always in agreement with prescribed ethical norms, a social order unbuttressed by a sense of moral obligation in its members would enjoy precious little stability.

Within recent years, a number of social anthropologists (Benedict, 1946; Leighton and Kluckhohn, 1947; Mead, 1949; Mead, 1950) have advanced the notion that guilt is not universally present or prominent as a sanction in mediating and sustaining the culture. Instead they have identified guilt as a unique property of the characterology of individuals who as children experience the kinds of relationships with parents allowing for "superego" formation, that is, typically of persons growing up in cultures adhering to the Judaic-Christian tradition. Thus, among the Samoans, Iatmul, and Balinese, Margaret Mead believes that the culture is primarily transmitted through such external sanctions as expediency in conforming to the rules (Mead, 1949, p. 514), shared, undifferentiated fear (Mead, 1950, p. 369), and anticipation of physical reprisals (Mead, 1950, p. 370), respectively. Ruth Benedict minimizes the importance of guilt and emphasizes the role of shame in regulating the social behavior of the Japanese (Benedict, 1946, p. 222). Leighton and Kluckhohn make the same point in reference to the Navaho: "Sensitivity to shame . . . largely takes the place that remorse and self-punishment have in preventing anti-social conduct in white society"

(1947, p. 106). And even in characterizing the moral development of adolescents in our own society who undergo peer-group rather than parent-regulated socialization, Margaret Mead comments that "shame, the agony of being found wanting and exposed to the disapproval of others, becomes a more prominent sanction behind conduct than guilt, the fear of not measuring up to the high standard which was represented by the parents" (Mead, 1949, p. 520).

In this paper we shall be concerned with a critical examination of the criteria that these anthropologists have used in differentiating between shame and guilt. We shall attempt to show that although the two kinds of sanctions are distinguishable from one another, they are nevertheless neither dichotomous nor mutually exclusive, and that the development of guilt feelings is not dependent upon highly specific aspects of a unique kind of parent-child relationship. Before turning to this task, however, it might be profitable to undertake a logical analysis of the developmental conditions under which the capacity for acquiring guilt behavior arises, as well as some of the basic relationships between shame and guilt. Because of the paucity of experimental or naturalistic evidence in this area of theoretical inquiry, it should be self-evident that the following paradigm is offered as a system of interrelated hypotheses rather than as an exposition of empirically established facts.

THE DEVELOPMENTAL ORIGINS OF GUILT

Guilt may be conceptualized as a special kind of negative self-evaluation which occurs when an individual acknowledges that his behavior is at variance with a given moral value to which he feels obligated to conform. It is a self-reaction to an injured conscience, if by conscience is meant an abstraction referring to a feeling of obligation to abide by all internalized moral values. The injury consists of a self-perceived violation of this obligation. Hence, in accordance with this formulation, one might hypothesize that before guilt feelings can become operative, the following developmental conditions must apply: (a) the individual must accept certain standards of right and wrong or good and bad as his own, (b) he must accept the obligation of regulating his behavior to conform to whatever standards he has thus adopted, and must feel accountable for lapses therefrom, and (c) he must possess sufficient self-critical ability to recognize when a discrepancy between behavior and internalized values occurs.

It goes without saying that none of these conditions can ever be satisfied at birth; under minimally favorable circumstances, however, all human beings should be potentially capable of acquiring the capacity for guilt behavior. Culture may make a difference in the form which this behavior takes and in the specific kinds of stimuli which instigate it; but the capacity itself should be so basically human and so fundamental to the sanctions by which social norms are maintained and transmitted to the young in any culture that differences among individuals within a culture would probably be as great as or greater than differences among cultures.

It is theoretically possible, of course, that in certain extreme cases a culture may be so anarchic and unstructured in terms of the obligations it engenders in its members that the potentiality for guilt experience is never realized, as, for example, among the Dobu (Benedict, 1934, p. 131). Ordinarily, however, we might expect that guilt feelings would be found universally; and, hence, the burden of proof regarding their alleged absence in a given culture more properly rests with the investigator making the allegation.

Despite the probable existence of many important culturally conditioned differences in children's acquisition of guilt behavior, there are presumptive grounds for believing that considerable communality prevails in the general pattern of sequential development. Such communality would be a product of various uniformities regarding (a) basic conditions of the parent-child relationship, (b) minimal cultural needs for socialization of the child, and (c) certain gross trends in cognitive and social growth that prevail from one culture to the next.

The cultural basis of conscience development in the individual may be found in the potent need of both parents and society to inculcate a sense of responsibility in the child. Not only the physical survival of its members, but also the perpetuation of its selective way of life is contingent upon the culture's degree of success in this undertaking. Thus, the attenuation of infantile irresponsibility might be considered part of the necessary process of ego devaluation and maturation that presumably characterizes personality development in all cultures. Socialization demands the learning of self-control and self-discipline, the subordination of personal desires to the needs and wishes of others, the acquisition of skills and self-sufficiency, the curbing of hedonistic and aggressive impulses, and the assimilation of culturally sanctioned patterns of behavior. It seems highly unlikely that any of these propensities could become thoroughly stable before conscience is firmly established.

We might postulate that the first step in the child's development of conscience involves his assimilation of parental values and standards. Having no other frame of reference for judgments of good and bad, the prestige suggestion of parents easily holds sway. But acceptance of these values does not obligate him—in the absence of a still undeveloped sense of moral responsibility—to regulate his own behavior accordingly. Lapses on the part of *other* persons are perceived as "bad," but such judgments have no relevance for similar behavior of his *own* when gratification of his *own* impulses is at stake. At this stage of development his behavior can only be directed into acceptable channels by punishment or by anticipation of punishment in the form of pain, deprivation, ridicule, threatened separation from the parent, etc. Conformity to ethical standards, therefore, is "devoid of moral implications because it is only indicative of submission to authority rather than acceptance of it" (Ausubel, 1952, p. 122).

Behavior can first be regarded as manifesting moral properties when a sense of obligation is acquired. The central hypothesis of the present formulation is that this development typically takes place in children who are accepted and intrinsically valued by parents, and who thereby acquire a derived or vicarious status in consequence of this acceptance. By the fiat of parental acceptance they are provided with intrinsic feelings of security and adequacy despite their manifest dependency and incompetence to fend for themselves. They accordingly become disposed to accept parental values implicitly and unconditionally out of loyalty to the individuals to whom they owe their status and self-esteem. Among other standards assimilated in this uncritical and subservient fashion "is the feeling of moral responsibility or accountability to conform to standards of behavior which have been given ethical implications. . . . Unlike other values which are ends in themselves, moral responsibility has [the] regulatory function of compelling adherence to internalized norms of behavior" (Ausubel, 1952, p. 135).

It is reasonable to suppose, however, that the inhibition of unacceptable behavior by feelings of personal loyalty and accountability, by the child's recognition of his parent's moral authority, and by his desire to avoid the self-punishing consequences of guilt develops relatively slowly. The old external sanctions of pain, punishment, threat, and ridicule continue to be applied, reinforced now by the more meaningful threat of withdrawal of love and approval. Delaying the consolidation of guilt behavior is the slow growth of both the self-critical faculty (making perception of discrepancies between precept and conduct difficult) and of the ability to generalize principles of right and wrong beyond specific situations.

During preadolescene and adolescence, as the child begins to lose his volitional dependence upon parents and becomes more concerned both with a primary status based upon his own competencies and with equal membership in the social order, the basis of conscience and guilt behavior apparently undergoes significant change. As Piaget has shown, greater experience in interpersonal relationships and in playing differentiated roles in complex social activities makes him more inclined to interpret rules of conduct as functional contrivances designed to facilitate social organization and interaction rather than as sacred and axiomatic givens (Piaget, 1932, p. 106). Concomitantly, he develops a notion of moral law based upon principles of equity and embodying a system of reciprocal as opposed to unilateral moral obligations (Piaget, 1932, p. 387). The absolutism of his moral standards also tends to be weakened by his greater need for self-enhancement as an individual in his own right—a need that no longer favors unconditional adherence to an uncompromisable set of parental standards, and places a greater premium on the value of expediency. Finally, once the individual acquires this functional concept of moral law, conceives of himself as an independent entity striving for primary status in a social community, and recognizes the reciprocal nature of obligation, he completes the process of transferring "his feeling of moral accountability from parents to the moral authority of society" (Ausubel, 1952, p. 482).

In heterogeneous cultures, values tend to acquire a wider social base during adolescence. The individual is exposed to a variety of ethical standards and can, within limits, choose between alternative moral systems. And where the peer group plays the major role in adolescent socialization, parents are replaced by peers as the chief interpreters and enforcers of the moral code and, to some extent, as the source of moral authority. But neither set of conditions is essential for the maturational changes in the nature of moral organization that take place during and subsequent to preadolescence (Mead, 1949, p. 519; Nichols, 1930, p. 96). In certain homogeneous cultures also, the source of moral values and authority is referred almost from the beginning to persons outside the immediate family circle (Leighton and Kluckhohn, 1947, p. 51).

ATYPICAL DEVELOPMENT OF GUILT BEHAVIOR

The above description of the original and subsequent development of guilt behavior is hypothesized as the more typical course of moral growth in most children. It presupposes that the latter can achieve derived feelings of status through the medium of a dependent parent-child relationship, and can consequently internalize both values and a sense of moral obligation on the implicit basis of personal loyalty. In all cultures, however, a variable number of parents are psychologically incapable of extending acceptance and intrinsic valuation to their offspring. Thus deprived of the self-esteem derived from the fiat of unconditional parental acceptance, such children are from the very beginning obliged to seek primary status and feelings of adequacy on the basis of their own competencies and performance ability. Accordingly, the basis on which they internalize values and moral obligations might be expected to be correspondingly different.

It would serve no useful purpose here to speculate further on the possible atypical courses that conscience development could take in rejected and extrinsically valued children (Ausubel, 1952). However, there is less reason to believe that rejecting and extrinsically valuing attitudes characterize *all* parents in a few rare cultures than that they may be found among *some* parents in almost all cultures. Hence, we would hypothesize that the probability of finding some conscienceless individuals in every culture is greater than that of finding conscienceless cultures.

CLASSIFICATION OF SHAME AND GUILT

Generally, shame may be defined as an unpleasant emotional reaction by an individual to an actual or presumed negative judgment of himself by others resulting in self-depreciation vis-à-vis the group. This definition of shame is inclusive of instances in which the persons passing judgment are valued either positively or negatively by the individual being judged (Mead, 1950, p. 367), and of both moral and nonmoral causes for the instigation of such negative judgments. Typical examples of nonmoral shame are embarrassment in committing a breach of propriety or in having one's bodily intimacy exposed to public scrutiny (Nuttin, 1950, p. 350), and "loss of face" resulting from exposure of ignorance or incompetency. Moral shame, on the other hand, is a reaction to the negative moral judgments of others. It is a prominent sanction in many cultures both before and subsequent to the development of conscience.

Moral shame can, in turn, be divided into two categories—internalized and noninternalized. The latter variety occurs when an individual reacts with self-depreciation to the moral condemnation of others, but does not accept the moral value to which he has failed to conform, e.g., a young child may be shamed by being caught in a lie even if he does not accept the judgment that lying is wrong. Essential for this type of shame is the presence of witnesses to or eventual discovery of the misdeed in question. When the value is internalized, e.g., when the child *really* believes that lying is opprobrious, actual discovery is unnecessary; shame can result merely from presumed or fantasied reproach. Under the influence of such unwitnessed shame, the Ojibway may commit suicide (Mead, 1950, p. 367). According to Margaret Mead, internalized shame only occurs when the parent is the interpreter and enforcer of the sanction (Mead, 1950, p. 366). Observation of closely-knit adolescent peer groups, however, seems to indicate that genuine shame may occur when adolescents perceive or fantasy the moral disapproval of their fellows for offenses against norms established and enforced by the group itself.

The shame associated with guilt may be considered a special case of moral shame. In addition to an internalized moral value, a personal obligation to abide by that value is at stake, e.g., the child not only believes that lying is wrong and feels shame by experiencing or imagining the censure of others, but also feels shame in fantasying the reproach of others for violating a moral obligation. In either case an actual audience is unnecessary, but a presumed or fantasied judgment by others is. However, it is important to emphasize at this point that shame is only one component of guilt, the component involving external judgment and sanction. Guilt also involves other *self-reactions* that are independent of the judgment of others, namely, self-reproach, self-disgust, self-contempt, remorse, lowered self-esteem, anxiety, and various characteristic and subjectively identifiable visceral and vasomotor responses. And conversely, the shame of guilt is only one of many kinds of shame. Thus, the presence of guilt-related shame does not preclude the simultaneous operation of other forms of moral or nonmoral shame unassociated with guilt; nor does the excitation of any of these kinds of shame (associated or unassociated with guilt) preclude the operation of the various self-judgments characterizing guilt feelings.

Shame relies on external sanctions alone. Guilt relies on both internal and external sanctions. The latter sanctions consist of the presumed judgments of others regarding one's lapses with respect to moral obligations and the resulting self-depreciation vis-à-vis the group, as well as the customary social reprisals associated with the misdemeanors arousing guilt. In addition, feelings of guilt have external reference in that they acknowledge accountability for a moral offense against the group.

In the following section we shall critically appraise (a) the views of Margaret Mead and of Leighton and Kluckhohn, who hold that the development of guilt behavior requires a parent-child relationship in which an omniscient parent is the referent for and the source of moral authority, in addition to personally administering and interpreting moral sanctions (Mead, 1950, pp. 366, 367); and (b) Ruth Benedict's position that guilt is shameless, involves no external sanctions, and is concerned with inner convictions of sin (Benedict, 1944, pp. 222–223).

ETHNOCENTRIC DISTINCTIONS BETWEEN SHAME AND GUILT

Superego Models of Guilt

The first ethnocentric conception of guilt referred to above equates the capacity for experiencing guilt feelings with neo-Freudian notions of superego formation. According to this conception, guilt feelings cannot arise unless the conditions essential for superego formation are not only present in childhood but are also maintained in subsequent years. Hence, guilt-like behavior in our own or other cultures that does not conform to these conditions is categorized as shame. The two basic conditions that are laid down for the development of guilt are: (a) the child must accept the parent or parent surrogate as omniscient or as qualitatively superior to himself in a moral sense, and (b) he must accept the parent as the source of moral authority, i.e., as the "referent" in whose name moral behavior is enjoined. In reference to the former condition Margaret Mead states:

> The adults in the society must think of the child as qualitatively different from themselves, in that the child has not yet attained their moral stature, but is subject to innate impulses which, if permitted unchecked expression, would eventuate in adult character different from and morally inferior to that of the parent (Mead, 1949, p. 514).

Leighton and Kluckhohn similarly characterize guilt feelings as representing an individual's acknowledgment that he is "unworthy . . . for not living up to the high standards represented by [his] parents" (1947, p. 106). In explaining why "Navaho sensitivity to shame takes the place of guilt in our society," they go on to say:

> "Conscience" is related to the belief in an omnipotent God who knows all. . . . In white society the child doesn't see the parent in many life situations. [But] in the circumstances of Navaho life a pose of omnipotence or omniscience on the part of parents would be speedily and almost daily exposed (Leighton and Kluckhohn, 1947, p. 106). Only rarely does one hear the utterances on the part of Navaho parents which are so usual among white parents: "Do it because I say it is right," "do it because I say so," "do it because I am your father and children must obey their parents" (Leighton and Kluckhohn, 1947, p. 53).

In the first place, one may legitimately question the assumption that children do not acquire moral obligations unless a highly authoritarian, paternalistic, and hierarchical parent-child relationship exists, unless the parent sets himself up and is perceived as a qualitatively superior paragon of virtue. As long as the conditions for acquiring derived status are fulfilled, it seems reasonable to suppose that moral obligations are incurred provided that parents or parent surrogates make such expectations unambiguously clear. It undoubtedly increases the prestige suggestion with which the standards and expectations of parents are endowed if the latter individuals are perceived as omniscient; but there is neither convincing logical nor empirical justification for designating this criterion as a *sine qua non* for the acquisition of guilt behavior.

A second difficulty confronting the proposition that qualitative hierarchical distinctions must prevail between preceptor and learner in order for guilt feelings to develop is the suggestive evidence of Piaget, referred to above, showing that as children approach adolescence in our culture they become increasingly concerned with moral obligations based on principles of reciprocity (Piaget, 1932, pp. 106, 387). Cooperative and functional relationships with peers engender notions of obligation reflecting mutual respect between equals which gradually displace unilateral feelings of obligation based on implicit acceptance of authority (Piaget, 1932, p. 106).

The second condition imposed by adherents of the superego model of guilt behavior, i.e., that parents or parent surrogates must serve as the source of moral authority, runs into similar difficulties posed by developmental shifts in the organization of conscience. It presupposes, in the words of Margaret Mead, that

> ... teachers, the clergy, judicial officials, etc., partake of the character of the judging parent who metes out reward to the individual child (or, later, adult) who makes a satisfactory approximation to the desired behavior, and punishment to him who does not (Mead, 1949, p. 514).

Such a requirement arbitrarily eliminates the possibility of guilt behavior developing in cultures like the Navaho where the authority for moral sanctions is from the earliest days of socialization referred to the group as a whole (Leighton and Kluckhohn, 1947, p. 51). The same criterion rules out the occurrence of guilt behavior among (a) adolescents in our own culture who accept the peer group as their major source of moral authority (see earlier quotation from Margaret Mead), (b) rejected and extrinsically valued children who never accept the moral authority of parents, but who may accept rational principles of equity and the moral authority of the group, and (c) adults in most cultures, who, in accordance with the developmental changes described above, transfer their allegiances from the moral authority of parents to the moral authority of society. The latter process does not necessarily require the intermediate adolescent step of repudiating adult authority and substituting peer standards. Sufficient for this outcome is a transformation of the basis upon which the authority of elders is accepted, i.e., a change from implicit acceptance of axiomatic truth by a dependent and ideationally subservient individual to a more rational acceptance of functionally necessary norms growing out of interpersonal relations by an independent member of adult society (Nichols, 1930, pp. 95–96).

To deny that guilt feelings can arise in the above four situations requires summary dismissal of the evidence of everyday experience with the behavioral content of others. It is admittedly difficult to evaluate the subjective emotional experience of other persons, particularly if they happen to be members of different cultures. Logical inference must always supplement the perceptions of even the most experienced observer. Nevertheless a decision regarding the meaning of behavior can never be reached on the basis of a priori criteria alone, especially when these lack irrefutable logical or face validity. An emotion is adjudged to be guilt or shame on the basis of its behavioral characteristics, its situational excitants, and its subjective properties, and not because it fails to meet certain arbitrary ethnocentric criteria that apply to a single culture or phase of development. In the next section we shall examine some ethnological materials presented by Leighton and Kluckhohn and by Ruth Benedict as illustrative of shame and show how such behavior can be more defensibly interpreted as guilt.

A conception of conscience or guilt behavior that makes no provision for developmental changes in the underlying personality structure upon which such behavior depends cannot be successfully integrated into any self-consistent theory of personality development. A theoretical framework must be found that is broad enough to encompass the guilt behavior of a child of eight and likewise of an adult of eighteen or eighty. We cannot conclude that eighteen-year-old guilt must be shame because it does not conform to an eight-year-old model of guilt.

Personality development is admittedly characterized by continuity as well as by change. A tendency to accept values and obligations uncritically, on the basis of personal allegiances, still continues in adult life. Similarly, early attitudes of unconditional loyalty to moral obligations tend to persist long beyond the span of childhood. Nevertheless although these continuing trends add much to the stability of conscience, they are largely supplanted by different moral orientations and enjoy only substrate existence in a generally changed gestalt. A precipitate of the experiences of the eight-year-old is represented in the behavior of the eighteen-year-old, but this precipitate has a phenomenologically different meaning and significance than its original form a decade earlier.

Pointing up the logical as well as the empirical untenability of a criterion of guilt that requires a qualitatively superior parent or parent surrogate as the source of moral authority is the discrepancy on this score between the two chief examples of allegedly "shaming cultures," i.e., certain North American Indian tribes and the Japanese. Leighton and Kluckhohn characterize the Navaho as a "shaming culture" in part because sanctions are applied laterally rather than from above, and are referred to group rather than to parental authority (Leighton and Kluckhohn, 1947, pp. 105–106). On the other hand, Ruth Benedict, using other criteria, regards the Japanese as a shaming culture despite the fact that the Japanese family is the ethnological example par excellence of unconditionally accepted, paternalistic (if not arbitrarily imposed) authority based upon hierarchical position (Benedict, 1946, pp. 55–57, 264). Obviously, then, this criterion for distinguishing between shame and guilt has little claim to universality.

Guilt as a Shameless, Wholly Internalized Conviction of Sin

The second major ethnocentric (and psychoanalytically oriented) conception of guilt assumes that guilt and shame are mutually incompatible and that genuine guilt must be devoid of shame and all external sanctions. Thus, in cultures where shame plays a more prominent role in behavioral control than in our own culture, ethnologists sharing this conception of guilt have insisted that guilt feelings must *ipso facto* be either nonexistent or of negligible significance. Among the Japanese, according to Gorer, "mockery is the most important and most effective sanction for obtaining conformity in social life" (Gorer, 1942, p. 20). Ruth Benedict espouses the same opinion in stating that "shame has the same place of authority in Japanese ethics that 'a clear conscience,' 'being right with God,' and avoidance of sin have in Western ethics" (Benedict, 1946, p. 224). Leighton and Kluckhohn claim that Navahos do not internalize the "standards of their parents and elders," and that shame ("I would feel very uncomfortable if anyone saw me deviating from accepted norms") is the major deterrent to antisocial behavior (Leighton and Kluckhohn, 1947, p. 106). Margaret Mead goes even further by ruling out the occurrence of both guilt and shame in the sanction systems of the Samoans (Mead, 1949, pp. 514–515), Balinese (Mead, 1950, p. 369), and Iatmul (Mead, 1950, pp. 369–370), and insisting that only such external sanctions as fear, expediency, and threat of physical reprisals are operative.

This dichotomization of shame and guilt, of internal and external sanctions, in addition to lacking logical self-consistency, simply does not conform to available naturalistic evidence. Both moral and nonmoral shame may be extremely important sanctions in a given culture, but they preclude the occurrence of neither the public (shame) nor the private (self-judgment) aspects of guilt. A culture so unstable and so anarchic that its members fail to respond to internal sanctions (i.e., feelings of moral obligation) is indeed an ethnological rarity. The inhabitants of Dobu (Benedict, 1934) may fit this description, but the case made out for the Samoans, Iatmul, and Balinese (Mead, 1949, 1950) is far from convincing; and descriptions of Japanese (Benedict, 1946; La Barre, 1948) and Navaho (Leighton and Kluckhohn, 1947) behavior tend to disprove the very contentions they are meant to illustrate. Conversely, a culture in which external sanctions are *not* applied at any stage of moral development is also rare enough to qualify as an ethnological oddity.

The evidence seems clear enough that although Japanese and Navaho individuals are more responsive to shame than we are, much of this shame is really the shame of guilt, i.e., the shame accompanying awareness of violated moral obligations. The predominant pattern of parent-child relationships in both cultures is one of acceptance and intrinsic valuation of the child, leading to the first or implicit stage of moral responsibility based upon personal loyalty (Benedict, 1946, Ch. 12; Leighton and Kluckhohn, 1947, Ch. 1). Navaho children acquire a sense of responsibility between five and eight years of age, learning assiduousness in executing their chores. They learn "that they cannot always indulge themselves and that they have duties toward others" (Leighton and Kluckholn, 1947, p. 58). Navaho parents are strikingly devoted and attentive to the needs of their children (Leighton and Kluckhohn, 1947, pp. 13–33), and children, in turn, even as adults, are very devoted to their parents and siblings (Leighton and Kluckhohn, 1947, pp. 94–100). The Navaho adult is capable of very responsible conduct in relation to his social group despite the fact that responsibility is "divided and shared" (Leighton and Kluckhohn, 1947, p. 107). If such behavior is not indicative of internalized moral obligation, what other credible explanation is there? Surely shame alone could not account for all of it.

Among the Japanese an even stronger case can be made for the importance of conscience and guilt behavior. Few other cultures lay greater stress upon the sanctity of moral obligations. "The strong according to Japanese verdict are those who disregard personal happiness and fulfill their obligations. . . . A man is weak if he pays attention to his personal desires when they conflict with the code of obligations" (Benedict, 1946, pp. 207–208). Obligations to others must be fulfilled even if one dislikes the latter personally (Benedict, 1946, p. 124). The Japanese sense of accountability is especially stringent. "Each man must accept responsibility for the outcome of his acts. He must acknowledge and accept all natural consequences of his weakness, his lack of persistence, his ineffectualness" (Benedict, 1946, p. 296).

What is even more impressive is the fact that in contrast to prevailing attitudes in our own culture, the self-discipline, the self-restraint, and any of the personal disadvantages incurred in honoring obligations are not regarded as self-sacrifice. The fulfillment of obligations is taken for granted on the grounds of reciprocity, and calls for no applause, reward, self-pity, or self-righteousness (Benedict, 1946, pp. 230–233). The notions of mutual dependence and indebtedness to one's society and one's past lie at the very heart of the Japanese concept of obligation. "One repays one's debts to one's forbears by passing on to one's children the care one oneself received" (Benedict, 1946, p. 122).

Despite this overwhelming evidence of conscience and guilt behavior, Ruth Benedict is misled by the dichotomized conception of shame and guilt, and insists upon referring to such behavior as shame on the grounds that guilt is supposedly shameless. But, as already pointed out above, what she calls "shame" is actually the shame component of guilt. La Barre paints essentially the same picture of Japanese character structure as she does and reaches a diametrically opposite conclusion. He asserts that the Japanese superego is exceedingly strong (La Barre, 1948, p. 329). Nevertheless, even while minimizing the role of guilt among the Japanese, Ruth Benedict is grudgingly obliged to admit the existence of moral self-judgments unrelated to external sanctions.

> They [the Japanese] are terribly concerned about what other people will think of their behavior, and they are also overcome by guilt when other people know nothing of their misstep. . . . Japanese sometimes react as strongly as any Puritan to a private accumulation of guilt (Benedict, 1946, pp. 2–3, 222).

We cannot escape the conclusion, therefore, that both guilt and shame, and internal and external sanctions, can and do exist side by side and mutually reinforce each other. The assertion that "true shame cultures rely on external sanctions for good behavior, not, as true guilt cultures do, on an internalized conviction of sin" (Benedict, 1946, p. 323) is unsupported by available evidence. The presence of the stock, the pillory, and the ducking stool in the public market place offers eloquent refutation to the statement that "the early Puritans who settled in the United States tried to base their whole morality on guilt" (Benedict, 1946, p. 223). Reinforcing most of the moral sanctions that we customarily assign to the domain of conscience is a parallel set of statutes and group pressures enforced by appropriate public reprisals. Even in cultures where moral obligations are highly internalized, we usually find a policeman on the corner giving a friendly nudge to sluggish consciences or a timely warning to impish consciences pondering a brief vacation from duty.

The regulation of conduct by moral self-judgment is also the *final* step in a long developmental process. In controlling the behavior of children in our own culture, parents may differ from Samoan, Balinese, and Iatmul parents in their propensity for premature sermonizing about right and wrong, filial duty, virtue, etc. But during the first few years of life such preachments are but empty verbalisms to our children, who actually respond as do children in all cultures to the accompanying external sanctions of reward and punishment. Guilt feelings also have external reference by virtue of their shame component which involves a self-deprecatory reaction to the presumed or actual moral censure of others for a transgression of moral obligation. Finally, the external reference of guilt is apparent in the fact that it is reduced by punishment and confession. It always implies an offense against the group which, therefore, can only be pardoned by group action.

Another source for ethnocentric misinterpretation of Japanese guilt behavior lies in their lack of preoccupation with sin. The idea of sin, however, is in no way indigenous to a conscience founded on moral obligation; it merely tends to be associated with a specific variety of guilt behavior that is influenced by certain religious traditions and notions about the original nature of man. Nevertheless, by equating guilt with "an internalized conviction of sin" (Benedict, 1946, p. 223), and conscience with "the avoidance of sin" (Benedict, 1946, p. 224), Ruth Benedict finds further "justification" for regarding the Japanese as relatively guiltless.

Japanese neglect of the problem of sin, however, stems from two other sources that can hardly be interpreted as detracting from the genuineness of their expressions of guilt. In the first place, since they do not regard indulgence in physical pleasure as inherently evil—providing that it is properly subordinated to moral obligation—they do not share our notion of "original sin" or our conception of human nature as constantly in need of redemption from inherently sinful desires (Benedict, 1946, pp. 191–192). Secondly, since the fulfillment of obligation is taken for granted and is not regarded as self-sacrifice or as a victory of virtue over innately evil propensities, Japanese good conscience is not burdened with the self-righteousness that comes from conquering sin; and, similarly, guilt is not "internalized conviction of sin," but simply awareness of the breakdown of moral obligation.

Because the Japanese lay great stress on certain "external" (shame) aspects of self-respect, such as acting with circumspection and paying scrupulous attention to the details of propriety, Western observers are prone to deduce that this precludes their association of the term *self*-respect with a criterion such as "consciously conforming to a worthy standard of conduct" (Benedict, 1946, p. 219). However, in the light of the foregoing description of Japanese concepts of moral obligation, we are only justified in concluding that *in addition* to sharing the meaning which is commonly placed on "self-respect" in our culture, the Japanese value other character traits (i.e., self-restraint, circumspection, respect for social niceties and for the feelings of others) sufficiently to dignify them by the same term that we usually reserve for moral uprightness.

Lastly, it is important to explain why confession and atonement are such relatively inconspicuous aspects of Japanese guilt behavior. The absence of these characteristics that so frequently accompany the expression of guilt in our culture does not prove, as Ruth Benedict suggests, that genuine guilt is lacking, since otherwise it would be relieved by confession (Benedict, 1946, p. 223). The Japanese does not, as alleged, avoid confession because his guilt is really only shame and, hence, would be aggravated rather than eased by being made public. The more credible explanation is that although confession would be guilt reducing it would also be too traumatic in view of the tremendous Japanese sensitivity to shame. Under such circumstances, overwhelming feelings of guilt can be relieved less painfully by suicide.

SUMMARY AND CONCLUSIONS

The capacity for experiencing guilt behavior (i.e., a constellation of negative self-reactions to the perceived violation of moral obligation) is conceived as so basically human and so fundamental to the sanctions by which social norms are maintained and transmitted to the young that under minimally favorable social conditions it should develop in all cultures. The only psychological conditions hypothesized as essential for the development of guilt behavior are (a) the acceptance of moral values, (b) the internalization of a sense of moral obligation to abide by these values, and (c) sufficient self-critical ability to perceive discrepancies between internalized values and actual behavior. The development of conscience typically embodies various sequential changes paralleling shifts in the individual's biosocial status. Ordinarily, greater differences in moral behavior may be anticipated among individuals within a culture than among different cultures.

Shame is a self-deprecatory reaction to the actual or presumed judgments of *others*. It may have moral or nonmoral reference. Guilt feelings always involve a special type of moral shame in addition to other negative *self*-judgments. In addition to the shame of guilt, conscience (guilt behavior) is customarily buttressed by such external sanctions as statutory law, public opinion, and ridicule. Thus, the sanctions of guilt are both external and internal in nature.

Various criteria have been advanced by different ethnologists for distinguishing between shame and guilt. It has been alleged (a) that guilt behavior can only arise when a hierarchically superior parent or parent surrogate serves as the source of moral authority, (b) that genuine guilt feelings can only exist when shame and other external sanctions are not operative, and (c) that, subjectively, guilt must be characterized by conviction of sin and need for atonement. Examination of Navaho and Japanese ethnological materials presented in support of these criteria shows that the latter lack both logical and empirical validity. Highly suggestive evidence of the operation of strong moral obligations and of guilt behavior was found in these supposedly prime examples of "shaming cultures."

The problem of shame and guilt is illustrative of a major methodological hazard in the cross-cultural investigation of personality traits, namely, of the ethnocentric tendency to define a given trait in terms of its *specific* attributes in one's own culture. This leads to a perversion of cultural relativism. Instead of demonstrating how a basic human capacity (e.g., guilt behavior) occurs under different conditions and assumes different forms in different cultures, this approach inevitably "discovers" that this very capacity is absent in other cultures because it does not conform to a specific set of ethnocentric criteria. The generalization is then made that the capacity is nonuniversal, culture-bound, and, hence, not basic. Cross-cultural investigations of personality must, therefore, start with definitions of traits that are both psychologically meaningful and general enough to encompass specific cultural variants.

It is also important to avoid the error of circularity—setting up *a priori conditions* for the emergence of a trait, finding these conditions absent in a given culture, and concluding "empirically" therefrom that the *trait itself* is absent. This error can be avoided in part by paying attention to the subjective and expressive content of behavior and not merely to the postulated determinants of the trait in question.

51. THE LEARNING OF SHARING BEHAVIOR

Dilman J. Doland & Kathryn Adelberg

After scientists have identified and described antecedent-consequent or cause-effect relationships in their laboratories, their natural curiosity frequently leads them to investigate the existence and generality of these newly discovered phenomena under seemingly comparable nonlaboratory conditions. The average scientist's curiosity may be even further stimulated by wondering whether his new finding may have some possible practical application, important to the welfare and happiness of his fellow men. In developmental and educational psychology, for example, it is often the scientist's hope that findings derived from his laboratory experiments may advance in some measure the perennial search for better and more reliable methods of aiding, guiding, and educating our children. It is unfortunately well known in the sciences that, just because a particular consequent can be produced by a particular constellation of antecedents in the laboratory, this provides no reliable assurance that the same consequent can be produced by the same set of variables outside the laboratory. In other words, the variables manipulated toward such happy consequences within the laboratory may or may not have the same fortunate outcome in the natural environment which seems so similar to the laboratory conditions.

In the following interesting study by Doland and Adelberg, an attempt is made to show that sharing behavior among nursery school children is influenced by the special home backgrounds of socialization experience by

SOURCE. Adapted and abridged from Dilman J. Dolan and Kathryn Adelberg, "The Learning of Sharing Behavior," *Child Development*, 1967, Vol. 38, 695–700. (With permission of the authors and the Society for Research in Child Development.)

the children. Fortunately, the authors demonstrate that it is possible through controlled social reinforcements to augment and modify the effects of these different backgrounds of socialization. As an incidental outcome the findings of this investigation show, as do the results of so many other research studies, that social learning among boys does not proceed nearly as rapidly as it does among girls. Some of the possible reasons for these sex differences are also discussed in a number of the other reports included in this book.

The willingness, given appropriate circumstances, to share one's possessions with others is commonly regarded in our culture as a mark of maturity, and empirical studies have demonstrated a relation between sharing behavior and chronological age (Handlon & Gross, 1959; Moore & Ucko, 1961). Very little is known about how a child learns to share or why some individuals find it difficult or impossible to do so. The present investigation was prompted by the observation of apparent differences in sharing behavior between nursery school children from a favored environment and a chronologically similar group at a child welfare center. Sharing of materials, toys, and equipment appeared quite common among the nursery school children, while it was rarely observed among the children at the child welfare center.

Viewed within the context of the social-learning theory of Bandura and Walters (1963), it is possible to hypothesize that sharing is an aspect of the child's behavior that is learned through social reinforcement. The presence of sharing behavior in the child's repertoire would then have two implications: first, that he is responsive to social reinforcement and, second, that he has at some time been in the appropriate learning situation, that is, one in which he has received social reinforcement upon exhibiting the sharing response. Failure to exhibit sharing behavior when faced with an appropriate situation might signify either a lack of responsiveness to social reinforcement or insufficient exposure to relevant learning situations.

To test the validity of the initial observation of apparent differences between the two groups, it was hypothesized in the present study that (1) a higher percentage of nursery school than welfare-center children would exhibit sharing behavior in the pretraining situation. Within the group of initial nonsharers it was hypothesized that (2) a higher percentage of nursery school children would learn to share under conditions of social reinforcement. This prediction was based on the theoretical assumptions concerning sharing behavior outlined above and on the expectation that welfare-center children, in comparison with nursery school children, are both less responsive to social reinforcement and less frequently exposed to appropriate learning situations.

METHOD

Subjects

One group consisted of ten boys and ten girls, all white, at a private nursery school in an upper middle-class suburb. The other group consisted of nine boys and seven girls, the majority Negro, at a child welfare center for dependent and neglected children. The mean age of both groups was 4½ years.

Experimenter and Confederates

All experimental sessions were conducted by the junior author. She had no contact with the children prior to the time of the study, and it is probable that she was perceived by them as an unfamiliar but friendly female adult, fairly typical of the white middle class.

The experimental design utilized confederates of the E. These consisted of two boys and a girl, all white, of approximately the same age as the Ss. Each of them accompanied the E to a session at both the nursery school and the child welfare center. An effort was made to have them dressed in clothes similar to those of the children with whom they were to interact. Sex of the confederate was not controlled, so in some instances E's confederate and the S were of the same sex, while in other instances they were of opposite sex.

Procedure

To provide each child with an opportunity to share, either spontaneously or following learning trials, a "game" was devised which involved both S and a confederate of E. Each child was given a stack of mimeographed, outline drawings of animals which had been traced from children's books. Both children were instructed to spread out their pictures and see what they had. The pictures were either of dogs, birds, cats, or fish, each species clearly distinguishable from the others, even by 4-year-olds. The confederate had received seven pictures of the same category, for example, all birds. The S, however, had received five pictures of a contrasting category, but two of the same category as those of the confederate.

The E then presented to each child a large piece of manila paper on which he was to arrange his pictures. The children were told that E would tape the pictures in place and they could later color them. Each sheet of manila paper already had one picture taped on it which corresponded to the particular child's category. The E first gave the confederate his, saying, "This piece has a bird on it already, and you have all birds, so you arrange your pictures on this." The S was then told, "This piece has a cat on it, and you have a lot of cats, so you arrange your pictures on this. You may want to share your bird pictures with Johnny. You may want to give them to him, as he seems to be collecting birds and you have more cats."

An important aspect of sharing behavior is the willingness of the individual, under appropriate circumstances, to give to another person something which he would like to keep for himself. If, in this pretraining situation, S handed the pictures which did not correspond to his category to the confederate, it was concluded that sharing behavior was a part of his repertoire, and his part in the study was completed. Failure to give the appropriate pictures to the confederate was considered a nonsharing response. If a child did not share during the pretraining situation, E returned 2 days later with a different confederate. The same game was played, but with several modifications. The S received a different category of animal than he had the first time. This was to insure that he would still have reason to want to keep the pictures. Moreover, there was a change in the actual condition of the sharing situation. This time E clearly indicated that S would receive social reinforcement if he shared. "I think that it would be *very nice* if you would share your dogs with Jimmy. That would be the really nicest thing to do." Learning-trial 1 thus differed from the pretraining situation in that E had made it explicit that a sharing response was desired and had clearly indicated that exhibition of the desired response of sharing would lead to approval by E. The incentive of social reinforcement had been added, in contrast to the more neutral set provided by instructions in the pretraining situation.

If S shared following learning-trial 1, his part in the study was completed. If not, E returned 2 days later with a third confederate. Again the game was played, with several modifications. A new combination of the animal categories was used, to insure that S never received the same kind more than once. This time, however, the confederate received the mixed collection of animals, while S received all of one kind. The E suggested to the confederate that he share with S, and indicated that this response would lead to her approval. The confederate, having been previously instructed to do so, readily shared, and was profusely socially reinforced by E. In this situation S was able to observe a model receive reinforcement for exhibiting the desired response. Thus, vicariously, he was able to experience the complete learning situation.

Immediately following this, both children were again presented with stacks of pictures, using still another combination of animals. The S again received the mixed collection and was again given the opportunity to share, with the incentive of social reinforcement for doing so.

RESULTS

Results pertaining to hypotheses 1 and 2 are summarized in Table 1. The initial difference in sharing behavior between the two groups, before any modification of that behavior was undertaken, was very large. Ten out

TABLE 1

Number Who Shared, Categorized by Sex, Group, and Experimental Condition

	Boys		Girls	
	Nursery School (N = 10)	Welfare Center (N = 9)	Nursery School (N = 10)	Welfare Center (N = 7)
Pretraining trial	5	1	5	1
Learning-trial 1	2	1	4	5
Learning-trial 2	3	3	1	0
Failed to share	0	4	0	1

of 20 of the nursery school children shared, as contrasted with 2 out of 16 of the welfare-center children. The difference in proportions of successes is statistically significant (χ^2 for 1 df, with Yates' correction for continuity, is 4.06, $p < .05$) and lends empirical support to the original observation upon which the first hypothesis was based.

Of the initial nonsharers, all 10 of the nursery school group, and 9 out of 14 of the welfare-center group, learned to share by the conclusion of learning trials. The difference in proportions of successes is statistically significant (Fisher Exact Probability Test, $p < .05$) and thus supports the second hypothesis.

Although no hypotheses were made regarding sex differences in sharing behavior, analysis of the data revealed interesting findings. At the conclusion of the study there were five subjects who had not shared, all of whom were welfare-center children, and all but one were boys. Out of a total group of nine welfare-center boys, one shared initially, four learned to share, and four failed to learn to share within the conditions of the present study. Welfare-center girls were comparable to the welfare-center boys at the initial stage, in that only one shared, but by the conclusion of the study all had learned to share except one.

Categorization by sex also revealed differences between boys and girls in the stage at which learning occurred. Eighty-two per cent of initially nonsharing girls learned to share in learning-trial 1, and the proportion was as high among welfare-center girls as nursery school girls. Only 23 per cent of initially nonsharing boys learned in the corresponding trial, although 60 per cent of the remaining group learned subsequently in trial 2 (the model situation). This difference is not attributable to welfare-center boys alone. Even in the group of initially nonsharing nursery school boys the majority (3 out of 5) learned after witnessing the model situation.

DISCUSSION

The learning trials presented the child with an appropriate situation for sharing and used the incentive of social reinforcement to induce behavioral modification. Although it is assumed that degree of responsiveness to social reinforcement is an important variable in sharing behavior, it cannot be assumed that the training undertaken in this study modified the child's initial degree of responsiveness to social reinforcement. It utilized the already existing level of responsiveness, increased his exposure to appropriate situations, and, if necessary, made increasingly explicit the offer of reinforcement. The variation introduced in learning-trial 2, observation of a model, was essential, since up to that point no actual reinforcement had been possible since no sharing response had been made.

The superiority of the nursery school children in the pretraining situation may be a function of a higher degree of social responsiveness, greater previous exposure to appropriate situations, or both. At the theoretical level it is possible to present plausible arguments that the welfare-center children are handicapped in both respects. In the experimental design here employed, the two variables are interrelated in their presentation, and no conclusion can be drawn about isolated effects of either.

Analysis of the data yielded support for the hypothesis that within the group of initial nonsharers a higher percentage of nursery school children would learn to share under conditions of social reinforcement. Categorization by sex, however, indicates that the poorer performance of the welfare-center group was more characteristic of the boys, since five out of six of the initially nonsharing welfare-center girls learned to share.

The fact that more initially nonsharing girls than boys changed after the first learning trial is provocative but inconclusive. It suggests that girls are more responsive to the incentive of social approval from an adult, and this is consistent with results found in previous studies. Bridges (1931), rating preschool children on a social-development scale, found that boys more often resisted adult suggestions and ignored adult disapproval. Hattwick (1937) also found that preschool boys ignored the requests of adults more frequently than preschool girls, while the latter more frequently sought praise from adults. It should be noted, however, that sex, age, color, and prestige of the

E have not been varied in the present investigation, so that the results cannot be generalized beyond responsiveness to the incentive of social approval when offered directly by a strange, female, friendly, middle-class adult.

The majority of initially nonsharing boys who learned to share did so after witnessing the confederate receive social reinforcement. The experimental design of the present investigation does not permit an unequivocal explanation of this. It may be that the boys were merely slower to learn, that is, required an additional learning trial. Or it may be that observing a model perform the desired response and receive reinforcement facilitated learning for the boys. Which of these explanations is most relevant can be determined only by systematically varying the different types of learning trial. Sex and color of the child playing the role of confederate-model should also be systematically varied, if the effectiveness of learning from a model is to be adequately understood. In the present study all of the confederates were white, and sometimes S interacted with a model of the same sex and sometimes with a model of the opposite sex. It was the impression of the E that there was no significant difference between the effects produced by same sex model and opposite sex model, but this needs to be checked by a more carefully controlled study.

The "game" devised to study sharing behavior with the assistance of a child as a confederate-model proved to be highly successful. Materials involved are economical and easy to assemble. Children are eager to participate, and there is little risk of a satiation effect. It should be a valuable technique in future studies of sharing behavior.

CHAPTER 10

Striving Toward Idealized Goals

It is a high compliment to the majority of us who are parents when someone whose opinion we value and whose judgment we trust says something similar to the following: "Your son has grown up to be a fine young man," or "What a splendid young woman your daughter has grown to be." We usually interpret such welcome evaluations as meaning more than the fact that our mature, or almost mature, offspring are successfully avoiding open conflicts related to the morals, mores, and customs of the general culture and of the specific subcultures within which we would like our family to be accepted and approved.

It must be recognized, of course, that not all parents have equal concern or equally high aspirations for the future success and happiness of their sons and daughters. Some simply don't give the matter very serious consideration, and a few literally abandon what most people regard as their proper responsibilities as parents. There is ample evidence in the psychological and sociological research literature that the latter child-rearing attitudes and related practices can be damaging to the psychological development and eventual socialization of boys and girls; although it is, for most of us, remarkable how many youngsters who fall within this category of parental neglect find their own ways to comparatively high levels of happiness-success and that ultimate accomplishment that some psychologists have called self-actualization. But that is another story—one that is not specifically dealt with in the present book.

Our concern in the present chapter is to sample some of the antecedents and concomitants of children's strivings toward idealized goals in their daily behavior and their hoped-for futures. The majority of the parents of the children included in the investigations being reviewed in the present book want their children to grow up to enjoy the richest rewards that can be bestowed on them by society and to be maximally happy throughout their life spans. Some parents have even higher aspirations in hoping that their sons and daughters can be especially creative in enriching their own and their associates' modes of living.

Although the research evidence is scanty and the findings far from clearcut, and even in a state of serious conflict in some instances, most parents, social scientists, and educators are convinced that both the quality and quantity of parent-child interactions have substantial influences on the individual child's present and future happiness and success. The evidence collected thus far is often interpreted as providing support for Socrates' recommendation of the "golden mean," or that everything in life should be pursued in moderation. As suggested by the theory advanced in Eysenck's paper, too much of parental threat and punishment in the most easily influenced children (most easily "conditioned" in Eysenck's terms) may result in an overly-oppressive conscience that dominates all dimensions of later psychological adaptation. Children, adolescents, and adults who suffer these consequences expend the bulk of their energies trying to avoid the possible disapproval of others. On the other hand, there are children who experience too little anxiety about how their actions are evaluated by their peers and elders. In extreme instances of this type, the individual has little happiness, or even peace, because society is continually punishing him in one way or another for violating its established rules for conduct.

When child-rearing has proceeded in moderation with respect to engendering anxiety in the young, then it is often possible for the adolescent and adult to strive toward idealized goals of self-fulfillment and social service. As stated so clearly in the report in this chapter by Haan, Smith, and Block, there is a difference in both the behavior and social backgrounds of young adults who may be classified as "principled young people" and those who may best be described as "conventionally moral." The latter group may be expected to try most of the time to do the "right" thing as it is typically defined by traditions and customs. The former group appear to be striving for something "better" for all concerned; they seem dissatisfied to accept the status quo in human affairs; they desire the "best" and achieve their happiness (if not always social success) by persistently striving toward improved conditions for civilized living. Some succeed during their lifetimes in making progress toward such ideal goals and are rewarded by the praise of their contemporaries; some fail and immediately retreat to a conventionally moral level of conduct; and some strive valiantly for a lifetime without social recognition but receive their social commendation posthumously. According to theory, the creative person whose activities may not be socially rewarded can still find happiness through the intrinsic rewards inherent in his work. But, as is well documented in historical accounts, not all creative persons have been so fortunate. The research by Haan, Smith, and Block is an example of a relatively neglected type of inquiry. Much more research in this general area is needed in order for the findings of the social sciences to provide reliable and valid guides for educational procedures that have the greatest probability of influencing boys and girls to build upon the best features of their cultural past and present.

In his report, Eysenck reminds us that man in his various stages of development has deep biological roots that cannot be overlooked or undervalued in any adequate account of the acquisition of moral values during childhood. Some boys and girls are easier to socialize than others on the basis of those physical properties that they have inherited as biological organisms. It is Eysenck's thesis that we should be prepared to find that innate biological factors (such as ease of conditioning) play a major role in determining an individual's standards for conduct.

Some examples of representative research into the structure and dynamics of children's ideals and moral persuasions are presented in the reports by Durkin and by McDonald. Durkin substantiates Piaget's hypothesis that children gradually acquire a concept of social justice that is increasingly flexible and contingent on the circumstances related to a particular instance. It must be noted, however, that some of Durkin's findings are not consistent with some of Piaget's postulates. This is to be expected in science. No theorist, however brilliant his works may be, can ever satisfactorily account for all happenings in the realm of his scientific interest. All theories and all presently established invariances in nature are subject to change as the quality and scope of methodology improve.

McDonald's findings again illustrate the developmental nature of morality and the pursuit of idealized goals. His data are not consistent with Piaget's reasoning that children become increasingly flexible in their moral judgments around ten to twelve years of age. Rather, McDonald concludes that morality taught on the basis of categorical principles leads to categorical-type moral decisions—at least throughout middle childhood and early adolescence. The slightly different findings for boys and girls and between different socioeconomic classes point up some of the limitations that restrict generalizing in this area of development and socialization.

In his report, Elkind considers the possible invariances of Piaget's concept of egocentrism as it may apply to the self-consciousness and social sensitivity of the typical adolescent. He hypothesizes that it is only when the growing adolescent develops to the point where he can decenter from his egocentric concern with the evaluations of his several imagined audiences that he can rely on his own ideals and restraints of conscience as socially safe and sure guides for an adequate philosophy for living. Elkind's thesis provides a fresh approach to understanding the teenager, and provides a potentially useful theoretical base for research designed to further our understanding of the antecedents and concomitants of adolescent dissent, exhibitionism, rebellion, and other dimensions of behavior that so often remain baffling to adults during the second decade of the young person's development.

In his report, Hoffman performs the valuable service of summing up of what little is known about the influence of different aspects of child-rearing on the moral development of children. This review reveals the many gaps in our research on this important part of the socialization process. This area of research suffers from numerous conceptual and methodological deficiencies, many of which are discussed in Hoffman's excellent summary. It is hoped that the current resurgence of interest in finding out more and more about the determinants of human morality can be sustained, and that the findings can be translated into useful guides for all who are attempting to contribute to the eventual happiness and success of our young. New and improved theories, methods, and research strategies are greatly needed in this important domain of psychological development and environmental influence.

52. MORAL REASONING OF YOUNG ADULTS: POLITICAL-SOCIAL BEHAVIOR, FAMILY BACKGROUND, AND PERSONALITY CORRELATES

Norma Haan, M. Brewster Smith, & Jeanne Block

Social and political historians may be in a better position during some subsequent decade to interpret the background and significance of the violent dissent, extreme withdrawal, and militant "activism" that has characterized substantial proportions of America's young men and women during the middle and late 1960's. At the present time, with the current knowledge that is always incomplete and myopic, it is possible to interpret such dissent, withdrawal, and activism in many different ways. For example, it is possible to conclude that such youthful activities are nothing new, but merely a somewhat different variation of rebellion that is seen in each new generation. Or, as another of several possibilities, one can conclude that today's young men and women are aspiring toward superior ideals and trying to build more useful social institutions, or at least make much needed changes in the old outmoded institutions. Perhaps they hope that modern man can move on to higher levels of ethical responsibility, brotherly love, peace, and happiness.

If one does not write off the quest of today's youths for social and political reforms as just the usual, impractical, ephemeral, idealized meanderings of "immature" minds which will fade away as soon as the activists have grown to maturity, then it is reasonable to attempt a scientific explanation for the apparently greater fervor and ethical dedication of this

SOURCE. Adapted and abridged from Norma Haan, M. Brewster Smith, and Jeanne Block. "Moral Reasoning of Young Adults: Political-Social Behavior, Family Background, and Personality Correlates," *Journal of Personality and Social Psychology*, 1968, Vol. 10, 183–201. (With permission of the authors and the American Psychological Association.)

generation of young people. It should be of scientific interest to attempt an identification of the differential developmental antecedents of dissenters and activists of various degrees of moral commitment and ethical persuasion. It is the latter which defines the aims and goals for the following interesting study by Haan, Smith, and Block. In this investigation, a provocative schema for classifying levels of moral judgment previously developed by Kohlberg was usefully employed. The details of this influential classificatory approach may be of special interest to the reader.

Although there are many interesting findings in this study, the contrast between "principled young people" and the "conventionally moral" youths stands out as a major outcome. The authors show how the conventionally moral young people are insulated from conflicting values by their "harmonious, nonskeptical relations with traditional institutions." In contrast, the "principled youths" are characterized by a "firm sense of autonomy in their life patterns and idiological positions." The latter are more concerned with their inner-personal obligations, and thereby reject traditional values which, to the authors, seem implicit in the Protestant Ethic. The authors conclude that the findings show strong associations between political protest, social action, and principled reasoning. They note, however, that premoral men also protest. And it may be difficult to separate the sheep from the goats.

Activist youth maintain that there are moral necessities for their social-political protest; this assertion bears upon a current, major research issue concerned with the relationship of moral judgment to behavior. If such a connection between moral reasoning and protesting behavior were found, and the activists were actually morally distinctive, a second issue concerned with the nature and context of the socialization experiences associated with morality and its related behavior would be of immediate interest.

The morality of young children has been studied more thoroughly than later morality, but a clearer understanding of the latter is crucial since it is the more critical issue for society. Various theoretical positions diverge in their assumptions about the kind of antecedent experiences that lead to a capability for principled judgments and behavior. In Kohlberg's (1964) developmental perspective the role of socializing agents and institutions is primarily that of providing role-taking opportunities since the young individual is viewed as developing morality in his own terms. On the other hand, various social learning points of view, for example, Aronfreed (1968), Bandura and McDonald (1963), generally ascribe moral attainment to selective reinforcement experiences and modeling behavior by the young and thereby suggest roles for socializing agents in children's development that are better characterized as countervening.

Conformity to the value content of some current social ideal, for example, the Protestant Ethic, or even "activism," is frequently taken as evidence of high morality. The value content of such orientations are clearly subject to considerable historical and cultural specificity, and the present generation's conceptualization of the "good man" is probably different from past ones. Moral philosophy draws attention, however, to the "calculus" (Baier, 1958) of moral reasoning, its processual properties, such as objectivity, generality, inclusiveness, universalizability, and impersonalness. The form of reasoning may likely have greater predictability and wider application than time-and-group-bound content; simple knowledge of socially approved ideals is known to be only a weak predictor of moral behavior. The present study focuses primarily on process criteria as indexed by the Kohlberg Moral Judgment Scale, but it also brings the Kohlberg typology of moral reasoning into relation with contemporary features of value content as indexed by descriptions of the ideal self.

This investigation identifies moral types based on the reasoning of college youth and Peace Corps volunteers in response to moral dilemmas of the Kohlberg Moral Judgment Scale and analyzes the differences between the types in political-social behavior, family background, perceptions of mother and father, and self-and ideal description. Other analyses from the larger study, of which this is part, have been reported by Block, Haan, and Smith (1968).

METHOD

Subjects

The original pool of 957 subjects who responded to the Kohlberg Moral Judgment Scale included University of California and San Francisco State College students and Peace Corps volunteers in training. The sexes were about equally divided; freshman and graduate students were excluded and Peace Corps volunteers were somewhat older. Most student subjects were contacted by letters sent to the membership of various organizations and to students randomly drawn from the registration files on the two campuses. Materials were subsequently sent to willing persons and returned by them through the mail. Berkeley campus groups included arrestees in the Free Speech Movement (FSM), Young Democrats, Young Republicans, California Conservatives for Political Action; San Francisco State College groups were the student-body-sponsored Community Involvement Program, Tutorial Group, and Experimental College. Some Peace Corps volunteers were tested in group meetings; others completed the tasks individually. The sample is not representative, since the subjects were volunteers and the participation rate was uneven from one contact group to another (cf. Smith et al., 1969, for a discussion of response rates). This analysis is concerned only with

54% of the responding sample who could be assigned to one or another of five "pure" moral types according to their responses to the Moral Judgment Scale.

Kohlberg Moral Judgment Scale

Kohlberg has identified three general levels of moral judgment with two types in each stage according to an age-developmental scheme which was demonstrated both longitudinally (Kohlberg, 1964; Kramer, 1968) and with cross-sectional age groups (Kohlberg, 1968; Turiel, 1969). The general levels and the specific stages are described in Table 1 and the alpha abbreviations identifying the various types are shown.

TABLE 1

Classification of Moral Judgment into Levels and Stages of Development

Levels	Basis of Moral Judgment	Stages of Development
I	Premoral Moral value resides in external, quasi-physical happenings, in bad acts, or in quasi-physical needs rather than in persons and standards.	Stage 1: Obedience and punishment orientation. Egocentric deference to superior power or prestige, or a trouble-avoiding set. Objective responsibility. Stage 2: Instrumental Relativists (IR) Naively egoistic orientation. Right action is that instrumentally satisfying the self's needs and occasionally others'. Awareness of relativism of value to each actor's needs and perspective. Naive egalitarianism and orientation to exchange and reciprocity.
II	Conventional Moral value resides in performing good or right roles, in maintaining the conventional order and the expectancies of others.	Stage 3: Personal Concordance (PC) Good-boy orientation. Orientation to approval and to pleasing and helping others. Conformity to stereotypical images of majority or natural role behavior, and judgment by intentions. Stage 4: Law and Order (LO) Authority and social-order maintaining orientation. Orientation to "doing duty" and to showing respect for authority and maintaining the given social order for its own sake. Regard for earned expectations of others.
III	Principled Moral value resides in conformity by the self to shared or shareable standards, rights or duties.	Stage 5: Social Contract (SC) Contractual legalistic orientation. Recognition of an arbitrary element or starting point in rules or expectations for the sake of agreement. Duty defined in terms of contract, general avoidance of violations of the will or rights of others, and majority will and welfare. Stage 6: Individual Principles (IP) Conscience or principle orientation. Orientation not only to actually ordained social rules but to principles of choice involving appeal to logical universality and consistency. Orientation to conscience as a directing agent and to mutual respect and trust.

Note.—Adapted from Kohlberg (1967).

Five of the 10 Kohlberg stories were chosen for use in this study (a sixth story concerned with the FSM sit-in of 1964 was included for Berkeley students, but is not considered in this paper). The stories pose classical moral dilemmas and are followed by questions which elicit the subject's resolution of the quandry, but more importantly ask for his supporting reasons. One situation concerns a husband who steals a drug for his wife because she is dying of cancer; the husband is unable to afford the drug, and all other means of his securing it are closed. Subsequent questions are concerned with the rightness or wrongness of his decision, the drug owner's rights, a husband's duties, one's obligations to nonrelatives, and the appropriate punishment for the husband. Sample answers for various stages and dilemmas can be found in Kohlberg (1964, p. 401).

Scoring. Three judges were trained by Kohlberg in a 4-day session. Scoring was based on sentence responses and relied upon a detailed manual worked out by Kohlberg. Each story was scored for approximately 200 subjects before the judges moved to the next in the series. A major overall type score, and a minor when needed, was assigned for each story. All stories were scored independently by two judges, and they did not know the sample membership or sex of the subjects.

Assignment of moral type. Subjects were mechanically assigned to their final "pure" type in accordance with a rule which required that the assigned type score must have twice the summed weight of any other for all five stories and two judges; major scores were weighted "2," or "3" if no minor was given, and minors, "1." This is a stringent criterion since there are 20 opportunities for a particular type score to appear. As a result the types are quite homogeneous; for example, Stage 2 men have the following mean scores across the six stages: .8, 18.5, 3.9, 2.9, 6.1, 1.5. Only one subject representing Stage 1 was found, and he is not included in this report.

Reliability. Reliability of scoring was calculated in two main ways. A first estimate of reliability was based upon the percentage of agreement between the two judges in their individual modal designations. (Note this procedure, based upon individual judges, is different from the assignment of the final consensus type just described.) The agreement between the two judges' modal type designations was 85%, with agreement defined as either complete (both major and minor), major code only, or reversals of major and minor designations.

In the second instance, a subject's weighted score for each story was summed for each judge. The reliability estimate which resulted from correlating the first judge's total scores with the second was .82 for all 957 subjects.

The Kohlberg instrument is usually administered in an interview and the paper-and-pencil version probably caused some subjects to abbreviate their responses to these troublesome dilemmas. This may have lowered reliability and led to an inflated proportion of mixed types. The low incidence of Instrumental Relativism and Individual Principles in this large sample is an interesting indication of the restrictions in extreme types with a bright, college-age population and corroborates Kohlberg's observation that modal morality is conventional. Despite their small numbers, these two extreme types are included in all analyses because of their relevance to the outer limits of morality. The results for these groups particularly need to be tested with other samples.

Other Measurements

The subjects filled out a five-page Biographical Questionnaire which asked for checks, ratings, and rankings. Questions concerned college status, political-social activity and commitments, demographic information and parents, agreement with parents about issues commonly in dispute between generations, and the degree of influence attributed to different agents with respect to the person the subject now is, his political-social views, and his ethics and morality.

A 63-adjective Q sort, adapted from one previously constructed by Jeanne Block, was sorted twice by the subjects to describe both their perceived and ideal selves. Adjectives were chosen to represent qualities which are deemed positive from various points of view.

Another Q sort, the 91-item Child-Rearing Practices Report, developed by Block (1965), was used by the participants to give their description of the mother's child-rearing practices, and an identical set with an altered stem, the father's child-rearing practices. All Q sorts were done with a forced rectangular distribution of seven steps, so that group comparisons reflect an accumulation of differences in degrees of variable saliency within the individuals who make up contrast groups.

RESULTS

The results of this study are best presented as a series of integrated summaries for each moral level. Some descriptive information for the various types is reported as percentages, but a probability level of $\leq .05$ is adopted as the cutting point for reporting other results with χ^2 or F ratio being the test of significance. The authors recognize the strict inapplicability of probability statistics to these data. A few findings at the .10 level are presented when they are of special interest, and in this case the probability level is noted. The summaries start with the principled Social Contract (SC) and Individual Principles (IP) groups which are first considered as one. Differences between them are subsequently discussed. After the results for the typologies are presented several summary analyses specifically concerned with moral judgment and behavior and family milieu are reported.

Principled Morality Groups

Biographical information. The principled groups are more likely to have interrupted their college careers, live in apartments and houses on their own, are politically more radical, were strongly in support of the Free Speech Movement (FSM), more frequently indicate that they are agnostics, atheists, or areligious, were frequently raised in Jewish or areligious homes, tend to have politically liberal parents with mothers being comparatively better educated. (The fathers' education and occupational levels did not approach significance for any of the groups.) Even though the parents of these young people are liberals, their sons, and even more, their daughters, indicate that they are absolutely more discrepant and left wing than their parents. They moderately disagree with their parents in regard to political-social issues. Sons report that their fathers have influenced them less, personally and politically, while their close friends have been more influential. The principled women report strong influences from close friends in all domains, political influence from organized groups, and altogether less parental influence.

The political-social activity of the principled groups is the highest. They not only have affiliated with more organizations and movements but have also been much involved in them. Greater numbers have engaged in a large variety of activities with a heavy emphasis upon political protest. Social service activity does not significantly distinguish between groups, but further details show that principled youth have not devoted themselves solely to jarring the establishment.

Adjective Q sorts. *Idealistic* is the only self-characteristic common to both the male SC and IP groups (common refers to characteristics that are either highest or lowest for *both* the SC and IP groups). The principled men's distinctive conceptualization of the ideal, good man emphasizes both their commitment to taking the roles of others by the high value they place on *perceptive, empathic,* and *altruistic* and their rejection of *stubborn* and to self-expressiveness implied by *creative.* Their censure of contemporary society is evidenced by their idealization of *rebellious* and their rejection of *conventional.* The principled women described themselves dysphorically as *guilty, doubting, restless, impulsive,* and with the clearly moral word, *altruistic.* They do not see themselves as *foresightful, ambitious,* or *stubborn.* Both groups feel they are less *feminine* than any of the others ($p < .10$). The shared ideal conceptualization of the women is being *rebellious* and *free,* but not *ambitious, practical, responsible,* or *sociable.*

Perceptions of parental practices. The principled males reported that their mothers teased and made fun of them and that the relationship was the most conflicted. Fathers were seen as most willing to let their sons take chances and try new things. The mothers of the principled women are seen as most disappointed in their daughters, likely to let them know about maternal sacrifices, and least likely to comfort them when they are upset. They were least likely to take away privileges for punishment or to give extra ones for good behavior. Fathers did not take away privileges when their daughters were bad and least approved of competitive games, according to their daughters.

SC and IP differences. Scheffé tests were calculated for all significant *F* ratios but none significantly separated the SC and IP groups (except for SC males' self-description of being more practical). The Scheffé is a very conservative test of group contrasts, but there are a number of other nonsignificant differences which do form coherent patterns. IPs more than SCs have interrupted their college careers, live on their own, are more radical, and more pro-FSM. The men are more frequently agnostic. The IP women are more areligious, their mothers are more radical, but even so, their political discrepancy with parents is greater. More SC women are from Jewish backgrounds. IPs generally agree with their parents less (the IP men, however, are in greatest agreement with both parents about occupational choice), and report less influence from parents and more from friends. The IPs have been the more politically-socially active.

Other differences where one group occupied an extreme position while the other had a middle rank show that the IP men see themselves as especially open to experience (*curious, sympathetic, responsive,* and not *reserved*) and less tradition oriented (not *conventional* and *practical*). The SCs described themselves as the most *foresightful*. The IP's ideal conceptualizations include a sense of interpersonal involvement: *idealistic, sensitive,* and *loving,* while devaluing *competitive, self-controlled, orderly, practical, aloof,* and *sociable*. The SCs only saliently value *self-controlled* while they reject *self-confident, uncompromising,* and *playful*.

Only a single self-difference separated the women: the SCs are highest for *fair,* whereas the IPs see themselves as the lowest. The IPs, like their male counterparts, uniquely combine their dissent from society with an idealization of interpersonal reactivity: they value *rebellious* and *individualistic* but also *sensitive* and *empathic* ($p < .10$), and place the least weight on *foresightful, orderly,* and *stubborn*. The more pragmatic SCs value *idealistic* least.

The parents of the SC men appear to place more emphasis on affection. The mothers of SC men were placed lowest in feeling that affection weakens a child. Their fathers openly express affection by kissing and hugging and are seen as too wrapped up in their children. On the other hand, the families of the IP boys seem to emphasize individuation, are less pressuring and rather factual with each other; the mothers were lowest in encouraging their sons to always do their best. The fathers seem like self-individuated men with clear standards for their sons. They most wanted time for themselves, felt too much affection would harm children, and were least wrapped up in their sons. (Note that the IP fathers were seen to be much more likely than any other group to let their sons take chances and try new things.)

The mothers of the SC and IP women are not differentiable; however, differences between fathers parallel the results for the males. The IP women were not given responsibilities by their fathers and feel they have disappointed their fathers.

Summarization for principled groups. The principled groups seem to have developed an autonomous sense of themselves. Their descriptions of the good man are a leitmotif of interpersonal responsiveness and self-expressiveness. Their dissonant political stands appear relatively ego-syntonic and tension free since they have the smallest discrepany between self and ideal on rebelliousness which is placed approximately at the absolute $\overline{X}$ on both Q sorts. They seem to have been permitted, and perhaps were encouraged by their parents, to be importantly affected by their own life experiences in their own time and place. The result seems to be that these young people, having interacted with a different and highly fluid social context, are not in high political-social agreement with their elders nor do they give them credit for what they are today. It is more likely that they feel self-made.

These parents of principled youth are not seen by their offspring as permissive; instead they are viewed as actively involved and even conflict producing. They insist on their own rights as people at the same time that they respect the needs of their children. The mothers of the IP women emphasized their sacrifices, clearly an officially disapproved way for a "good mother" to act. The fathers of the men felt free to insist on time for themselves. The familial relationships are not seen as being importantly defined by formal powers of parents to give and take-away. SC families are characterized as more concrete, loving, reactive, and conflicted, whereas IP families are seen as less expressive but clearer and more factual about the individuation and the responsibilities of its members.

The women's dysphoric self-descriptions, particularly the IPs, suggest that the development of autonomous morality—perhaps even autonomous ego functioning—may be a more arduous task for girls than boys and one that is not accomplished with comfort by this age group. There is a particular flavor of self-honesty and self-condemnation, consistent with Kohlberg's formulation of IPs, reflected in their report of guilt and lack of fairness.

In summary, principled young people are characterized by a firm sense of autonomy in their life patterns and ideological positions. They appear candid about themselves and their families and espouse both new values and their new politics. They are concerned with their interpersonal obligations while they reject traditional values implicit in the Protestant Ethic.

Conventionally Moral Groups

Biographical information. The Personal Concordance (PC) and Law-Order (LO) groups of both sexes share many characteristics indicating that they conduct their lives in expected ways: they least often interrupt their college careers, predominantly live in institutional, adult-approved arrangements, are politically more conservative (the means are in the moderate to conservative range), have small political difference with their most conservative parents, and were least in support of FSM (their absolute means are still in the range of approving). Their religious upbringing was often Protestant or Catholic, and they more often retain the religious beliefs of their childhood and still attend church. Their mothers are the least educated of all groups.

Family harmony and strong parental influence are reported: the men are in the highest agreement with their fathers in regard to most issues sampled and with their mothers in regard to friends. Moreover, they attribute considerable influence to their fathers, both politically and personally, and the least to close friends. Fathers and daughters agree politically and are in harmony with regard to the subjects' vocational choice. Mothers and daughters agree on both politics and religion. These women attribute considerable political, personal, and ethical influence to their mothers and political and ethical influence to their fathers. The clergy and older relatives have also influenced them while close friends and boyfriends have not.

The conventional groups have affiliated with few political-social organizations and were relatively inactive. Only small proportions engaged in political-social activities of any sort, except for attending meetings.

Adjective Q sorts. The self-descriptions for the male groups reflect traditional virtues: they see themselves as comparatively *conventional, ambitious, sociable, practical,* and *orderly,* and not as *curious, individualistic,* or *rebellious.* The women describe themselves as *ambitious* and *foresightful* and not as *guilty, restless,* or *rebellious.*

The shared conceptualizations of the good person by both sexes include values that emphasize efficient control of the self and social skillfulness, rather than the self-expressiveness and interpersonal responsiveness valued by the principled groups. The men value *ambitious, competitive, practical, foresightful, orderly, conventional,* and with other people they would be *responsible, self-confident, sociable,* and *needing approval.* They devalue *doubting, rebellious, idealistic*; self-expressiveness as reflected in *creative, free,* and *artistic*; and interpersonal responsiveness as reflected in *sensitive, perceptive,* and *empathic.* Although the women's conceptualizations of the ideal person have less commonality, the pattern is still like the men's. They value *orderly, logical, responsible,* and, paradoxically, both *competitive* and *self-denying. Rebellious* and *sensitive* are placed low.

Perceptions of parental practices. Father-son relations are reported as the least conflictual and angry, and fathers were seen as always believing that their sons told the truth and placed least emphasis on making a good impression. The mother-son relationships also were described as less conflicted; mothers expected the least from their sons, wanted the least time for themselves, but felt most that too much affection would weaken a child.

The women's descriptions of their parents have fewer shared characteristics. Nevertheless the commonalities reflect the use of parental power: their mothers gave extra privileges when they were good; fathers had firm, well-established rules, their daughters did not disappoint them, and they did not want their daughters to be different.

PC and LO differences. A systematic difference between the PC and the LO groups shows that the LOs are more exaggerated in their traditionalism than the PCs. The LOs and their parents are the more conservative; there is both greater agreement with and influence from their parents. Their parents are less consciously ambivalent. The self- and ideal descriptions of the LOs more strongly emphasize the aggressive self-sufficiency and the interpersonal exteriorizing implied in the Protestant Ethic.

Scheffé tests between groups were calculated for the significant F ratios: the PC men are politically less conservative ($p \leq .10$) than the LOs, describe themselves as less reserved ($p \leq .10$), are more valuing of responsivity ($p \leq .05$), and their mothers were more likely to give extra privileges for good behavior ($p \leq .05$). Other differences where the LOs were in an extreme position and the PCs in the middle show that the LOs see themselves as most foresightful and put the least value on loving, responsive and impulsive. Their mothers least often teased them, most often knew where they were and what they were doing, and encouraged them always to do their best. Their fathers were seen as not expressing affection openly and wanting the least time for themselves while feeling reluctant to see their sons grow up, whereas the PC fathers were the least reluctant ($p \leq .10$).

Scheffé tests showed that the PC women, significantly more than the LOs, attribute close friends ($p \leq .05$) and boyfriends ($p \leq .10$) with having influence on their morals and ethics, see themselves as less foresightful ($p \leq .10$), and also value this characteristic less ($p \leq .05$). Of all groups, the LOs see themselves as least aloof and doubting and place the lowest value on individualism. LO fathers gave their daughters family responsibilities and took away privileges when they were bad. The PC women most value sociability and ambitiousness.

Summarization for the conventionally moral groups. The context for the moral reasoning of these young people is clear: they have harmonious, nonskeptical relations with traditional institutions—school, church, and politics—and with personal authorities—father, mother, and clergy. In this way they are probably well-insulated from conflicting values, and thus the impact of current political pressures and dilemmas upon them is attenuated. In this way, and consistent with the theory's expectations, the moral choices of the LOs can be guided by the rules of existing authorities and institutions while the PCs can consider the immediate wishes and good intentions of authorities in their attempt to maintain smooth role relationships, sociability, and to avoid guilt.

In summary, these young people describe their parents as relating to them in a manner consistent with the strategies generally recommended by social learning theory for the development of morality—clear rules, punishments, and rewards. There is ample evidence that they have modeled themselves after their parents and have accepted the traditional values of American society. It is clear that the child-rearing practices and the nature of the parent-child relationship described by the conventionalists make for a high degree of familial harmony, personal confidence, and political inactivity—even within the sphere of their own conventional ideology.

Premoral Instrumental Relativists

Biographical information. The Instrumental Relativists (IRs) of both sexes were more likely to have interrupted their college careers. The men more frequently live on their own, generally consider themselves political liberals or radicals, are now most nontheistic, do not attend church, but are disproportionately from Jewish backgrounds. Both men and women most strongly supported FSM, although the women are only moderate liberals. Mothers of both are the best educated and are politically liberal; their fathers are more conservative. Discrepancies with the parents in political attitudes are the greatest for the men while women are in complete harmony with the political beliefs of their mothers. The men least agree with their fathers in regard to generational gap issues but acknowledge moderate paternal personal and political influence; they disagree with their mothers about the personal concerns of friends and occupational choice. The women, more than other groups, agree with their mothers about politics and attribute strong political influence to them, but religion is a cause of discord. They attribute opposite sex peers with stronger political, personal, and ethical influence than any other group.

IR men have belonged to only a moderate number of organizations, but their participation has been the most intense; their activity has involved both protest and politics. Conversely, the women have joined the most organizations but have been the most inactive.

Adjective Q sorts. Both men and women describe themselves as the most *rebellious*, but their rebellion is not ego-syntonic as reflected by their greatest discrepancy between self- and ideal item placements. The men's self-reports generally reflect a lack of involvement with others and an emphasis on personal freedom. The men see themselves as *reserved* and *nonresponsive*, but also *creative* and *individualistic*; they idealize the traits of *aloof*, *stubborn*, and *uncompromising* but also would like to be *responsive*, *playful*, *free*, and *artistic*. They reject most traditional virtues and place a lower value than any group on *altruism*. The women also reject interpersonal obligations but seem more intent on securing their own ends than on being personally expressive. They describe themselves as *stubborn* and *aloof* and report that they are neither *altruistic* nor *impulsive*. They place a low value on *self-denying*, *free*, and *empathic* ($p \leq .10$) and idealize a contradictory pattern of *practical* and *stubborn* coupled with *idealistic* and *sensitive*. They describe themselves as the most *feminine* ($p \leq .10$), consistent with their heterosexual commitment as reflected in the influence accorded their boyfriends.

The relations of the IR men with their fathers involve greater conflict and anger than any other group. In addition, the IRs most felt that their fathers expected them to make a good impression, doubted their reliability, discouraged trying new things if failure might result, and were the least concerned that too much affection was harmful. In terms of these emphases, it is of some interest that 5 of these 16 fathers were salesmen. Their well-educated mothers seem to have a detached, laissez-faire, indulging attitude; they were the lowest in teasing them, least often gave extra privileges when the sons were good, least often knew where they were, and most liked time for themselves. They, too, were not concerned that excess affection would weaken their sons. They held the highest aspirations for them, but with ambivalence suggested by the fact that they were not particularly encouraging.

The IR women described their mothers in unrelieved, positive terms: they comforted their daughters when they were afraid, found it interesting to be with them, were not disappointed by them, did not remind them of maternal sacrifice, and did not take away privileges as punishment. Fathers were seen as uninvolved and permissive: they did not establish firm rules or family duties, did not think scolding or criticism helped ($p \leq .10$), least cared if their daughters were different, but believed competitive games were good. Five of these seven fathers were engineers.

Summarization for the IRs. Male IRs are politically radical, active, and protesting; the women are political moderates and inactive, even though they are "joiners" and strongly supported FSM. In spite of these behavioral differences, there is commonality in their intrapsychic descriptions. Both see themselves as rebellious but wish they were less so. Both disclose in their self- and ideal descriptions (by the use of such words as aloof, reserved, stubborn, uncompromising, and most importantly, altruistic and self-denying) that they do not endorse the neccessity or the interpersonal obligation to take the roles of others and are, instead, more concerned with personal fulfillment—the women by a stubborn practicality and the men for personal flair and expressiveness. These findings are consistent with the Kohlberg conceptualization of Stage 2 which emphasizes self-enhancement and rejects reciprocal obligations and satisfactions.

The IR families did not seem to encourage their children to evolve a sense of responsibility and autonomy. The IR men seem to have been alternately pressured, neglected, and indulged; the women's relationships with their mothers seem somewhat immature and suggest that these women are still quite dependent on their mothers. Taken altogether, there seems to be evidence to suggest that the IRs may have been indulged as children for purposes of maternal convenience in the case of the men and for enhancing the child's dependency in the case of the women. The problem with indulgence is that it can never be unambivalent, since the competition of rights between children and parents is inevitable, giving rise to the recrimination expressed by IR men. Because indulgence is often motivated by parental convenience and self-interest, there is unpredictability and a lack of clarification of rights and responsibilities, an unlikely context for moral development.

Since these educated and advantaged young people presumably have had opportunity for cognitive development, if not moral development, their premorality may be due more to affective disruption with social units and institutions than to experiential retardation. It is possible that the IR's present level of moral reasoning might be only temporarily regressive, due to personal crises, since Kramer (1968) did find such phenomena characterizing a small sample within a longitudinal study.

A Comparison of the IR and IP Groups

The reader will have noted that the male IR and IP groups have a number of similarities. Both groups, more than any of the others, report frequent interruption of their college careers, independent living arrangements, political liberalism-radicalism, pro-FSM positions, political involvement, and a lack of religious comment. Their self- and ideal descriptions both express the mode of present-day "liberated" youth. There are other considerations, however, which indicate that the distinction between the two types is valid and that their seemingly similar protesting and politicized behavior arises from different sources.

First, there is sufficient commonality between the intrapsychic descriptions of male and female IRs to suggest that the classification has meaning. Second, the behavior of the IR and IP women is in contrast; the former are inactive, merely joiners of organizations and politically moderate, whereas the IPs are active, protesting, and radical. Third, the fact that both IP men and women are active dissenters in this sample suggests a connection between this behavior and level of moral reasoning. However, the similarity of the male IR and IP groups needs to be examined.

There are pivotal differences. The following synopsis of the differences between IR and IP males follows the rule of citing only those contrasts where these two groups are at the opposite extremes of a dimension defined by all five groups. The rated occupational focus of the IPs is highest ($p \leq .10$), and their fathers agree with them about their choice. IRs and IPs belong to radical organizations in about equal numbers, but the IPs have the highest membership in liberal organizations; the IRs have none ($p \leq .05$). There are twice as many social science majors in the IP group (56%) as in the IR group (25%), but twice as many humanities majors in the IR (25%) as in the IP (12%).

The IRs describe themselves as most stubborn ($p \leq .10$) and *reserved*; the IPs see themselves as most *responsive* and *perceptive* ($p \leq .10$). The IRs idealize *aloof* and *stubborn* ($p \leq .10$) and *reserved*; the IPs *self-denying*. The correlations between the self and ideal Q sorts is highest for the IPs, .59, and lowest for the IRs, .43. The IPs see themselves as more *uncompromising* than they ideally would like to be, but the IRs have little wish for change in this respect ($p \leq .05$). The IR fathers were lowest in letting their sons take chances and try new things, lowest in trusting them to behave when they were not around ($p \leq .10$), and lowest in thinking that too much affection harms a child. The mothers of the two groups could not be distinguished by the criterion being used.

Altogether, this pattern of results indicates a distinct difference between the male IRs and IPs and suggests that ego effectiveness is a cleaving dimension. IR and IP women not only behave differently but are different intrapsychically. IR men and women behave differently but share some pivotal self- and ideal characteristics that are consistent with the theory's conceptualization of this type.

The two groups differ in their relationship to society and to authority. The IPs are independent and critical, but also involved, giving and responsive to others. The IRs are angry, also critical, but disjointed, uncommitted to others, and potentially narcissistic. It should not be surprising to find moral heterogeneity among protestees. Protest which opts for change and accommodation in the social order should draw support from individuals who question the justice of the status quo and are committed to improving it, as well as from those who want to win an issue simply because it is theirs.

Conflict and Disagreement with Parents

In the moral types' relations with their parents the role of conflict and disagreement seems central. Since moral decisions are imminently conflictual, the way that families and institutions view, structure, and resolve conflict

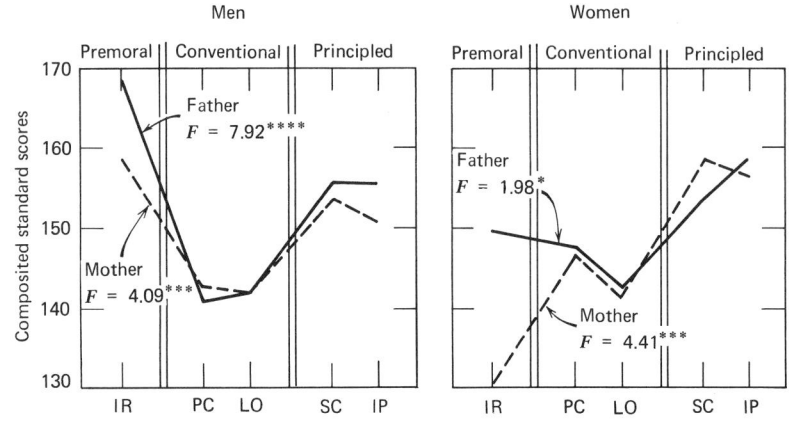

FIGURE 1. Index of parental conflict and disagreement for various moral types.

should have important connections with the development of morality in the young. Figure 1 shows the position of the moral types on separate indexes of mother and father conflict generated by converting three measures of conflict to standard scores and compositing. The dimensions included: (a) subjects' discrepancy with each parent in political commitment, (b) mean disagreement between subject and parents on the generational gap issues, and (c) placement of the Q-sort item referring to degree of conflict with the parent. For the men, there is a curvilinear relationship between conflict and moral reasoning: intense family conflict, particularly with the father, being associated with premorality, least conflict with conventional morality, and moderate conflict with principled morality. For women, conflict with mother is positively related to increasing morality, whereas conflict with father is less important but is still positively related. The relationship with the same-sex parent is the more determinative. A difference between parents in level of conflict is most evident in the IR families.

The findings for men are generally consistent with Kohlberg's (1966) suggestions that moral development is promoted by the cognitive reorganizations that occur when the moral conflicts of naturalistic social interactions are openly examined and negotiated. Langer (1969) has posited a similar vehicle for cognitive development—cognitive disequilibrium. Both the degree of conflict and its quality—affective rather than cognitive—may have retarded or disrupted the moral development in the IR men. This finding is consistent with well-accepted observations that intense or chronic affective states are stressful and disruptive of ego processes. In the female sample, conflict is positively related to moral maturity. Undoubtedly there would be an upper limit but it was not reached in this sample. The social milieu and expectations for women encourage dependency, which is one form of irresponsibility. Consequently, the development of autonomous, principled morality may be a more difficult task for girls because it involves conflict with the culturally defined feminine role. The principled women's dysphoria and their admission of disappointing their parents may be a manifestation of their moral growing pains.

The FSM Situation

The FSM sit-in provides us with an opportunity to view the public behavior of the University of California students in response to the same, well-publicized incident (cf. Lipset & Wolins, 1965, for a good chronology of the event and statement of the issues). Since this conflict took months to develop and public debate took place daily before thousands of students, the ultimate choice for most individuals can be assumed to have been an informed one. Table 2 reports the proportions of the total University of California sample who were arrested for sitting in.

TABLE 2

Percentages of Pure Moral Types Arrested in the FSM Sit-in

	IR	PC	LO	SC	IP
Men	60	18	6	41	75
	(10)	(22)	(50)	(27)	(8)
Women	33	9	12	57	86
	(3)	(32)	(41)	(14)	(7)

Note.—UC students only. N's in parentheses.

These findings, based on a public behavior, are consistent with the subjects' reported activities and substantiate the general relationships of moral reasoning to behavior. The variety of moral reasons that can lead to the same behavior, civil disobedience in this instance, is shown by the fact that some conventionally moral people were also arrested. Most of these students supported their choice of sitting-in (which they reported in the special story concerned with the FSM situation) by reasoning which referred to their supposition that the University of California administrators had failed in their role of authorities—as good authorities for Stage 3, and as actual violators of proper legal understandings for Stage 4. Principled arrestees were more concerned with the basic issues of civil liberties and rights and the relationship of students as citizens within a university community. The IRs' reasons were more often concerned with their individual rights in a conflict of power.

They frequently included the indubitable fact that the sit-in had worked to bring social-political reforms on the campus.

DISCUSSION

That there are comparatively few women in the extreme IR and IP groups, that the source samples, were not representative, and that the Moral Judgment Scale is better administered in an interview have already been noted as limitations of this study. The reliance upon the subjects' descriptions of themselves and their view of their parents means that these results are to be regarded as descriptions of the subjects' present views—including defensive, wishful, or hostile distortions—of their history and current relationships.

Perceptions of parents are undoubtedly subject to developmental changes, and these subjects have described them during a period when separation from the family usually occurs. To the extent that the present results depend upon the character of concurrent relations and upon levels of moral reasoning that may still be evolving, the findings must be understood in a special light. Young people who have already become principled regard themselves as separated from their parents; those who are still conventionally moral, or who will remain conventionally moral, see themselves as stably attached to their parents; premoral men view their familial relationships as chaotically conflicted and indulging, and premoral women see theirs as mother-centered. Little is known about whether adult experiences affect moral development. Kramer (1968) did find continued growth in the late adolescent and young adult years, characterized by a decrease in lower stages rather than an increase in higher stages. This finding suggests that the premoral subjects might be the ones most likely to change.

Within these limitations and qualifications the results also show strong associations between political protest, social action, and principled reasoning —qualified by the finding that premoral men also protest—and that young people of conventional moral reasoning are inactive. Note that these findings do not suggest that protest in itself is moral. That judgment would have to depend upon the nature of the individual's reasoning and the specific aspects of the situation.

This finding and those concerned with parental relations raise a number of questions: What conceptualizations account for the association between the form of moral reasoning and related political-social behavior, since there is no political content in the Kohlberg stories? How can the family and social context of these young people be understood to support these outcomes? Can the Kohlberg conceptualization of moral reasoning account for the shift away from parental values that the principled protestors report?

Subsequent discussion of the above questions necessarily interweaves two concepts: the relation of moral thinking to the existing order of things and the individual's capability of taking another's or society's point of view when he is engaged in moral thought.

The frame of reference for the middle, conventional level of moral reasoning is that of maintaining society. Thus, the morally conventional individual—as he structures the interlocking pros and cons of a moral problem and considers its ramifications, consequences, and alternative solutions—views himself and his decisions as immanently within society. He will see and choose the good in those terms. Consequently, conventional moralizing does not often come to doubt the status quo, unless representatives of that order disappointingly and clearly prove themselves unworthy of their positions. In this way conventional morality circumscribes thinking and choosing the good, and it follows that such individuals are not likely to protest.

The IR must reject the status quo since it often does not comply with his egoistic view of his relationship to others and society and with his personally referenced definition of the good. His self-view does not permit him to see or take the roles of others including those in authority. This inability undoubtedly becomes an increasingly unworkable mode of choosing for people as they grow older.

Conventional, and particularly principled, morality is made possible by the capacity to take another's role which depends upon the ability to extend one's self and move from one's fixedness. The empathy of the PC moralist, although not equivalent to principled or IP role taking, is a precursor of it, as is the understanding respect the LO pays to representatives of society. When a principled person, particularly an IP, temporarily takes the position of another in a moral conflict situation—he may still end up rejecting the primary or legitimacy of the others' rights, such as the drug owner's in the story cited in this paper—considerable cognitive interplay and work is involved. Here thought has the properties of consistency, objectivity, universality, and impersonalness. The thought of the premoralist, however, does not show these characteristics; that is, he cannot objectively take another person's position, irrespective of who he is, and understand that ultimately the other has basic human needs that are roughly consistent with his own.

Political-social protest and premoral reasoning are probably not consistently linked across many samples, as the results for women suggest. Since the IR's concern about society is personally referenced, a generally politicized milieu is undoubtedly required for the IR to protest, and his ultimate criterion would often be whether it would work or not. Political protest itself is likely a fine expression of politicized IRs' personal battles with a society which is seen as ungiving rather than immoral.

The principled individual is not automatically limited by the extant characteristics of a specified social order or arrangement. The SC, however, with his stronger sense of being contractually obligated, may not clearly or smoothly separate himself from the social order, even when he cognizes covenanted injustices. The IP's allegiance in a moral confrontation will be to universal and logically consistent, ideal principles of justice which necessarily include existing social agreements, but his principles will be primary if these two considerations should conflict. Kohlberg (1968) has observed that one cannot be at Stage 6 without first having been at Stage 5, that is, one cannot reject a social contract *on the basis of individual principles* without first understanding the essential contractual nature of social orders and human affairs. The IP takes the role of others in a most inclusive, abstract, and ideal sense. The "others" may frequently be all mankind and are not only those personally known or directly observed as with the PC, or occupants of formal positions as with the LO, or parties to contractual understandings as with the SC. The IP's sense of personal responsibility causes him to take roles in double sense, not only understanding the position of others, but also questioning what he would have others do to him if the tables were turned. This highly developed sense of interpersonal obligation was reflected in the IPs' description of the person he would like to be—sensitive, empathic, and altruistic or self-denying. Principled thinking may or may not support the status quo, but since societies (and people) are only proximate representations of the good at any one time and place, the principled with his sense of obligation and his sense of himself as a chooser, and again the IP more than the SC, is the most likely to protest, as this study has shown.

Most studies that have related behavior to moral judgment have chosen behavior such as cheating, which is "bad" by everybody's agreement, and the required, criterion moral action is prohibitive (cf. Kohlberg, 1964; Maccoby, 1968 for reviews; also Krebs, 1967). The behavior studied here better represents "promotive" or "affiliative" morality as declaratory acts were analyzed. Only one other similar study has been reported. Kohlberg (1968) gave the Moral Judgment Scale to the students who were subjects in Milgram's pseudo-learning experiments. They were asked by the experimenter (an authority) to violate the universal dictate of not hurting others for insufficient reasons by shocking victims who did not learn rapidly. Since the subjects needed to take emphatic and disobedient action to solve their dilemma, the situation is similar to ones that the student protestors often believe they are in. Kohlberg found that 75% of the subjects who used some Stage 6 thinking quit the experiment compared to only 13% of conventional or Pure Stage 5 subjects. Milgram (1965) has commented that most people are without a language of disobedience when confronted with such situations. Kohlberg's study and the present one show, however, that Stage 6 individuals are the least likely to comply with requirements they regard as morally indefensible.

The relationships between the conventionally moral subjects, particularly the LOs, and their parents are consistent with moral replacement, a process Maccoby (1968) has labeled and used to describe the intergenerational process of value transmission as it is conceptualized by social learning theory. The conventionally moral report that their parents used child-rearing strategies which are consistent with social learning's recommendations for the development of morality—clear rules, punishments, and rewards—and there is ample evidence that they have modeled themselves after their parents. The present results suggest that these procedures do not release young people to be affected by their own experiences or to shift in response to social change as Maccoby had already deduced. The principled subjects, while not rejecting their parents with ambivalent anger as do the male premoralists, have adopted political-social and personal values that reflect contemporary leitmotif. Their responsiveness to social change, however, had a history of preparedness within politically liberal families who frankly experienced and examined conflict, and with parents who exercised their own rights as people, rather than the power and control that society automatically ascribes to them.

The families of the conventional moralists were probably not as conflict-free as their offspring describe, and were more likely reported to be conflictless because this was an important family value (an ideal parent sort would have provided certain information). When harmony is an ultimate value, individuals are prone to base their decisions on the approved solutions. Furthermore, conflictless experiences are probably inconsistent with both moral and cognitive growth. Both Turiel (1969) and Kohlberg (1968) have recently reported work which shows that moral development can be accelerated by moral arguments presented to children along with contradictory solutions and different levels of moral thought. The present authors have previously pointed out (Block et al., 1968), in accord with Inhelder and Piaget (1958), that adolescent cognitive development is characterized by the growth of capacities to entertain hypothetical ideas of what might be and to engage in reciprocity—there but for good fortune, go you or I. In this fluid, abstract, and person-oriented context moral disequilibriums undoubtedly occur and may result in change.

Undoubtedly new settings and new experiences, such as those encountered on a college campus, make for cognitive disequilibriums and the reexamination of moral commitments. Late adolescents who are open to experience are more likely to change than those who protect themselves from disharmonies. At the same time they may be the more vulnerable to temporary or permanent regressions, but then all growth is a chance. One does not know whether the stress and moral conflict of the FSM crisis and other Bay Area protests have affected the moral judgments of young people, but they may very well have. One does not know whether the net effect would be progressive or regressive, but it may be surmised that both occurred.

53. THE DEVELOPMENT OF MORAL VALUES IN CHILDREN: THE CONTRIBUTION OF LEARNING THEORY

H. J. Eysenck

A contemporary British psychologist, Eysenck is well known to the scientific world because of the theoretical consistency of his many research papers and his numerous popular and professional books. He has been regarded by many in the United States as a rebel (a reputation we suspect and like to believe he enjoys) because of his sharp criticism of the effectiveness of traditional psychoanalytic and neo-psychoanalytic methods of psychotherapy. He dared, in the days in which it was not nearly so popular to do so, to challenge the allegorical psychoanalytic conception of man and to offer in its stead a far more plebeian version based on Pavlovian conditioning principles. Eysenck has made much theoretical use of the experimental finding that some individuals seem far easier to condition than others.

In the following report, Eysenck builds his argument that values are acquired through processes of learning and conditioning that fall within the general domain of all behavior modification. For example, conscience comes from nothing more than "a conditioned anxiety response to certain types of situations and actions." Some people have stronger consciences than others simply because they condition more easily.

Old concepts of introversion and extroversion are given new life and salience through the conceptual creativity enjoyed by Eysenck. It is his staunch belief and conviction, presented forcefully and unequivocally in

SOURCE. Adapted and abridged from H. J. Eysenck, "The Development of Moral Values in Children: The Contribution of Learning Theory," *British Journal of Educational Psychology*, 1960, Vol. 30, 11–21. (With permission of the author and the British Journal of Educational Psychology.)

many of his writings, that we should be prepared to discover *"innate biological factors* determining in some degree the moral or immoral, criminal or noncriminal reactions of human beings to certain types of situations." Although he appears to believe that much can be done to better man's lot by education and training, Eysenck reaffirms in this paper his belief in the primacy of man as a biological organism.

There is little doubt that attitudes, interests and values are acquired through some process of learning or conditioning during the course of the individual's development, and it seems almost certain from the great deal of evidence accumulated by psychologists, and reviewed by earlier contributors to this symposium, that much of this process of learning takes place during childhood and possibly adolescence. If it is agreed that responses indicative of moral values, whether verbal or behavioural, are indeed, learned responses, then it would seem that modern learning theory, which is probably the most advanced part of psychology, should have a contribution to make to our understanding of their development. In what follows I have tried briefly to indicate the direction which such a contribution might take, and also to quote some experimental data which seem to support the position taken here.

There is an obvious dualism involved in talking about "moral values." We may be concerned with the *knowledge* of existing values in a society, and this can be verbally expressed in a questionnaire or an interview; this knowledge is not necessarily related to conduct although there does appear to be a slight tendency for such correlations to exist. Nevertheless, the delinquent child as well as the criminal adult is usually only too well aware of the *fact* that his conduct is contrary to moral precept; his evil-doing is not by and large due to ignorance.

The alternative method of defining the moral values of a person deals with his conduct, rather than with his knowledge, and it would seem that this approach is probably more fundamental and more fruitful than the other. Here also, however, we have a choice to make. We can deal with the matter at the observational and naturalistic level, i.e., by studying actual delinquencies as has been done for instance by Ackerson (1942), or by Hewitt and Jenkins (1946). Alternatively, we can make use of the experimental method, and study delinquent behaviour in the laboratory, in the classroom, or in strictly controlled conditions, as was done for instance in the famous Character Education Enquiry. In either case we discover that among children, adolescents and adults, there appears to be a range of delinquent behaviour from the person who never commits a delinquent or dishonest act, to the person who almost invariably does so. The task of the learning theorist is to account for this gradation in behaviour along the well established lines of learning theory.

Many people interested in the social consequences of crime put the fundamental question in the following way. They ask: "How is it that some people commit crimes when they know perfectly well that their acts are anti-social, and when they have also been taught that crime does not pay?" Such a way of looking at the problem appears to be the matter of putting the cart before the horse. Delinquent behaviour, i.e., the tendency to act out immediately and without restraint one's instinctual impulses, whether sexual, aggressive or predatory, is surely the natural way to act for animals and for young children; the question is: "Why and how do human beings learn to act in conformity with the dictates of society, however inconvenient and distressing these dictates may be, and however much they may conflict with the individual's biological needs and drives?"

It is often suggested that people refrain from immoral acts because of the fear of punishment. It is unlikely that this hypothesis can be taken very seriously. We know from learning theory that the effectiveness of reward and punishment is an *inverse function* of the time interval between act and reinforcement, and a *direct function* of the proportion of reinforcements. Now the one thing we do know about social punishment is that on both counts it fails to provide the necessary mechanism. Punishment usually occurs a long time after the event, sometimes years after, and it only occurs in a small proportion of cases. It is difficult, if not impossible, to give accurate figures about the relative numbers of crimes discovered and punished, as compared with those where the culprit goes free, but the ratio of reinforcement is almost certainly very low.

There are other reasons for doubting the effectiveness of punishment. The well-known and well substantiated Yerkes-Dodson Law tells us that while an increase in drive usually leads to an improvement in performance and learning, there is an optimal point beyond which an increase in drive leads to a *decrement* in performance and learning. The law also states that the more complex the task, the lower is the drive level at which this reversal occurs. Now the kind of punishment meted out by society is usually rather harsh and, therefore, has a high drive level, whereas the task to be learnt, i.e., behaving in conformity with the precepts of society, is obviously a very complex one. Conditions are, therefore, highly unfavourable for punishment to exert its desired influence.

THE BASIS OF "CONSCIENCE"

These and many other reasons make it unlikely that the threat of punishment is the only or even the main reason for moral behaviour. The alternative suggested by many writers has been a kind of interiorised policeman variously named conscience, "inner light," or *super-ego*.[1] This is usually conceived as some kind of *deus ex machina* implanted in the human being in some mysterious way, which ceaselessly keeps an eye on his activities, and gives him a sharp tweak, whenever he deviates from the straight and narrow path of duty. Descriptively, this is probably not entirely an inaccurate account; the difficulty with it is that there is no known mechanism by means of which such an inner policeman could be called into being, and that the description does not give us any clues about the reasons why some people have a strong and tender conscience while others seem to be completely lacking in it. It is sometimes suggested that environment and teaching are responsible for the apparent individual differences, or that there might be an intellectual deficit which makes some people fail to respond to moral teaching. There is, of course, no doubt that environmental pressures play an important part in the growth of moral ideas and conduct, but such a hypothesis would not account for the frequently observed fact that even the best environment often produces psychopathic individuals apparently lacking completely in any "inner guiding light," while the very poorest environment does not by any means invariably produce criminals. Similarly, there is not very much relationship between lack of intelligence and criminality; what relation there is is more likely between low intelligence and likelihood of being found out!

The suggestion made here is a relatively simple one, namely, that *conscience is a conditioned anxiety response to certain types of situations and actions*. In the typical Pavlovian experiment, the dog, through simple pairing of conditioned stimulus (bell) and unconditioned stimulus (meat powder) learns to salivate to the bell, whereas previously it only salivated to the meat powder. Everyone is familiar with this experimental paradigm, and with the fact that similar conditioned responses, particularly of the autonomic nervous system, can be quite easily produced in human beings as well. There is ample evidence to show that anxiety is a conditioned fear response attached

---

[1] The Freudian conception is concisely given in Freud's "General Introduction": "It is not to be doubted for a moment that one may recognize in the Oedipus-complex one of the most important sources for the consciousness of guilt with which neurotics are so often harassed . . . Perhaps mankind as a whole has, at the beginning of its history, come by its consciousness of guilt, the final source of religion and morality, through the Oedipus complex." Perhaps. Even if the first part of this quotation had some factual reference, it would still not be clear how a phenomenon assumed to be of universal occurrence, like the Oedipus complex, could be used to account for individual differences in proneness to guilt feelings. Nor is it at all clear how such a theory could be experimentally or even observationally tested. Possibly one might deduce that boys brought up by widowers whose wives died in childbirth should all develop into psychopaths. At least they should stand in little danger of developing neurotic guilt feelings!

to a previously neutral stimulus. Watson's famous experiment with little Albert is probably too well known to need extensive retelling; he induced a phobia for furry animals in an 11-month-old infant "Albert," who previously had been fond of such animals, by banging a metal bar with a hammer behind Albert's head whenever the infant reached out to pat a white rat (Watson and Raynor, 1920). Learning theory has formalised the rules according to which this conditioning takes place, but we need not be concerned with anything but the bare fact that *anxiety and fear responses can be conditioned in human beings with very great ease.* It is also to be noted that such conditioned responses, once they are formally established, do not extinguish by themselves in the course of time, but require an experimental process of *extinction* (Osgood, 1953).

The application of this well-documented process to the development of moral behaviour can be briefly indicated in the following way. A young child behaves in a socially undesirable manner, i.e., by being aggressive, by indulging in overt sexual activity, by stealing, lying and cheating, or in whatever way anti-social behaviour is defined in a given society. There is an immediate sharp punishment—a slap, withdrawal of some privilege, "shaming," exclusion from the family circle or whatever it may be. This punishment produces pain and fear and the associated autonomic disturbances; these in turn become attached to the *type of situation* and the *type of action* which called forth the punishment, thus producing a conditioned anxiety reaction whenever similar situations and actions re-occur.

It might be argued that surely identical situations never occur, but this objection is taken care of by the well-known fact of *stimulus generalisation.* Little Albert was taught to be afraid of a rat, but this conditioned fear generalised to rabbits and other furry animals. Stimulus generalisation, therefore, will account for the fact that not only identical but similar situations and actions will also call forth the conditioned anxiety response in the child which has been punished once or several times for certain types of misdemeanour. This process of generalisation is undoubtedly aided by the fact that parents often draw attention to similarities between different anti-social acts by a process of *labelling.* There is ample experimental evidence to show that generalisation of conditioned responses does proceed along verbal lines. Thus the subject who has formed a conditioned P.G.R. response to the word "cow," because this word was in the past followed by an electric shock, will now have a conditioned P.G.R. response also to the names of other animals, such as "goat"; he will not, however, generalise responses to words such as "how" which are, apparently, much more similar to the original conditioned stimulus from the point of view of sound.

We thus have a growing child in whom conditioned anxiety responses have been built up to anti-social behaviour in situations involving aggression, sex, etc. When temptation arises, there also arises the conditioned anxiety, and we, consequently, have some form of hedonic calculus involving not *present* satisfaction and *future* punishment (in which present satisfaction would almost certainly win), but rather *present satisfaction* in opposition to *present discomfort* as produced by the anxiety reaction in response to overt anti-social behaviour. If the conditioning has been strong enough, "conscience" will win the day, and the individual will withdraw from the situations without giving way to "temptation." Even if he does give way to "temptation" there will still be a strong anxiety reaction to detract from his enjoyment, thus making it less likely for him to react anti-socially on the next occasion.

It might be queried whether anxiety is in effect strong enough for this proposed role. When we consider that many people have committed suicide rather than suffer strong anxiety, and when we consider that criminals have, on many occasions, preferred to give themselves up and take their punishment, rather than continue to bear the anxiety produced by their crime, we may not feel so doubtful about the efficacy of the proposed mechanism or its strength. However, such facts, of course, do not provide proof of the hypothesis in question; they merely illustrate the strength which feelings of anxiety can reach. We must now turn to the evidence firmly supporting our hypothesis.

INDIVIDUAL DIFFERENCES

It is well-known that there is a group of people, not sharply segregated from the rest, but presumably continuous with the remainder of humanity, which is characterised by anti-social behaviour in almost pure culture. I am referring, of course, to the so-called *psychopaths,* i.e., to children, adolescents and adults, who, in spite of often high intelligence and good up-bringing, seem to be completely lacking in moral sense—so much so that they have even been called *moral imbeciles.* They will lie, cheat, steal, rape, and indulge in any form of anti-social activity without apparent regard for consequence, and without regard for their victims. Such people will often commit criminal acts for the slightest of gains, and in situations where discovery and severe punishment are practically certain. Here is a group of people for whose behavior no adequate theory has been put forward. Can our theory do better?

Let us note, first of all, that Pavlov already discovered very great individual differences in respect of *conditionability* between his dogs. Some dogs are very easy to condition, others very difficult, with the remainder inbetween. This finding has been universally verified in the case of other animals, and also in the case of human beings. Differences in conditionability are by and large unrelated to such factors as age, sex and intelligence. If our theory is accurate, then we might be able to explain the behaviour of psychopaths by postulating that such people are endowed with a nervous system which is largely resistant to the formation of conditioned responses. If this were so, then the course of upbringing would not suffice to produce in them the requisite anxiety responses, which we have postulated to lie as the basis of "conscience." It should be easy to test this hypothesis by attempting to condition psychopaths in the laboratory, and by comparing their success or failure with the responses made by an average group of people put in the same experimental situation. When this is done, the results very strongly bear out the hypothesis, and it is found that compared with a normal group of people, psychopaths are, indeed, very difficult to condition, requiring many more pairings of conditioned and unconditioned stimulus before any effect is seen (Lykken, 1957; Eysenck, 1957). Results, therefore, are in accordance with our hypothesis.

We might put forward another hypothesis to complement the previous one. There is a group of people in society who are suffering from unduly strong anxieties related to stimuli which, in the normal person, do not arouse anxieties at all. These people suffer from fears of open spaces, fears of enclosed spaces, fears of animals, and so forth, without being able to give any rational account of their fears. Such people constitute the main group of neurotics, whether in-patients or out-patients, at our hospitals and clinics; they are sometimes known as "anxiety states." Such people also frequently show strong guilt feelings about actions which few people would regard as immoral or anti-social in any real sense of those terms. In other words, these people appear to have a conscience much more tender than the average person. In terms of our hypothesis we would expect such people to be particularly easy to condition; their symptoms and their behaviour could then be accounted for in terms of a too ready conditioning of fear responses to a large number of previously neutral conditioned stimuli.

Again, the evidence strongly supports this view. The work of Spence (1956), Franks (1956, 1957), and many others (cf. Eysenck, 1957) shows that people suffering from anxiety states are more easily conditionable than the average run of people, and accordingly, we have a complementary piece of evidence showing that we can arrange human beings in a continuum of "conditionability" from high to low, a continuum which runs parallel with a continuum of behaviour patterns going from hyper-moral through average to psychopathic and immoral. There is more evidence in favour of this hypothesis, and some of it has been quoted elsewhere (Eysenck, 1957). Instead of going into this additional evidence I would prefer to draw attention to another extension of this general scheme.

I have argued that the personality dimension, at the one extreme of which we have the psychopath, and at the other extreme of which we have the anxiety state, can be found not only in the emotional, anxious and neurotic

Striving Toward Idealized Goals 625

type of personality, but also in the population as a whole, and I have suggested that we are, in fact, here dealing with the well-known extravert-introvert typology transferred into the field of neurosis and maladaptation. Figure 1 will illustrate this notion; it is quoted from "The Structure of Human Personality" (Eysenck, 1960) and it is a diagrammatical presentation of a factor analysis of fifty traits which had been correlated by Ackerson (1942)

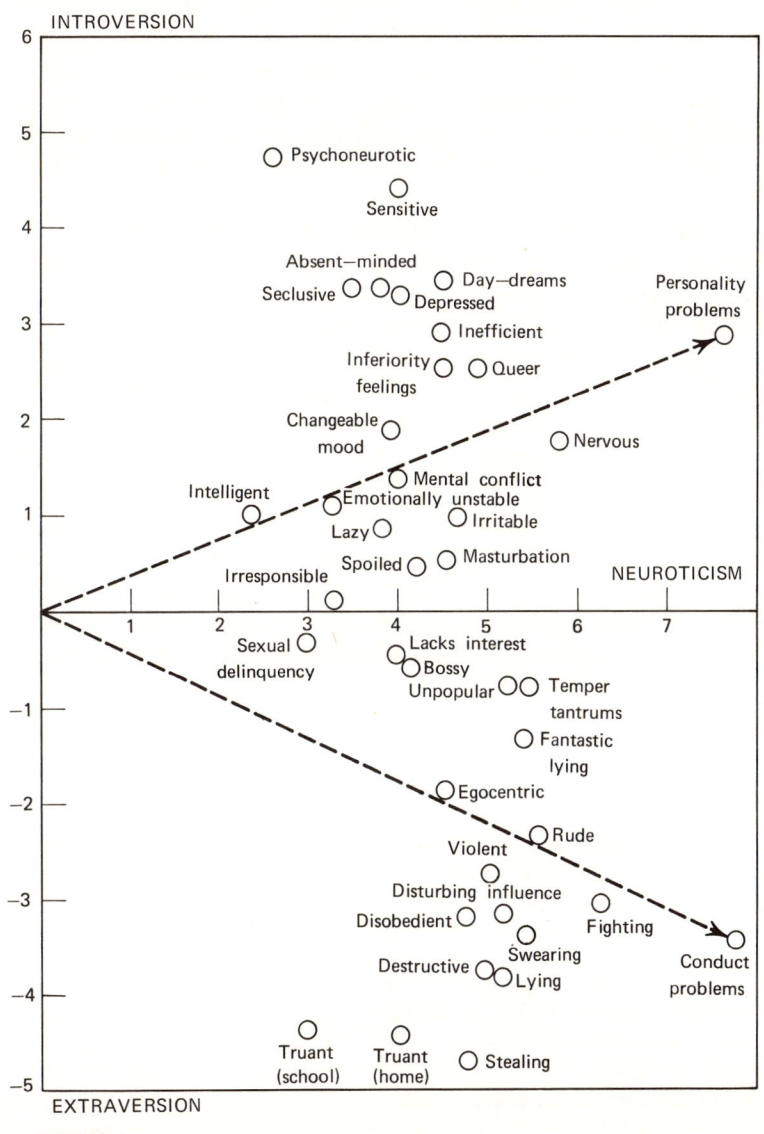

FIGURE 1.

among several thousand children who had been studied at the Illinois Institution for Juvenile Research. It will be seen that of the items included, all have correlations with the general factor of neuroticism or emotional instability, but that there is a division along the lines of the second factor into *personality problems* characteristic of the introvert, and *conduct problems* characteristic of the extravert.

Much the same kind of result was found by Hewitt and Jenkins (1946) in a study of 500 problem children. When they correlated various notations from the case histories of these children, they found three main characteristics, ranging from "unsocialized aggression" (the extraverted end) through "socialized delinquency" to "over-inhibited behaviour" (the introverted end). Other data are quoted in "The Structure of Human Personality," to support the existence of a general dimension of this nature. There is no direct evidence of a relationship between these behaviour patterns in children and their conditionability; here would seem to be an area of research which could, with advantage, be pursued by those responsible for the moral welfare of children and for their disposal after they have come in contact with the law.[2]

Among adults, however, there is considerable evidence in the work of Franks (1956, 1957), and others (Eysenck, 1957) to show that there does exist a significant relationship between introversion and conditionability, even when extreme cases of psychopathy are not included in the neurotic sample, and even when quite ordinary normal subjects are being tested. In so far as our hypothesis deals with conduct and patterns of observable behaviour it must, I think, be concluded that we are on relatively safe ground in putting forward the hypothesis that *differences in conditionability determine in part the socialized or anti-social behaviour of children and adults alike.*

---

[2] The reader may wonder why both personality problems and conduct problems have such high loadings on neuroticism, and whether adult criminals too would be found to be neurotic. It would appear from some recent work done with the Maudsley Personality Inventory on recidivist criminals, that their neuroticism is indeed almost as high as that of hospitalized neurotics. Some learning theorists, particularly Spence, regard neuroticism or emotionality as a kind of drive variable (D), which according to Hull's theory, is multiplied by habit ($_sH_R$) to produce behaviour ($_sE_R$). If we regard, in a very rough-and-ready fashion, the extravert as a person in whom "temptation" $>$ "conscience," whereas in introvert "temptation" $<$ "conscience," then the added drive produced by the emotionality-neuroticism variable might be thought to produce a much stronger reaction in the direction determined by the respective weight of these two influences. This is a highly speculative consideration and it would require a considerable amount of experimental work to decide if any real meaning is attached to it.

IMPLICATIONS OF THE THEORY

Does the theory have anything to say about the more verbalized type of values and attitudes? An attempt has been made in *The Psychology of Politics* (Eysenck, 1954) to make certain deductions from the theory, and to test these objectively. It would seem to follow from the theory developed here that introverts would be more concerned with ethical and moral prohibitions, with religious ideas and quite generally with the erection of barriers against the direct and immediate satisfaction of instinctual and libidinal impulses. Conversely, it would seem to follow that extraverts would be more likely to favour the direct expression of sexual, aggressive, and other anti-social impulses and to be less concerned with ethical, moral and religious ideas. The proof of this hypothesis requires two series of studies. In the first series, a number of correlation studies were carried out on the attitudes of quite large numbers of subjects towards a number of variegated social issues. When these attitudes were inter-correlated, they invariably gave rise to two main factors, the ever present one of radicalism-conservatism, which does not concern us here, and a second factor, independent of the first, the two poles of which were entitled tough-mindedness and tender-mindedness. The factor structure is illustrated in Figure 2, and it will be seen that tender-mindedness is a factor which appears to be characterised by those attitudes theoretically described as introverted, while tough-mindedness is made up of attitudes theoretically attributable to the extravert. Thus, a tough-minded person favours the overt expression of aggression (by flogging, death penalty, birching, etc.), towards out-groups (criminals, Jews, coloured people, etc.), and the overt indulgence in sexual activities (companionate marriage, easier divorce laws, the abolition of abortion laws). The tender-minded person has strongly favourable ideas towards religion and ethical ideals such as pacifism, etc. The first step in our proof, therefore does not seem to contradict the hypothesis (Eysenck, 1954).

As the second step, several studies have been carried out, as I have mentioned in the *Psychology of Politics*, showing that correlations do indeed exist between tender-mindedness and introversion on the one hand, and tough-mindedness and extraversion on the other. Some of these studies have been criticised because of the non-representative nature of the samples, and consequently, I have in a recent investigation, repeated this work on a random sample of the population (Eysenck, 1960). The results were fully in line with those previously reported and seem to leave little doubt about the existence of some such relationship as that postulated. It would appear, therefore, that in the field of verbally expressed moral attitudes and ideas also the general hypothesis here put forward can make possible verifiable predictions.

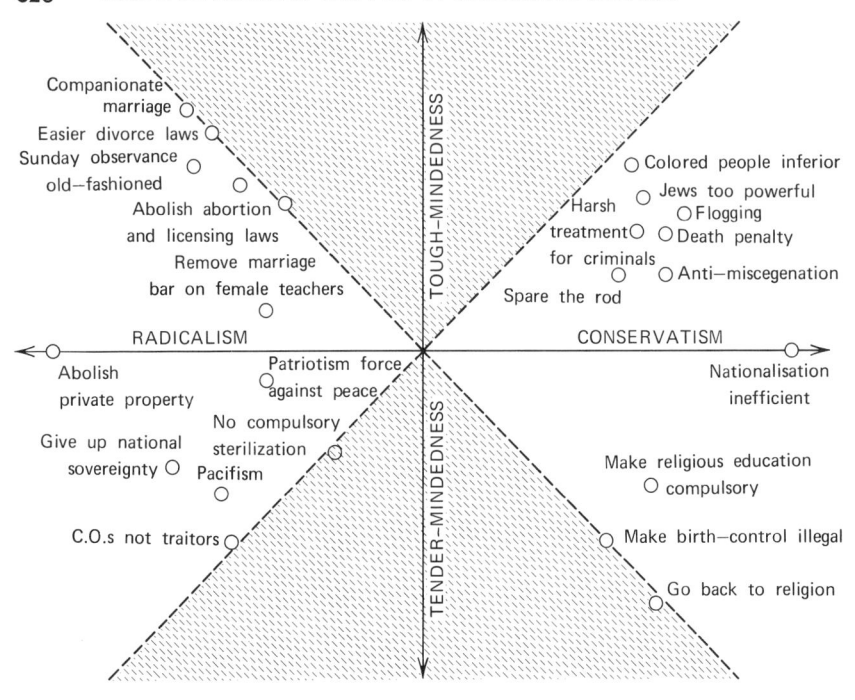

628 SOCIAL DEVELOPMENT: READINGS IN EDUCATIONAL RESEARCH

```
                    TOUGH-MINDEDNESS
Companionate
  marriage
Easier divorce laws
Sunday observance
old–fashioned                              Colored people inferior
    Abolish abortion                        Jews too powerful
    and licensing laws          Harsh        Flogging
        Remove marriage      treatment    Death penalty
        bar on female teachers for criminals
                                            Anti-miscegenation
                              Spare the rod
←   RADICALISM      Patriotism force          CONSERVATISM    →
    Abolish          against peace                     Nationalisation
    private property                                   inefficient
                    No compulsory
Give up national      sterilization
sovereignty    Pacifism                      Make religious education
                                                 compulsory

C.O.s not traitors                           Make birth–control illegal

                                                  Go back to religion
                    TENDER-MINDEDNESS
```

FIGURE 2.

It will, of course, be obvious to the reader that there is no intention, in sketching out this theory, to account for all criminal or immoral behaviour. The nature of such behaviour, and the manifold determining causes which are involved are too complex for any single factor theory to be acceptable to students of the field. It is obvious that individual differences in conditionability are important in deciding whether a particular conditioned response will or will not be established; it is equally obvious that for such a response to be established, even in the most easily conditioned person, there must first of all occur a *process of conditioning,* i.e., of pairing the conditioned and the unconditioned stimulus. Thus, in conditioning we are obviously involved in what one vaguely calls the *social factors* of character building, and it is clear that these differ from person to person, and probably quite generally from class to class. Thus, there is some evidence from American researches, particularly the work of Kinsey (1948) and the Chicago school, that lower-class groups lay far less emphasis on the extinction of overt aggressive and sexual reactions than do middle-class groups. In these circumstances we would expect quite a different pattern of behaviour in middle and working class boys, even if there were no differences in conditionability between them, and these differences are, indeed, found. (Cf. also Eysenck, 1951.)

Another point where environmental influences are clearly of the greatest importance is that relating to the strength of a given temptation which has to be overcome by the conditioned anxiety response we call "conscience." If, indeed, a person's reactions are determined by the respective strength of "conscience" and "temptation," then clearly the same person may act morally on one occasion and immorally on another, depending on the degree of desire, hunger, anger, or whatever may be involved in the situation. A poor man, as has often been pointed out, is more likely to steal a loaf of bread than a rich man, because the temptation for him is so very much stronger; from comparing the actions of the rich and the poor in respect of stealing a loaf of bread, obviously no deductions can be made as to their likelihood to form conditioned responses easily. All these considerations will be obvious, but I have mentioned them briefly to avoid criticisms sometimes made of theories of this kind, to the effect that they do not take into account all the conditions of a complex social phenomenon.

Nevertheless, our theory demands that at least to some extent we should recognize, and be prepared to discover, *innate biological factors* determining in some degree the moral or immoral, criminal or non-criminal reactions of human beings to certain types of situations. Conditionability, presumably, is a function of certain features of the central nervous system, and as such is likely to owe much to heredity. Is there any evidence about the hereditary determination of crime? The important and, indeed, fundamental work of Lange (1931), Stumpfl (1936), and Kranz (1936) has shown that such hereditary determination can, indeed, be demonstrated very clearly. As is well-known, these investigators located prisoners who had a like-sexed fraternal or identical twin. They then investigated this twin to see whether or not he also had been convicted of a crime, and if so, whether his crime was similar to that of his sibling. They found a very considerable degree of concordance for identical twins, and much less for fraternal twins; it is difficult to interpret the evidence in any other way, but as a strong confirmation of the heredity hypothesis. This conclusion is well expressed in the title which Lange gave to his book: *Crime as Destiny*. It may be noted that J. B. S. Haldane wrote an introduction to this book in its English translation, in which he fully concurred with the author's conclusions; this is relevant and important because of his expert knowledge in the field in genetics and because of his well-known political sympathies which would make him less likely to accept such conclusions with enthusiasm.

Do any practical suggestions follow from the theory here developed? Two points seem to be worth making. In the first place, there has been far too little work of an experimental nature directly related to this problem to make it possible to decide with any degree of conviction as to the adequacy of the theory here presented. What is needed is a decade of concentrated experimentation before we shall be able to come to a conclusion with any degree of confidence. It would, therefore, appear to be premature to make any detailed practical suggestions; these must await further qualification of theoretical issues and further experimental verification.

In the second place, however, it does seem to me that if there is any degree of truth at all in the theory here presented, then it does lend some support to the slogan that punishment should not fit the crime but the criminal. Perhaps we might amplify this a little and say that character education cannot and should not be a uniform process, but that it should take into account the individual personalities involved. This saying, of course, is a truism which has often been repeated; what I am suggesting is that it can only cease to be a truism, and become a guide to action, when we know what are the parameters directly involved in moral actions, and how these parameters can be measured, and if possible, affected by our actions. If it were true that conditionability plays as important a role as I have suggested, then it would seem to follow that the maxim "spare the rod, spoil the child" could with advantage, be applied to the extraverted, possibly psychopathic, non-conditioner, whereas the modern free-and-easy methods of up-bringing would be much more appropriate to the introverted, anxious, easy-to-condition type of child. It may be possible that the acceptance of some such general rule might reduce the number of both behaviour problems and personal problems, which at the moment, appear to be increasing to such an alarming extent. However, on this point also much further research, possibly of an applied nature and carried out in the classroom, will be required before we can say for certain whether this suggestion is likely to have the consequences envisaged.

54. CHILDREN'S CONCEPTS OF JUSTICE: A COMPARISON WITH THE PIAGET DATA

Dolores Durkin

The most influential investigation of moral *judgment* of our century was conducted in Switzerland by Piaget some 35 years ago. It is of interest that the most influential investigation of moral *behavior* was conducted only slightly earlier in the United States by Hartshorne and May. It is also interesting that there is no indication that these investigators had any important influence on each other. Of course, their purposes were different and this may have combined with the language differences to reduce meaningful communication. Hartshorne and May were searching for a possible nuclear core of character traits that would dictate moral behavior in a majority of social settings. Piaget's was a quite different interest. He hoped to conceptualize *how children change* in their moral judgments, as a function of development and experience. On the basis of data collected with his game-like situations and clinical-like questions, Piaget concluded that there is a natural evolution in the moral development of the child.

Piaget saw ethnic heteronomy being replaced during development by ethnic autonomy. Justice which the child at first defines as submission to adult authority is eventually superseded during development by an equalitarian definition of justice. Furthermore, equalitarianism is eventually tempered in the direction of relativity, which means that moral judgments become increasingly dependent upon the particular circumstances defining the judgmental situation.

SOURCE. Adapted and abridged from Dolores Durkin, "Children's Concepts of Justice: a Comparison with the Piaget Data," *Child Development*, 1959, Vol. 30, 59–67. (With permission of the author and the Society for Research in Child Development.)

The following research by Durkin is a replication of Piaget's earlier work and a slight extension in the direction of seeing whether or not intelligence, as well as chronological age, may be predictive of the advent of equalitarianism and equity.

The findings of Durkin's investigation generally substantiate Piaget's postulated relationship between chronological age and the acquisition of concepts of justice. The findings of the present study emphasize the complexity of the reciprocity principle as it relates to personal aggression. Intellectual level, as measured by standardized intelligence tests, appears not to be significantly related to any of the dimensions of moral judgment involved in this study. But then one must remember that Piaget's conception of intelligence bears very little relationship to intelligence as defined by our standardized tests.

This is an investigation of children's concepts of justice, in particular, of justice regarding one's person. It is specifically designed to examine developmental trends, with age, in these concepts, and to compare the trends with those described by Piaget in *The Moral Judgment of the Child* (1932). It also examines the relationship between the intelligence of children and their justice-concepts.

In the Piaget investigation 167 subjects, ranging in age from 6 to 12 years, were questioned about what should be done "if someone punches you." They generally proposed two quite different solutions. Younger subjects favored reporting to an authority person, older subjects, a return of the aggression. Piaget saw in this trend of responses evidence for his theory concerning "the existence of a sort of law of evolution in the moral development of the child" (1932, p. 225).

According to Piaget's exposition of the theory, this law is of psychological origin being rooted in child-adult social relationships. For the child of about 7 or 8 the relationship is necessarily one of unilateral respect, hence, of constraint. And, Piaget maintains, the fruit of this constraint in moral-judgment development is twofold: (a) an ethic of heteronomy wherein the good is defined by submission to adult authority, and (b) moral realism, "the tendency . . . to regard duty and the value attaching to it as self-subsistent and independent of the mind, as imposing itself regardless of the circumstances in which the individual may find himself" (1932, p. 106). At this first stage, then, justice is defined by submission to adult authority and, further, moral judgments are made without concern for the particular circumstances of the situation being judged.

Among children ranging in age from about 3 to 11, the child-adult relationship changes; it becomes one of mutual respect because "as the child grows up, his relations with adults approximate to equality . . ." (1932, p. 84). Now, an ethic of autonomy or cooperation begins to make itself felt, and it is at this second stage that the equalitarian notion of justice emerges. Here, maintains Piaget, "reciprocity stands so high in the eyes of the child that he will apply it even where to us it seems to border on crude vengeance" (1932, p. 215).

Later, in a period which begins at approximately 11 to 12 years, a new attitude develops parallel with the equalitarian notion of justice. It is an attitude Piaget calls "equity" which is "the development of equalitarianism in the direction of relativity" (1932, p. 310). At this stage, then, moral judgments are made on the basis of the particular circumstances of a situation and, too, justice continues to be defined in terms of reciprocity.

The theory of Piaget and the findings he puts forth as substantiating the theory suggest the following problem for consideration: If subjects different in nationality and economic status from those included in the Piaget study, but similar in terms of chronological age, were questioned about an act of physical aggression, would their responses reflect stages in moral judgment identical to those outlined by Piaget? Or has he, on the basis of interviews with children "from the poorer parts of Geneva (Switzerland)" made too sweeping generalizations about children in general? Studies evaluating other aspects of Piaget's work (Abel, 1941; Bruce, 1941; Deutsche, 1937; Harrower, 1934; Lerner, 1937; McCarthy, 1946; MacRae, 1950; Oakes, 1947) indicate that he has.

A second problem, suggested by Piaget's emphasis on chronological age, concerns the function of intelligence in moral-judgment development. Might it not be that intelligence, rather than chronological age, is the significant factor in the development of both equalitarianism and equity?

The present study considers both of these problems.

PROCEDURE

School-Community Setting

The locale of the present study was a midwestern community with a population of about one thousand, all of whom were white and, with the exception of three Catholic families, also Protestant. The primary income-source for the community was farming. Three large factories were other important sources of income.

The school from which subjects were chosen was of the community-consolidated type. It was the only elementary school in the area and included grades 1 through 8. The total enrollment was 271.

Subjects

The subjects were 101 boys and girls in grades 2, 5, and 8. All of the children in each of the grades chosen were included. These particular grade-levels were selected because in them it would be more likely to find chronological ages of 7, 10, and 13, the age-groups that correspond to what Piaget designates as "three great periods in the development of the sense of justice in the child" (1932, p. 314). The actual mean ages of the three groups were 7.8, 10.9, and 13.9.

Since Piaget described the background of his subjects only in terms of their being poor, subjects in the present study were also classified in terms of economic status. The first-grade teacher in the school rated each subject as being "poor," "average," or "rich." She was chosen as the person most likely to have such information on the bases of life-long residence in the community, acquaintance with all of its families, and 35 years of teaching experience in this particular school. For the purpose of verification, her ratings were later compared with those independently given by the school clerk, also a resident of the community. In three instances their judgments showed classification differences; in each of these they decided together which of the ratings was more accurate and realistic.

Examination of their judgments showed that the economic rating "average" had been given to 75.0 per cent of the second graders, 68.4 per cent of the fifth graders, and 80.0 per cent of the eighth graders. Ratings of the remaining subjects were fairly equally divided between "rich" and "poor." It is on the basis of the total distribution of ratings that subjects in the present investigation are assumed to be different from Piaget's in terms of economic status.

Instrument

Following Piaget's procedure, an attempt was made to arrive at children's concepts of justice regarding one's person through their responses to questions about story-situations which depict possible violations of justice.

The following story-situation and questions were presented to male subjects:

(A) One day when they were out at recess Bennett hit Van.
What should Van do?
Why?

To those subjects who, in their responses to question (A), appeared to subscribe to an equalitarian or "eye for an eye" concept of justice, the following situation and questions were also presented:

(B) What if Van hit Bennett back and gave him a push besides?
What would you think about that?
Why?

Situation (B) was included for the purpose of evaluating Piaget's finding that children who accept an "eye for an eye" concept of justice do not accept "a sort of arbitrary punishment whose content bears no relation to the punishable act" (1932, p. 299).

Story-situations and questions identical to (A) and (B), but involving girls ("Adla" and "Hannah"), were presented to female subjects.

Interviews

Subjects' oral responses to questions about the story-situations were obtained through tape-recorded interviews. For each interview only the investigator, acting as interviewer, and one subject were present.

At the beginning of each interview the investigator explained to the subject that she was interested in finding out what children really thought about certain kinds of things. She promised that nothing of what he said would be told to parents, principal, or teacher; and she also explained that he, as a respondent, would remain anonymous.

Because of the intentionally brief, almost skeleton-like form of the story-situations, it was expected that at least some of the subjects would ask questions in response to those of the interviewer. Certainly to be expected, for example, were such questions as "How old is he?" or "Did he do it on purpose?" or "Did he ever do that before?" If and when such questions were posed, the interviewer's standard response was, "Would that make a difference?" and "Why?"

Administration of Intelligence Test

Once all of the interviews were completed, the investigator administered the Kuhlmann-Anderson Intelligence Test to 100 of the subjects. IQ scores in grade 2 ranged from 92 to 114. The mean score was 103.4; the standard deviation, 5.1. In grade 5, scores ranged from 69 to 122. The mean was 101.6, and the standard deviation was 13.2. For grade 8, scores ranged from 77 to 148. The mean was 103.4; the standard deviation, 11.4.

FINDINGS

Responses and Grade Level

Kinds of responses given to the problem of what a child should do if another child hits him, and the number of subjects at each grade level giving these responses, are summarized in Table 1.

To test the hypothesis that, within each grade, the different kinds of responses were chance occurrences, a chi square test was used. For grade 8, the hypothesis can be rejected with confidence at the 5 per cent level, the criterion of significance used throughout this paper. For grades 2 and 5,

TABLE 1

Kinds of Responses and Number of Subjects Giving Them

Kind of Response	Grade 2	Grade 5	Grade 8
Tell authority person	15	13	27
Return identical aggression	8	15	4
Other	5	10	4
Ignore aggression		6	1
Withdraw from situation	3		2
Have aggressor apologize		2	
Tell aggressor to stop		2	
Exclude aggressor from play	1		
Do nothing			1
Undecided	1		

however, the hypothesis cannot be rejected ($.05 < p < .10$; and $.50 < p < .70$, respectively).

Testing the hypothesis of no relationship between age, as defined by the three grade-levels, and kind of response, a chi square of 13.76 was obtained ($.005 < p < .010$). The data thus suggest that the different kinds of justice-concepts are significantly related to different CA levels.

As can be seen in Table 1, 27 subjects responded to Situation A in favor of a return of aggression. None in the group, however, approved of returning "a push besides" (Situation B). They unanimously denounced this behavior in such terms as: "It makes the fight unfair." "That other guy never pushed him." "He's asking for more."

Six fifth graders and 12 eighth graders showed, through the questions they asked, concern for the particular circumstances of the situation being judged. They questioned the motive for the aggression ($N = 13$), the deliberativeness ($N = 3$), and the severity ($N = 2$) of the aggression. Testing the hypothesis of no relationship between age, as defined by grade-level, and this overt concern for particular circumstances, a chi square of 12.0 was obtained ($.001 < p < .005$). The data thus show a significant relationship between a subject's concern for particulars and his CA level.

Responses and IQ Level

Table 2 shows the number of subjects at two different IQ levels giving the various kinds of responses. It also lists the value of chi square and the level of significance obtained when hypotheses of no relationship between kind of response and IQ level were tested. On the basis of the chi square values, there appears to be no significant relationship between IQ level and kind of justice-

TABLE 2

Kinds of Responses and Number of Subjects at Two Different IQ Levels Giving Them

IQ Level	Tell	Hit Back	Other	Chi Square	p
Grade 2 (N = 27)				1.84	<.50
Above Median	5	5	3		
Below Median	9	3	2		
Grade 5 (N = 38)				7.42	<.05
Above Median	3	8	8		
Below Median	10	7	2		
Grade 8 (N = 35)				1.04	<.70
Above Median	14	1	2		
Below Median	13	3	2		
Grades 2, 5, 8				6.17	<.05
Above Median	21	16	13		
Below Median	33	11	6		

concept in grades 2 and 8. A statistically significant relationship does exist, however, in grade 5 and again when the three grade-levels are combined.

A chi square of 0.89 was obtained when the hypothesis of no relationship between IQ level and overt concern for particular circumstances was tested ($.25 < p < .50$). On the basis of this finding, the emergence of what Piaget calls "equity" does not appear to be significantly related to intelligence.

DISCUSSION

While subjects' responses in the present study do substantiate Piaget's contention of a relationship existing between chronological age and concepts of justice, they do not substantiate his more specific proposal that "children maintain with a conviction that grows with their years that it is strictly fair to give back the blows one has received" (1932, p. 301). Only between grades 2 and 5 is there evidence of an increasing acceptance of reciprocity; eighth grade subjects, like those in grade 2, tend to seek justice in the authority person. This is not to say, of course, that similarity in grade 2 and grade 8 proposals reflects similarity in the two groups' disposition toward such a proposal. For the second graders, telling an authority person was a quick and apparently obvious solution to the problem at hand. For eighth graders, on the contrary, it was a solution that was proposed with neither haste nor enthusiasm. The kind of reasoning that led to their acceptance of it is graphically depicted in the verbatim response of one subject:

> You're not supposed to hit the guy, but you can't walk away from him or he'll always be doing that. You have to defend yourself, and

if you tell the teacher they'll all be after you for telling. And if you hit him, the teacher will get mad at you. I don't rightly know exactly. I guess he should tell the teacher or report him in some way so it won't happen all the time.

Another kind of difference that was evident in the older subjects' responses was their overt concern for possible mitigating factors in the situation being judged. This finding substantiates Piaget's contention that older children's moral judgments are characterized by equity. It can be conjectured, of course, that many or even most of the subjects at all three grade-levels were actually concerned about the particulars of the situation they were judging; however, none of the second graders, six of the fifth graders (15.8 per cent), and 12 of the eighth graders (34.3 per cent) were sufficiently concerned to ask questions about them. For this total group of 18 subjects, hitting another child was not an aggressive act, and therefore not subject to punishment, if it were accidental, if it were lacking in severity, or if it represented a return of aggression previously received. But these conditions not being present, the group unanimously responded in favor of some punishment. It is these latter responses that are included in the summaries in Tables 1 and 2.

Findings concerning the function of intelligence in moral-judgment development suggest no clear-cut conclusions. When IQ scores are divided into above-the-median and below-the-median levels, the data show no significant relationship between intelligence and kind of justice-concept held at the grade 2 and grade 8 levels, but do suggest a relationship at the grade 5 level, and again when all three grade levels are combined. Even where the relationship is significant the trends are not consistent. At the grade 5 level, for example, there is a tendency for the less intelligent subject to seek justice in an authority person, and for the more intelligent subject to avoid both "telling" and hitting back. When the three grade levels are combined, however, it is the more intelligent subject who tends to solve the problem by telling an authority person while the less intelligent subject tends to favor either reciprocity or some other solution.

When IQ scores of the subjects showing concern for details were examined, again no significant relationship between intelligence and such concern was evident. Eleven in the group had IQ scores above the median; seven, below the median.

On the basis of these various findings it would seem that no definite conclusions can be drawn concerning the function of intelligence in the development of moral judgment until other studies involving more subjects are carried out. Other studies in this general area might also provide evidence to substantiate two incidental but nonetheless consistent findings in the present study, namely:

1. Children tend to be much more certain about what they should not do than they are about what they should do. Perhaps this finding reflects an emphasis on the negative side of moral codes to such an extent that the path to goodness is left highly undefined for the child.

2. Children tend to be greatly perplexed about what constitutes rightful self-defense and what constitutes unlawful aggression. Perhaps this finding only reflects the highly complicated and often conflicting attitudes toward physical aggression preached and practiced by adults.

SUMMARY AND CONCLUSIONS

Middle-class subjects of three different age-groups were questioned about the problem of restoring right order in instances of physical aggression between children. Their responses were examined in order to identify possible developmental trends in kinds of solutions proposed and, further, to compare such trends with those suggested by Piaget as being basic to the evolution of a sense of justice in the child. The function of intelligence in moral-judgment development was also examined.

Findings in the present study show that:

1. Piaget's contention of a relationship existing between chronological age and justice concepts is substantiated. However, the data do not support his more specific proposal that acceptance of reciprocity as a justice-principle increases with age.

2. In no instance did acceptance of reciprocity include approval of returning aggression that was different from the aggression received. This unanimous reaction duplicates the Piaget finding that children who approve of reciprocity do not accept "a sort of arbitrary punishment whose content bears no relationship to the punishable act."

3. Older children tend to show concern for possible mitigating factors in the situation being judged. This bears out Piaget's finding concerning the emergence of "equity" with increase in age.

4. The role of intelligence in moral-judgment development remains undefined. Data concerning the relationship of intelligence and kind of justice concept are conflicting. However, findings do support the hypothesis of no relationship between intelligence and "the feeling of equity."

55. CHILDREN'S JUDGMENTS OF THEFT FROM INDIVIDUAL AND CORPORATE OWNERS

Frederick J. McDonald

We generally assume, because it seems so naively reasonable, that moral principles which appear to be acquired gradually by children during the acculturation process serve as guidelines for moral-ethical actions. Of course, in order to be very useful, moral principles must possess a capacity for being applied to slightly varying social situations. A scientific study of the application of moral principles to different social situations has a potential for throwing light on the functioning of cultural values. The following study by McDonald does just this.

Children were presented with pairs of stories describing acts of theft. In the one instance, the object was taken from an individual, and in the other from an anonymous corporate entity. Some 792 public school children between the ages of 8 and 15 were asked to choose which child did the "worst thing" and to indicate why.

Among the findings is the especially interesting one that the majority of children judged both actions as equally serious because both constituted stealing. The author's interpretation seems reasonable that children in our culture are "taught categorically and unequivocally" that taking another person's property without his knowledge and/or his consent is stealing and that stealing is *always* wrong. Girls were slightly more likely than boys to judge both actions as equally serious. Boys considered theft of more valuable objects as being more serious. There are also some suggestions in these findings of social class differences in attitudes toward theft. For ex-

SOURCE. Adapted and abridged from Frederick J. McDonald, "Children's Judgments of Theft from Individual and Corporate Owners," *Child Development*, 1963, Vol. 34, 141–150. (With permission of the author and the Society for Research in Child Development.)

ample, lower social class position was associated with the making of categorical, nondiscriminating judgments. The author's conclusion is that those child-rearing antecedents "that determine the strength of conscience also determine its content when the content is conceptualized as the acquisition of the valuative labeling responses." In other words, as the strength of conscience is being developed, so is the range of content in situations to which it may be applied. Children respond to their experiences in the real world and child-rearing cannot take place in a social vacuum.

This study reports an analysis of the judgmental criteria children use in evaluating the comparative moral reprehensiveness of acts of theft from an individual or corporate owner. It seemed reasonable to assume that such factors as the age, sex, social class position, and intellectual status of children would be associated with their moral judgmental responses. For that reason, information concerning these factors was obtained and related to kinds of moral judgments made in evaluating theft of individually or corporately owned property.

In studying conscience development one might focus on the content of conscience or its strength (Sears, Maccoby, and Levin, 1957). In the study of the content, which was the focus of this investigation, attention is directed toward the kinds and variety of events or actions to which value standards are applied and in relation to which the child is likely to experience inhibitory and guilt responses.

The content of conscience may be viewed as evaluative labeling responses learned through the pairing of certain actions and positive or negative consequences. The child learns, for example, that certain acts are regularly labeled by others as "good" or "bad." The performance of the "good" act is likely to be rewarded, performance of the "bad" act to be punished. Evaluative labeling is also used to develop anticipatory inhibition responses. Through such pairings, response correlated and independent environmental cues elicit anxiety or guilt which inhibits certain acts.

Depending on the nature of the discrimination and generalization training provided, a variety of actions or events come to be labeled by the child as reprehensible. Some children will label a wide variety of actions as unequivocally and categorically reprehensible. Other children will learn to make distinctions among actions which enable them to label some as relatively more serious than others.

The critical discrimination involved in judging an action to be stealing is the discrimination of rightful ownership. However, the cues that identify ownership are relatively complex. Initial learning in this respect probably consists in associating objects with individuals. Awareness of group ownership occurs as the child moves out of the immediate home environment and sees objects that are not to be taken though they do not belong to an individual.

The child may recognize the property rights of a corporate owner but may evaluate as less serious a theft from the corporate owner. Early training on property rights is largely if not exclusively concerned with individual property. Theft from the individual is more likely to be detected, may be identified as more consequential to the individual owner, and is likely to be followed by punishment. In brief, the pairing of evaluative labeling and consequences is more likely to occur in conjunction with acts against individual owners, and, hence, the child is more likely to learn that theft from an individual is more serious. For these reasons, it was predicted that, if a child made a distinction in the seriousness of the two kinds of actions, he would regard theft from the individual owner as more serious.

However, a substantial percentage of evaluative labeling acts by adults is categorical in character—"you shouldn't steal," "it's wrong to take other people's property." With this kind of discrimination training the child learns that the significant discriminative cue is the act of taking another's property. Consequently, some children will make no distinction between the actions of stealing from an individual or corporate owner, labeling both actions "stealing" and equally reprehensible. Stendler found that 12 per cent of her sample of junior high school age children made no distinction between these two kinds of theft (Stendler, 1949).

The antecedents of these two response modes, making and not making a distinction, are unknown. It is reasonable to assume that these response tendencies may be associated with such factors as the age, sex, social class position, and intellectual status of the child. Associations between these factors and other kinds of moral judgments have been reported (Beller, 1949; Durkin, 1959; Eberhart, 1942; Hartshorn and May, 1928; Lerner, 1937; MacRae, 1954; Peck and Havighurst, 1960; Piaget, 1932; Tudor-Hart, 1926). Since the direction of the association can be supported only by tenuous theoretical considerations, it was decided simply to examine the associations in this study. The presence and direction of association will, however, suggest hypotheses about the antecedents of the judgments children make. Further, this study, though involving a modification of Stendler's classification procedures, provides a replication of her study and extends it by increasing the age range and size of sample and by including a social class analysis of variations in judgmental responses.

METHODOLOGY

The methodology employed to evoke a moral judgment consisted in presenting a child with a pair of stories describing acts of theft by children. The owner of the object taken was an individual in one story and an anonymous corporate entity in the other story. The child was asked to choose which child did the "worse thing," and to indicate why. The stories were presented to the child in booklet form, and responses to both questions were written in the booklet. A pilot study indicated that substantial numbers of children were highly resistant to a force-choice technique and ignored directions by stating that "both" were equally wrong. Since some children probably do not regard one offense as more serious than the other, a "both" choice was permitted, but children were encouraged to choose one action as the more serious.

The stories described acts of theft which differed only in the source of ownership of the object stolen. In each story in a pair the motives for stealing were identical (necessity, opportunity, "fun" of getting away with it), and the value of the objects taken was objectively comparable (pieces of cloth, a wrench, and a screwdriver) or identical (a dime). The stories were those used by Stendler except that the sex of the subjects in the first story was made the same, and a sixth story was added so that an equal number of boys and girls were represented in the subjects of the stories (Stendler, 1949).

When a child picks one of the children in a story pair as "doing the worse thing," he is picking a child who has stolen from an individual or a corporate group. This selection could be used to decide which of the two kinds of theft he regarded as more serious (this procedure was used by Stendler). However, analysis of the reasons given for choices revealed numerous discrepancies between selections and reasons since many children apparently were not responding to the individual-corporate discrimination. The consistency in reasons given across stories indicated that the pattern of reasons reflected the child's stable judgmental response tendencies. This pattern of reasons was used to classify the types of judgments children made.

Each reason for each story was originally classified in one of 29 categories. The pattern of reasons across stories was then categorized by the dominant theme of the reasons. Ten categories, labeled "reason-types" subsumed the data and are described in Table 1. Each child was classified in one of these reason-types.

An independent categorizer classified each of the reasons and the reason-patterns for a subsample. With minimal training (10 stories) rater agreement on a sample of 100 children was 73 per cent for the original categorization and 85 per cent for classifications by reason-types.

Stability of response patterns was determined by administering a second set of stories to a subsample of 147 children from the original sample. These stories, administered 3 to 4 weeks after the first set, were highly similar to the original set. Only the names of the children in the stories and the objects taken were changed; but the objects substituted were comparable, for ex-

TABLE 1
Categories Used in Classifying Children's Judgments

Reason-Type	Dominant Theme in Stated Reasons
1	Both actions are equally wrong because stealing always wrong. Critical cue: stealing.
2	Harm to individual from theft more serious. Critical cue: effect on individual.
3	Harm to corporate group from theft more serious. Critical cue: effect on corporate group.
4	Theft from more deprived owner more serious action. Critical cue: owner more likely to suffer by theft.
5	Greater value of object taken more serious theft. Critical cue: value of object taken.
6	No single theme. Critical cue: variable.
7	Two dominant themes, equally used. Critical cue: variable.
8	Likelihood of punishment associated with more serious action. Critical cue: probability of punishment.
9	Actions which cannot be rationalized by introducing irrelevant element more serious. Critical cue: unknown.
10	Unnecessary theft more serious. Critical cue: necessity of theft.

ample, "hammer" being substituted for "screwdriver." Responses were classified as before. Percentage agreement between classifications ranged from 16 per cent for reason-type 5 ($N = 6$) to 73 per cent for reason-type 2 ($N = 15$). The most stable response patterns were reason-types 1, 2, 3, and 10, and the least stable, 4, 5, 6, and 7.

Sample

The sample consisted of 792 public school children between the ages of 8 and 15. Twelve subjects were eliminated because they did not supply reasons for their choices. The schools from which the children were chosen were located in two communities which provided a range of socioeconomic status.

Age, sex, occupation of father, and intelligence test data were obtained on each child. Children were classified by intelligence into three categories —high (.7 SD above the mean, IQ 111 and above), middle, and low (.7 SD below mean, IQ 89 approximately and below). Three categories of socioeconomic status were established using father's occupation as an index—high (professional and executive occupations), middle (white collar workers), and low (skilled, semiskilled, and unskilled workers).

RESULTS

Distribution of Reason-Types

Table 2 reports the number and percentage of children classified in each category on the basis of the generalization each child used in evaluating the actions described in the stories. Half the children made no discrimination

TABLE 2
Number and Percentage of Children in Each Reason-Type ($N = 780$)

Reason-Type	Frequency	Percentage
1	388	49.7
2	50	6.4
3	58	7.4
4	45	5.8
5	30	3.8
6	96	12.3
7	56	7.2
8	4	.5
9	2	.3
10	51	6.5

between the two events described, utilizing the principle, "stealing is always wrong." The next most frequent category was reason-type 6, varied pattern of reasons. This category was one of the less stable categories on retest.

Individual-Corporate Choices

Table 2 shows that 6 per cent of children chose stealing from the individual as more serious, and 7.5 per cent chose theft from the corporate group as more serious. It may be concluded that 14 per cent of the children made this discrimination.

These two categories were among the most reliable on retest. Further, 80 per cent of the children classified in reason-type 2 also had more selections of a child who stole from an individual. Of children in reason-type 3, 96.5 per cent actually picked the child stealing from the corporate group as the more serious offense.

Sex Differences

The association between sex and reason-type was significant. Table 3 reports the number and percentage of children in each reason-type by sex and the significance of the differences in each category. A significantly

TABLE 3
Sex of Child and Classification by Reason-Type*

	Males		Females	
Reason-Type	Frequency	Percentage‡	Frequency	Percentage‡
1†	179	44.2	209	55.7
2	28	6.9	22	5.8
3	34	8.4	24	6.4
4	22	5.4	23	6.1
5†	26	6.4	4	1.1
6	53	13.1	43	11.5
7, 8, 9	36	8.9	26	6.9
10	27	6.7	24	6.4
N	405		375	

* $\chi^2 = 23.67$, $df = 7$, $p < .01$.
† Differences between sexes significant, $p < .01$.
‡ Percentage of sex group.

larger percentage of girls made no distinction between the actions (reason-type 1), and significantly more boys decided in terms of the value of the object taken.

Social Class Differences

Since an association between sex and reason-type had been found, subsequent analyses were separated by sex of subject. Tables 4 and 5 report

TABLE 4
Social Class Position of Males and Classification by Reason-Types ($N = 405$) *

	Social Class					
	Upper		Middle		Lower	
Reason-Type	Frequency	Percentage†	Frequency	Percentage†	Frequency	Percentage†
1	34	35.8	60	50.8	85	44.3
2	9	9.5	6	5.1	13	6.7
3	12	12.6	12	10.2	10	5.2
4	10	10.5	4	3.4	8	4.2
5	8	8.4	10	8.5	8	4.2
6	12	12.6	13	11.0	28	14.6
7, 8, 9	8	8.4	9	7.6	19	9.9
10	2	2.1	4	3.4	21	10.9
N	95		118		192	

* $\chi^2 = 29.14$, $df = 14$, $p < .01$.
† Percentage is of the class group.

TABLE 5
Social Class Position of Females and Classification by Reason-Types ($N = 375$)*

Reason-Type	Upper Frequency	Upper Percentage†	Middle Frequency	Middle Percentage†	Lower Frequency	Lower Percentage†
1	48	54.5	51	47.7	110	61.1
2	11	12.5	3	2.8	8	4.4
3	6	6.8	8	7.5	10	5.6
4	9	10.2	8	7.5	6	3.3
5	0	0.0	1	0.9	3	1.7
6	8	9.1	21	19.6	14	7.8
7, 8, 9	5	5.7	10	9.3	11	6.1
10	1	1.1	5	4.7	18	10.0
N	88		107		180	

* $\chi^2 = 35.37$, $df = 12$, $p < .01$.
† Percentage is of the class group.

social class differences in reason-types for males and females, respectively. The largest proportion both of males and females classified as reason-type 1 (no difference—"stealing is always wrong") fell in the lower socioeconomic group (21 and 29 per cent of the respective groups).

A direct test of the interaction between sex and social class and reason-types is not possible with the data in frequency form. However, subjects were separated by social class and sex, and chi square tests made for each of the resulting contingency tables. A significant association between sex and reason-type was found for upper class children ($p < .05$) and for middle class children ($p < .05$).

To determine the source of these differences, the percentage of males and females in each social class in each reason-type was computed (see Tables 4 and 5). Among females, the largest frequency for reason-type 2 ("individual-minded") occurred in the upper class; among males the largest frequency for reason-type 3 ("corporate-minded") occurred in the upper class. The largest frequencies for reason-type 10 (justification in terms of necessity) occurred in the lower class for both males and females. The largest frequency for reason-type 1 was found in the lower class female category, though the differences between lower class males and females across all 10 types were not significant.

Intellectual Status

Intelligence level and reason-type were not significantly associated for males, but the association for females was significant (chi square = 24.39,

$df = 12$, $.05 > p > .01$). The largest percentages occurred in reason-type 1 and the upper and middle intelligence ranges (29 and 24 per cent, respectively). Seventeen per cent of the low range subjects were classified in reason-type 10. No association was found between intelligence level and reason-type when subjects were also classified by social class.

Age Differences

Subjects were classified in three age groups, 8 to 10, 11 and 12, and 13 to 15. The association between age and reason-type was not significant for either sex. A significant association between age and reason-type was found for upper class females ($p < .05$) when subjects were also classified by social class. This association seems to be accounted for by the significantly fewer 8- to 10-year-old upper class females who were classified in reason-type 1 (35 per cent).

DISCUSSION

The prediction that children will judge theft from an individual as more serious was not supported. Individual or corporate ownership was a critical cue for only 14 per cent of the children in the sample studied. If reason-types 2, 3, and 4 are combined, each reflecting a concern for the victim of theft, only 20 per cent of the children utilized effect on owner as a discriminative cue.

The majority of children (50 per cent) of both sexes, across a wide range of socioeconomic and intellectual status, and between the ages of 8 and 15 judged both actions as equally serious because both are stealing. The simplest explanation of this result is that children are taught categorically and unequivocally that taking another person's property without his knowledge and/or consent is stealing and that stealing is always wrong. This explanation is supported by Eberhart's data (1942) in which it was found that children labeled as more serious those offenses that could be identified as "stealing" rather than "borrowing."

However, the sex and social class differences in judgmental response tendencies are suggestive for a social learning conception of the development of conscience. Girls were more likely to judge both actions as equally serious. Boys judged by an assumed difference in the value of the object taken, considering theft of the more valuable object as more serious.

These differences may reflect generalized orientation and evaluative responses which are a part of differential sex-role behavior. The learning of sex role behaviors requires learning the discriminations that identify sex-appropriate behavior. This discrimination learning is also mediated by evaluative labeling behaviors enacted by the teaching model. Generalization training mediated in this process would facilitate the acquisition of generalized evaluative tendencies. Judgmental standards by which sex-appropriate behaviors are evaluated then become standards for evaluating a variety of actions.

Similarly, the differences associated with social class membership may be accounted for by systematic variations in child-rearing practices across social classes. In this study the tendency to make categorical judgments was associated with lower social class membership. It has been found that "working class" mothers are more likely to use punitive techniques in disciplining their children, are less permissive and less "warm" (Sears, Maccoby, and Levin, 1957). They are more likely to use object-oriented rather than love-oriented techniques in discipline. Disciplining is also discrimination training mediated in part through evaluative labeling of behavior. One of the cognitive effects of these procedures may be the acquisition of categorical judgment response tendencies. It would then be predicted that the use of object-oriented discipline techniques by parents is likely to be associated with the tendency to make categorical moral judgments.

The content as well as the strength of conscience are likely to be the direct product of antecedent child-rearing practices. The hypothetical explanations proffered for the data obtained in this study suggest that the antecedents which are prepotent in determining the strength of conscience are equally critical in determining its content. This explanation would also account for the lack of association between age of child and judgmental response pattern, since these suggested antecedents are more likely to be related to parent-child interactions than age of child.

It should be noted that the percentage of children making categorical judgments in this study was significantly different than that obtained by Stendler. The modification of the classification procedure and sample differences probably account for some of this difference. These variations, however, probably account for only a portion of the variation in results, and there is no obvious explanation for any remaining difference.

SUMMARY

Seven hundred and ninety-two children were asked to judge which of two actions, stealing from an individual or from a corporate owner, was more reprehensible and why. These two kinds of theft were described to the children in pairs of stories in which the value of the objects taken was comparable and the motivations for the theft were identical. The children's judgments were classified into 10 types on the basis of the reasons given for their choices.

Fifty per cent of the children across a wide range of socioeconomic, intellectual, and age differences judged that both actions were equally serious because both were stealing. When children made a distinction in the relative seriousness of the actions, they judged the more serious action by the presumed effect on the owner, the assumed differences in the value of the objects taken, or the greater possibility of detection of one action. Only 14 per cent of the children discriminated systematically on the basis of the source of ownership.

The tendency to discriminate the relative seriousness of the actions was associated with the sex and social class position of the child. Girls were more likely to evaluate the actions categorically as stealing and to judge them as equally serious. Boys judged on the value of the object stolen. Lower social class position was associated with categorical, nondiscriminating judgments. Higher social class position for boys was associated with judging theft from the corporate group as more serious; for girls, higher social class position was associated with judging theft from the individual as more serious. Age was not associated with the type of judgment. Intellectual status was associated with type of judgment for girls and in the same direction as the association with social class position.

It was hypothesized that the child-rearing antecedents that determine the strength of conscience also determine its content when the content is conceptualized as the acquisition of evaluative labeling responses.

ception (Charlesworth, 1966; Piaget, 1954). The egocentrism of this stage corresponds, therefore, to a lack of differentiation between the object and the sense impressions occasioned by it. Toward the end of the first year, however, the infant begins to seek the object even when it is hidden, and thus shows that he can now differentiate between the object and the "experience of the object." This breakdown of egocentrism with respect to objects is brought about by mental representation of the absent object. An internal representation of the absent object is the earliest manifestation of the symbolic function which develops gradually during the second year of life and whose activities dominate the next stage of mental growth.

Pre-operational Egocentrism (2–6 Years)

During the preschool period, the child's major cognitive task can be regarded as *the conquest of the symbol*. It is during the preschool period that the symbolic function becomes fully active, as evidenced by the rapid growth in the acquisition and utilization of language, by the appearance of symbolic play, and by the first reports of dreams. Yet this new capacity for representation, which loosened the infant from his egocentrism with respect to objects, now ensnares the preschool children in a new egocentrism with regard to symbols. At the beginning of this period, the child fails to differentiate between words and their referents (Piaget, 1952b) and between his self-created play and dream symbols and reality (Kohlberg, 1966; Piaget, 1951). Children at this stage believe that the name inheres in the thing and that an object cannot have more than one name (Elkind, 1961a, 1962, 1963).

The egocentrism of this period is particularly evident in children's linguistic behavior. When explaining a piece of apparatus to another child, for example, the youngster at this stage uses many indefinite terms and leaves out important information (Piaget, 1952b). Although this observation is sometimes explained by saying that the child fails to take the other person's point of view, it can also be explained by saying that the child assumes words carry much more information than they actually do. This results from his belief that even the indefinite "thing" somehow conveys the properties of the object which it is used to represent. In short, the egocentrism of this period consists in a lack of clear differentiation between symbols and their referents.

Toward the end of the pre-operational period, the differentiation between symbols and their referents is gradually brought about by the emergence of concrete operations (internalized actions which are roughly comparable in their activity to the elementary operations of arithmetic). One consequence of concrete operational thought is that it enables the child to deal with two elements, properties, or relations at the same time. A child with concrete operations can, for example, take account of both the height and width of a glass of colored liquid and recognize that, when the liquid is poured into a differently shaped container, the changes in height and width of the liquid compensate one another so that the total quantity of liquid is conserved (Elkind, 1961b; Piaget, 1952a). This ability, to hold two dimensions in mind at the same time, also enables the child to hold both symbol and referent in mind simultaneously, and thus distinguish between them. Concrete operations are, therefore, instrumental in overcoming the egocentrism of the preoperational stage.

Concrete Operational Egocentrism (7–11 Years)

With the emergence of concrete operations, the major cognitive task of the school-age child becomes that of *mastering classes, relations, and quantities*. While the preschool child forms global notions of classes, relations, and quantities, such notions are imprecise and cannot be combined one with the other. The child with concrete operations, on the other hand, can nest classes, seriate relations, and conserve quantities. In addition, concrete operations enable the school-age child to perform elementary syllogistic reasoning and to formulate hypotheses and explanations about concrete matters. This system of concrete operations, however, which lifts the school-age child to new heights of thought, nonetheless lowers him to new depths of egocentrism.

Operations are essentially mental tools whose products, series, class hierarchies, conservations, etc., are not directly derived from experience. At this stage, however, the child nonetheless regards these mental products as being on a par with perceptual phenomena. It is the inability to differentiate clearly between mental constructions and perceptual givens which constitutes the egocentrism of the school-age child. An example may help to clarify the form which egocentrism takes during the concrete operational stage.

In a study reported by Peel (1960), children and adolescents were read a passage about Stonehenge and then asked questions about it. One of the questions had to do with whether Stonehenge was a place for religious worship or a fort. The children (ages 7–10) answered the question with flat statements, as if they were stating a fact. When they were given evidence that contradicted their statements, they rationalized the evidence to make it conform with their initial position. Adolescents, on the other hand, phrased their replies in probabilistic terms and supported their judgments with material gleaned from the passage. Similar differences between children and adolescents have been found by Elkind (1966) and Weir (1964).

What these studies show is that, when a child constructs a hypothesis or formulates a strategy, he assumes that this product is imposed by the data rather than derived from his own mental activity. When his position is challenged, he does not change his stance but, on the contrary, reinterprets the data to fit with his assumption. This observation, however, raises a puzzling question. Why, if the child regards both his thought products and the givens of perception as coming from the environment, does he nonetheless give preference to his own mental constructions? The answer probably lies in the fact that the child's mental constructions are the product of reasoning, and hence are experienced as imbued with a (logical) necessity. This "felt" necessity is absent when the child experiences the products of perception. It is not surprising, then, that the child should give priority to what seems permanent and necessary in perception (the products of his own thought, such as conservation) rather than to what seems transitory and arbitrary in perception (products of environmental stimulation). Only in adolescence do young people differentiate between their own mental constructions and the givens of perception. For the child, there are no problems of epistemology.

Toward the end of childhood, the emergence of formal operational thought (which is analogous to propositional logic) gradually frees the child from his egocentrism with respect to his own mental constructions. As Inhelder and Piaget (1958) have shown, formal operational thought enables the young person to deal with all of the possible combinations and permutations of elements within a given set. Provided with four differently colored pieces of plastic, for example, the adolescent can work out all the possible combinations of colors by taking the pieces one, two, three and four, and none, at a time. Children, on the other hand, cannot formulate these combinations in any systematic way. The ability to conceptualize all of the possible combinations in a system allows the adolescent to construct contrary-to-fact hypotheses and to reason about such propositions "as if" they were true. The adolescent, for example, can accept the statement, "Let's suppose coal is white," whereas the child would reply, "But coal is black." This ability to formulate contrary-to-fact hypotheses is crucial to the overcoming of the egocentrism of the concrete operational period. Through the formulation of such contrary-to-fact hypotheses, the young person discovers the arbitrariness of his own mental constructions and learns to differentiate them from perceptual reality.

ADOLESCENT EGOCENTRISM

From the strictly cognitive point of view (as opposed to the psychoanalytic point of view as represented by Blos [1962] and A. Freud [1946] or the ego psychological point of view as represented by Erikson [1959]), the major task of early adolescence can be regarded as having to do with *the conquest of thought*. Formal operations not only permit the young person to construct all the possibilities in a system and construct contrary-to-fact propositions (Inhelder & Piaget, 1958); they also enable him to conceptualize his own thought, to take his mental constructions as objects and reason about them. Only at about the ages of 11–12, for example, do children spontaneously introduce concepts of belief, intelligence, and faith into their definitions of their religious denomination (Elkind, 1961a, 1962, 1963). Once more, however, this new mental system which frees the young person from the egocentrism of childhood entangles him in a new form of egocentrism characteristic of adolescence.

Formal operational thought not only enables the adolescent to conceptualize his thought, it also permits him to conceptualize the thought of other people. It is this capacity to take account of other people's thought, however, which is the crux of adolescent egocentrism. This egocentrism emerges because, while the adolescent can now cognize the thoughts of others, he fails to differentiate between the objects toward which the thoughts of others are directed and those which are the focus of his own concern. Now, it is well known that the young adolescent, because of the physiological metamorphosis he is undergoing, is primarily concerned with himself. Accordingly, since he fails to differentiate between what others are thinking about and his own mental preoccupations, he assumes that other people are as obsessed with his behavior and appearance as he is himself. *It is this belief that others are preoccupied with his appearance and behavior that constitutes the egocentrism of the adolescent.*

One consequence of adolescent egocentrism is that, in actual or impending social situations, the young person anticipates the reactions of other people to himself. These anticipations, however, are based on the premise that others are as admiring or as critical of him as he is of himself. In a sense, then, the adolescent is continually constructing, or reacting to, *an imaginary audience*. It is an audience because the adolescent believes that he will be the focus of attention; and it is imaginary because, in actual social situations, this is not usually the case (unless he contrives to make it so). The construction of imaginary audiences would seem to account, in part at least, for a wide variety of typical adolescent behaviors and experiences.

The imaginary audience, for example, probably plays a role in the self-consciousness which is so characteristic of early adolescence. When the young person is feeling critical of himself, he anticipates that the audience —of which he is necessarily a part—will be critical too. And, since the audience is his own construction and privy to his own knowledge of himself, it knows just what to look for in the way of cosmetic and behavioral sensitivities. The adolescent's wish for privacy and his reluctance to reveal himself may, to some extent, be a reaction to the feeling of being under the constant critical scrutiny of other people. The notion of an imaginary audience also helps to explain the observation that the affect which most concerns adolescents is not guilt but, rather, shame, that is, the reaction to an audience (Lynd, 1961).

While the adolescent is often self-critical, he is frequently self-admiring too. At such times, the audience takes on the same affective coloration. A good deal of adolescent boorishness, loudness, and faddish dress is probably provoked, partially in any case, by a failure to differentiate between what the young person believes to be attractive and what others admire. It is for this reason that the young person frequently fails to understand why adults disapprove of the way he dresses and behaves. The same sort of egocentrism is often seen in behavior directed toward the opposite sex. The boy who stands in front of the mirror for 2 hours combing his hair is probably imagining the swooning reactions he will produce in the girls. Likewise, the girl applying her makeup is more likely than not imagining the admiring glances that will come her way. When these young people actually meet, each is more concerned with being the observed than with being the observer. Gatherings of young adolescents are unique in the sense that each young person is simultaneously an actor to himself and an audience to others.

One of the most common admiring audience constructions, in the adolescent, is the anticipation of how others will react to his own demise. A certain bittersweet pleasure is derived from anticipating the belated recognition by others of his positive qualities. As often happens with such universal fantasies, the imaginary anticipation of one's own demise has been realized in fiction. Below, for example, is the passage in *Tom Sawyer* where Tom sneaks back to his home, after having run away with Joe and Huck, to discover that he and his friends are thought to have been drowned:

> But this memory was too much for the old lady, and she broke entirely down. Tom was snuffling, now, himself—and more in pity of himself than anybody else. He could hear Mary crying and putting in a kindly word for him from time to time. He began to have a nobler opinion of himself than ever before. Still, he was sufficiently touched by his aunt's grief to long to rush out from under the bed and overwhelm her with joy—and the theatrical gorgeousness of the thing appealed strongly to his nature too—but he resisted and lay still.

Corresponding to the imaginary audience is another mental construction which is its complement. While the adolescent fails to differentiate the concerns of his own thought from those of others, he at the same time overdifferentiates his feelings. Perhaps because he believes he is of importance to so many people, the imaginary audience, he comes to regard himself, and particularly his feelings, as something special and unique. Only he can suffer with such agonized intensity, or experience such exquisite rapture. How many parents have been confronted with the typically adolescent phrase, "But you don't know how it feels. . . ." The emotional torments undergone by Goethe's young Werther and by Salinger's Holden Caulfield exemplify the adolescent's belief in the uniqueness of his own emotional experience. At a somewhat different level, this belief in personal uniqueness becomes a conviction that he will not die, that death will happen to others but not to him. This complex of beliefs in the uniqueness of his feelings and of his immortality might be called *a personal fable,* a story which he tells himself and which is not true.

Evidences of the personal fable are particularly prominent in adolescent diaries. Such diaries are often written for posterity in the conviction that the young person's experiences, crushes, and frustrations are of universal significance and importance. Another kind of evidence for the personal fable during this period is the tendency to confide in a personal God. The search for privacy and the belief in personal uniqueness leads to the establishment of an I-Thou relationship with God as a personal confident to whom one no longer looks for gifts but rather for guidance and support (Long, Elkind, & Spilka, 1967).

The concepts of an imaginary audience and a personal fable have proved useful, at least to the writer, in the understanding and treatment of troubled adolescents. The imaginary audience, for example, seems often to play a role in middle-class delinquency (Elkind, 1967). As a case in point, one young man took $1,000 from a golf tournament purse, hid the money, and then promptly revealed himself. It turned out that much of the motivation for this act was derived from the anticipated response of "the audience" to the guttiness of his action. In a similar vein, many young girls become pregnant because, in part at least, their personal fable convinces them that pregnancy will happen to others but never to them and so they need not take precautions. Such examples could be multiplied but will perhaps suffice to illustrate how adolescent egocentrism, as manifested in the imaginary audience and in the personal fable, can help provide a rationale for some adolescent behavior. These concepts can, moreover, be utilized in the treatment of adolescent offenders. It is often helpful to these young people if they can learn to differentiate between the real and the imaginary audience, which often boils down to a discrimination between the real and the imaginary parents.

THE PASSING OF ADOLESCENT EGOCENTRISM

After the appearance of formal operational thought, no new mental systems develop and the mental structures of adolescence must serve for the rest of the life span. The egocentrism of early adolescence nonetheless tends to diminish by the age of 15 or 16, the age at which formal operations become firmly established. What appears to happen is that the imaginary audience, which is primarily an anticipatory audience, is progressively modified in the direction of the reactions of the real audience. In a way, the imaginary audience can be regarded as hypothesis—or better, as a series of hypotheses—which the young person tests against reality. As a consequence of this testing, he gradually comes to recognize the difference between his own preoccupations and the interests and concerns of others.

The personal fable, on the other hand, is probably overcome (although probably never in its entirety) by the gradual establishment of what Erikson (1959) has called "intimacy." Once the young person sees himself in a more realistic light as a function of having adjusted his imaginary audience to the real one, he can establish true rather than self-interested interpersonal relations. Once relations of mutuality are established and confidences are shared, the young person discovers that others have feelings similar to his own and have suffered and been enraptured in the same way.

Adolescent egocentrism is thus overcome by a twofold transformation. On the cognitive plane, it is overcome by the gradual differentiation between his own preoccupations and the thoughts of others; while on the plane of affectivity, it is overcome by a gradual integration of the feelings of others with his own emotions.

SUMMARY AND CONCLUSIONS

In this paper I have tried to describe the forms which egocentrism takes and the mechanisms by which it is overcome, in the course of mental development. In infancy, egocentrism corresponds to the impression that objects are identical with the perception of them, and this form of egocentrism is overcome with the appearance of representation. During the preschool period, egocentrism appears in the guise of a belief that symbols contain the same information as is provided by the objects which they represent. With the emergence of concrete operations, the child is able to discriminate between symbol and referent, and so overcome this type of egocentrism. The egocentrism of the school-age period can be characterized as the belief that one's own mental constructions correspond to a superior form of perceptual reality. With the advent of formal operations and the ability to construct contrary-to-fact hypotheses, this kind of egocentrism is dissolved because the young person can now recognize the arbitrariness of his own mental constructions. Finally, during early adolescence, egocentrism appears as the belief that the thoughts of others are directed toward the self. This variety of egocentrism is overcome as a consequence of the conflict between the reactions which the young person anticipates and those which actually occur.

Although egocentrism corresponds to a negative product of mental growth, its usefulness would seem to lie in the light which it throws upon the affective reactions characteristic of any particular stage of mental development. In this paper I have dealt primarily with the affective reactions associated with the egocentrism of adolescence. Much of the material, particularly the discussion of the *imaginary audience* and the *personal fable* is speculative in the sense that it is based as much upon my clinical experience with young people as it is upon research data. These constructs are offered, not as the final word on adolescent egocentrism, but rather to illustrate how the cognitive structures peculiar to a particular level of development can be related to the affective experience and behavior characteristic of that stage. Although I have here only considered the correspondence between mental structure and affect in adolescence, it is possible that similar correspondences can be found at the earlier levels of development as well. A consideration of egocentrism, then, would seem to be a useful starting point for any attempt to reconcile cognitive structure and the dynamics of personality.

57. CHILD-REARING PRACTICES AND MORAL DEVELOPMENT: GENERALIZATIONS FROM EMPIRICAL RESEARCH

Martin L. Hoffman

When historical accounts are finally written, long after a series of loosely related events have taken place, the chronicler can often rationalize a high degree of logical interrelatedness among such happenings, even though they undoubtedly seemed largely circumstantial and adventitious to contemporary observers. Only through the passage of time do clearly discernible patterns emerge from natural events and from our scientific efforts to interpret and influence them.

There do, however, appear to be especially propitious times in the sciences, as well as in the other affairs of man, for logical reckoning, for summing up, for separating the valid and the useful from the irrelevant and the trivial.

In the following report Hoffman has done us the service of summarizing and interpreting our gropings toward a better understanding of moral development. With the advantage of at least a modest historical perspective he shows that we have made only minor progress toward exploiting what many psychologists still believe to be the inherently important theoretical properties of identification. Further research and theorizing in this vital dimension of socialization should eventually yield important knowledge for the social sciences and the related applied arts.

Hoffman also gives valuable perspectives on our attempts to understand the dynamics of transgressions against internalized controls over personal

SOURCE. Adapted and abridged from Martin L. Hoffman, "Child-Rearing Practices and Moral Development: Generalizations from Empirical Research," *Child Development*, 1963, Vol. 34, 295–318. (With permission of the author and the Society for Research in Child Development.)

conduct, as well as child-rearing correlates and antecedents of such guides and restraints. This comprehensive summing-up can serve as a fresh beginning for the research and theorizing that surely lie ahead in this interesting sector of man's eternal journey toward becoming civilized.

In complex areas such as that of morality and its antecedents no single research can supply the answers to all important questions. Each study can do no more than shed light on a small facet of the problem, especially in the early stages of research when measuring instruments and experimental procedures are cumbersome and inefficient. Progress therefore requires many research efforts, along with systematic attempts to assess methods and integrate results. This paper is such an attempt. Its purpose is to pull together the research findings on parental practices and the child's moral development so as to point up tentative generalizations, gaps, and inconsistencies which can be used as guides in further research. The studies examined are those which were designed primarily to investigate parental antecedents of moral variables and which meet current methodological standards. The focus is substantive although methodological points are made where necessary in interpreting contradictory findings and suggesting directions for further research.

THEORETICAL FOUNDATIONS OF THE RESEARCH

Most of our theoretical knowledge about moral development derives from the works of Piaget and Freud. Piaget and his followers have focused on the cognitive aspects of the child's moral orientation, and their empirical investigations have centered on the child's concepts of justice, his attitudes toward rules, and toward violations of moral norms (Kohlberg, 1958; Lerner, 1937; Piaget, 1932). In these studies the child's moral perspective has been probed with great depth, and a number of valuable concepts bearing on the cognitive aspects of morality have been contributed to the field, e.g., moral realism, immanent justice, and the role of cognitive processes in moral growth. Although considerable importance is assigned to decreased adult constraint and increased interaction with peers, the main interest of these investigators is to establish developmental sequences which are more or less universal, fixed, and intrinsic to the organism, rather than to study individual differences and the antecedent role of the parent. The one exception, a study of the effects of parental restriction on the child's moral judgment (MacRae, 1954), produced inconclusive results.

Psychoanalytic theory, on the other hand, is concerned primarily with the emotional and motivational aspects of personality structure. And although this theory too was initially intended as a universal explanation of the processes underlying the formation of conscience rather than a source of hypotheses about individual differences, it has provided the main inspiration and the over-all direction for most of the research on the role of parental practices in shaping and determining moral character.

Although Freud did not organize the theory into a coherent whole, its concepts are unveiled in scattered references throughout the literature and it may be reconstructed briefly as follows: The young child is inevitably subjected to many frustrations, some of which are due to parental control and some of which have nothing directly to do with the parent, e.g., illness and other physical discomforts. All of these frustrations contribute to the development of hostility toward the parent. The child's anxiety over counter aggression by the parent or over the anticipated loss of the parent's love leads him to repress his hostility, incorporate the parent's prohibitions, and generally model his behavior after that of the parent. Among the important parental characteristics adopted by the child is the capacity to punish himself when he violates a prohibition or is tempted to do so—turning inward, in the course of doing this, the hostility which was originally directed toward the parent. This self-punishment is experienced as guilt feelings which are dreaded because of their intensity and their resemblance to the earlier fears of punishment or abandonment by the parent. The child, therefore, tries to avoid guilt by acting always in accordance with the incorporated parental prohibitions and erecting various mechanisms of defense against the conscious awareness of impulses to act contrary to the prohibitions.

This theory is thus far unchallenged as a comprehensive account of the role of family dynamics in the moral development of the child. Although many researchers in the field disagree with some of its details, most have accepted its basic premise: that sometime in early childhood the individual begins to model his behavior after that of the parent and through this process of identification codes of conduct such as moral standards and values, which are originally externally enforced, become part of the child's own set of standards.

Because of the complexity of the theory no investigator has attempted to test it in its entirety. Instead, each study has focused on one or another of its concepts—such as identification or guilt—often modifying it somewhat in line with other theoretical approaches, e.g., reinforcement learning theory.

IDENTIFICATION

The psychoanalytic concept that has received the most attention from theorists and researchers is identification. Two general types of identification are discussed in the literature. In one—referred to as identification with the aggressor or defensive identification—the child, treated punitively by the parent but fearful of further punishment if he fights back, avoids the conflict and gains further parental approval by taking on the characteristics and point of view of the parent. Although Freud considered this type of identification to be central to the development of a conscience, especially in the male, it is now often thought of as a more or less temporary mechanism or one which leads to an aggressive, hostile outlook toward the world rather than a process which underlies the development of an inner conscience (Freud, 1946). The other type, referred to as developmental or anaclitic identification (Bronfenbrenner, 1960), is based on the child's anxiety over the loss of the parent's love. To get rid of this anxiety and assure himself of the parent's continued love, the child strives to become like the parent—to incorporate everything about him including his moral standards and values. This type of identification, seen by Freud as especially characteristic of females, is assumed by most present-day writers to underlie the development of an inner conscience.

Numerous attempts have been made in recent years to clarify these concepts (e.g., Brodbeck, 1954; Bronfenbrenner, 1960; Jacobson, 1954; Mowrer, 1950; Sanford, 1955; Stoke, 1950) and to place them within broader theoretical frameworks (e.g., Kagan, 1958; Seward, 1954; Slater, 1961; Whiting, 1960). In each case the concepts are modified somewhat in line with the author's theoretical preference, resulting in a variety of subtly different notions that have guided the empirical research on identification. With each investigator stressing one or another aspect, e.g., motivation to emulate the parent, actual similarity between parent and child, or similarity as perceived by the child, the measures used have been many and varied and there has been little overlap between those used in the different studies.

In a study of 5-year-old boys (Sears, 1953), the manipulation of the father doll in a structured doll play situation was used as an index of father identification and was found to relate positively to the father's warmth and affection toward the boy, as reported by the mother. Further evidence that paternal warmth contributes to the boy's identification with the father comes from a study of high school juniors and seniors (Payne and Mussen, 1956) in which an "actual similarity" measure of identification was used—the extent to which the boys responded to personality and attitude tests the same way their fathers did. Here a positive relationship was obtained between identification and the perception of the father as warm, helpful, and kind— as revealed by the boy's completion of a number of stories dealing with family interaction, e.g., one in which an adolescent boy wants to use the family car. The results of these two studies are generally taken as support for the anaclitic view of identification. Although they demonstrate that identification relates to *receiving* parental love—rather than being *threatened with its loss,* as the anaclitic view would predict—it seems reasonable to assume that discipline by a loving father is more apt to elicit anxiety over love-withdrawal than discipline by a nonloving one.

Seemingly contradictory findings were obtained in another study, using high school senior boys as subjects (Cava and Raush, 1952). This study was guided by the Freudian notion that the boy, motivated by fears and anxieties related to hostility toward his father, shifts his identification from the mother to the father during the Oedipal phase of development. Identification with the father was measured in terms of the similarity between the boy's responses on a vocational interest blank and the responses he thought his father would make. In accordance with the theory, identification was found to relate positively to intensity of castration anxiety, as measured by the Blacky Test—a projective device using dogs to represent family figures. On the assumption that castration anxiety in boys signifies the fear of a physically punitive father, this finding is viewed as providing some empirical support for the notion of identification with an aggressive parent rather than with a loving one.

Thus, although the aggressive and anaclitic conceptions of identification dynamics are quite different, each has some empirical support. It is difficult to assess which receives the greater support, since the identification measures used in these studies differ widely and we do not know which are more valid. While these measures leave much to be desired (Bronfenbrenner, 1958), they all have a certain amount of face validity since they tap aspects of behavior which are manifestly close to the concept of parent identification. Thus, two deal directly with the similarity—real or perceived—between the child and his own parent.[1,2] The third is less direct and makes the assumption that taking the father role projectively reflects identification with the

---

[1] It should be noted that identification is largely unconscious according to psychoanalytic theory. From this standpoint, actual similarity may be preferable to perceived similarity as a measure since it may include characteristics shared with the parent of which the child is not aware. On the other hand, actual similarity measures are limited in that similar institutional influences which impinge on both the parent and child very likely account for a good part of their resemblance (Newcomb, 1937).

[2] Bronfenbrenner (1958) has criticized measures like these on the grounds that they may be tapping no more than the child's similarity with adults of the same sex. To support this point he cites findings by Helper and Lazowick that children show little or no more similarity to their same-sexed parent than to adults of the same sex selected at random. Helper's measures deal with the relation between the child's ideal for himself and the parent's ideal for the child; and Lazowick's, with the "semantic similarity" existing between parent and child. Although these measures differ from those under discussion, it is possible that further investigation will show the latter to be subject to the same limitation.

father, and not merely with adult males in general or with an abstract conception of the paternal role. But the subjects in this study seem young enough to justify this assumption.

The other studies of the antecedents of identification generally support the view that love rather than punitiveness is the significant parent variable, but the evidence provided is limited since the identification measures used are highly indirect and therefore of questionable validity. These measures deal with personality characteristics such as sex-role typing (Bronson, 1959; Levin and Sears, 1956; Mussen and Distler, 1959; Mussen and Distler, 1960) and conscience (Sears, Maccoby, and Levin, 1957) which are sometimes presumed on theoretical grounds to be consequents of parent identification and therefore adequate as measures of identification. However, they may also result from other developmental processes including identification with persons other than the same-sexed parent.

A possible explanation for the support given both the aggressive and anaclitic conceptions is that the significant antecedent of father identification is the father's *salience* in the child's experience, which can be heightened by *either* affection or punitiveness. Another possible explanation, suggested by the predominantly lower class sample in the study finding father identification related to punitiveness (Cava and Raush, 1952), is that identification may have different bases in different segments of the population. Identification with the aggressor may more often be the underlying process in the lower class setting with its more traditional orientation toward obedience and more frequent use of physical discipline (Allinsmith, 1960; Aronfreed, 1961; Bronfenbrenner, 1958; Hoffman, 1960; Kohn, 1959). In the more psychologically oriented middle class, on the other hand, the parental pattern may be more conducive to anaclitic identification.

These explanations are conjectural and further work on the antecedents of identification is needed. With no evidence for the superiority of any particular approach to the measurement of identification, investigators might consider using a battery. Each test would tap a different aspect of identification and subjects would be scored on how consistently they identified. The practices used by the parents of subjects who consistently identify, identify primarily with aggressive and power-oriented characteristics, and consistently do not identify could then be compared. Such a procedure might provide the necessary data for generalizing with confidence about the optimum antecedents of each type of identification. It might also provide appropriate criterion groups for validating more practical measures of identification.

Knowing the antecedents of identification, however, would still leave us a long way from our goal of understanding the dynamics of conscience formation. For one thing, there is no empirical support for the implicit assumption made by some researchers that identification is total, i.e., that the child strives to emulate the parent in all respects. It is therefore theoretically possible for a highly motivated child to adopt certain valued parental characteristics like mechanical skills, social prestige, sense of humor, and power, but not others, values and moral standards included. Even assuming identification in the moral realm, the child's moral structure would still be unknown unless the particular parental standards internalized could be ascertained. Another reason for not inferring conscience from parent identification is that parents' consciences vary in strength and in content. The child who identifies with his parent is not necessarily more moral than one who identifies with a teacher, minister, or older sibling. The general problem of the relation between the process of identification and what aspect of the parent model is internalized is highlighted by the finding, reported by McCord and McCord (1958), that boys whose fathers are criminals are less apt to become criminals if accepted by their fathers than if rejected by them. Apparently paternal acceptance may operate *against* identification when the parent model is opposed to the norms of the larger society.

Perhaps the precise role of parent identification in moral development would be clarified by developing measures of the child's identification with the parent's moral standards and using these in conjunction with independent indices of what the parent's moral standards actually are. These measures might then be studied in relation to the child's identification in other areas than the moral and in relation to parental practices.

REACTIONS TO TRANSGRESSION

A more profitable approach to the role of the parent in the child's moral growth is to drop, tentatively, the assumption that identification is the intervening process and study the various manifestations of conscience more directly. The focus of our research efforts would then become the parent's role in developing a child whose motives are generally to behave in a morally acceptable way; who, when under pressure from external forces or inner desires to violate a moral standard, can generally exercise the controls necessary to resist these pressures; who, when he does submit to temptation or accidentally violates a standard, can generally be expected to recognize the wrong, be aware of his own responsibility, experience an appropriate amount of guilt or remorse, and attempt to make reparations where possible. Further, to react in all these ways can be assumed not due to fear of external consequences but due to an inner moral sense.

Some work along these lines has already been done, mainly on the child's reactions after committing a transgression. Allinsmith (1960) designed a study to test the hypothesis derived from psychoanalytic theory that harsh treatment in infancy creates excessive aggression, which must later be turned inward by the child in the course of identifying with the parent and which therefore leads eventually to experiencing severe guilt upon violating a prohibition. The prediction was that early weaning and harsh toilet training, data on which were obtained in interviews with the mothers, would relate to severe guilt reactions by the child in later life. His subjects were junior high school boys whose guilt severity was assessed by having them complete a number of stories, each one having a central figure who violates a commonly held moral standard, e.g., disobeys his mother, steals, or has hostile thoughts about an authority figure. The assumption underlying this technique is that the child tends to identify with the central figure of the story and to express his own characteristic guilt reaction pattern in his completions, without being aware that his own reactions are the focus of study. The stories are so phrased that the infraction can neither be detected nor attributed to the central figure unless he gives himself up or inadvertently gives himself away. Therefore, responses in which the central figure confesses, makes reparation, or feels remorse can be assumed to reflect an inner sense of guilt rather than fear of external consequences.

Allinsmith's findings provide evidence for the effect of early infant experience on later guilt severity. But the direction of the findings varies depending on which particular transgression—that is, which story—is being considered. Thus, the severity of guilt over hostile thoughts relates in a curvilinear fashion to severe weaning and severe toilet training—the more severe practices in each case relating to moderate guilt and the less severe practices, to high and low guilt. The stealing and disobedience findings were more clear cut and linear but in the opposite direction from that predicted: severe infant training related *negatively* to guilt severity. In the main, then, Allinsmith's findings suggest that severe infant practices are associated with low or moderate guilt. This is at variance with the findings reported in a study by Heinicke (1953) using 5-year-old boys as subjects and a cross-cultural study by Whiting and Child (1953). Heinicke used as a measure of guilt the children's responses to interview questions dealing with their conceptions of right and wrong and how they feel and act when they have done something wrong. He found severe weaning to relate to high guilt. Whiting and Child's approach was to study a large number of cultures and relate their predominant child-rearing patterns to a cultural index of guilt severity, the prevalence in the culture of self-recrimination as a response to illness. The assumption underlying this measure was that blaming oneself for being ill is a reflection of guilt. They found, like Heinicke, that severe weaning related positively to the severity of guilt. For toilet training, neither study gave a consistent trend.

There are many possible reasons for the discrepancy between the Allinsmith and Heinicke findings. The measures of guilt were different. The ages of the subjects varied, which meant among other things that the parents in the Allinsmith study had to recall the practices used 12 years earlier, while those in the Heinicke study only had to think back about 4 years. And, although both investigators used the same index of toilet training severity, which considered both the age of onset and the duration of training, their measures of weaning severity differed. Allinsmith used the age of completion, whereas Heinicke's measure considered both age of completion and duration. With no further empirical evidence to draw upon, we cannot determine which measures are better or draw any firm conclusions about how infant training relates to later guilt severity. Nor can we be sure that the true antecedent variable is the particular infant practice reported by the parent or some other related aspect of infancy and early childhood. The Whiting and Child findings are of little help in interpreting the over-all results since we cannot even be sure of their relevance to the parent-child relationship. For one thing, cultural influences other than the assumed socialization processes might account for the relation obtained between discipline and guilt. This possibility is increased by the fact that the guilt measure was not based on child data. Even if it were, however, a general methodological problem would still apply: relations obtained with groups as the unit of analysis are not necessarily the same as those obtained with individuals as the unit (for relevant discussion *see* Hills [1957] and [Kendall and Lazarsfeld, 1955]).[3] There is some empirical evidence on this point: Hollenberg (1952) and Faigan (1952) found a lack of agreement between relations obtained cross-culturally and those obtained with parents and children within the same culture.

The above studies as a group, then, seem to provide empirical support for the general hypothesis that early experiences can have a bearing on the child's later moral response. Just what kind of bearing, however, remains a matter for further study.

The Allinsmith and Heinicke studies also investigated the relation between

---

[3] This point also applies to social class findings. Knowing, for example, that in the lower class the parents use more physical discipline and the children are more openly aggressive than in the middle class tells us nothing about how physical discipline and aggressiveness relate in either class.

A related criticism can also be made of relationships obtained between parent and child variables even within culturally homogeneous samples. That is, such relationships might be accounted for by other aspects of home life than the ones studied. But in this case we would at least be sure the parent and child variables were related. To find the true antecedent variables may ultimately require studies which include the entire range of parental behaviors—reduced perhaps by factor analysis to a relatively small number of independent influences. Until such studies are done, our inferences must be based largely on the amount of agreement among different investigators—the approach used in this paper.

the parent's current discipline practices and the child's guilt severity. Allinsmith distinguished between two broad types of discipline: corporal discipline, which includes spanking, whipping, slapping, and beating the child, and psychological discipline, which includes manipulation of the child by shaming, appeals to pride and guilt, and expressions of disappointment. His hypothesis that psychological discipline would contribute to guilt severity, especially around aggression, was derived from the theory that in disciplining the child psychologically the parent provides a model of self-restraint about aggression and about the manner in which to express disapproval, thus contributing to the child's tendency to inhibit and feel guilty about his own hostile tendencies. Further, in psychological discipline the punishment is not likely to be gotten over and done with, and the parent's anger is apt to smolder unexpressed and thus convey strong disapproval, thereby increasing the child's anxiety about displeasing the parent. The parent who favors corporal punishment, on the other hand, was viewed as providing a model of aggression and as condoning it implicitly, if not explicitly, and also as providing the child with a suitable target for the direct expression of aggression. Allinsmith found no relationship between the two discipline categories and the child's guilt, but in a later study (1955), using a more homogeneous middle class college sample, he found that male students who recalled both parents (especially their mothers) as having used mainly psychological discipline, obtained higher guilt-over-aggression scores on a story completion measure than those whose parents used corporal punishment. The female subjects only showed a slight tendency in the same direction, but, as the authors point out, this may be due to the fact that the story-beginning used was designed for boys and had a masculine theme. Heinicke found a similar pattern with his 5-year-olds. The frequent use of praise and the infrequent use of physical punishment and isolation related to high guilt. Heinicke also found that the parent's expression of affection toward the child is positively related to the child's guilt.

Further evidence for the relation between psychological discipline and guilt severity comes from the Whiting and Child cross-cultural study (with due regard for the precautions mentioned earlier that are necessary in interpreting these findings). They found a positive relation between their cultural index of guilt and the prevalence in a culture of "love-oriented" techniques of discipline. These techniques overlap considerably with those fitting Allinsmith's "psychological" category. However, whereas Allinsmith views these techniques as providing a model of restraint, Whiting and Child's theory is that they contribute to guilt by keeping the child oriented toward the goal of affection and at the same time arousing uncertainty as to the attainment of this goal. Examples are rewarding by praise, punishing by isolation, and punishing by the withdrawal of love.

Sears, Maccoby, and Levin (1957) found similar results with kindergarten children using as a measure of conscience another aspect of the child's behavior following a transgression: whether he characteristically confesses, hides, or lies—as reported by the parent. This index related positively to the mother's reported use of love-oriented techniques and negatively to the use of object-oriented techniques (tangible rewards and incentives, physical punishment, deprivation of privileges as punishment). But the love-oriented discipline pattern was found to relate to the child's conscience only in conjunction with the frequent expression of love and affection. That is, mothers who were both warm and used love-oriented techniques produced children who tended to confess to their deviations rather than hide or deny them. The author's explanation for this finding is that the effectiveness of love withdrawal depends somewhat upon the amount of love that is being taken away. That is, the child who generally experiences a warmly affectionate relationship with his parents is more affected by the threat that this relationship will be broken than the child who has never enjoyed such parental warmth. In response to the pressure to devise habitual means of insuring the continuation of the parent's love, the child adopts as his own the parent's restrictions and ideals.

Aronfreed (1961) investigated still another aspect of the child's post-transgression behavior: whether it is motivated by internal or external forces. He studied sixth grade children, using a projective story completion technique. In each story-beginning the central figure commits an act of aggression, the stories varying with respect to the person toward whom the aggression is directed and in the type of aggression expressed. The story completions were coded according to whether the central figure, without any reliance on outside forces or events, accepts responsibility for his action and actively seeks to correct the situation, for example, by making reparation or modifying his future behavior in the direction of social acceptability; or whether the events following the transgression are dominated by external concerns, mainly in the form of accidents or other unpleasant fortuitous happenings. Data on parent discipline were obtained by interviewing the mothers about how they handled aggression in the child. The discipline techniques reported were classified as "induction" techniques or "sensitization" techniques. The "induction" category is similar to Allinsmith's "psychological" one, but in his theory about the effects of this type of discipline Aronfreed focuses not so much on its relevance for the kind of behavior model presented the child, as Allinsmith does, but more directly on its capacity to arouse unpleasant feeling reactions in the child about his misbehavior, reactions which are seen as being independent of external threat. Certain induction techniques (asking the child why he behaved as he did, insisting that he correct the damage he has done, or refraining from punishment when he takes the moral initiative) are also seen as encouraging the child to accept responsibility for his actions. And others, especially the use of explanations or reasoning, are viewed as "utilizing a verbal and cognitive medium of exchange that can provide the child with his own resources for evaluating his behavior" (1961, p. 226). The "sensitization" category resembles Allinsmith's "corporal" techniques but also includes attempts to control the child through direct verbal assault (yelling, shouting, bawling-out, etc.). These techniques are viewed as attempting only to extinguish or control the child's inacceptable behavior and as tending "not to be translated into a set of independent moral functions because they emphasize only the painful external consequences of the child's transgression and the importance of external threats or demands in carrying out moral actions" (1961, p. 226). Aronfreed found, as he hypothesized, that the use of induction techniques is positively related to a high degree of internally motivated self-corrective action in the child stories and with the absence of punishment from external forces. Mothers who used more sensitization techniques, on the other hand, had children whose stories contained more external punishment.

Hoffman and Saltzstein (1960) obtained similar results with seventh grade children. The children were asked to make moral judgments about norm violations (e.g., stealing, lying, violating a trust) committed under different conditions and to give the reasons for their judgments. Their responses were classified as expressing an internalized standard or merely the fear of detection and punishment by external authorities. The data on parental practices were obtained from the children's responses to highly structured objective items bearing on the parent's current disciplinary pattern in several types of situations, expressions of affection toward the child, and participation in child-centered activities. The results were that the more internalized boys as compared to those who were more externally oriented reported that both parents were more permissive in their discipline; that their mothers less often used techniques which openly asserted their power over the child (this category included the use of force, threat of force or deprivation, and direct commands, and therefore resembles Allinsmith's "corporal" and Aronfreed's "sensitization" categories); that their mothers more often used techniques indicating the painful consequences of the child's act for the parents; and that their mothers were more affectionate. The only significant findings for girls were that the internalized girls less often reported their mothers as threatening to have the father discipline them and more often reported their fathers as using rational appeals in their discipline. The internalized subjects of both sexes also gave more consistently severe guilt responses than the externals on a story completion measure. Thus, although the above findings are more directly relevant to the child's conscious moral orientation, they also have a bearing on his reactions to transgression.

Despite the diversity of theoretical approaches, measuring instruments, and moral content areas involved in the studies discussed in this section, their results have a common core of agreement that is encouraging. The relatively frequent use of discipline which attempts to change the child's behavior by inducing internal forces toward compliance appears to foster the development of an internalized moral orientation, especially as reflected in the child's reactions to his own transgressions. The use of coercive measures that openly confront the child with the parent's power, on the other hand, apparently contributes to a moral orientation based on the fear of authority.

Further, the studies in this group that include data on parental affection (Heinicke, 1953; Hoffman and Saltzstein, 1960; Sears, Maccoby, and Levin, 1957) suggest that this variable, too, contributes to internalization. Putting all of this together, we may tentatively conclude that an internalized moral orientation is fostered by an affectionate relationship between the parent and child, in combination with the use of discipline techniques which utilize this relationship by appealing to the child's personal and social motives.

RESISTANCE TO PRESSURES TO DEVIATE

Perhaps a more important index of conscience than the child's reaction to transgressing is the degree to which he behaves in accordance with his standards and avoids transgressing in the first place. The ability to resist pressures to deviate from one's standards may be a better test of their strength and integration with the personality than the experiencing of guilt after having transgressed. Pressures to deviate may be external (e.g., peer-group pressures) or internal (e.g., desires for objects which are themselves forbidden or which require prohibited action for their attainment). Some research has been done on parental antecedents of the child's response to external pressures (Hoffman, 1953; Mussen and Kagan, 1958), but not where the pressures were opposed to the child's values and standards. The latter is an important aspect of the larger social problem of how the individual learns to resolve conflicts between inner- and other-directed pressures (Riesman, Denney, and Glaser, 1953). There is need for empirical research on this problem, for example, on the antecedents of the moral strength or courage necessary to resist social pressures to deviate from one's internalized standards, and, more generally, on the antecedents of how one copes with conflict between moral norms internalized in the home and opposing pressure from peers.[4]

---

[4] There is empirical evidence that at least in communities not characterized by rapid social change, peer pressures tend to reinforce parentally inculcated norms rather than

Although external pressures against moral standards have been neglected in research, considerable work has been done on resistance to inner temptation. In the Allinsmith study already cited, two additional story-beginnings were included, one dealing with theft and the other with disobedience, in which the hero has not yet transgressed but is tempted to do so. The subject's resistance-to-temptation score was determined by whether or not in his story-completions the hero transgressed. One of the several parental background variables investigated, the use of explained requests rather than arbitrary demands, was found to be positively associated with the resistance-to-temptation scores obtained for both stories. In an earlier study MacKinnon (1938) used a more direct behavioral index of resistance to temptation. His subjects, all college students, took a written test under conditions of no tangible reward. Cheaters were detected without their knowledge by observations through a one-way screen. Data on early parental practices were obtained from questionnaires filled out by the student. The findings showed a positive relation between physical punishment and cheating and between psychological punishment—defined as techniques which indicate that the child has fallen short of some ideal in some way or hurt the parents and therefore that they love or approve of him less—and not cheating. Although these results are broadly consistent with Allinsmith's findings, the latter's own measures of psychological and corporal discipline did not relate to resistance to temptation.

Further confusion as to the antecedents of resistance to temptation is apparent when we examine the results of the three most recent studies in this area. Two used preschool age children (Burton, Maccoby, and Allinsmith, 1961; Sears, Rau, and Alpert, 1960) and the other, 11- to 12-year-olds (Grinder, 1960). All three used the child's behavior in an experimental test situation as the index of his ability to resist temptation. The test consisted of placing the child in a situation in which he was tempted to violate the rules of the game in order to win a prize and then leaving him to play alone. Although the child thought no one was watching him, his reactions were observed through a one-way-screen, as in the MacKinnon study; and he was assigned scores indicating whether or not and to what degree he cheated or resisted the temptation to do so. All three studies used parent interviews consisting of a large number of structured and unstructured items, and there is considerable overlap in the items used. Despite the similarities in conceptual approach, the way in which resistance to temptation was measured,

oppose them (Peck and Havighurst, 1960) and that most adolescents favor parental advice over peer advice (Remmers and Radler, 1957). Still, in a national sample one third of the boys and one sixth of the girls replied to the question, "When do you think a (boy) (girl) might break a rule?" by stating that they might do so under the influence of the group (Douvan, 1955; Douvan and Kaye, 1956).

and the parent interview items used, the findings in the three studies have little in common. Each investigator found several parent variables to relate to the child's ability to resist temptation, but there was little agreement among them as to which of the many parent variables used were the ones which related significantly to the child measure. Further, in those few cases in which the parent variables relating significantly to the child's resistance to temptation were similar, the direction of the relations were as likely to be discrepant as not. Here are two examples: Burton et al. and Grinder each found the severity with which the child was weaned to relate positively to resistance to temptation, but Sears et al. found the same variable to relate negatively; and, whereas the general pattern of the Grinder and the Sears et al. findings was for resistance to temptation to relate to verbal rather than physical means of control, the Burton et al. findings tended to be in the opposite direction. Finally, none of these three studies replicated MacKinnon's findings of a positive relation between psychological discipline and not cheating, although all three had obtained psychological and physical discipline scores roughly comparable to those used by MacKinnon.

Such discrepant results among studies using similar methodologies cannot be ignored in our efforts to pull together and find meaning in the research in this area. A possible explanation for the inconsistencies lies in the choice of a situation involving success and failure in a task as the behavioral index of resistance to temptation. Such a measure is open to the damaging influence of unequal motivation to do well on the task, i.e., the temptation to cheat may not be the same for all subjects. Not cheating for some, for example, may signify disinterest in the prize or perhaps low achievement strivings in general rather than a strong conscience. Some of the investigators (especially Grinder) indicate awareness of this problem and attempt in one way or another to take cognizance of it in interpreting their findings. But none of the studies actually control the child's general needs for achievement or his desire for the particular prize.

Although the studies of resistance to temptation were undertaken with the expectation that its parental antecedents would roughly approximate those obtained for guilt, we have seen that this did not turn out to be the case. The expectation of a generally positive relation between the two variables is based on the notion that a person with a strong conscience generally tends to resist temptation and that, when he does transgress for some reason, he experiences relatively severe guilt. Or, adhering more closely to the psychoanalytic formulation, that the person capable of experiencing severe guilt resists temptations in order to avoid guilt. Correspondingly, the person with little guilt potential—or one with smoothly functioning defenses against guilt—has little reason to resist temptation.

The assumption of a positive relation between resistance to temptation and guilt is thrown into question not only by the lack of empirical evidence for their having common parental antecedents, but more directly by the fact that they have not been found to relate to each other with any consistency. Thus, while MacKinnon (1938), Grinder (1960), and Sears et al. (1960) report low positive relations between resistance to temptation and guilt (for girls, Sears et al. find a slight negative relation), Allinsmith (1960) and Maccoby (1959) report no relation and Burton et al. (1961), a negative one. The lack of a clear-cut relation suggests that the motivation to avoid guilt is insufficient for resisting temptation and that other personality and situational variables should be considered. For example, a person might become so highly involved in striving for highly desired objectives that, though he wishes to avoid guilt, he actually fails to anticipate it and acts accordingly. This is especially likely in the young child who is too immature cognitively to discriminate relevant cues and anticipate consequences. Or the person might be fully aware of the consequences at all times, yet lack the ego controls necessary to resist gratifying the impulse or need in question. Another possibility is that he might both foresee the consequences and have the necessary controls, yet be quite willing to tolerate considerable guilt in order to attain his objectives. Finally, a guilt-prone individual might violate a standard because of an unconscious wish for punishment. Simply because a person has strong moral concerns then does not necessarily mean he will *behave* morally; whether he resists or submits to temptation is a function of a complex balance of forces between his achievement needs and specific goal strivings, guilt and other aspects of his moral structure, his system of ego controls, and various aspects of the immediate situation. Conversely, resistance to temptation need not necessarily imply guilt but might be done in the service of a value or ideal, e.g., masculine self-control, which—like guilt—competes with the gratification of the impulse in question.

Such considerations highlight the complexities of doing empirical research on resistance to temptation. Very likely the closer our concepts approach the level of overt behavior which is subject to conscious volitional controls, the more multidetermined they become and the more difficult it becomes empirically to institute the various methodological controls that are necessary for establishing specific antecedent-consequent relations. Internal states like guilt, on the other hand, may be more unitary and less subject to such complexities. This line of argument may explain why the studies dealing with guilt and guilt-related reactions to transgressions reviewed above have a great deal of agreement despite the diversity of approaches used, while the resistance-to-temptation studies, which used similar concepts and methods, have little agreement. It may also account in part for the low relations obtained in the classical studies by Hartshorne and May (1929) between different manifestations of morality, since these investigators used mainly overt behavioral indices and did not control for such variables as motivation and fear.

Several suggestions for further research on resistance to temptation seem to follow from this discussion. First, every effort should be made not only to control on motivation but, more specifically, to make certain that all the subjects are highly motivated. To measure resistance to temptation adequately obviously requires that there be temptation. Otherwise we could only be sure, at best, of measuring the absence of cheating or of whatever unacceptable behaviors were under study. Studies of resistance to pressure from peers might for the same reason need to control on the subject's needs for affiliation and fears of rejection as well as his needs to continue behaving in the manner opposed by the group.

Secondly, resistance to temptation scores should probably be based on a battery of measures dealing with different kinds of moral standards. This might pose new problems, e.g., the ethics of inducing children, even in the service of science, to commit acts more strongly prohibited in our culture than cheating, such as stealing and physical violence. This may be why a relatively harmless (and, from the experimenter's standpoint, passive) test situation has been used in all the experimental studies of resistance to temptation. Perhaps compromise solutions can be found, e.g., using a complex index based on a carefully controlled experimental cheating situation, in conjunction with a projective measure dealing with temptation in areas more difficult to study in the laboratory. From a large sample children who consistently resist temptation on both the experimental and projective measures might then be compared with those who consistently do not resist.

Thirdly, since the relation between resistance to temptation and guilt is variable and apparently unpredictable, it must be assumed in any given sample that the resistance to temptation measure may be confounded with guilt. Studies having the theoretical goal of isolating out the specific antecedents of resistance to temptation per se may, therefore, have to control on guilt, e.g., by comparing children who are high on both guilt and resistance to temptation with those who are high on guilt but low on resistance to temptation.

GENERALIZATIONS ABOUT PARENTAL ANTECEDENTS

Though definite conclusions cannot be drawn from the work on parental antecedents of moral development done thus far, several tentative generalizations can be made which may help serve as a guide for future research in this area. The first is that the research generally supports the view that the frequent expression of warmth and affection toward the child helps promote identification with the parent, although there is some evidence that a threatening and punitive approach might in some cases also contribute to identification. Second, the use of discipline techniques which attempt to change the child's behavior by inducing internal forces toward compliance (e.g., by appealing to the child's needs for affection and self-esteem and his concern for others), especially in the context of an affectionate parent-child relationship, appears to foster the development of an internalized moral orientation at least with respect to one's reactions following the violation of a moral standard. The use of techniques that involve physical coercion or that directly assert the parent's power over the child, on the other hand, are more conducive to the development of a moral orientation based on fear of external detection and punishment. The third and most tentative generalization is that the particular kind of psychological techniques used, i.e., the particular aspect of the child's need system to which appeal is generally made, may affect the type of internalized morality that develops, e.g., whether it is oriented predominantly toward human need or conventional authority, and the degree to which it is integrated with the rest of the personality. Summarizing and stating these generalizations most broadly, we would offer the following tentative synthesis of the research findings to date: affection contributes to identification; psychological discipline which capitalizes on the affectionate relationship (and its resulting identification) fosters the development of internalized moral structures in general; and variations in type of psychological discipline may then account for the particular kind of internalized moral structure that develops.

Sex Differences

To the extent that these generalizations are valid, they apply mainly to males since most of the studies on which they are based deal only with males; and, further, when both sexes are used as subjects, the findings are usually more pronounced for males than females. The explanation may lie in the fact that psychoanalytic theory has always been better articulated and understood with respect to males and that as a result our concepts are clearer for boys. The paucity of realistic female items in most studies of moral development may also reflect the degree to which many of our moral values are masculine tinged; and this in turn may reflect actual sex differences in the likelihood of engaging in the acts that are most strongly prohibited in our society. For example, women are less likely than men to destroy property or use physical violence. This may not mean that they are more moral than men, but that their role exerts less pressure toward deviation and also provides less opportunities for it. Another possible explanation is that in our culture the pressures on girls toward "self-definition and investment in a personal identity" come later than for boys and that, "when such broader identity issues are postponed, the issues that might lead to differentiation of moral standards and values are also postponed" (Douvan, 1960). If true, this would suggest that studies of morality in girls should perhaps be done with older subjects. Clearly, we have much to learn about the processes of moral growth in women. The research done thus far tells us very little, especially about the role of parental practices.

This is not to say that our understanding of the male pattern is entirely clear. The findings in general, for example, appear to contradict the Freudian view that castration anxiety is responsible for identification and conscience formation in males, since this view would lead us to expect a more physically punitive parental pattern to relate to male internalization. This contradiction suggests that Freud might have been wrong—perhaps because his theory was based on the observations of a sample of men who were not representative and whose neuroses may have been due largely to excessive severity in their early upbringing. Another possibility is that Freud was right—for his time and place; but that in our society, especially in the middle class, the parental treatment of boys has become more psychological and love oriented, having shifted in this direction to the point where it now has much in common with the treatment generally accorded girls (Bronfenbrenner, 1961). As a result, the kind of physically harsh treatment discussed by Freud may be rare, and conscience formation today may be based more on parental practices which increase the boy's anxiety over losing the parent's love. Further research will hopefully throw light on this question as well as provide us with needed insight into the general problem of six differences in morality and its familial antecedents.

The Role of the Father

In the studies reporting data on the discipline used by both parents, father discipline emerges as relatively unimportant in young children but as taking on increased significance with older ones. Perhaps it is only after the child has attained a relatively advanced level of cognitive maturity that the father's discipline can have important effects despite his absence most of the day from the child's immediate life space.

The influence of the father is most pronounced in the two studies using college students as subjects: in one (Allinsmith and Greening, 1955), discipline by the father as well as the mother related to guilt, and, in the other (MacKinnon, 1938), discipline by the father and not the mother related to resistance to temptation. In addition to highlighting the increased importance of the father with age, these findings, together with those obtained in the studies of younger children, also seem to suggest that mothers and fathers may be particularly influential with respect to different aspects of moral development. That whereas the mother may be the main socializing agent with respect to guilt,[5] the father may play the more important role in the development of resistance to pressures to deviate from moral standards. At least this may be true for boys—perhaps, because of the importance that self-control, a masculine ideal in our culture, has for this aspect of morality.[6] Thus, early discipline by the mother may contribute more to guilt and later discipline by the father, to the controls necessary for resisting pressures to transgress.

Intervening Processes

Aside from establishing empirical generalizations, another goal of research is to increase our understanding of the processes intervening between the parent's pattern and the child's moral development. We need to know, for example, not only that psychological discipline contributes to internalization but the manner in which it does so. Is it because this type of discipline provides the child with a model of self-restraint, because it provides the child with information needed at the cognitive level for evaluating the rightness or wrongness of his act, or because it induces unpleasant feelings about the act? And if the last, which feelings aroused in the child are the most significant: anxiety over the loss of parental love, guilt over the harmful consequences of his act for the parent, or shame over his inability to attain a standard of excellence or maturity?

Several approaches to this problem suggest themselves. The most obvious is to refine the definitions of the parent concepts. For example, broad concepts like "psychological discipline" might more often be broken down into several more homogeneous ones like techniques which threaten love withdrawal, point out harmful social consequences of the child's action, and interpret the child's misbehavior as evidence of incompetence or immaturity— and each of these in turn related to the child variables under study. This procedure should enable the investigator to reduce the possibility of unknown cancellation effects and, if followed by other researchers, to increase the comparability of different studies, thereby making it possible to draw more

---

[5] That the mother is the main disciplinary agent with respect to guilt is also suggested by the finding that subjects who say they would blame themselves, in hypothetical interaction situations involving harm to another person, are more likely to perceive the mother in the principal disciplinary role than subjects who say they would not blame themselves (Henry, 1956).

[6] If delinquency and overt aggressiveness are, at least in part, manifestations of low control, then further empirical support exists for the suggestion that socialization by the father may be especially important in the development of control in older boys. In several recent studies the father-son relationship has been found to be more crucial than the mother-son relationship in the development of these antisocial behavior patterns (Andry, 1960; Bandura and Walters, 1959; Gold, 1961).

reliable conclusions about the aspects of parent discipline most responsible for moral development. Similarly, to assess whether parent discipline affects the child more by reinforcing morally relevant behaviors or by building the child's ego-control system may require sharpening the conceptual distinction between discipline that follows the child's action and discipline that is oriented more toward the initiation and prevention of action.[7]

Another approach to the search for intervening processes, that might be used in conjunction with the above, is to compare the backgrounds of subjects who show conformity to a theoretical expectation with those who deviate from it. An example would be to compare the parental practices of children who identify with their parents and have internalized moral reactions to transgressions with children who identify but are not internalized. Controlling for identification in this manner would permit the more precise study of the antecedents of internalization and perhaps suggest the processes that contribute to internalization over and above those needed for identification. Closely related would be the study of children having different moral patterns, for example, the comparison suggested earlier between children who are internalized but nonetheless show weakness in the face of pressures to deviate and internalized children who successfully resist these pressures.

The study of the child's immediate reactions to various kinds of discipline techniques may also provide clues as to the psychological effects of these techniques, especially if different age levels are investigated. The same technique that at a very early age arouses anger and resentment at being frustrated might, later on, arouse anxiety over the loss of parental love; and, still later, when the child has attained the necessary level of cognitive and emotional maturity, the same technique might arouse guilt over the harmful consequences of his behavior. Knowing the reactions typically elicited by various techniques at different age levels might suggest new theoretical formulations about the processes linking parental practices to the child's moral development. Such knowledge should also help in the evaluation of the soundness of hypotheses already advanced since these hypotheses invariably make assumptions, usually implicitly, about the immediate impact of parental discipline on the child at a certain age.

These three approaches should complement each other in providing the knowledge at different levels necessary for further theoretical advance and increased understanding of the manner in which parental methods affect the child.

---

[7] Allinsmith (1960) has suggested, for example, that rewards and punishment may be primarily responsible for how the child behaves after a transgression, whereas the techniques used to initiate action or prevent it may have more relevance to the development of controls and hence play a larger role in resistance to temptation.

Behavioral Generality and Dynamic Consistency

Although the focus of this paper has been on parental influences, we have at several points, mainly in discussing resistance to temptation, found it necessary to touch upon a long-standing issue in moral development research: that of the generality or specificity of moral behavior. Since none of the studies discussed here include observations of moral behavior in a variety of contexts, they contribute little over and above the classical demonstration by Hartshorne and May (1929) that children who behave in accord with one moral standard may not do so with respect to another. The findings on the relation between guilt and resistance to temptation have a bearing on a related issue, however, one that might be called "dynamic consistency." This refers to the degree of consistency *at different personality levels* with respect to *a particular moral standard*. Is there a relation between having a strong conscious moral standard in a particular area, resisting pressures to behave contrary to that standard, and experiencing guilt when it is violated? At first glance, the findings reported in this paper would seem to suggest a negative answer to this question and the general conclusion that dynamic consistency, like behavioral generality across different standards, is the exception rather than the rule. Upon closer inspection, however, we find that the major inconsistencies occur only at the preschool level. Further, the only two studies using college students as subjects yield findings that are dynamically consistent: psychological discipline by the parent contributes to both guilt (Allinsmith and Greening, 1955) and resistance to temptation (MacKinnon, 1938). These studies also suggest that behavioral generality too might be more pronounced at this older age level, since different content areas were used, cheating and expressing aggression.

From the over-all pattern we would tentatively conclude that, while in early childhood there may be little behavioral generality and little dynamic consistency, both tend to increase with age. The morality of the young child may then be more a matter of the rote learning of relatively specific acts and avoidances, learnings which may not cut across different standards and which, in the absence of the ability to discriminate relevant cues and anticipate consequences, may not consistently offer strong competition to the drives and "pulls" of moral conflict situations. As the child grows older, on the other hand, his standards tend to become more integrated around broader principles and are therefore more likely to be generalized from one situation to another. In addition, these principles (if they exist at all) may have relatively deep roots within the personality and thus offer a more dependable challenge to the momentary needs and desires with which they conflict.

This interpretation, though based on a barely discernible trend in a small number of studies, seems reasonable in terms of what we know about psychological, especially cognitive, development. One qualification is needed, however. The amount of behavioral generality even at the older age levels may necessarily be limited since different moral standards merely reflect, to some extent, specific familial or subcultural values. The significant question for study, then, might be that of the antecedents of dynamic consistency with respect to particular moral standards.

References

Abel, T. M. Moral judgments among subnormals. *Journal of Abnormal and Social Psychology*, 1941, **36**, 378–392.

Aberle, D., and Naegele, K. Middle-class fathers' occupational role and attitudes toward children. *American Journal of Orthopsychiatry*, 1952, **22**, 366–378.

Ackerson, L. *Children's behavior problems.* Chicago: University of Chicago Press, 1942.

Adler, A. Characteristics of the first, second, third child. *Children*, 1928, **3**, 14–52.

Adorno, T. W., Frenkel-Brunswik, E., Levinson, D. J., and Sanford, R. N. *The authoritarian personality.* New York: Harper, 1950.

Allee, W. C. Dominance and hierarchy in societies of vertebrates. In P. P. Grass (Ed.), *Structure et Physiologie des Societes Animales.* Paris: Centre Nat. Recherche Scientifique, 1952.

Allen, K. E., Hart, B., Buell, J. S., Harris, F. R., and Wolf, M. M. Effects of social reinforcement on the isolate behavior of a nursery school child. *Child Development*, 1964, **35**, 511–518.

Allinsmith, B. B. Expressive styles: II. Directness with which anger is expressed. In D. R. Miller and G. E. Swanson (Eds.), *Inner conflict and defense.* New York: Holt, 1960. Pp. 315–336.

Allinsmith, W. The learning of moral standards. In D. R. Miller, G. E. Swanson, et al., *Inner conflict and defense.* New York: Holt, 1960. Pp. 141–176.

Allinsmith, W., and Greening, T. C. Guilt over anger as predicted from parental discipline: A study of superego development. *American Psychologist*, 1955, **10**, 320. (Abstract)

Allport, G. W. *Personality: A psychological interpretation.* New York: Holt, 1937. Pp. 159–166.

Altus, W. D. Birth order and scholastic aptitude. *Journal of Consulting Psychology,* 1965, **29**, 202–205.

———. Birth order and its sequelae. *Science,* 1966, **151**, 44–49.

Amsel, A., and Roussel, J. Motivational properties of frustration. I: Effect on a running response of the addition of frustration in the motivational complex. *Journal of Experimental Psychology,* 1952, **43**, 363–368.

Anderson, H. H. Domination and social integration in the behavior of kindergarten children and teachers. *Genetic Psychology Monographs,* 1939, **21**, 287–385.

Anderson, R. L., and Bancroft, T. A. *Statistical theory in research.* New York: McGraw-Hill, 1952.

Andry, R. *Delinquency and parental pathology.* Springfield, Ill.: Charles C Thomas, 1960.

Angrilli, A. F. The psychosexual identification of preschool boys. *Journal of Genetic Psychology,* 1960, **97**, 329–340.

Anisfeld, M., Munoz, S. R., and Lambert, W. E. The structure and dynamics of the ethnic attitudes of Jewish adolescents. *Journal of Abnormal and Social Psychology,* 1963, **66**, 31–36.

Argyle, M. *The scientific study of social behavior.* London: Methuen, 1957.

Aronfreed, J. Moral behavior and sex identity. In D. R. Miller, G. E. Swanson, et al., *Inner conflict and defense.* New York: Holt, 1960. Pp. 177–193.

———. The nature, variety, and social patterning of moral responses to transgression. *Journal of Abnormal and Social Psychology,* 1961, **63**, 223–240.

———. The effects of experimental socialization paradigms upon two moral responses to transgression. *Journal of Abnormal and Social Psychology,* 1963, **66**, 437–448.

———. Imitation and identification: An analysis of some affective and cognitive mechanisms. Paper presented at the biennial meeting of the Society for Research in Child Development, New York, March, 1967.

———. The concept of internalization. In D. A. Goslin (Ed.), *Handbook of socialization theory and research.* Chicago: Rand-McNally, 1968. Ch. 4.

———. *Conduct and conscience: The socialization of internalized control over behavior.* New York: Academic Press, 1968.

Aronfreed, J., Cutick, R. A., and Fagan, S. A. Cognitive structure, punishment, and nurturance in the experimental induction of self-criticism. *Child Development,* 1963, **34**, 281–294.

Asch, S. E. Effects of group pressure upon the modification and distortion of judgments. In E. E. Maccoby, T. M. Newcomb, and E. L. Hartley (Eds.), *Readings in social psychology.* New York: Holt, 1958. Pp. 174–183.

Atkinson, J. W. Motivational determinants of risk-taking behavior. *Psychological Review,* 1957, **64**, 359–372.

References

Atkinson, J. W. (Ed.) *Motives in fantasy, action, and society.* Princeton, N.J.: Van Nostrand, 1958.

Ausubel, D. P. *Ego development and the personality disorders.* New York: Grune and Stratton, 1952.

———. *Theory and problems of child development.* New York: Grune and Stratton, 1958.

Ausubel, D. P., and Ausubel, P. Ego development among segregated Negro children. In A. H. Passow (Ed.), *Education in depressed areas.* New York: Bureau of Publications, Teachers College, Columbia University, 1963. Pp. 109–141.

Ayllon, T., and Michael, J. The psychiatric nurse as a behavioral engineer. *Journal of Experimental Analysis of Behavior,* 1959, **2**, 323–334.

Azrin, N. H., and Lindsley, O. R. The reinforcement of cooperation between children. *Journal of Abnormal and Social Psychology,* 1956, **52**, 100–102.

Bach, G. R. Father-fantasies and father-typing in father-separated children. *Child Development,* 1946, **17**, 63–80.

Baer, D. M., and Harris, F. R. Control of nursery school children's behavior by programming social reinforcement from their teachers. *American Psychologist,* 1963, **18**, 343. (Abstract)

Baer, D. M., Peterson, R. F., and Sherman, J. A. The development of imitation by reinforcing behavioral similarity to a model. *Journal of the Experimental Analysis of Behavior,* 1967, **10**, 405–416.

Baier, K. *The moral point of view: a rational point of ethics.* Ithaca: Cornell University Press, 1958.

Bain, R. The self-and-other words of a child. *American Journal of Sociology,* 1936, **41**, 767–775.

Baldwin, J. M. *Social and ethical interpretations in mental development.* New York: Macmillan, 1897. P. 7.

Bandura, A. Social learning through imitation. *Nebraska Symposium on Motivation: 1962.* Lincoln: University of Nebraska Press, 1962, **10**, 211–269.

———. Social-learning theory of identificatory processes. In D. A. Goslin (Ed.), *Handbook of socialization theory and research.* Chicago: Rand-McNally, 1968. Ch. 3.

Bandura, A., and Huston, A. C. Identification as a process of incidental learning. *Journal of Abnormal and Social Psychology,* 1961, **63**, 311–318.

Bandura, A., and Kupers, C. J. Transmission of patterns of self-reinforcement through modeling. *Journal of Abnormal and Social Psychology,* 1964, **69**, 1–9.

Bandura, A., and McDonald, F. Influence of social reinforcement and the behavior of models in shaping children's moral judgments. *Journal of Abnormal and Social Psychology,* 1963, **67**, 274–281.

Bandura, A., Ross, D., and Ross, S. A. A comparative test of the status envy, social power, and secondary reinforcement theories of identificatory learning. *Journal of Abnormal and Social Psychology*, 1963, **67**, 527–534.

———. Imitation of film-mediated aggressive models. *Journal of Abnormal and Social Psychology*, 1963, **66**, 3–11.

———. Vicarious reinforcement and imitative learning. *Journal of Abnormal and Social Psychology*, 1963, **67**, 601–607.

Bandura, A., and Walters, R. H. *Adolescent aggression.* New York: Ronald Press, 1959.

———. *Social learning and personality development.* New York: Holt, Rinehart, and Winston, 1963.

Barker, R. G., Dembo, T., and Lewin, K. Frustration and regression. In R. G. Barker, et al. (Eds.), *Child behavior and development.* New York: McGraw-Hill, 1943. Pp. 441–458.

Barker, R. G., and Wright, H. F. *Midwest and its children.* Evanston, Ill.: Row, Peterson, 1954.

Beach, F. A., and Jaynes, J. Studies of maternal retrieving in rats. III. Sensory cues involved in the lactating females' response to her young. *Behavior*, 1956, **10**, 104–125.

Beck, R. C. On secondary reinforcement and shock termination. *Psychological Bulletin*, 1961, **58**, 28–45.

Bell, R. Q. Some factors to be controlled in studies of behavior of newborns. *Biologia Neonatorum*, 1963, **5**, 200–214.

———. The effect on the family of a limitation in coping ability in a child: A research approach and a finding. *Merrill-Palmer Quarterly*, 1964, **10**, 129–142.

———. A reinterpretation of the direction of effects in studies of socialization. *Psychological Review*, 1968, **75**, 81–95.

Beller, E. K. Dependence and independence in young children. Doctoral dissertation, State University of Iowa, 1948.

———. Two attitude components in younger boys. *Journal of Social Psychology*, 1949, **29**, 137–151.

———. Dependency and autonomous achievement striving related to orality and anality in early childhood. *Child Development*, 1957, **28**, 287–315.

Benedict, R. *Patterns of culture.* Boston: Houghton Mifflin, 1934.

———. *The chrysanthemum and the sword.* Boston: Houghton Mifflin, 1946.

Bennett, E. M., and Cohen, L. R. Men and women: Personality patterns and contrasts. *Genetic Psychology Monographs*, 1959, **59**, 101–155.

Berenda, R. W. *The influence of the group on the judgments of children.* New York: Kings Crown Press, 1950.

Berg, I. A., and Bass, B. M. (Eds.) *Conformity and deviation.* New York: Harper, 1961.

Berger, S. Conditioning through vicarious instigation. *Psychological Review,* 1962, **69,** 450–466.

Berkowitz, L. *Aggression: A social psychological analysis.* New York: McGraw-Hill, 1962.

———. Aggressive cues in aggressive behavior and hostility catharsis. *Psychological Review,* 1964, **71,** 104–122.

———. Some aspects of observed aggression. *Journal of Personality and Social Psychology,* 1965, **2,** 359–369.

———. A laboratory investigation of social class and national differences in helping behavior. *International Journal of Psychology,* 1966, **1,** 231–240.

Berkowitz, L., and Daniels, L. Responsibility and dependency. *Journal of Abnormal and Social Psychology,* 1963, **66,** 429–436.

———. Affecting the salience of the social responsibility norm: Effects of past help on the response to dependency relationships. *Journal of Abnormal and Social Psychology,* 1964, **68,** 275–281.

Berkowitz, L., and Friedman, P. Some social class differences in helping behavior. *Journal of Personality and Social Psychology,* 1967, **5,** 217–225.

Berkowitz, L., and Geen, R. G. Film violence and the cue properties of available targets. *Journal of Personality and Social Psychology,* 1966, **3,** 525–530.

Berkowitz, L., Klanderman, S. B., and Harris, R. Effects of experimenter awareness and sex of subject and experimenter on reactions to dependency relationships. *Sociometry,* 1964, **27,** 327–337.

Berkowitz, L., and Rawlings, E. Effects of film violence on inhibitions against subsequent aggression. *Journal of Abnormal and Social Psychology,* 1963, **66,** 405–412.

Bertrand, F. L. Contribution à l'étude psychogenetique de l'attention. *Année Psychologie,* 1925, **26,** 155–158.

Bettelheim, B. Individual and mass behavior in extreme situations. *Journal of Abnormal and Social Psychology,* 1943, **38,** 417–452.

Bibby, C. *Race, prejudice, and education.* London: William Heineman, Ltd., 1959.

Biber, B., Zimilies, H., Minuchin, P., and Shapiro, E. A study of the psychological impact of school experience: A series of papers on selected findings. Papers read at New England Psychological Association, Boston, November, 1962.

Bing, E. Effect of child-rearing practices on development of differential cognitive abilities. *Child Development,* 1963, **34,** 631–648.

Bitterman, M. E., and Holtzman, W. H. Conditioning and extinction of the galvanic skin response as a function of anxiety. *Journal of Abnormal and Social Psychology,* 1952, **47,** 615–623.

Block, J. H. The child-rearing practices report. Institute of Human Development, University of California, 1965. (Mimeo)

Block, J. H., Haan, N., and Smith, M. B. Activism and apathy in contemporary adolescents. In J. F. Adams (Ed.), *Understanding adolescence: Current developments in adolescent psychology.* Boston: Allyn and Bacon, 1968. Pp. 198–232.

Blos, P. *On adolescence: a psychoanalytic interpretation.* New York: Free Press, 1962.

Boehm, L. The development of independence: a comparative study. *Child Development,* 1957, **28**, 85–92.

Bott, H. Observation of play activities in a nursery school. *Genetic Psychology Monographs,* 1928, **4**, 44–88.

Bott, M. McM. *Personality development in young children.* University of Toronto Studies, Child Development Series #2. Toronto: University of Toronto Press, 1934.

Brady, J. P., and Lind, D. L. Experimental analysis of hysterical blindness. *Archives of General Psychiatry,* 1961, **4**, 331–339.

Brady, J. V., Schreiner, L., Geller, I., and Kling, A. Subcortical mechanisms in emotional behavior: The effect of rhinencephalic injury upon the acquisition and retention of a conditioned avoidance response in cats. *Journal of Comparative and Physiological Psychology,* 1954, **47**, 179–186.

Brehm, J. W. Increasing cognitive dissonance by a fait-accompli. *Journal of Abnormal and Social Psychology,* 1959, **58**, 379–382.

Brehm, J. W., and Cohen, A. R. *Explorations in cognitive dissonance.* New York: Wiley, 1962.

Bridges, K. M. B. *The social and emotional development of the pre-school child.* London: Kegan Paul, Trench, Trubner and Co., 1931.

Brodbeck, A. J. Learning theory and identification: IV. Oedipal motivation as a determinant of conscience development. *Journal of Genetic Psychology,* 1954, **84**, 219–227.

Bronfenbrenner, U. Socialization and social class through time and space. In E. E. Maccoby, T. M. Newcomb, and E. L. Hartley (Eds.), *Readings in social psychology* (3rd Ed.). Henry Holt and Co., 1958. Pp. 400–424.

———. The study of identification through interpersonal perception. In R. Tagiuri and L. Petrullo (Eds.), *Person perception and interpersonal behavior.* Stanford, Calif.: Stanford University Press, 1958. Pp. 110–130.

———. Freudian theories of identification and their derivatives. *Child Development,* 1960, **31**, 15–40.

———. The changing American child: A speculative analysis. *Journal of Social Issues,* 1961, **17**, 6–18.

———. Some familial antecedents of responsibility and leadership in adolescents. In L. Petrullo and B. M. Bass (Eds.), *Leadership and interpersonal behavior.* New York: Holt, Rinehart, and Winston, 1961. Pp. 239–272.

———. Toward a theoretical model for the analysis of parent-child relationships in a social context. In J. Glidewell (Ed.), *Parental attitudes and child behavior*. Springfield, Ill.: Charles C Thomas, 1961. Pp. 90–109.

———. Upbringing in collective settings in Switzerland and the USSR. Paper presented to the XVIIth International Congress of Psychology, Washington, D.C., 1963.

Bronson, W. C. Dimensions of ego and infantile identification. *Journal of Personality*, 1959, **27**, 532–545.

Brookover, W. B., and Gottlieb, D. *A sociology of education*, Revised Edition. New York: American Book Company, 1964.

Brown, D. G. Sex-role preference in young children. *Psychological Monographs*, 1956, **70**, No. 14.

———. Sex-role development in a changing culture. *Psychological Bulletin*, 1958, **55**, 232–242.

Bruce, H. M. Observations on the suckling stimulus and lactation in the rat. *Journal of Reproduction and Fertility*, 1961, **2**, 17–34.

Bruce, M. Animism vs. evolution of the concept "alive." *Journal of Psychology*, 1941, **12**, 81–90.

Brush, F. R., Brush, E. S., and Solomon, R. L. Traumatic avoidance learning: The effects of CS-US interval with a delayed-conditioning procedure. *Journal of Comparative and Physiological Psychology*, 1955, **48**, 285–293.

Buchanan, G. The effects of various punishment-escape events upon subsequent choice behavior of rats. *Journal of Comparative and Physiological Psychology*, 1958, **51**, 355–362.

Bühler, C. The social behavior of the child. In Carl Murchison (Ed.), *Handbook of child psychology*. Worcester, Mass.: Clark University Press, 1931. Pp. 392–431.

Burnstein, E., Stotland, E., and Zander, A. Similarity to a model and self-evaluation. *Journal of Abnormal and Social Psychology*, 1961, **62**, 257–264.

Burris, R. The effect of counseling on achievement motivation. Unpublished doctoral dissertation, Indiana University, 1958.

Burton, R. V. The generality of honesty reconsidered. *Psychological Review*, 1963, **70**, 481–499.

Burton, R. V., Maccoby, E. E., and Allinsmith, W. Antecedents of resistance to temptation in four-year-old children. *Child Development*, 1961, **32**, 689–710.

Buss, A. *The psychology of aggression*. New York: Wiley, 1961.

Byrne, D. Interpersonal attraction and attitude similarity. *Journal of Abnormal and Social Psychology*, 1961, **62**, 713–715.

Byrne, D., and Wong, T. J. Racial prejudice, interpersonal attraction, and assumed dissimilarity of attitudes. *Journal of Abnormal and Social Psychology*, 1962, **65**, 246–253.

Campbell, D. T. Conformity in psychology's theories of acquired behavioral dispositions. In I. A. Berg and B. M. Bass (Eds.), *Conformity and deviation.* New York: Harper, 1961. Pp. 101–142.

———. Ethnocentric and other altruistic motives. In D. Levine (Ed.), *Nebraska symposium on motivation: 1965.* Lincoln: University of Nebraska Press, 1965. Pp. 283–312.

Capra, P. C., and Dittes, J. E. Birth order as a selective factor among volunteer subjects. *Journal of Abnormal and Social Psychology,* 1962, **64,** 302.

Cartwright, D., and Robertson, R. J. Membership in cliques and achievement. *American Journal of Sociology,* 1961, **66,** 441–445.

Caruso, I. La notion de responsabilité et de justice immanente de l'enfant. *Archives de Psychologie,* 1943, **29,** No. 114.

Cattell, J. M. Families of American men of science. *Scientific Monthly,* 1917, **5,** 368–377.

Cava, E. L., and Raush, H. Identification and the adolescent boy's perception of his father. *Journal of Abnormal and Social Psychology,* 1952, **47,** 855–856.

Charlesworth, W. R. Development of the object concept in infancy: Methodological study. *American Psychologist,* 1966, **21,** 623. (Abstract)

Charlesworth, R., and Hartup, W. W. Positive social reinforcement in the nursery school peer group. *Child Development,* 1967, **38,** 993–1002.

Child, I. L. Socialization. In G. Lindzey (Ed.), *Handbook of social psychology.* Vol. II. Cambridge, Mass.: Addison-Wesley, 1954. Pp. 655–692.

Child, I. L., Potter, E. H., and Levine, E. M. Children's textbooks and personality development: An exploration in the social psychology of education. *Psychological Monographs,* 1946, **60,** No. 3.

Child, I. L., Storm, T., and Veroff, J. Achievement themes in folk tales related to socialization practice. In J. W. Atkinson (Ed.), *Motives in fantasy, action, and society.* Princeton, N.J.: Van Nostrand, 1958.

Church, R. M. Transmission of learned behavior between rats. *Journal of Abnormal and Social Psychology,* 1957, **54,** 163–165.

Church, R. M., Brush, F. R., and Solomon, R. L. Traumatic avoidance learning: The effects of CS-US interval with a delayed-conditioning procedure in a free-responding situation. *Journal of Comparative and Physiological Psychology,* 1956, **49,** 301–308.

Clark, B. S. The acquisition and extinction of peer imitation in children. *Psychonomic Science,* 1965, **2,** 147–148.

Clark, K. B. Educational stimulation of racially disadvantaged children. In A. H. Passow (Ed.), *Education in depressed areas.* New York: Bureau of Publications, Teachers College, Columbia University, 1963. Pp. 142–162.

———. *Prejudice and your child.* Boston: Beacon Press, 1963.

Clark, K. B., and Clark, M. P. Racial identification and preference in Negro children. In T. M. Newcomb and E. L. Hartley (Eds.), *Readings in social psychology.* New York: Holt, 1947. Pp. 169–178.

Clarke, E. L. *American men of letters, their nature and nurture.* New York: Columbia University Press, 1916.

Cohen, A. R., Greenbaum, C. W., and Mansson, H. H. Commitment to social deprivation and verbal conditioning. *Journal of Abnormal and Social Psychology*, 1963, **67**, 410–421.

Cohen, D. J. Justin and his peers: An experimental analysis of a child's social world. *Child Development*, 1962, **33**, 697–717.

Coleman, J. S. *The adolescent society.* Glencoe, Ill.: Free Press, 1961.

Coles, R. *The desegregation of Southern schools: A psychiatric study.* Anti-Defamation League of B'nai B'rith, New York, and the Southern Regional Council, Atlanta, 1963.

Collier, R. O., Jr. Analysis of variance for correlated observations. *Psychometrika*, 1958, **23**, 223–236.

Conners, C. K. Birth order and needs for affiliation. *Journal of Personality*, 1963, **31**, 408–416.

Couch, A., and Keniston, K. Yeasayers and naysayers: Agreeing response set as a personality variable. *Journal of Abnormal and Social Psychology*, 1960, **60**, 151–174.

Cowan, P. A. Cognitive egocentrism and social interaction in children. *American Psychologist*, 1966, **21**, 623. (Abstract)

Cowan, P. A., and Walters, R. H. Studies of reinforcement of aggression. I. Effects of scheduling. *Child Development*, 1963, **34**, 543–551.

Crandall, V. C. Reinforcement effects of adult reactions and nonreactions on children's achievement expectations. *Child Development*, 1963, **34**, 335–354.

———. Personality characteristics and social and achievement behaviors associated with children's social desirability response tendencies. *Journal of Personality and Social Psychology*, 1966, **4**, 477–486.

Crandall, V. C., Crandall, V. J., and Katkovsky, W. A children's social desirability questionnaire. *Journal of Consulting Psychology*, 1965, **29**, 27–36.

Crandall, V. C., Good, S., and Crandall, V. J. Reinforcement effects of adults' reactions and nonreactions on children's achievement expectations: A replication study. *Child Development*, 1964, **35**, 485–497.

Crandall, V. J., Soloman, D., and Kellaway, R. A comparison of the patterned and nonpatterned probability learning of adolescent and early grade school-age children. *Journal of Genetic Psychology*, 1961, **99**, 29–39.

Crowne, D. P., and Marlowe, D. A new scale of social desirability independent of psychopathology. *Journal of Consulting Psychology*, 1960, **24**, 349–354.

Crutchfield, R. S. Conformity and character. *American Psychologist*, 1955, **10**, 191–198.

Cumming, W. W., and Berryman, R. The complex discriminated operant: Studies of matching-to-sample and related problems. In D. I. Mostofsky (Ed.),

Stimulus generalization. Stanford: Stanford University Press, 1965. Pp. 284–330.

D'Amato, M. R., and Gumenik, W. E. Some effects of immediate versus randomly delayed shock on an instrumental response and cognitive processes. *Journal of Abnormal and Social Psychology*, 1960, **60**, 64–67.

Daniels, L., and Berkowitz, L. Liking and response to dependency relationships. *Human Relations*, 1963, **16**, 141–148.

Darby, C. L., and Riopelle, A. J. Observational learning in the rhesus monkey. *Journal of Comparative and Physiological Psychology*, 1959, **52**, 94–98.

Darlington, R. B., and Macker, C. E. Displacement of guilt-produced altruistic behavior. *Journal of Personality and Social Psychology*, 1966, **4**, 442–443.

Davids, A., Holden, R. H., and Gray, G. B. Maternal anxiety during pregnancy and adequacy of mother and child adjustment eight months following childbirth. *Child Development*, 1963, **34**, 993–1002.

Davis, A. American status systems and the socialization of the child. *American Sociological Review*, 1941, **6**, 345–354.

———. Child training and social class. In R. G. Barker, et al. (Eds.), *Child behavior and development*. New York: McGraw-Hill, 1943. Pp. 607–619.

———. *Social class influence upon learning.* Cambridge, Mass.: Harvard University Press, 1948.

Davis, A., and Havighurst, R. J. Social class and color differences in child rearing. *American Sociological Review*, 1946, **11**, 698–701.

———. *Father of the man.* Boston: Houghton Mifflin, 1947.

———. Social class and color differences in child rearing. In G. E. Swanson, T. M. Newcomb, and E. L. Hartley (Eds.), *Readings in social psychology*. New York: Henry Holt, 1952.

Davitz, J. R., Mason, D. J., Mowrer, O. H., and Viek, P. Conditioning of fear: A function of the delay of reinforcement. *American Journal of Psychology*, 1957, **70**, 69–74.

Dean, D. A. The relation of ordinal position to personality in young children. Unpublished master's thesis, State University of Iowa, 1947.

Dennis, W. Animism and related tendencies in Hopi children. *Journal of Abnormal and Social Psychology*, 1943, **38**, 21–36.

Deutsh, H. *The psychology of women.* Vol. I: *Girlhood*. New York: Grune and Stratton, 1944.

Deutsche, J. M. The development of children's concepts of causal relations. *University of Minnesota Institute of Child Welfare Monograph*, 1937, No. 13.

Dinsmoor, J. A. Punishment. 1. The avoidance hypothesis. *Psychological Review*, 1954, **61**, 34–46.

Dollard, J., Doob, L. W., Miller, N. E., Mowrer, O. H., and Sears, R. R. *Frustration and aggression.* New Haven: Yale University Press, 1939.

Doob, L. W., and Sears, R. R. Factors determining substitute behavior and the overt expression of aggression. *Journal of Abnormal and Social Psychology,* 1939, **34,** 293–313.

Douvan, E. *A study of adolescent boys.* Institute for Social Research, University of Michigan, 1955.

———. Sex differences in adolescent character processes. *Merrill-Palmer Quarterly,* 1960, **6,** 203–211.

Douvan, E., and Kaye, C. *Adolescent girls.* Institute for Social Research, University of Michigan, 1956.

Duffy, E. Tensions and emotional factors in reaction. *Genetic Psychology Monographs,* 1930, **7,** 1–79.

———. The relationship between muscular tension and quality of performance. *American Journal of Psychology,* 1932, **44,** 535–546. (a)

———. Muscular tension as related to physique and behavior. *Child Development,* 1932, **3,** 200–206. (b)

———. *Activation and behavior.* New York: Wiley, 1962. Duncan, O. D. A socioeconomic index for all occupations. In A. J. Reiss, Jr. (Ed.), *Occupations and social status.* New York: Crowell-Collier, 1961. Pp. 109–138.

Duncan, O. D., and Davis, B. An alternative to ecological correlation. *American Sociological Review,* 1953, **18,** 665.

Durkin, D. Children's acceptance of reciprocity as a justice principle. *Child Development,* 1959, **30,** 289–296.

———. Children's concepts of justice: A comparison with the Piaget data. *Child Development,* 1959, **30,** 59–67.

Duvall, E. N. Conceptions of parenthood. *American Journal of Sociology,* 1946, **52,** 195–203.

Eberhart, J. C. Attitudes toward property: A genetic study by the paired-comparisons rating of offenses. *Journal of Genetic Psychology,* 1942, **60,** 3–35.

Ehrlich, D. Determinants of verbal commonality and influencibility. Unpublished doctoral dissertation, University of Minnesota, 1958.

Elkind, D. The child's conception of his religious denomination, I: The Jewish child. *Journal of Genetic Psychology,* 1961, **99,** 209–225. (a)

———. The development of quantitative thinking: a systematic replication. *Journal of Genetic Psychology,* 1961, **98,** 37–46. (b).

———. The child's conception of his religious denomination, II: The Catholic child. *Journal of Genetic Psychology,* 1962, **101,** 185–193.

———. The child's conception of his religious denomination, III: The Protestant child. *Journal of Genetic Psychology,* 1963, **103,** 291–304.

———. Conceptual orientation shifts in children and adolescents. *Child Development,* 1966, **37,** 493–498.

———. Middle-class delinquency. *Mental Hygiene,* 1967, **51,** 80–84.

Emmerich, W. Parental identification in young children. *Genetic Psychology Monographs,* 1959, **60,** 257–308.

Engel, M., and Raine, W. J. A method for the measurement of the self-concept of children in the third grade. *Journal of Genetic Psychology*, 1963, **102**, 125–137.

English, H. B., and English, A. C. *A comprehensive dictionary of psychological and psychoanalytical terms.* New York: McKay, 1958.

Epstein, R. Aggression toward outgroups as a function of authoritarianism and imitation of aggressive models. *Journal of Personality and Social Psychology*, 1966, **3**, 574–579.

Epstein, R., and Komorita, S. S. The development of a scale of parental punitiveness towards aggression. *Child Development*, 1965, **36**, 129–142. (a)

———. Parental discipline, stimulus characteristics of outgroups, and social distance in children. *Journal of Personality and Social Psychology*, 1965, **2**, 416–420. (b).

———. Childhood prejudice as a function of parental ethnocentrism, punitiveness, and outgroup characteristics. *Journal of Personality and Social Psychology*, 1966, **3**, 259–264.

Epstein, W. Experimental investigations of the genesis of visual space perception. *Psychological Bulletin*, 1964, **61**, 115–128.

Erickson, M. T. Effects of social deprivation and satiation on verbal conditioning in children. *Journal of Comparative and Physiological Psychology*, 1962, **55**, 953–957.

Erikson, E. H. *Childhood and society.* New York: W. W. Norton, 1950.

———. *Identity and the life cycle.* New York: International Universities Press, 1959. (Also, *Psychological Issues*, 1959, **1**, 1–171.)

Eron, L. D. Relationship of TV viewing habits and aggressive behavior in children. *Journal of Abnormal and Social Psychology*, 1963, **67**, 193–196.

Eron, L. D., Banta, T. J., Walder, L. O., and Laulicht, J. H. Comparison of data obtained from mothers and fathers on child-rearing practices and their relation to child aggression. *Child Development*, 1961, **32**, 457–472.

Eron, L. D., Walder, L. O., Toiga, R., and Lefkowitz, M. M. Social class, parental punishment for aggression, and child aggression. *Child Development*, 1963, **34**, 849–867.

Estes, W. K. An experimental study of punishment. *Psychological Monographs*, 1944, **57**, No. 3.

Estes, W. K., and Johns, M. D. Probability learning with ambiguity in the reinforcing stimulus. *American Journal of Psychology*, 1958, **71**, 219–228.

Etzel, B., and Gewirtz, J. Experimental modification of caretaker-maintained high rate operant crying in a 6- and a 20-week-old infant (Infans Tyrannotearus). *Journal of Experimental Child Psychology*, 1967, **5**, 303–317.

Eysenck, H. J. Primary social attitudes as related to social class and political party. *British Journal of Sociology*, 1951, **2**, 198–209.

———. *The psychology of politics.* London: Routledge and Kegan Paul, 1954.

———. *The dynamics of anxiety and hysteria.* London: Routledge and Kegan Paul, 1957.

———. *The structure of human personality* (2nd ed.). London: Methuen, 1960.

———. Personality and social attitudes. *Journal of Social Psychology,* 1961, **53,** 243–248.

Faigin, H. Child rearing in the Rimrock community with special reference to the development of guilt. Unpublished doctoral dissertation. Harvard University, 1952.

Farber, I. E. Response fixation under anxiety and non-anxiety conditions. *Journal of Experimental Psychology,* 1948, **38,** 111–131.

Fauls, L. B., and Smith, W. D. Sex-role learning of five-year-olds. *Journal of Genetic Psychology,* 1956, **89,** 105–117.

Ferreira, A. J. The pregnant woman's emotional attitude and its reflection on the newborn. *American Journal of Orthopsychiatry,* 1960, **30,** 553–561.

Ferster, C. B., and DeMyer, M. K. The development of performance in autistic children in an automatically controlled environment. *Journal of Chronic Disease,* 1961, **13,** 312–345.

Festinger, L. *A theory of cognitive dissonance.* Evanston, Ill.: Row, Peterson, 1957.

Flavell, J. H., and Draguns, J. A microgenetic approach to perception and thought. *Psychological Bulletin,* 1957, **54,** 197–217.

Franks, C. M. Conditioning and personality: A study of normal and neurotic subjects. *Journal of Abnormal and Social Psychology,* 1956, **52,** 143–150.

———. Recidivism, psychopathy and personality. *British Journal of Delinquency,* 1956, **6,** 192–201.

———. Personality factors and the rate of conditioning. *British Journal of Psychology,* 1957, **48,** 119–126.

Freed, A., Chandler, P., Mouton, J., and Blake, R. Stimulus and background factors in sign violation. *Journal of Personality,* 1955, **23,** 499.

French, J. R. P., Jr., Morrison, H. W., and Levinger, G. Coercive power and forces affecting conformity. *Journal of Abnormal and Social Psychology,* 1960, **61,** 93–101.

French, J. R. P., Jr., and Raven, B. The bases of social power. In D. Cartwright (Ed.), *Studies in social power.* Ann Arbor, Mich.: Institute for Social Research, 1959. Pp. 150–167.

Freud, A. *The ego and the mechanisms of defense.* London: Hogarth, 1937. (Also, New York: International Universities Press, 1946).

Freud, A., and Burlingham, D. *Infants without families.* New York: International Universities Press, 1944.

Freud, S. *A general introduction to psychoanalysis.* Garden City, N.Y.: Garden City Publishing Company, 1920.

———. *New introductory lectures in psychoanalysis.* New York: Norton, 1933. (Also, London: Hogarth, 1933.)

———. *The ego and the id.* London: Hogarth, 1935.

———. *The problem of anxiety.* New York: Norton, 1936.

———. *Group psychology and the analysis of the ego.* London: Hogarth, 1949.

Fuchs, S. H. On introjection. *International Journal of Psychoanalysis,* 1937, **18,** 269–293.

Galton, F. *English men of science.* London: Macmillan, 1874.

Gardner, R. W., and Long, R. I. Control, defence, and centration effect: A study of scanning behavior. *British Journal of Psychology,* 1962, **53,** 129–140.

Gewirtz, J. L. Dependent and aggressive interaction in young children. Doctoral dissertation, State University of Iowa, 1948.

———. Mechanisms of social learning: Some roles of stimulation and behavior in early human development. In D. A. Goslin (Ed.), *Handbook of socialization theory and research.* Chicago: Rand-McNally, 1969. Ch. 2.

Gewirtz, J. L., and Baer, D. M. The effect of brief social deprivation on behaviors for a social reinforcer. *Journal of Abnormal and Social Psychology,* 1958, **56,** 49–56. (a).

———. Deprivation and satiation of social reinforcers as drive conditions. *Journal of Abnormal and Social Psychology,* 1958, **57,** 165–172 (b).

Gewirtz, J. L., and Stingle, K. G. Learning of generalized imitation as the basis for identification. *Psychological Review,* 1968, **75,** 374–397.

Gillespie, J. M., and Allport, G. W. *Youths' outlook on the future.* New York: Doubleday, 1955.

Glanzer, M., and Clark, W. H. Accuracy of perceptual recall: An analysis of organization. *Journal of Verbal Learning and Verbal Behavior,* 1963, **1,** 289–299.

———. The verbal loop hypothesis: Conventional figures. Unpublished master's thesis, University of Maryland, 1965.

Gleitman, H. Place learning without prior performance. *Journal of Comparative and Physiological Psychology,* 1955, **48,** 77–79.

Glueck, S., and Glueck, E. *Unraveling juvenile delinquency.* Cambridge, Mass.: Harvard University Press, 1950.

Gold, M. Social class, family structure, and identification process as related to juvenile delinquency. Paper read at American Psychological Association, New York City, September, 1961.

Goldberg, M. L. Factors affecting educational attainment in depressed areas. In A. H. Passow (Ed.), *Education in depressed urban areas.* New York: Bureau of Publications, Teachers College, Columbia University, 1963, Pp. 68–99.

Goldberg, M. L., et al. A three-year experimental program at Dewitt Clinton High School to help bright underachievers. *High Points,* 1959, **41,** 5–35.

Goldstein, A. Aggression and hostility in the elementary school in low socioeconomic areas. *Understanding the Child*, 1955, **24**, 20.

———. *Therapist-patient expectancies in psychotherapy.* New York: Pergamon Press, 1962.

Goldstein, K. *The organism.* New York: American Book, 1939.

Goodenough, E. W. Interest in persons as an aspect of sex difference in early years. *Genetic Psychology Monographs*, 1957, **55**, 287–323.

Goodenough, F. L. The use of pronouns by young children: A note on the development of self-awareness. *Journal of Genetic Psychology*, 1938, **52**, 333–346.

Goodman, M. E. *Race awareness in young children* (Revised Ed.). New York: Collier Books, 1964.

Goodson, F., and Brownstein, A. Secondary reinforcing and motivating properties of stimuli contiguous with shock onset and termination. *Journal of Comparative and Physiological Psychology*, 1955, **48**, 381–386.

Goranson, R., and Berkowitz, L. Reciprocity and responsibility reactions to prior help. *Journal of Personality and Social Psychology*, 1966, **3**, 227–232.

Gordon, J., and Cohn, F. Effect of fantasy arousal of affiliation drive on doll play aggression. *Journal of Abnormal and Social Psychology*, 1963, **66**, 301–307.

Gore, P. M., and Rotter, J. B. A personality correlate of social action. *Journal of Personality*, 1963, **31**, 58–64.

Gorer, G. *Japanese character structure.* New York: Institute for Intercultural Studies, 1942.

Gough, H. G. *California psychological inventory—manual.* Palo Alto, Calif.: Consulting Psychologists Press, Inc., 1956.

Gouldner, A. The norm of reciprocity: A preliminary statement. *American Sociological Review*, 1960, **25**, 161–178.

Gourevitch, V., and Feffer, M. H. A study of motivational development. *Journal of Genetic Psychology*, 1962, **100**, 361–375.

Gray, S. W. Perceived similarity to parents and adjustment. *Child Development*, 1959, **30**, 91–107.

Gray, S. W., and Klaus, R. The assessment of parental identification. *Genetic Psychology Monographs*, 1956, **54**, 87–114.

Green, A. W. The middle-class male child and neurosis. *American Sociological Review*, 1946, **11**, 31–41.

Grim, P. F. Reaction time set effects and the GSR in relation to age and behavior ratings. Unpublished doctoral dissertation, University of Chicago, 1965.

———. A sustained attention comparison of children and adults using reaction time set and GSR. *Journal of Experimental Child Psychology*, 1967, **5**, 26–38.

Grim, P. F., and Anderson, R. A. A system for recording the orienting reflex: A photo-electric plethysmograph and transistor amplifier. *American Journal of Psychology*, 1965, **78**, 672–676.

Grim, P. F., and White, S. H. Effects of stimulus change upon the GSR and reaction time. *Journal of Experimental Psychology*, 1965, **69**, 276–281.

Grinder, R. E. Behavior in a temptation situation and its relation to certain aspects of socialization. Unpublished doctoral dissertation, Harvard University, 1960.

Grosser, D., Polansky, N., and Lippitt, R. A laboratory study of behavioral contagion. *Human Relations*, 1951, **4**, 115–142.

Gwinn, G. T. The effects of punishment on acts motivated by fear. *Journal of Experimental Psychology*, 1949, **39**, 260–269.

Haeberle, A. Interactions of sex, birth order and dependency with behavior problems and symptoms in emotionally disturbed preschool children. Paper read at Eastern Psychological Association, Philadelphia, Pennsylvania, 1958.

Hall, J. C. Some conditions of anxiety extinction. *Journal of Abnormal and Social Psychology*, 1955, **51**, 126–132.

Hallworth, H. J. Sociometric relationships among grammar school boys and girls between the ages of eleven and sixteen years. *Sociometry*, 1953, **16**, 39–70.

Handlon, B. J., and Gross, P. The development of sharing behavior. *Journal of Abnormal and Social Psychology*, 1959, **59**, 425–428.

Harman, H. H. *Modern factor analysis.* Chicago: University of Chicago Press, 1960.

Harris, D. B. A scale for measuring attitudes of social responsibility in children. *Journal of Abnormal and Social Psychology*, 1957, **55**, 322–326.

Harris, F. R., Johnston, M. K., Kelley, C. S., and Wolf, M. M. Effects of positive social reinforcement on regressed crawling of a nursery school child. *Journal of Educational Psychology*, 1964, **55**, 35–41.

Harrower, M. R. Social status and the moral development of the child. *British Journal of Educational Psychology*, 1934, **4**, 75–95.

Hart, B. M., Allen, K. E., Buell, J. S., Harris, F. R., and Wolf, M. M. Effects of social reinforcement on operant crying. *Journal of Experimental Child Psychology*, 1964, **1**, 145–153.

Hartley, E. L. *Problems in prejudice.* New York: Kings Crown Press, 1946.

Hartley, R. E. Children's concepts of male and female roles. *Merrill-Palmer Quarterly*, 1960, **6**, 83–91.

———. A developmental view of female sex-role definition and identification. *Merrill-Palmer Quarterly*, 1964, **10**, 3–16.

Hartley, R. E., Frank, L. K., and Goldenson, R. M. *Understanding children's play.* New York: Columbia University Press, 1952.

Hartshorne, H., and May, M. A. *Studies in the nature of character.* Vol. 1. *Studies in deceit.* New York: Macmillan, 1928.

Hartshorne, H., May, M. A., and Maller, J. B. *Studies in the nature of character.* Vol. 2. *Studies in service and self-control.* New York: Macmillan, 1929.

Hartshorne, H., May, M. A., and Shuttleworth, F. K. *Studies in the nature of character.* Vol. 3. *Studies in the organization of character.* New York: Macmillan, 1930.

Hartup, W. W. Social behavior of children. *Review of Educational Research,* 1965, **35**, 122–129.

Hartup, W. W., and Coates, B. Imitation of a peer as a function of reinforcement from the peer group and rewardingness of the model. *Child Development,* 1967, **38**, 1003–1016.

Hartup, W. W., Glazer, J., and Charlesworth, R. Peer reinforcement and sociometric status. *Child Development,* 1967, **38**, 1017–1024.

Hattwick, L. A. Sex differences in behavior of nursery school children. *Child Development,* 1937, **8**, 343–355.

Havighurst, R. J., and Davis, A. A comparison of the Chicago and Harvard studies of social class differences in child rearing. *American Sociological Review,* 1955, **20**, 438–442.

Havighurst, R. J., and Neugarten, B. L. *American Indian and white children.* Chicago: University of Chicago Press, 1955.

———. *Society and education.* Boston: Allyn and Bacon, 1957.

Heinecke, C. M. Some antecedents and correlates of guilt and fear in young boys. Unpublished doctoral dissertation, Harvard University, 1953.

Helper, M. M. Learning theory and the self-concept. *Journal of Abnormal and Social Psychology,* 1955, **51**, 184–194.

Henry, A. F. Family role structure and self-blame. *Social Forces,* 1956, **35**, 34–38.

Hetherington, E. M. A developmental study of the effects of sex of the dominant parent on sex-role preference, identification, and imitation in children. *Journal of Personality and Social Psychology,* 1965, **2**, 188–194.

Hewitt, L. E., and Jenkins, R. L. *Fundamental patterns of maladjustment.* Chicago: D. H. Green, 1946.

Hill, K. T., and Stevenson, H. W. Effectiveness of social reinforcement following social and sensory deprivation. *Journal of Abnormal and Social Psychology,* 1964, **68**, 579–584.

Hill, W. F. Learning theory and the acquisition of values. *Psychological Review,* 1960, **67**, 317–331.

Hills, J. R. Within-groups correlations and their correction for attenuation. *Psychological Bulletin,* 1957, **54**, 131–133.

Himmelweit, H., Oppenheim, A., and Vince, P. *Television and the child: An empirical study of the effect of television on the young.* New York: Oxford University Press, 1958.

Hoffman, M. L. Some psychodynamic factors in compulsive conformity. *Journal of Abnormal and Social Psychology*, 1953, 48, 383–393.

———. Power assertion by the parent and its impact on the child. *Child Development*, 1960, 31, 129–143.

———. Child-rearing practices and moral development: Generalizations from empirical research. *Child Development*, 1963, 34, 295–318.

Hoffman, M. L., and Saltzstein, H. D. Parent practices and the child's moral orientation. Paper read at American Psychological Association, Chicago, September, 1960.

Hollenberg, E. H. Child training among the Zeepi with special reference to the internalization of moral values. Unpublished doctoral dissertation, Harvard University, 1952.

Hollenberg, E. H., and Sperry, M. S. Some antecedents of aggression and effects of frustration in doll play. *Personality*, 1951, 1, 32–43.

Hollingshead, A., and Redlick, F. C. Social stratification and psychiatric disorders. *American Sociological Review*, 1953, 18, 163–169.

Homans, G. C. *The human group.* New York: Harcourt, Brace and World, 1950.

Homme, L. E., DeBaca, P. C., Devine, J. V., Steinhorst, R., and Rickert, E. J. Use of the Premack principle in controlling the behavior of nursery school children. *Journal of the Experimental Analysis of Behavior*, 1963, 6, 544.

Horowitz, E. L. Spatial localization of the self. *Journal of Social Psychology*, 1935, 6, 379–387.

———. The development of attitude toward the Negro. *Archives of Psychology, New York*, 1936, 28, No. 194.

Horowitz, R. E. Racial aspects of self-identification in nursery school children. *Journal of Psychology*, 1939, 7, 91–99.

Hull, C. L. *Principles of behavior.* New York: Appleton-Century-Crofts, 1943.

Hunt, J. M. *Intelligence and experience.* New York: Ronald Press, 1961.

Hurlock, E. B. An evaluation of certain incentives used in school work. *Journal of Educational Psychology*, 1925, 16, 145–159.

Huston, P. E., Shakow, D., and Riggs, L. A. Studies of motor function in schizophrenia: II. Reaction time. *Journal of Genetic Psychology*, 1937, 16, 39–82.

Inhelder, B., and Piaget, J. *The growth of logical thinking from childhood to adolescence.* New York: Basic Books, 1958.

Iscoe, I., Williams, M., and Harvey, J. Modification of children's judgments by a simulated group technique: A normative developmental study. *Child Development*, 1963, 34, 963–978.

Jacob, P. E. *Changing values in college.* New York: Harper Brothers, 1957.

Jacobson, E. Contributions to the metapsychology of psychotic identification. *Journal of American Psychoanalytic Association*, 1954, 2, 239–262.

James, W. *Principles of psychology.* New York: Holt, 1890.

Jenkins, R. L. Guilt feelings—their function and dysfunction. In M. L. Reymert (Ed.), *Feelings and emotions.* New York: McGraw-Hill, 1950.

Jenkins, W. O. A temporal gradient of derived reinforcement. *American Journal of Psychology,* 1950, **63**, 237–243.

Jersild, A. T. *In search of self.* New York: Bureau of Publications, Teachers College, Columbia University, 1952.

Johnson, M. M. Instrumental and expressive components in the personalities of women. Unpublished doctoral dissertation, Radcliffe College, 1955.

Jones, M. H., and Liverant, S. Effects of age differences on choice behavior. *Child Development,* 1960, **31**, 673–680.

Jones, V. *Character and citizenship training in the public schools.* Chicago: University of Chicago Press, 1936.

Jost, H. Some physiological changes during frustration. *Child Development,* 1941, **12**, 9–15.

Kagan, J. The child's perception of the parent. *Journal of Abnormal and Social Psychology,* 1956, **53**, 257–258.

———. The concept of identification. *Psychological Review,* 1958, **65**, 296–305.

———. Socialization of aggression and the perception of parents in fantasy. *Child Development,* 1958, **29**, 311–320.

———. Acquisition and significance of sex typing and sex role identity. In M. L. Hoffman and L. W. Hoffman (Eds.), *Review of child development research.* New York: Russell Sage Foundation, 1964. Pp. 137–167.

———. On the need for relativism. *American Psychologist,* 1967, **22**, 131–142.

Kagan, J., and Moss, H. A. *Birth to maturity.* New York: Wiley, 1962.

Kagan, J., Moss, H. A., and Sigel, I. E. Psychological significance of styles of conceptualization. In J. C. Wright and J. Kagan (Eds.), *Basic cognitive processes in children.* Lafayette, Ind.: Child Development Publications, 1963. (Also, *Monograph for the Society for Research in Child Development,* 1963, Serial No. 86.)

Kahl, J. A. Adolescent ambition. Unpublished doctoral dissertation, Harvard University, 1952.

Kamin, L. J. The delay-of-punishment gradient. *Journal of Comparative and Physiological Psychology,* 1959, **52**, 434–437.

Kardiner, A., and Ovesey, L. *The mark of oppression.* New York: Norton, 1951.

Karon, B. P. *The Negro personality.* New York: Springer, 1958.

Katz, J. *Report of the student development study.* (Mimeo) Stanford University, Stanford, California: Institute for the Study of Human Problems, 1966.

Kelley, H., and Volkart, E. The resistance to change of group-anchored attitudes. *American Sociological Review,* 1952, **17**, 453–485.

Kelly, G. *The psychology of personal constructs.* Vol. 1. New York: Norton, 1955.

Kendall, P. L., and Lazarsfeld, P. F. The relation between individual and group characteristics. In P. F. Lazarsfeld and M. Rosenberg (Eds.), *The language of social research*. Glencoe, Ill.: Free Press, 1955. Pp. 290–297.

Kessen, W., and Kessen, M. L. Behavior of young children in a two choice guessing problem. *Child Development*, 1961, **32**, 779–788.

King, M. G. Peck frequency and minimal approach distance in domestic fowl. *Journal of Genetic Psychology*, 1965, **106**, 35–38.

———. Social reflexes Nos. 1 and 2 in relation to approach and avoidance tendencies. *Journal of Genetic Psychology*, 1966, **109**, 101–107.

Kinsey, A. C., Pomeroy, W. B., and Martin, C. E. *Sexual behavior in the human male*. Philadelphia: Saunders, 1948.

Kluckhohn, C. Universal categories of culture. In A. L. Kroeber (Ed.), *Anthropology today*. Chicago: University of Chicago Press, 1953. Pp. 507–523.

———. Culture and behavior. In G. Lindzey (Ed.), *Handbook of social psychology*. Cambridge, Mass.: Addison-Wesley, 1954. Pp. 921–976.

Knight, R. P. Introjection, projection, and identification. *Psychoanalytic Quarterly*, 1940, **9**, 334–341.

Koch, H. L. Attitudes of young children toward their peers as related to certain characteristics of their siblings. *Psychological Monographs*, 1956, **70**, No. 19.

———. Sissiness and tomboyishness in relation to sibling characteristics. *Journal of Genetic Psychology*, 1956, **88**, 231–244.

Kohl, J. A., and Davis, J. A. A comparison of indexes of socioeconomic status. *American Sociological Review*, 1955, **20**, 317–326.

Kohlberg, L. The development of modes of moral thinking and choice in the years 10 to 16. Unpublished doctoral dissertation, University of Chicago, 1958.

———. Moral development and identification. In H. W. Stevenson (Ed.), *Child psychology: The sixty-second yearbook of the National Society for the Study of Education*. Chicago: University of Chicago Press, 1963. Pp. 277–332.

———. Development of moral character and moral ideology. In M. L. Hoffman and L. N. Hoffman (Eds.), *Review of child development research*. Vol. 1. New York: Russell Sage Foundation, 1964.

———. A cognitive-developmental analysis of children's sex-role concepts and attitudes. In E. E. Maccoby (Ed.), *The development of sex differences*. Stanford: Stanford University Press, 1966. Pp. 82–173.

———. Cognitive stages and preschool education. *Human Development*, 1966, **9**, 5–17.

———. Moral and religious education and the public schools: A developmental view. In T. R. Sizer (Ed.), *Religion and public education*. New York: Houghton-Mifflin, 1967.

———. Education for justice: A modern statement of the Platonic view. Ernest Burton Lecture on moral education, Harvard University, April 23, 1968.

———. Stage and sequence: A cognitive-developmental approach to socialization. In Goslin (Ed.), *Handbook of socialization theory and research*. New York: Rand-McNally, 1969. Pp. 347–480.

Kohlberg, L., and Jensen, J. Assessment of a Montessori program with culturally disadvantaged children. Unpublished monograph, Chicago, 1966. (Mimeo)

Kohn, M. Social class and the exercise of parental authority. *American Sociological Review*, 1959, **24**, 352–366.

———. The importance of beginning: kindergarten. *National Elementary Principal*, 1962, **41**, 18–22.

———. Analysis of two kindergarten settings. In A. A. Bellack (Ed.), *Theory and Research in Teaching*. New York: Bureau of Publications, Teachers College, Columbia University, 1963.

———. The child as a determinant of his peers' approach to him. *Journal of Genetic Psychology*, 1966, **109**, 91–100.

Kolb, D. A. Achievement motivation training for underachieving high school boys. *Journal of Personality and Social Psychology*, 1965, **2**, 783–792.

Kounin, J. Experimental studies of rigidity: I. The measurement of rigidity in normal and feebleminded persons. *Character and Personality*, 1941, **9**, 251–272.

Kramer, C. Y. On the analysis of variance of a two-way classification with unequal sub-class numbers. *Biometrics*, 1955, **11**, 441–452.

Kramer, R. B. Changes in moral judgment response pattern during late adolescence and young adulthood: Retrogression in a development sequence. Unpublished doctoral dissertation, University of Chicago, 1968.

Kranz, H. *Lebensschicksale Krimineller Zwillinge*. Berlin: Springer, 1936.

Krebs, R. The development of internalized moral judgments in the years four to eight. Unpublished master's thesis, University of Chicago, 1965.

———. Some relations between moral judgment, attention, and resistance to temptation. Unpublished doctoral dissertation, University of Chicago, 1967.

Kuhlen, R. G. *The psychology of adolescent development*. New York: Harper, 1952.

La Barre, W. Some observations on character structure in the Orient: The Japanese. *Psychiatry*, 1945, **8**, 319–342.

Lacey, J. I., and Lacey, B. C. The relationship of resting autonomic activity to motor impulsivity. *Research Publications of the Association for Nervous and Mental Disease*, 1958, **36**, 144–209.

Lange, J. *Crime as destiny*. London: Allen and Unwin, 1931.

Langer, J. Disequilibrium as a source of development. In P. Mussen, J. Langer, and M. L. Covington (Eds.), *New directions in developmental psychology*. New York: Holt, Rinehart and Winston, 1969.

Lashley, K. S. Conditional reactions in the rat. *Journal of Psychology*, 1938, **6**, 311–324.

Lasko, J. K. Parent behavior toward first and second children. *Genetic Psychology Monographs*, 1954, **49**, 97-137.

Lawson, E. D., and Boek, W. E. Correlations of indexes of families' socioeconomic status. *Social Forces*, 1960, **39**, 149-152.

Lazarsfeld, P. F., and Menzel, H. On the relation between individual and collective properties. In A. Etzioni (Ed.), *Complex organization: a sociological reader.* New York: Holt, Rinehart and Winston, 1961. Pp. 422-440.

Lazowick, L. M. On the nature of identification. *Journal of Abnormal and Social Psychology*, 1955, **51**, 175-183.

Leary, T. How to change behavior. Paper read at the XIVth International Congress of Applied Psychology, Copenhagen, 1961. (a)

Lefcourt, H. M., and Ladwig, G. W. The American Negro: A problem in expectancies. *Journal of Personality and Social Psychology*, 1965, **1**, 377-380.

Lefkowitz, M. M., Blake, R., and Mouton, J. Status factors in pedestrian violation of traffic signals. *Journal of Abnormal and Social Psychology*, 1955, **51**, 704-706.

Lefkowitz, M. M., Walder, L. O., and Eron, L. D. Punishment, identification and aggression. *Merrill-Palmer Quarterly*, 1963, **9**, 159-174.

Leighton, D., and Kluckhohn, C. *Children of the people: The Navaho individual and his development.* Cambridge, Mass.: Harvard University Press, 1947.

Lerner, E. *Constraint areas and the moral judgment of children.* Menosha, Wisc.: George Banta, 1937.

———. The problem of perspective in moral reasoning. *American Journal of Sociology*, 1937, **43**, 249-269.

Levin, H., and Sears, R. R. Identification with parents as a determinant of doll play aggression. *Child Development*, 1956, **27**, 135-153.

Levy, D. M. *Behavioral analysis: Analysis of clinical observations of behavior; as applied to mother-newborn relationships.* Springfield, Ill.: Thomas, 1958.

Lewin, K. *Dynamic theory of personality: Selected papers.* New York: McGraw-Hill, 1935.

———. *Principles of topological psychology.* New York: McGraw-Hill, 1936.

———. The conceptual representation and the measurement of psychological forces. *Contributions to Psychological Theory*, 1938, **1**, No. 4.

———. Field theory and experiment in social psychology: Concept and methods. *American Journal of Sociology*, 1939, **44**, 868-896.

———. Experiments in social space. *Harvard Educational Review*, 1939, **9**, 21-32.

Lewin, K., and Lippitt, R. An experimental approach to the study of autocracy and democracy: A preliminary note. *Sociometry*, 1938, **1**, 292-300.

Lewis, M. A review of children's binary choice behavior. Unpublished manuscript, Fels Research Institute, 1963.

———. Social isolation: A parametric study of its effect on social reinforcement. *Journal of Experimental Child Psychology*, 1965, **2**, 205-218.

Lewis, M., and Richman, S. Social encounters and their effect on subsequent social reinforcement. *Journal of Abnormal and Social Psychology*, 1964, **69**, 253–257.

Lewis, M., Wall, A. M., and Aronfreed, J. Developmental change in the relative values of social and nonsocial reinforcement. *Journal of Experimental Psychology*, 1963, **66**, 133–137.

Lindquist, E. F. *Design and analysis of experiments in psychology and education.* Boston: Houghton Mifflin, 1956.

Lindsley, O. R. Operant conditioning methods applied to research in chronic schizophrenia. *Psychiatric Research Reports*, 1956, **5**, 118–139.

Lippitt, R. An experimental study of authoritarian and democratic group atmospheres. *University of Iowa Studies: Child Welfare*, 1940, **16**, 43–195.

Lipset, S. M., and Wolin, S. S. (Eds.) *The Berkeley student revolt: Facts and interpretations.* Garden City, N.Y.: Doubleday, 1965.

Littman, R. A., Moore, R. C. A., and Pierce-Jones, J. Social class differences in child rearing: A third community for comparison with Chicago and Newton. *American Sociological Review*, 1957, **22**, 694–704.

Littman, R. A., and Wade, E. A. A negative test of the drive-reduction hypothesis. *Quarterly Journal of Experimental Psychology*, 1955, **7**, 56–66.

Litwin, G. H., and Ciarlo, J. A. *Achievement motivation and risk-taking in a business setting, technical report.* Ossining, N.Y.: General Electric Company, Behavioral Research Service, 1961.

Long, B. H., and Henderson, E. H. Self-social concepts of disadvantaged school beginners. *Journal of Genetic Psychology*, 1968, **113**, 41–51.

Long, B. H., Henderson, E. H., and Ziller, R. Developmental changes in the self-concept during middle childhood. *Merrill-Palmer Quarterly of Behavior and Development*, 1967, **13**, 201–215.

Long, D., Elkind, D., and Spilka, B. The child's conception of prayer. *Journal for the Scientific Study of Religion*, 1967, **6**, 101–109.

Lovaas, O. I. A behavior therapy approach to the treatment of childhood schizophrenia. In J. P. Hill (Ed.), *Minnesota symposia on child psychology.* Vol. I. Minneapolis: University of Minnesota Press, 1967. Pp. 108–159.

Lovaas, O. I., Berberich, J. P., Perloff, B. F., and Schaeffer, B. Acquisition of imitative speech by schizophrenic children. *Science*, 1966, **151**, 705–707.

Lykken, D. T. A study of anxiety in the sociopathic personality. *Journal of Abnormal and Social Psychology*, 1957, **55**, 6–10.

Lynd, H. M. *On shame and the search for identity.* New York: Science Editions, 1961.

Lynn, D. B. A note on sex differences in the development of masculine and feminine identification. *Psychological Review*, 1959, **66**, 126–135.

Lynn, D. B., and Sawrey, W. L. The effects of father-absence on Norwegian boys and girls. *Journal of Abnormal and Social Psychology*, 1959, **59**, 258–262.

Maccoby, E. E. The generality of moral behavior. *American Psychologist*, 1959, **14**, 358. (Abstract)

———. Role-taking in childhood and its consequences for social learning. *Child Development*, 1959, **30**, 239–252.

———. Development of moral values and behavior in childhood. In J. Clausen (Ed.), *Socialization and society*. Boston: Little, Brown, 1968. Pp. 227–269.

Maccoby, E. E., Gibbs, P. K., et al. Methods of child rearing in two social classes. In W. E. Martin and C. B. Stendler (Eds.), *Readings in child development*. Harcourt, Brace, 1954. Pp. 380–396.

Maccoby, E. E., and Wilson, W. C. Identification and observational learning from films. *Journal of Abnormal and Social Psychology*, 1957, **55**, 76–87.

Macfarlane, J. W. Studies in child guidance. I. Methodology of data collection and organization. *Monographs of the Society for Research in Child Development*, 1938, **3**, No. 6.

MacKinnon, D. W. Violation of prohibitions. In H. A. Murray, et al. (Eds.), *Explorations in personality*. New York: Oxford University Press, 1938. Pp. 491–501.

MacRae, D., Jr. The development of moral judgment in children. Unpublished doctoral dissertation, Harvard University, 1950.

———. A test of Piaget's theories of moral development. *Journal of Abnormal and Social Psychology*, 1954, **49**, 14–18.

Maier, N. R. F. *Frustration: The study of behavior without a goal*. New York: Holt, 1949.

Marple, C. H. The comparative susceptibility of three age levels to the suggestion of group versus expert opinion. *Journal of Social Psychology*, 1933, **10**, 3–40.

Marshall, H. R., and McCandless, B. R. A study in prediction of social behavior of preschool children. *Child Development*, 1957, **28**, 149–159.

Martin, W. E. Learning theory and identification: III. The development of value in children. *Journal of Genetic Psychology*, 1954, **84**, 211–217.

Masling, J. M. How neurotic is the authoritarian? *Journal of Abnormal and Social Psychology*, 1954, **49**, 316–318.

McCarthy, D. Language development in children. In L. Carmichael (Ed.), *Manual of child psychology*. New York: Wiley, 1946. Pp. 492–630.

McClelland, D. C. *Personality*. New York: Sloane, 1951.

———. *The achieving society*. Princeton, N.J.: Van Nostrand, 1961.

McClelland, D. C., Atkinson, J. W., Clark, R., and Lowell, E. *The achievement motive*. New York: Appleton-Century-Crofts, 1953.

McClelland, D. C., and Friedman, G. A. A cross-cultural study of the relationship between child-training practices and achievement motivation, appearing in folk tales. In G. E. Swanson, T. M. Newcomb, and E. L. Hartley (Eds.), *Readings in social psychology*. New York: Holt, 1952.

McCord, J., and McCord, W. The effect of parental role model on criminality. *Journal of Social Issues,* 1958, **14,** 66–75.

McCord, J., McCord, W., and Thurber, E. Some effects of paternal absence on male children. *Journal of Abnormal and Social Psychology,* 1962, **64,** 361–369.

McCoy, N., and Zigler, E. Social reinforcer effectiveness as a function of the relationship between child and adult. *Journal of Personality and Social Psychology,* 1965, **1,** 604–612.

McKee, J. P. The relationship between maternal behavior and the aggressive behavior of young children. Unpublished doctoral dissertation, State University of Iowa, 1949.

McKee, J. P., and Leader, F. B. The relationship of socioeconomic status and aggression to the competitive behavior of preschool children. *Child Development,* 1955, **26,** 135–142.

McNemar, Q. *Psychological statistics.* New York: Wiley, 1955.

Mead, M. (Ed.) *Cooperation and competition among primitive peoples.* New York: Macmillan, 1937.

Mead, M. Social change and cultural surrogates. In C. Kluckhohn and H. A. Murray (Eds.), *Personality in nature, society and culture.* New York: Knopf, 1948.

———. Some anthropological considerations concerning guilt. In M. L. Reymert (Ed.), *Feelings and emotions.* New York: McGraw-Hill, 1950.

Medinnus, G. R. An investigation of Piaget's concept of moral judgment in six- to twelve-year-old children from the lower socioeconomic group. Unpublished doctoral dissertation, University of Minnesota, 1957.

Melikian, L. Preference for delayed reinforcement: An experimental study among Palestinian Arab refugee children. *Journal of Social Psychology,* 1959, **50,** 81–86.

Mengert, I. G. A preliminary study of the reactions of two-year-old children to each other when paired in a semi-controlled situation. *Journal of Genetic Psychology,* 1931, **39,** 393–398.

Merrill, B. A measurement of mother-child interaction. *Journal of Abnormal and Social Psychology,* 1946, **41,** 37–49.

Metzner, R. Preference for delayed reinforcement: Some complications. Harvard Psychological Clinic, 1960. (Mimeo)

Midlarsky, E., and Bryan, J. H. Training charity in children. *Journal of Personality and Social Psychology,* 1967, **5,** 408–415.

Miles, K. A. Sustained visual fixation of preschool children to a delayed stimulus. *Child Development,* 1933, **4,** 1–5.

Milgram, S. Some conditions of obedience and disobedience to authority. *Human Relations,* 1965, **18,** 57–76.

Miller, D. R., and Swanson, G. E. *The changing American parent.* New York: Wiley, 1958.

———. *Inner conflict and defense.* New York: Holt, 1960. Pp. 141–176.

Miller, N. E. Liberalization of basic S-R concepts: Extensions to conflict behavior, motivation and social learning. In S. Koch (Ed.), *Psychology: A study of a science.* Vol. 2. *General systematic formulations, learning, and special processes.* New York: McGraw-Hill, 1959. Pp. 196–292.

Miller, N. E., and Bugelski, R. Minor studies in aggression: II. The influence of frustrations imposed by the in-group on attitudes expressed toward outgroups. *Journal of Psychology,* 1948, **25,** 437–442.

Miller, N. E., and Dollard, J. *Social learning and imitation.* New Haven: Yale University Press, 1941.

Minuchin, P., and Shapiro, E. *Patterns of mastery and conflict resolution at the elementary school level.* New York: Bank Street College of Education, 1964. (U.S. Office of Education Coop. Research Project No. 1401)

Minuchin, P., Shapiro, E., Dinnerstein, D., and Biber, B. The psychological impact of school experience: Methodological report of a study in progress. Unpublished manuscript. New York: Bank Street College of Education Library, 1961.

Mischel, W. Preference for delayed reinforcement: An experimental study of a cultural observation. *Journal of Abnormal and Social Psychology,* 1958, **56,** 57–61.

———. Preference for delayed reinforcement: Further cross-cultural applications. Harvard Psychological Clinic, 1959. (Mimeo)

———. Delay of gratification, need for achievement, and acquiescence in another culture. *Journal of Abnormal and Social Psychology,* 1961, **62,** 543–552.

———. Preference for delayed reinforcement and social responsibility. *Journal of Abnormal and Social Psychology,* 1961, **62,** 1–7.

———. A social-learning view of sex differences in behavior. In E. E. Maccoby (Ed.), *The development of sex differences.* Stanford: Stanford University Press, 1966. Pp. 56–81.

Montgomery, K. C., and Galton, B. B. A test of the drive-reduction explanation of learned fear. Paper read at Eastern Psychological Association, Philadelphia, April 1955.

Moore, T., and Ucko, L. E. Four to six: Constructiveness and conflict in meeting doll play problems. *Journal of Child Psychology and Psychiatry,* 1961, **2,** 21–47.

Moreno, J. L. *Who shall survive? A new approach to the problem of human interrelations.* Washington, D.C.: Nervous and Mental Disease Publishing Co., 1934.

Morgan, C. *Introduction to psychology.* New York: McGraw-Hill, 1956.

Morgan, J. J. B. Effect of non-rational factors on inductive reasoning. *Journal of Experimental Psychology,* 1944, **34,** 159–168.

Morland, J. K. Racial recognition by nursery school children in Lynchburg, Virginia. *Social Forces*, 1958, **37**, 132–137.

———. Racial acceptance and preference of nursery school children in a southern city. *Merrill-Palmer Quarterly of Behavior and Development*, 1962, **8**, 271–280.

———. The development of racial bias in young children. *Theory into Practice*, 1963, **2**, 120–127.

———. Racial self-identification: A study of nursery school children. *The American Catholic Sociological Review*, 1963, **24**, 231–242.

———. *Southern schools: Token desegregation and beyond.* Anti-Defamation League of B'nai B'rith, New York, and the Southern Regional Council, Atlanta, 1963.

Morris, C. *Varieties of human value.* Chicago: University of Chicago Press, 1956.

Morris, J. F. The development of moral values in children. *British Journal of Educational Psychology*, 1958, **28**, 1–14.

Mosher, D. L., and Scodel, A. Relationships between ethnocentrism and authoritarian rearing practices of their mothers. *Child Development*, 1960, **31**, 369–376.

Moss, H. A. Sex, age, and state as determinants of mother-infant interaction. *Merrill-Palmer Quarterly*, 1967, **13**, 19–36.

Moss, H. A., and Kagan, J. Stability of achievement and recognition seeking behaviors from early childhood through adulthood. *Journal of Abnormal and Social Psychology*, 1961, **62**, 504–513.

Mowrer, O. H. Identification: A link between learning theory and psychotherapy. In *Learning theory and personality dynamics: Selected papers.* New York: Ronald Press, 1950. Pp. 573–616.

———. *Learning theory and personality dynamics: selected papers.* New York: Ronald Press, 1950.

———. On the psychology of talking birds. In *Learning theory and personality dynamics: Selected papers.* New York: Ronald Press, 1950. Pp. 688–707.

———. *Learning theory and behavior.* New York: Wiley, 1960. (a)

———. *Learning theory and the symbolic processes.* New York: Wiley, 1960. (b)

Mowrer, O. H., and Aiken, E. G. Contiguity vs. drive-reduction in conditioned fear: Temporal variations in conditioned and unconditioned stimulus. *American Journal of Psychology*, 1954, **67**, 26–38.

Mowrer, O. H., and Lamoreaux, R. R. Avoidance conditioning and signal duration—a study of secondary motivation and reward. *Psychological Monographs*, 1942, **54**, No. 5.

Mowrer, O. H., and Viek, P. An experimental analogue of fear from a sense of helplessness. *Journal of Abnormal and Social Psychology*, 1948, **43**, 193–200.

Murchison, C. The experimental measurement of a social hierarchy in *Gallus Domesticus*: I. The direct identification and direct measurement of Social

Reflex No. 1 and Social Reflex No. 2. *Journal of Genetic Psychology*, 1935, **12**, 3–39.

———. The experimental measurement of a social hierarchy in *Gallus Domesticus*: II. The identification and inferential measurement of Social Reflex No. 1 and Social Reflex No. 2 by means of social discrimination. *Journal of Social Psychology*, 1935, **6**, 3–30.

Murray, H. A., Jr., et al. *Explorations in personality*. New York: Oxford, 1938.

Mussen, P., and Distler, L. Masculinity, identification, and father-son relationships. *Journal of Abnormal and Social Psychology*, 1959, **59**, 350–356.

———. Child rearing antecedents of masculine identification in kindergarten boys. *Child Development*, 1960, **31**, 89–100.

Mussen, P., and Jones, M. C. Self-conceptions, motivations, and interpersonal attitudes of late- and early-maturing boys. *Child Development*, 1957, **28**, 243–256.

Mussen, P., and Kagan, J. Group conformity and perceptions of parents. *Child Development*, 1958, **29**, 57–60.

Mussen, P., and Rutherford, E. Parent-child relations and parental personality in relation to young children's sex-role preferences. *Child Development*, 1963, **34**, 589–607.

Mutterer, M. An investigation of generality in moral behavior across contrived temptation conflicts. Unpublished master's thesis, University of Wisconsin, 1965.

Nefzger, M. D. The properties of stimuli associated with shock reduction. *Journal of Experimental Psychology*, 1957, **53**, 184–188.

Newcomb, T. M. *Personality and social change*. New York: Dryden Press, 1943.

Newcomb, T. M., and Svehla, G. Intra-family relationships in attitude. *Sociometry*, 1937, **1**, 180–205.

Nichols, C. A. *Moral education among the North American Indians*. New York: Teachers College, Columbia University, 1930.

Noirot, E. Changes in responsiveness to young in the adult mouse. III. The effect of immediately preceding performances. *Behavior*, 1965, **24**, 318–325.

Nuttin, J. Intimacy and shame in the dynamic structure of personality. In M. L. Reymert (Ed.), *Feelings and emotions*. New York: McGraw-Hill, 1950. Pp. 343–352.

Nye, F. I. *Family relationships and delinquent behavior*. New York: Wiley, 1958.

Oakes, M. E. Children's explanations of natural phenomena. *Teachers College Contribution to Education*, 1947, No. 926.

Orne, M. T. On the social psychology of the psychological experiment: With particular reference to demand characteristics and their implications. *American Psychologist*, 1962, **17**, 776–783.

Osgood, C. E. *Method and theory in experimental psychology*. New York: Oxford University Press, 1953.

———. Studies on the generality of affective meaning systems. *American Psychologist*, 1963, **17**, 10–28.

Osgood, C. E., Suci, G., and Tannenbaum, P. H. *The measurement of meaning.* Urbana, Ill.: University of Illinois Press, 1957.

Ottinger, D. R., and Simmons, J. E. Behavior of human neonates and prenatal maternal anxiety. *Psychological Reports*, 1964, **14**, 391–394.

Parsons, T. Age and sex in the social structure of the United States. *American Sociological Review*, 1942, **7**, 604–616.

———. Consciousness and symbolic processes. In H. A. Abramson (Ed.), *Problems of consciousness.* New York: Josiah Macy Foundation, 1954.

———. The incest taboo in relation to social structure and the socialization of the child. *British Journal of Sociology*, 1954.

———. Social structure and the development of personality: Freud's contribution to the integration of psychology and sociology. *Psychiatry*, 1958, **21**, 321–340.

———. The school class as a social system: Some of its functions in American society. *Harvard Educational Review*, 1959, **29**, 297–316.

Parsons, T., and Bales, R. F. *Family, socialization and interaction process.* Glencoe, Ill.: The Free Press, 1955.

Parsons, T., Bales, R. F., and Shils, E. A. *Working papers in the theory of action.* Glencoe, Ill.: The Free Press, 1953.

Parten, M. B. Social participation among preschool children. *Journal of Abnormal and Social Psychology*, 1932, **27**, 243–269.

Pasamanick, B., Rogers, M. E., and Lilienfeld, A. M. Pregnancy experience and the development of behavior disorder in children. *American Journal of Psychiatry*, 1956, **112**, 613–618.

Passow, A. H. *Education in depressed areas.* New York: Bureau of Publications, Teachers College, Columbia University, 1963.

Patel, A. S., and Gordon, J. E. Some personal and situational determinants of yielding to influence. *Journal of Abnormal and Social Psychology*, 1960, **61**, 411–418.

Payne, D. E., and Mussen, P. H. Parent-child relations and father identification among adolescent boys. *Journal of Abnormal and Social Psychology*, 1956, **52**, 358–362.

Peck, R. F., and Havighurst, R. J. *The psychology of character development.* New York: Wiley, 1960.

Peel, E. A. *The pupil's thinking.* London: Oldhourne, 1960.

Peterson, D. R. Scope and generality of verbally defined personality factors. *Psychological Review*, 1965, **72**, 48–59.

Pettigrew, T. F. *A profile of the Negro American.* Princeton, N.J.: D. Van Nostrand, 1964.

Piaget, J. *Judgment and reasoning in the child.* New York: Harcourt, Brace, 1928.

———. *The child's conception of the world.* New York: Harcourt, Brace, 1929. (Also, London: Routledge and Kegan Paul, 1951.)

———. *The child's conception of physical causality.* New York: Harcourt, Brace, 1930.

———. *The moral judgment of the child.* Glencoe, Ill.: The Free Press, 1932. (Also, Harcourt, Brace, 1932; also, Basic Books, 1954.)

———. *Play, dreams, and imitation in childhood.* New York: Norton, 1951.

———. *The child's conception of number.* New York: Humanities Press, 1952. (a)

———. *The language and thought of the child.* London: Routledge and Kegan Paul, 1952. (b)

———. *The construction of reality in the child.* New York: Basic Books, 1954.

———. Comments on Vygotsky's critical remarks concerning "*The language and thought of the child*" and "*Judgment and reasoning in the child.*" Cambridge, Mass.: M.I.T. Press, 1962.

Rabban, M. Sex-role identification in young children in two diverse social groups. *Genetic Psychology Monographs,* 1950, **42,** 81–158.

Radke, M., and Trager, H. G. Children's perceptions of the social roles of Negroes and whites. *Journal of Psychology,* 1950, **29,** 3–33.

Rainwater, L. *And the poor get children.* Chicago: Quadrangle Books, 1961.

Reckless, W. T., Dinitz, S., and Kay, B. The self-component in potential delinquency and potential non-delinquency. *American Sociological Review,* 1957, **22,** 566–570.

Remmers, H. H., and Radler, D. H. *The American teenager.* Indianapolis, Ind.: Bobbs-Merrill, 1957.

Ressler, R. H. Parental handling in two strains of mice reared by foster parents. *Science,* 1962, **137,** 129–130.

Rheingold, H. L. (Ed.). *Maternal behavior in mammals.* New York: Wiley, 1963.

Rheingold, H. L. The development of social behavior in the human infant. In H. W. Stevenson (Ed.), Concept of development: A report of a conference commemorating the fortieth anniversary of the Institute of Child Development, University of Minnesota. *Monographs of the Society for Research in Child Development,* 1966, **31,** No. 5.

Riesman, D. Permissiveness and sex roles. *Human Development Bulletin,* 1958, 47–57.

———. The uncommitted generation. *Encounter,* 1960, **15,** 25–30.

Riesman, D., Denney, R., and Glazer, M. *The lonely crowd: A study of changing American character.* New York: Doubleday, 1953.

Riessman, F. Workers' attitudes toward participation and leadership. Unpublished doctoral dissertation, Columbia University, 1955.

———. *The culturally deprived child.* New York: Harper, 1962.

Robinson, W. S. Ecological correlations and the behavior of individuals. *American Sociological Review,* 1950, **15,** 351.

Roe, A. A psychological study of eminent psychologists and anthropologists, and a comparison with biological and physical scientists. *Psychological Monographs,* 1953, **67,** No. 2.

Rokeach, M. (Ed.) *The open and closed mind.* New York: Basic Books, 1960.

Rokeach, M. Belief versus race as determinants of social distance: Comment on Triandis' paper. *Journal of Abnormal and Social Psychology,* 1961, **62,** 187–188.

Rokeach, M., Smith, P. W., and Evans, R. I. Two kinds of prejudice or one? In M. Rokeach (Ed.), *The open and closed mind.* New York: Basic Books, 1960. Pp. 132–168.

Rosekrans, M. A. Imitation in children as a function of perceived similarity to a social model and vicarious reinforcement. *Journal of Personality and Social Psychology,* 1967, **7,** 307–315.

Rosen, B. C., and D'Andrade, R. The psychosocial origins of achievement motivation. *Sociometry,* 1959, **22,** 185–218.

Rosenbaum, M. The effect of stimulus and background factors on the volunteering response. *Journal of Abnormal and Social Psychology,* 1956, **53,** 118–121.

Rosenbaum, M., and Blake, R. Volunteering as a function of field structure. *Journal of Abnormal and Social Psychology,* 1955, **50,** 193–196.

Rosenberg, M. *Society and the adolescent self-image.* Princeton, N.J.: Princeton University Press, 1964.

Rosenhan, D. L. *Cultural deprivation and learning: An examination of method and theory.* (Research Memo. 65-4) Princeton, N.J.: Educational Testing Service, 1965.

———. Effects of social class and race on responsiveness to approval and disapproval. *Journal of Personality and Social Psychology,* 1966, **4,** 253–259.

Rosenhan, D., and White, G. M. Observation and rehearsal as determinants of prosocial behavior. *Journal of Personality and Social Psychology,* 1967, **5,** 424–431.

Rosenthal, R. On the social psychology of the psychological experiment: The experimenter's hypothesis as the unintended determinant of experimental results. *American Scientist,* 1963, **51,** 268–283.

———. Experimenter outcome-orientation and the results of the psychological experiment. *Psychological Bulletin,* 1964, **61,** 405–412.

Rotter, J. B. Generalized expectancies for internal versus external control of reinforcement. *Psychological Monographs,* 1966, **80,** No. 1.

Ryan, T. A. Multiple comparisons in psychological research. *Psychological Bulletin,* 1959, **56,** 26–47.

Sanford, N. The dynamics of identification. *Psychological Review*, 1955, **62**, 106–118.

———. Personality development during the college years. *Journal of Social Issues*, 1956, **12**, 4.

———. Changing sex roles, socialization and education. *Human Development Bulletin*, 1958, 58–75.

———. *The American college*. New York: Wiley, 1962.

Schachter, S. *The psychology of affiliation*. Stanford, Calif.: Stanford University Press, 1959.

———. Birth order, eminence and higher education. *American Sociological Review*, 1963, **28**, 757–768.

Schaefer, E. A circumplex model for maternal behavior. *Journal of Abnormal and Social Psychology*, 1959, **59**, 226–235.

Schaefer, E., and Bayley, N. Maternal behavior, child behavior, and their intercorrelations from infancy through adolescence. *Monographs of the Society for Research in Child Development*, 1963, **28**, No. 3.

Schaffer, H. R., and Emerson, P. E. Patterns of response to physical contact in early human development. *Journal of Child Psychology and Psychiatry*, 1964, **5**, 1–13.

Schilder, P. On the development of thoughts. In D. Rapaport (Ed.), *Organization and pathology of thought: Selected sources*. New York: Columbia University Press, 1951.

Schoenfeld, W. N., Antonitis, J. J., and Bersh, P. J. A preliminary study of training conditions necessary for secondary reinforcement. *Journal of Experimental Psychology*, 1950, **40**, 40–45.

Schwitzgebel, R. Analysis and evaluation of the experimenter-subject role relationship in the reduction of known male adolescent crime. Unpublished doctoral dissertation, Harvard University, 1962.

Schwitzgebel, R., and Slack, C. *A handbook: Reducing adolescent crime in your community*. Cambridge, Mass.: Authors, 1960.

Scott, P. M., Burton, R. V., and Yarrow, M. R. Social reinforcement under natural conditions. *Child Development*, 1967, **38**, 53–63.

Sears, P. S. Doll play aggression in normal young children: Influence of sex, age, sibling status, father's absence. *Psychological Monographs*, 1951, **65**, No. 6.

———. Child rearing factors related to the playing of sex-typed roles. *American Psychologist*, 1953, **8**, 431. (Abstract)

Sears, R. R. Ordinal position in the family as a psychological variable. *American Sociological Review*, 1950, **15**, 397–401.

———. Identification as a form of behavior development. In D. B. Harris (Ed.), *The concept of development*. Minneapolis: University of Minnesota Press, 1957. Pp. 149–161.

———. Relation of early socialization experiences to aggression in middle childhood. *Journal of Abnormal and Social Psychology*, 1961, **63**, 466–492.

Sears, R. R., Maccoby, E. E., and Levin, H. *Patterns of child-rearing.* Evanston, Ill.: Row, Peterson, 1957.

Sears, R. R., Pintler, M. H., and Sears, P. S. Effect of father separation on preschool children's doll play aggression. *Child Development*, 1946, **17**, 219–243.

Sears, R. R., Rau, L., and Alpert, R. Identification and child training: The development of conscience. Paper read at American Psychological Association, Chicago, September, 1960.

———. *Identification and child rearing.* Stanford, Calif.: Stanford University Press, 1965.

Sears, R. R., Whiting, J. W. M., Nowlis, V., and Sears, P. S. Some child-rearing antecedents of aggression and dependency in young children. *Genetic Psychology Monographs*, 1953, **47**, 135–236.

Seward, J. P. Aggressive behavior in the rat: IV. Submission as determined by conditioning, extinction, and disuse. *Journal of Comparative Psychology*, 1946, **39**, 51–76.

———. Learning theory and identification: II. The role of punishment. *Journal of Genetic Psychology*, 1954, **84**, 201–210.

Shakow, D. Segmental set. *Archives of General Psychiatry*, 1962, **6**, 1–17.

Shallenberger, P., and Zigler, E. Rigidity, negative reaction tendencies, and cosatiation effects in normal and feebleminded children. *Journal of Abnormal and Social Psychology*, 1961, **63**, 20–26.

Shaw, M. C., Edson, K., and Bell, H. M. The self-concept of bright underachieving high school students as revealed by an objective check list. *Personnel and Guidance*, 1960, **39**, 193–196.

Sherif, C. W. Adolescence: Motivational, attitudinal, and personality factors. *Review of Educational Research*, 1966, **36**, 437–449.

Sidman, M., and Boren, J. The relative aversiveness of warning signal and shock in an avoidance situation. *Journal of Abnormal and Social Psychology*, 1957, **55**, 339–344.

Sidman, M., Herrnstein, R. J., and Conrad, D. G. Maintenance of avoidance behavior by unavoidable shocks. *Journal of Comparative and Physiological Psychology*, 1957, **50**, 553–557.

Siegel, G. M. Adult verbal behavior with retarded children labeled as "high" or "low" in verbal ability. *American Journal of Mental Deficiency*, 1963, **68**, 417–424.

Siegel, S. *Nonparametric statistics for the behavioral sciences.* New York: McGraw-Hill, 1956.

Silverman, A. S., Cohen, S. I., and Shmavonian, B. M. Investigation of psychophysiologic relationships with skin resistance measures. *Journal of Psychosomatic Research*, 1959, **4**, 65–87.

Singer, J. E. Motivation for consistency. In S. Feldman (Ed.), *Cognitive consistency: Motivational antecedents and behavioral consequents.* New York: Academic Press, 1966.

Skinner, B. F. *Science and human behavior.* New York: Macmillan, 1953.

Slater, P. Toward a dualistic theory of identification. *Merrill-Palmer Quarterly*, 1961, **7**, 113–126.

Sokolov, Y. N. *Perception and the conditioned reflex.* New York: Macmillan, 1963.

Solomon, R. L., and Brush, E. S. Experimentally deprived conceptions of anxiety and aversion. In M. R. Jones (Ed.), *Nebraska symposium on motivation: 1956.* Lincoln: University of Nebraska Press, 1956. Pp. 212–305.

Solomon, R. L., and Turner, L. H. Discriminative classical conditioning in dogs paralyzed by curare can later control discriminative avoidance responses in the normal state. *Psychological Review*, 1962, **69**, 202–219.

Solomon, R. L., and Wynne, L. C. Traumatic avoidance learning: The principles of anxiety conservation and partial irreversibility. *Psychological Review*, 1954, **61**, 353–385.

Somers, R. H. The mainsprings of the rebellion: A survey of Berkeley students in November. In S. M. Lipset and S. S. Wolin (Eds.), *The Berkeley student revolt.* New York: Doubleday, 1965.

Sopchak, A. L. Parental "identification" and "tendency toward disorders" as measured by the MMPI. *Journal of Abnormal and Social Psychology*, 1952, **47**, 159–165.

Spence, K. W. *Behaviour theory and conditioning.* New Haven: Yale University Press, 1956.

Spock, B. *The common sense book of baby and child care.* New York: Duell, Sloan, and Pearce, 1957.

Springer, D. Awareness of racial differences by preschool children in Hawaii. *Genetic Psychology Monographs*, 1950, **41**, 215–270.

Stagner, R., and Congdon, C. S. Another failure to demonstrate displacement of aggression. *Journal of Abnormal and Social Psychology*, 1955, **51**, 695–696.

Stechler, G. A longitudinal follow-up of neonatal apnea. *Child Development*, 1964, **35**, 333–348.

Stendler, C. A study of some socio-moral judgments of junior high school children. *Child Development*, 1949, **20**, 15–28.

Stevenson, H. W. Social reinforcement with children as a function of CA, sex of E, and sex of S. *Journal of Abnormal and Social Psychology*, 1961, **63**, 147–154.

———. Social reinforcement of children's behavior. In L. P. Lipsitt and C. C. Spiker (Eds.), *Advances in child development and behavior.* New York: Academic Press, 1965. Pp. 97–126.

Development of a peer-rating measure of aggression. *Psychological Reports*, 1961, **9**, 497–556. (Monogr. Suppl. 4-V9)

Waldrop, M., and Bell, R. Q. Relation of preschool dependency behavior to family size and density. *Child Development*, 1964, **35**, 1187–1195.

———. Effects of family size and density on newborn characteristics. *American Journal of Orthopsychiatry*, 1966, **36**, 544–550.

Walters, J. C., Pearce, D., and Dahms, L. Affectional and aggressive behavior of preschool children. *Child Development*, 1957, **28**, 15–26.

Walters, R. H., and Karal, P. Social deprivation and verbal behavior. *Journal of Personality*, 1960, **28**, 89–107.

Walters, R. H., and Parke, R. D. Social motivation, dependency, and susceptibility to social influence. In L. Berkowitz (Ed.), *Advances in experimental social psychology*. New York: Academic Press, 1965. Pp. 232–272.

Walters, R. H., and Ray, E. Anxiety, social isolation and reinforcer effectiveness. *Journal of Personality*, 1960, **28**, 358–367.

Walters, R. H., Thomas, E. L., and Acker, C. W. Enhancement of punitive behavior by audio-visual displays. *Science*, 1962, **136**, 872–873.

Warner, W. L., Meeker, M., and Eells, K. *Social class in America*. Chicago: Science Research Associates, 1949.

Watson, J. B., and Rayner, R. Conditioned emotional reactions. *Journal of Experimental Psychology*, 1920, **3**, 1–14.

Weir, M. W. Development changes in problem solving strategies. *Psychological Review*, 1964, **71**, 473–490.

Weller, G. M., and Bell, R. Q. Basal skin conductance and neonatal state. *Child Development*, 1965, **36**, 647–657.

Werner, H. The concept of development from a comparative and organismic point of view. In D. B. Harris (Ed.), *The concept of development*. Minneapolis: University of Minnesota, 1957.

Wheeler, L. Toward a theory of behavioral contagion. *Psychological Review*, 1966, **73**, 179–192.

White House Conference on Child Health and Protection. *The young child in the home: A survey of 3000 American families*. Appleton-Century, 1936.

White, S. H. Evidence for a hierarchical arrangement of learning processes. In L. P. Lipsitt and C. C. Spiker (Eds.), *Advances in child development and behavior*. Vol. 2. New York: Academic Press, 1965. (a)

———. Training and timing in the generalization of a voluntary response. *Journal of Experimental Psychology*, 1965, **69**, 269–276. (b)

White, S. H., and Grim, P. F. Investigations of a voluntary generalization paradigm. *American Psychologist*, 1962, **17**, 378. (Abstract)

Whiting, J. W. M. Sorcery, sin, and the superego: A cross-cultural study of some mechanisms of social control. In M. R. Jones (Ed.), *Nebraska symposium on motivation: 1959*. Lincoln: University of Nebraska Press, 1959. Pp. 174–195.

———. Resource mediation and learning by identification. In I. Iscoe and H. W. Stevenson (Eds.), *Personality development in children.* Austin, Texas: University of Texas Press, 1960. Pp. 112–126.

———. Social structure and child rearing: A theory of identification. Paper read at Tulane University as part of the Mona Brorsman Sheckman Lectures in Social Psychiatry, March 17–19, 1960.

Whiting, J. W. M., and Child, I. L. *Child training and personality.* New Haven: Yale University Press, 1953.

Williams, C. D. The elimination of tantrum behavior by extinction procedures. *Journal of Abnormal and Social Psychology,* 1959, **59**, 269.

Wilson, A. B. Social stratification and academic achievement. In A. H. Passow (Ed.), *Education in depressed urban areas.* New York: Bureau of Publications, Teachers College, Columbia University, 1963. Pp. 217–236.

Winch, R. F. Further data and observations on the Oedipus hypothesis: The consequence of an inadequate hypothesis. *American Sociological Review,* 1951, **16**, 784–795.

Witkin, H. A., Dyk, R. B., Faterson, H. F., Goodenough, D. R., and Karp, S. A. *Psychological differentiation.* New York: Wiley, 1962.

Wolf, M., Risley, T. R., and Mees, H. L. Application of operant conditioning procedures to the behavior problems of an autistic child. *Behavioral Research and Therapy,* 1964, **1**, 305–312.

Wright, B. A. Altruism in children and perceived conduct of others. *Journal of Abnormal and Social Psychology,* 1942, **37**, 218–233.

Wright, E. Constructiveness of play as affected by group organization and frustration. *Character and Personality,* 1942, **11**, 40–49.

Wylie, R. C. *The self-concept.* Lincoln: University of Nebraska Press, 1961.

Yarrow, L. J. Research in dimensions of early maternal care. *Merrill-Palmer Quarterly,* 1963, **9**, 101–114.

Zigler, E. Social deprivation and rigidity in the performance of feeble-minded children. *Journal of Abnormal and Social Psychology,* 1961, **62**, 413–421.

———. Rigidity and social reinforcement effects in the performance of institutionalized and non-institutionalized normal and retarded children. *Journal of Personality,* 1963, **31**, 258–269.

Zigler, E., Hodgden, L., and Stevenson, H. W. The effect of support and nonsupport on the performance of normal and feeble-minded children. *Journal of Personality,* 1958, **26**, 106–122.

Zimbardo, P. G. The cognitive control of motivation. *Transactions of the New York Academy of Sciences,* 1966, **28**, 902–922.

Zimmerman, E. H., and Zimmerman, J. The alteration of behavior in a special classroom situation. *Journal of Experimental Analysis of Behavior,* 1962, **5**, 59–60.

Zipf, S. G. Resistance and conformity under reward and punishment. *Journal of Abnormal and Social Psychology,* 1960, **61**, 102–109.

Author Index

Abel, T. M., 633
Aberle, D., 364
Acker, C. W., 462
Ackerson, L., 619, 625
Adelberg, K., 506, 585
Adler, A., 70
Adorno, T. W., 430
Aiken, E. G., 558
Allee, W. C., 409
Allen, K. E., 194, 195, 243, 244, 502
Allinsmith, B. B., 470, 471, 476, 477, 554, 565, 666, 667, 668, 669, 670, 671, 672, 674, 676, 679, 681, 682
Allinsmith, W., 470, 471, 476, 477, 554, 565, 666, 667, 668, 669, 670, 671, 672, 674, 676, 679, 681, 682
Allport, G. W., 509
Alpert, R., 674
Altus, W. D., 52, 67, 70, 73
Amsel, A., 212
Anderson, H. H., 97
Anderson, R. A., 533
Andry, R., 680
Angrilli, A. F., 366
Anisfeld, M., 430
Antonitis, J. J., 559
Argyle, M., 87
Aronfreed, J., 65, 214, 268, 282, 505, 554, 555, 565, 598, 666, 671, 672
Asch, S. E., 304
Atkinson, J. W., 115, 122, 149, 159, 161, 162, 491
Ausubel, D. P., 503, 505, 506, 568, 572, 573
Ayllon, T., 244, 498
Azrin, N. H., 87, 498

Bach, G. R., 389
Baer, D. M., 214, 215, 255, 269, 270, 271, 278, 309, 498
Baier, K., 599
Bales, 359
Bandura, A., 62, 65, 224, 255, 256, 268, 275, 291, 295, 296, 333, 338, 447, 448, 451, 462, 468, 470, 498, 564, 586, 598, 680
Barker, R. G., 27, 28, 36
Bass, B. M., 303
Bayley, N., 64
Beach, F. A., 58
Beck, R. C., 558
Bell, H. M., 323
Bell, R. Q., 51, 52, 55, 56, 64, 66
Beller, E. K., 391, 642
Benedict, R., 505, 568, 569, 571, 575, 578, 579, 580, 581, 582

723

724 Author Index

Berg, I. A., 303
Berger, S., 282
Berkowitz, L., 332, 333, 339, 447, 448, 461, 462, 463, 464, 465, 467, 468
Berryman, R., 269
Bersh, P. J., 559
Bertrand, F. L., 546
Bettelheim, B., 564
Biber, B., 373
Bing, E., 63
Bitterman, M. E., 560
Blake, R., 333
Block, J., 594, 595, 597, 598, 599, 602, 617
Blos, P., 655
Boehm, L., 504, 517, 518, 519, 524
Boren, J., 562
Bott, H., 531, 546
Bott, M. M., 97
Brady, J. P., 244
Brady, J. V., 556
Bridges, K. M. B., 590
Brodbeck, A. J., 363, 664
Bronfenbrenner, Urie, 2, 3, 13, 14, 43, 360, 364, 372, 477, 559, 564, 565, 664, 665, 666, 679
Bronson, W. C., 666
Brown, D. G., 35, 300, 385, 391
Brown, P., 449, 497, 498
Browning, 384
Brownstein, A., 558
Bruce, H. M., 57
Bruce, M., 633
Brush, E. S., 556, 560
Brush, F. R., 556, 559, 560
Bryan, J. H., 319, 331, 332, 333, 341
Buchanan, G., 557-558
Buell, J. S., 194, 243, 244, 502
Bugelski, R., 425
Burlingham, D., 395
Burnstein, E., 282, 289
Burris, R., 159
Burton, R. V., 194, 233, 234, 243, 529, 674, 675, 676
Buss, A., 430
Byrne, D., 433, 434, 435, 439, 442

Campbell, D. T., 430
Capra, P. C., 71
Cartwright, D., 170
Caruso, I., 518

Cattell, J. M., 72
Cava, E. L., 665, 666
Chandler, P., 333
Charlesworth, R., 225, 231
Charlesworth, W. R., 653
Child, I. L., 118, 122, 136, 453, 470, 495, 553, 560, 564, 565, 668, 669, 670
Church, R. M., 354, 556, 559, 560
Ciarlo, J. A., 160, 161, 163
Clark, B. S., 224
Clark, K. B., 197, 425, 430
Clark, R., 149, 491
Clark, W. H., 325, 326
Clarke, E. L., 68
Coates, B., 193, 222
Cohen, D. J., 53, 86
Cohen, S. I., 532
Cohn, F., 490, 496
Coleman, J. S., 169
Congdon, C. S., 425
Conners, C. K., 64
Conrad, D. G., 561
Costanzo, P. R., 257, 302, 303
Couch, A., 156
Cowan, P. A., 498, 652
Crandall, V. C., 80, 310, 313, 315
Crandall, V. J., 221, 310
Crowne, D. P., 310
Cruse, D. B., 212
Crutchfield, R. S., 304
Cumming, W. W., 269
Cutick, R. A., 555

Dahms, L., 499
D'Amato, M. R., 562
D'Andrade, R. G., 118, 121, 122
Daniels, L., 332, 333, 339
Darby, C. L., 556
Darley, 341
Darlington, R. B., 332
Davids, A., 60
Davis, A., 43, 470, 476, 525
Davis, H., 398, 401
Davitz, J. R., 559
Dean, D. A., 71, 72
DeBaca, P. C., 498
Dembo, T., 36
DeMyer, M. K., 244
Denney, R., 673
Dennis, W., 518

Deutsche, J. M., 633
Devereux, E. C., Jr., 2, 13
Devine, J. V., 498
Dickens, 384
Dinitz, S., 323
Dinnerstein, D., 373
Dinsmoor, J. A., 562
Distler, L., 293, 369, 390, 564, 666
Dittes, J. E., 71
Doland, D. J., 506, 585
Dollard, J., 260, 261, 275, 344, 451, 470, 556
Doob, L. W., 470
Dorwart, 214, 215, 216, 220
Douvan, E., 674, 679
Draguns, J., 529
Duffy, E., 532, 533, 543
Duncan, O. D., 478
Durkin, D., 518, 595, 631, 632, 642
Duvall, E. N., 476
Dyk, R. B., 530

Eberhart, J. C., 642, 648
Edson, K., 323
Eells, K., 160, 198
Elkind, D., 595, 596, 651, 653, 654, 656, 658
Elliott, R., 449, 450, 497, 498
Emerson, P. E., 61
Emmerich, W., 369, 385
Engel, M., 376
English, A. C., 197
English, H. B., 197
Epstein, R., 257, 308, 309, 400, 417, 424, 425, 426, 429, 431
Epstein, W., 56
Erickson, M. T., 214, 215, 309
Erikson, E. H., 323, 655, 659
Eron, L. D., 62, 256, 448, 450, 469, 470, 471, 478, 496
Estes, W. K., 562
Etzel, B., 59
Evans, R. I., 433
Eysenck, H. J., 594, 595, 618, 619, 624, 625, 626, 627, 628
Ezerman, 214

Fagan, S. A., 555
Fahel, L. S., 191, 204, 205
Faigin, H., 669

Farber, I. E., 562
Faterson, H. F., 530
Fauls, L. B., 35
Feffer, M. H., 652
Ferreira, A. J., 60
Ferster, C. B., 244
Festinger, L., 308, 309
Flavell, J. H., 529
Frank, L. K., 36
Franks, C. M., 624, 626
Freed, A., 333
French, J. R. P., Jr., 293
Frenkel-Brunswik, E., 430
Freud, A., 261, 263, 264, 274, 279, 395, 562, 621, 655, 662, 663, 664, 679
Freud, S., 264, 274, 275, 360, 505, 553, 559, 562
Friedman, G. A., 122
Friedman, P., 332, 339
Fuchs, S. H., 276

Galton, B. B., 556, 558
Galton, F., 67, 68, 69
Gardner, R. W., 530
Geen, R. G., 447, 448, 461, 462, 463, 464, 467
Geller, I., 556
Gewirtz, J. L., 59, 214, 215, 255, 267, 271, 272, 309
Gibbs, P. K., 470, 477
Gillespie, J. M., 509
Gilmer, 546
Glanzer, M., 325, 326
Glazer, J., 231
Glazer, M., 673
Gleitman, H., 556
Glueck, E., 470
Glueck, S., 470
Goethe, W. von, 658
Gold, M., 680
Goldberg, M. L., 159
Goldenson, R. M., 36
Goldstein, A., 159, 470
Goldstein, K., 264
Goodenough, D. R., 530
Goodenough, E., 363
Goodenough, F. W., 60
Goodson, F., 558
Goranson, R., 339
Gordon, J. E., 449, 489, 490, 495, 496

Gore, P. M., 332
Gorer, G., 579
Gouldner, A., 332
Gourevitch, V., 652
Gray, G. B., 60
Gray, S. W., 366, 367
Green, A. W., 360
Greening, T. C., 679, 682
Greenwald, 203
Grim, P. F., 505, 528, 531, 532, 533, 543, 545
Grinder, R. E., 674, 675, 676
Gross, P., 332, 586
Grosser, D., 224
Gumenik, W. E., 562
Gwinn, G. T., 561, 562

Haan, N., 594, 595, 597, 598, 599
Haldane, J. B. S., 629
Hallworth, H. J., 170
Handlon, B. J., 332, 586
Hardyck, J. A., 400, 432
Harman, H. H., 15, 22
Harris, D. B., 151, 153
Harris, F. R., 194, 243, 244, 498, 502
Harris, R., 333
Harrower, M. R., 633
Hart, B., 194, 243, 502
Hart, B. M., 244
Hartley, E. L., 43, 425, 430
Hartley, R. E., 36, 386
Hartshorne, H., 105, 137, 529, 533, 534, 542, 545, 547, 553, 631, 642, 676, 682
Hartup, W. W., 193, 195, 222, 225, 231
Hattwick, L. A., 590
Haughton, 244
Havighurst, R. J., 43, 169, 518, 524, 525, 642, 674
Heinicke, C. M., 564, 668, 669, 670, 673
Helper, M. M., 361, 367, 665
Henderson, E. H., 319, 322, 323, 328
Henry, A. F., 680
Herrnstein, R. J., 561
Hetherington, E. M., 321, 388, 389, 390
Hewitt, L. E., 619, 626
Hicks, 224
Hill, K. T., 312
Hill, W. F., 159, 557
Hills, J. R., 669
Himmelweit, H., 496

Hodgden, L., 77, 205
Hoffman, M. L., 62, 596, 661, 666, 672, 673
Holden, R. H., 60
Hollenberg, E. H., 470, 669
Hollingshead, A., 124
Holtzman, W. H., 560
Homans, G. C., 169
Homme, L. E., 498
Hovland, 453
Hull, C. L., 265, 626
Hunt, J. M., 73
Hurlock, E. B., 190
Huston, A. C., 295, 296, 564
Huston, P. E., 530

Inhelder, B., 524, 617, 652, 655, 656
Irons, N. M., 75

Jacob, P. E., 509
Jacobson, E., 664
James, W., 505, 529, 549, 551
Jaynes, J., 58
Jenkins, R. L., 619, 626
Jenkins, W. O., 559
Jensen, J., 547
Jersild, A. T., 323
Johnson, M. M., 320, 357, 368, 372, 454
Johnston, M. K., 244
Jones, M. C., 323
Jones, M. H., 221
Jones, V., 137, 538
Jost, H., 533

Kagan, J., 66, 97, 159, 254, 259, 290, 380, 389, 530, 543, 547, 563, 664, 673
Kahl, J. A., 166, 167
Kamin, L. J., 559
Karal, P., 214
Kardiner, A., 390
Karon, B. P., 390
Karp, S. A., 530
Katkovsky, W., 310
Katz, J., 509
Kay, B., 323
Kaye, C., 674
Keen, R., 65
Kellaway, R., 221
Kelley, C. S., 244
Kelly, G., 159

Kendall, P. L., 411, 669
Kenniston, K., 156
Kessen, M. L., 221
Kessen, W., 221
King, M. G., 399, 408, 409, 414
Kinsey, A. C., 44, 45, 628
Klanderman, S. B., 332
Kling, A., 556
Kluckhohn, C., 14, 569, 573, 575, 576, 577, 578, 579, 580
Knights, R. M., 65
Koch, H. L., 71, 265
Kohl, J. A., 472
Kohlberg, L., 275, 276, 505, 518, 528, 529, 546, 547, 550, 554, 598, 599, 600, 601, 602, 605, 612, 614, 616, 617, 653, 662
Kohn, M., 53, 96, 97, 98, 666
Kolb, D. A., 119, 158, 159
Komorita, S. S., 400, 417, 424, 425, 426, 429, 431
Kounin, J., 77, 83, 211
Kramer, R. B., 600, 610, 614
Kranz, H., 629
Krebs, R., 533, 535, 542, 547, 548, 550, 616
Kupers, C. J., 224

LaBarre, W., 579, 580, 581
Lacey, B. C., 532, 543
Lacey, J. I., 532, 543
Ladwig, G. W., 431
Lambert, W. E., 430
Lamoreaux, R. R., 559
Lange, J., 629
Langer, J., 612
Lashley, K. S., 269
Lasko, J. K., 57, 64
Latané, 341
Lawson, E. D., 472
Lazarsfeld, P. F., 478, 669
Lazowick, L. M., 665
Leary, T., 160
Lefcourt, H. M., 431
Lefkowitz, M. M., 62, 333, 469, 471
Leighton, D., 569, 573, 575, 576, 577, 578, 579, 580
Lerner, E., 518, 633, 642, 662
Levin, H., 2, 4, 71, 202, 360, 364, 372, 425, 454, 458, 470, 475, 490, 519, 526, 553, 641, 649, 666, 671, 673

Levine, E. M., 118, 136
Levinger, G., 293
Levinson, D. J., 430
Levy, D. M., 66
Lewin, K., 36, 116, 323, 448, 453, 479, 480, 485, 486, 487
Lewis, M., 192, 193, 213, 214, 215, 216, 217, 220, 221
Libby, 548
Lilienfeld, A. M., 60
Lind, D. L., 244
Lindquist, E. F., 81
Lindsley, O. R., 87, 88, 498
Lindzey, 453
Lippitt, R., 224, 448, 453, 479, 480, 482, 487, 488
Lipset, S. M., 613
Littman, R. A., 470, 558
Litwin, G. H., 160, 161, 163
Liverant, S., 221
Long, B. H., 318, 319, 322, 323, 328
Long, D., 658
Long, R. I., 530
Lovaas, O. I., 270, 277, 278
Lowell, E., 122, 149, 491
Lykken, D. T., 624
Lynd, H. M., 657
Lynn, D. B., 276, 389

McCandless, B. R., 231
McCarthy, D., 633
McClelland, D. C., 73, 117, 118, 122, 124, 149, 150, 152, 159, 162, 491
Maccoby, E. E., 2, 4, 43, 71, 202, 293, 319, 320, 343, 354, 360, 364, 372, 425, 454, 458, 470, 475, 477, 490, 519, 526, 553, 563, 616, 617, 641, 649, 666, 671, 673, 674, 676
McCord, J., 389, 667
McCord, W., 389, 667
McCoy, N., 52, 75, 193
McDonald, F. J., 595, 598, 640
Macfarlane, J. W., 106
McKee, J. P., 470, 476
Macker, C. E., 332
MacKinnon, D. W., 565, 674, 675, 676, 679, 682
McNemar, Q., 438
MacRae, D., Jr., 518, 633, 642, 662
Maier, N. R. F., 562

Author Index

Maller, J. B., 105
Marlowe, D., 310
Marshall, H. R., 231
Masling, J. M., 425
Mason, D. J., 559
May, M. A., 105, 137, 529, 533, 534, 542, 545, 547, 553, 631, 642, 676, 682
Mead, M., 505, 568, 569, 570, 573, 574, 575, 576, 577, 579
Medinnus, G. R., 518, 524
Meeker, M., 160, 198
Mees, H. L., 244
Melikian, L., 149
Mendel, G., 1
Mengert, I. G., 100
Merrill, B., 65
Metzner, R., 150
Michael, J., 244, 498
Midlarsky, E., 332
Miles, K. A., 531
Milgram, S., 616
Miller, D. R., 41, 360, 372, 559
Miller, N. E., 260, 261, 275, 344, 409, 425, 553, 556, 560, 562
Miller, 453
Minuchin, P. P., 320, 321, 371, 372, 373, 381
Mischel, W., 119, 148, 149, 151, 152, 153, 156
Mischel, W. A., 276
Montgomery, K. C., 556, 558
Moore, T., 586
Morgan, C., 41
Morgan, J. J. B., 324
Morland, J. K., 399, 400, 416, 417
Morris, C., 433
Morris, J. F., 518, 524, 526
Morrison, H. W., 293
Mosher, D. L., 431
Moss, H. A., 59, 60, 66, 97, 389, 530
Mouton, J., 333
Mowrer, O. H., 222, 223, 224, 231, 254, 255, 260, 261, 263, 274, 279, 293, 358, 554, 556, 558, 559, 562, 564, 664
Moyer, 546
Munoz, S. R., 430
Murchison, C., 408
Murray, H. A., Jr., 117, 139
Mussen, P. H., 62, 293, 323, 369, 390, 564, 664, 666, 673

Mutterer, M., 542

Naegele, K., 364
Nass, M. L., 504, 517
Nefzger, M. D., 558
Neugarten, B. L., 169, 518, 524
Newcomb, T. M., 43, 514, 665
Nichols, C. A., 573, 577
Nichols, R. C., 69, 73
Noirot, E., 57
Nowlis, V., 391, 453
Nuttin, J., 574
Nye, F. I., 564

Oakes, M. E., 633
Oppenheim, A., 496
Orne, M. T., 159, 341
Osgood, C. E., 23, 365, 366, 367, 622
Ottinger, D. R., 60
Ovesey, L., 390

Parke, R. D., 215
Parsons, T., 162, 293, 358, 359, 372
Parten, M. B., 28, 35
Pasamanick, B., 60
Passow, 197
Patchen, M., 282, 289
Pavlov, 623
Payne, D. E., 664
Pearce, D., 499
Peck, R. F., 642, 674
Peel, E. A., 654
Peterson, D. R., 23
Peterson, R. F., 269, 271
Piaget, J., 253, 303, 344, 345, 346, 352, 353, 504, 517, 518, 519, 522, 524, 526, 527, 553, 572, 573, 576, 577, 595, 617, 631, 632, 633, 634, 637, 638, 639, 651, 652, 653, 654, 655, 656, 662
Pintler, M. H., 389
Polansky, N., 224
Potter, E. H., 118, 136

Rabban, M., 372, 385
Radke, M. A., 398, 399, 401, 425
Raine, W. J., 376
Rainwater, L., 44
Rau, L., 674
Raush, H., 665, 666
Raven, B., 293

Rawlings, E., 462, 465
Ray, E., 214, 309
Raynor, R., 622
Reckless, W. T., 323
Redlick, F. C., 124
Ressler, R. H., 58
Rheingold, H. L., 57, 59
Richman, S., 214, 215, 216, 217, 220, 221
Rickert, E. J., 498
Riesman, D., 372, 509, 673
Riessman, F., 3, 38, 42, 197, 198
Riggs, L. A., 530
Riopelle, A. J., 556
Risley, T. R., 244
Robertson, R. J., 170
Robinson, W. S., 478
Rodgers, R. F., 2, 13
Roe, A., 68, 69
Rogers, M. E., 60
Rokeach, M., 432, 433, 434, 438, 441, 442
Rosekrans, M. A., 256, 281, 282
Rosen, B. C., 118, 121, 122
Rosenbaum, M., 333
Rosenberg, M., 323
Rosenhan, D. L., 191, 196, 197, 203, 214, 224, 230, 333
Rosenthal, R., 159, 236
Ross, D., 65, 256, 291, 333, 462
Ross, S. A., 65, 256, 291, 333, 462
Rotter, J. B., 314, 332
Roussel, J., 212
Rutherford, E., 62
Ryan, T. A., 19

Salinger, J., 658
Saltzstein, H. D., 672, 673
Sanford, N., 254, 260, 261, 372, 504, 507, 508, 664
Sanford, R. N., 430
Sawrey, W. L., 389
Schachter, S., 70, 71, 73
Schaefer, E., 64
Schaefer, E. A., 63
Schaffer, H. R., 61
Schilder, P., 529
Schoenfeld, W. N., 559
Schreiner, L., 556
Schwitzgebel, R., 159
Scodel, A., 431
Scott, P. M., 194, 233, 234, 236, 243

Sears, P. S., 265, 363, 364, 389, 391, 664
Sears, R. R., 2, 4, 71, 202, 223, 263, 265, 268, 274, 360, 364, 372, 389, 391, 425, 453, 454, 458, 470, 475, 490, 492, 493, 494, 495, 519, 526, 553, 560, 564, 565, 641, 649, 666, 671, 673, 674, 675, 676
Seward, J. P., 275, 470, 664
Shakow, D., 530, 549
Shallenberger, P., 78, 84
Shapiro, E., 373, 381
Shaw, M. C., 323
Shaw, M. E., 257, 302, 303
Sherif, C. W., 323
Sherman, J. A., 269, 271
Shmavonian, B. M., 532
Shure, M., 2, 26
Sidman, M., 561
Siegel, G. M., 65
Siegel, S., 217, 219, 412, 525
Sigel, I. E., 530
Silverman, A. S., 532
Simmons, J. E., 60
Singer, J. E., 313
Skinner, B. F., 225
Slack, C. A., 159
Slater, P., 664
Smith, E., 449, 489, 495
Smith, M. B., 400, 432, 594, 595, 597, 598, 599
Smith, P. W., 433
Smith, W. D., 35
Snyder, L. C., 80
Sokolov, Y. N., 532
Soloman, D., 221
Solomon, R. L., 554, 556, 559, 560, 561, 562
Somers, R. H., 511
Sopchak, A. L., 367
Spence, K. W., 624
Spilka, B., 658
Spock, B., 40, 41
Stagner, R., 425
Stechler, G. A., 60
Stein, D. D., 400, 432
Steinhorst, R., 498
Stendler, C., 642, 643, 649
Stevenson, H. W., 65, 77, 80, 85, 191, 193, 195, 204, 205, 212, 221, 309, 312, 425
Stewart, E. C., 425
Stewart, M., 70

Stingle, K. G., 255, 267
Stoke, S. M., 664
Stolz, L. M., 389, 470
Storm, T., 122
Stotland, E., 282, 289
Stott, L. H., 57
Strang, R., 323
Stumpfl, F., 629
Sugarman, B., 119, 168, 169, 170, 175
Swanson, G. E., 41, 360, 372
Szurek, 454

Tasch, R. J., 364
Terman, L. M., 69, 73
Test, M. A., 319, 331, 332, 333, 341
Thomas, E. L., 462
Thorndike, 75
Thurber, E., 389
Tiller, P. O., 389
Toigo, R., 469, 471, 473
Torgerson, W. S., 412
Trager, H. G., 398, 401, 423, 425
Triandis, H. C., 432, 433, 434, 440, 441, 442
Tuddenham, R. D., 53, 54, 104
Tudor-Hart, B. E., 642
Turiel, E., 600, 617
Turner, L. H., 556
Turner, R. H., 119, 179, 180

Ucko, L. E., 586
Ugurel-Semin, R., 332, 518, 526

VanAlstyne, D., 531, 546
Veroff, J., 122
Viek, P., 559, 562
Vince, P., 496
Vincent, C., 44

Wade, E. A., 558
Walder, L. O., 62, 469, 471
Waldrop, M., 64
Wall, A. M., 214
Walters, J. C., 499, 501

Walters, R. H., 62, 214, 215, 275, 309, 333, 447, 448, 451, 462, 468, 470, 498, 564, 586, 680
Warner, W. L., 160, 161, 198
Watson, J. B., 622
Weir, M. W., 221, 654
Weller, G. M., 64
Werner, H., 529
Wheeler, L., 333, 342
White, G. M., 224, 230, 333
White, R. K., 448, 453, 479, 480, 488
White, S. H., 505, 528, 529, 531, 532, 543, 545
Whiting, J. W. M., 292, 350, 391, 453, 495, 553, 554, 560, 563, 564, 565, 668, 669, 670
Williams, C. D., 498
Wilson, A. B., 169
Wilson, W. C., 354
Winterbottom, M. R., 117, 121, 123, 491
Witkin, H. A., 530
Wolf, M. M., 194, 243, 244, 498, 502
Wolin, S. S., 613
Wong, T. J., 433, 434, 439, 442
Wright, B. A., 332
Wright, E., 36
Wright, H. F., 27, 28, 36
Wright, 453
Wynne, L. C., 556, 561, 562

Yarrow, L. J., 57, 66
Yarrow, M. R., 194, 233, 234, 243, 401, 423

Zander, A., 282
Zigler, E., 52, 75, 77, 78, 79, 84, 193, 205, 211
Zigler, E. F., 221
Ziller, R. C., 319, 322, 323, 328
Zimbardo, P. G., 309, 314
Zimilies, H., 373
Zimmerman, E. H., 498
Zimmerman, J., 498
Zipf, S. G., 293

Subject Index

Achievement Motivation Training Program, 160
Achievement training, 158-167
  achievement imagery, 117
  affiliation and, 158-159, 163, 167
  expectations and, 158, 159, 161, 167
  games, 160, 161, 163, 166, 167
  responsibility, 162, 167
  risk-taking, 162, 163, 165-167
  role construct, 159-160, 162, 166-167
  school performance and, 164-167
  social status and, 163-167
Acquiescence, achievement motivation and, 148-157
  delayed gratification and, 148-157
Activity-passivity, 23, 53
Aggression, 147, 360, 455-502
  age and, 475, 487, 488, 491-492, 498
    adolescents, 454-460
  anxiety and, 453, 455-456, 459, 470, 475-476
  apathy and, 484, 487, 488
  behavior theory and, 470, 475, 480
    instrumental, 447, 452-453
  communications media and, 447, 461-468, 496
  development of, 447, 451-454
  frustration and, 445-446, 447, 451-452, 460, 475, 488, 491, 494
  groups and, 479-488
    discipline and, 480, 481, 482, 484, 486, 487
    scapegoats, 483, 485
    tension, 485-488
  hostility and, 455, 459, 460, 482
  imitation and, 261, 263-264, 274, 356, 447-448, 461-468, 494-495, 496
    cues, 462, 463, 467
    effectiveness of, 462
    identification, 494-495
  indirect, 453, 454, 455-456, 457
  individual differences and, 449-450, 496
  meaning of, 445, 452, 484, 486
  morality and, 520, 526-527, 622, 626, 627, 632, 636, 639, 663, 670, 671
  parents and, 447-448, 454-455, 456-459, 489-496
    child rearing, 52, 55, 56, 448, 451, 457-459, 469-478, 490-496
    as targets, 456-457, 469, 474
  toward peers, 453, 457, 459, 469, 474
  physical, 455, 456
  punishment and, 41, 62, 448, 453, 456, 457-458, 469-478
    physical, 474-475, 489-495
    psychological, 470, 474-475

731

732 Subject Index

sex differences, 469, 472-474, 475, 476, 477-478, 489-490, 493-496, 498
socialization and, 446, 450, 453, 477, 478, 496, 498
  by affiliation motive, 490-492, 496
  control, 449, 453, 497-502
  inhibition and, 456, 465, 468
  reinforcement, 449, 497-502
  school, 446-447, 448-449
  teachers, 446-447, 450, 479, 497-502
social status and, 469-478, 487, 492
verbal, 455, 456, 501
Alienation, 38
  in disadvantaged children, 47, 48
  students and, 507, 512, 516, 697-717
Ambition, 179-188
  eminence, 180, 181-182, 186-187
  marginal man and, 179-181
  material, 182, 186-187
  mobility, 179-182, 183, 185, 187
  peer groups and, 181, 187
  sex differences, 185-188
  social context, 179-188
    stratification, 182-183, 184-185
  socialization and, 180, 187
  types, 181
  women and, 185-188
  youth and, 179, 180-181, 187-188
  see also Motivation, achievement
Anxiety, aggression and, 453, 455-456, 459, 470, 475-476
  anticipatory, 505, 546, 552, 555-556, 558-559, 562-563
  conditioned, 621, 622-623, 624, 629
  guilt and, 566-567, 641
  moral development and, 548, 552-567, 594, 663, 664
  social reinforcement and, 203, 213, 215, 220, 221, 223, 224, 231

Behavior theory, aggression and, 470, 475, 480
  identification and, 275
  instrumental, 447, 452-453, 552-567
  morality development and, 505
  neo-behaviorist concepts, 2, 4, 505
Bennington College, 514
Birth order, 67-74
  congenital factors, 64
  conscience development and, 519

first-born children, 67-74
  college attendance, 69-70
  education, 52, 67, 68, 70, 72-73
  eminence and, 51, 52, 68, 72, 73
  graduate school attendance, 52, 67, 70
  intelligence, 69, 73
  personality characteristics, 52, 70-72
  sex of, 67-69, 71
  social behavior, 71
parental behavior and, 64, 67-68, 71-73
  fathers, 71
younger children, 64
see also Siblings
Blacky Test (castration anxiety), 665
Brothers Test (Piaget), 352-353

Child personality, aggression, 360, 361
  social development, 104-114
  sex differences, 106, 107-110
  see also Social behavior in children
Child rearing, 4-12, 72
  aggression and, 448, 451, 458-459, 469-478, 490-496, 520, 526-527, 622, 626, 627, 632, 636, 639, 663, 670, 671
  cultural differences, 13
  discipline, 365, 680-681
  effect on behavior, 6-7, 9-11, 360
  imitation and, 257-258, 320, 321
  morality development and, 62, 505, 506, 526, 569, 573, 575-576, 593, 594, 596, 602, 630, 641, 649, 650, 662-683
  motivation training, 10-11, 116, 117-118, 121-135, 184
  sex differences, 364-365, 679-680
  socialization and, 50, 51
    prejudices and, 400, 425
    social reinforcement, 222-223
  toilet training, 50, 355, 668-669
  weaning, 668-669, 675
  see also Socialization; Punishment; Parental behavior
Children's Social Desirability Questionnaire, 310
Circular reflex principle (Holt), 344
College students, first-born children, 52, 69-70
  moral judgments, 597-617
  radicalism, 511, 613-617
  social awareness of, 507-516, 597-617

Subject Index

Common-law marriage, 44
Communications media, aggressive behavior and, 447, 461-468, 496
Conscience, *see* Moral behavior

Declaration of Independence, 397, 508
  Bill of Rights, 397
Developmental psychology, 585
  imitation and, 253
    age and, 302, 303, 358
  socialization and, 50
Disadvantaged, 506
  achievement motivation training and, 158-167
  aggression and, 41-42
  alienation, 47, 48
  broken homes, 39, 44, 48
  children, 38-48
  extended family, 39-40, 48
    discipline, 40-42
  functional responsibility, 43-44
  illegitimacy, 44, 45, 390
  obedience and, 42
  psychotherapy and, 47-48
  punishment and, 40-42, 47
  self-image, 326
  sexual attitudes, 44-46
  social reinforcement and, 196-198, 200-203
  teacher and, 46-47
Duncan Multiple Range Test, 466

Education, aggression and, 446-447, 448-449
  behavior reinforcement, 138-147
  moral behavior and, 504
  personality development and, 136-138
  see also Schools; Socialization
Egocentrism, in adolescence, 651, 655-659, 660
  in childhood, 653-655
  cognition and, 651-660
  in infancy, 352-353, 652-653
Eminence, ambition and, 180, 181-182, 186-187
  birth order and, 51, 52, 68, 73
  scientists, 68
Environment, ecology, 3, 26
  "psychological ecology," 3, 26, 27
  of nursery school, 26-37

response qualities of, 9
Ethnocentrism, moral behavior and, 506, 508, 575-584
  in social research, 568-569, 575-584
Extended family, 38, 39, 43
  delinquency and, 46
  description, 39-40, 48
  education and, 46
  security and, 39
  sibling rivalry and, 40

Family, socialization by, 388-389
  structure effects, birth order, 51, 52, 57, 64, 67-74, 519
    sibling rivalry, 40-48, 90-95
    size and density, 64
Fathers, absence of, 388-395
  daughters and, 320, 357, 364, 366-370
  morality development and, 679-680
  motivation training by, 124, 131, 134-135
  sex typing by, 320, 357-370
  sons and, 62-63, 124, 134-135
Field-Gestalt theory, motives and, 116
Fisher Exact Probability Test, 589
Fleming, penicillin and, 528
Foster mothers, 57, 66
Free Speech Movement (University of California at Berkeley), 511, 603, 608, 609, 610, 613-614, 617
Freudian psychology, *see* Psychoanalytic theory

Graduate school, first-born children and, 52, 67, 70
Group behavior, aggression and, 479-488
  culture and, 487
  discipline and, 480, 481, 482, 484, 486, 487
  freedom of movement, 485, 487
  scapegoats, 483, 488
  tension, 485-488
Guilt, 568-584, 621, 663, 668-672, 675-677
  anxiety and, 566-567, 641
  crosscultural study of, 568, 569, 574, 575-584, 669, 670
  development of, 570-574, 679-680
  shame and, 568, 569-570, 574-584

Hollingshead Index of Social Position, 124

Subject Index

Identification, 259-290
  aggression and, 494-495
  anaclitic, 360-361, 664, 665
  in children versus adults, 282-290
    adolescents, 326-330
  defensive, 261, 274, 279-280, 562, 663-664, 665
  dependence and, 268, 278-279, 327-330
  developmental, 260-261, 274, 358
  generalized theory of, 274-278
  imitation and, 254, 256, 259-290
  introjection, 276
  learning and, 283, 289-290, 291-301
    attentiveness, 289-290
  meaning of, 261-262, 274-275
  in moral development, 554, 559-560, 663-667, 677-678, 679, 681
  motivation and, 262-265
  negative, 290
  psychoanalytic theory of, 237, 274-275
  schizophrenic children and, 277-278
  self-image and, 318, 319, 326
  sexual, 358, 365-367
    cross-sex, 358
    with father, 328-330, 358, 664-666
  vicarious effect, 261, 281-290
Illegitimacy, among disadvantaged, 44, 45
  teen-age, 44, 45
Imitation, 253-315
  age and, 257, 265, 302-307
  aggression and, 261, 263-264, 274, 356, 447-448, 461-468, 494-495, 496
  anxiety and, 255, 261, 264
  child rearing and, 257-258, 320, 321
  in children versus adults, 282-290
  conformity, 314
    age level and, 302-307
  covert, 343-356, 557
    effectiveness of, 343-345, 352-355
  generalized theory of, 267-280
    versus identification, 274-278
    influences on, 270-274
    values in, 273-274
  identification and, 254, 256, 259-290
    dependence and, 268, 278-279
    developmental, 260-261, 274
    introjection, 276
    meaning of, 261-263, 274-275
    motivation and, 262-265
    negative, 290
    psychoanalytic theory of, 231, 274-275
    vicarious effect, 261, 281-290
  isolation and, 257, 308-315
    cognitive dissonance and, 308-310, 312-315
    voluntary, 313-315
  learning and, 253-258, 260, 267-280, 291-301, 344
    attentiveness, 289-290
    versus performance, 283, 289-290
    prohibition learning, 260, 261
    schools, 258
  models and, 253, 254, 261, 277, 284, 292-293
    absence of, 272-273
    effectiveness, 255-257, 262, 265, 331-342
    power theory, 291, 292, 293, 298, 299, 300
    in prejudice, 398, 399, 404, 405, 424-431
    secondary reinforcement theory, 291, 292, 293
    status envy theory, 291, 292-293
  in moral development, 553, 556, 557, 564, 590
  motivation and, 254, 262-265, 266
  need for approval, 308-309, 310, 315
  parents and, 257-258, 270-271, 272
  peers and, 222-224, 229-232, 257, 302-307
  reinforcement and, 222-232, 254-256, 260-261, 263, 265, 266, 282, 308-315
    extrinsic, 268, 270, 278
    negative, 292, 293
    secondary, 254, 291, 292, 293
    types of, 256
    vicarious, 256, 267, 281-290
  role practice and, 300, 344-347
  schizophrenic children and, 277-278
  sex differences in, 256, 272, 292, 305
  sex roles and, 257-258, 264-265, 272, 276, 292, 298-301
    cross-sex imitation, 300, 358
  socialization and, 255, 270-271, 301, 306
  teachers and, 259
Imprinting behavior, motivation and, 118
Improbable Achievement Tests, 533-534
Improbable Achievement Speed Test, 534
Incentives, see Motivation
Infants, contact avoidance, 59

effect on parents, 59-61
egocentricity, 352-353, 652-653
imitation, 344-346
irritability, in males, 59
learning, 344-346
maternal treatment, 57, 668-669
  foster mothers, 57, 66
  influenced by child, 57, 59-60
sex differences, 59-60
  social orientation, 59-60
social behavior, 59-60
  congenital influences on, 59-60
  effect of pregnancy and delivery on, 60
Institutionalization, 190, 191-192, 205-212
social deprivation and, 192
stimulus deprivation and, 191-192, 212, 215
see also Isolation
Interaction, 49-114
adult-child, 212, 355-356
child effect (on parents), 50-54, 55-56, 76-78, 83-85, 96-103
among children, 13-25, 30, 33, 37, 51, 53-54
  activity-passivity, 23, 53
  parallel play, 34, 35
conflict, 76
effect of, frequency, 343
  on reinforcement, 75-85, 208
  on social behavior, 83-85, 87, 95, 343
egocentrism, 653, 656-659
imitation and, 254
parent-child, 4-12, 49-54, 55-66, 272, 552-567
  identification and, 300-301
  infants, 57, 59-61, 344-346
  moral development, 593, 594
  in motivation training, 123-126, 133-134
  negative child reactions, 58-59, 76-78
  peer groups, 86-114, 168-178, 193, 222-251, 302-307
in sex typing, 371-372, 388-389
social learning and, 343-356
Iowa Test of Basic Skills, 325
Isolation, 205-221
cognitive dissonance and, 308-310, 312-315
duration of, 220
imitation and, 257, 308-315

institutionalization, 190, 191-192, 205-212
from peers, 243-251
social deprivation, 191-192, 212, 215
social reinforcement and, 190-192, 205-221, 308-315
stimulus deprivation, 192
voluntary, 313-315
It Scale for Children, 369, 391

Jefferson, Thomas, social legislation and, 397
Juvenile delinquency, 46, 619, 620

Koh's block patterns, 125
Kruskal-Wallis test (analysis of variance), 219
Kuhlmann-Anderson Intelligence Test, 635

Learning, circular reflex principle, 344
as conditioning, 344-345, 618-623, 628
imitation and, 253-258, 260, 267-280, 291-301, 344-346
instrumental, 344, 351, 356, 552-567
moral development, 618-630
versus performance, 283, 289-290
prohibition learning, 260, 261
social, 343-356, 498, 586
Lie Test (Hartshorne and May), 534, 536, 537, 538
Litwin-Ciarlo Business Game, 161, 163, 166, 167

Mandler-Sarason Test Anxiety Scale, 161
Mann-Whitney U Test, 163, 164, 217, 219, 220, 365
Marginal man, adolescent as, 323
ambition and, 179-181
definition, 179
Marlowe-Crowne Social Desirability Scale, 310, 315
Mental patients, self-conception, 325, 326
see also Schizophrenics
Moral behavior, 503-683
age and, 518, 519, 523, 524-525, 527, 530-531, 535-546, 548-551, 578, 586, 632-634, 637-639, 648, 679
aggression and, 520, 526-527, 622, 626, 627, 632, 636, 639, 663, 670, 671
antisocial conduct, 622, 623, 624,

626, 630
delinquency, 619, 620
anxiety and, 548, 552-567, 594, 663, 664
  anticipatory, 505, 546, 552, 555-556, 558-559, 562-563
  conditioned, 621, 622-623, 624, 629
  guilt and, 566-567, 641
attention processes and, 528-551
  impulsiveness, 529-530, 532, 533, 543, 545
  psychomotor control, 530, 533, 535, 542-546, 548-549, 551
  reaction time, 530-532, 536-541, 544-550
  in schizophrenics, 530-531, 549
  will, 529, 549-551
biological roots of, 595, 619, 623-624, 626, 628-630
college students, 507-516, 597-617
  Free Speech Movement, 511, 603, 608, 609, 610, 613-614, 617
conscience development, 504-505, 517-527, 550, 570-574, 618-639
  adolescence, 570, 573, 576-577, 595-596, 600, 603-610, 651, 655-659, 660
  autonomy, 631, 632
  child rearing and, 62, 505, 506, 526, 569, 573, 575-576, 593, 594, 596, 602, 630, 641, 649, 650, 662-683
  conditioning, 618-623, 628
  content, 641, 649, 651, 661-683
  equity, 633, 637, 638, 639
  origins, 503, 505, 552-567
  relativity, 631, 633
consistency, 682-683
cultural differences, 505-506, 518, 566, 568-584, 586, 589-598
  ethnocentrism, 506, 508, 568-569, 575-584
egocentrism, 595, 651-660
gratification delay and, 505, 529, 530
guilt, 566-567, 568-584, 621, 641, 663, 668-672, 675-677
  crosscultural study of, 568, 569, 574, 575-584, 669, 670
  development of, 570-574, 679-680
  shame and, 568, 569-570, 574-584
honesty, 529-530, 533-534, 536-544, 547, 550, 674, 675
idealized goals, 594, 595, 596, 600, 603-606
identification and, 554, 559-560, 663-667, 677-678, 679, 681
  anaclitic, 664, 665
  defensive, 562, 663-664, 665
  with father, 664-666
imitation and, 553, 556, 557, 564, 590
individual differences, 525, 531, 623-627, 630
  conditionability, 623-624, 626, 628-630
  emotional stability, 529
  extravert versus introvert, 625-627
  motor steadiness, 533
intelligence and, 518, 519, 529-531, 536-537, 539-543, 632-633, 635, 636-639, 647-648, 650
judgments, 597-617, 631-633, 637
  conventional, 598, 600, 606-608
  parents and, 603-605, 607-610, 612, 614, 617
  premoral, 600, 608-610
  principled, 600, 603-606
learning theory and, 618-630
material values, 526, 527
obedience, 533, 536-541, 543, 544
peers versus authority, 521, 524, 525, 570, 573, 673-674, 677
psychoanalytic theory and, 505, 621, 662-663, 665, 667, 678
  ego strength, 528, 529, 530, 545, 546, 551
  superego, 505, 546, 555, 575, 581, 621
punishment, 522, 552-567, 572, 594, 620, 622, 635, 664, 666, 670, 672, 674
  nurturance and, 563-566
  physical, 670, 671
  reproduction of, 561-563, 676
  withdrawing affection, 565-566, 664, 670, 671
research in, 504, 506, 517, 568-569, 661-683
resisting temptation, 673-677, 679, 681, 682
  versus guilt, 675-677
self-criticism, 505, 552-567, 570, 575, 580, 581, 583, 663
  acquisition of, 554-560, 670
  cognitive processes and, 554, 566-567
  maintenance of, 560-561
  meaning of, 555

sex differences, 518, 522, 523, 524, 525, 526-527, 530, 586, 589-590, 591, 640, 645-650, 678-679
sharing, learning of, 585-591
sin, 579-582
socialization and, 503, 506, 549, 571, 572, 585-586
  interaction, 511-512, 593, 594, 596
  punishment, 557-560
  teaching and, 515-516
social reinforcement and, 554, 556, 557-558, 560, 586, 588, 590, 620, 663
social responsibility, 503, 507-516, 573, 577, 581, 597-617
  versus alienation, 507, 512, 516, 597-617
  college and, 508-511, 512-516
  conformism, 509, 513, 515, 542, 546, 550, 598, 600, 606-608
  dissent, 597-598
  ethnocentrism, 508, 509, 512, 513
  ideals and, 508, 512, 514, 516, 594-595, 600, 603-606
  participation, 509-511
social status and, 505, 517-527, 586, 589-590, 628, 640-641, 646-647, 649, 650, 666, 669
stages, 518, 597-617, 634
  authoritative constraint, 522, 525-527, 569, 571, 575-576, 577, 578-579, 632, 637, 673
  cooperation-reciprocity, 522, 527, 572-573, 576-580, 632-633, 638, 639
  internalization, 506, 522, 542, 550, 552-567, 573, 574, 579-582, 583, 667-673, 678, 681
theft, 640-650
  from individual versus corporation, 640, 642, 645, 649, 650
trustworthiness, 533, 536-541, 543-544
Moral Judgment Scale (Kohlberg), 599, 600-602
Mothers, demanding, 63, 64, 132, 134-135
  interaction with child, 4-12, 49, 93-94
  determined by infant, 59-60
  hostility-aggression, 52, 55, 66
  identificatory learning, 300
  inconsistency, 57
  motivation training, 116, 117-118, 121, 123-135
  personality differences and, 11-12, 62
  problems, 11, 59
  morality development and, 680
  in Negro family, 45
  pregnancy and delivery, 64
  effect on child, 60
  sons and, 134-135
  verbal child and, 63
Motivation, 115-188
  achievement, 115-135, 179
    delayed gratification and, 119, 148-157, 181
    independence motive and, 122-123, 126, 129-130, 133-134
    training in, 121-124, 126, 128-130, 133-135, 158-167
  affiliation, 115-116, 158-159, 163, 167
  ambition, 179-188
  derivation of, 10-11, 116-118, 120, 121-135
  of institutionalized children, 204, 212
  meaning of, 115, 117
  modification of, 158-167
  parental influence on, 121-135
    expectations, 127-129, 133
    types of, 126
  power, 115
  versus primary drives, 115-116, 118
  reinforcement and, 123, 126, 130, 135
  school texts and, 118, 137, 139-141
  social drive, 214, 221
  social status and, 124, 133, 163-167
  types of, 115-116
  underachievers and, 119, 158-167
Motor skills, learning of, 343, 352

National Merit Scholarships, 69
Negro children, 197, 198-203, 388-395, 399, 400, 405, 406, 417, 419-431
Negro family, 39
  matriarchal, 45, 390
  sexual attitudes, 45
Nuclear family, sex roles in, 357-370
Nursery school, behavior in, 27, 29-37
  categories, 27-28, 29-30
  constructiveness, 27, 29-30, 32-33, 34, 36, 37
  preferred activity, 29, 30-31, 34, 35, 36
  relevant, 31-32, 33, 34, 36-37
  social participation, 27, 30, 33, 34, 37

imitation and, 291-301
parallel play in, 34, 35
physical environment, 35-36
sex differences in, 27, 30-31, 33-34, 35, 36-37
social reinforcement and, 194-195, 223-251

Oedipus complex, 40, 48, 358, 621, 665
Overachievers, in peer groups, 171, 177
Overprotection, 39, 40

Parental behavior, toward aggression, 447, 448, 451, 454-455, 456-459, 469-478, 489-496
in animals, 57-58
control, lower-limit, 61, 63
upper-limit, 61, 62, 63
variance, 63-64
effect on child, 49-53, 56, 61-62
prejudice, 399, 404, 405, 424-431
reinforcement, 75-85, 202-203
influenced by child, 50-54, 55-66, 96
birth order, 57-58, 67-68, 71-73
congenital factors, 58-59, 60, 61, 66
negative child reactions, 58-59
sex difference, 57, 59-60
motivation training, 121-135
types of, 126
neglect, 593
sex-typing, 357-370
Pavlovian conditioning, 618, 621, 623
Peace Corps, 509, 599
Peer groups, 86-114, 168-178
adolescent, English, 168-178
aggression and, 453, 457, 459, 469, 474
ambition and, 181, 187
competition versus cooperation, 86-95
test of, 87-94
contacts, frequency, 97, 99-103
initiation of, 100-103
quality of, 97, 99, 100-103
effect of, on socialization, 14, 22, 168
imitation and, 222-224, 229-232, 257, 302-307
individual and, 96-103, 169, 172, 318, 319, 324, 326
leadership, 90-95, 174-175, 187-188
morality and, 521, 524, 525, 570, 573, 673-674, 677

motivation and, 119
reinforcement and, 193, 222-224, 229-232, 234-242, 243-251
Reputation Test, 104-114
diagnostic potential, 110-114
function of, 106-107
results, 107-112
sex differences, 107-110
standards, 108
school performance and, 168-178
status in, 51, 53-54, 62, 104-114, 173-175
values, 175-176, 180-181
Perceived Similarity Test, 284, 285, 286
Personality development, aggression and, 41-42
ambition and, 180
birth order and, 51, 52, 70-72
cultural differences, 14, 19-20, 22-25
identification and, 358
imitation and, 253-315
motives and, 115-135
parents and, 49-53, 121-135
peer-group behavior and, 97
school texts and, 137-138
Pintner-Cunningham Intelligence Test, 519
Play, imitation in, 273
Prejudice, 397-443
aggression and, 424, 425, 426
childhood origins, 398-399, 402-403, 405, 406-407
child rearing, 400, 425
generalized misanthropy, 430
identification, 425
dominance and, 408-415
distance and, 399, 412-415
pecking order, 408-409, 414
friendliness and, 433, 437-439
imitative, 425, 430-431
models, parents, 399, 404, 405, 424-431
teachers, 398, 399
toward nationalities, 427
in Negroes, 399, 400, 417, 419, 421, 424-431
self-rejection and, 400, 405, 406, 420, 422, 424-431
in Northern and Southern children, 400, 416-423
parental punitiveness and, 424-431
religious, 402-406
schools and, 398, 401, 407, 422-423

self-image and, 399, 400, 405, 406, 419-420, 422, 424-431
shared beliefs and, 398, 432-443
  versus race difference, 439, 442-443
social awareness and, in adolescents, 400, 432-443
  age and, 404-405
  cultural context and, 403-404, 421-422, 425, 430
  group affiliation, 398, 399, 405-406, 419-420
  group differentiation, 400, 402-403, 420
  racial, 400, 402-403
  status concern, 398, 405-406, 419, 421
  social distance scale, 427, 439-442
  social status influence, 426, 427, 428, 431, 441-442
Premarital intercourse, 44
"Privatism," 509
Problem children, case studies, 111-114
  peer groups and, 110-114
Psychoanalytic theory, 618, 655
  castration anxiety, 665, 679
  concepts, 2, 4
  ego strength, 528, 529, 530, 545, 546, 551
  identification theory, 231, 274-275, 495, 665
  moral development and, 505, 621
  motivation theory, 116
  Oedipus complex, 40, 48, 358, 621, 665
  superego development, 261, 361, 505, 546, 555, 575, 581, 621
Psychotherapy, 618
  disadvantaged persons, 47-48
Puberty, conformity and, 306-307
Punishment, aggression and, 41, 62, 448, 453, 456, 457-458, 469-478
  effects of, 4, 8-9, 41, 75, 76
  deleterious, 40
  learning and, 8-9
  meaning, 8
  mixed, 41
  moral development and, 522, 552-567, 572, 594, 620, 622, 635, 664, 666, 670, 672, 674
  physical, 40-42, 47, 58, 59, 62, 202-203, 474-475, 489-495, 670, 671
  psychological, 470, 474-475

responses to, 9, 52-53, 62
rewards and, 52-53
school, 47, 177
  textbooks, 139, 140, 145, 146
withdrawing affection, 565-566, 664, 670, 671

Radicalism, 511
  college students and, 511
Reading, children's, 138-139
Reed College, 514
Reinforcement, behavior and, 75
  in competition and cooperation, 87-94
  delayed gratification, 119, 148-157, 181
    achievement motivation and, 148-157
    social responsibility and, 149, 151, 153, 156
    work motivation and, 150
  in motivation training, 123, 126, 130, 135
  recency of exposure, 289, 297
  theory, 241-242
  see also Social reinforcement
Reputation, sex differences, 107-110
  test of, 104-114
    function, 106-107
    results, 107-110
    standards, 108
Research, extra-experimental effects, 95
Research methods, achievement imagery, 117
  comparative psychological methods, 408
  cosatiation index, 77-78
  experimenter, bias, 236-237
    sex of, 221
  with institutionalized children, 205
  naturalistic setting, 331-343, 497-502
  in parent-child interaction, 64-66
    with parent versus stranger, 64-65, 76, 78-85, 92
  reinforcement, 86-95
  Reputation Test, 104-114
  socialization theory, 51
  types, 86
Retarded children, 65
  personality structure, 211
  social reinforcement and, 193, 205-212
Roles, 317-356
  achievement training and, 159-160, 162, 166-167
  in adolescence, 318-319

altruism and, 319, 333-342
  motivation, 322-333, 339, 340
  versus racial feeling, 338-341
appropriateness, 343, 347-349, 351-352, 354
child rearing and, 320, 321
covert practice of, 343-356
  effectiveness, 343-345, 352-355
development of, 317
imitation and, 344-347
  contiguity and, 346, 348
  limitations on, 345-346, 348-349, 352-355
interaction and, 343, 349-351
  context of, 320
  frequency of, 320, 343, 350, 351
  power and, 350-351
  reciprocity of, 332
  teacher-child, 321
learning of, 318, 343, 350-351
meaning of, 346-347
models and, 319, 331, 333-342, 354
  in adult behavior, 333-342
  shame and, 342
parental influence on, 319-320, 343-356
  age and, 321, 327-330, 389, 392-393
  father, 318, 320, 321, 328-330, 355, 357-370
  mother, 320, 355
  versus teacher, 318, 319, 320, 329, 330, 355
social learning and, 319, 343-356
  instrumental, 344, 351, 356
social status and, 321, 371-387
see also Sex roles; Self-image
Rorschach test, 482

St. John's College (Annapolis), 514
Schizophrenics, attention processes and, 530-531, 549
  children, 277-278
School-Community Coordinator, 46
  Puerto Rican Coordinator, 46
Schools, disadvantaged children and, 46-47
  English, 119, 170
  Guidance Study, 106-114
  personality development, 136-138
  social behavior and, 21, 23
    in elementary classes, 105-114
    in high school, 120
  in kindergarten, 96-103
  nursery school, 26-37
  prejudice and, 398, 401, 407, 422-423
  textbooks, 136-147
  Trinidad, 148-157
Self-image, 317-318, 322-330
  age and, 327-330
  centrality, 318, 325
  complexity, 318, 325
  dependency, 318, 325, 327-330
  derogation, 318
  versus group identification, 318, 319, 326
  individuation, 318, 322-323, 325-326, 327-330
  learning of, 343, 355
  power of self, 318, 325
  self-esteem, 318, 324, 330, 355
  race and, 399, 400, 405, 406, 419-420, 422, 424-431
  sex differences, 326, 327-330, 367
Self-Social Symbols Task Test, 318, 323-326
Sex roles, 318-321, 357-395
  child rearing and, 320, 360-361, 364-365, 372, 375, 386
  children, 16-24, 118, 142-144, 363, 366-367
    international comparisons, 16-24
    kindergarten, 369
    masculinity and, 16-24, 62-63, 111-112, 300, 328-329, 356, 366, 369, 389-395
    nursery-school age, 27, 363-364, 369
    opposite sex and, 376-380
    in play and fantasy, 380-385
  congenital influence, 63
  development, 62-63, 387
  disruption of, 389-390, 395
    age and, 321, 389, 392-393
  family influence, 321, 372-375, 377-381, 384-387, 388
  father and, 62-63, 328-329, 356
    absence of, 388-395
    for both sexes, 320, 357-370
    girls' femininity and, 362, 367-368
    nurturance, 369-370
  identification and, 358, 365-367, 390
  imitation and, 257-258, 264-265, 272, 276, 292, 298-301
  modern versus traditional, 321, 371-387
    changing attitudes, 371-374, 386-387

for girls, 375, 377, 379, 380, 384-386
morality and, 648-649
mother and, 358-359, 362, 366, 390
personality and, 107-110, 362, 365
  adjustment, 366-367, 368
  aggression, 360, 361, 364, 365, 380-382, 384-386, 390-395
  dependence versus independence, 391-395
  expressivity versus instrumentality, 358-362, 365, 368
school influence, 373-374, 377-379, 382-383, 386-387
  textbooks, 118, 142-144
social status and, 371-387
Sharing, learning of, 585-591
  age and, 586
  imitation, 590
  meaning of, 588
  race and, 587, 590, 591
  sex differences, 586, 589-590, 591
  social reinforcement and, 586, 588, 590
  social status and, 586, 589-590
Siblings, identification and, 265
  parental treatment, 57
  rivalry, 40, 48, 90-95
  see also Birth order; Family, structure effects
Social attitudes, *see* Prejudice
Social behavior in children, 13-25
  age and, 22, 100-101
  assertiveness, 58-59, 62, 63
  in boarding schools, 21, 23
  broken homes and, 22, 23, 39, 388-395
  competition versus cooperation, 86-95
    test of, 87-94
  congenital factors, 58-61, 62
  disadvantaged, 38-48
  effect on parents, 55-66
  hyperactivity, 60, 62, 66
  infants, 59-61
    male, 59-60
  international comparisons, 13-25
  moral development, 62, 503-683
  negative, 234-242
  parental effect on, 52, 55, 56
  peer groups, 86-114
  person orientation, 59, 60, 62, 63
  punishment and, 4, 8-9, 40, 51-53, 62, 75, 76, 139, 140, 145, 146

reaction tendency, positive versus negative, 76-78, 84-85, 102-103, 193
retarded, 211
sex differences, 16-21, 23, 24, 107-109, 118, 142-144, 586, 589-590, 591
  infants, 59-61
sharing, learning of, 585-591
standards of, 14-25, 108, 140
  masculinity, 14-25, 62-63
teen-age, British, 168-178
type of school and, 21, 23
see also Aggression; Prejudice
Socialization, achievement motivation and, 115-120, 124
  aggression and, 446, 450, 453, 477, 478, 496, 498
  affiliation motive, 490-492, 496
  control of, 449, 453, 497-502
  inhibitions, 456, 465, 468
  reinforcement and, 449, 497-502
  school and, 446-447, 448-449
  teachers, 446-447, 450, 479, 497-502
  altruism, 222-223, 224, 228-231, 331-342
  ambition and, 180, 187
  conformity and, 306-307
  cultural differences, 2, 13-25
  education, textbooks, 136-137, 138, 139-140, 145
  environmental response qualities, 3, 9
  imitation, 255, 270-271, 301, 306
  influences on, 49-54, 204
    age, 302, 306-307
    birth order, 51, 52, 57, 71
    by child, 50-54, 55-66
    congenital, 58-61
    environmental, 50, 52
    parental, 49-114
  interaction, 49-114
    peer groups, 86-114, 168-178
    social reinforcement, 65, 75-85, 87, 95
  learning and, 398-400, 498
  moral development and, 503, 506, 549, 571, 572, 585-586
    interaction and, 511-512
    punishment, 557-560
    teaching and, 515-516
  neo-behavioristic concepts, 2, 4
  parents' role, 2, 4-12, 49-114
  peer group behavior, 86-114, 168-178
  personality and, 49, 53

Subject Index

personal relations, 11, 398
primary dimensions of, 1-48
  efforts to define, 1-3
  social environment and, 3, 50
  in theory, 2
reciprocity, 332
reinforcement and, 192-193, 194, 195, 223, 224, 230, 232, 313
sex roles and, 360
social disturbances and, 3
social origins, 3, 5
social responsibility, 333, 341
social skills, 49-50, 241-242, 244-245, 250
  behavioral tendencies and, 49
  see also Interaction; Child rearing
Social reinforcement, 65, 75-85, 87, 95, 189-251, 308-315
  academic performance and, 197-198, 202
  by adults, 75-85, 205, 208-209, 211-212, 233-242
    negative, 76-77, 84-85, 198
    parents, 52-53, 58, 76, 84-85, 123, 126, 130, 135
    positive, 87, 190-203, 205, 207-208
    teachers, 196, 234, 237, 241, 242, 243-251
    test of, 78-83
  age and, 193, 221
  aggression and, 449, 497-502
  alienation and, 196-198, 203
  anxiety and, 203, 213, 215, 220, 221, 223, 224, 231
  cross-sex effect, 193
  effectiveness, 190-203, 213, 222-223
    on altruism, 222-223, 224, 228-231, 332, 337, 338, 342
    in changing behavior, 194-195, 205, 209, 212, 214, 233-251
    individual differences, 193, 219-221, 222, 313-315
    interaction and, 75-85, 208
    model and, 223-224, 229-231
    prior history and, 223, 224, 230-232
    research in, 190-195, 308, 313, 315
    reward value, 196
    sex differences, 216-221, 223, 240
    skills and, 241-242, 244-245, 250
  of interaction, 243-251
  isolation and, 213-221, 308-315
    duration of, 220
  institutionalization, 190, 191-192, 205-212
  from peers, 243-251
  social deprivation, 191-192, 212, 215, 311-312, 315
  stimulus deprivation, 192
  learning and, 214, 253, 254
  model imitation and, 222-232, 260-261, 263, 308-315
    peers, 222-224, 229-232
  moral development and, 554, 556, 557-558, 560, 586, 588, 590, 620, 663
  need for approval and, 308-309, 310, 315
  versus nonsocial, 214, 215
  nursery school and, 194-195, 223-251
  peers and, 193, 222-224, 229-232, 234-242
  race and, 197, 198-203
  reaction tendencies and, 193
  retarded children, 193, 205-212
  in school texts, 138-147
  secondary, 222, 223, 231
  socialization and, 194, 195, 243-251
    history of, 192-193, 223, 224, 230, 232
  social status and, 190-191, 196-203
    disadvantaged children, 196-198, 200-203
  verbal, 75, 76, 80-81, 198-203, 235, 247
  see also Reinforcement
Stanford Achievement Test, 160, 161, 163
Stanford-Binet test, 547

Taylor Manifest Anxiety Scale, 161
Test of Insight, 161, 162
Textbooks, 136-147
  as behavior reinforcers, 138-147
  adjustment problems, 141-142
  asocial tendencies, 141, 145-146
  standards, 140
  submissiveness, 141-142
  motivation and, 118
  punishment in, 139, 140, 145, 146
  realism, 146-147
  sex roles in, 118, 142-144
  socialization and, 136-137, 138, 139-140, 145
Thumb-sucking, 41
Trinidad, 151
  achievement motivation in, 148-157
  delayed gratification, 148-157

Underachievers, motivation training and, 119, 158-167
   in peer groups, 169, 171-172
Underprivileged, *see* Disadvantaged
United States Supreme Court, social rights and, 397

Verbal skills, 63

   effect on parental behavior, 65
   learning of, 271, 343, 344-345, 352
   mother's role in, 63

Women, ambition and, 185-188
   materialist, 186-187

Yerkes-Dodson Law (drives), 620